Illustrated World Encyclopedia

1975

BOOK OF THE YEAR

Bicentennial Edition

vol. 11

Editor: Robert Halasz
Associate Editors: Barbara Mackowiak, Nancy Ruth
Contributing Editors: Anne Neigoff, Emma Redmond
Graphic Design: Willis Proudfoot
Picture Research: Adrienne Coleman

Bobley Publishing Corp.

WOODBURY, NEW YORK

The 1975 ILLUSTRATED WORLD ENCYCLOPEDIA
BOOK-OF-THE-YEAR is divided into four parts, one
for each quarter of the year. Section I starts on page
3; section II on page 135; section III on page 267;
and section IV on page 399. Each begins with a feature article on an important topic of the day, followed
by current news reports entered in alphabetical order
from A through Z, and concludes with the NEWS IN
BRIEF in which supplementary news stories are
highlighted. At the very end of each quarterly division
is a cumulative index covering information found up
to that point in the book. (The index at the back of the
book therefore covers the events of the entire year.)
This format combines the advantages of chronolog-
ical arrangement with those of alphabetical organization. That is, while giving the reader a feeling for
the natural progression of the news, it still enables
him to look up individual items alphabetically.

report
on the oil
industry

The OIL
COMPANIES

Mounting criticism over the scarcity and rising cost of gasoline is prompting investigation of the nation's petroleum industry.

As U.S. oil companies tallied their 1973 profits, mounting criticism from consumers over the scarcity and rising cost of gasoline prompted congressional investigations into the operations of the nation's huge petroleum industry. The companies responded with a massive advertising campaign defending their returns as necessary for the future development of vital energy resources. A large segment of the public, however, became convinced that fuel shortages were being engineered by the major petroleum corporations to force a rise in prices and drive independent competitors out of business.

A Very Profitable Year

The 10 largest petroleum companies, often referred to as the "majors," reported profits for 1973 up 51.2 per cent over 1972, to a total of $7.8 billion; for the top 24, profits were up 53 per cent. Exxon, the world's largest oil company, reported that its profits for the last quarter of 1973 (when Arab nations imposed an oil embargo on the United States) and for 1973 as a whole were up 59 per cent, setting a record. Reports presented to a Senate hearing of the Permanent Subcommittee on Investigations showed that the seven largest companies operating in the United States increased their profits 46 per cent during the first nine months of 1973 (at a time when prices were rising sharply), even though the volume sold was only 6 per cent higher than during the first three-quarters of the previous year.

Industry representatives explained the sudden rise in profits as primarily the result of oil-price increases in Europe, where American petroleum companies have a large share of the market. (An oil glut had suppressed prices on the Continent until 1971.) Statistics gathered on 30 corporations by the Chase Manhattan Bank tend to support this contention: Earnings on the foreign operations of these companies nearly doubled from

5

The petroleum industry has been handicapped by what may be the worst public image in American business.

$3.2 billion in 1972 to an estimated $6.1 billion in 1973. By contrast, earnings on domestic oil rose from $3.6 to about $4.4 billion. A smaller amount of the increased profits was attributed to accounting gains made by U.S.-based companies abroad on the devaluation of the dollar and to price increases permitted by the Nixon Administration during 1973 to alleviate the fuel shortage.

Industry representatives testifying before a Senate subcommittee that opened hearings on the energy crisis explained that the recent profit surge was based largely on the fourfold rise in prices for crude oil during 1973. (See Feature Article in the Winter, 1973, issue.) These prices were passed on from company refineries to wholesalers and, ultimately, to consumers. John Sawhill, the new director of the Federal Energy Office, said that on January 1, 1973, the typical profit on a barrel of Middle East crude oil was 79 cents. On January 1, 1974, it had jumped to $3.73, he said.

The petroleum industry defended its 1973 returns as high only in comparison with several recent years of depressed earnings. But data submitted by Secretary of the Treasury George P. Shultz to the House Ways and Means Committee (which began hearings in February on taxation of the oil industry) seemed to contradict this assertion. According to his study, average oil profits among 22 large companies for 1973 were the highest in 11 years. The rate of return on stockholders' equity averaged 15.1 per cent in 1973 (based on the first three quarters), compared with 10.9 per cent for the previous 10 years. The average for previous years ranged from a low of 9.7 in 1972 to a high of 11.8 per cent in 1968.

Some petroleum executives have also maintained that higher earnings in 1973 enabled oil's lagging return on equity (total investment) to pull up even with other manufacturing industries. But, according to the Federal Trade Commission, the rate of return on equity for oil has averaged the same as that for manufacturing—about 10.3 per cent. Only 1972 was exceptional, when oil's rate of return was 8.5 per cent, as compared with 12.0 for manufacturing. It was estimated that for 1973 both oil and other industries earned about 12 per cent on their investments.

Another measurement of profitability, often considered a better indicator in an industry with rapid turnover such as gasoline marketing, is profit taken as a percentage of sales. According to this measure, oil-industry profits for the first three quarters of 1972 were 6.5 per cent, compared with 4.2 for all manufacturing. During 1973, oil profitability rose to 7.4 per cent, compared with 4.7 for all manufacturing.

Big Oil's Bad Image

In attempting to refute allegations of windfall profits at a time of national emergency, the petroleum industry has been handicapped by what may be the worst public image in American business. A Gallup poll taken in January indicated that more Americans (25 per cent) blamed the oil industry for the fuel shortage than any other cause, including the Arab boycott. By cultivating close relationships with political leaders and ignoring the public, oilmen had developed a false sense of security—which was rapidly dissipated as congressmen, spurred by angry constituents, called for regulation of the "oiligarchy."

Major petroleum companies tried to improve the industry's image by blanketing the mass media with a multimillion-dollar public-relations campaign. In a radical departure from past policies of secrecy, executives held press conferences and gave interviews to explain their earnings and persuade consumers that higher profits are necessary for the development of future sources of energy.

As a capital-intensive industry, oil requires (in the view of its executives) a higher rate

6

A pattern of complacency and a lack of long-range government planning have contributed to heating-oil and gasoline shortages.

of return on investment than the average—perhaps 16 per cent instead of 12. Traditionally, the petroleum industry has financed its investments primarily through retained earnings (unlike other industries, which rely more heavily on borrowing for this purpose).

The industry anticipates a need for $800 billion in capital for 1970 through 1985 to finance exploration for new pools of oil, constructing plants to process oil shale and tar sands, building new pipelines and refining capacity, and developing coal-gasification and -liquefaction techniques. But many of the oil companies have indicated that increasing dividends to their stockholders has a higher priority in their plans than increasing investment.

An increasing proportion of new investment is going into domestic operations. The profitability of overseas investments has been jeopardized by several recent trends. Oil-producing members of the Organization of Petroleum Exporting Countries (OPEC) have acquired expanding shares in the ownership of companies operating within their territories. (See *Persian Gulf* in the 1974 yearbook.) Marketing agreements are being made directly between the governments of oil-consuming and OPEC nations, bypassing the lucrative role the petroleum companies have played in wholesaling crude oil from the Middle East to refiners and other customers in Europe and Japan. Through these bartering arrangements, the consuming nations trade their own products for petroleum (saving their stocks of foreign reserves, such as dollars) while the OPEC governments pocket what would have been the oil companies' marketing profits.

OPEC hiked the posted price of crude oil from $2.59 to $11.65 per barrel during 1973. (The posted price is an artificial price used by oil-producing countries to compute taxes and royalties on their crude oil. In recent years, it has run about 40 per cent above the actual market price.) The higher prices may dampen the rate of growth in demand for petroleum abroad. If so, the oil companies could find their profits cut in Europe and Japan.

A Shortage of Policy

An investigation by the New York *Times* into national energy policies revealed that a pattern of complacency and a lack of long-range government planning have contributed more to the recent heating-oil and gasoline shortages than any conspiracy on the part of the petroleum industry.

Past policies toward energy consumption were based on the concept of unlimited economic growth and virtually limitless natural resources. As a result, the annual consumption of petroleum in the United States shot up from 1.9 billion barrels in 1947 to 5.6 by 1972, with the United States using one-third of the world's production of energy. In 1952, the president's Materials Policy Commission had warned of the "extraordinarily rapid rate at which we are utilizing our materials and energy resources," but this report and other early warnings of an impending energy shortage were disregarded.

Federal tax policies during the 1950's encouraged investment abroad, rather than domestic exploration, drilling, and refining. Special tax allowances granted to the petroleum industry included deductions for drilling costs, the 22 (formerly 27.5) per cent depletion allowance, and foreign tax credits.

The drilling deduction reduces the expense of exploring for new wells. The depletion allowance, which is also granted to producers of other minerals, is based on the theory that the producers' assets are being depleted as minerals are removed from the ground. In the case of the oil industry, 22 per cent of the profits derived from the production of crude oil are exempt from income taxes.

The foreign tax credit permits oil com-

Most U.S. citizens are paying almost 50 per cent more for their gasoline than they were in 1970. The oil companies are making less money on foreign oil—but, as the graphs show, are making more on domestic oil.

panies to deduct taxes or royalties paid to the producer governments from their United States income taxes. A secret agreement made in 1950 by the Treasury and State departments allowed the companies to credit part of the royalty against their U.S. income taxes, on a dollar-for-dollar basis. Thus, in 1950, Aramco paid federal taxes of $50 million, and paid $66 million to the government of Saudi Arabia. In 1951, the company turned over $110 million to Saudi Arabia, but its federal taxes dropped to $6 million.

Under the profit-sharing system that came into use at this time, a "posted price"—originally tied to the higher cost of oil produced in the Gulf of Mexico—was established by the companies for oil from the Middle East. After subtracting production costs and a royalty to the producer governments of 12.5 per cent, the remaining profit was divided evenly between the governments and the corporations. The 50-per-cent foreign "income tax" could then be deducted from U.S. tax liabilities.

Critics of the oil foreign-tax credit believe that it has served primarily to prop up reactionary regimes abroad, while subsidizing the petroleum companies at the expense of the American taxpayer. According to the Petroleum Industry Research Foundation, most of the major oil companies have paid little or no U.S. income taxes on foreign earnings since the mid-1960's. In fact, they have accumulated surplus tax credits which are unusable except through the creation of subsidiary industries, such as shipping. A transfer of excess tax credits from the production of crude oil thus allows subsidiary businesses to pay reduced taxes on their profit-making operations.

Throughout the 1950's and most of the 1960's corporate profits rose, due to expanded output, declining production costs, and tax benefits. As more and more producers entered the field, however, the world-

wide supply of petroleum increased to a point that threatened to depress the international price the major companies had established.

Defense planners worried about reliance on foreign energy sources and U.S. oil producers without overseas interests were becoming alarmed at the growing volume of cheaper foreign petroleum entering the United States. These pressures led the Eisenhower Administration in 1959 to place mandatory import restrictions on petroleum for "national security" purposes.

The imposition of import quotas protected the higher price of domestic petroleum, but it had unforeseen political and economic consequences. The international market became flooded with petroleum from a host of new producers frozen out of the U.S. market. Because of the oil glut the majors took steps to lower their posted prices and thus keep their oil competitive in Europe. But this move angered the producing governments because it reduced their income. It led directly to the formation in 1960 of the Organization of Petroleum Exporting Countries (OPEC), a kind of producers' cartel established by Venezuela and the oil-rich Middle East nations.

A number of other policy decisions made by the federal government during the 1950's came to be seen as errors during the 1970's. The oil industry had persuaded the Eisenhower Administration to abandon research on fuel conversion, such as the gasoline-from-coal experiments begun by the Germans during World War II. In 1956, work began on the 42,000-mile interstate-highway system. As money was poured into the promotion of airliners and large cars, means of transportation that were more energy-efficient, such as railroads, were going bankrupt.

By the late 1960's it was becoming clear that the United States was facing an unanticipated shortage of oil-refinery capacity. Mobil, for example, increased its U.S. refining by only 25 per cent between 1963 and 1972, while its refining operations abroad rose 137 per cent during the same period. Industry spokesmen cite uncertainty whether supplies of crude oil would be adequate as a major reason for their failure to step up domestic refinery capacity. But when the Nixon Administration's Task Force on Import Controls recommended that import quotas on oil be lifted, the petroleum industry registered a vehement complaint. President Nixon rejected the task-force report in August, 1970.

Administration officials have generally agreed with the oil companies that price controls and increased demand were the immediate cause of the heating-oil and gasoline shortages that struck the nation. When President Nixon imposed wage and price controls in August, 1971, gasoline prices were frozen at seasonal highs, while heating oil remained stuck at off-season lows, creating a disincentive for the production of heating oil for the coming winter. The first effects of the energy crisis became evident a few months later, as spot shortages of heating oil occurred around the country.

In the first half of 1972, industry profits declined nearly 5 per cent, although sales and demand were up. Domestic crude production began to decline, and refinery production was below the level of the same period in 1971. As summer approached, the output of gasoline was stepped up, but this delayed the production of heating oil for the following season.

In September, 1972, President Nixon increased allowable imports of foreign oil for the second time in five months and appealed to the industry to produce heating oil at maximum capacity. (Stocks of heating oil and supplies of crude oil had by this time fallen to the lowest level since World War II.) Yet, for reasons that are not entirely clear, the industry imported only one-third of the addi-

The dramatic jump in Middle East crude prices

Period	Posted price*	tax	Total cost [production cost plus tax]
1960-65	$1.80	$0.82	$0.92
1966-67	1.80	0.85	0.95
1968-69	1.80	0.68	0.98
Jan. 1—Nov. 14, 1970	1.80	0.91	1.01
Nov. 15, 1970—Feb. 14, 1971	1.80	0.99	1.10
Feb. 15—May 31, 1971	2.18	1.26	1.37
June 1, 1971—Jan. 19, 1972	2.28	1.32	1.43
Jan. 20, 1972—Jan. 1, 1973	2.48	1.44	1.55
Jan. 1—Mar. 31, 1973	2.59	1.51	1.62
Apr. 1—May 31, 1973	2.75	1.61	1.71
June, 1973	2.90	1.70	1.80
July, 1973	2.95	1.74	1.84
Aug., 1973	3.07	1.80	1.90
Oct. 1—Oct. 15, 1973	3.01	1.77	1.87
Oct. 16—Dec. 31, 1973	5.12	3.05	3.15
Jan. 1, 1974	11.56	7.00	7.10

*Posted price is the base on which OPEC countries figure their tax; it bears little relationship to the producers' selling price.

Data: International Crude Oil & Product Prices
Source: *Business Week*

Where the money goes (per gallon of gasoline)

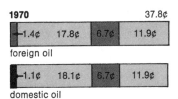

1970   37.8¢
1.4¢ 17.8¢ 6.7¢ 11.9¢
foreign oil

1.1¢ 18.1¢ 6.7¢ 11.9¢
domestic oil

1974   54.9¢
21.3¢ 9.4¢ 10.0¢ 14.2¢
foreign oil

2.1¢ 28.6¢ 10.0¢ 14.2¢
domestic oil

■ U.S. landowner
▨ foreigners
□ oil company
▨ service station
□ taxes

tional allowance and ran most refineries below capacity for the remainder of the year. This made the gasoline shortages of 1973 inevitable, even before the Arab oil boycott.

After the Middle East war of October, 1973, the price of both foreign and domestic petroleum skyrocketed. This was due in large part to successful efforts by OPEC to raise the posted price of their crude oil. But the average price of domestic oil rose almost as fast, doubling to an average of $7 per barrel in the 12-month period that ended February, 1974. For the consumer, these price hikes were reflected in the cost of gasoline, which rose 19.7 per cent in 1973, fuel oil (48.6 per cent), and propane and some other distillates (300 per cent).

Structure of the Industry

Widespread suspicion that the major oil companies had profited from shortages at the expense of their independent competitors has focused new attention on the structure of the petroleum industry. In the United States, 18 corporations produce about 80 per cent of the refinery capacity and market 72 per cent of the gasoline sold.

These huge companies are vertically integrated—that is, involved in all stages of the petroleum business, from exploration, drilling, and production, to transport, refining, and marketing. Critics of the majors charge that they have maintained a cartel which has enabled them to set artificially high prices at the oil-production level, where most of the tax breaks are concentrated. At the same time, they maintain rock-bottom margins in the refining and marketing phases of the business, to reduce competition from the independents (many of whom must purchase their crude supplies from the majors).

Although the majors insist that their operations are fully competitive against one another, they are horizontally integrated in various ways. Through their joint ventures,

The oil companies are involved in all stages of the petroleum business, from exploration, drilling, and production, to transport, refining, and marketing.

for example, the risk of exploring a new field or building a pipeline is divided between several companies. In the Middle East, every concession after 1954 has been operated by two or more of the seven largest multinational firms (Royal Dutch-Shell, Mobil, Gulf, British Petroleum, California Standard, Texaco, and Exxon, formerly Standard of New Jersey).

Through long-term supply contracts, the companies match up producers of crude oil with appropriate marketing areas. Other examples of horizontal cooperation include joint bids on multimillion-dollar leases of government oil reserves, and reciprocal processing agreements, which enable one company to have its crude oil refined in a place where it lacks facilities, in exchange for a similar favor to the other company.

Just as international markets have often been divided among the majors through agreements designed to reduce competition, a similar trend toward regional-market specialization has been observed in the United States during the past few years. Nearly all of the majors have cut back their operations in certain regions to increase efficiency and profits on transport and marketing operations. For instance, ARCO sold its Florida service stations to Mobil, Gulf pulled out of the West Coast, and Exxon left Illinois.

According to a study completed by the Federal Trade Commission in the summer of 1973, this rearrangement of the domestic market may have the effect of preventing further growth in competition from independent marketers. Independent dealers had increased their share of the national gasoline retail market from 10 to 25 per cent between 1960 and 1972. They were able to do so by cutting advertising costs, selling gas in volume at 3¢ to 6¢ less per gallon than the majors, and operating no-frills self-service stations.

But all of the independent marketers were dependent upon the majors for their supplies of gasoline, either directly or through independent refiners. When the oil shortage began, the majors cut back deliveries to their independent customers on the grounds that they needed available supplies for their own distributors. (It was also reported in February that some major oil companies unhappy with the government's allocation program were actually diverting much of their available foreign crude oil to refineries in Europe, Japan, and the Caribbean, rather than sell some of it to their competitors, as required by federal regulations.)

Thousands of independent stations were forced to shut down or lose their competitive edge by raising prices. The number of gasoline stations in the nation peaked in 1969 at about 222,000 and has since declined to 216,000. Although the total impact of the oil shortage on station closings is as yet not known, some preliminary studies have indicated that the failure rate has been much higher for independents than for the majors' outlets.

On the basis of its investigation, the Federal Trade Commission instituted an antitrust suit against eight major oil companies in 1973, accusing them of collusion to monopolize the petroleum industry. In its suit, the FTC alleges that these companies "maintained and reinforced a noncompetitive market structure in the refining of crude oil into petroleum products" by "pursuing a common cause of action to abuse and exploit the means of gathering and transporting crude oil to refineries . . . participating in restrictive or exclusionary transfers of ownership of crude oil among themselves and with other petroleum companies . . . using their vertical integration to keep profits at the crude level artificially high and profits at the refining level artificially low . . . to the exclusion or detriment of independent refiners." The suit also maintains that similar practices have

enabled the firms to gain "monopoly power" over the marketing of petroleum products.

The FTC action (and similar suits filed by the states of Florida and Connecticut) is expected to result in years of litigation. One possible result would be a form of divestiture under which different segments of the business would be split up. (There is a precedent in a 1948 edict which separated the production and distribution sectors of the motion-picture industry.)

Governmental Regulation

One by-product of the energy shortage will be increased federal regulation of the petroleum industry. The Federal Energy Office created by the Nixon Administration to deal with the crisis has become involved in nearly every phase of the business, from price controls on crude oil to directives on the size of inventories and the distribution of refined products.

But federal efforts to supervise the petroleum industry have been hampered by the complete dependence of government agencies on information provided by the industry through trade associations, the American Petroleum Institute, and reports to other organizations and to state governments. As a preliminary corrective measure, the Federal Energy Office and the Internal Revenue Service have taken steps to audit the price, profit, and supply records of every petroleum refinery in the nation to verify recent price increases (which must be limited to increased costs).

A more formal reporting system will probably be developed to provide federal agencies with accurate information on the country's energy supplies and needs. (The FTC has turned up evidence of such abuses as systematic underreporting of natural-gas reserves by the petroleum industry.) Senators Henry Jackson of Washington and Gaylord Nelson of Wisconsin have co-authored a bill

> **During the coming years, Americans must decide to what extent, and for whose benefit, publicly owned resources will be developed.**

to create a Bureau of Energy Information, which would collect data on the profits, costs, reserves, production, and inventories of energy companies.

Congressional investigations into the oil companies' spectacular 1973 profits generated a number of other regulatory proposals, from imposition of an "excess-profits" tax to calls for virtual nationalization of the industry. Many critics of the industry would like to see the depletion allowance and the drilling deductions repealed. (However, elimination of the depletion allowance would hurt the small independents far more than the majors.)

Senator Jackson has called for the charter of all large oil companies by a federal agency. This body would prescribe certain rules of operation, place a public representative on the board of each company, and require clearance for such actions as acquisitions and market withdrawals. Under these conditions, the petroleum industry would be regulated much like a public utility.

Senator Adlai Stevenson III of Illinois and eight other senators have co-sponsored a bill under which a federal oil and gas corporation would be set up to explore federal lands and waters, which contain most domestic petroleum reserves. To promote competition in the petroleum industry, any crude oil produced by the public corporation would be sold to independent refiners. While Stevenson calls the bill an alternative to Jackson's proposal, the oil industry views it as a step toward nationalization.

The uncertain economic conditions in the Middle East and Europe are expected to result in a shift of petroleum capital back to the United States in 1974. At the same time, higher prices for domestic oil have opened up many new prospects for domestic production. Expensive secondary and tertiary techniques of production, which utilize water flooding and chemical treatment to recover a larger proportion of oil from a well, became worthwhile when the price of decontrolled oil rose to $10 per barrel. As a result, a 15-year downward trend in domestic drilling is being reversed. New leases obtained by petroleum companies on offshore-oil tracts in the Gulf of Mexico and government-owned oil shale lands in the Rocky Mountains will bolster this expansion of domestic drilling.

The goals of environmentalists will receive a lower priority than in the past decade. After a three-year delay, the industry received congressional approval, at the height of the Arab oil embargo, for construction of the trans-Alaska pipeline. President Nixon has recommended expansion of the federal offshore leasing program, which was curbed following the Santa Barbara oil spill in 1969.

The need for expanded domestic production has also placed the Environmental Protection Agency under heavy pressure from the petroleum industry to loosen the tough pollution-abatement restrictions established by the Clean Air (1965) and Environmental Policy (1969) acts. The petroleum industry has frequently attributed the energy shortage to increased demand for gasoline created by auto emission-control devices and to obstacles to refinery construction created by conservationists.

During the coming years, Americans must decide to what extent, and for whose benefit, publicly owned resources will be developed. The petroleum industry has indicated its interest by diversifying its investment into natural gas, oil shale, coal, and uranium, as well as oil. The public interest is more difficult to define. National self-sufficiency in petroleum, a goal which has been proclaimed by President Nixon, may or may not prove to be the most desirable energy policy for the United States. But certainly, as Exxon's M. A. Wright has said, "the ad hoc, diffuse, and often conflicting approaches to individual energy issues that have characterized the past will not be adequate for the future."

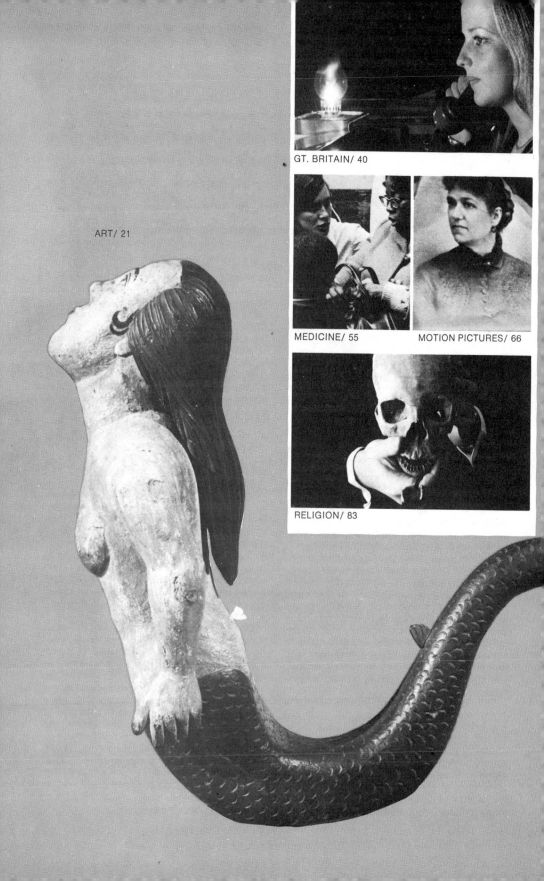

Spring 1974

Agriculture. Only a few years ago, farmers in the United States were paid not to plant certain crops, yet surpluses still piled up. Food was relatively cheap, but billions of dollars were paid to farmers in subsidy payments.

Now the "farm problem" has become to increase production fast enough to meet demand at home and abroad. For the year ending June 30, 1974, the federal government was estimating total agricultural sales to foreign customers of $20 billion. With government blessing, U.S. farmers are returning 40 million idle acres to production. And food prices have shot up—20 per cent in 1973—as Americans compete with foreigners for available supplies.

The Farm Boom

Net income for farmers rose 32 per cent in 1973. They planted about 24 million acres more than in 1972. Partly because of this added acreage, and partly because of the higher prices they are getting for their products, farmers are buying tremendous amounts of new equipment and supplies. County-seat towns, the primary trading centers for many farmers, have shared in the boom. Other sectors of the economy gain too; for example, an estimated 5,000 jobs are created to handle each $100 million of grain exports. And rising exports help the nation's balance of payments.

Increased food exports, once seen as the result of one-shot transactions such as the Soviet wheat deal or such transient phenomena as bad weather in other parts of the world, are now seen as a permanent feature of the 1970's. Rising world population and increasing affluence in many parts of the world have created a growing demand for meat and the feed grains necessary to raise poultry and livestock. A government economist says, "There are simply too many consumers in too many countries bidding for better diets to let world farm prices drop back to the levels that prevailed until the past two years."

Apparently, American consumers will be bidding against foreign consumers for some time to come. Foreign demand for soybeans boosted prices so high in 1973 that the government imposed an embargo on sales abroad for 2½ months. High prices for soybeans and other feed grains add to the expense of feeding livestock and poultry, and eventually to the cost of chicken and meat.

In February, the American Bakers Association sought to slow record exports of wheat lest the nation run out of supplies before the end of the crop year (June 30); the ABA warned that the price of bread could reach $1 a loaf. Government officials, though rejecting the association's analysis as alarmist, conceded that wheat reserves were at their lowest since the end of World War II. On January 25, President Nixon lifted import quotas in effect since 1941 in order to enable U.S. customers to expand their orders of Canadian wheat.

To save on feed costs, some ranchers were reducing their herds; others were buying cheaper grades of animal feed. These measures were likely to result in a decline in beef and milk production for 1974 (milk production had already dropped in 1973). Higher prices would follow if demand remained constant.

Farmers, in spite of their higher earnings, were disturbed at having to pay 17

Agribusiness. Arizona-Colorado Land & Cattle Corporation is engaged in the production of beef "from range to range"—grazing range to cooking range. The feedlot at right is one of the largest in the United States. The ranch at left, located adjacent to a company-developed recreational community, typifies its strategy of holding land both for ranching and future real-estate development.

per cent more for their supplies in 1973. And some were finding that supplies were not available at any price.

A shortage of fertilizer threatened to cut 1974 crop yields. The farm boom caught fertilizer producers, many of whom went out of business in the 1960's, a period of overexpansion, by surprise. With supplies scarce, fertilizer prices rose 81 per cent between the time federal controls were lifted in October, 1973, and mid-March, 1974. The demand for farm machinery was also outstripping production.

Farmers were getting fuel on a top-priority basis in spite of the oil shortage. But prices had increased by a third overall during the past year, and the price of liquefied-petroleum gas, needed to dry crops, had doubled.

Producing More Food

The sudden need for higher food production has caused concern that future food shortages could develop even more suddenly than in 1973 and that the United States might find itself unable to respond as readily. Agricultural economists figure that U.S. farms will have to increase their production of food and fiber by 32 per cent to meet demand in 1985.

Some authorities believe that there will be little difficulty in expanding U.S. farm output by 20 to 25 per cent in the next several years, if crop prices stay high, by tilling more acreage. Production could be further augmented by farming acres now under cultivation more intensively.

But there are some limits to available land. Each year more than one million acres are covered by new housing subdivisions, shopping centers, highways, and other forms of urbanization. Another 2 million acres are given over to recreation and wildlife. A few states and local governments have become so concerned over the disappearance of farmland that they have passed laws discouraging its commercial development.

And in some areas the farmland that can be brought into production is less than desirable. More land can be irrigated in the West, for example, and old cotton fields and timberland in the South can be cleared and planted with grass for cattle grazing, but these methods are expensive and may not be profitable at today's prices.

Some segments of agriculture may actually be squeezed out. Gale Johnson, an agricultural economist at the University

of Chicago, believes the dairy industry could not compete with foreign products if import quotas and other trade barriers were removed—steps favored by the Nixon Administration.

Environmentalists may limit food production. Much of the growth in agricultural production has come from farming fewer acres more intensively through the heavy use of fertilizers and other chemicals that are coming under increased scrutiny and challenge. For instance, DDT and other pesticides have been banned or restricted. Some states have limited the amounts and types of fertilizers that farmers can apply because of runoffs of the chemicals into streams. Some areas are imposing strict water-pollution controls on cattle feedlots. A growth-stimulating hormone commonly fed to cattle was banned by the federal government in 1973 because it caused cancer in some experimental animals.

The development of hybrid corn in the 1930's was probably the most dramatic advance in agriculture of this century, raising yields by more than 40 per cent. Research on hybrid wheat, hybrid soybeans, multiple calf births, and other ways of boosting production is under way, but is still in an experimental stage.

A grain-company executive concludes, "Increased production is the only way to halt the rise in food prices for the consumer . . . But with limits on acreage available for expansion, the difficulties in developing hybrids, and other problems, it's not going to be as easy as we might wish."

Agribusiness

Companies and cooperatives with $140 billion in assets supply farmers with machinery, process and distribute farm products, and in some cases raise food. These organizations include farm-equipment manufacturers, fertilizer producers, seed producers, grain processors, and meat packers.

Fears that corporations would crowd out family farmers have faded as a number of companies have lost money and dropped out of agricultural production. Still, some persist. Superior Farming Corporation is probably the most technologically advanced such company. It employs about 1,200 people to raise 27 crops on 35,000 acres in California and Arizona.

Superior Farming has a computer-programmed and monitored irrigation system in which water trickles to roots through taps installed at each plant's base. The company has a 13-acre, plastic-enclosed "tomato factory" in Tucson, Arizona, in which every agronomic variable is strictly controlled. The operation is said to produce eight times as many tomatoes as comparably sized field operations. Such innovations, however, are expensive, and the company has yet to turn a profit.

Arizona-Colorado Land & Cattle Corporation owns or leases 1.1-million acres that are to be developed into a variety of ventures, such as shopping centers and residential areas. Currently, however, much of the land is used for cattle ranching, feedlots, and meat packing. Company profits have risen handsomely, with most of the earnings from agribusiness and the remainder from land sales and development.

Charles McQuoid, a Chicago businessman, plans to start a 6,000-acre hog farm in northeastern Missouri. It would employ 2,000 people to raise and slaughter 2.5 million hogs yearly—a third of the state's total.

There are 7,700 farmer-owned cooperatives, and while most are small, six are among the nation's 500 largest corporations in sales. All told, the co-ops account for 17 per cent of all agribusiness sales. FS Services Inc., a large supply co-op, owns six feed mills, three petroleum terminals, and four seed-processing plants.

Agriculture is becoming increasingly concentrated. There are 155,000 cattle feedlots, but 711 house half of the nation's 27 million cattle annually fed in lots. About 14 per cent of the nation's crops and 36 per cent of its livestock are sold under some contractual arrangement rather than on the market, including 95 per cent of the chickens and processed vegetables. The food-processor corporations have learned that they cannot take their food supplies for granted, and the farmers and co-ops have found they need the help of large corporations to reach foreign markets.

AMERICAN FOLK ART

Among the first of dozens of exhibits planned to explore the nation's artistic heritage in celebration of its bicentennial was "The Flowering of American Folk Art 1776-1876." The exhibit opened at the Whitney Museum of American Art in New York City February 1. After leaving the Whitney, it was scheduled to be shown at the Virginia Museum of Fine Arts in Richmond from April 22 to June 2, then at the M. H. De Young Memorial Museum in San Francisco from June 24 to September 15.

Displayed were some 300 objects produced by nonacademic artists and artisans during the first century of independence. Paintings were only a portion of the display. There were also rugs, toys, pottery, furniture, weathervanes, shop signs, ships' figureheads, carvings on whale's teeth, quilts, embroidery, gravestones—nearly everything that touched the lives of 19th-century Americans.

Jean Lipman, former editor of *Art in America*, and Alice Winchester, former editor of *Antiques* magazine, organized the show. They chose, from more than 10,000 pieces in museums and private collections, objects that display competence, ingenuity, a spirit of independence, and a feeling for materials. The exhibit presented works of folk art as objects that could be viewed as worthy in themselves and not merely as reminders of a simpler time.

An appreciation for folk art has been slow in coming. Only since the 1930's have the products of amateurs and untrained artisans come to be collected and admired. Even today, as critic Hilton Kramer remarks, "when the effigies of distant African tribesmen and the carvings of obscure Pacific islanders are a regular part of our basic courses in art appreciation, American folk art is not always given its due."

Folk Carving. This garden fountain in the form of a mermaid resembles the wooden figureheads on sailing ships. The plentiful supply of wood made it the most widely used sculptural material.

21

Painting and sculpture were regarded as useful trades— and conversely, the trades were regarded as arts.

Jean Lipman believes that the best folk art "compares with the best academic art of its time and in some instances is better." To modern taste, the academic art of the 19th century, heavily influenced by European styles, sometimes appears belabored. The folk arts and crafts seem fresher and more diverse.

"The new nation had the . . . advantage of unashamed variety, fluidity and cultural anarchy," explains Daniel J. Boorstin, senior historian of the Smithsonian Institution's Museum of History and Technology. "Americans were luckily free of the Royal Academies and National Academies that tended to cast cultures in respectable molds." Moreover, there were few art schools and no effective guilds.

Crafts and "fine art" were not firmly separated. Painting was generally regarded as a useful trade—and conversely, the trades were regarded as arts. In old records one reads references to "butchers, bakers . . . barbers, millers, masons, with all other artists," and of choosing an "artist . . . to lay our towne bounds." Painting and sculpting were practical arts: the painter recorded a likeness or painted a house, the sculptor carved a grave marker or made a figure that drew customers to a store.

Recent Interest in Folk Art

Artists interested in experimentation were the 20th century's first audience for early folk art. They were attracted to the free mixing of media and the dominance of design and abstraction. They, and modernist collectors, were the first serious buyers of American folk art.

Characteristics of folk art, such as flat patterns, repeated motifs, arbitrary color, and sharp-edged shapes, appeared in the work of experimenting artists, influencing the public's taste. The modern viewer therefore brings to the work of naive artists different habits of taste than earlier viewers had.

Traditional patterns for quilts, used over and over with slight modifications, were for years dismissed as repetitive craft exercises. Today, the geometric patterns and brilliant colors seem to foreshadow the work of later abstract painters and to compete with the work of contemporary graphic designers. Common motifs of flags, eagles, and flowers provided a genuine popular imagery that, for contemporary viewers, is almost a put-down of the pop-art movement. The folk artist was not expressing a personal view; his style and designs reflected communal taste.

Painting

Untrained artists began to be active in America in the mid-18th century. It has been said that during the first half of the 19th century there was more painting done, in proportion to the population, than at any other time in the history of the country.

The early artists used a variety of materials and techniques. Their vibrant colors often were made from natural substances, such as berries and brick dust. Still lifes sometimes combine stencil techniques with free-hand drawing. One portrait artist posed her subjects in profile, traced their shadows on paper, and filled in the details.

What look like paintings from a distance can turn out to be collages. In an effort at realism, artists affixed to their paintings pieces of gold and silver paper cut in the shapes of brooches, rings, but-

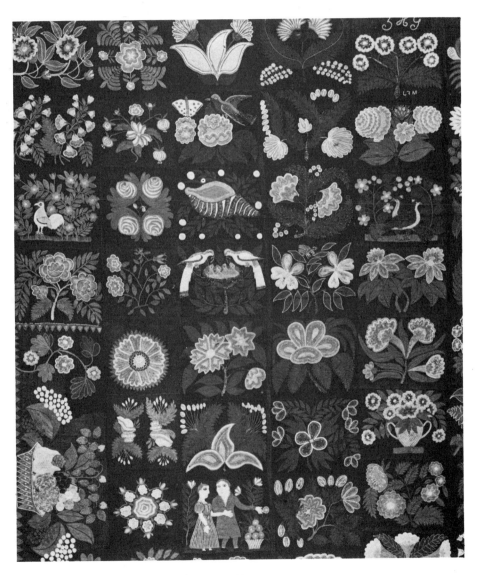

Family Portrait. Untrained artists traveled from town to town, satisfying the need of people at all levels of society to see themselves immortalized in paint.

tons, or earrings. A landscape painted in oils or watercolors might have paper figures pasted down among the trees. Compositions created with needle and thread have details added in ink.

Portraiture. Before about 1800, wealthy patrons living in cities were the main purchasers of paintings. Afterwards the market expanded, and people at virtually all levels of society began to want to see themselves immortalized in paint. The demand was so great that there were not enough trained portraitists and a class of self-taught "primitives" arose to meet the need.

These full-time painters travelled the countryside on foot or horseback soliciting business along the way. Often the painter settled briefly in a small town to do portraits of the townspeople and nearby farmers. He also supplied whatever other painting a buyer might want done, such as walls or signboards. When the commissions were filled, he moved on. When he had no commissions, or during winter when the weather made traveling difficult, he filled his time painting copies of prints, scenes from literature, and portraits of national heroes, which he took along to sell.

Differences in size and medium allowed a range in price so broad that virtually anyone could afford a portrait. Oil portraits were most expensive because they required the longest working time and the materials were costly. Watercolors and drawings were cheaper. For those at the bottom of the economic scale there were paper cutouts of silhouettes. Many portraits were only a few inches high.

Because the untrained artist had trouble with perspective, foreshortening, and composition, he usually learned a few sim-

ple poses and used them again and again. The watercolorist worked in the easiest and most direct manner, usually outlining and filling the spaces with even washes of color, then adding details in ink. The commissioner of a portrait in the early 19th century was generally uncritical of the artist's work. He had little acquaintance with art other than shop signs and was happy to see any likeness of himself and his family in paint.

Later, books and magazines illustrated with prints made their way into even the rural areas and people became more familiar with the academic art of Europe. Copies and diluted versions of woodcuts, engravings, paintings, and sculpture also appeared as illustrations on playing cards and advertisements for fairs. The folk artist often borrowed from these prototypes, imitating a style but also adapting, accentuating, or simplifying different elements to meet his patron's requirements or to fit his own abilities.

By the middle of the century, photography had become commonplace. Portraiture suffered most from the new invention. The photographic likeness seemed much more accurate, and as a result portrait-painting declined quickly.

Fraktur. Fraktur was a folk art of Germany brought to America by immigrants in the middle of the 18th century. It was an adaptation of manuscript illumination based on Gothic script. Here, among the Pennsylvania Dutch, it developed into a fresh and independent art form.

Borders of birds, flowers, animals, hearts, and angels enclosed hand-lettered passages from the Bible or other important texts. The designs were drawn in ink

Blanket Chest,
made of painted wood.

Abraham Lincoln. A more skillful sculptor than the anonymous Illinois whittler might have produced a more graceful work, but the straightness of the block of hard wood from which it was carved lends a feeling of uprightness and patriotism to the figure.

and filled in with washes of bright colors. Originally the designs were used to enhance a text, but eventually pictures were done in the same style without a text. The Fraktur style was even used to decorate chests, tables, and household utensils.

Birth and baptismal certificates were the most popular form of Fraktur. They were hung on walls or kept in family Bibles, and the large number that survived are valued today for their genealogical information as well as their aesthetic appeal. Another common Fraktur was a handwriting specimen used by schoolchildren learning to write.

Originally, the Fraktur artist was a local minister or schoolteacher; later itinerant artists went from town to town inquiring about recent births and offering certificates to parents. Because the basic text and decoration were prepared in advance and only the names and dates were filled in later, they could offer a variety of designs.

The printing of birth certificates, which became practical at the beginning of the 19th century, caused the art of Fraktur to diminish. During the 1830's Frakturs of all kinds began to be lithographed, and these were neater, cheaper, and more accurate than the ones done by hand. By the Civil War, the Fraktur artist had disappeared.

Sculpture

The plentiful supply of wood made it the most widely used sculptural material. Shop signs and figures, carved furniture, decoys, architectural ornaments, and small toys came from the hands of professional and amateur woodcarvers. Weathervanes and sometimes shop signs were done in metal.

Common motifs of flags, eagles, and flowers provided a genuine popular imagery.

Woodcarving and metalwork, being usually utilitarian, were not in competition with the products of academic artists—as was painting—so they could more easily develop in their own styles. Weathervanes are vigorous and original, duck decoys beautifully simplified.

For the folk carver, the nature of the material did not dictate the form. Forks of limbs and direction of grain were often ignored. Logs were bolted together, knotholes filled in rather than worked into the design.

Sometimes, even when the craftsmanship is crude, the result is still forceful and appealing. A standing figure of Abraham Lincoln is straight and squared, revealing the block of hard wood from which it was carved. A more skillful sculptor than the anonymous Illinois whittler might have produced a more graceful work, but here the straightness lends a feeling of uprightness and patriotism to the figure.

The carving of ships' figureheads developed into a major art form. A few examples that survive suggest the high quality that must have prevailed, though most of the work produced during the early 19th century has been lost. The art came to an end as the iron steamship and the railroad replaced the sailing ship with its carved wooden figurehead.

Gravestone carving was also a major sculptural form. The designs and shapes of gravestones were brought from England, and a strong artisan tradition developed in New England. The stones produced at populous centers like Boston and Newport were sophisticated works with elegant lettering and decorative carving, while in isolated places locally developed

styles flourished. The stones of this period—particularly around the turn of the century—were a highly original form of art; by the second half of the 19th century the traditional artistry had been replaced by carvings of urns, weeping willows and other reflections of academic sculpture.

Other Crafts

Many of the items on display were made by professionals—that is, by people who made a living by their art or craft. Furniture, portraits, and gravestones were products of respected artisans, some of whom have been identified.

Other objects are by amateurs or part-time craftsmen whose names are not known. They may be one-time efforts, like the gate made by a farmer in the pattern of the American flag. The design, with its horizontal wooden slats painted alternately red and white, adapts perfectly to the low rectangular shape of a pasture gate and is unforced.

Perhaps the largest group of anonymous artists of the period were the women who created the quilts, rugs, tablecloths, and samplers that filled their homes. One painting at the exhibit commemorates a gathering of neighbors to work on a quilt. The hours of labor spent with traditional patterns and methods produced works of utility and great craftsmanship, many of which are regarded today as masterpieces of art.

This exhibit of folk art in a museum usually associated with the most advanced art of modern times represents a significant change in attitude. Craft items that used to be left to antique shops and historical restorations are being viewed for their own intrinsic qualities.

Early Pop Art. This painted wooden gate was
made by a farmer a century ago in the pattern
of the American flag. The geometric patterns
and brilliant colors make the work
strikingly contemporary.

Business and Finance. On February 1, Nixon Administration spokesmen asked Congress to let the Economic Stabilization Act expire April 30 and thereby end wage and price controls for all but two industries —health care and petroleum products. The Cost of Living Council would remain in existence, equipped with fact-finding powers and summoning industries to public hearings, if necessary, to explain why they had raised prices. CLC Director John Dunlop was negotiating "decontrol agreements" with large companies in various industries in order to limit future price increases, with the understanding that the Administration might ask Congress to re-impose controls on industries that refused to go along with such agreements.

Business leaders said that controls, first imposed in August, 1971, had discouraged investment, dried up supplies, created black markets, and generally disrupted orderly business. A poll taken by the National Association of Manufacturers showed that more than 90 per cent of the companies contacted favored an immediate end to controls. Another survey found that more than 60 per cent of corporate purchasing agents contacted said supply problems had been caused or aggravated by price controls. Large quantities of raw materials were said to have been shipped to Europe because prices were higher there than in the United States.

Immediately exempted on February 1 from price and wage curbs were all retailers still under controls except those that sell food, motor vehicles and parts, and petroleum products. The decision left only about 25 per cent of retail sales under controls, which allow prices to rise only to reflect wholesale price increases in merchandise, and not those of an operating nature, such as labor, taxes, and insurance.

The Cost of Living Council obtained commitments from the 10 largest retail chains that, through August 1, they would hold pretax operating profit margins to levels no higher than those realized through the fiscal year that ended January 31, 1974.

Auto Sales Drop

The oil shortage (see PETROLEUM in this section) led to a slump in automobile sales. By early March, the auto industry had laid off more than 80,000 workers, and March production was expected to fall 30 per cent below the levels of a year earlier.

A desire for small cars with better gas mileage was affecting at least eight auto plants throughout the country. Reconversion to small-car production was said to constitute the biggest change the industry had made since the World War II switch to military production and would cost the Big Three automakers hundreds of millions of dollars.

General Motors, with its product line consisting mainly of large cars, saw its sales drop 47.5 per cent in February, 1974, compared to February, 1973. Ford and Chrysler slipped in sales by 29.5 per cent and 22.8 per cent, respectively. American Motors, which specializes in small cars, reported a gain of 4.7 per cent. The total decline in domestic sales was 36.8 per cent.

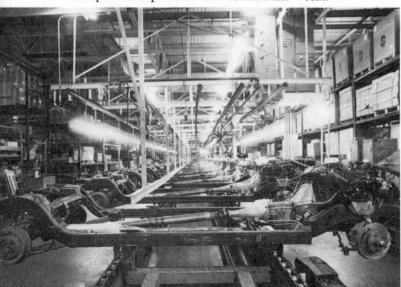

Closed Ford Plant. Several auto-assembly factories cut back production or converted to small-car manufacturing as sales of large automobiles plummeted.

Shortage of Materials

American manufacturers were faced with a shortage of vital petrochemical products as a result of the oil shortage. The textile industry was short of polyesters and acrylics, which have largely supplanted natural fibers. The plastics industry was suffering from a lack of benzene, the principal raw material. Transportation, construction, and the manufacture of furniture, toys, electronic products, and phonograph records were also affected.

Farmers feared a shortage of fertilizers, resulting not only from a lack of petroleum-product feedstocks, but also because of the effect of price controls, which made selling fertilizer abroad more profitable than selling it at home. Strikes in Canada, price controls that made added production unprofitable, and soaring demand were blamed for shortages of newsprint and coarse paper.

Price of Gold Soars

Gold was sold at a record $186 an ounce on February 26 in the London market—more than double its value a year earlier and $60 an ounce higher than the price at the end of 1973. (The rate for official transactions between governments is $42.22 an ounce.) The demand for gold was due to a lack of confidence in paper currencies. Inflation in the Common Market nations was averaging 10 per cent a year, and the pound had lost 20 per cent of its value since late 1971.

On January 19, the French government in effect devalued the franc by 4 to 5 per cent by allowing it to float for six months. The government decided not to support the franc although France had been an advocate of fixed rates and had joined with five other Common Market nations in an agreement to keep their currencies aligned.

Foreign Investment in U.S.

New foreign investment in the United States amounted to only $385 million in 1971 and $708 million in 1972. But in 1973 the sum rose to $3 billion, bringing total foreign investment to a minimum of $17 billion by 580 overseas firms.

By contrast, American investment abroad is worth at least $100 billion. IBM dominates the computer market in Europe. Du Pont operates 80 plants in 70

New Gold Rush. The U.S. $20 gold piece—the double eagle—jumped in value from $175 to $375 in three months. The demand for gold was due to a lack of confidence in paper money by people worried about inflation. It is illegal for U.S. citizens to own gold bullion, but they can hold gold in the form of coins, jewelry, works of arts, or nuggets.

countries. American interests own or control 45 per cent of Canada's manufacturing operations. Even large countries such as France and Britain have feared that they would become American colonies.

It was ironic, therefore, that in early 1974 three congressional committees were studying whether foreign control of U.S. corporations should be outlawed or more tightly controlled. Aside from laws limiting foreign ownership of radio and television stations, air carriers, and merchant ships, the United States has no protective statutes. Almost every other major country in the world has laws allowing the government to veto foreign acquisitions in key sectors of the economy.

In recent years British interests have bought into such well-known companies as Gimbel Brothers, Grand Union supermarkets, and TraveLodge Motels. Switzerland's Nestlé Alimentana acquired Litton Industries from Stouffer Foods for $100 million in 1973. Michelin, the French tiremaker, plans to build a $200-million plant in the Carolinas.

Japanese firms have invested more than $250 million in Hawaii alone, including acquisition of 11 hotels and 2 Honolulu golf courses. The Sony Corporation is making television sets in San Diego. The Japanese have also bought farmland in the Midwest, are opening a steel mill in Auburn, New York, and are buying into U.S. coal mines. Arab interests (see PETROLEUM, subtitle *Middle East Oil Wealth*)

are expected to invest at least $1 billion in American real estate in 1974 and 1975.

Foreign investors say there are many excellent values in American stocks, and businesses abroad find it easy to borrow dollars in Europe. In some industries, it is possible to produce goods as cheaply in the United States as overseas. Moreover, by manufacturing goods in the United States, foreign companies can sell to the U.S. market without the burden of trade barriers.

Senator Adlai Stevenson III of Illinois has voiced concern over the possibility that foreign ownership of natural resources such as coal mines, timber, and farmlands could result in diversion of scare foodstuffs and materials overseas. Representative John Moss of California has introduced a bill designed to prevent foreign takeovers in the energy and defense industries. Representative John Dent of Pennsylvania would go even further, prohibiting foreign ownership of more than 5 per cent of any U.S. corporation's voting stock.

The Nixon Administration argues against any legislative restrictions on foreign investment. The flow of money to the United States helps improve the national balance of payments. It provides capital for industrial expansion, which in turn creates jobs. Moreover, restrictions would invite retaliation against U.S. investment in other countries.

See also AGRICULTURE.

TraveLodge Motels is one of several big companies that British interests have bought into. Foreign investors say there are many excellent values in American stocks.

China. On February 2, the official Communist party newspaper *Jenmin Jih Pao* announced "a serious class struggle and a thoroughgoing revolution in the realm of ideology in China." The paper said that the campaign involved "consolidating and carrying to a higher stage" the gains of the Cultural Revolution of 1966-69. Support for the campaign was being mobilized by groups of activists. The theme also was being sounded by official press and broadcasts, which told of mass rallies of students, soldiers, and workers in many provinces.

Although some foreign observers believed the campaign had been launched by ultraleftists as part of a power struggle, the only prominent Chinese denounced by name were former defense minister Lin Piao and the sage Confucius. The phrase used repeatedly was "Criticize Lin Piao, criticize Confucius," who were called "jackals from the same lair." Lin, once heir to party chairman Mao Tse-tung, was reportedly killed while trying to flee to the Soviet Union in 1971 and had been denounced as a traitor. The denunciation of Confucius, who lived about 2,500 years ago, seemed to be aimed at traditional Chinese concepts of right conduct, such as fulfilling family obligations and respecting education, particularly the classics. Lin was said to have been infatuated with traditional Confucian ideals.

An indication that the campaign might take a violent turn appeared in an editorial of *Hung Chi,* the Communist theoretical journal. It declared that "without destruction there can be no construction." It vowed that "all reactionary elements of the reactionary classes who dare to resist" would be "resolutely mercilessly suppressed."

The campaign appeared to be disciplined, however, with the intention of avoiding the excesses of the Cultural Revolution. This earlier effort to instill revolutionary fervor began with a purge of high officials accused of "taking the capitalist road." Soon after, shock troops of young enthusiasts called the Red Guards began intimidating teachers and industrial managers whose politics were suspect. Widespread fighting broke out between the zea-

Courtesy, Museum of Fine Arts, Boston

Confucius. The ancient Chinese sage was the target of a new campaign intended to uproot traditional Chinese concepts of right conduct.

lots and their opponents, and eventually the military was called in to restore order.

Mao was said to have been maneuvering ever since the end of the Cultural Revolution to curb the extraordinary power of the military and reestablish civilian party leadership. On New Year's Day, the government announced changes in the commands of 8 of the 11 military regions in China. Most of the commanders shifted had also been party secretaries and chairmen of provincial revolutionary committees, giving them party and government, as well as military, authority.

The 80-year-old Mao was known to fear that, without periodic reform campaigns, the party bureaucrats and industrial managers would form a new "bourgeois" class and adopt the "revisionism" of the Soviet Union. Significantly, newspapers cited examples almost every day of party officials who used their influence to save their own children from being exiled to remote rural communes to "integrate with the masses." Examples were also given of influential members of the Communist party who pulled strings to get their children admitted to college.

Confucius was denounced for holding that a man's worth is determined by the breadth of his education rather than by his class origins, for expressing disdain for physical labor, and for his belief that only an educated elite is fit to govern. China's most eminent academic philosopher, Professor Yu-lan of Peking University, had previously argued that communism was an appropriate system for modern China because it preserved the Confucian ideal of harmony. But in three articles, he repudiated Confucian thought. "The understanding of intellectuals is really not understanding at all," he concluded.

Wall posters in Chinese factories denounced the "evil tendency" to offer overtime payments and other material incentives to workers in order to stimulate higher production. The posters attacked "economism"—the argument that incentives rather than ideological fervor stimulate output. There were no published accounts of managers losing their posts, as had happened during the Cultural Revolution, but many managers were said to have been aroused from their "revisionist" thinking by delegations of workers.

Although some foreign observers believed the campaign was really aimed at Premier Chou En-lai, others thought the 76-year-old premier had adroitly joined it and had even deflected it against his opponents (some of whom had been allies of Lin). On February 24, Chou addressed a dinner attended by the diplomatic and foreign-press corps and said that the criticism of Lin Piao and Confucius was of "great immediate significance . . . in strengthening and expanding the great achievements of the great proletarian cultural revolution, consolidating the dictatorship of the proletariat, and preventing a capitalist restoration."

Foreign Influences Denounced

Hung Chi cautioned against tendencies to "worship things foreign," and many of those criticized were foreigners. Some observers saw a sharp reversal of the "Ping-Pong diplomacy" inaugurated in 1971 that led to ties with the United States, and they predicted a new tendency toward isolation and belligerence.

Owen Lattimore, an American specialist on the Far East who was one of the first Americans invited by Chou in 1971 to visit China, was called "an American reactionary historian" and "an international spy." The Italian film director Mi-

Troops Attend Rally. Mass rallies of students, soldiers, and workers were organized to denounce "reactionary elements." Premier Chou En-lai said the campaign was intended to prevent a capitalist restoration.

chelangelo Antonioni, who had made a documentary on China in 1972, was denounced for "a wild provocation against the Chinese people." The Antonioni movie was widely distributed abroad but never shown in China. Nevertheless the press featured charges by outraged workers, peasants, and soldiers that he had pointed his cameras to evoke a false impression of grim drudgery and despair.

Also attacked were such Western composers as Beethoven, called a "German capitalist composer," and Schubert, who was described as "petit bourgeois." Respighi's *Pines of Rome*, which had been performed in Peking by the Philadelphia Orchestra in September, 1973, was said to express "nasty, rotten life and decadent sentiments."

Jonathan Livingston Seagull—published in Taiwan in a Chinese-language translation—was described as "an elitist bird." A Shanghai journal said, "He is only talking about unlimited liberty for the bourgeoisie to do what they like best—to enslave, suppress, and exploit the working people."

Some observers saw indications of a more bellicose foreign policy in the Chinese occupation of the disputed Paracel Islands in January. (See VIETNAM in this section.) Simultaneously, China expelled three Soviet diplomats and the wives of two January 19, after charging them with espionage and subversion. The Chinese government had not before publicly aired charges of Soviet espionage, although it had privately expressed concern over unofficial activities by the large embassy staff, according to the London *Times*.

Disasters. All 346 persons aboard a Turkish Airlines DC-10 jumbo jet were killed March 3 when it plunged into a forest 26 miles northeast of Paris. It was the worst disaster in aviation history.

The plane was fully loaded. Turkish Airlines said that 216 passengers had boarded the jet in Paris. The flight orig-

Worst Aviation Disaster took the lives of all 346 persons aboard a DC-10 jumbo jet. The accident was blamed on the blowing out of a cargo door, causing the cabin floor to buckle downward and jam vital control cables.

inated in Istanbul, and the final destination was London.

The aft cargo door, and the bodies of six persons evidently whisked out the door opening, were found six or seven miles from the main crash site. Officials tentatively concluded that the blowing off of the door was responsible for the crash. In 1972 a DC-10 nearly crashed over Canada when the door to the left cargo compartment flew off. The sudden difference in air pressure between the pressurized passenger cabin and the cargo area below caused the cabin floor to buckle downward, breaking or jamming vital control cables from cockpit to tail. The pilot was able to land safely although the tail engines were shut down and a jammed rudder veered the plane dangerously to the right.

Soon after the Canadian incident, the McDonnell Douglas Corporation, manufacturer of the DC-10, issued a number of "service bulletins" recommending "fixes" to the system for latching the cargo door. However, the Federal Aviation Administration did not make the changes mandatory for U.S. airlines. Turkish Airlines said that the suggested improvements were made, but investigators who examined the ejected cargo door reportedly were convinced that they had not been made. On March 14, McDonnell Douglas announced an accelerated program of changes designed to make the cargo-door locking system "foolproof."

Other disasters that occurred in December, 1973, and January, February, and early March, 1974, included the following:

Bank-Building Fire in São Paulo, Brazil, took at least 189 lives. Many people panicked in the heat and jumped to their deaths from the upper floors of the 25-story building.

Aviation. All 106 persons aboard a charter flight from Paris to Tangier and Casablanca perished December 23 when the plane crashed in the Rif Mountains near Tangier. Most of the passengers were Moroccan workers or students returning home from France.

Thirty-nine of 43 persons aboard an Italian jetliner were killed January 1 when the craft crashed near Turin on a flight from Cagliari, Sardinia, while trying to land in rain and fog.

All 40 persons were killed on January 10 when a Colombian airliner crashed in the Andes Mountains. The plane was traveling from Florencia to Bogotá.

A Turkish jetliner crashed and burst into flames on takeoff from Izmir's military airport January 26, killing 63 of the 73 persons aboard. The jetliner, a Dutch-made Fokker 28 on a flight to Istanbul, rose about 400 feet and then crashed onto the runway.

A Pan American World Airways jet crashed January 31 at Pago Pago, American Samoa, killing 96 of the 101 persons aboard. An airline spokesman said the plane crashed 1,000 yards short of the runway during heavy rain squalls. The flight originated in Auckland, New Zealand, and was to have terminated in Los Angeles.

All 31 persons aboard a flight to Burbank, California, were killed March 13 when the plane crashed in the Sierra Nevadas near Bishop, California. The passengers were members of the cast and film crew of the "Primal Man" television series, returning from a film location near a mountain lake.

A Danish airliner caught fire March 15 as it taxied toward takeoff from the airport at Teheran, Iran. At least 16 persons were killed.

Fire. Twenty-three teen-age boys were killed January 23 in Heusden, Belgium, in a Catholic school-dormitory fire that police sources said might have been caused by a youth smoking in bed. About 40 boys escaped from the smoking dormitory.

At least 189 people were killed February 1 when fire spread through a 25-story bank building in São Paulo, Brazil. The injured numbered more than 100.

The fire started with a short circuit in a 12th-floor air conditioner and spread upward through the wiring system. Fire ladders were unable to reach beyond the 13th and 14th floors of the building. An air force helicopter landed on the roof and rescued at least 80 persons, but many others panicked in the heat and jumped to their deaths.

The building, completed in 1972, did not have certain safety features considered essential in the United States. The stair shaft was not sealed off at different levels, and there was no outside fire escape or sprinkler system.

Flood. At least 60 persons were killed and more than 100,000 were evacuated from their homes in three northwestern provinces of Argentina in the wake of severe flooding during three weeks of almost continuous rain in late January and early February. Damage to crops and homes was expected to reach millions of dollars. Worst hit was Santiago del Estero Province; officials reported that virtually the entire cotton harvest—one of the area's most important cash crops—had been ruined.

Marine. At least 109 persons drowned December 24 when a ferryboat carrying about 300 people—double its capacity—capsized in the Pacific Ocean off Guayaquil, Ecuador. The 167-ton vessel was on its way to Guayaquil from Puerto Bolívar.

One hundred fifty-seven South Korean navy trainees were missing and presumed dead February 22 after a tugboat carrying them capsized in the harbor of Chungmu, South Korea. A navy spokesman said 159 others who were on the 120-ton boat were pulled from the icy waters, but that two of them died later in a hospital.

Stampede. Forty-nine persons were killed and 47 injured in Cairo February 17 when thousands of Egyptian soccer fans crashed through iron gates into a stadium where the national team was about to play. Eighty thousand people were already jammed into the stadium, which officially has a capacity of 45,000, and the thousands outside were angry at being unable to gain admission.

Egypt. See MIDDLE EAST.

Energy. See PETROLEUM.

Emperor Haile Selassie has held virtually unlimited powers during his long reign in Ethiopia. But an army mutiny and civilian strikes and demonstrations forced him to dismiss his cabinet and agree to a constitutional conference that was expected to limit the powers of the monarchy.

Ethiopia. An army mutiny that began on February 25 forced 81-year-old Emperor Haile Selassie to dismiss his cabinet, give costly pay raises and benefits to the armed forces, and agree to a constitutional conference that was expected to limit the powers of the monarchy. On March 5, the emperor said that a convention would be called at an unspecified date to create a new system with more democracy. "Basic changes" were promised in economic and political life.

A 3,000-Year-Old Monarchy

According to tradition, the Ethiopian empire is 3,000 years old, and the first emperor was the son of King Solomon and the Queen of Sheba. Haile Selassie, who ascended the throne in 1930 as the 255th emperor, is said to be a direct descendant of the first emperor.

The constitution promulgated in 1955 states that "the person of the emperor is sacred, his dignity is inviolable, his power indisputable." There is a parliament, but only the lower house is elected. The cabinet is appointed by the emperor and is not responsible to the parliament. The judiciary has little independence. There are no political parties.

Despite his virtually unlimited powers, Haile Selassie has had a turbulent reign. Mussolini's troops occupied Ethiopia in 1935 and held it until 1941, when Haile Selassie returned with the support of British troops and native resistance forces. His years in power have been marked by plots, assassination attempts, provincial and ethnic revolts, and a full-scale attempt to depose him in 1960.

About 90 per cent of Ethiopia's 26 million people are farmers or herders, and 90 per cent of these are tenants on estates owned by the nobility, the royal family, or the Ethiopian Orthodox Church. The clergy and nobles have blocked the emperor's land-reform proposals.

Mutiny and New Government

The army mutiny followed four days of disorders in Addis Ababa, the capital. Demonstrators were protesting unemployment and the rising cost of living; the sharp increase in the price of oil had set off steep rises in the prices of other goods. A police statement said three people were killed in the riots, 22 wounded, and 558 arrested, and that 75 buses and 69 automobiles had been damaged.

Another cause of discontent was a reform of educational policy that was poorly explained and was seen by the middle class as a threat to their children's chances of receiving secondary schooling. (Less than 5 per cent of the people are literate, and only about a quarter of the nation's schoolchildren receive any education.) Teachers also viewed the reform as a threat to their livelihoods, since the plan proposed bringing new, less-qualified teachers into the system.

On February 25, troops in Asmara, the second largest city, mutinied, demanding pay raises. The revolt spread to other units of the 35,000-man army, and the list of grievances and demands was broadened to 22, including better housing and fringe benefits. Some soldiers also demanded political changes, such as free elections, a free press, and appointment of a new cabinet.

Haile Selassie responded by raising the pay of privates from $41 to $50 a month, but the increase was rejected as too small. Although the emperor maintained that the government could not afford further pay increases (per-capita income in Ethiopia averages only $60 a year), he later reversed himself and again raised wages. He also appointed a new army commander and a new minister of defense.

The emperor dismissed the cabinet on February 28 and appointed Ednalkatchew Makonnen, a member of the nobility who had been serving as minister of posts and communications, to be the new premier. The choice was acceptable to the army and police, although bitterly criticized by students and other radicals. Makonnen avoided any specific promises and vowed only "improvement and reform."

The army appeared anxious to quell further civilian agitation. Ethiopia is made up of diverse groups, many of which resent the dominance of the Amhara, who are concentrated in the north central high-

Army Mutiny. *Below,* the emperor's personal guard stands outside the barracks near the royal palace. Soldiers won costly pay raises and benefits. Some also demanded political changes, such as free elections and a free press.

lands. An insurgency by Moslems in Eritrea has been in existence for more than 10 years.

Civilian labor unrest followed the mutiny, however. A four-day general strike in March forced important concessions from the government. The labor-union movement won the right to organize workers in essential services such as power and communications, as well as other demands, including a readjustment after two months of the minimum wage of 50 cents a day. In addition, the government promised nationwide price controls and abolition of school fees for children of the poor.

The settlement did not end labor unrest. Teachers remained on strike and air-traffic controllers walked out on March 11. The Orthodox Church's 200,000 priests, who earn only $1.50 a month, plus food and lodging, threatened to strike.

The devastating drought, which had taken a heavy toll in lives and suffering (see DISASTERS, sidehead *Famine,* **fourth section, 1973**. was not an issue, although governmental neglect was a factor in the extent of the famine. Foreign observers concluded that the unrest had not touched the peasants and was limited to the approximately 2 million people living in towns and cities.

More changes seemed inevitable. A foreign diplomat said, "It will probably no longer be acceptable for the cabinet to appear to be merely palace servants . . . . They will have to be responsible to somebody, but since they are not elected, the question is—to whom?"

Fashion. The romantic look was favored in both haute couture and ready-to-wear styles for spring and summer. In winter haute-couture showings in Paris, the accent was on femininity and the revival of the dress. Bias-cut, unlined fabrics such as silk, crepe de chine, georgette, and shantung were favored for a soft, elegant effect. The 1930's look appeared in lower necklines and hemlines, and lighter, more delicate accessories. Skirts were often pleated, trousers always wide, and shirts cut full, with tie-necks, or bands at the wrist and elbow.

Ready-to-wear designs, which were shown in the fall of 1973 for spring, also emphasized the softer, more feminine look of the 1930's. Few pants or short skirts were shown, but below-the-knee lengths appeared in nearly every collection. The "new-old" look was complemented by floppy hats, flat shoes, and shorter hairstyles.

The New Proportion

The longer skirt lengths aroused consternation among buyers—many of whom approved of what designers called "the new proportion," but weren't so sure about their customers. The new styles reminded them of the midi-skirt, which failed to catch on in 1970. The new hemlines, which varied in length from two to four or more inches below the knee, were being promoted by *Women's Wear Daily* as "Big-Skirts." Other observers just called them "baggy."

In retail outlets, the longer skirts appeared to be selling, but in addition to both mini- and ankle-length designs. Most stores decided to offer customers an assortment of lengths. A typical viewpoint was taken by retailer Stanley Korshak of Chicago, who bought styles which hovered conservatively around the kneecap: "I can see skirts getting a little longer each season, maybe a half-inch or so at a time until they could end up two or three inches below the knee."

As it turned out, many women preferred somewhat longer skirts and dresses, but had been unable to obtain them during the midi-skirt backlash of the past few years. Others saw the new styles as a gimmick to lure women away from pant-suits and slacks. Among younger customers, popular sentiment was probably expressed by a New Jersey secretary who commented that she would substitute a skirt for pants only if the skirt stopped at least two inches above the knee.

The St. Tropez Skirt

The first romantic-looking item to catch on in a big way was the "swirl" skirt, a calf- or ankle-length flared skirt made of narrow panels and cut on the bias to swirl around the body. The panels usually alternate between solid color and a print (or two different patterns) in such materials as cotton, denim, wool, or velveteen.

The shape of the skirts differs from the

Spring Fashions. Designers showed longer skirts, including the swirl, *above*, which became a favorite on the Riviera during the summer of 1973. Also being promoted was the Great Gatsby look, inspired by the 1920's fashions shown in the motion picture that starred Robert Redford and Mia Farrow.

bias skirts of the 1930's, the pleated models of the 1950's, or the A-line of the 1960's. The swingy style originated in London, but became a summer favorite around the Riviera, especially in St. Tropez. Introduced in the United States by Saks Fifth Avenue, the swirl skirt quickly became available everywhere, even at pattern counters for the home sewer.

The Great Gatsby Look

In 1973, *Women's Wear Daily* attempted to capitalize on the Paramount Pictures remake of F. Scott Fitzgerald's *The Great Gatsby* by promoting "The Great Gatsby Look" in sportswear, evening dress, and even children's clothes. The GG label was first assigned to blue-and-red-trimmed tennis sweaters and white flannel slacks offered by ready-to-wear designer Kenzo Takada in the spring of 1973.

Besides pleated flannel slacks, the 1920's look for men included starched Panama hats, wing-tip shoes, bow ties, and sleeveless sweaters. For women, the GG look featured pleated white skirts, cloche hats, argyle sweater-vests, and hip-hugging cardigans. Makeup manufacturers jumped on the bandwagon by coming out with new pink lipsticks and blushers.

The Great Gatsby look was not expected to supersede the blue-jeans and sportswear favored by most Americans. "The Gatsby look is from the same glorious people who gave us the midi," snorted the women's editor of the New York *Times*. "It simply creates a credibility gap between the fashion industry and the real people." On the other hand, the new-old look would undoubtedly influence accessories and top-of-the-line sportswear. The clunky, chunky look in shoes, bags, jewelry, and other accessories was definitely out.

Great Britain. Prime Minister Edward Heath's Conservative government lost its majority in the House of Commons and was ousted from office as a result of parliamentary elections held on February 28. Harold Wilson, leader of the Labour party, formed a new government on March 4 although no party had secured a majority of seats. It was the first minority government in Britain in 45 years.

Heath had decided to seek a new man-

date from the voters in the midst of a national economic crisis that resulted from a coal miners' strike. A three-day work week had been imposed by the government on December 31 in order to conserve the nation's supply of coal.

In elections held in the 635 House of Commons districts, Labour candidates won 301 seats, a gain of 14 from the 1970 elections. Conservatives won 296 seats, a loss of 26. Liberals won 14, a gain of three. The other 24 seats went to smaller parties and independents. Since 318 seats were needed for a majority, the election results meant that either a Labour or Conservative government would be dependent on support from the smaller parties.

The Conservatives, though they won five fewer seats than Labour, polled 300,-000 more votes. They received 38.1 per cent of the vote while Labour won 37.2 per cent. The biggest gains were scored by the Liberals, who won 19.3 per cent of the vote compared to only 7.5 per cent in 1970. However, the Liberals won few seats since their strength was spread evenly throughout the country while the Labour and Conservative parties could count on large numbers of safe districts.

Hard-line Protestants who opposed the 1973 power-sharing agreement between Protestants and Catholics in Northern Ireland won 11 of the 12 Ulster seats. Scottish Nationalists won 7 of Scotland's 71 seats, their best showing ever. Welsh Nationalists won two seats.

Immediately following the elections, Heath attempted to stay in power. He resigned on March 4, however, after failing to persuade the Liberals to join in a governing coalition. Queen Elizabeth II then asked Wilson to form a new government.

Three-Day Work Week

The economic crisis began on November 12, when the National Union of Mineworkers banned overtime work in the coal mines. The government declared a state of emergency on the following day, thus giv-

Harold Wilson became prime minister of a minority government after his Labour party won a narrow victory in British parliamentary elections held February 28. No party was able to secure a majority of seats.

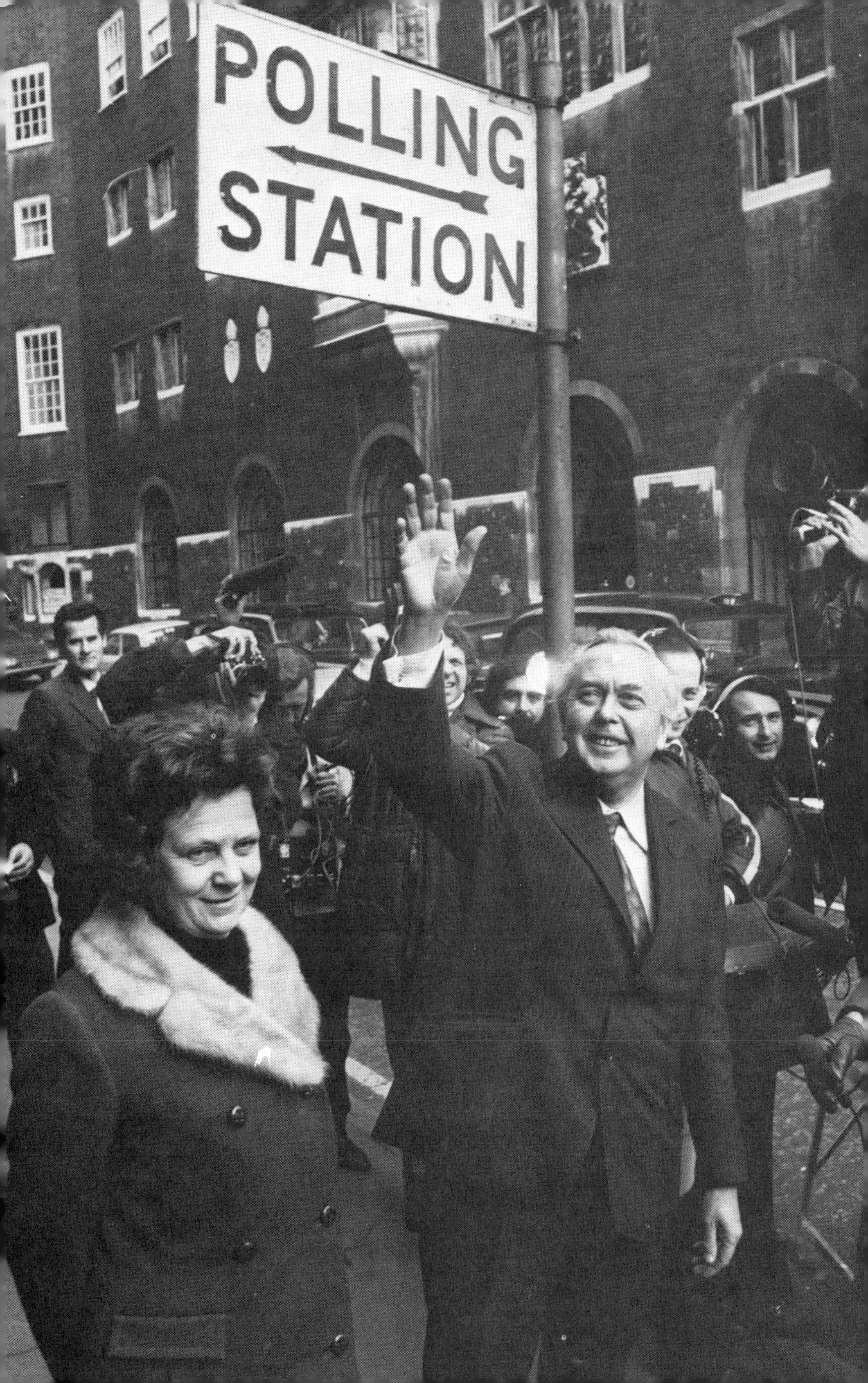
POLLING
STATION

Coal Miners first refused to work overtime, then voted to strike, in seeking a wage increase in excess of the government's guidelines. A three-day work week was imposed to conserve coal. Some stores and offices stayed open full-time, however, by using kerosene lanterns and other emergency lighting.

ing itself the power to regulate fuel distribution.

Britain's coal mines are government-owned. The miners were seeking a pay increase in excess of the government's 7-percent wage-increase guidelines. They maintained that they were underpaid relative to industrial workers. The basic wage was $55 a week for surface workers, $62 for underground miners, and $84 for the most skilled miners at the coal faces. During the campaign, government statisticians found that miners' pay had been overstated in relation to other workers; the miners were actually 8 per cent behind other manual workers in their wages.

The fuel situation became more serious when 29,000 railway engineers and firemen began a slowdown on December 12 in seeking a pay boost. Working "by the book"—that is, following all work rules strictly—and manning only trains in perfect working order, the railwaymen disrupted the distribution of coal supplies, which are generally carried by rail. The engineers also refused to work overtime or on Sundays and periodically walked off their jobs for 24 hours, stranding commuters.

With coal production cut by 40 per cent, Britain faced an energy crisis, particularly in the generation of electricity. Coal-fueled furnaces generate about 70 per cent of Britain's power. In addition, many homes are still heated by coal-burning furnaces, fireplaces, and stoves.

A three-day work week was imposed December 31 to conserve coal. Roughly half of the work force began working Monday through Wednesday and the other half from Thursday through Saturday. (In late January, Wednesday was made an overlapping day so that the second shift of workers could avoid having to work on Saturdays.) Power cutbacks were made on a geographic basis, with one area operating Monday through Wednesday, another Wednesday through Friday. The heat in almost all public buildings was turned off, and lighting for advertising signs was banned.

Food markets and vital businesses or services such as hospitals and pharmacies, dentists' and doctors' offices, laundries, mortuaries, and fuel dealers were exempted from having to curtail operations. All businesses that could remain open full time without using electric power were allowed to do so, and many companies and stores kept working with kerosene lanterns and heaters. "Continuous process" producers, such as steel or glass manufacturers, were not shut down, but they were required to reduce their power consumption by 35 per cent, which meant reducing production and laying off workers.

The curb on electricity was not applied to residences, and pubs, restaurants, movies, theaters, clubs, and bingo parlors were among the exempted "essential" industries. But television stations were shut down at 10:30 P.M. each evening.

Manufacturing production fell to between 70 and 80 per cent of normal. About 700,000 people were laid off their jobs. Ten million of the 25 million people employed in Britain were believed to be covered by guaranteed weekly wage agreements, but even many of these workers suffered a loss of income, because there was no compensation for overtime lost.

The government presented an offer that it said would increase the miners' pay by about 16.5 per cent, but the basic across-the-board increase was still only 7 per cent, and the union demanded a larger increase. On January 21, the Trades Union Congress, whose 10 million members include the 270,000 coal miners, proposed that the government grant the miners a larger pay increase in return for a pledge that other unions would not increase their pay demands commensurately. But Prime Minister Heath maintained that the TUC had not given adequate guarantees of the compliance of individual unions with this proposal, although officials of more than 100 unions endorsed it.

By a 4-to-1 margin, the miners on January 31 and February 1 authorized a full-fledged strike. Three days later, Heath asked union officials to accept the government's pay offer and await the findings of a new impartial board that was expected to suggest additional pay. But the mineworkers' union replied that it wanted more money promised immediately. The miners went out on strike February 10.

On March 6, the new Labour government and the miners reached agreement on a pay increase that met the union's demands virtually in full. The miners received an average wage increase of 35 per cent—their most generous settlement ever. The increase was expected to cost the government $230 million more a year to run the coal industry and would undoubtedly mean higher prices to consumers. The Trades Union Council renewed its earlier promise that the settlement would not be used by other unions as an argument for more pay.

The miners went back to work on March 11. Industry then returned to a normal work week.

The Campaign

In calling for new elections, Heath said the choice was one between a "strong government" willing to wage an effective anti-inflation fight or "a government which will abandon the struggle against rising prices under pressure from one particular powerful group of workers." He urged a vote against union "militants and extremists" who "want to bring down the whole democratic way of life."

The Conservatives charged that Com-

munist influence was behind the labor unrest. Michael McGahey, a vice president of the National Union of Mineworkers and one of six Communists on the NUM's 27-man executive board, had said the struggle was "not simply a question of wages but a campaign against a declining capitalist society." He said that if troops were used to move coal he would appeal to them to disobey orders. The Labour party, which had given cautious support to the miners, issued a statement repudiating "any attempt by Communists or others to use the miners as a political battering ram." NUM President Joseph Gormley also said he opposed using the dispute for political purposes.

The Conservative platform included a provision to force unions to pay strike benefits to members' families. Under the present system, the government in effect subsidizes strikes by making payments available to workers out on strike.

The Labour party vowed to nationalize or enter the government in participation in such key industries as shipbuilding, aircraft manufacturing, machine toolmaking, and "profitable sectors" of companies in the pharmaceutical field. It also called for public control of offshore oil and gas.

The Liberal party, hoping to increase sizably its 11 seats, put up candidates in more than 500 of the 635 House of Commons constituencies. Jeremy Thorpe, the party leader, said his party would support whichever of the two major parties was willing to draw up an agreed minimum program, but he said the Liberals would not enter a coalition government.

Inflation was the chief campaign issue. Prices had risen by about 10 per cent in 1973; food prices led the way, having increased by 18 per cent in 1973 and 53 per cent since Heath took office in 1970. While Heath argued that strict limits on wage increases were necessary to control

Campaign Rivals were, *top, left to right,* Edward Heath, Jeremy Thorpe, and Harold Wilson, leaders of the Conservative, Liberal, and Labour parties, respectively. Another important figure was Joseph Gormley, *above,* president of the National Union of Mineworkers, although he said he opposed using the miners' strike for political purposes.

inflation, Labour spokesmen said his pro-gram had failed and called for controls on prices and profits, but not on wages.

British entry into the Common Market was another campaign issue. Labour party leader Wilson had pledged to renegotiate the terms of entry if his party was voted into power. Enoch Powell, a right-wing Conservative leader, urged his followers to vote Labour in order to protest mem-bership in the Common Market. Many voters wanted to see Britain out because market membership bars importation of cheap food from the Commonwealth countries.

Britain's trade deficit was another area of discussion. The nation ran a trade defi-cit of $5.2 billion in 1973—the largest ever in any one year. Austerity measures such as budget reductions, restrictions on con-sumer credit, and higher taxes were an-nounced on December 17 in order to but-tress the pound. The coal strike would af-fect Britain's balance of payments to the extent that goods for export could not be produced. Sharp increases in the price of imported oil were expected to add at least $5 billion to the cost of British imports in 1974.

Indochina. See VIETNAM.

Indonesia. Violent anti-Japanese dem-onstrations occurred in Jakarta on the oc-casion of Japanese Prime Minister Kakuei Tanaka's visit January 14-17. It was the first eruption of public discontent in Indo-nesia since 1967, when President Sukarno was formally replaced by General Suharto, following a series of anti-Communist dis-turbances.

Riots in Jakarta

Indonesia was the last—and roughest—stop on a five-nation tour of Southeast Asia undertaken by Tanaka in January. (He had encountered more than 2,000 anti-Japanese demonstrators in Bangkok, Thailand, the previous week.) On his ar-rival in Jakarta January 14, Tanaka's route from the International Airport was temporarily blocked by 800 students who broke through an armed guard.

On January 15, thousands of Indone-sians, many of them high-school and uni-versity students, roamed the streets of Ja-karta tearing down Japanese flags, looting stores with Japanese signs, and burning Japanese-made cars, trucks, and motor-bikes. Furniture from Japanese-owned of-fice buildings was tossed onto bonfires by

Unrest in Indonesia. A mob roamed the streets of Jakarta, burning Japanese-made cars and looting Japanese-owned stores and offices. It was the first eruption of public discontent in Indonesia since 1967 and indicated anger over government corruption as well as ill feelings toward foreigners.

the mob, which numbered up to 100,000 at times. At least 650 cars were wrecked, 50,000 stores damaged, and many buildings set afire.

Although police fired shots over the heads of the crowd, little effort was made to quell the disturbance at first. General Sumitro, chairman of the National Security Agency, and Adam Malik, the foreign minister, were cheered when they appeared in the streets to call for order. But when the rampage continued past nightfall, police and soldiers cracked down, killing 11 of the demonstrators, wounding 101, and arresting more than 150.

At a dinner held in Tanaka's honor, President Suharto apologized for the incidents, which had forced Tanaka to cancel his schedule for the day. (Japan later filed a formal protest with Indonesia, requesting protection for Japanese lives and property in Indonesia, and seeking compensation for damages inflicted.)

The violence in Jakarta diminished the next day, but about 500 students returned to the streets, denouncing "Japanese economic imperialism" in Indonesia and attacking both Japanese and Chinese places of business.

Sources of Discontent

Anti-Japanese sentiment in Indonesia and other parts of Southeast Asia appears to be caused more by the way the Japanese do business than by the economic activities themselves. (Japanese investment in Indonesia accounts for only 15 per cent of foreign investment—a smaller share than that of Americans.) Many Indonesians believe that the Japanese are unscrupulous, pay Indonesians less than Japanese for the same work, and try to keep Indonesians out of important positions. They point out, for example, that 70 per cent of Japanese businessmen met the Indonesian government's requirements for joint ventures by taking ethnic Chinese as partners. (Most Indonesians are Malays.)

Trade between the two nations, which amounts to $2 billion annually, is interdependent. Indonesia relies on Japan for ma-

Oil from wells on Sumatra and Borneo may help relieve Indonesia's economic woes.

chinery, processed industrial goods, and economic and technical aid. Japan imports 12 per cent of its vital oil supply from Indonesia.

Many Indonesian and foreign observers interpreted the recent unrest in Indonesia as reflecting widespread public disenchantment with the performance of Suharto's government, particularly in the economic sphere. There was also a feeling that large payoffs by Japanese businessmen had contributed to the corruption which is rampant among Indonesian officials.

However, corruption has been a pervasive feature of Indonesian life since independence was acquired from the Netherlands in 1949. Recent exploitation of Indonesia's vast oil, mineral, and timber resources has increased the scale of corruption but has not led to a more equal distribution of national wealth. Bribes, graft, and influence-peddling were estimated by a leading Indonesian economist to account for 30 per cent of the Indonesian national income. The pay scales of the white-collar groups—including teachers, clerks, policemen, and government employees—have traditionally been so low as to presuppose graft.

In the wake of the riots, Suharto removed several generals from key posts. Students charged that these men had been collecting payoffs from foreign businessmen in return for government approval of trade and investment deals.

Economic Advancement

When Suharto came to power in the mid-1960's, he inherited economic chaos from the administration of President Sukarno, who wasted huge amounts of foreign aid. By encouraging a climate of political stability, Suharto was able to attract foreign economic assistance (some $600 million from the United States, Japan, and western Europe), and private capital to develop the country's rich natural resources.

The influx of foreign investment has helped Indonesia's economic position improve markedly in recent years. While in 1968 there were no foreign-exchange reserves, by 1974, there was a surplus of $800 million. Under a new contract, sales of natural gas to Japan alone were ex-

pected to pay all Indonesia's foreign debts for a period of 20 years.

Oil, Indonesia's largest earner of foreign exchange, was expected to bring in $3 billion in 1974. Other resources include large pockets of natural gas in Borneo and Sumatra, rubber plantations, large timber stands, and big deposits of tin, bauxite, nickel, copper, and iron ore. Among new enterprises planned are a $700-million natural-gas project for East Kalimantan (Borneo) and northern Sumatra, and a $500-million hydroelectric-power and aluminum-smelter development, both sponsored by Japan.

Indonesia's petroleum exports have provided the generals and a few others with access to extravagant life-styles, but the average villager continues to subsist on about 25 cents a day. On January 7, Suharto announced a new five-year plan which quadrupled the development budget and shifted emphasis to problems of food, clothing, housing, and employment. (The first five-year plan had concentrated on building up the country's industrial and communications infrastructure.) Suharto's new plan had been anticipated, but students and other critics doubted that improvements in social welfare could occur fast enough to reduce the national feeling of malaise.

The unchecked growth of population and accompanying unemployment are Indonesia's greatest obstacles to economic progress. With 120 million people, Indonesia is the world's fifth largest country in both area and population, but 85 per cent of its inhabitants are squeezed onto the small island of Java. Overcrowding in rural areas forces thousands of peasants to migrate to the cities in search of work, but most can find employment only as trash-pickers or, at best, pedicab pedalers.

Expanding at the rate of 2.5 per cent annually, Indonesia's population is likely to double by the end of the century. Thus, despite the nation's wealth of natural resources, Indonesia's leaders are expected to encounter difficulty maintaining even existing living standards for the majority of the citizens.

Israel. See MIDDLE EAST.

Secretary of State Kissinger sought to improve relations between the United States and other Western Hemisphere nations. *Above,* he signed an eight-point agreement with Panama to serve as a guide in drawing up a new Panama Canal treaty. *Right,* he called for "a new spirit in our relations" at a meeting of the foreign ministers of 25 hemispheric nations.

BIENVENIDOS CANCILLERES DE AMERICA

Latin America. U.S. Secretary of State Henry Kissinger, speaking at a three-day meeting of Western Hemisphere nations held in Mexico City in late February, called for "a new spirit in our relations." The meeting was marked by a feeling of new self-confidence among the 24 Latin American and Caribbean foreign ministers attending, due to a widespread belief among them that the hemispheric nations had grown in their importance to U.S. foreign policy.

Latin American leaders had noted a shift in the balance of power from countries controlling capital to those that possess natural resources. Venezuela supplies 10 per cent of the oil imported by the United States. Chile has 40 per cent of the world's copper and vast supplies of nitrates, a key ingredient of fertilizer and explosives. Bolivia is a major source of the world's tin and Jamaica is a leading supplier of bauxite, or aluminum ore. At the hemispheric meeting Venezuelan Foreign Minister Aristides Calvani urged his colleagues to follow the lead of the Arab world and form producer cartels to exploit their resources to the fullest.

While no formal agreements resulted from the meeting, Kissinger outlined areas for cooperation. The United States had prepared the way for a conciliatory session by concluding an agreement with Panama on principles for the operation of the Panama Canal and a settlement with Peru concerning compensation for nationalized U.S. properties.

Among the issues discussed in Mexico City were the following:

Trade. Kissinger said the United States would "do its utmost to avoid raising new tariff barriers against Latin American imports" and would empower the U.S.-financed Inter-American Development Bank to ease payments deficits created by the oil shortage. Brazil, South America's leading exporter, wants a relaxation of trade barriers and preferential treatment for Latin American goods.

Aid. Kissinger said that the Nixon Administration would maintain current development-aid levels, Congress willing. But he said that the American nations should explore other possibilities, such as private loans, concessions, and trade credits.

Multinational Companies. The Latin American nations, led by Mexico, Peru, Argentina, and Colombia, voiced their belief in the need for international legislation to control the power of these companies. Most Latins feel that U.S. influence is maintained primarily by multinational corporations.

Energy. The United States expressed willingness to share research for developing new sources of energy. But even Washington's close hemispheric ally, Brazil, refused to support any move to form a Western front against Arab oil producers.

Cuba. A dozen countries, led by Mexico, Argentina, and Peru, favored normalizing relations with Cuba, but Brazil, Chile, and other countries with right-wing regimes remained adamantly opposed to a lifting of sanctions. Argentina pressed a demand that the United States allow Ford and General Motors subsidiaries in Argentina to sell vehicles to Cuba as part of a large bilateral trade deal. U.S. diplomats let it be known privately that they would not stand in the way.

Agreements with Panama and Peru

On February 7, Kissinger and Panamanian Foreign Minister Juan Antonio Tack signed an agreement that established eight principles as a guide in drawing up a new Panama Canal treaty. The most important of these stated that "the concept of perpetuity will be eliminated." A 1903 treaty gave the United States a perpetual lease over the 553-square-mile Canal Zone.

The agreement stated that the 1903 treaty would be abrogated with the conclusion of an entirely new interocean canal treaty. This treaty would have a fixed termination date and provide for the ultimate reversion of the canal and the adjoining Canal Zone to Panama.

Panama would grant for the duration of the new interoceanic canal treaty the right of the United States to use "the lands, water, and airspace which may be necessary for the operation, maintenance, protection, and defense of the canal and the transit of ships." Panama would have a "just and equitable share of the benefits" derived from the operation of the canal, would "participate in the administration of the canal" and its defense, and would assume total responsibility for the operation of the canal.

On February 19, Peru agreed to pay $76 million, almost all of it borrowed from U.S. private banks, in compensation for the Peruvian properties of U.S. companies expropriated in recent years. This sum was in addition to $74 million that Peru had previously agreed to pay directly to five companies.

The Cerro Corporation, whose large mining operations were taken over in January, said the agreement was "reasonable under the political realities in Peru today." Privately, however, some business executives were bitter and expressed their belief that the compensation was inadequate. One said the agreement was made hastily in preparation for the hemispheric meeting in Mexico City. Another said the State Department wanted a solution to protect heavy U.S. investment in the Peruvian oilfields as well as in the remaining mining operations.

Literature. Among the books published during late 1973 and early 1974 were the following:

Fiction

The Case Worker, by George Konrád, translated from the Hungarian by Paul Aston. In this highly regarded first novel, a Budapest civil servant who works for a welfare agency gropes for a humane solution to the plight of his clients. (Harcourt Brace Jovanovich—$6.95)

A Crown of Feathers, by Isaac Bashevis Singer. Twenty-four stories by this accomplished author recall the vanished world of Polish Jewry and its exasperating but memorable people. (Farrar, Straus and Giroux—$8.95)

The Eye of the Storm, by Patrick White. A wealthy, sadistic invalid woman in her eighties—once an imperious beauty—continues to dominate her middle-aged children in this gracefully written novel by the 1973 Nobel laureate. (Viking—$8.95)

Jaws, by Peter Benchley. A Long Island seaside resort town is faced with a moral dilemma when a 20-foot great white shark rises from the depths and threatens the local economy as well as the bathers. (Doubleday—$6.95)

Malevil, by Robert Merle. Seven Frenchmen emerge from a subterranean wine cellar to find they are among the few survivors of an atomic holocaust. The plot allows the au-

49

Best Selling Books

FICTION
Burr, by Gore Vidal
Jaws, by Peter Benchley
The Snare of the Hunter,
    by Helen MacInnes
Watership Down, by Richard Adams
The Partners, by Louis Auchincloss
The Eye of the Storm, by Patrick White

NONFICTION
Plain Speaking, by Merle Miller
You Can Profit from a Monetary Crisis,
    by Harry Browne
How To Be Your Own Best Friend,
    by Mildred Newman, et. al.
Alistair Cooke's America, by Alistair Cooke
Times to Remember,
    by Rose Fitzgerald Kennedy
Management, by Peter Drucker

thor to recapitulate human history, which he argues must inevitably repeat itself. Law and order, he contends, are n cessary; monogamy a luxury; science and technology must return, regardless of their abuses; and even killing one's fellow man is sometimes necessary. (Simon & Schuster—$10)

Nickel Mountain, by John Gardner. Henry Soames, the proprietor of an all-night diner in the Catskills, is the unlikely but authentic hero of this moral tale of a man who truly cares about his fellow man. (Knopf—$6.95)

The Oath, by Elie Wiesel, translated from the French by Marion Wiesel. The dilemma of Jews in a hostile world and the impact of violence on the human consciousness are themes of this allegorical tale. (Random House—$7.95)

The Partners, by Louis Auchincloss. The world of well-born and wealthy New Yorkers is the author's chosen landscape. In this series of stories he examines the lives of the men and women who work for a Wall Street firm. (Houghton Mifflin—$6.95)

A Woman in the Sky, by James Hanley. Lena and Brigid, two elderly London women, fight an unequal battle against bureaucrats whose well-meaning efforts to "help" them intrude on the autonomy of their lives. (Horizon Press—$6.95)

Nonfiction

The American Food Scandal, by William Robbins. Food processors, supermarket chains, and government agencies all conspire to sell the consumer adulterated food at high prices, according to this indictment of the industry. (William Morrow & Co.—$6.95)

An American Verdict, by Michael Arlen. Edward Hanrahan, Cook County state's attorney, was indicted for conspiracy to obstruct justice in connection with the 1969 raid of a Chicago apartment in which two Black Panthers were killed and several wounded. This account of the trial is also a drama of the confrontation between blacks and police and of the cultural, social, and political life of Chicago. (Doubleday—$6.95)

Defeated: Inside America's Military Machine, by Stuart H. Loory. The author paints a disturbing picture of a military weakened by lax discipline, racial division, corruption, and complacency. He concludes that "the American military machine today is not qualified to protect the nation's vital interests in situations short of nuclear exchange." (Random House—$10)

The Empty Mirror, by Janwillem van de Wetering. A Dutchman who spent a year and a half in a Japanese Zen Buddhist monastery describes his unsuccessful attempt to adjust to rigorous Zen training and achieve *satori*—a feeling of oneness with existence. But his depression lifted when, on his parting, his master said, "You have been forged in this monastery . . . your training continues." (Houghton Mifflin—$5.95)

Four Reforms—A Guide for the Seventies, by William F. Buckley, Jr. Among the proposals of this conservative thinker are a flat tax of 15 per cent on all income in place of higher tax rates for higher incomes; elimination of the corporation tax; amending the Constitution to permit public aid to non-public schools; and repeal of the Fifth Amendment against self-incrimination. (Putnam—$4.95)

Grandma Moses, by Otto Kallir. In 1937, when she was 77 and could no longer run her farm, Grandma Moses took up painting because she had never learned to do nothing. Her 1,600 paintings, some reproduced here, show the world as it appeared to her—births and deaths, changing seasons, holidays and harvests, and their accompanying pleasures and chores. (Abrams—$40)

Grandmasters of Chess, by Harold C. Schonberg. Some have called chess a concrete illustration of abstract thought; others compare it to art or music. Many of the men who have excelled at the game have been monsters of egotism—perhaps because they must project their brains and personality into 16 pieces and expose them to attack. (Lippincott—$10)

The Living Presidency, by Emmet John Hughes. In addition to his own analysis of the history and changing character of the presidency in its various aspects, the author offers an appendix in which a dozen alumni of past administrations appraise the qualities of presidential leadership. Although the book was largely written before the Watergate scandal, he observes, "The judgments of all historians of the presidency concur that the loss of the people's trust is the one mortal disaster from which there can be no real recovery." (Coward, McCann & Geoghegan—$10.50)

Obedience to Authority: An Experimental View, by Stanley Milgram. A social psychologist hired 100 "ordinary people" and found that more than 60 per cent administered electric shocks when told to do so by "scientists" even when the "patient"—actually a trained actor—screamed in agony. The author concluded, "A substantial proportion of people do what they are told to . . . without limitations of conscience, so long as they perceive that the command comes from a legitimate authority." (Harper & Row—$10)

Plain Speaking: An Oral Biography of Harry S. Truman, by Merle Miller. The 33rd president spoke bluntly and forcefully to the author when interviewed in retirement during the winter of 1962. In this work Truman defends his record, settles scores with his political rivals, and delivers judgments on his predecessors and successors in the White House. (Berkley/Putnam—$8.95)

The Political Criminal, by Stephen Schafer. History is filled with illegal acts that are now regarded as praiseworthy. But who precisely is a "political criminal?" Are there any absolute definitions of justice, law, and morality? These are questions examined, but not solved, in this study. (The Free Press/Macmillan—$7.95)

The Saturday Night Special, and Other Guns With Which Americans Won the West, Protected Bootleg Franchises, Slew Wildlife, Robbed Countless Banks, Shot Husbands Purposely and by Mistake and Killed Presidents—Together With the Debate Over Continuing Same, by Robert Sherill. The title tells the story, as with grim humor, bitter sarcasm, and outright despair, the author concludes that Americans are not ready to abandon their gun-toting ways. (Charterhouse—$8.95)

Tristes Tropiques, by Claude Lévi-Strauss, translated from the French by John and Doreen Weightman. A new translation of this classic work, which is the story of the making of an anthropologist, his search for "natural" man in the jungles of Brazil, an appreciation

Harry S. Truman does the talking in *Plain Speaking,* a biography by Merle Miller based on Truman's own blunt and forceful comments.

of other cultures on their own terms, and a lamentation that the richness of the past is giving way to one global but debased culture. (Atheneum—$12.50)

Viet Journal, by James Jones. A war novelist sent to South Vietnam just before American troops were pulled out writes pungently and dramatically about the fighting he saw and the people—Vietnamese and Americans —he spoke to. (Delacorte—$7.95)

Word Play, by Peter Farb. A Melanesian tribe is said to be incapable of metaphor, and several New Guinea tribes have only two basic color words—roughly "black" and "white." A tribe in the Philippines chooses its leaders according to how much verbal skill they display while drinking rice beer. Taboo words, linguistic theories, psychoanalyst-patient exchanges—all are grist for the author's mill as he examines the uniquely human faculty of language. (Knopf—$8.95)

Working, by Studs Terkel. For three years, the author wandered around the country, getting people to "talk about what they do all day and how they feel about what they do." The 130 people in this book generally echo the complaint voiced by one woman: "Most of us . . . have jobs that are too small for our spirit." (Pantheon—$10)

The Writer's Craft, edited by John Hersey. Writers here reflect on writing. Included are selections from Tolstoy, Poe, Flaubert, Henry James, George Orwell, E. M. Forster, and Thomas Mann, and many others. (Knopf— $10)

Literature for Children

Picture Books and Easy-to-Read Books

The Adventures of Stanley Kane, by Stan J. Goldberg and Victoria Chess. Stanley lived in a purple house with a dog, two cats, and a pig, and remarkable things happened. Did you ever talk to a knock or listen to the moon? Stanley did! (Harcourt—$5.95)

African Treehouse, by James Tasker, illustrated by Kathleen Elgin. Funny, informative verses about African animals from aardvark to zebra. (Harvey—$6.00)

Benjy's Dog House, by Margaret Bloy Graham. When a resourceful puppy decides he does not want to sleep in a dog house, anything can happen. (Harper—$4.50)

The Brownstone, by Paul Scher, pictures by Stan Mack. How can a bear family find a quiet place for their winter sleep in a crowded apartment house? (Pantheon—$4.50)

Buzz Buzz Buzz, by Byron Barton. A bee stings a bull, the bull scares a cow, the cow kicks . . . who? What happens next makes a rollicking guessing tale. (Macmillan—$4.95)

Don't You Remember? by Lucille Clifton, illustrated by Evaline Ness. Tate was a small girl who thought her family never remembered anything they promised. (Dutton—$4.95)

I Do Not Like It When My Friend Comes to Visit, by Ivan Sherman. Friends are fun, but not when they come to visit and you have to do everything their way! (Harcourt—$4.95)

If You'd Been Born in India, by Gail Ranadive, pictures by Paul Frame. A warm and evocative portrayal of how a baby lives and grows in a family of Bombay. (Albert Whitman—$3.95)

It's Raining Said John Twaining, translated and illustrated by N. M. Bodecker. Children will enjoy chanting these delightful Danish nursery rhymes. (Atheneum—$4.95)

Jasmine, by Roger Duvoisin. A nonconformist cow creates havoc in the barnyard. (Knopf—$4.50)

Kiviok's Magic Journey, by James Houston. An Eskimo legend about a hero who makes a strange journey to rescue his enchanted wife. (Atheneum—$5.25)

The Little Park, by Dale Fife, pictures by Janet La Salle. Three children find a way to save the last bit of empty land in their town. (Albert Whitman—$3.25)

Little Yellow Fur, by Wilma Putchford Hays, illustrated by Richard Cuffari. An easy-to-read tale of a pioneer girl who made friends with the Indians. (Coward—$3.86)

Lucky Wilma, by Wendy Kindred. Every Saturday Wilma and her father explored places—but one wonderful Saturday they discovered each other! (Dial—$4.95)

Martha Ann and the Mother Store, by Nathaniel and Betty Jo Charnley, illustrated by Jerome Snyder. An enterprising little girl goes shopping for the perfect mother. (Harcourt—$4.95)

The Mermaid and the Whale, by Goergess McHargue, pictures by Robert Andrew Parker. When a mermaid falls in love with a reluctant whale, who will win? (Holt—$5.95)

Once a Bright Red Tiger, by Alex Whitney, illustrated by Charles Robinson. Red is the color of danger—especially if you are a forgetful tiger in the jungle. (Walck—$4.95)

Pig Tale, by Henel Oxenbury. The hilarious misadventures of two pigs who find that money can't buy happiness . . . at least for pigs. (Morrow—$4.95)

Poor Richard in France, by F. N. Monjo, pictures by Brinton Turkle. Beginning readers will chuckle over Benjamin Franklin's adventures in France, as seen by his young nephew. (Holt—$4.95)

Somebody's Dog, by Miska Miles, illustrated by John Schoenherr. A lost, hungry little dog finds where he really belongs. (Little—$4.95)

Suppose You Met a Witch, by Ivan Seraillier, illustrated by Ed Emberley. A resourceful boy and girl prove that even the wickedest witch can be defeated. (Little—$5.95)

The Travels of Atunga, by Theodore Clymer, illustrated by John Schoenherr. When hunger stalked the land of the Eskimos, so the legend goes, brave Atunga dared the wrath of the gods to seek help for his people. (Little—$4.95)

Fiction (8 to 12 Years Old)

A Book of Ogres and Trolls, by Ruth Manning-Sanders. Ogres and trolls of many kinds troop mischievously through these stories, working good and evil. (Dutton—$4.95)

The Cat Sitter Mystery, by Carol Adorjan. Lonely in her new home, Beth didn't expect a haunted house to bring her a friend. (O'Hara—$3.95)

A Dream of Ghosts, by Frank Bonham. Her scientific mind told Gwen there were no ghosts, but what was the reason for the spooky happenings in the old French castle? (Dutton—$4.95)

Emma's Search for Something, by Mary Anderson. Emma was a city pigeon with a remarkable gift—she could read. And that

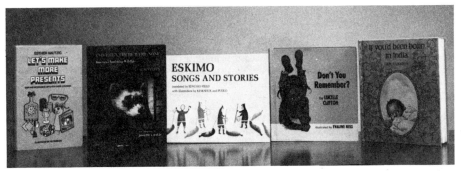

led her into surprising adventure. (Atheneum —$5.95)

The Foundling and Other Tales of Prydain, by Lloyd Alexander. Enchantments and sorcery, wizards and princesses, make these tales an enchantment of their own. (Holt—$4.95)

Men From the Village Deep in the Mountains, translated by Garrett Bang. Funny, scary, exciting, are these delightful folk tales from old Japan. (Macmillan—$4.95)

The Spring on the Mountain, by Judy Allen. Did an eerie power draw the three children to the ancient track that led up the mountain? (Farrar—$4.95)

Think About It, You Might Learn Something, by Robyn Supraner. The adventures and misadventures Jennifer records are funny or painful, but always heartwarming. (Houghton—$4.95)

What the Witch Left, by Ruth Chew. What would you do if you found a box that held magical charms—and you could make the charms work? (Hastings—$4.95)

Nonfiction (8 to 12 Years Old)

Animals that Frighten People, by Dorothy E. Shuttlesworth. A new look at wolves, bats, and other animals that people have feared through the ages. (Dutton—$4.95)

Let's Make More Presents, by Esther Hautzig. Simple and easy instructions that will help children make many different kinds of presents inexpensively. (Macmillan—$5.95)

Let's Start a Puppet Theatre, by Benny E. Andersen. Here are clear and exciting ways to make and use puppets of many kinds. (Van Nostrand—$4.95)

This Is an Orchestra, by Elsa Z. Posell. Newly revised is this invaluable introduction to the instruments and players that comprise an orchestra. (Houghton—$5.95)

What Can She Be? A Newscaster, by Gloria and Esther Goldreich. The busy and exciting day of a TV newscaster is described in this career book. (Lothrop—$3.95)

The Wonderful World of Mammals, Adventuring with Stamps, by Roger Caras. An unusual invitation to collect stamps and so learn about the fascinating mammals represented on them. (Harcourt—$6.95)

Yoga for Children, by Erene Cheki Haney and Ruth Richards. For fun, relaxation, and building supple bodies, here are easy-to-do yoga exercises. (Bobbs-Merrill—$4.95)

Fiction (11 to 14 Years Old)

The Cheese Stands Alone, by Marjorie M. Prince. Always before, Daisy had been a leader of the pack, but suddenly she was left out, left behind. Could she ever catch up again? Every girl and boy who has had growing-up problems will share Daisy's dilemma. (Houghton—$4.95)

The Court of the Stone Children, by Eleanor Cameron. A lonely girl meets a stranger from another time and fights to solve an ancient mystery. (Dutton—$5.50)

Eskimo Songs and Stories, translated by Edward Field. A fascinating collection of creation tales, magic tales, and songs that will help young readers begin to understand the beliefs of Eskimos of the past and today. (Delacorte—$6.95)

The Golden Shadow, by Leon Garfield and Edward Blishen. An exciting tale that weaves together the immortal Greek myths. (Pantheon—$5.50)

The Juniper Tree and Other Tales from Grimm, selected by Lore Segal and Maurice Sendak. This distinguished edition in two volumes is an illuminating translation of the beloved folk tales and a selection that combines the best of Grimm. (Farrar—$12.95; 2 vols.)

Lyncoya, by Margery Evernden. Based on fact is this dramatic story of the two brothers, one white, one Indian, who were the adopted sons of Andrew Jackson. (Walck—$5.95)

Supernatural Tales of Terror and Suspense, selected by Alfred Hitchcock. Vampires, ghosts, and other ghastly apparitions make these tales a shuddery delight. (Random—$3.95)

The Way Home, by Joan Phipson. An automobile accident catapults three young people into a fantastic journey through time and space. (Atheneum—$5.50)

Weland, Smith of the Gods, by Ursula Synge. The fierce, courageous saga of Weland, who married a Swan Maiden, dared the wrath of the Norse gods, and fought to a strange victory. (Phillips—$5.95)

Nonfiction (11 to 14 Years Old)

And Then There Were None, by Nina Leen, with commentary by Joseph A. Davis. These striking photographs of America's vanishing wildlife by Nina Leen, and the graphic notes by Davis, are a compelling plea for protection of our endangered species. (Holt—$8.95)

Bill Severn's Big Book of Magic. Amateur magicians—and their audiences—will find this book entertaining and a temptation to try magic tricks themselves. (McKay—$5.95)

Bold Leaders of the American Revolution, by Colonel Red Reeder. Brief, stirring biographies of Ethan Allen, Deborah Sampson, Thaddeus Kosciuszko, and other fighters for and against American freedom. (Little—$5.95)

Life Battles Cold, by Lucy Kavaler. The incredible ways living things adapt to and battle freezing cold are presented. (John Day—$6.50)

Mental Magic Tricks, by Geoffrey Lamb. Would you like to read minds—or pretend to? Here are easy-to-follow directions for mental trickery of many kinds. (Nelson—$4.95)

A Skyscraper Goes Up, by Carter Harman. The step-by-step building of a huge skyscraper from idea to completion is presented in vivid text and pictures. (Random—$4.95)

The Way Things Work, an Illustrated Encyclopedia of Technology, by T. Lodewijk and others. How do things work in our modern technology? Why do things work? Here are clear and concise answers. (Simon & Schuster—$9.95)

Fiction (Teen-age)

Cosmic Laughter, compiled by Joe Haldeman. Lively and humorous stories by science-fiction masters. (Holt—$5.95)

The Friends, by Rosa Guy. A powerful and provocative story of a West Indian girl who must come to terms with a new life in Harlem and her own needs and pride. (Holt—$5.95)

Here Abide Monsters, by Andre Norton. Nick and Linda are projected into a strange space-time era where ancient magic still rules, and they must choose between alien forces. (Atheneum—$5.95)

The Life and Death of Yellow Bird, by James Forman. Half-Indian, half-white in blood, all Indian in his dreams and loyalty,

Yellow Bird fights for the freedom of his people. (Farrar—$5.95)

The Other Side of Tomorrow, edited by Roger Elwood. Original and thought provoking are these science-fiction stories of life on the other side of tomorrow. (Random—$3.95)

The Outback and Beyond, edited by Hope Harshaw Evans. This anthology of Australian writing is rich in warmth and humor and courage as it portrays the peoples of this last frontier. (Doubleday—$4.95)

Smith Valley, by Florence Crannell Means. An absorbing novel of a girl of the early 1900's who fought for her own independence. (Houghton—$5.95)

Three-Point Hero, by Joe Archibald. Brad has to fight his father's fame on the football field as well as the opposing team. (Macrae—$4.75)

A Time to Choose, by Richard Parker. Stephen discovers he can cross over into a new dimension, a new world. But soon he must choose between his two worlds . . . finally and forever. (Harper—$5.50)

Nonfiction (Teen-age)

African Slavery, by Edwin P. Hoyt. A vivid and compelling account of the African slave trade from its inception to its end, and the influence it exerted on our modern world. (Abelard—$5.95)

ESP, the Search Beyond the Senses, by Daniel Cohen. An absorbing exploration of extrasensory perception and the scientific investigations that are trying to prove or disprove psychic phenomena. (Harcourt—$5.95)

The Heavyweight Champions, by John Durant. A swiftly moving panorama of the ring, its history, and its champions. (Hastings—$6.95)

Joy in Stone, by Sabra Holbrook. As exciting as fiction is this story of the cathedral of Reims, and the people—saints, sinners, kings, peasants—who made it the heart of France. (Farrar—$5.95)

The New Malaysia, by I. G. Edmonds. This new Southeast Asian country was created in 1963. Here is the story of its peoples and their struggle to build a nation. (Bobbs-Merrill—$5.00)

We Elect a President, by David E. Weingast. As timely as tomorrow's headlines is this clear and perceptive account of how our presidential campaigns are run. (Messner—$5.50)

Why We Do What We Do. A Look at Psychology, by Elizabeth Hall. Psychology, the science of behavior, touches every part of our daily lives. Here is a lively introduction to it. (Houghton—$5.95)

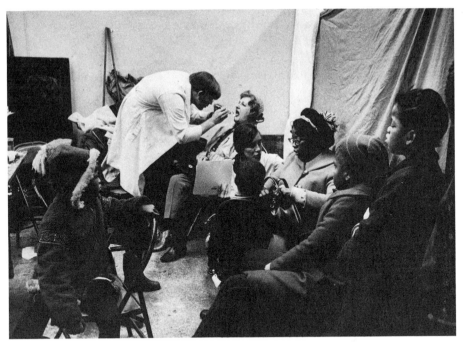

Free Clinic. Neighborhood health centers are attempting to fill the gap until national health insurance is adopted. At present, perhaps 20 million Americans have no protection at all against the often-ruinous costs of illness.

Medicine. Both the Nixon Administration and the 93rd Congress agreed in early 1974 that national health insurance was a priority goal. The reasons why national health insurance ranks high among issues of vital importance are many, but they boil down to two: soaring medical costs and serious shortcomings in the present health-care delivery system.

A study by the Health Insurance Institute of America, a New York-based group made up of most of the private companies writing medical and hospital policies, showed that hospitalization costs have tripled in the last decade. At the end of 1972, these costs were up to $105.40 per patient day (an increase of 14.2 per cent over 1971). Despite the fact that the average hospital stay was somewhat shorter in 1972 than in 1971—7.9 days compared to 8.0 days—the average cost of a hospital stay was up 12.8 per cent, to $832.66 at the end of 1972.

And yet this same study showed that the typical health-insurance policy pays for less than half the cost of medical care and that approximately 10 per cent of Americans under 65 years of age have no protection at all against the often-ruinous costs of a serious illness. Information from the National Center for Health Statistics, a federal agency, suggests that this number is greatly underestimated and that nearly 20 million persons actually may be uninsured.

National health insurance has been prescribed as a cure for these problems, but there is no agreement as to what kind of program should be enacted. By March, six major bills had been introduced in Congress.

Among the various proposals are widely divergent approaches to such important matters as (1) the role of the federal government in administering and financing a national health-insurance program, (2) the people who would be covered under the program, (3) the scope of the bene-

National health insurance: four proposals

Administration. Coverage for costs of basic health insurance and catastrophic illness through three programs—one for the employees, a second for low-income families and nonworkers, and the present Medicare program. Increased federal costs estimated at $5.9 billion.

Kennedy-Mills. Unlike Administration plan, coverage is compulsory and federal government, not private insurance carriers, would pay out and collect money. Sponsors claim it would cost no more than the Administration plan, but that individuals would pay less in out-of-pocket costs.

Kennedy-Griffiths. Broader benefits and fewer out-of-pocket expenses for individuals, with new revenue raised from significantly higher federal taxes. Participation compulsory; no role for private health-insurance carriers.

Long-Ribicoff. Basic health-insurance coverage for low-income persons and protection from costs of catastrophic illness for all. No restructuring of private health-insurance industry. Increased federal costs estimated at $3.7 billion.

fits, (4) the extent of involvement by private health insurers, (5) the methods of reimbursement, and (6) the effect on overall organization and delivery of healthcare services. Following is a summary of the major bills, who backs them, what coverage each would provide, who would be covered, and how the plan would be administered and financed.

Administration Plan

President Nixon, in his January 30 State of the Union address, declared that "the time is at hand this year to bring comprehensive, high-quality health care within the reach of every American." A week later, the Administration's Comprehensive Health Insurance Plan was placed before Congress for consideration.

Under this proposal, health insurance would be offered in three broad ways: an employer plan, under which employers would buy basic policies for full-time employees; a government plan that would pay all or part of the cost of insurance for low-income families, nonworkers, and others unable to buy group insurance on their own; and the present Medicare program, with some liberalized changes for those over 65 years of age.

The coverage would include all physician and hospital bills, prescription drugs, laboratory tests and X-rays, ambulance services, treatment for mental illness, alcoholism and drug addiction, certain nursing-home and convalescent services, and a broad package of preventive care and health examinations for children. The scope of benefits provided would be the same under either the employer or the government plan.

The employer plan would be financed by premiums charged to employers and their employees, with employees paying 35 per cent and employers the rest for three years. After that, the employees' share would be 25 per cent. Employees earning more than $10,000 a year would pay the first $150 of annual medical bills; those in lower income brackets would pay less. Then the insurance would take over and cover 75 per cent of all additional medical bills until a family ran up a specified amount of out-of-pocket expenses in any year. This amount for a family with an income of $10,000 would be $1,500. Beyond that figure, the insurance would cover all costs of catastrophic illness.

According to the president, "every American participating in the program would be insured for catastrophic illnesses that can eat away savings and plunge individuals and families into hopeless debt for years."

For the self-employed and those who

buy into the government plan, the amount of premiums paid would rise with the purchaser's income. The government would foot the bill for the rest.

Private insurance plans and nonprofit organizations, such as Blue Cross and Blue Shield, would run the program under government regulation of cost and quality control. Employees would have the option of joining group-practice plans (health-maintenance organizations) that offer comprehensive medical care at a prepaid, fixed fee.

President Nixon said that his plan would add about $5.9 billion a year to federal spending and would not require additional taxes. The total cost to employers and employees was not determined, but some experts have estimated that it might be upwards of $37 billion during the first year.

The main objections voiced against the Nixon proposal were that the plan places too heavy a burden on both the employer and the employee and that it enriches private insurance carriers without adequate supervision. Senator Edward Kennedy said that the proposal does little to stop health costs from climbing steadily or to keep insurance companies from making ever-increasing profits. The United Auto Workers criticized the bill as being very expensive without providing comprehensive coverage and as totally ignoring the issues of reimbursement methods, quality control, and health-manpower shortages.

Other unions objected strenuously to a provision that calls for an employee to pay income tax on both his employer's contribution and his own. They pointed out that the changes would raise health-care costs for some workers currently covered by employer health insurance while employers would continue deducting their payments as a cost of doing business. Since health insurance has been a popular tax-free fringe benefit, changing its tax status would upset countless long-standing collective-bargaining agreements and would require renegotiation of almost all union contracts.

Dr. Herbert S. Denenberg, health-insurance commissioner of Pennsylvania, assailed the proposal's reliance on state governments for enforcement of the insurance regulations. "The states have absolutely no ability to regulate the insurance industry and their track record proves it," he said. "To turn national health insurance over to the states for supervision would be disastrous."

Kennedy-Mills Bill

In 1968, Senator Kennedy co-sponsored a bill that provided for near-total "cradle to grave" protection for everyone, with costs financed from general revenues and from a boost in Social Security payroll taxes. It provided for the Department of Health, Education, and Welfare to monitor the performance of hospitals, physicians, and other personnel through professional panels. Opponents said it would be "too expensive"—$60 billion in the first year—and called it "unrealistic" in seeking to restructure the nation's entire health-care delivery system.

On April 2, Kennedy and Representative Wilbur Mills of Arkansas unveiled a new plan that the two lawmakers said would cost no more than the Nixon Administration's version. Senator Kennedy said he still supports the principle of totally comprehensive health insurance but declared the new proposal "represents a practical embodiment of these principles that can be enacted into law in the next year or two."

The Kennedy-Mills plan would make participation compulsory, while the Administration plan leaves it up to the individual. Individuals would have to pay somewhat less out of their own pockets under the Kennedy-Mills plan.

Under the Kennedy-Mills bill, an individual would have to pay $150 a year in medical-care costs, with a maximum of $300 per family, before receiving benefits, compared to a maximum of $450 per family under the Administration plan. Both plans would require beneficiaries to pay 25 per cent of additional medical-care costs, but up to only $1,000 a year under the Kennedy-Mills bill rather than $1,500 under the Nixon plan.

The Kennedy-Mills bill would take the Social Security Administration out of the Department of Health, Education, and Welfare and create a new independent agency to administer various income-maintenance programs, including health insurance and Medicaid. While private-insurance companies would not administer the program, as under the Nixon plan, Senator Kennedy said they would be left a "lucrative business" in supplementary insurance to pay deductibles and other costs that the bill would not cover.

Kennedy-Griffiths Bill

But some of Senator Kennedy's staunchest supporters refused to switch to the Kenendy-Mills plan and continued to back the plan introduced in 1968 by him and Representative Martha Griffiths of Michigan. It is the most liberal plan before Congress and one that has strong backing from organized labor. It provides for near-total "cradle-to-grave" protection for everyone.

This plan would pay all hospital and doctor bills; ancillary services, such as X-rays, lab tests, and drugs in the hospital; up to 120 days in a skilled nursing home; up to 45 days in a hospital for mental illness; home health services; and rehabilitation.

The patient would have very little to pay under this plan; for example, there are no deductibles. Costs would be financed from general revenues and from a boost in the Social Security payroll taxes. The government would operate the program through a five-man Health Security Board appointed by the president to set policy and standards of care. Private insurance carriers would have no role. The Department of Health, Education, and Welfare would monitor the performance of hospitals, physicians, and other personnel through professional panels. The use of health-maintenance organizations to furnish comprehensive health care also would be encouraged.

President Nixon, in a February speech before the American Hospital Association, criticized the plan as one that "would appeal to demagogues." HEW Secretary Caspar Weinberger denounced it as "saddling the taxpayer with $75 billion in new taxes." This figure is misleading, however, because funds collected and disbursed by the government would take the place of premiums now paid by individuals and employers to private insurance carriers.

Long-Ribicoff Plan

The Catastrophic Health Insurance and Medical Assistance Reform Act, sponsored by Senator Russell Long of Louisiana and Senator Abraham Ribicoff of Connecticut, is designed chiefly to provide protection against the cost of catastrophic illnesses. Under this plan, everyone collecting or paying Social Security, plus their dependents, would be eligible for coverage. After 60 days of hospitalization and $2,000 in family medical expenses in a single year, the government would step in and pay 80 per cent of additional expenses now covered by Medicare—hospital charges, doctors' fees, X-rays, lab tests—without Medicare's limit on the number of days covered.

Another element of the bill would replace Medicaid with a medical assistance plan for low-income families, under which the government would finance 60 days of hospital care, doctors' expenses, nursing services, and home health care. Basic insurance protection would be provided for most Americans through the present private carrier system. Most insurance companies would be required to offer to the public policies that would cover families to the point where the catastrophic insurance program would take over.

Both the catastrophic and medical assistance plans would be administered by the Social Security Administration through the private system. Two trust funds would be set up—one for catastrophic coverage, financed by an increase in Social Security taxes, the other for the medical-assistance plan, financed from general Treasury revenues and state contributions.

This plan would cost approximately $8.9 billion, including the $5.2 billion already being spent on Medicaid. It has the strong backing of the Senate Finance Committee, of which Senator Long is chairman. The bill has relatively few enemies and has been deemed "realistic" by most health-care experts, mainly because it would be fairly inexpensive and relatively easy to implement.

AMA Plan

The Health Care Insurance Act (Medicredit) introduced by Representative Richard Fulton of Tennessee, Representative

Delivery of Health Care is as important an issue as soaring medical costs. Critics of the Administration's health-insurance plan say that it totally ignores the issues of reimbursement methods, quality control, and health-manpower shortages.

Joel Broyhill of Virginia, and Senator Vance Hartke of Indiana, is supported by the American Medical Association. It is called Medicredit because it includes income-tax credits for costs of private health insurance.

Every American would be eligible for coverage under this plan, except those over 65 years of age, who are covered by Medicare. The bill would cover virtually every type of medical care, including preventive and rehabilitative treatment. People would buy their own private health-insurance policies or join a health-maintenance organization.

Premiums or enrollment costs could be claimed as income-tax credits on a sliding scale—10 per cent of premiums deducted directly from taxes for taxpayers owing $890 or more, up to 99 per cent for those owing $1 to $10 in taxes. Persons owing no income tax would get from the government certificates to be used to pay for health insurance. Federal funds would be used to pay for full insurance against catastrophic illness for everyone.

This program would be administered, on the national level, by a health advisory board, which would be responsible for determining policy and regulations and for establishing minimum federal standards on the qualifications of private health-insurance plans. On the state level, state insurance departments would be responsible for determining whether insurance carriers and policies met program standards set by the national board.

Medicredit does not call for changing or improving any segment of the nation's health-care system. The AMA thinks other programs should be legislated (or present programs improved) to deal with problems of utilization of health personnel, such as increasing health manpower and resources in rural and inner-city areas, moderating the costs of care, and meeting the need for custodial and home care for the elderly and disabled.

Wilbur Mills, *right,* greets Secretary of Health, Education, and Welfare Caspar Weinberger prior to the start of House committee hearings on national health insurance. The Administration and Mills have proposed rival plans.

AHA Plan

The American Hospital Association backs the National Health Care Services Reorganization and Financing Act, which was introduced in the House by Representative Al Ullman of Oregon. This plan would offer three insurance packages: one would provide standard benefits resembling those of Medicare, with added coverage in such areas as maternity and child care; another would provide health-maintenance care, including annual physical checkups, immunization shots, and dental services for children; and the third would protect against catastrophic illness.

To get the health-maintenance and catastrophic-illness benefits, an individual would first have to subscribe to a private health-insurance plan that offered standard benefits. A person also would have to enroll in a health-care corporation, which would be created as a community-based, nonprofit organization capable of providing comprehensive health services to all residents in defined geographic areas.

The poor and aged now covered by Medicaid would be insured for all three packages of benefits at public expense, with costs paid by the federal government out of general revenues. People who could afford to buy standard health insurance would do so in the same manner as they do at present. Employers would be required to pay at least 75 per cent of premium costs for the required coverage, with the remaining 25 per cent paid by employee contributions. The federal government would pay 10 per cent of premium costs for all employees registered with health-care corporations.

A special Department of Health would be split off from Health, Education, and Welfare to administer all health-care programs. The federal government would administer the insurance program for the aged and low-income groups and would contract directly with carriers or health-care corporations to provide covered benefits. Employer-employee plans would be administered through approved carriers or health-care corporations. Estimated cost of the program is $18 billion in the first year.

The basic intent of this bill is to tie together, in a somewhat coordinated fashion, the major necessary changes in the three primary areas of the health-care field: regulations and administration, health-delivery systems, and financing elements.

Insurers' Plan

The National Healthcare Act, introduced by Senator Thomas McIntyre of New Hampshire, and Representative Omar Burleson of Texas, is backed by the Health Insurance Association of America, which represents the major companies selling private health coverage.

The plan is similar to AMA's Medicredit in that it offers income-tax credits for the cost of health insurance in private programs approved by the federal government. The bill stresses the development of centers for ambulatory health care and provides the means to gradually replace Medicaid. For a start, the insurance would cover physicians' services, 30 days of hospital care for each illness, dental services, prescribed drugs, prosthetic devices, pregnancy costs, and health services at home or in an extended-care facility. Benefits

60

would be expanded in succeeding years. The bill also provides that once an individual incurred $5,000 in medical expenses in a single year, whether out-of-pocket or covered by insurance, the insurer would pay catastrophic costs up to $250,000.

When an employer and employee shared the costs of the insurance, each would take an income-tax deduction for the amount he had paid. Policies covering the poor, near-poor, and persons previously uninsurable for health reasons would be subsidized by federal and state funds. Sponsors say this bill would cost $8.1 billion in additional tax revenues in the first year of operation.

The Healthcare plan basically is aimed at protecting the private health-insurance industry in its role as sellers of insurance and as private carriers. It provides increased funding and authority to state and local planning agencies and requires state agency approval before projects would be able to receive federal funds.

Other Plans

• The National Health Insurance and Health Services Improvement Act, introduced by Senator Jacob Javits of New York, would extend a broadened Medicare program to the entire population and provide federal assistance for the development of improved health care delivery systems.

• The Health Rights Act, introduced by Senator Hugh Scott of Pennsylvania and Senator Charles Percy of Illinois, is a two-part program providing for major-illness in-patient coverage through a federal program covering costs above an income-related "health-cost ceiling," and an out-patient health-maintenance plan, financed by the purchase of private insurance, with federal supplements for purchase for low-income families.

• The Health Benefits and Health Services Distribution and Education Act, introduced by Senator Claiborne Pell of Rhode Island and Senator Walter Mondale of Minnesota, would require employers to provide a basic package of health benefits, would provide federally financed benefits for the needy, and would require federally chartered regional, for-profit community health and education corpora-

tions to manage the planning and delivery of health services.

Hearings on the various national health insurance bills were scheduled for late spring, with some sort of system expected to be adopted in 1974. The question no longer was whether national health insurance would come—but when and in what form. Health-care experts say that whatever proposal emerges from congressional debate will almost certainly combine elements of more than one plan.

Middle East. Israeli forces withdrew from their bridgehead on the west bank of Egypt's Suez Canal and from their corridor on the east bank after a disengagement accord was signed January 18. The pact was negotiated through the mediation of U.S. Secretary of State Henry Kis-

Disengagement Agreement provided for Israeli withdrawal from Egyptian territory occupied in the Yom Kippur War and a buffer zone patrolled by UN forces. The accord was called "a first step toward a final, just, and durable peace."

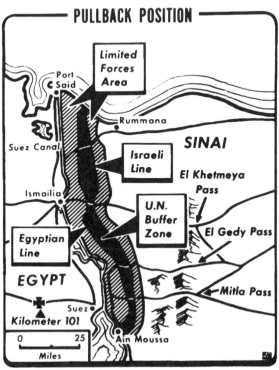

Israeli Forces, *above,* furled their flag and withdrew from occupied territory on both sides of the Suez Canal. They remained in possession of the passes that control the routes into the heart of the Sinai Peninsula. The disengagement agreement freed the supply lines of the Egyptian Third Army, *below,* which was east of the canal.

singer, who shuttled between Aswan and Jerusalem for a week, consulting the leaders of the two countries.

One part of the accord dealt with the pullback of troops and the establishment of disengagement zones; the other, details of which were not officially disclosed, provided for limitations of troops and arms in the zones. The agreement was said to constitute "a first step toward a final, just, and durable peace." It was signed at Kilometer 101 on the Suez-Cairo highway by the Egyptian and Israeli chiefs of staff.

Israeli troop withdrawal formally got under way on January 25 and was completed on March 4. Egyptian forces were allowed to remain on the east bank of the canal in a zone 5 to 7½ miles wide. Immediately adjacent to this force was a buffer zone 3½ to 5 miles wide, patrolled by 2,000 United Nations Emergency Force troops. Immediately to the east of the buffer zone, Israeli troops occupied a third zone 5 to 7½ miles wide. This deployment of forces left the Israelis in continued possession of the Mitla and Gidi passes, which control the routes into the heart of the Sinai Peninsula.

While the limitation of forces was not officially announced, unofficial reports said that each side was obligated to reduce its forces in its zone to 7,000 troops and 30 tanks. Missiles, artillery, and other heavy military equipment were to be removed.

A senior U.S. State Department official disclosed January 21 that the United States had informed Israel that it assumed Egypt would reopen the Suez Canal to international shipping, including Israel-bound vessels. The Israelis reportedly had insisted that Egypt agree to start work soon on rebuilding cities in the canal zone as proof of Egypt's peaceful intentions. However, Egyptian President Anwar el-Sadat said on January 23 that such a decision would "in no way" be linked to the disengagement accord.

The United States and Egypt announced on February 28 immediate resumption of full-scale diplomatic relations, which were severed by Egypt in 1967. The decision to resume diplomatic relations had been made in principle on November 6.

Syrian Front

By contrast, little progress was made toward negotiating a disengagement of forces along the other battlefront of the 1973 war, the Golan Heights. There were hundreds of incidents along the truce line between Israeli and Syrian forces, with exchanges of artillery, tank, and rifle fire.

The Israelis wanted to limit their withdrawal to the 300 square miles that Israel captured in 1973, while the Syrians wanted it to involve at least some of the land Israel captured in 1967. The Syrians also wanted Israel to allow 170,000 residents who had fled the Golan Heights area in 1967 and 1973 to return to their homes.

On January 30, Israeli Premier Golda Meir said her country had no intention of retaining territory captured in the 1973 war. But she told Israeli settlers in the Golan Heights February 8 that she considered the territory captured in 1967 "an inseparable part of Israel." Plans for building a city on the heights were announced by the government two days later.

Progress toward a disengagement pact was evidenced on February 27, when Kissinger turned over a list of 65 Israeli soldiers captured by Syria in the 1973 war to Mrs. Meir. International Red Cross officials were allowed March 1 to visit the captives for the first time. Israel had refused to discuss disengagement until Syria met these conditions. The 386 Syrians, 10 Iraqis, and 6 Moroccans captured by Israel on the Syrian front had been visited regularly by Red Cross representatives.

Suez Canal Reopening Planned

Egypt reportedly planned to reopen the Suez Canal, closed since the 1967 war, by the end of 1974, and to widen and deepen it so that 150,000-ton tankers could pass through by 1978. A long-range plan called for the war-devastated canal cities to be rebuilt and for industry and agriculture to be tied into a giant development plan at a cost of $7 billion.

The first priority was to remove thousands of unexploded bombs, shells, and mines from the canal zone, a process which was expected to take months. The canal would have to be cleared of 10 large sunken ships and 75 smaller vessels. Work crews would also have to dismantle the

New Israeli Government was once again headed by Premier Golda Meir, ending nine weeks of stalemate that followed parliamentary elections on December 31. But Mrs. Meir resigned in April, and a new period of political instability was expected.

concrete-block causeways that both Egypt and Israel built across the waterway during the most recent war.

The Pentagon announced March 19 that 500 U.S. navy and army men would be dispatched to clear the canal of mines and train Egyptians to remove tons of unexploded munitions that had been planted in the waterway. The United States would finance the operation, which the Pentagon estimated at "tens of millions of dollars."

According to a long-range scheme, Port Said and Suez would be rebuilt as modern free ports, like Hong Kong and Singapore, and 1 million acres of desert would be irrigated. Before the 1967 war, 280,000 people lived in Suez and about 350,000 in Port Said. But, in two wars, 80 per cent of the buildings in Suez were destroyed or damaged beyond repair; 70 per cent in Port Said; and 60 per cent in Ismailia.

American construction companies were expected to play a major part in the reconstruction of the canal zone. Private investors in general—Arabs, Europeans, and Japanese as well as Americans—were eyeing Egypt as potentially the most lucrative market in the Arab world. Sadat had shifted the country away from the socialist policies of Nasser, who brought 70 per cent of the economy under government control and nationalized practically all foreign holdings.

Israeli Government Formed

Premier Golda Meir formed a new Israeli cabinet on March 6, ending nine

weeks of political stalemate that followed parliamentary elections on December 31. Most of the ministers were carryovers from the outgoing cabinet. The new government won a vote of confidence on March 10 by 62 to 46, with nine abstentions.

On March 3, Mrs. Meir had announced that she would not head a new government, but after repeated visits by her top ministers she relented and agreed to try again. Citing reports of the threatening Syrian build-up, Defense Minister Moshe Dayan on March 5 reversed his earlier decision not to serve in the new cabinet. Dayan had called for a national-unity government that would embrace the right-wing opposition bloc, Likud, with 39 parliamentary seats, as well as Labor, with 51 seats. Dayan's refusal to serve would have meant withdrawal of support for the government by the faction in the Labor party that supports him.

The governing coalition was fully restored on March 5 when the National Religious party, with 10 seats, agreed to support Mrs. Meir. Earlier, the party refused to join the government unless it received assurances that legislation would be passed providing that immigrants who are converts to Judaism would not be listed as Jews and thus automatically eligible for Israeli citizenship unless their conversions were carried out according to Orthodox ritual, rather than Reform or Conservative rites. The party settled for a promise that the problem would be studied and that meanwhile questionable conversions would not be registered.

Labor party sources said that Mrs. Meir agreed to a demand by the National Religious party that new elections be held before any agreement was signed to relinquish the West Bank area, captured from Jordan in 1967. The party considers the West Bank part of the historic Jewish homeland.

Fighting in Iraq

Iranian and Iraqi forces engaged in heavy fighting along their 600-mile common border in February and March, with each side blaming the other for the clashes. The two countries had been involved in frontier disputes and clashes for several years. In 1969 Iran cancelled a treaty giving Iraq control of navigation rights along the Shatt al-Arab, a large waterway formed by the confluence of the Tigris and Euphrates rivers that flows into the Persian Gulf. Iranian tankers must use it to gain access to their oil ports.

On February 10, Iran gave its casualties as 41 killed and 81 wounded, and Iraq's at 22 dead; Iraq claimed that 70 Iranians were killed or wounded and gave its own losses as one dead and 22 wounded. After three days of fighting in early March, Iran said 50 to 100 Iraqi troops had been killed, but made no mention of its own casualties.

Fighting also broke in northern Iraq between government troops and Kurdish mountaineers after General Mustafa al-Barzani, the leader of Kurdish rebels, rejected an offer of self-rule that fell far short of Kurdish demands. The Kurds are Moslems, but not Arabs. It is estimated that there are at least 800,000 Kurds in Iraq, and many more in neighboring areas of Iran and Turkey, as well as the Soviet Union. The Kurds say they number a quarter to a third of Iraq's 10 million people.

The government decree was issued on the fourth anniversary of a cease-fire proclaimed March 11, 1970. It granted the Kurdish language official status, established a special regional budget, and provided for the election of a legislative council for the Kurdish region. However, the president of Iraq retained the power to select the head of the region's executive council and the right to dissolve the legislative council. Moreover, the government refused to include Kirkuk, an important oil-producing center, in the Kurdish region.

Outbursts of fighting were reported after Barzani ignored the government's 15-day deadline to accept the autonomy plan. Kurdish forces were said to control all of the Iraqi-Turkish frontier and a 250-mile stretch of the frontier with Iran. Iran reportedly was sending provisions to the Kurdish forces, although it discourages its own Kurdish minority from seeking self-rule.

See also PETROLEUM.

Mustafa al-Barzani is the leader of a movement that seeks Kurdish self-rule within Iraq. The Kurds, who are Moslems but not Arabs, say that they number a quarter to a third of Iraq's 10 million people.

MOTION PICTURES

The Sting, starring Paul Newman and Robert Redford as confidence men in Chicago during the 1930s, was voted best feature film of 1973 by the Academy of Motion Picture Arts and Sciences. The film was also honored with six other Oscars: best director (George Roy Hill); best original screenplay (David S. Ward); best scoring; best costume design; best art direction; and best film editing. The awards were presented in Los Angeles on April 2.

Jack Lemmon won the best-actor award for his role as a businessman struggling to survive in *Save the Tiger*. Glenda Jackson won her second Oscar as best actress for her performance as a London divorcee having a romance with a married man in *A Touch of Class*.

Nine-year-old Tatum O'Neal was named best supporting actress for her role as the daughter of a confidence man (played by her father, Ryan O'Neal), in *Paper Moon*. She was the first juvenile to receive an Oscar other than an honorary one. The award for best supporting actor went to 71-year-old John Houseman, a veteran stage director and movie producer, for his role as a law professor in *The Paper Chase*. He had previously appeared in only one film.

The Exorcist, the current box-office sensation, received 10 nominations, but only two Oscars, one for best screenplay adaptation (by William Peter Blatty, from his own novel), and the other for best achievement in sound.

Costume designer Edith Head won her eighth Oscar for the wardrobe in *The Sting*. She holds the record of 33 Oscar nominations.

Marvin Hamlisch won three Academy Awards—for composing the best song, *The Way We Were,* from the picture of the same name; for best dramatic score in the same picture; and for best scoring, in *The Sting*.

Day for Night was voted the best foreign-language film of 1973.

New York Film Critics. *Day for Night,* a French comedy-drama dealing with the filming of a movie, was voted best picture of 1973 in the 39th annual poll of the New York Film Critics Circle on January 8. François Truffaut and Valentina Cortese were named the best director and supporting actress for their contributions to *Day for Night*.

Joanne Woodward was voted best actress for her performance as a restless, middle-aged housewife in *Summer Wishes, Winter Dreams*. Marlon Brando won the best-actor award for his role as a troubled American in the sexually explicit *Last Tango in Paris*. Robert De Niro was named best supporting actor for his performance as a small-time hoodlum in *Mean Streets*.

National Society of Film Critics. *Day for Night* was voted best film of 1973 by the National Society of Film Critics on January 6. The representatives of 21 magazines and newspapers also chose François Truffaut the year's best director and Val-

entina Cortese the best supporting actress for their contributions to the film.

Marlon Brando was named best actor for his performance in *Last Tango in Paris,* Liv Ullman was voted best actress for her role as a Swedish immigrant to the United States in *The New Land,* and Robert De Niro was named best supporting actor for his role in *Mean Streets*. The cinematography award was presented to Vilmos Zsigmond for his filming of *The Long Goodbye*.

Movies Today

Only six major film studios are actively functioning in the United States. Even a studio as venerable as MGM has folded

Paul Newman plays poker with a powerful New York racketeer aboard the 20th Century Limited in *The Sting*. The picture was voted best feature film of 1973 by the Academy of Motion Picture Arts and Sciences.

Movies tend to run in cycles as studios work a theme to death.

its film operations, and Columbia Pictures is in debt $160 million.

Movie attendance dropped off rapidly more than two decades ago with the advent of television. Today, the usual ticket price for a first-run show in big cities is $3; paying for parking and a babysitter in addition makes a night out a significant investment. Understandably, most people stay home and watch television. The studios, in turn, make far more films for television than for theaters; "Television has become the bread-and-butter operation today," says a studio executive.

Movies tend to run in cycles as studios work a theme to death. Many high-budget productions flopped trying to duplicate the success of *The Sound of Music.* A series of "youth" movies failed to capitalize on the popularity of *The Graduate* and *Easy Rider.* The box-office hit *The French Connection* inspired an excess of cops-and-robbers movies.

2001 inspired science-fiction films such as *Zardoz, Sleeper, Westworld, THX 1138, Silent Running,* and *Soylent Green.* *Summer of '42* was perceived as appealing to a craving for nostalgia, and was succeeded by "period" films such as *American Graffiti, The Way We Were, The Sting,* and *The Great Gatsby. Enter the Dragon* was followed by a horde of kung-fu movies until, an executive says, people grew "tired of seeing gallons of blood spilled on the screen and scenes of constant slaughter."

Many of the acclaimed recent films, such as *Serpico, Sounder,* and *Mean Streets,* were independently financed and began production without a guarantee of distribution by the studios. For a director, the main attraction of independent financing is the chance to make unconventional films with a greater degree of freedom than a studio will allow.

Distribution also is becoming more independent of the studios. *Billy Jack* has grossed between $40 and $50 million by "four-walling." Instead of the usual percentage deal, the producers rent the theater for a week and become in effect the exhibitor, paying a flat fee to the theater owner in exchange for the entire box-office take. The producers spent several hundred thousand dollars in saturation advertising and rented enough theaters—62 in southern California alone—so that almost everyone would be within five to six miles of a theater. *Jeremiah Johnson* was re-released in the same way.

A mass-audience blockbuster, like *The Godfather* (which is approaching a global gross of more than $150 million), *Love Story,* or *The Exorcist,* makes up for a dozen duds. But movie executives increasingly believe that the mass market is lost to television and that most films must be geared to separate, specialized audiences. William Friedkin, director of *The Exorcist,* says, "Today there's a black audience, a youth audience, what you might call a Middle American audience that sees Disney pictures. There are redneck films that do very well in the South."

Melvin Van Peebles startled the industry by grossing $11 million for *Sweet Sweetback's Baadasssss Song,* which was distributed completely outside established industry channels. The "stick-it-to-the-Man" theme and heavy emphasis on sex and violence proved highly popular among blacks. Soon other black films, such as *Shaft* and *Super Fly,* were doing big box

For Blacks. Priest (Ron O'Neal), a cocaine pusher in *Super Fly*, becomes socially conscious in *Super Fly TNT*, running guns to African rebels fighting a repressive colonial regime.

Nostalgia. Jay Gatsby's guests cool off after doing a "hot Charleston."

American Film Theatre. Fredric March and Robert Ryan in Eugene O'Neill's *The Iceman Cometh*.

"Boy Meets Boy." Steve McQueen and Dustin Hoffman as prisoners on Devil's Island in *Papillon*.

office in downtown theaters. Some black films, like *Lady Sings the Blues* and *Sounder*, appeal to white audiences as well.

Once moviegoers went to see actresses of the caliber of Greta Garbo, Joan Crawford, and Bette Davis. Now men dominate the box office; Barbra Streisand is the only woman among the 10 most popular stars. In recent years there have been a number of "boy-meets-boy" pictures such as *Midnight Cowboy, Scarecrow, Butch Cassidy and the Sundance Kid, Papillon,* and *The Sting,* in which women are irrelevant and the story concerns the friendship between two men.

Feminists say more women must be allowed the opportunity to be producers, directors, and screenwriters so that films will show women as people instead of, in the words of Molly Haskell, "prostitutes, jilted mistresses, emotional cripples, drunks, daffy ingenues, Lolitas, kooks, sex-starved spinsters, psychotics, icebergs, zombies." She urges films in which "a woman, however small her part, is seen to have an interior life."

The most audacious recent experiment in movies is the American Film Theatre. During the winter of 1973-74, subscribers paid $24 (for matinees) or $30 (for evening performances) to see filmed versions of eight modern plays on Mondays or Tuesdays in more than 500 motion-picture theaters. The films included Edward Albee's *A Delicate Balance* and Eugene O'Neill's *The Iceman Cometh.* Critics felt that in many cases the transition from stage to film was successful, with the lack of physical action and of exciting visual material compensated by challenging content, literate dialogue, and outstanding acting.

Obituaries. December, 1973, and January, February, and early March, 1974.

ALDRICH, WINTHROP W., former board chairman of the Chase National Bank and ambassador to Britain under President Dwight D. Eisenhower; February 25, age 88.

ALLEN, WILLIAM C., Associated Press photographer who covered the White House from Presidents Franklin D. Roosevelt to Lyndon Johnson; February 7, age 60.

ANDERSON, DILLON, special assistant to President Eisenhower for national-security affairs (1955-1956); January 28, age 67.

ANOKHIN, PYOTR K., Soviet physiologist and brain specialist; March 6, age 76.

BATES, H. E., British novelist whose works include *The Darling Buds of May;* January 29, age 68.

BEN-GURION, DAVID, first prime minister of Israel who read the declaration proclaiming the creation of the nation. Before independence, he was a leader in the world Zionist movement; December 1, age 87.

BLUNDEN, EDMUND, English poet and writer who was professor of poetry at Oxford University from 1966 to 1968; January 20, age 77.

BOHLEN, CHARLES, influential U.S. government adviser on Soviet relations for more than 30 years. He helped open the U.S. embassy in Moscow in 1934 and served as presidential interpreter at the summit conferences at Teheran, Yalta, and Potsdam; January 1, age 69.

BRISLIN, JOHN, journalist whose four-year campaign against labor terrorists won him a Pulitzer Prize for local reporting in 1959; December 20, age 62.

BROGAN, D. W., British historian and expert on France and the United States; January 5, age 73.

BROWN, PRENTISS M., senator from Michigan (1936-42) and former director of the Office of Price Administration; December 19, age 84.

BURCKHARDT, CARL J., Swiss historian, diplomat and author; March 3, age 82.

BUSSER, HENRI, French composer and former director of the Paris Opera; December 30, age 101.

BUTTS, WALLY, former University of Georgia football coach who won a sensational libel suit in 1963 against the Curtis Publishing Company, which printed a story suggesting that he had participated in a fixed game; December 17, age 68.

CAMPBELL, PERSIA, economist and consumer advocate; March 2, age 75.

David Ben-Gurion

CANNON, JIMMY, syndicated sports columnist; December 5, age 63.

CHOTINER, MURRAY M., controversial campaign advisor to Richard Nixon since 1946 who played a variety of behind-the-scenes roles for the Nixon Administration; January 30, age 64.

CHU K'O-CHEN, vice president of the Chinese Academy of Sciences and one of the first to introduce 20th-century science to China; February 14, age 84.

CICOGNANA, AMLETO GIOVANNI CARDINAL, dean of the Roman Catholic College of Cardinals who served for 25 years as apostolic delegate in Washington; December 17, age 90.

CLAIRE, HELEN, actress on stage, radio, and television; January 12, age 68.

COLBERT, RICHARD G., former commander in chief of the Allied forces in Southern Europe; December 2, age 58.

COLE, JACK, dance choreographer who introduced the jazz style that became the U.S. dance trademark; February 17, age 60.

CORD, ERRETT LOBBAN, designer of the luxury Cord car of the 1930's. The car was discontinued after 1937, but many of its features were adopted by later autos, such as front-wheel drive, bucket seats, and retractable convertible top; January 2, age 79.

CORDINER, RALPH J., management expert who formulated the policy that decentralized General Electric's corporate management; December 5, age 73.

DALEY, ARTHUR, sports columnist for the New York *Times* who won a Pulitzer Prize in 1956 for his columns; January 3, age 69.

DARIN, BOBBY, popular singer; December 20, age 37.

DART, RAYMOND O., first director of the Armed Forces Institute of Pathology (1946-50); February 2, age 83.

DAUGHERTY, JAMES H., non-objective artist and a writer and illustrator of children's books; February 21, age 84.

DE WOLFE, BILLY, comedian and actor whose films include *Call Me Madam;* March 5, age 67.

DEL SESTO, CHRISTOPHER, former governor of Rhode Island and an associate justice of the state's Superior Court; December 27, age 66.

DILWORTH, RICHARDSON, mayor of Philadelphia (1955-62); January 23, age 75.

DOUGLAS, LEWIS W., director of the budget in the early days of the New Deal and ambassador to Britain (1947-50); March 7, age 79.

DOYLE, LARRY, captain of the New York Giants under manager John McGraw; March 1, age 87.

EMMET, CHRISTOPHER T., political writer who actively opposed both Nazi and Communist totalitarianism; February 13, age 73.

FREMONT-SMITH, FRANK, former president of the World Federation for Mental Health; February 27, age 78.

FULLER, ALFRED C., founder of the Fuller Brush Company and one of the foremost promoters of door-to-door salesmanship; December 4, age 88.

GARAND, JOHN C., inventor of the .30-caliber M-1 rifle used in World War II; February 16, age 86.

GENSOUL, MARCEL-BRUNO, French admiral who defied a World War II order by Winston Churchill to surrender warships anchored in the bay of Oran, Algeria, leading to a battle in which they were sunk or damaged; December 30, age 93.

GERARD, RALPH WALDO, biologist noted for his contributions to the understanding of the brain and nervous system. He presented evidence that schizophrenia is caused by faulty body chemistry, challenging the theory that the disease has psychological and cultural origins; February 17, age 73.

GIBERGA, MANUEL RAFAEL, prominent Cuban economist, refugee leader, and White House aide; January 16, age 58.

GOLD, HARRY, convicted spy and key prosecution witness in the trial of Julius and Ethel Rosenberg for atomic espionage. His death on August 28, 1972, was kept secret until it was uncovered by a journalist and reported February 14; age 60.

GOLDWYN, SAMUEL, Hollywood producer whose career spanned half a century. One of the flashiest and most controversial producers, he was a tyrant on the set and an industry legend. His films, always on a grand scale, were respected for their quality and taste. Among them were *Wuthering Heights, Guys and Dolls,* and *Porgy and Bess;* January 31, age 91.

GOLENPAUL, DAN, creator of the radio show *Information Please,* which ran from 1938 to 1952; February 13, age 73.

GOTTLIEB, ADOLPH, a founder of the New York School of abstract expressionism and a major figure in American art for more than 30 years; March 4, age 70.

GRIVAS, GEORGE, general who helped lead Cyprus to independence from Britain in 1960 and then led a campaign of terrorist attacks in an effort to bring about union with Greece; January 27, age 75.

GRUENBERG, SIDONIE MATSNER, a leading authority on the rearing of children; March 11, age 91.

HARRISON, BURR P., congressman from Virginia (1946-63); December 29, age 69.

HORTON, TIM, hockey defenseman with the Buffalo Sabres and president of Tim Donut, Ltd., Canada's third-largest doughnut chain; February 21, age 44.

HUROK, SOL, one of the world's foremost impresarios. He sponsored a vast number of singers and musicians, dance groups, and theatrical groups, including Marian Anderson, André Segovia, the Bolshoi Ballet with Galina Ulanova, the Old Vic, and Kabuki players from Tokyo; March 5, age 85.

INONU, ISMET, first premier of modern Turkey and its second president. He administered a number of reforms that helped transform Turkey from an oriental sultanate to a Western-style state, including introducing the Roman alphabet and the Gregorian calendar, and establishing new civil and penal code; December 25, age 89.

JOHNSON, EARL J., editor for 30 years of the news operations of United Press International and its predecessor, the United Press; January 3, age 73.

JORDAN, B. EVERETT, former Democratic senator from North Carolina who led the 1964 investigation into the activities of Bobby Baker; March 15, age 77.

JUDGE, ARLINE, movie star of the 1930's; February 7, age 61.

KALLEN, HORACE, philosopher and educator who founded the New School for Social Research in New York City; February 16, age 91.

Lewis Douglas

Samuel Goldwyn

KOMINEK, BOLESLAW CARDINAL, Polish archbishop of Wroclaw (Breslau) since 1956; March 10, age 70.

KRISHNAMACHARI, TIRUVALLUR THATTAI, former finance minister of India and a close associate of the late prime minister Nehru; March 7, age 74.

KUIPER, GERARD P., internationally known astronomer and one of the foremost authorities on the moon. He played an important role in the United States' early space program; December 23, age 68.

LEE, HAROLD B., president of the Church of Jesus Christ of Latter-Day Saints since July, 1972; December 26, age 74.

LEECH, MARGARET, historian who won Pulitzer prizes for *Reveille in Washington* (1940) and *In the Days of McKinley* (1959); February 24, age 80.

LENTZ, ARTHUR, former director of the U.S. Olympic Committee; January 25, age 65.

LENZ, MAURICE, internationally known radiotherapist who specialized in the treatment of cancer; January 4, age 83.

LINK, THEODORE C., investigative reporter for the St. Louis *Post-Dispatch* who helped publicize crime syndicates throughout the country; February 14, age 69.

LOEB, HAROLD A., publisher of *Broom,* an influential literary magazine of the early 1920's; January 20, age 82.

LOVEJOY, CLARENCE E., editor of the series of popular school and college guides that bear his name; January 16, age 79.

McGRAW, DONALD C., former president of McGraw-Hill, Inc., publishers; February 7, age 76.

McKINNEY, FRANK E., SR., Democratic party national chairman in 1951 and 1952; January 9, age 69.

McMASTER, LAWRENCE W., executive of the United Presbyterian Synod of the Covenant, which covers the central states; February 2, age 44.

MERROW, CHESTER E., Republican representative from New Hampshire (1943-1963); February 10, age 67.

MORRIS, GLENN, Olympic decathlon champion in 1936 and star of several Tarzan movies; January 31, age 62.

MUNRO, Sir LESLIE, former president of the UN General Assembly and New Zealand's ambassador to the United States; February 13, age 72.

MYERBERG, MICHAEL, stage and screen producer; January 6, age 67.

NILSSON, ANNA Q., one of the first Swedish film actresses to attain stardom in Hollywood; February 11, age 85.

ODRIA, MANUEL A., president of Peru (1948-56) who made some improvements for the working class but suppressed political opposition; February 18, age 77.

PITTS, LUCIUS H., president of Paine College in Atlanta, Georgia, since 1971; February 25, age 59.

POPE-HENNESSY, JAMES, official biographer of British royalty; January 25, age 57.

POSTON, TED, one of the first black reporters hired to work for a major New York daily newspaper; January 11, age 67.

POWERS, MARIE, contralto acclaimed for her roles in the operas of Gian Carlo Menotti; December 28, believed to be in her 60's.

RAHV, PHILIP, literary critic who was a founding co-editor of *Partisan Review;* December 22, age 64.

RITTER, TEX, country-music star in movies and on records; January 2, age 67.

ROUSSEAU, THEODORE, curator in chief and vice director of the Metropolitan Museum of Art; December 31, age 61.

RUBY, HARRY, composer of popular songs, including "Three Little Words" and "Who's Sorry Now?"; February 23, age 79.

RUIZ CORTINES, ADOLFO, president of Mexico (1952-58) who presided over extensive changes in the country's economy and was regarded by many as having restored confidence in the government; December 3, age 82.

SCHLAG, FELIX, sculptor who designed the Jefferson nickel in 1938; March 9, age 82.

SEATON, FRED A., secretary of the interior under Dwight D. Eisenhower and owner of a network of newspapers in the Midwest; January 16, age 64.

SHAKESPEARE, WILLIAM V., star halfback for the University of Notre Dame in the 1930's; January 17, age 61.

SHAW, JOHN P., diplomat and specialist on Soviet affairs who helped draft one of the basic SALT documents in 1971; January 20, age 50.

SIQUEIROS, DAVID ALFARO, Mexican muralist whose works dealt with the struggles of the poor and made use of native culture and traditions. He was the last of three Mexican muralists—the others were Diego Rivera and Clemente José Orozco—regarded as having profoundly influenced Western art. After the artist's death, President Luis Echeverría Alvarez praised him for having "contributed to a better understanding of the independence process of the Mexicans"; January 7, age 77.

SMITH, ALBERT COWPER, commander of

the 14th U.S. Armored Division in Europe during World War II; January 23, age 80.

SMRKOVSKY, JOSEF, close associate of Alexander Dubcek, the Czechoslovakian reformist leader; January 14, age 62.

SOKOLOVA, LYDIA (born Hilda Munnings), a leading dancer of the Diaghilev Ballet; February 2, age 77.

SPECTER, EDWARD, a founder and manager of the Pittsburgh Symphony Orchestra and a former Broadway producer; March 13, age 73.

STEINBERG, BENJAMIN, founder of the Symphony of the New World; January 29, age 58.

STRAUSS, LEWIS, former chairman of the Atomic Energy Commission and a key figure in shaping U.S. thermonuclear policy. He was a strong advocate of America's development of the hydrogen bomb; January 21, age 77.

STRUMILIN, STANISLAV G., dean of Soviet scholars in economics; January 25, age 96.

SUTHERLAND, EARL W., JR., biologist who won the 1971 Nobel Prize in physiology or medicine for his basic research on hormones; March 9, age 58.

TANAKA, KOTARO, former chief justice of the Supreme Court of Japan and a former judge of the International Court of Justice in The Hague; March 1, age 83.

TOMLINSON, EDWARD, a prominent reporter and author of books on Latin-American politics and economics; December 29, age 82.

VAN WATERS, MIRIAM, pioneering prison director, penal reformer, and social worker; January 17, age 86.

VOISIN, GABRIEL, French air pioneer who made his first flight in a glider in 1904 and the following year founded the world's first airplane factory; December 25, age 93.

VOLKOV, LEON, Soviet air force pilot who defected in 1945 and spent his last 20 years as a specialist on Soviet affairs for *Newsweek* magazine; January 21, age 59.

WANG CHIA-HSIANG, China's first post-revolutionary ambassador to the Soviet Union; January 25, age 68.

WASHBURN, WATSON, Davis Cup tennis star in the 1920's; December 2, age 79.

WATSON-WATT, Sir ROBERT, developer of the world's first practical radar system, which proved vital during the Battle of Britain in 1940; December 5, age 81.

WHEELER, RAYMOND A., chief of the Army's corps of engineers from 1946 to 1949 who directed the clearing of the Suez Canal for the UN after the 1956 Sinai campaign; February 8, age 88.

ZWICKY, FRITZ, astronomer and jet-propulsion expert; February 8, age 74.

Adolfo Ruíz Cortines

David Siqueiros

Petroleum. Arab oil ministers meeting in Vienna, Austria, agreed on March 18 to lift the five-month embargo on oil deliveries to the United States for a period ending June 1. Libya and Syria dissented, saying they would continue to enforce the boycott.

The oil ministers made it clear that the Arabs expected the United States to put further pressure on Israel to withdraw from occupied territories. No mention was made of lifting the embargo against Denmark, the Netherlands, Portugal, South Africa, or Rhodesia.

Saudi Arabia's oil minister, Ahmed Zaki Yamani, said the United States could expect to receive at least a million more barrels a day from his country. The Arabs, who had cut back oil production in October as well as putting an embargo on the United States, said output would be raised significantly to accommodate most major consuming nations but refrained from committing themselves to a full restoration of production. (Arab oil production was running 10 to 15 per cent below the levels of September, 1973.)

President Nixon said March 19 that stations would no longer have to close on Sundays and that gasoline rationing could be ruled out. But Federal Energy Office Director William Simon warned that gas supplies would remain tight due to conditions—such as the shortage of refining capacity in the United States—that preceded the embargo.

The Federal Energy Office had predicted in late February that for the first quarter of 1974 oil supplies in the United States would be 13.6 per cent below unconstrained needs, a shortfall of 2.7 million barrels of oil per day. After the first quarter, inventories of excess oil would be virtually depleted, and the estimated shortage would be 3 million barrels a day. Senior officials of the FEO said February 23 that if the Arab oil embargo were not lifted by the end of April, a gasoline drought could hit wide areas of the country by late spring or early summer.

Gasless Sundays, lower speed limits, higher prices, and long lines at service stations resulted from the oil shortage. A dozen states adopted rationing programs. Most of them restricted sales of gas to alternate days; cars with license plates ending with an even number were served on days ending with an even number, and cars with plates ending with an odd number were given gas on odd-numbered days. The auto and travel-related industries were the worst hit by the gasoline shortage. (See BUSINESS AND FINANCE in this section.)

The United States was suffering about three-fourths of the total world oil shortage. Surplus oil was available abroad, but

Frustrated Motorists endured gasless Sundays, lower speed limits, higher prices, and long lines at service stations as a result of the gasoline shortage. The Arab oil boycott was lifted on March 18.

the FEO conceded that the government's allocation program had made the oil shortage worse. FEO Director Simon conceded that the shortfall could have been reduced by 800,000 to 1 million barrels daily, or by 7 to 9 per cent of the nation's needs, if it had not been for disincentives in the program.

The major oil companies were required to share their crude oil with competitors experiencing a shortage when their own refineries were filled to 76 per cent of capacity. Many of the companies, rather than bid on available oil and then share it with competitors at government-controlled prices, decided not to import oil at all. The allocation program also required oil companies to distribute to their service stations only 81 per cent of the gasoline that the stations had received in 1972, in order to conserve supplies. But many stations had closed since 1972, and the number of cars had increased. As a result, less gasoline was reaching consumers than expected.

Truckers' Strike

Independent truckers halted deliveries of perishable goods and other items throughout much of the nation for 12 days in demanding a fuel price rollback. Most of the trucks returned to the highways February 11, indicating their acceptance of an agreement negotiated with the aid of Governor Milton Shapp of Pennsylvania and Administration officials.

Independent truckers number 100,000 and deliver 70 per cent of the nation's perishable goods. Self-employed, they use their own rigs to haul goods on a contract basis for trucking companies. The truckers complained that the increase in the price of diesel fuel—from 27 cents to 45 cents a gallon in the last six months—had cut their incomes by one-third or more. They also protested the fuel allocation—limited to 110 per cent of their 1972 consumption

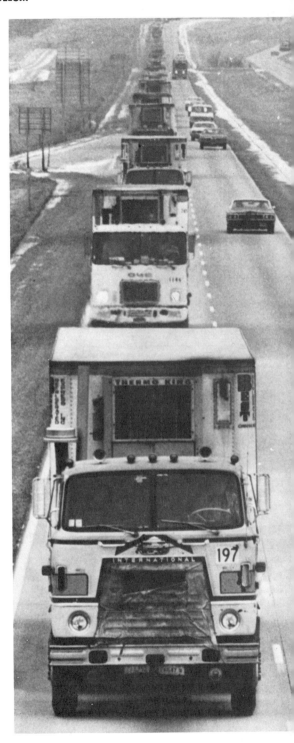

Trucking Dispute. National Guard units were called up in eight states to patrol the highways and provide convoy protection for nonstriking drivers during a 12-day strike by independent truckers. The independents, who deliver 70 per cent of the nation's perishable goods, demanded a fuel price rollback.

—and driving time wasted by reduced highway speed limits.

The strike was loosely organized by a coalition of 18 regional groups that demanded a price rollback to the levels of May 15, 1973, and a public audit of diesel-fuel supplies held by the major oil companies. At least 75,000 workers were laid off as the flow of supplies dwindled around the nation.

Truckers set up pickets around oil depots and harassed nonstriking truck drivers. Violent incidents involving gunfire, stonings, beatings, burned rigs, and bomb threats were reported in more than 20 states. Two truckers were killed, and there were scores of injuries. National Guard units were called up in eight states to patrol the highways and provide convoy protection for nonstriking drivers.

On February 6, President Nixon ordered a 30-day freeze on fuel prices and promised to give the truckers all the fuel they needed. The following day, agreement was reached on a 6-per-cent surcharge on freight rates to cover increased fuel costs; truckers buying their own fuel would get this sum. The truckers were exempted from the ban on Sunday fuel sales.

Oil in Europe

By contrast, the cutbacks in oil production had minimal impact in Europe, although Arab producers were, at least in theory, pumping less oil than before the Yom Kippur war of October, 1973. Unseasonably warm weather helped to reduce energy consumption. Prices of gasoline rose sharply, but supplies were adequate. Lower speed limits imposed on most highways were hailed as a blessing for cutting accident rates.

The Arab producers had imposed a total oil embargo on the Netherlands, but oil companies allocated the supply from all sources in such a way that there was no great difference in the amount of oil each European country was receiving. Gasoline rationing in the Netherlands ended after 23 days, and the ban on Sunday driving was lifted after 10 weeks. Gas rationing was ended in Sweden on January 29 after only 22 days. In West Germany, Sunday driving was banned only from November 25 to December 16, when the restriction was lifted.

Gasless Sundays in Rome. A ban on Sunday driving was in effect in Italy for most of the winter because a government ceiling on gasoline prices led to diversion of oil to countries willing to pay more. In general, the cutbacks in oil production caused only minor disruption in Europe; prices of gasoline rose sharply, but supplies were adequate.

Italy suffered the most, because a government ceiling on gasoline prices led to diversion of oil to countries willing to pay more. A ban on Sunday driving continued through the winter, heating in public buildings was curtailed, and curfews were in effect in restaurants and bars.

On February 13, the United States and 11 other major oil-consuming nations overrode strong French objections and agreed in Washington on "a comprehensive action program" to deal with the energy crisis. The communiqué called for joint action in conserving energy, allocating oil supplies in times of emergency, accelerating research, and searching for new energy sources. U.S. officials had expressed their opposition to bilateral deals between individual oil-producing and oil-consuming nations, saying such accords would tend to drive up the price of oil.

The 12 nations also said that they favored financial and monetary measures to avoid competitive depreciation of currencies because of the impact of higher oil prices on the balance of payments. They announced plans for a conference of oil-consuming and oil-producing countries "at the earliest possible opportunity."

On March 4, however, the nine Common Market countries agreed to separate talks with the Arab nations on a number of issues, including oil. A U.S. State Department spokesman said that it "remains to be seen" whether the action had undermined the validity of the decisions made at the Washington energy conference.

A number of nations were negotiating bilateral deals for oil. The New York Times reported January 27 that in the last few months Western and Japanese government and business delegations had concluded $6 billion worth of agreements with the Middle East exporters of oil, including loans, services, and investment in return for long-term oil contracts. However, the bulk of these agreements were letters of intent rather than hard-and-fast contracts.

On January 25, Great Britain agreed to buy about 5 million tons of crude oil from Iran in 1974 for about $7 a barrel, in return for textiles, steel, paper, petrochemicals, and other industrial goods.

Franco-American Dispute. U.S. Secretary of State Henry Kissinger and French Foreign Minister Michel Jobert did not see eye-to-eye on ways to deal with the energy crisis during a conference of major oil-consuming nations. Later, American officials accused France of urging Arab governments not to lift their embargo on oil deliveries to the United States.

Britain also agreed to sell Iran ground-to-air missiles.

Earlier, France agreed to buy 27 million tons of Saudi Arabian oil over three years in return for weapons and industrial machinery. Italy reached an agreement in principle with Saudi Arabia to set up a Fiat assembly plant there. Japan was to receive 160 million tons of Iraqi oil over 10 years in return for carrying out re-

fining, petrochemical, and other industrial projects in Iraq valued at $1 billion.

Middle East Oil Wealth

In 1973, oil revenues received by Middle East nations amounted to about $22 billion; in 1974 the sum was expected to run anywhere between $85 billion and $110 billion. Most of the consuming nations were faced with massive balance-of-payments deficits unless they could attract the revenue back to their own countries. For example, the Common Market countries expected to be paying $17 to $18 billion more in 1974 for oil, of which perhaps only a third would come back to Europe.

The New York *Times* reported February 12 that the Middle East oil exporters were spending huge amounts for refineries, natural-gas processing plants, petrochemical industries, arms, industrial goods, and nonoil-based industrial plants and projects. These projects would give the producers a much stronger position in competing with oil companies for a major share in world markets for petroleum products and industrial raw materials derived from petroleum. Meanwhile, the consuming nations would earn money by supplying the engineering, equipment, and technology for these ventures.

But, it was calculated, the oil producers would still be able to spend less than half of their 1974 earnings for capital equipment and consumer goods. Most of the remaining $50 billion was expected to be deposited, lent, or invested in major Western capital markets. The rest would go into corporate stocks or real-estate investments in the developed countries.

Traditionally, the Arabs have been cautious investors, putting money heavily into short-term government bonds. But Arab institutions were showing new interest in buying hotels, apartments, and office buildings abroad, and buying interests in

Arab Know-How. Saudi Arabians study the petroleum business at the Arabian American Oil Company's College of Petroleum and Minerals. Nearly every oil-producing nation is planning to market its oil in order to compete with the companies for a major share of the world market.

foreign banks. Oil revenue was expected increasingly to flow to Arab-affiliated banks, such as the newly established Union des Banques Arabes et Françaises, which has 60 per cent of its assets owned by Arab nations and 40 per cent by French banks.

Worst hit by the sharp rise in oil prices were the developing countries, which have little to attract investors. But Saudi Arabia was setting up an Arab African Bank in Cairo to ch. nnel Arab funds to African countries.

Nearly every producing nation was entering the oil business. The National Iranian Oil Company holds interests in India and South Africa and was contracting to sell oil to Ashland Oil Company in return for a half-interest in 180 service stations in New York State and a refinery in Buffalo. Petromin plans ultimately to market Saudi Arabian oil worldwide and to expand into petrochemicals. Kuwait National Petroleum Company operates a refinery and markets oil and refined products internationally through offices in the United States, Britain, Japan, and Singapore.

Portugal. Portugal's worst political crisis in 13 years was touched off by the dismissal of General António de Spínola, deputy chief of the general staff, and his immediate superior, General Francisco de Costa Gomes, on March 14. A small group of junior officers and enlisted men sympathetic to Spínola staged a brief rebellion two days later.

Officers Purged

General Spínola was a popular figure who had served four years as governor of the West African colony of Portuguese Guinea and as commander of Portuguese forces there. In 1973 he returned to Portugal, where he was decorated with highest honors and given a post created especially for him. But the publication in February of a book by Spínola criticizing Portuguese policy in its African territories created a furor among right-wing officers and government officials, who forced Premier Marcello Caetano to fire him.

Spínola's book, *Portugal and the Future,* argued the necessity of a political settlement with guerrillas who have been fighting the Portuguese army in Mozambique, Angola, and Portuguese Guinea for nearly 13 years. (See AFRICA in the first 1973 section.) General Costa Gomes reportedly had authorized Spínola's book and had praised it in a confidential memo circulated in Lisbon.

The ouster of other officers favoring an early political accommodation with the African guerrillas was also reported. On

War-Weariness. Smiling mannequins on display in Lisbon were designed to attract volunteers for the fighting in Portugal's colonies. But unrest in the armed forces was a clear indication that the nation was tiring of the colonial wars which had sapped Portugal's treasury and manpower for so long.

March 14, the naval secretary of the armed forces defense staff, Admiral Tierno Bagulho, was dismissed.

Military Rebellion Fails

A brief insurrection by about 200 members of the army's 5th Infantry Regiment took place March 16. At Calhas de Rainha, regimental headquarters 50 miles north of Lisbon, armed soldiers locked up their commanding officers and began traveling toward the capital in a convoy of 10 trucks. The mutinous troops had hoped to gather support from other military units as they moved on Lisbon. Instead, they were confronted with a mobilized 7th Armored Regiment (based at Santarem, 30 miles northeast of Lisbon) and surrendered without bloodshed.

The revolt was led mainly by junior officers who were partisans of the ousted chief of staff, General Spínola. Following the rebels' return to Calhas de Rainha, 33 officers and 180 enlisted men were arrested, and a state of alert was imposed to confine remaining troops to barracks. The alert was lifted on March 18.

The military academy in Lisbon had become a particular center for dissenting young officers. Late March 15, the academy was surrounded by military police during a meeting called to protest the firings of Spínola and Costa Gomes. The officers were allowed to leave, but there were reports of later arrests. Dismissal of the academy's commandant, Reserve General Amaro Romau, was announced by the government on March 18.

Portugal and the Future

When General Spínola's book *Portugal and the Future* was released February 22, it became an instant best-seller. In part, this response reflected widespread public desire for an end to the colonial wars which had sapped Portugal's treasury and manpower for so long. But Spínola's attack on official policy was especially devastating because the author's credentials as a soldier and a patriot were beyond reproach.

The expression of opposition to government policies has been sharply limited by the rightist forces which have controlled the country's political, military, and economic life for half a century. Critics of

the African war have been imprisoned and tortured. In the 1973 elections campaign, candidates for the National Assembly who had criticized colonial policies were compelled to withdraw.

According to the government's official position, the African provinces of Angola, Mozambique, and Portuguese Guinea (also known as Guinea-Bissau) are integral parts of Portugal. This position is based largely on the fear that Portugal without its colonies would have little influence in Europe, or might even be swallowed up by Spain. But perpetuation of the African fighting has drained the country's resources, consuming nearly one-half of the national budget, and has contributed to Portugal's political isolation in the world.

Spínola proposed that the African impasse be resolved through the formation by referendum of a federation in which Angola, Mozambique, and Portuguese Guinea would be given equal status with Portugal. He suggested the impossibility of a military victory and pointed to Portugal's increasing economic ills. Inflation is severe (about 19 per cent in 1973) and one-tenth of the population has emigrated to look for employment. The appearance of domestic prosperity is maintained by tourism, government spending, and remittances from workers abroad.

Premier Caetano asserted March 15 that there would be no change in the government's policy toward the African territories. "We have full confidence in our capacity to win [a military victory]," he said. "I have faith that unity, serenity, and the national awareness of the people will finally triumph over this crisis." However, the fact that the government did not ban Spínola's book aroused wide speculation that Caetano was not in complete disagreement with his views.

Increased public pressure for a political settlement of the African conflict appeared inevitable. Only three days after Caetano's speech, a paper circulated among some 300 military officers appeared, calling for "a political solution that safeguards national honor and dignity but which takes into account the incontestable and irreversible reality of the deep aspirations of the African peoples."

Religion: Rise of the Occult

William Blatty's novel *The Exorcist* was published in 1971 and remained on the best-seller lists for over a year. By early 1974 sales had passed 9 million. The opening of the motion picture at the end of 1973 brought a public response that *Newsweek* described as an "exorcism frenzy."

Nearly 4 million people rushed to see the film during the first month, many waiting in line for hours. Reports of viewers fainting or vomiting over what took place on the screen, or having to walk out in the middle of the movie, seemed only to attract greater crowds. One newscaster called the movie the most talked about subject in the country, overtaking even Watergate and the energy crisis.

Blatty's story is based on a case that made the newspapers in 1949 concerning the alleged demonic possession of a boy in Mt. Ranier, Maryland. After illness—physical or mental—was explored and rejected as the reason for the boy's behavior, the parents agreed to his conversion to Catholicism for the purpose of exorcism, and the boy was "cured."

Blatty got much of his information from a diary kept by one of the priests involved in the boy's case. He changed the victim to a girl and added some subplots, such as the younger priest's crisis of faith, but the main action concerns the deterioration of the possessed child into a raving, tormented creature under the influence of the devil.

Exorcism Rite is performed by two priests in *The Exorcist*. The film, which was seen by nearly 4 million people during its first month on exhibit, capitalized on and added to a mounting interest in psychic phenomena, witchcraft, Satanism, and the occult in general.

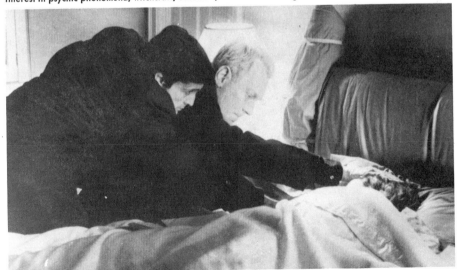

Pope Paul calls evil "a living spiritual being... a terrible reality."

The movie capitalized on and added to a mounting interest in psychic phenomena, witchcraft, Satanism, and the occult in general. Many critics and clergy called *The Exorcist* sensational, theologically unsound, and philosophically simplistic. Yet priests reported an increased number of inquiries about and requests for exorcisms. A few interpreted the public reaction as signaling a renewed interest in religion. For some viewers the fear engendered by the movie was apparently more than the thrill provided by a good horror film; it reflected a remnant—or a beginning—of belief in a literal devil.

Growth of the Devil

The devil that comes with Christianity has his roots in Old Testament Judaism, but the image has influences from other cultures. Satan, the Hebrew word for adversary, occurs only a few times in the Old Testament, as in the naming of Job's tormentor. That being was not the embodiment of evil that he later became

Medieval Image of the Devil shows him with horns, bat's wings, and a hairy body. But sometimes, in deference to his origin as a fallen angel, he is painted or described as a handsome man dressed attractively in a black cape.

but clearly a subject of God—more a tester of man than a temptor. God remained the originator of both good and evil; He both blessed and punished.

Later, under Persian influence, a dualism of good and evil developed, increasing the devil's power significantly and giving him a host of lesser demons to aid his work. By the time of the New Testament, Satan had acquired quite an independent stature, as when he tempts Christ in the desert.

Early and medieval Christian writers showed great concern over the problems raised by belief in such a powerful evil spirit in a universe controlled by an all-wise and loving God. Satan came to play an important part in explanations of the nature of evil and the meaning of salvation. Through art the theologians' devil came within the grasp of everyone; the gargoyles on European cathedrals and the representative of hell conjured up by the knowledge-seeking Faust are aspects of the same spirit of evil.

Many of the more picturesque characteristics of the devil derive from pagan dieties. The cloven hooves, horns, and tail are found in the Greek nature god Pan. The image of a winged and clawed demon occurred in ancient Mesopotamia, where Pazuzu was a malaria-bearing demon, a "king of the evil spirits of the air." Set, an early Egyptian god associated with violent aspects of nature, such as thunder and earthquakes, was represented as a snake or a crocodile and eventually became the personification of all evil.

An obnoxious or animal-like appearance appropriately represents a devil responsible for chaos and evil. Sometimes, in deference to his origin as a fallen angel, the devil is painted or described as a courteous and handsome man, dressed attractively in a black cape, and with perhaps only the nubs of horns to suggest his evil identity. Also, to reflect his once exalted status, he is often depicted as clever and quick-tongued—valuable talents in the bargaining for souls.

Despite the riches of demonic mythology, most progressive theologians do not believe that Satan is a real being prowling the earth. The majority of Biblical scholars suggest that the New Testament writers, embellishing Old Testament references, used mythological and religious conventions of their time to describe the constant struggle between good and evil.

Others, however, keep the traditional Christian view that Satan really exists. Among those who so believe is Pope Paul VI. In an address in November, 1972, he said, "Evil is not merely a lack of something, but an effective agent, a living spiritual being, perverted and perverting. A terrible reality." He specifically objected to efforts to explain the devil as "a conceptual and fanciful personification" of misfortune.

Satanism

As churchmen argue or hedge on the existence of a satanic personage, the explicit acknowledgement and worship of him spreads. Probably the most prominent formal group is the First Church of Satan, founded in 1966 by Anton Szandor La Vey. It was organized in San Francisco and is incorporated and protected under California law.

La Vey's *Satanic Bible* includes the beatitude "Blessed are the strong, for they shall

The Satanic church is a mirror image of the traditional beliefs of Christianity.

Satanism. Anton Szandor La Vey founded the First Church of Satan in 1966. Members are openly committed to self-gratification and the pursuit of material wealth.

possess the earth," and such injunctions as "If a man smite you on one cheek, SMASH him on the other!" As the Black Mass is said to be a reversal of the Catholic celebration, the Satanic church is a mirror image of the traditional beliefs of Christianity. The Satanic church has held satanic baptisms and a "black wedding," and it has a hierarchy. La Vey stopped giving out membership figures when his followers reached 10,000.

Despite the occult trappings of the Church of Satan—inverted pentagrams, vestments of red and black, a nude woman stretched on the altar during services—members do not really invoke Satan as a supernatural being; in fact, they look down on those who believe in supernatural beings, evil or good. But they seem to have taken his message to heart, being most unspiritual in their open commitment to self-gratification and the pursuit of material wealth.

Appointments to the various ranks of the church's hierarchy are based not only on proficiency in Satanist doctrine but also on the candidate's "dining preferences," the "style of decor" in his home, and the "make, year and condition" of his car. La Vey claims the church's goal is the establishment of a police state in which the weak are weeded out and the "achievement-oriented leadership" is permitted to pursue the mysteries of black magic.

More spiritually minded are members of the Process Church of the Final Judgment. They believe in Satan, Jehovah, and Lucifer as a divine triumverate representing different aspects of human nature which are unified in Christ. Young members have openly proselytized in major cities, distributing a colorful magazine and asking donations.

There also exists a more malevolent form of Satanism, of which the Charles Manson "family" is a well-known example. Other cases occasionally make the news. In 1971 a 22-year-old Satanist killed a 62-year-old friend, stabbing him 46 times. When she drew a seven-year sentence for manslaughter, she thanked the devil for the light sentence and said that she had enjoyed the killing.

In another incident, a 20-year-old Satanist was killed by two friends at his own request. His studies in black magic led him to believe that a loyal worshipper of Satan who is murdered by his friends will be reborn as a captain of devils. Ministers who worked with young people in the New Jersey town estimated that dozens of them were witches and warlocks.

Witchcraft

The practice of witchcraft experienced a revival in the 1950's and 1960's after a couple of centuries of dormancy. In the Christian tradition, witchcraft has been considered the exercise of supernatural power for evil purposes. During the early centuries of the church the claim to such power was considered delusion or superstition and was forbidden. Later, practitioners were believed to be in league with the devil, and hundreds of thousands of alleged witches suffered torture and death. Witch trials, popular at various times throughout Europe and in the United States, finally ended in the 18th century.

The repeal, in 1951, of old laws against witchcraft in England may have spurred its revival there. Cases of black magic were reported in England, the Soviet Union, and Germany, as well as in Mexico

Witchcraft. Self-proclaimed witch Morgan McFarland says "Witchcraft is a very Christian religion, the oldest in the world." Scholars view witchcraft as a vestige of pagan nature worship. For centuries, practitioners were believed to be in league with the devil and suffered torture or death, but so-called white witches like Miss McFarland say they do good, not evil.

Witches believe that they can affect events through hexes, spells, and collected human energy.

and Guatemala where witchcraft never completely lost its hold.

Although witches are commonly believed to derive their power from the devil, in 1921 anthropologist Margaret Murray advanced the theory that witchcraft was actually a vestige of pagan nature worship. So-called white witches hold this belief. Whereas black magic causes harm, white magic heals, works for good for others, or attempts to lift spells cast by black magic. (This distinction is also made in many cultures where magic is still practiced openly and believed in by most people.) A philosophy instructor in Chicago estimates that there are some 80,000 white witches in the United States.

Sybil Leek, who was born in Britain, claims to be a hereditary witch whose lineage goes back to 1134. She prefers to call her craft by the Anglo-Saxon name *wicca,* meaning sorcerer or wise one. The term suggests that power comes through knowledge of the forces of nature, rather than from the devil.

In "pure witchcraft," she says, "the life force is all important. Satanism is death. *Wicca* is a religion designed to preserve life." She has made her home in the United States for several years and has made a comfortable living from the sale of her many books (including *Diary of a Witch* and *Cast Your Own Spell*).

A number of covens have arisen in cities and suburbs around the country. In keeping with tradition, the covens have as many as 13 members, who gather when the moon is full and perform rituals. Often the participants are "sky-clad"—witch terminology for nude—except for symbolic ornaments such as an athame, or magic

knife, tied at the waist. Special ceremonies are celebrated on witches' sabbaths, such as Halloween and the spring equinox.

The recent publication of scores of books on various aspects of the occult—ranging from serious histories to astrological cookbooks—feeds what Owen Rachleff calls "library witchcraft." Rites and chants are picked up from numerous sources and combined with new inventions. The result might be a worship ritual performed in elaborate costume or a drug and sex orgy.

Most members of the new covens are said to be professionals—office managers, social workers, chemists. One coven member is an air force captain, another teaches a college course in witchcraft, another is a clergyman. To neighbors and co-workers they appear as ordinary middle-class people.

When one engineer was asked what draws a modern scientist to an anachronistic cult like witchcraft, he replied, "The computer age is one of incredible boredom to most of us. The sense of wonder and awe has been lost and replaced by programmed learning and living. Now people are seaching for something more personal, more intimate, more stimulating—something with deep roots and ancient mystery."

Witches believe that they can affect events through hexes, spells, and collected human energy. Gerald Gardner, who did much to publicize witchcraft in England, said that in 1940 witches of several covens had joined together to form a "Cone of Power," directing their energies toward preventing Hitler from invading Britain. He said similar energies had been directed against Napoleon and against the Spanish Armada.

Magic Medicine. Witch doctors have been recognized in tribal cultures around the world as persons of power, able to affect both body and spirit. Western medicine and psychiatry have generally ignored or explained away the results of traditional ceremonials, and under Western influence many ancient practices wither away.

In the Navajo culture the medicine man was in danger of dying out because potential students needed to work at paying jobs and did not have time to devote to learning. To prevent the loss of this knowledge, the National Institute of Mental Health began two years ago providing scholarships for Navajo Indians to study "curing ceremonials" under tribal medicine men on the federal reservation at Rough Rock, Arizona.

In treating a patient, a Navajo medicine man creates a symbolic pattern in the sand using pollen, meal, and crushed flowers. The patient is directed to sit on this "painting" during part of the ceremony, after which the painting—and the patient's problems—are destroyed. The ceremony also includes ritual singing and dancing with the patient and his relatives and friends.

Psychiatrist Robert Bergman explained that the ceremonials are based on a belief that disease is "caused by disharmony with the universe, including the universe of other men." Bergman was impressed with the approach when he met a Navajo medicine man who had apparently cured a psychotic Indian woman after a modern psychiatric hospital had failed to help her. He pointed out that Navajo medicine and psychoanalysis have much in common: both hold that much behavior is shaped by unconscious processes and both have an "ordered method of establishing intense, helpful relationships" between doctor and patient.

Don Juan. Among the scores of books that have encouraged or taken advantage of the interest in the occult are the best-selling "Don Juan books" by anthropologist Carlos Castaneda. The author, then a graduate student, went to Mexico to

African Witch Doctor. Mrs. Anna Sithole helps her patients find lost possessions, communicate with the dead, and regain the affections of straying spouses. Witch doctors have been recognized in tribal cultures around the world as persons of power, able to affect both body and spirit. The "cure" often includes ritual singing and dancing.

gather information on hallucinogenic plants for his master's thesis. There he met Juan Matus, an old Yaqui Indian, who presented the plants to him as keys to an entirely different system of reality. Castaneda began an apprenticeship in the ways of Indian sorcery that was to extend over 10 years.

The books which have so fascinated readers in the United States are a record of Castaneda's efforts, under the tutelage of Don Juan, to become a "man of knowledge," to penetrate the "non-ordinary reality" of the sorcerer's world. *The Teachings of Don Juan: A Yaqui Way of Knowledge* (1968) describes his first steps in the process, through experiences with natural drugs such as the peyote cactus and a preparation made from psilocybin mushrooms. *A Separate Reality* (1971) deals with Castaneda's efforts to learn to "see" the world directly—to experience it without interpreting. In *Journey to Ixtlan* (1972) Castaneda talks about "seeing" without the use of drugs.

Teachings achieved its first popularity as a counterculture classic since it dealt with drug experiences, but readers were later to realize—as Castaneda himself had to learn—that drugs were only a step to something deeper and more complete. "A sorcerer takes hallucinogens for a different reason than heads do," he said, "and after he has gotten where he wants to go, he stops taking them."

A sorcerer, a man of knowledge, is a "warrior" in Don Juan's term. He is wholly at one with his environment, disciplined, capable of acting with "controlled abandon." He is alone. Death is always over his left shoulder, so he performs each act "impeccably," as though it were his last.

Don Juan frequently prods Castaneda to free himself from daily routines, which dull perception, and from his past, his constantly reinforced concepts of himself. He explains, "Nobody knows who I am or what I do. Not even I .... We either take everything for sure and real, or we don't. If we follow the first path, we get bored to death with ourselves and the world. If we follow the second and erase personal history, we create a fog around us, a very exciting and mysterious state."

Occult Studies

In response to student demand, many high schools and universities offer courses in the occult. Popular classes have dealt with extrasensory perception, numerology, hypnotism, yoga, witchcraft, and astrology. Oakland University in Rochester, Michigan, offers a course in ethnopsychiatry, the healing of mental disorders through witchcraft and similar means.

Some professors acknowledge that they are offering such courses only because that is what the students are interested in. Students, in turn, have complained that some teachers are too biased toward hard science to admit the possibility of the very phenomena under study.

Educators and others have connected the increased interest in the occult with the diminishing role of the established religions and a general "breakdown in society." "Cults represent a response to . . . the powerlessness of individuals to control their own destiny," said one professor. "Get yourself a little cult group and pretty soon you're convinced that you can control your own life."

Exiled. Aleksandr Solzhenitsyn, recipient of the 1970 Nobel Prize for literature, was deported to West Germany after being stripped of Soviet citizenship. He and his family settled in Switzerland. An outspoken critic of the regime, Solzhenitsyn had charged that Stalin's rule of terror was not an aberration of communism but inherent in the system.

Soviet Union. Aleksandr Solzhenitsyn, recipient of the 1970 Nobel Prize for literature, was deported to West Germany February 13 after being stripped of his Soviet citizenship. An outspoken critic of the regime, he was believed to be the first Soviet citizen forcibly expelled from the country since Leon Trotsky in 1929.

Solzhenitsyn had been arrested the day before at his wife's Moscow apartment by seven policemen. (He was staying in the apartment although officially barred from living in Moscow.) After being held overnight and told he was being charged with treason, he was placed aboard a Soviet airliner that landed in Frankfurt.

The Soviet news agency Tass said that Solzhenitsyn had been deprived of citizenship by the presidium of the Supreme Soviet (the nation's parliament) for "performing systematically actions that are incompatible with being a citizen." The regime reportedly feared that a trial and imprisonment would have severely damaged Soviet interests abroad. Tass said that Solzhenitsyn's wife and their three children would be allowed to join him in exile. (They did so in April.)

Upon arrival in West Germany, Solzhenitsyn was taken to the home of his friend and fellow Nobel laureate, novelist Heinrich Böll. After a stop in Switzerland, he left a week later for Norway, having been granted a three-month tourist visa. On March 12 he announced his intention to settle in Zurich, Switzerland.

Only one of Solzhenitsyn's novels had been published in the Soviet Union; the others were sent abroad to be published. They also circulated among Russian intellectuals in the form of typewritten manuscripts. *One Day in the Life of Ivan Denisovich* (1962) and *The First Circle* (1968) were based on his experiences in labor camps. Solzhenitsyn, while an officer during World War II, was arrested for criti-

The Gulag Archipelago.
Solzhenitsyn's newest work, published in Paris, is a history of the Soviet penal system, based on his own experiences, letters, and interviews with others. He charged that labor camps once housed 12 million people, of whom half were political prisoners, and called for the punishment of the more than 250,000 people he estimated were guilty of the crimes he detailed in the book.

cizing Stalin in a letter to a friend. He spent 11 years, first in prison and later in internal exile, before being exonerated of all charges in 1956.

The Gulag Archipelago

For years Solzhenitsyn had been working on a history of the Soviet penal system, based on his own experiences, letters from ex-prisoners, and interviews that he conducted with 227 survivors of the camps. He sent the manuscript overseas and entrusted parts to close friends. In the fall of 1973, his typist surrendered a copy of the manuscript after interrogation by security policemen; later she hanged herself. Once the manuscript was in the hands of the police, Solzhenitsyn could no longer shield his informants, most of whom he had named, and he gave permission for the book to be published abroad.

A 606-page volume, comprising only two of seven parts of the work, was published December 28 in the original Russian-language version by the YMCA-Press in Paris. "Gulag" is an acronym composed of the initials of the Central Corrective Labor Camp Administration, and the "archipelago" consists of the labor-camp "islands" strung out over the entire Soviet Union. In his work Solzhenitsyn charged that just before Stalin's death the camps housed 12 million people, of whom half were political prisoners. He said that the number of arrests, executions, and prison terms under the Communist regime ranged from 10 to 1,000 times greater than during the preceding period of Czarist rule.

(The New York *Times* reported on January 10 that Western experts believe 1 million citizens, including 10,000 political prisoners, are currently kept in about 900 prisons and labor camps; by comparison, the prison population of the United States is 425,000. Present political prisoners are said to include those arrested for circulating dissident documents, those who seek to practice their religion outside the officially approved system of worship, and those who have engaged in activities in support of minority nationalities.)

Solzhenitsyn charged that Stalin's rule of terror was not an aberration of communism but inherent in the system itself, with its roots stemming from the early days of Bolshevik rule under Lenin. In the two-part work he sought to discredit the Communist system by citing the large-scale collaboration of Soviet citizens with the enemy during World War II, when millions of soldiers and civilians captured by the Germans went straight from Nazi prisons to Stalin's labor camps.

More than 500,000 Soviet citizens served in the German army, according to Solzhenitsyn. He conceded that some were true Nazi collaborators, but said that many more felt compelled to serve the Germans in order to survive, particularly since the Soviet government refused to sign the Geneva convention protecting the rights of prisoners of war. Solzhenitsyn denounced Winston Churchill and Franklin D. Roosevelt for turning over to the Soviet government hundreds of thousands of prisoners liberated by the Western allies who did not wish to return to Russia.

Solzhenitsyn called for the punishment of the more than 250,000 people he estimated were guilty of the crimes he detailed in the book. In postwar Germany, he said, more than 78,000 persons had been convicted of Nazi brutalities. In the Soviet Union, there had been only two dozen convictions for similar crimes, he said.

Soviet Reaction

Tass described *The Gulag Archipelago* as an "unfounded slander against the Soviet people" and charged Solzhenitsyn with being a Nazi sympathizer. Soviet newspapers and magazines carried letters denouncing him, and an eight-foot poster portraying him as a traitor was displayed in a major Moscow thoroughfare. The official position was that the abuses of the Stalinist era had already been dealt with satisfactorily.

A few well-known dissidents backed him, among them physicist Andrei Sakharov and historian Roy Medvedev. Ten dissidents, including Sakharov, issued a statement, saying: "His so-called 'treason' consists of his disclosure to the whole world, with shattering force, of the monstrous crimes committed in the U.S.S.R. not very long ago." Poet Yevgeny Yevtushenko defended him for raising the issue of Stalinist terror.

A New Manifesto

In March, Solzhenitsyn released a revised version of a 15,000-word letter that he had written to Soviet leaders the previous fall. In it he urged that the Soviet Union be split into its 15 ethnic components. Russians were urged to settle in and exploit the resources of relatively undeveloped Siberia.

Solzhenitsyn condemned Marxism-Leninism, Western-style democracy, and faith in progress through industrialization as philosophies pernicious to Russia. He expressed concern over pollution and distress at the "cancerous tumors" of the cities. Democracy in its "last decline" has no ethical foundation, he contended, and consists only of "parties and social classes engaged in a conflict of interests . . . nothing higher." He acknowledged that Russia is authoritarian, said it would remain so, but urged a benevolent despotism guaranteeing freedom of expression.

Solzhenitsyn's manifesto distinguished his views from those of other Soviet dissenters. Medvedev, who seeks reform of communism from within, said that Solzhenitsyn's utopia would turn into "the worst kind of theocratic state." Sakharov believes that Marxism and capitalism are drawing closer to each other.

Space Exploration. *Mariner 10,* a U.S. interplanetary space probe, flew by Venus on February 5 and Mercury on March 29. Pictures and other data transmitted by the probe revealed considerable new information about the two planets.

Venus. *Mariner 10* came within 3,585 miles of Venus. Preliminary analysis of data by scientists of the Jet Propulsion Laboratory in Pasadena, California, indicated that the planet probably is not closely related to the earth, although they are of similar size.

Radio signals sent back to earth revealed at least three distinct layers of the clouds that enshroud Venus, with the topmost layer extending 38 miles above the surface. The temperature on the planet's surface reaches as high as 890° F., although on top of the cloud decks it is −9°.

Data indicated that hydrogen is the major element in the cloud decks, and that the likeliest source of the hydrogen is the solar wind—gases blown from the sun— rather than water from the planet itself. This finding suggested that Venus and the earth are not similar, and that the solar wind blew away the hydrogen that might otherwise have been bound into the planet as it was congealing in the distant past. Thus water may never have existed in quantity despite abundant hydrogen.

Magnetic detectors on *Mariner 10* confirmed the virtual absence of a magnetic field to ward off solar winds. The magnetic fields of the earth and Jupiter protect their surfaces from solar winds by deflecting them, but the winds reach all the way down to the ionized layer in the upper atmosphere of Venus. Scientists believe Venus lacks a magnetic field because of its slow rotation on its axis, which gives it a "day" 243 times as long as a day on earth, which revolves around its axis every 24 hours.

The slow rotation also affects the circulation of the atmosphere, since there is additional time for heat to accumulate. The winds, primarily composed of carbon dioxide, move at speeds of up to 200 miles per hour, carrying heat energy from the warmer equatorial regions to the cooler poles, then back to the equator at lower levels in the atmosphere. (The clouds move around the planet every four days,

in the direction of the spin but 60 times as fast.) However, there is little air flow at the lower levels since the atmosphere there is 90 times as dense as that of the earth.

Pictures revealed an "eye," or break in the cloud cover, about 4,200 miles wide and 1,200 miles long. This eye is a permanent marker of the spot at which the sun's heat falls vertically on the clouds.

Mercury. On March 29, *Mariner 10* passed within 438 miles of Mercury, sending back pictures, some of which showed features on the planet's surface no more than several hundred yards wide. The pictures showed many resemblances between Mercury and Mars or the moon, including a surface pockmarked by craters and strange-looking valleys of unknown origin. Gouges on the surface were presumably torn and blasted by space debris and by proximity to the sun.

Mercury, the closest planet to the sun, comes as near to the sun as 29 million miles, compared to 93 million miles for the earth. The planet is obscured from earth by the sun's rays, and even such fundamental facts as its size and shape have not been clearly known. Carl Sagan, director of Cornell University's Laboratory for Planetary Studies, predicted that *Mariner 10* would provide "the greatest advance in knowledge of a single planet from a space mission."

Probably the biggest surprise was the indication that Mercury has a magnetic field of about 1 per cent that of earth— stronger than any field observed near Venus, Mars, or the moon. The rotation of Mercury on its axis is so slow that little or no field was expected.

Another surprise was the presence of a tenuous but perceptible atmosphere formed of helium, neon, and argon, with some hydrogen present. Apparently there is no oxygen, carbon dioxide, or nitrogen in the atmosphere. Mercury's atmosphere presumably is blasted away by intense solar radiation and would have to be constantly renewed, either through volcanic activity within the planet, the breakdown of surface materials under solar bombardment, or the capture of atomic particles from the solar wind.

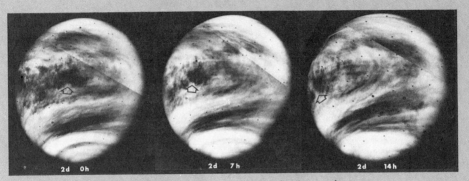

2d 0h   2d 7h   2d 14h

Venus and Mercury. *Mariner 10* revealed that the clouds enshrouding Venus, *above*, move completely around the planet every four days, 60 times faster than the planet's rotation on its own axis. (The three pictures show the planet at seven-hour intervals.) Mercury, *below*, was revealed to be heavily pockmarked by craters, like the moon and Mars.

It was long assumed that Mercury always kept one side toward the sun, as the moon does toward the earth. But radar observations showed the planet revolves on its own axis every 56.8 days, while it takes 88 days to make one trip around the sun. The dark side of Mercury cools to several hundred degrees below zero, while the sunlit side reaches hundreds of degrees above zero.

Mariner 10, after passing Mercury, began orbiting the sun. Its orbital path was expected to bring it close to Mercury again in late September. If the craft survived the heat and other hazards, it would send back more data about the planet.

Mars Probes

The Soviet Union launched four Mars space probes in the summer of 1973. One went into orbit around the planet, but another suffered a braking-rocket malfunction which caused it to speed past. A third apparently failed to make a landing attempt. The fourth, *Mars 6,* touched down on Mars March 12, but radio contact broke off as it neared the surface. Although specific data were not released, the news agency Tass reported that the probe's descent had revealed the presence of "several times more water vapor in the atmosphere of Mars over some areas of its surface than was thought so far."

Skylab 3 Mission Ends

Three U.S. astronauts completed a record 84 days in space on February 8 as the third and final crew to man the U.S. orbiting Skylab space station. The flight was launched on November 16 (see SPACE EXPLORATION, subtitle *Mission of Skylab 3,* in the fourth section,1973.) In addition to setting a record for duration of flight, the crew circled the earth a record 1,214 times and traveled an unprecedented 34.5 million miles in orbit.

Activities. One of the scientific activities of the mission was to study the comet Kohoutek, which passed around the sun December 28, 1973, and headed out again into far space. Although the comet proved to be a disappointment to ground observers because it never became bright enough for naked-eye viewing, the astronauts were able to see it well and to take many photos of it.

The Skylab 3 astronauts, like the two previous crews, complained that the food was bland. The Skylab 3 crewmen had been given strips of papers with varying sweet, sour, and salty tastes, to discover their "taste thresholds." Doctors said the crew was tasting things differently in space than it had on earth. This finding convinced medical men that better diet planning is necessary for future flights, because, as astronaut William Pogue reported from space, bland food was becoming "highly detrimental to morale."

All three astronauts suffered vertigo during their initial hours back on earth, but the symptoms soon passed. They soon lost their "growth" in height of an inch to an inch and three-quarters that had resulted from the slight separation of spinal discs in the weightlessness of space.

Space physicians said that although there appeared to have been some deterioration in the cardiovascular systems of the astronauts during the early weeks of the mission, an improvement started after about six weeks. Their muscular condition showed little or no deterioration, which was ascribed to the fact that the crew had followed a much heavier program of exercise than the earlier crews. Dr. Charles Berry, NASA director of the life sciences, said the missions had disclosed no medical reason to bar a two-year manned mission to Mars.

Achievements of Skylab. The three-mission program cost $2.5 billion but produced more practical results than the Apollo program, which was 10 times more costly. Overall, the crews obtained some 182,800 astronomical photos, plus 46,148 pictures of earth and 54 miles of magnetically taped data about the earth.

The Earth Resources Experiments Package (EREP), using an array of six sensors, investigated various earth phenomena. Utilizing the heat-sensing aspects, astronauts scanned the western United States for "hot spots"—geothermal-energy outlets in the earth's crust that could be used to generate electricity. Other photos helped agricultural experts track fruit flies and fire ants that had been ravaging crops along the Texas-Mexico border.

Pockets of cold water in the Caribbean

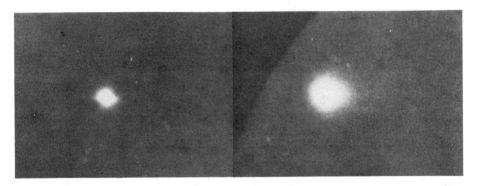

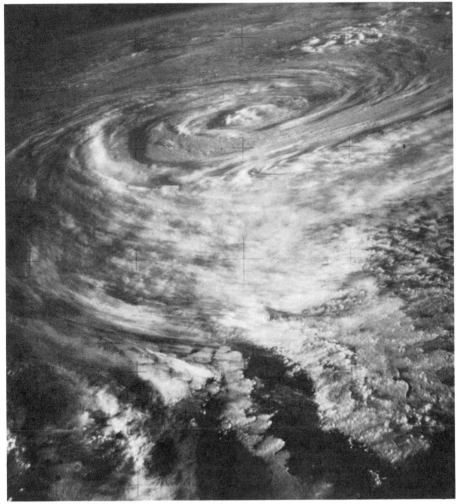

Pictures from Skylab 3 Mission. The comet Kohoutek, *top,* is shown increasing in ultraviolet-light intensity as it approached the earth over a month-long period. The picture above shows the vortex of a typhoon in the Pacific Ocean, southeast of New Zealand.

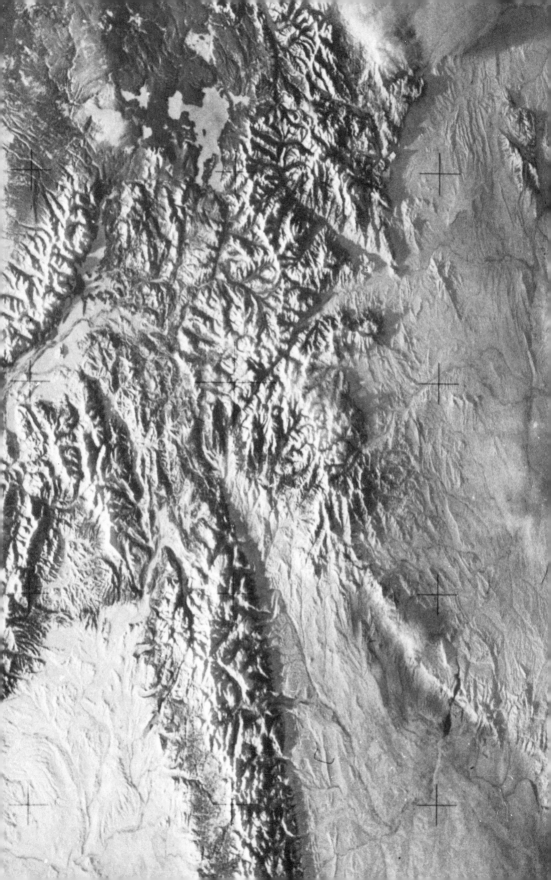

were discovered that could aid weather forecasting and fishing. The cold-water eddy apparently draws rich nutrients to the surface, making it an exceptional fishing ground.

Other achievements included the following:

• Astronaut Ed Gibson traced the development of a flare on the western half of the sun from the moment of its birth to its final expiration. One of the mysteries of solar physics concerns the process whereby energy is transformed from the sun's magnetic field into heat energy.

• Experiments with metals and other materials confirmed that processes such as welding, melting, and purification can be carried out in the absence of gravity far more efficiently than on earth. Scientists believe that eventually electronic parts will be manufactured in gravity-free orbiting space factories.

• With the help of Skylab pictures, Leroy Jensen of the University of Utah spotted a probable vein of copper relatively close to the surface in Nevada. An oil company began actively exploring for oil in some 20 areas indicated by Skylab data. Photos taken of U.S. metropolitan areas may provide faster, cheaper information on population movements than traditional surveys.

Snow-Covered Northwest Corner of Wyoming is shown in this picture from the Skylab space station in earth orbit. The dark area is Yellowstone National Park, and the largest body of water is Yellowstone Lake. The Absaroka Range of the Rocky Mountains is immediately east and northeast of Yellowstone Lake. Using heat-sensing devices, astronauts scanned the western United States for "hot spots"— geothermal-energy outlets in the earth's crust that could be used to generate electricity.

Spain. A political and administrative upheaval of unusual proportions appeared to be taking place following the installation of Spain's new premier, Carlos Arias Navarro, on January 4. In a speech before the Cortes—the Spanish parliament—on February 12, Arias presented a number of bills intended to liberalize Spain's authoritarian system by expanding opportunities for political participation. However, the continued repression of opposition spokesmen indicated that increased public dissent would not be tolerated by the new regime.

New Administration

Arias Navarro had been designated by the head of state, Generalissimo Francisco Franco, to succeed Premier Luis Carrero Blanco, who was assassinated in December, 1973. (See NEWS IN BRIEF in the fourth section, 1973.) Although not previously considered a political leader, the former minister of the interior quickly made extensive changes in the upper levels of the administration. Eleven of the 19 cabinet members were replaced. In all, more than 100 positions changed hands, as new cabinet ministers nominated their candidates for lower posts.

Most of the new ministers were considered to be (like Arias himself) generally conservative professionals whose primary loyalties were to Franco and the National Movement, Spain's only legal political organization. But the new appointees also included several prominent liberals.

Laureano López Rodó, a powerful figure who had directed Spain's economic development before becoming foreign minister in 1973, was excluded from the new government. López Rodó had been the most prominent member of Opus Dei (a Catholic laymen's group) in Carrero Blanco's cabinet; his departure signaled that organization's loss of influence.

Opus Dei technocrats and businessmen had played a major role in modernizing the Spanish economy and in improving relations with western European and Communist nations. But the organization's power had aroused resentment among anti-Communist military men.

Two prominent right-wing members of Carrero Blanco's government were also dropped—Gonzalo Fernández de la Mora,

Carlos Arias Navarro was appointed by Generalissimo Francisco Franco to succeed the assassinated Luis Carrero Blanco as premier of Spain. The new government's policy on questions of law and order was one of firmness, tempered with a hint of liberalization.

former minister of public works, and Torcuato Fernández Miranda, who was deputy premier and head of the National Movement.

Political Reforms Promised

The new government's policy on questions of law and order was one of firmness, tempered with a hint of liberalization. In a speech January 4, Arias pledged that his cabinet would "give great importance to the development of political participation," in light of "the proved civic maturity of the people." But the premier emphasized that his government would "make use of all its authority—with severity and calmness—to defend the common good and to maintain an order in whose framework Spaniards can develop their rights and liberties."

In an 80-minute message to the parliament on February 12, Arias introduced a program of political reforms which would enable "34 million Spaniards" to participate in political and economic life. One of the bills called for the election of mayors and presidents of provincial assemblies. These officials have been appointed by provincial and national authorities.

If enacted, a bill to be offered by June 30 would prohibit government officials from holding seats in the parliament. Since many members of parliament occupy other posts in the government, this measure would promote clearer separation of the executive and legislative branches.

Other proposals dealt with the formation of political and economic organizations. One would permit the establishment of national political associations—the term "political party" has been avoided since the Spanish Civil War. The right to form associations was seen by such groups as the Socialists and Christian Democrats as a test of the government's sincerity on questions of political reform.

But skeptics noted that such bills had been promised before, and that Arias had not specified in his speech which groups might be considered "subversive" and forbidden to form associations. It also remained uncertain whether any political association would be allowed to operate independently of the National Movement or to slate candidates for office.

The same day Arias announced his legislative proposals, a bill regulating associations of professionals (such as lawyers) was passed by the Cortes. The measure was widely interpreted as an effort by the government to exercise greater control over groups which had spoken out on public issues.

The legitimacy of work stoppages or strikes was a key question left unanswered in Arias' remarks. All work stoppages are criminal offenses in Spain, and labor unrest is not normally publicized. But it was revealed that hundreds of factory workers had been dismissed, suspended, or locked out for taking part in strikes, work stoppages, or work-to-rule actions in January. Strikes had occurred in many cities, including Pamplona, El Ferrol, Bilbao, San Sebastian, Valladolid, Barcelona, and Madrid.

Workers who organized unions outside of the official syndicates were also treated harshly. In December, 10 labor leaders convicted of forming workers' commissions parallel to the official associations were sentenced to long prison terms. The new workers' groups were considered by the government to be subversive extensions of the Communist party.

Although many of his suggested reforms were familiar, the new language and tone of Arias' address were encouraging to moderate opposition forces in Madrid. Most startling to his audience were references to Franco's mortality. Remarking on the past leadership of the 81-year-old head of state, Arias noted that in the future, the government he himself headed would assume primary responsibility for political innovation.

Catalonian Anarchist Executed

The new regime's treatment of its opposition was seen as a test of its liberal intentions. But, in Barcelona, an execution with political overtones took place for the first time since 1963.

Salvador Puig Antich, a 26-year-old anarchist associated with an obscure group called the Iberian Liberation Movement was garroted on March 2. He had been convicted of killing a policeman during a gunfight in Barcelona. (The garrote is a metal collar that, when tightened, kills the victim through strangulation or by breaking the spine where it joins the base of the neck. The method of execution dates from the 14th century.)

In an apparent attempt to depoliticize the incident, the government also executed a 33-year-old stateless person named Heinz Chez. He had been convicted of killing a guard near Tarragona in 1972. At the same time, clemency was extended to a civil guard who had killed a superior officer during an argument in Huelva.

Widespread appeals for clemency made on humanitarian grounds by individuals and groups both in Spain and abroad failed to save Puig. Entreaties on his behalf had been made during February and early March by several European governments, the Geneva section of the Human Rights League, the Spanish Council of Lawyers, and some 300 Madrid intellectuals. Thousands of people had demonstrated in Barcelona and Paris on February 21 to demand clemency for Puig Antich.

In his February 12 address, Premier Arias had reiterated Spain's desire to become a member of the European Economic Community. But, two weeks after Puig's execution, the European Parliament passed a resolution condemning the act and asserting that "the repeated violations of the fundamental rights of many by the Spanish regime . . . preclude the entrance of Spain into the European Community."

Following Puig's execution, student demonstrators clashed with police in Barcelona, Madrid, and other university communities. The main universities in Madrid and Barcelona were virtually paralyzed and heavily patrolled. Protests continued for weeks in both Spain and France, where two branches of Spanish banks and a Spanish tourist office were bombed with Molotov cocktails.

At least 13 demonstrators were arrested during protests in two working-class neighborhoods of Barcelona March 7, in which hundreds of people shouted anti-Franco slogans. On March 10, police broke up another demonstration in Barcelona's main square. Earlier in the day, some 2,000 people had attended a memorial service for Puig held in a Barcelona church.

Catalonia, a formerly autonomous region of which Barcelona is the capital, has long been a focal point for political unrest in Spain. Although it is a major publishing and intellectual center, the government does not allow the publication of a daily paper, or the broadcast of radio programs, in Catalan, the regional language.

The Añoveros Affair

Regional aspirations in another corner of Spain, the Basque country, helped precipitate Spain's worst church-state crisis since the end of the Civil War. The bishop of Bilbao, Antonio Añoveros Ataún, was placed under house arrest February 27. A strongly-worded sermon issued by Añoveros had been read at masses in Vizcaya Province the preceding Sunday.

In his homily Añoveros had called for

a "just freedom" for the Basque people, charging that "in present circumstances" Basques were denied freedom in Spain and that their language and teaching were "subjected to severe restrictions." He noted that the Basques' "spiritual and cultural characteristics" and "ancient language" had given them a "specific personality within the Spanish state."

The government tried unsuccessfully to expel Añoveros March 3 on a charge of undermining national unity. A deadlock with church authorities was resolved when the Permanent Commission of the Spanish Episcopal Conference issued a statement supporting the bishop and denying the regime's right to try him. (Under Spain's 1953 concordat with the Vatican, Spanish churchmen were given immunity from arrest and prosecution without Vatican approval.)

The Arias regime retreated in the face of a lobbying campaign that was said to have won the support of Franco's wife. In Añoveros' diocese, some 12,000 signatures on his behalf were collected. Pope Paul VI and most Spanish diocesan priests also backed him. No further actions were taken against Añoveros.

Sports and Athletics. Among the outstanding sporting events of the first quarter of 1974 were the following:

Auto Racing

Richard Petty won the Daytona 500 on for a record fifth time on February 17 in Daytona Beach, Florida, outdueling Donnie Allison. The $275,000 race—richest in stock-car history—was cut to 450 miles in order to conserve fuel. Petty's average speed of 140.894 miles an hour was the slowest since the 1960 race as high winds spread debris over the track. Fifty-three of the 180 laps were run under caution, and only 17 of the 40 starters finished.

In Grand Prix racing, Denis Hulme won the Argentine race, Emerson Fittipaldi the Brazilian race, and Carlos Reutemann the South African event.

Baseball

Yankee stars Mickey Mantle and Whitey Ford were voted into baseball's hall of fame on January 16. The Veterans Committee selected players Jim Bottomley and Sam Thompson, and umpire Jocko Conlan on January 28. A special committee on Negro leagues elected James (Cool Papa) Bell, who was acclaimed the "Black Ty Cobb" during his career.

Basketball

College. North Carolina State won the NCAA championship on March 25 in Greensboro, North Carolina, defeating Marquette, 76-64. David Thompson of North Carolina State was voted player of the season in an Associated Press poll.

North Carolina State lost only one game all year, to UCLA, but avenged its defeat by beating the Bruins, 80-77 in double overtime, in the NCAA semifinals. This defeat snapped UCLA's record of seven consecutive NCAA championships. The Bruins' record of 88 consecutive victories was ended earlier in the season by Notre Dame.

Purdue won the National Invitational Tournament in New York City on March 24, defeating Utah, 87-81. In other postseason tournaments, Morgan State won the NCAA College Division, Immaculata the women's championship, and Jacksonville the AAU crown.

Professional. Milwaukee, Chicago, Detroit, Los Angeles, Boston, New York, Buffalo, and Capital qualified for the National Basketball Association playoffs. Bob McAdoo of the Buffalo Braves led the league in scoring, averaging 30.6 points per game. Kareem Abdul-Jabbar of Milwaukee was chosen the league's most valuable player for the third time in four years.

The New York Nets and Utah Stars won divisional titles in the American Basketball Association. Jules Erving of New York led the league in scoring, averaging 27.3 points per game. Erving was voted the league's most valuable player.

Bowling

Larry Laub won the $85,000 U.S. Open in New York City in February, defeating Dave Davis.

Boxing

Heavyweight. George Foreman retained his title in Caracas, Venezuela, on March 26, knocking out Ken Norton in the second round of their bout. The unbeaten Foreman registered his 40th victory and 37th knockout, the last 24 in succession.

Sports Stars. David Thompson, *right,* led North Carolina State to the NCAA basketball championship; he was voted college player of the season. George Foreman, *below,* KO'd Ken Norton in the second round of their bout and retained the world heavyweight title.

The Martial-Arts Craze

Fueled by the popularity of Bruce Lee movies and the television series "Kung Fu," the Asian martial arts are experiencing a boom in the United States. The Yellow Pages of major cities are filled with advertisements offering instruction in judo, jujitsu, kendo, kempo, aikido, karate, kung fu, tai chi, and the like.

In general, the martial arts have, in their home countries, been considered more of an art form than a practical means of self-defense; just as the greatest samurai, it is said, never has to fight, and his sword has rust on its scabbard from never being drawn. But in the United States, many are attracted to the martial arts in the hopes of fending off street crime. Others practice the martial arts for body conditioning, sport, or as "meditation in motion."

The martial arts enable a person to turn an opponent's strength against him so that he is thrown to the ground. Training also enables one to counter with hands and feet against the vulnerable body areas of the opponent. A heavily conditioned hand, favored in some kung-fu and karate systems, becomes a lethal weapon. Also fearsome are nunchakus, used by some karate clubs. These are two 12-inch sticks of hardwood joined together by several inches of rope, leather, or chain; they can be swung out with great speed and power or used to throttle an opponent.

Most teachers of the martial arts prefer to emphasize the nonviolent aspects. The exercises contribute to suppleness and muscle tone. Skill can be tested in competition in which kicks and punches must be delivered at maximum velocity, yet stopped on contact to avoid injury.

For some, the meditative aspects are important, although the tendency to view the martial arts as a "way of life" may be mere faddism. "Before the TV show," says one instructor, "we had to force-feed the kung-fu philosophy. Now, if they don't hear some fancy little parable or Chinese saying, they think they're being cheated."

Among the forms of the Asian martial arts are the following:

Jujitsu has been traced to 16th-century Japanese warriors. It consists of a number of techniques, including kneeing, striking, throwing, holding, choking, and locking joints.

Judo, adapted from jujitsu in the late 19th century, is based on scientific principles of leverage and balance. It is now an official Olympic sport.

Karate has been traced to Okinawa, although the basic concept comes from Chinese boxing. It employs punching, kicking, and blocking techniques.

Kung fu is a general term referring to all of the many styles of Chinese boxing. Like karate, it uses punching, kicking, and blocking techniques.

Aikido, founded in Japan in 1925, uses principles of leverage and balance. Holds and throws are applied in circular rather than linear movements.

Tae kwon do, developed in Korea, is usually considered a form of karate.

Tai chi chuan is often referred to as Chinese shadow boxing because of its slow-motion circular movements. It consists of 108 forms based on animal movements.

In a widely followed bout between two former champions, Muhammad Ali scored a 12-round decision over Joe Frazier in New York City on January 28.

Middleweight. Carlos Monzon of Argentina retained his title in Paris in February, when welterweight champion José Napoles of Mexico was unable to come out for the seventh round.

Lightweight. Roberto Duran of Panama knocked out Esteban DeJesus in the 11th round of their fight in Panama City, Panama, in March to retain his title.

Commonwealth Games

Australia won the most medals, 82, at the British Commonwealth Games, held in Christchurch, New Zealand, in January; England was second with 80. Filbert Bayi of Tanzania set a new track record for the 1,500 meters of 3:32.2 minutes.

Curling

The United States won the world championship in Berne, Switzerland, in March, defeating defending champion Sweden 11-4 in nine ends.

Football

College. In bowl games played on New Year's Day, Ohio State defeated Southern California in the Rose Bowl, 42-21; Nebraska defeated Texas, 19-3, in the Cotton Bowl; and Penn State ended its season undefeated and untied by beating Louisiana State, 16-9, in the Orange Bowl.

Professional. The Miami Dolphins became the first National Football League team to win two championships in succession, defeating the Minnesota Vikings in the Super Bowl, 24-7. The game, held in Houston on January 13, was no contest as Miami forged to a quick 17-0 lead. The Dolphins made almost no mistakes—no lost fumbles, no intercepted passes, and only one minor penalty. Larry Csonka set a Super Bowl record by rushing for 145 yards.

O. J. Simpson of the Buffalo Bills, who set a season record by running for 2,003 yards, was named NFL offensive player of the year in an Associated Press poll. Safety Dick Anderson of Miami was chosen best defensive player. Minnesota running back Chuck Foreman and defensive end Wally Chambers of the Chicago Bears were named rookies of the year. Chuck Knox of the Los Angeles Rams was voted coach of the year.

In February, four former NFL players were named to professional football's hall of fame in Canton, Ohio—Green Bay fullback Tony Canadeo, Chicago Bears linebacker Bill George, Cleveland Browns placekicker and tackle Lou (the Toe) Groza, and defensive back Dick (Night Train) Lane.

Golf

In January, Johnny Miller became the

Larry Csonka ran for 145 yards as the Miami Dolphins became the first National Football League team to win two championships in succession, defeating the Minnesota Vikings in the Super Bowl, 24-7.

first to win three straight Professional Golfers Association tournaments since Arnold Palmer in 1962. Miller won the Bing Crosby tournament, the Phoenix Open, and the Dean Martin-Tucson Open.

Horse Racing

An American-bred and -owned mare, Delmonica Hanover, won the world's richest trotting race, the $250,000 Prix d'Amérique, on January 27 in Paris.

Ice Skating

Figure Skating. East Germany's Christine Errath won the women's world championship in Munich, West Germany, in March; Dorothy Hamill of the United States was second. Jan Hoffman of East Germany won the men's title. Irina Rodnina and Aleksandr Zaitaev of the Soviet Union won their second consecutive pairs title.

The U.S. championships were won on February 9 by Dorothy Hamill and Gordon McKellen in Providence, Rhode Island.

Speed Skating. Atje Keulen-Deelstra of the Netherlands won her fourth world championship, sweeping three of the four events. The 500-meter race was won by Sheila Young of Detroit.

Norway's Per Bjoerang won the men's world sprint championship in Innsbruck, Austria, in February. Tatiana Averina of the Soviet Union won the women's championship.

Skiing

Annemarie Proell of Austria won her fourth straight World Cup Alpine skiing championship for the best overall performance during the skiing season. Piero Gros of Italy won the men's title.

East Germany won 11 medals, five of them gold, to win the world Nordic championship in Falun, Sweden, in February. Galina Kulakova of the Soviet Union was the outstanding individual performer with three gold medals in women's events.

Tennis

Australian Open titles were won on January 1 by Evonne Goolagong of Australia and Jimmy Connors of the United States.

Rod Laver of Australia defeated Arthur Ashe of the United States on January 27 to win the $100,000 U.S. professional indoor championships, 6-1, 6-4, 3-6, 6-4.

Transportation. During 1973, a steady decline since 1945 in public-transit passengers was checked. Between 1945 and 1972, the number of riders had dropped 60 per cent, but in 1973 ridership increased by 1.4 per cent.

Transit systems almost invariably operate at a deficit because, given freedom of choice, people choose the personal flexibility and comfort of the automobile. But, spurred by the gasoline shortage, the Nixon Administration is proposing increased federal aid to make mass transportation more appealing. Cities, too, are increasing aid to their transit systems in order to stimulate business in downtown stores and counter traffic congestion and air pollution.

Bus Service

Free Rides. In 1973 Seattle became the first major U.S. city to offer free bus rides. The "Magic Carpet" bus service offers free rides to anyone traveling within a 105-square-block area containing most of the city's major department stores, office buildings, hotels, theaters, and restaurants. Transit officials say the number of downtown bus riders has almost doubled, to about 11,000 a day.

The one-year experiment is being subsidized by a city appropriation of $64,000 to the transit agency. The original idea was to keep cars off the streets, partly to help meet strict air-quality standards set by the U.S. Environmental Protection Agency. But office workers and downtown merchants, who say business has picked up, are also enthusiastic.

Riders rarely have to wait more than a minute for a bus in the free area. Persons who board buses before they get into the free area pay their fare when they get on; those who board inside the free zone and get off outside pay when they get off. Besides the free-service experiment, the transit agency has greatly expanded suburban service, has established 12 park-and-ride lots where outlying residents can park and take express buses downtown, and operates special buses to ski areas, college football games, and race tracks. There is a freeway express-bus lane and a special 10-cent fare for senior citizens.

Rural areas are also experimenting with free fares. Kearney, Nebraska, using

Better Bus Service. It looks like any city bus, but it offers Seattle's "Magic Carpet" service—free rides to anyone traveling within a 105-square-block area containing most of the city's department stores, offices, hotels, and restaurants. Above, one of several metropolitan bus lines that use freeway express-bus lanes to speed commuters to and from work.

funds from the U.S. Office of Economic Opportunity, provides free minibus service for the poor, the old, and the handicapped in a five-county area.

Fare Reductions. Atlanta has rolled fares back from 40 cents to 15 cents, leading to a 15-per-cent increase in riders. Cincinnati cut the basic fare from 55 cents to 25 cents, resulting in a 42-per-cent increase in ridership. San Francisco has adopted a Sunday unlimited-use fare of 50 cents. An annual subsidy has allowed the transit system for the St. Louis area to cut the basic fare from 45 cents to 25 cents. Reduced fares for the elderly are in effect in many cities.

Ridership on the Denver Metro Transit has grown about 15 per cent a year since 1971. The fare was cut from 40 cents to 35 cents, with special rates for the elderly

and students, and minibuses that drive passengers around the downtown area for 10 cents. The annual deficit of $2.5 million is made up through an increased sales tax.

Many economists advocate fare reductions in off-peak hours. As many as 20 per cent of the riders during rush hours are on shopping trips or errands that could be diverted to other times with price incentives. But most economists are dubious about wholesale fare cuts. Often the increased number of riders is drawn from former pedestrians rather than motorists, and traffic congestion remains unaffected.

One consulting firm suggests that the reduction in auto trips that free transit would be expected to produce in Boston could be achieved at a fraction of the cost simply by offering more extensive and convenient routes. "Good service—comfortable, fre-

Mass-Transit Statistics

Population and Ridership

Urban area	Population	Riders
New York City	16,300,000	9,000,000
Los Angeles	8,300,000	550,000
Chicago	6,700,000	1,600,000
Philadelphia	4,000,000	1,000,000
San Francisco	2,900,000	850,000*
Boston	2,600,000	430,000
Washington	2,500,000	400,000
Cleveland	1,900,000	330,000
Baltimore	1,600,000	350,000
Atlanta	1,200,000	200,000

Travel preference

	Auto	Rail	Bus
New York City	50.6%	26.7%	12.3%
Los Angeles	88.8	0.1	4.7
Chicago	66.3	9.3	15.1
Philadelphia	66.2	8.6	16.0
San Francisco	74.7	0.7	15.3
Boston	67.4	8.1	12.0
Washington	73.2	0.2	17.4
Cleveland	79.0	0.8	13.3
Baltimore	74.5	0.2	16.7
Atlanta	84.2	—	10.4

Mass-Transit Units Available

	Buses and trolleys	El and subway cars	Commuter rail cars
New York City	8,230	7,300	2,400
Los Angeles	1,900	—	—
Chicago	3,100	1,100	850
Philadelphia	2,400	575	400
San Francisco	2,000	250	100
Boston	1,600	350	125
Washington	1,800	—	—
Cleveland	855	120	—
Baltimore	800	—	—
Atlanta	600	—	—

*Before BART opened
Source: *Business Week.* Data: Urban Mass Transportation Administration and 1970 census.

quent and fast—is what will get people
out of their cars and into buses and trains,"
says Ronald Kirby of the Urban Institute.

Dial-A-Bus. Dial-a-bus systems are in
service in more than 30 U.S. communities,
plus others in Canada, Britain, and Sweden, with three to five new ones started
every month. The first system was
launched in 1971 in Regina, Saskatche-
wan. Each subsequent one has been a success, and none has yet been abandoned.

The patron phones a control center that
tells him when to expect a bus at his door
and then dispatches a bus to pick him up.
Once aboard, the rider—along with other
passengers—is carried to his exact destination. In some places, the service ties in
with rail or bus routes; in others, the service is the only public transportation available.

Most of the cities with dial-a-bus systems are small or medium-sized. However,
Los Angeles has "dial your ride" service
in low-income areas. For a 15-cent fee,
the passenger is picked up and driven anywhere within the system's operating zone
of 42 square miles.

Rail Transit Lines

Some of the larger cities plan to build
or expand rail rapid-transit lines. Rail systems have the largest passenger capacity—
between 40,000 and 70,000 riders per
hour.

The Bay Area Rapid Transit (BART)
system, opened in 1972, will eventually
link the entire San Francisco-Oakland
metropolitan area. New York City is building a new 13-mile Second Avenue subway
line. Subway systems are under construction or in an advanced stage of planning
in Atlanta, Baltimore, Buffalo, and Washington, D.C. Boston, Philadelphia, and
Chicago are planning expansion of their
existing rail-transit systems.

Toronto has North America's most
highly integrated urban-transit network.
Two subways link with each other and
with electric buses, trolleys, and motor

Rail Transit. A subway system is being
constructed for the Washington, D.C., area. Rail
transit systems have the largest passenger
capacity—between 40,000 and 70,000
riders per hour.

109

buses covering 660 miles of routes that feed the subways from outlying areas. Transfers are free; for 25 cents a rider can go anywhere within the 240-square-mile metropolitan area. Trains run every three minutes during rush hours and every five minutes at other times. The system, which is subsidized, lost $8 million in 1972.

Federal Aid

The highway trust fund is being tapped for the cost of mass-transit capital improvements. Up to $200 million from this fund, which is supported by taxes on gasoline, will be available for bus projects in fiscal 1975. During fiscal 1976, $800 million can be used for any type of transit project, bus or rail.

In February, the Nixon Administration asked Congress to take urban transportation programs out of the Highway Act and to combine them with the Urban Mass Transportation's capital-assistance program. Money would also be added for operating assistance to transit systems, representing a reversal of the Administration's long-standing opposition to this form of aid. Administration officials predicted that the net effect should be to make about 30 per cent more money available for urban transportation.

United States of AMERICA. Among events of note during December, 1973, and the first quarter of 1974 were the following:

Presidency

President Nixon faced in early 1974 a serious effort in Congress to have him impeached and removed from office. (See WATERGATE SCANDAL in this section.)However, in a series of speeches and nationally televised news conferences, he vowed not to resign. Earlier, in his State of the Union address, he told Congress, "I want you to know that I have no intention whatever of ever walking away from the job that the people elected me to do for the people of the United States."

State of Union Address. Before a joint session of Congress January 30, the president pledged that there would be no recession, that inflation would be checked, and that "we will break the back of the energy crisis." He said the federal government would spend $10 billion for research and development over the next five years in seeking to make the nation self-dependent in energy by 1980. He also pledged a "sweeping new program . . . to assure comprehensive health-insurance protection." (See MEDICINE in this section.)

Budget. On February 4, Nixon submitted a budget for fiscal 1975 with total federal outlays of $304.4 billion—$29.8 billion higher than in fiscal 1974. Receipts for fiscal 1975 were estimated at $295 billion, leaving a projected deficit of $9.4 billion. Ninety per cent of the increase in outlays was attributed to mandatory-spending areas such as interest on the national debt and maintenance of the Social Security system.

The new budget contained few new initiatives and, unlike its controversial predecessor, few cutbacks of existing programs. There was, however, a significant increase allotted in federal aid to mass transit. (See TRANSPORTATION in this section.) Funds for two major new initiatives, a nation health-insurance plan and welfare reform, were not in the budget, their starting dates still in the fiscal future.

The largest increases were for defense, pollution control, and payments to retired persons, veterans, the poor, and the unemployed. The $86 billion allotted to defense and $63 billion for Social Security comprised about half the total budget.

Economic Report. In his annual economic message to Congress, submitted February 1, Nixon called the outlook for 1974 "highly uncertain" but said "there will be no recession." The companion report prepared by the Council of Economic Advisers forecast an increase in the gross national product of 8 per cent for 1974. However, only 1 per cent of that would be real growth, since inflation was expected to advance by 7 per cent.

CEA Chairman Herbert Stein said that by the second half of 1974 inflation would be at an annual rate of less than 5 per cent as food and fuel price increases were put "behind us." Unemployment, he said, would average a little above the current rate of 5.5 per cent but would not reach 6 per cent.

Appointments and Resignations. Melvin Laird resigned December 19 as Nixon's

Chief domestic adviser. He had joined the White House staff June 6 to replace John Ehrlichman. Reportedly, however, the president seldom sought his counsel on means to repair the damage done the Administration by the Watergate scandal. Kenneth R. Cole, Jr., replaced Laird on January 16 while keeping his post as executive director of the Domestic Council.

Secretary of the Treasury George Shultz, the last remaining member of the original Nixon cabinet, resigned his position on March 14, effective in May. No successor was immediately named.

Congress

Among the bills passed by Congress in December, 1973, and the first quarter of 1974 were the following:

Manpower Training. Congress, after reaching a compromise with the Administration, approved on December 20 a multibillion-dollar comprehensive manpower act including an emergency public-employment program that would hire perhaps 40,000 people. The bill was to be funded at $1.8 billion in fiscal 1974 and close to $2 billion in fiscal 1975. Part of the money was to be used for state and local public-employment programs in areas where unemployment rates have reached 6.5 per cent.

The bill also provided for about 500 manpower training programs, with states, counties, and cities acting as prime contractors. A few of the old federal programs, such as the Job Corps, would be retained, but most of the others, including the Neighborhood Youth Corps and Mainstream, would be dropped.

Health Maintenance. Congress on December 19 passed a bill authorizing the spending of $375 million over five years to help set up and evaluate health-maintenance organizations in communities throughout the country. Subscribers would pay a predetermined flat fee monthly or yearly and in return would be entitled to basic health-care services. The new law was expected to be an adjunct to the national health-insurance program proposed by the Administration.

Foreign Aid. On December 20, Congress appropriated $5.8 billion in foreign aid. The sum included emergency aid of $2.2

Vows Not to Resign. President Nixon told Congress in his State of the Union address that he had "no intention whatever of walking away from the job that the people elected me to do." He submitted a budget that contained few new initiatives and, unlike its controversial predecessor, few cutbacks of existing programs.

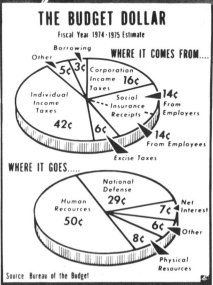

THE BUDGET DOLLAR
Fiscal Year 1974-1975 Estimate

WHERE IT COMES FROM....

Borrowing
Other
5¢ 3¢
Corporation Income Taxes 16¢
Individual Income Taxes 42¢
Social Insurance Receipts 6¢
14¢ From Employers
14¢ From Employees
Excise Taxes

WHERE IT GOES.....

National Defense 29¢
Human Recources 50¢
Net Interest 7¢
6¢ Other
8¢
Physical Resources

Source Bureau of the Budget

billion for Israel, $150 million for Cambodia, and $150 million for disaster relief.

Railway Reorganization. On December 21, Congress authorized the establishment of an independent federal agency to reorganize the railway system in the Northeastern states and a new railway corporation to operate it. Routes would be purchased from the seven bankrupt railways encompassed by the system. Funding of $558.5 million over two years was authorized, and the agency was authorized to issue up to $1.5 billion in federally guaranteed loans.

Daylight Saving Time. On December 14, Congress approved year-round daylight saving time for two years, effective January 6, 1974. Alaska and Hawaii were exempted. Proponents of the measure said the added daylight in the late afternoon would save 95,000 barrels of fuel a day, or 3 per cent of the estimated shortage of fuel.

Social Security. Congress gave final approval December 21 to an 11-per-cent increase in Social Security benefits for some 29 million retired persons. Under the bill, which superseded a 5.9-per-cent cost-of-

living increase in benefits enacted earlier in 1973, recipients would receive a 7-percent increase in their checks as of April, 1974, and a further 4-per-cent increase as of July, 1974. To help pay for the increased benefits, the amount of a person's annual income subject to the Social Security tax would rise to $13,200 in 1974, with the maximum tax $772.20. The bill also increased federal welfare payments for the aged, blind, and disabled.

Energy. On February 27, Congress sent to the White House an emergency energy bill that contained a provision opposed by the Administration—a rollback in the price of crude oil from "new" wells and "stripper" wells producing less than 10 barrels a day. This oil, amounting to about 30 per cent of domestic production, had been exempt from price controls and was selling for as high as $10.35 a barrel; the bill rolled back the price to $5.25 a barrel.

Also included in the bill was authority for the Federal Energy Office to order further energy-conservation measures subject to a six-month time limit and a veto by either house of Congress; standby authority for the president to order gasoline ra-

Year-Round Daylight Saving Time was approved by Congress as a means of combating the energy crisis. Proponents of the measure said the added daylight in the late afternoon would save fuel, but many parents did not like their children leaving for school in the dark of early winter mornings.

tioning; authority for regulatory agencies to make fuel-saving cutbacks in transportation; authority for the FEO to order increased domestic oil production and make generating plants convert from oil to coal burning; and grants of limited immunity from antitrust prosecution for retailers and the oil industry.

President Nixon vetoed the bill March 6. He said the price rollback would "set domestic crude-oil prices at such low levels that the oil industry would be unable to sustain its present production of petroleum products." The Senate fell eight votes short of the two-thirds majority needed to override the veto.

Supreme Court

Police Search. The Supreme Court ruled by a 6-to-3 vote December 11 that a person who had been properly arrested for a minor offense might subsequently be searched for evidence pertaining to a more serious but unrelated crime. The ruling applied to two separate cases in which the appellants were first stopped for traffic violations and then searched, with illegal narcotics found.

Grand Jury Evidence. Similarly, the high court ruled 6 to 3 on January 8 that grand juries could use illegally obtained evidence as the basis for questioning witnesses without violating their constitutional rights. The result would be that a grand jury could use evidence that later would be inadmissible in the suspect's trial.

Maternity Leave. The Court ruled 7 to 2 on January 2 that a public-school system could not force a pregnant teacher to take a maternity leave until a few weeks before she was due to bear a child.

English Instruction. The Supreme Court ruled unanimously January 21 that the San Francisco public-school system was in violation of the 1964 Civil Rights Act if it did not provide English-language instruction for 1,800 non-English-speaking Chinese. A federal attorney said the government would use the decision to ensure equal educational opportunities for 2 million U.S. school students whose first language is Spanish.

Cable TV. The high court ruled 6 to 3 on March 4 that cable-television systems are not subject to U.S. copyright laws when they import distant television signals and broadcast them to paid subscribers. In 1968, the Court had exempted cable TV from payments of royalties for copyrighted programs originating locally. As in 1968, the majority held that reception and retransmission of signals is "essentially a viewer function."

Flag Display. On March 25, the Supreme Court by a vote of 6 to 3 struck down as unconstitutionally vague a Massachusetts law that made it a crime to treat the U.S. flag "contemptuously." In so doing they overturned a six-month jail sentence imposed on a man for wearing a four-by-six-inch flag sewn on the seat of his jeans.

Kidnappings

Patricia Hearst, 19-year-old granddaughter of the late newspaper publisher William Randolph Hearst, was kidnapped February 5 and held for ransom by members of a radical group called the Symbionese Liberation Army. The action resembled some kidnappings in Latin America and other parts of the world. It was followed by others across the nation that had no avowed political motive, plus countless threats and a few hoaxes.

Miss Hearst was abducted from her Berkeley, California, apartment by at least two women and two men. They belonged to a group of both blacks and whites who call for violent revolution to overturn "all forms of racism, sexism, ageism, capitalism, fascism, individualism, possessiveness, and competitiveness."

The kidnappers demanded that her father, Randolph A. Hearst, president and publisher of the San Francisco *Examiner,* provide as a prelude to further negotiations $70 worth of top-quality free meat, vegetables, and dairy products over a four-week period to "all people [in California] with welfare cards, Social Security pension cards, food-stamp cards, disabled veteran cards, medical cards, parole or probation papers, and jail or bail-release slips." Tape recordings were mailed of Miss Hearst's voice and of a speaker who called himself Field Marshal Cinque—reportedly an escaped convict named Donald DeFreeze.

Estimates of the cost of providing the food ran as high as $400 million. Hearst said February 19 that he would contribute $500,000 to a food-giveaway program, and that $1.5 million more would be donated by the William Randolph Hearst Foundation. Later, he said the Hearst Corporation would put up an additional $4 million to continue the program, but only after his daughter was released.

Another demand later added by the kidnappers was that Russell Little and Joseph Remiro, two SLA members arrested and

charged with the 1973 slaying of Marcus Foster, Oakland superintendent of schools, be allowed to conduct a nationally televised news conference. Two judges refused to sanction the request.

By late March there had been five distributions of free food in the Bay Area to thousands of people. The first four were considered unsatisfactory by the kidnappers because crowds had to wait for hours at a few distribution points to receive bags valued at $4 to $6 of such goods as frozen turkey parts, saltine crackers, and milk cartons. The last distribution, on March 25, was made at 17 points. Boxes valued at $25 each contained up to five steaks as well as frozen fish, chicken, and turkey, eggs, milk, rice, and fresh fruit. The last distribution reportedly exhausted the funds available.

On April 4, Miss Hearst's parents received a tape recording in which she said that she had rejected them and would stay with the Symbionese Liberation Army. The recording strengthened earlier speculation that she had been a party to her "kidnapping." But the FBI said it would continue its investigation on the premise that a crime had indeed been committed.

On February 20, J. Reginald Murphy, editor of the Atlanta *Constitution*, was kidnapped and held for a ransom of $700,-000 by a self-styled "colonel" in an al-

Patty Hearst was kidnapped and held for ransom by members of an organization called the Symbionese Liberation Army; later, the SLA released the picture of her above in front of the organization's insignia and a tape recording in which she said she was joining the group. *Left*, some of the thousands of people who received free groceries from funds donated by her father in the hope of securing her return.

leged right-wing "army." He was returned unharmed two days later after Murphy's employer paid the ransom; a couple was subsequently arrested and the money recovered.

In most of the cases that followed the Hearst kidnapping, the kidnappers were quickly arrested, the victims released unharmed, and the bulk of the ransom money recovered. FBI Director Clarence Kelley said the conviction rate in cases involving the bureau was close to 100 per cent. He called quick arrests and stiff sentences the best deterrents to such crimes.

Detective agencies across the country reported a surge in requests for bodyguards. A number of large corporations took out ransom insurance on key executives. Other firms urged their top officers to vary their routes to and from work.

Amnesty Hearings

Thirty-two witnesses testified during three days of hearings in March before a House subcommittee that was considering the question of granting amnesty to men who deserted the armed forces or evaded the draft during the Vietnam war. According to government statistics, 423,422

Americans deserted the armed forces between 1966 and 1972, of which 32,557 remain at large. Nearly 5,000 of more than 24,000 men considered draft dodgers during this period remain at large. Of this figure, 2,300 are believed to be in Canada and 1,700 living underground in the United States.

President Nixon opposes amnesty, and a poll taken in 1973 indicated that two of three Americans were against pardon for draft evaders. The testimony reflected deep division between the advocates and opponents of amnesty. After the hearings ended, subcommittee chairman Robert Kastenmeier said, "It will take some time to get a consensus. There will have to be some changes of heart."

The maximum federal penalty for desertion and draft evasion is five years in prison. However, the military services often have permitted deserters to surrender voluntarily and serve out their commitments without prosecution. The Justice Department's policy on draft evaders has been to allow criminal charges to be dropped if the draftee agrees to a preinduction physical examination. There has

Amnesty for men who evaded the draft or deserted the armed forces during the Vietnam war was debated in congressional hearings. The picture below shows members of a group in Canada that claims to represent between 70,000 and 100,000 fellow exiled Americans and rejects "alternative service" as a condition for amnesty.

never been a general amnesty for draft evaders or deserters, although some have been pardoned by presidential act and practically all Confederate soldiers received full and unconditional amnesty.

Among those testifying was Senator Robert Taft of Ohio, who has introduced legislation that would create a board to consider amnesty for draft evaders on a case-by-case basis. Under this proposal, amnesty would be granted in exchange for two years' service in a civilian agency such as VISTA or in the armed forces. Also appearing was Robert Froehlke, secretary of the army from 1971 to 1973, who proposed a similar board to consider amnesty for deserters on an individual basis. Froehlke said he had opposed amnesty while the United States was still fighting in Vietnam. "Now is the time to begin mending the heartbreak and wounds left by the war," he said.

Speaking against amnesty, a Justice Department official said Congress lacked the power to pass appropriate legislation. Lieutenant General Leo Benade said it would undermine military discipline by encouraging desertion or draft evasion in some future war. He also produced figures from an army study purporting to show that only a small percentage of the deserters were motivated by idealistic opposition to the Vietnam war.

Among those who testified in favor of amnesty was former Alaska senator Ernest Gruening. He said immediate, unconditional amnesty should be granted to deserters and draft evaders with a "declaration of appreciation for their decency and humanitarianism."

Many draft evaders have received defacto amnesty. Of 3,495 draft-evasion cases that the government prosecuted in 1972, only 977 ended in conviction and only 260 men actually went to jail. In many cases a young man's draft records were destroyed after his 26th birthday—Selective Service's cutoff date for induction—making prosecution impossible. Other draftees had their induction dates moved up by local boards in retaliation for engaging in antiwar activities, a practice that the Supreme Court has ruled unconstitutional.

Yeoman Charles Radford told a Senate committee that he had stolen top-secret papers and had passed them on to high Pentagon officials.

Spy Ring Revealed

The presence of a military spy ring operating wtihin the National Security Council during 1970 and 1971 was reported by the New York *Times* in January. David R. Young, Jr., a former member of the White House "plumbers" unit, reportedly uncovered the group while investigating information leaks to columnist Jack Anderson concerning the India-Pakistan war of 1971.

Implicated in the theft of classified documents were Rear Admiral Robert Welander, who served in 1971 as military liaison officer between the National Security Council and the joint chiefs of staff, and his chief aide, Yeoman Charles Radford. According to the *Times'* sources, Radford confessed under interrogation in December, 1971, that he had begun pilfering top-secret papers in the fall of 1970 at the re-

National Guardsmen sent to the campus of Kent State University in 1970 opened fire on students, killing four and wounding nine. In March, one present member and seven former members of the Ohio National Guard were indicted on federal charges of violating the civil rights of the slain and wounded students by willfully assaulting them.

quest of the late Rear Admiral Rembrandt Robinson, Welander's predecessor.

Radford's job as stenographer-clerk for the NSC had given him regular access to classified information. He had also served as an aide on overseas missions of Henry Kissinger (then head of the NSC) and Kissinger's former deputy, General Alexander M. Haig. (Welander's post was later eliminated, and both men were transferred to other assignments.)

The documents, which pertained to sensitive U.S. discussions with China, Russia, and North Vietnam, were allegedly supplied to the office of Admiral Thomas H. Moorer, chairman of the joint chiefs of staff since 1970. Moorer had reportedly been frustrated by White House secrecy over diplomatic initiatives affecting the military.

In testimony before the Senate Armed Services Committee, Moorer and Welander denied directing Radford to steal documents. Both conceded that they had received purloined material but said they originally thought the material had been obtained by Radford in the regular course of his clerical duties.

Kent State Guardsmen Indicted

On March 29, a federal grand jury in Cleveland indicted one present member and seven former members of the Ohio National Guard on charges of violating the civil rights of four Kent State University students who were shot to death and nine others who were wounded. They were charged with willfully assaulting and intimidating demonstrators on the Kent State campus who were protesting on May 4, 1970, against the U.S. invasion of Cambodia (See EDUCATION, subtitle *Kent State* in the second section, 1970.) The grand jury found no conspiracy among the guardsmen to shoot the students, a theory that had been previously raised.

A host of investigations—public and private, federal, state, and local—followed the incident. In 1971, a state grand jury indicted 25 students, faculty members, and outsiders on riot charges and accused the university administrators of permissiveness. Two defendants subsequently pleaded guilty, one was convicted on a minor charge, one was acquitted, and charges against the 21 others were dropped for lack of evidence.

117

An 8,000-page FBI report concluded that the assertion by the national guardsmen "that their lives were endangered by the students was fabricated subsequent to the event." U.S. Attorney General John Mitchell declined to bring charges against the guardsmen, but his successor, Elliot Richardson, reopened the case.

See also AGRICULTURE; ART; BUSINESS AND FINANCE; DISASTERS; FASHION; LATIN AMERICA; LITERATURE; MIDDLE EAST; MOTION PICTURES; OBITUARIES; PETROLEUM; RELIGION; SPACE EXPLORATION; SPORTS AND ATHLETICS; and VIETNAM, in this section.

Vietnam. In the year following the January 27, 1973, cease-fire agreement, nearly 13,000 South Vietnamese soldiers and 2,150 civilians were killed. According to Saigon, 44,850 North Vietnamese and Vietcong soldiers were killed in South Vietnam.

Saigon reported an average of 80 incidents a day. South Vietnamese authorities said Hanoi had sent south 30,000 troops in 1973, bringing its total to 170,000 in South Vietnam. To support these forces, Hanoi had committed 700 heavy artillery pieces and 300 tracked vehicles, including heavy tanks. The Communists had built a network of roads from the demilitarized zone to within 100 miles of Saigon, had refurbished 12 former U.S. airfields in Communist-controlled territory, and had set up missiles sites along the former U.S. Marine airfield at Khesanh.

Communist forces had come close to cutting South Vietnam in half at the Central Highlands and had threatened the Mekong river delta rice harvest. They were destroying bridges, blockading key arteries, attacking outposts, and terrorizing local officials. They appeared to have stockpiled enough arms to sustain major fighting for at least 12 months.

Both sides had moved civilians into sparsely settled regions and villages abandoned in earlier fighting. In many government areas farmers were paying "taxes" to the Vietcong, usually in the form of food. Vehicles on roads and boats on canals were also being stopped to collect "taxes."

The United States contributed almost $1 billion in military aid to South Vietnam in 1973, and $600 million more in economic aid. Americans were playing an important role in the supply, transport, and intelligence systems of the armed forces. A total of 4,155 U.S. citizens were engaged in military-related jobs, including 2,800 civilians employed by defense contractors and 1,150 in the defense attaché's office.

Although South Vietnam's soldiers fought well in 1973, the economic situation was causing concern. Prices rose by 65 per cent during the year; rice doubled in cost. The standard of living reportedly

Last-Ditch Defense was constructed by South Vietnamese peasants 22 miles north of Saigon with the aim of halting any thrust by North Vietnamese tanks on the capital. The government reported an average of 80 incidents a day and said almost 60,000 people had been killed since the 1973 "cease-fire."

fell by more than 5 cent for the second straight year.

One of the few clauses of the cease-fire agreement to be implemented was the exchange of prisoners; on March 8, the last prisoners officially listed as captured before the cease-fire were released, culminating four weeks of exchanges. This brought to 31,502 the number of prisoners released by Saigon since the cease-fire agreement, of which 26,880 were soldiers. The Vietcong released 5,942, of whom 5,336 were military men. But officials on both sides said as many people had been captured since the cease-fire agreement as had been released.

Disputed Islands

China occupied the Paracel Islands on January 19 and 20 after a clash with South Vietnamese forces. Both countries had claimed the island group, which lies in the South China Sea about 200 miles east of South Vietnam and 175 miles southeast of the Chinese island of Hainan.

The islands have no permanent settlers. Pattle, the largest, is only 1,000 yards long by 500 yards wide. The only economic resources are guano deposits for fertilizer and swallows' nests, which are used with pigeon or crabmeat to make a dish called yen sao. However, oil deposits may lie under the seabed near the islands.

On January 11, Peking renewed earlier claims of sovereignty over the Paracels and the Spratly Islands, which lie 500 miles south of the Paracels. A group of 20 Chinese fishermen subsequently landed on one of the Paracels, Robert Island, and planted the Chinese flag.

South Vietnam sent six gunboats to the area. On January 18, navy commandos reportedly forced the fishermen off the island.

Heavy fighting erupted January 19 as South Vietnamese troops landing on Duncan Island encountered a larger force of Chinese soldiers and had to retreat. In a naval clash that followed, a South Vietnamese patrol boat carrying 82 men was sunk (only 23 survivors were picked up) and several other vessels were hit. A Chinese patrol boat was also reportedly sunk. On January 20, a force of about 600 Chinese, supported by MIG aircraft and 14

Disputed Islands. Chinese forces occupied the Paracel Islands after a clash with South Vietnamese forces. Both nations claim the island group, which has no permanent settlers. Both countries also claim the Spratly Islands, which lie 500 miles south of the Paracels.

warships, stormed Pattle, Robert, and Money islands and overwhelmed the defenders.

Peking captured and later freed 43 South Vietnamese. Also captured and released was an American, Gerald Kosh, who had been serving as an observer with the South Vietnamese navy.

The Vietnam Press Agency reported February 22 that South Vietnamese forces had completed their "program for consolidation of sovereignty" in the Spratly Islands after occupying 5 of the 11 islands. South Vietnam had reasserted sovereignty over the Spratlys as well as the Paracels on February 14 and had warned it would go to war if necessary with China, Taiwan, or the Philippines. The Philippines was believed to have troops on three of the islands and Nationalist China reportedly had troops on one.

Watergate Scandal. On March 1, former Nixon Administration aides H. R. Haldeman, John Ehrlichman, Charles Colson, and Gordon Strachan; former attorney general John Mitchell; and campaign aides Robert Mardian and Kenneth Parkinson were indicted on charges of covering up the 1972 break-in of Democratic National Committee headquarters in the Watergate Office Building. The grand jury also gave Judge John Sirica a sealed report believed to deal with Nixon's role in the cover-up, with the recommendation that it be forwarded to the House Judiciary Committee for inclusion in its impeachment investigation.

The defendants were variously charged with conspiracy, obstruction of justice, perjury, and making false statements and false declarations. At a brief arraignment hearing, the seven pleaded not guilty. The trial was scheduled to begin September 9; Sirica announced that he had assigned himself to hear the case.

The overall conspiracy charge involving all seven defendants detailed a complex scenario in which the defendants, along with others, arranged "hush money" pay-offs for those charged in the Watergate burglary and wiretapping. They were also charged with offering executive clemency, destroying documents, and lying to various investigative bodies. According to the 45 "overt acts" of conspiracy cited by the grand jury, the cover-up began within hours after the break-in June 17, 1972, and continued through March 22, 1973.

The grand jury's account of the alleged conspiracy generally followed the damaging testimony offered to the Senate Watergate committee in 1973 by several witnesses, especially former White House counsel John Dean, who had pleaded guilty to one count of conspiracy and was cooperating with the prosecution. (See the feature article in the second section, 1973, for an account of the Watergate scandal.) The grand jury also heard a number of tape recordings of presidential conversations involving the Watergate case.

President Nixon was not mentioned except for a reference in one of three counts of perjury against Haldeman. Dean had told the Watergate committee that on March 13, 1973, the president had told him that it would be "no problem" to

Indicted. Seven former Nixon Administration and 1972 campaign aides were indicted March 1 on charges of covering up the Watergate break-in. The grand jury also issued a sealed report believed to deal with President Nixon's role in the cover-up; it was forwarded to the House Judiciary Committee for inclusion in its impeachment investigation.

raise the $1 million that Dean estimated it might cost to buy the silence of the Watergate defendants. Haldeman, who was present at this meeting, said the conversation had taken place on March 21, 1973, and that a recording of the conversation showed that Nixon added "it would be wrong." Haldeman said the tape of the meeting—which was among those later surrendered by the White House to the prosecution—confirmed his recollection. But the grand jury charged that these statements "as he then and there well knew, were false."

A sealed two-page report and covering letter, accompanied by a bulging briefcase of documents, were turned over to Sirica by the grand jury. On March 18, Sirica ordered this material turned over to the House Judiciary Committee. Attorneys for the seven indicted men had urged him not to do so on the grounds that it could lead to leaks of the contents and generate pretrial publicity affecting their clients. But, on March 20, the U.S. Court of Appeals rejected their appeal from Sirica's ruling by a vote of 5 to 1.

In a 22-page written opinion, Sirica made it clear that the secret grand-jury report as well the briefcase of material dealt with President Nixon's acts "in his public capacity" during the period under investigation. Prosecution sources said special prosecutor Leon Jaworski had advised the jurors that they could not indict a president in office.

More Tapes Sought

Jaworski said on February 1 that it was "clear that evidence I deem material to our investigations will not be forthcoming" from the White House. He said that he had requested 27 additional recordings of conversations that he called material to his investigation. On March 15, he issued a subpoena for the release of evidence dealing with the alleged sale of ambassadorships in return for campaign contributions. On March 30, the White House agreed to surrender the subpoenaed material.

On February 25, the House Judiciary Committee asked for 42 White House tapes with regard to its inquiry into impeachment. Nixon replied March 6 that

Seeking Evidence. House Judiciary Committee Chairman Peter Rodino, left, shown with John Doar, the committee's chief counsel, asked for 42 White House tapes with regard to the inquiry into impeachment.

he had turned over to Jaworski 19 tapes and more than 700 documents and that he would furnish the committee with all these tapes and documents, but he indicated that he would not comply with requests for further material.

The 42 tapes sought by the House committee covered six areas not commonly associated with the Watergate scandal but rather with charges that decisions concerning environmental questions, oil imports, and antitrust cases were influenced by political contributions or friendship. White House Press Secretary Ronald Ziegler expressed the Administration's position in saying "the mere fact of an impeachment inquiry does not give Congress the right to back up a truck and haul off White House files."

Panel Reports on Tape

On January 15, the panel of technical experts examining the tapes surrendered by the White House in October reported on the inaudible 18½-minute gap found on a tape for June 20, 1972. (See WATERGATE SCANDAL, subtitle *The Tapes Crisis: Missing Tapes,* in the fourth section, 1973.) The panel said that the gap had been caused by at least five separate erasing and recording operations, and not by a single accidental erasure, as the White House had contended.

White House lawyers challenged the panel's conclusion. An electronics firm

Impeachment: The Issues

Article II, Section 4, of the United States Constitution states that "the President, Vice President and all civil officers of the United States, shall be removed from office on impeachment for, and conviction of, treason, bribery, or other high crimes and misdemeanors." The House of Representatives, acting as the equivalent of a grand jury, may impeach such officials by majority vote. The Senate, acting as the equivalent of a trial jury, may convict by a two-thirds vote.

Conviction means removal from office and disqualification from holding future office. Any other punishment requires criminal proceedings in the courts. The president is generally considered exempt from ordinary criminal proceedings while in office.

Impeachable Offenses

There exists wide latitude between the broadest and narrowest interpretations of impeachment. The broadest interpretation was expressed by Gerald Ford in 1970. When Republican leaders in the House of Representatives sought to impeach Supreme Court Justice William O. Douglas, Ford, then House minority leader, said, "An impeachable offense is whatever a majority of the House of Representatives considers it to be at a given moment in history." Similarly, former attorney general Richard Kleindienst, testifying before a congressional committee, said of impeachment, "You don't need facts. You don't need evidence. All you need is votes." Douglas' counsels argued, on the other hand, that an official can be impeached only for criminal offenses that would be indictable by a grand jury.

The White House makes a distinction between the impeachment of federal judges and of the president. The president, Nixon's attorneys contend, can only be impeached for criminal offenses; judges may be impeached on other grounds because Article III, Section 1, of the Constitution states "The judges . . . shall hold their offices during good behavior . . . "

Some White House counsels have even argued that Congress is not the final arbiter of impeachment, citing the opinion of Harvard University law historian Raoul Berger. In his book *Impeachment: The Constitutional Problem* (1973), Berger argues that an impeachment conviction can be appealed to the courts.

Most authorities take a middle position. Impeachment in the United States, wrote 19th-century Supreme Court Justice Joseph Story in a commentary, is "a proceeding purely of a political nature . . . not so much designed to punish an offender as to secure the state against gross official misdemeanors." In 1912, a federal judge was impeached and convicted in spite of his defense that he had committed no criminal acts. A federal judge was found guilty and removed from office by the Senate in 1936 for bringing his court "into scandal and disrepute" although he was acquitted of specific crimes.

Impeachment was originally a device used by the Parliament in England to prosecute royal advisers for offenses both criminal and non-criminal. Parliament removed magistrates on such charges as misleading their sovereign and appointing bad men to office. An admiral was impeached for neglecting to safeguard the sea, a lord chancellor for putting the seal of trust to a treaty judged to be ignominious.

The Founding Fathers took the phrase "high crimes and misdemeanors" from these parliamentary impeachments. (The prevailing assumption is that "misdemeanors" refers in impeachment cases to crimes connected with the conduct of office.) James Madison, one of the principal framers of the Constitution, objected to a proposal to make "maladministration" grounds for impeachment, saying "so vague a term will be equivalent to a tenure during the pleasure of the Senate." But he argued that the president was not only liable for his own actions but also for those of his assistants, being "responsible for their conduct and subject to impeachment himself, if he suffers them to perpetrate with impunity high crimes or misdemeanors against the United States, or neglects to superintend their conduct, so as to check their excesses."

The House of Representatives has impeached 13 officials; only four, all judges, have been convicted by the Senate and removed from office. The most famous impeachment case was that of President Andrew Johnson, who escaped removal from office in 1868 by only one vote. The principal charge against him was his defiance of an act of Congress that was later held by the Supreme Court to be unconstitutional. Most authorities regard the proceedings against Johnson as an abuse of the impeachment power.

Charges Against Nixon

Several groups have called for the impeachment of Richard Nixon. The American Civil Liberties Union lists 11 charges against him, the AFL-CIO 19. A "public-interest" law group lists "28 violations of law" committed by him "or persons answerable to him."

The charges include the following:

● Establishing within the White House a personal force (the plumbers) that engaged in such criminal acts as burglary, illegal wiretapping, and perjury.

● Approval of the "Huston plan" authorizing illegal acts, although approval was allegedly rescinded before the plan was put into action.

● Attempted use of federal investigations to harass political "enemies."

● Tampering with the process of justice, as evidenced by Administration contacts with the judge hearing the Ellsberg trial concerning a possible job offer.

● Obstruction of justice, as evidenced by the effort to limit the FBI investigation of the Watergate break-in and the payment of alleged "hush money" to the Watergate defendants.

● Authorization of more than 3,600 secret bombing sorties into Cambodia in 1969 and 1970, involving persistent falsification of Air Force records, and despite federal statutes requiring congressional approval of such military actions.

● Impoundment of funds appropriated by Congress despite an array of lower-court decisions holding such impoundment to be illegal.

● Questionable tax deductions, and home improvements at federal expense. The Constitution forbids the president to receive any emolument from the government beyond his specified salary and expenses.

The staff lawyers conducting the impeachment inquiry for the House Judiciary Committee were requesting specific information, documents, and tapes from the White House bearing on President Nixon's personal conduct. Refusal to comply with the request might be another ground for impeachment.

Impeachment trial of
President Andrew Johnson, 1868

issued a report arguing that the sounds and magnetic marks discovered by the panel on the inaudible segment could have all been caused in a single operation, by the sputtering on and off of the recorder's internal-power supply. (The technical-expert panel's finding of multiple erasures implied, by contrast, that the erasures were deliberate.)

Ellsberg Burglary Indictments

On March 7, Ehrlichman, Colson, G. Gordon Liddy, Bernard Barker, Eugenio Martinez, and Felipe DeDiego were indicted for conspiring to violate the civil rights of Daniel Ellsberg's psychiatrist (Dr. Lewis J. Fielding) by illegally breaking and entering into his office. A list of 19 "overt acts" was related. E. Howard Hunt, Egil Krogh, and David Young were named as unindicted co-conspirators. Ehrlichman was also charged with three counts of false declarations to the grand jury and one count of lying to the FBI. In a separate indictment, Liddy was charged with two counts of contempt stemming from his refusal to testify before a congressional committee.

Other Court Cases

Herbert Kalmbach, the president's personal lawyer, pleaded guilty February 25 to two violations of the federal law governing campaign funds. He admitted raising $3.9 million for a secret congressional campaign committee and promising an ambassador a better diplomatic post in return for a $100,000 campaign contribution. Jaworski indicated in a letter filed with the court that other charges against Kalmbach had been dropped in exchange for his cooperation with the Watergate investigation.

Herbert Porter, a former presidential campaign aide, pleaded guilty January 28 to a charge of making false statements to the FBI. He had admitted to the Senate Watergate committee telling lies to cover up the fact that funds for campaign "dirty tricks" had been given to Liddy. Jaworski's office told the court that Porter had cooperated fully with the prosecution; he was sentenced to 30 days in jail.

Egil Krogh, who headed the White House investigative unit known as "the plumbers" and who had pleaded guilty November 30 to a civil-rights violation arising from the burglary of the office of Ellsberg's psychiatrist, was sentenced to six months in prison on January 24. He said that he had "received no specific instruction or authority whatsoever regarding the break-in from the president, directly or indirectly."

NEWS

Energy Crisis Saves Lives

The National Safety Council reported February 1 that about 1,000 fewer persons were killed in traffic accidents in the United States in 1973 than in 1972. The largest portion of the reduction came during December, when the energy crisis reached its peak for the year. There were 55,600 traffic deaths in 1973 and 56,600 in 1972.

Twenty-four states adopted reduced speed limits effective December 10. The traffic-death reduction in those states during December was 22 per cent, compared to December, 1972.

The national motor-vehicle death rate for 1973 dropped to 4.2 deaths per 100 million vehicle-miles, compared to 4.5 in 1972. The 4.2 figure was the lowest on record.

Non to English Food

The Michelin Guide, long considered the ultimate arbiter of French cuisine, published its first guide to British and Irish restaurants in 40 years and found them mostly deplorable. Only 25 dining establishments were awarded a star, the coveted emblem that Michelin uses to designate "a good restaurant in its class," compared to 624 in France. None were deemed worthy of two stars, or the ultimate Michelin accolade, three stars. Nine establishments in France rate two stars and six carry three stars.

Giving support to those who believe that Michelin must be biased because it is a French company was the fact that seven of the nine London restaurants that received stars specialize in French cuisine; the other two were a Chinese restaurant and a chop house that denies entry to women. But the many caustic critics of British and Irish cooking believe the guide's evaluation was thoroughly justified. The Michelin people themselves blamed British diners. "They are too polite," said the concern's anonymous chief inspector. "They accept everything."

Kissinger Weds

Secretary of State Henry Kissinger was married to Nancy Maginnes on March 30 in a brief civil ceremony. It was his second marriage and her first. The couple left immediately after the ceremony for a honeymoon in Acapulco, Mexico.

Miss Maginnes is an aide on foreign-policy matters to former governor of New York Nelson Rockefeller and met Kissinger when he was serving as a part-time consultant to Rockefeller. They became frequent companions, and even though Kissinger had been photographed in the company of movie stars and other attractive women in the last five years, his close associates privately had predicted that if he remarried, it would be to Miss Maginnes.

New Bird Species Found

A previously unknown bird has been sighted by students in a remote rain forest of Hawaii. The bird, a member of the Hawaiian Honeycreeper family, is believed to be the first new genus and species of bird reported in 10 years, according to the National Science Foundation, which announced the discovery.

World's Oldest Song

Richard Crocker, *above,* a musicologist at the University of California, played for the press March 5 a song that is the oldest known piece of music in the world. Notes and words were found on a tablet dating from 1400 B.C. which was unearthed in ancient Ugarit, a city now known as Ras Shamra, on the Syrian coast.

Only three people have attempted to reconstruct the song, and all of them differ. The version that was played was the interpretation by Anne Kilmer of the University of California, who fitted the words—in Hurrian, one of the oldest and least-understood of the world's languages —to the music. The result, if she is correct, is a two-part composition for a singer and a musician, probably a lyre player. Crocker sang the words while playing the music on a reproduction of a 4,600-year-old Sumerian lyre. Reporters said it sounded like a lullaby, a hymn, or a gentle folk song. Kilmer has translated some of the words, including "father," "love," the phrase "beloved of the heart," and references to gods and goddesses.

Previously, the oldest known piece of music was a fragment of a setting for a song in Euripides' play *Orestes,* found on a fragment of Greek papyrus dated about 400 B.C.

Mindszenty Is Retired

Jozsef Cardinal Mindszenty, exiled primate of Hungary, was removed from the jurisdiction he nominally retained there on February 5 by Pope Paul VI. The papal decision on retirement for the 81-year-old cardinal, living in Vienna, was clearly aimed at improving church-state relations in Hungary. Cardinal Mindszenty spent more than 22 years in imprisonment or in asylum in the U.S. legation in Budapest. For years Communist officials in Hungary had told the Vatican that Mindszenty would have to be removed as primate before the Roman Catholic Church could expect to fill all vacant sees or hold religious classes in schools.

Election in Costa Rica

Government candidate Daniel Oduber Quiros was elected president of Costa Rica on February 3. He led seven other candidates in nationwide voting and received more than the 40 per cent minimum required for election without a runoff. His National Liberation party lost its majority in the National Assembly, however. The main issue in the campaign was inflation, although outgoing President José Figueres called the election "a plebiscite in favor of or against my government."

Wretched Excess

A plague of blackbirds, starlings, and grackles, estimated at about 10 million, roosted in a pine grove near the village of Graceham, Maryland, before Christmas and stayed there for three months, harassing the villagers and their livestock and pets. They were chased away March 23 by an assault of firecrackers, clay bombs, propane cannons, and high-pitched whistles.

Revised Rite of Penance

The Vatican published a revised liturgy for the sacrament of penance February 6 in an action expected to emphasize the social as well as personal consequences of sin. Under the new liturgy, parishes would be encouraged to hold regular "penitential celebrations" that could be attended by anywhere from a handful to hundreds of people. Individuals would still have the opportunity to confess their sins privately to a priest, and absolution would still be granted on an individual basis only. The document also provided for perpetuation of the present practice of private confession without the communal setting.

Many Catholics have argued in recent years that a strictly personal ritual is inadequate to deal with social evils such as racism or with the social consequences of a personal sin, such as adultery. Thus many parishes, acting on their own, have begun to hold communal penitential services of one kind or another.

Not Bad, Just Misunderstood

The wolf—in folklore and song a savage creature—is developing a growing reputation as a gentle, loving, sensitive animal, according to tentative findings by scientists. Not only do wolves, according to one researcher, devote a considerable amount of time to "being friendly, nice, and reassuring to each other," but they are "very sensitive to people's moods and they adjust their own behavior, depending upon whether you're feeling good or bad."

Independence for Grenada

The West Indian island of Grenada became an independent nation February 7, ending more than 200 years of British colonial rule. Prime Minister Eric Gairy appealed for an end to the conflict that had beset the island since November, 1973.

Opponents of Gairy charged that secret police, the core of which was allegedly a criminal gang known as the "Mongoose Squad," was terrorizing critics of the government, looting stores, and assaulting protesting demonstrators. A general strike that began January 1 with the aim of ousting the prime minister from power had virtually paralyzed the island, closing the port, halting most commercial activity, and shutting down all public utilities except potable water.

His War Ends—After 29 Years

A Japanese lieutenant emerged from the jungles of the Philippines March 10, 29 years after the end of World War II, and said he had not surrendered sooner because "I had not received the order." Shortly after, 52-year-old Lieutenant Hiroo Onoda formally handed over his samurai sword in Manila to Philippines President Ferdinand Marcos.

Several searches for Lieutenant Onoda had been conducted over the years, and twice he was declared dead. Japanese officials have estimated that hundreds of World War II soldiers could be hiding out in the jungles of Southeast Asia, either from ignorance of the war's end or out of loyalty to a military code that taught them death was preferable to surrender. Onoda's last order had been to continue guerrilla warfare, and he was not willing to surrender until a Japanese visitor brought him an order to do so from his old commander. For 30 years, Onoda and his three comrades—all of whom are now dead—burned the crops and houses of Filipino villagers. Local authorities estimate they may have killed as many as 30 Filipinos.

Bob Dylan Returns

Rock superstar Bob Dylan kicked off a six-week, 21-city concert tour—his first in eight years—on January 3 in the Chicago Stadium. Dylan and his backup group, The Band, performed 28 songs, all familiar Dylan material except for three new ones from his forthcoming album *Planet Waves*.

To the faithful, Dylan was the voice of the Sixties who articulated their thoughts during that turbulent decade. In interviews he dispelled any intention of taking up the mantle for a new generation. But he closed with "It's Alright Ma (I'm Only Bleeding)," and at the line "Even the President of the U.S. must have to stand naked," the crowd went wild.

Bangladesh Recognized

Pakistan recognized Bangladesh, its former eastern wing, as an independent nation on February 22. The action came at the opening of a major conference of Moslem nations. In late 1971 India defeated Pakistan in a three-week war and the province of East Pakistan became Bangladesh.

Moslem countries had urged both nations to heal the breach in the Islamic world. As a precondition, Pakistan had demanded that Bangladesh publicly cancel plans to try 195 Pakistanis for atrocities committed during the struggle that ended with the creation of Bangladesh. Bangladesh agreed April 9 to cancel the trials and to return all Pakistanis being held as prisoners of war.

Remains of *Monitor* Found

A researcher at Duke University reported March 6 that the long-sought wreck of the *Monitor*, the Union vessel in history's first duel between ironclads, during the Civil War, had been found on the bottom of the Atlantic Ocean off Cape Hatteras, North Carolina. The ship, which was compared to a cheesebox on a raft because of its unusual shape, fought the Confederacy's *Virginia*—popularly known as the *Merrimack*—to a draw in their historic encounter in Hampton Roads on March 9, 1862. Later the *Monitor* sank in a gale off Cape Hatteras.

The researcher said that the remains of the 172-foot vessel were lying in 220 feet of water and were probably not recoverable with equipment and technology currently available. He offered as evidence underwater television films of portions of the wreck, along with sonar readings, magnetometer records, and bits and pieces of wood and coal brought up by mechanical scoops.

Queen Still Tops Down Under

God Save the Queen is the national anthem preferred by 78 per cent of Australians, according to a poll conducted by the Sydney *Sun*. *Waltzing Matilda* received the support of only 2 per cent. The government has committed itself to replacing *God Save the Queen* as the national anthem in order to deemphasize Australia's links with Great Britain and, perhaps, as a prelude to eventually making Australia a republic.

Double-Deckers Will Return

The double-decker bus, once a fixture of Manhattan life, will return to New York City soon, according to the U.S. Department of Transportation. Federal sources said the department would finance a trial program to test the performance, economics, safety, and public acceptance of the buses in New York City and Los Angeles. Four British-built double-decker buses would be put into use in New York and two German-built buses in Los Angeles.

Double-deckers were in use in Manhattan from 1907 to 1953. Until 1946 many of the buses had open tops, offering a scenic view of the Hudson River and Central Park as they made their way down Riverside Drive and Fifth Avenue.

Guatemala Votes

General Kjell Laugerud Garcia of the ruling National Coalition was declared the winner of Guatemala's presidential election, held March 3. Since no candidate won an absolute majority of the votes, the outgoing Congress, dominated by the government, proclaimed Laugerud the winner on March 12. Official results gave him 41.2 per cent of the vote, compared to 35.7 per cent for retired general Efrain Rios Montt, his closest rival.

Rios Montt claimed victory and accused the government of vote fraud. Four of his supporters had been murdered immediately after the election. Also killed was a leftist lawyer who gave aid to an organization that holds the authorities responsible for the death or disappearance of hundreds of persons in recent years.

Solar Energy in Manhattan

An addition to the RCA Building in New York City's Rockefeller Center will utilize solar energy in the city for the first time as a pilot project in energy technology. The picture above shows a scale model of the facility, which will rise from a 12th-floor setback of the 70-story skyscraper. It will serve as a management conference center for the company.

The facility will make use of panels on its solid exterior surfaces to capture solar energy in the form of radiant heat, which will be stored and used to substitute for other forms of energy. It will make abundant use of insulated glass to enclose a large garden and bridge walkways as well as to cover much of its roof area. The cost is estimated at $6 million.

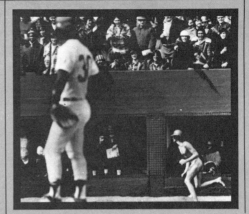

Be Fashionable: Wear Nothing

Streaking became the latest rite of spring as college students of both sexes touched off the fad of sprinting in the nude through campuses, shopping centers, factories, and sports arenas. Clad in the latest accessories—sneakers, neckties, masks, and body paint—streakers also appeared on bicycles, motorcycles, skis, and parachutes.

Although most streakers said they had turned out in the buff merely as a lark, author and communications theorist Marshall McLuhan called the phenomenon "an art form . . . Streaking has a political point, too." And a "Streak for Impeachment" rally drew a dozen participants on the campus of Fairleigh Dickinson University in Rutherford, New Jersey.

The Great American Ripoff

The 21,000 hotels and 43,500 motels in the United States estimate that pilferage of "souvenirs" such as towels, bedspreads, and ashtrays will cost them $500 million in 1974. They predict that one of every three people who stay at an American hotel or motel in 1974 will take part of it away. Thousands will steal lamps, television sets, and even whole suites of furniture.

Industry officials say ordinarily honest guests rather than professional thieves account for most of the losses. Most guests who steal have curious ways of rationalizing their behavior, one being that room rates are so high that only by pilferage can they get their money's worth. One motel operator calls this attitude "part of the new consumerism ripoff syndrome." Guests are rarely prosecuted unless the goods stolen are expensive.

Viking Map a Phony

Yale University announced January 25 that its "Vinland Map," *above,* which purported to show North America as discovered by Leif Ericson, had been found to be a forgery. The university had described the map in 1965 as "the most exciting cartographic discovery of the century" and had defended its authenticity ever since against criticism by skeptical scholars. In making the announcement, Yale said newly devised chemical tests had showed that the ink used to draw the map could not have been produced before the 1920's.

The map, which was said to have been copied about 1440 from earlier documents, was the only known map of New World lands drawn up before the voyages of Christopher Columbus. It shows Iceland, Greenland, and an island labeled "Vinlandia" that appears to correspond to Labrador.

The Yale University Press sold 10,000 copies of the map and related works (two 15th-century books whose authenticity is not in doubt, says the university) at $15 each. It also contracted with the Book-of-the-Month Club to print an additional 40,000 copies for its members. There are no plans to offer refunds to those who purchased the bogus material.

Scholars pointed out that the map was not necessary to prove the pre-Columbian presence of the Vikings in America. In 1963 a Viking settlement established about 1000 was unearthed in northern Newfoundland. Its authenticity has been confirmed by several historical societies.

Khrushchev Memoirs on Tape

Time, Inc. disclosed March 6 that it had in its possession 180 hours of tape-recorded memoirs dictated by the late Soviet leader Nikita Khrushchev. The corporation said it was presenting the tapes to the Oral History Collection of Columbia University. It was the first public disclosure of the existence of the tapes and their presence in the United States.

It was also announced that a second volume of the memoirs, drawn from the tapes and covering Khrushchev's years in power, from 1953 to 1964, would be published in June. The first volume, which appeared in 1970, focused on his rise to power during the Stalin era. It is presumed to have been based on the tapes.

The recordings were said to have been arranged by unidentified members of Khrushchev's family and by his friends and to have been sent abroad without the approval of the present Soviet leadership. Some experts on Soviet affairs have questioned the authenticity of the memoirs, but voiceprint experts are said to have identified the voice on the tapes as Khrushchev's.

What Next: Galley Slaves?

The British navy, its ships short of fuel, is experimentally going back to sail. In January, an 1,800-ton deep-sea diving vessel called the *Reclaim* was, like all other British warships, ordered to keep her engines at half-speed when possible in the interest of saving oil. Since at best the *Reclaim* can barely manage 10 knots, and to reduce this by half would make some operations difficult, officials decided to put sails on her two masts. With a good wind it is thought she might make about eight knots on half-power.

Elections in Belgium

The moderate Social Christians remained Belgium's largest party in general elections held March 10, winning 32 per cent of the vote. Their two partners in the outgoing coalition government—the Socialists and the Liberals—declined slightly in strength. But the federalist parties, which had demanded that the nation be split into a federation between areas predominantly French-speaking and Dutch-speaking, lost ground after gains in three previous elections. Federalism and economic policy were the major issues in the campaign.

The Yale Blues

Mory's, a New Haven restaurant-club that had been an all-male enclave for generations of Yale University students and faculty, agreed on March 29 to admit women to full-fledged membership. In return, women's-rights advocates agreed not to block the granting of a new liquor license; the old one had been revoked in 1972 because of sex discrimination. The restaurant, which has no official connection with Yale but which limits its membership to the "Yale Community," was immortalized by the "Whiffenpoof Song" in 1909.

Chopper Buzzes White House

An army helicopter on an unauthorized flight flew across the White House grounds before landing 100 yards from the building in the early morning of February 17. The pilot, Private Robert K. Preston, landed the craft after being struck and slightly injured by shotgun blasts from security forces. Neither President Nixon nor any member of his family was at the White House at the time.

Preston was serving as a helicopter-maintenance man at Fort Meade, Maryland, about 25 miles from Washington, when he commandeered the helicopter, an army "Huey." The craft hovered five minutes around the base of the Washington Monument and, according to some reports, made an earlier pass over the White House grounds before returning an hour later—at 2 A.M.—to meet a fusillade of gunshots from the security guards.

Return of the Windmill

Some researchers believe that windmills, grouped to form power stations, could meet a significant portion of U.S. energy needs. The National Science Foundation is spending more than $1 million in fiscal 1974 on wind research, at least five universities have windmill-research programs, and one company is putting windmills out to sea to provide power for offshore oil-drilling platforms. The Great Plains is thought to be one area where wind energy could become competitive with other energy sources once engineers figure ways to reduce construction costs and store power when the weather turns calm.

It is estimated that 6.5 million windmills, including the one above, were built in the United States between 1880 and 1930, mostly for pumping water and running sawmills. But some were built to generate small amounts of electricity before the rural-electrification program rendered them obsolete.

NSF researchers are planning to build the "perfect" windmill—one that will capture the maximum possible amount of power from the wind—on a tower more than 100 feet above a research lab near Sandusky, Ohio. The experimental 100-kilowatt machine will, it is hoped, pioneer a low-cost structural design that will make it possible to mass-produce very large windmills for power stations.

New President of Brazil

General Ernesto Geisel was elected president of Brazil on January 15 by a body consisting of representatives of Congress and of the state legislatures. He had been named as the candidate of the governing party, the National Renewal Alliance, by outgoing president General Emilio Mêdici, and he received 400 votes from the 503-member electoral body. He took office March 15 for a five-year term.

Geisel, 65, had formerly been head of the state oil monopoly. He made no commitments to restore democratic liberties or lift censorship of the press. The military has dominated all Brazilian governments since the overthrow of the last civilian president in 1964.

New Turkish Government

Turkey's first left-of-center government—a coalition between a moderately socialist party and an Islamic party—was formed on January 25; exactly 100 days after inconclusive elections. The coalition partners commanded a majority of eight in the 450-member National Assembly. Bulent Ecevit, leader of the Republican People's party, became the premier; Necmettin Erbakan of the National Salvation party was named deputy premier.

Help Wanted: Spies

The *Bundesnachrichtendienst* (BND), or Federal Intelligence Service, West Germany's equivalent of the CIA, is looking for men and women in more than 40 professions, according to an eight-page brochure available at government employment offices. Most of those hired will fill routine assignments at BND headquarters in Bavaria, but a few will be sent out into the cold as "spooks."

Such candor is unusual for the supersecret service, but staff shortages for the organization of 5,000 could not be filled by the traditional word-of-mouth method or by classified ads that called the BND a "multinational company." Intelligence officials reportedly feel they have little to lose by going public since the BND has been thoroughly infiltrated by Soviet agents.

Airships Again?

Once dirigibles, such as the German Zeppelin *Hindenburg*, roamed the skies. Some aircraft designers now consider airships an answer to the requirements of contemporary transportation since energy savings and environmental protection are important concerns. A recent report indicates that the Soviet Union is planning to build a nuclear-powered dirigible capable of carrying 180 tons of freight and 1,800 passengers at a cruising speed of 190 miles per hour.

Index

first section

INDEX

1975 BOOK-OF-THE-YEAR

Illustrated World Encyclopedia

Gerald R. Ford,
38th President
of the U.S.

The New President

At noon on Friday, August 9, Gerald R. Ford was sworn in as the 38th President of the United States. Declaring that "our long national nightmare is over," he called on Americans to join together to close the wounds inflicted by Watergate.

When he was named vice president in late 1973, he expressed the fear that "my friends might stop calling me Jerry." In his early addresses to the nation as president, he gave the same impression of unaffected candor as he stated that only honesty could wipe away the political disillusionment brought on by Watergate.

Early Years. The President's original name was Leslie King, Jr., but when his mother divorced his father and moved from Omaha to Grand Rapids, Michigan, and remar-

*Chief Justice Warren Burger administers
the oath of office as Mrs. Ford watches.*

ried, her husband, Gerald Ford, Sr., adopted the boy and
gave him his name. In his new family he was one of four
sons, and his early years were filled with his main passion—
football. Ford's glory days on the gridiron were spent at the
University of Michigan, where he was named the most valuable player in 1934 for his performance as center and linebacker. Declining offers to pursue a professional football
career, Ford entered Yale University's law school. He graduated in 1941.

After earning his degree, Ford returned to Grand Rapids,
where he began practicing law. He enlisted in the U.S. Navy
in 1942 and served a total of 47 months, rising to the rank
of lieutenant commander. Returning once again to Grand
Rapids, he resumed his practice. Soon after, he unseated

Ford as University of Michigan football player.

The Ford family. Clockwise from top left: Steven, Susan, Jack, Mr. Ford, Sugar, Mrs. Ford, Michael.

the incumbent congressman, an isolationist veteran, in the Republican primary. Ford won the general election in the largely Republican district and entered the House of Representatives in 1949. He was to remain there until October 12, 1973, when he was named by President Nixon as his choice to replace Spiro Agnew as vice president.

Before coming to Washington, Ford married Elizabeth Bloomer, a former model whose previous five-year marriage had ended in divorce. The Fords have three sons and a daughter, ages 24 to 16.

Foreign Policy. During his 25 years in Congress—the last eight as House minority leader—Ford compiled a record as a moderate-to-conservative Republican. His views on both domestic and foreign policy were virtually identical to those of Richard Nixon. He described himself as "a moderate on domestic issues, a conservative on fiscal affairs, and a dyed-in-the-wool internationalist in foreign affairs."

Like Nixon, Ford in his early days was adamant in his anti-communist stand. In recent years, though, he supported the Nixon Administration's moves towards détente, and his first actions as president were designed to assure world leaders that the Nixon policy would be maintained and that Secretary of State Henry Kissinger would retain his post in the Ford Administration.

Ford maintained a hawkish stand on the Vietnam war, opposing Lyndon Johnson's tactics because he felt they were militarily flawed. He regarded air attacks over North Vietnam, initiated in the Johnson years and escalated during the Nixon Administration, as the only way to "cripple the enemy's warmaking capability." Ford places great importance on national security and has stressed the need for the United States to maintain its military superiority. Nevertheless, he holds that defense expenditures should be closely scrutinized in the interest of budget cutting.

Despite his admitted lack of broad expertise in foreign affairs, Ford faces many critical decisions during his early months in office. First, he must immediately begin work on peace initiatives in the Middle East. Many observers have expressed a fear that unless negotiations continue, new fighting could break out. Ford has expressed support in the past for Israel but believes a "firm treaty" guaranteeing that country's independence in case of attack would be dangerous. At the same time, he has expressed concern over the possibility of increased Soviet influence in the Middle East.

Talks with the Russians were set to resume in Geneva in September, with the main topic of conversation being the elusive goal of limiting strategic arms. There had been rumors of disagreement within the Nixon Administration

*Ford leaves his
Alexandria,
Virginia, home for
the White House
to put in his first
full day as
president.*

*Even before
assuming office,
Ford announced
that Henry
Kissinger would
stay on as secretary
of state.*

*Nelson Rockefeller,
Ford's choice to
be vice president.*

about the proper U.S. position, and Ford was likely to be called on to reconcile varying viewpoints.

Ford's first priority concerning China was to assure its leaders that the United States would continue its policy of friendship. Regarding Europe, Ford was expected to confer with Continental leaders in order to maintain good relations.

Domestic Issues. "I don't want a honeymoon with you. I want a good marriage," quipped Ford in his first speech before Congress. The president claims not to have a single enemy on Capitol Hill, and while he admits clashing with a good many adversaries during his years in the House, he has pledged to cooperate fully with the legislators. By contrast, the Nixon Administration often locked horns in hopeless battle with the Democratic Congress.

First on the new Administration's domestic agenda was the economy. Observers of both Nixon and Ford expected subtle differences in the two leaders' approaches to dealing with inflation. Where Nixon often went all-out for a new plan, such as the wage-and-price controls which he later abandoned, Ford was expected to take a steadier and more pragmatic approach to the problem. The new Administration hoped to curb double-digit inflation with specific spending cuts designed to maintain a tighter money supply, and by applying presidential pressure to hold down prices and wages. Specifically, Ford called on Congress to strive for a balanced federal budget and to reactivate the Cost of Living Council as an advisory board without the power to control wages and prices. He pledged to preside over "a domestic summit meeting to devise a bipartisan action for stability and growth in the American economy."

Ford had surprised some observers by seeming less adverse to using federal funds to spur employment than his predecessor. Noting that those hardest hit by inflation are lower-income families, the unemployed, and those living on fixed incomes, he had declared shortly before becoming president that these groups might need government assistance.

During his years in Congress, however, Ford opposed a broad array of social-welfare programs, including food stamps for the needy, federal aid to elementary and secondary schools, rent subsidies, Model Cities programs, Medicare for the elderly, and the creation of the Office of Economic Opportunity. Organized labor gave him low scores. His record also drew criticism from civil rights leaders. While he consistently voted for key civil rights bills on their final passage, he did so only after voting for amendments that sought to weaken the bills. Ford has stated, however, that "every American, regardless of race, color, or creed, must be treated equally."

Nixon: The Last 40 Days

In the last 40 days of Nixon's presidency, his lines of defense crumbled as impeachment drew inexorably closer.

The first blow during this final period came on July 9, when the House Judiciary Committee made public its own transcripts of eight White House conversations. The committee's transcripts varied in many instances from the White House transcripts of the same talks, released to the public on April 30. (See WATERGATE SCANDAL in this section.) In nearly all cases where there were substantial differences, the White House version put the president in a better light.

The committee released a transcript of a conversation on

Nixon bids farewell to his staff in an emotional finale.

COMMITTEE	Ayes	Nays	Pres
MR. DONOHUE	✓		
MR. BROOKS	✓		
MR. KASTENMEIER	✓		
MR. EDWARDS	✓		
MR. HUNGATE	✓		
MR. CONYERS	✓		
MR. EILBERG	✓		
MR. WALDIE	✓		
MR. FLOWERS	✓		
MR. MANN	✓		
MR. SARBANES	✓		
MR. SEIBERLING	✓		
MR. DANIELSON	✓		
MR. DRINAN	✓		
MR. RANGEL	✓		
MS. JORDAN	✓		
MR. THORNTON	✓		
MS. HOLTZMAN	✓		
MR. OWENS	✓		
MR. MEZVINSKY	✓		
MR. HUTCHINSON		✓	
MR. McCLORY		✓	
MR. SMITH		✓	
MR. SANDMAN		✓	
MR. RAILSBACK	✓		
MR. WIGGINS		✓	
MR. DENNIS		✓	
MR. FISH	✓		
MR. MAYNE		✓	
MR. HOGAN	✓		
MR. BUTLER	✓		
MR. COHEN	✓		
MR. LOTT		✓	
MR. FROEHLICH	✓		
MR. MOORHEAD		✓	
MR. MARAZITI		✓	
MR. LATTA		✓	
MR. RODINO, Chairman	✓		
TOTAL	27	11	

House Judiciary Committee scorecard: all 21 Democrats voted for impeachment on Article I; 6 of 17 Republicans also did so.

March 22, 1973, between Nixon and former campaign director John Mitchell that was not in the White House version. During this conversation Nixon remarked: "I want you all to stonewall it, let them plead the Fifth Amendment, cover up or anything else, if it'll save it—save the plan. That's the whole point."

On July 24, the Supreme Court ruled 8 to 0 that the president must provide "forthwith" the tapes and documents relating to 64 White House conversations subpoenaed by special prosecutor Leon Jaworski for the pending Watergate cover-up trial of six former presidential aides. Chief Justice Warren Burger, writing the opinion, endorsed the concept of executive privilege as "constitutionally based" but said it "must yield to the demonstrated, specific need for evidence in a pending criminal trial." The high court left standing a grand-jury citation of Nixon as an unindicted co-conspirator in the cover-up case by declining to rule on the question.

Vote to Impeach. On July 27, the House Judiciary Committee voted 27 to 11 to impeach Nixon on Article I of its resolution. The article listed nine separate "means" by which Nixon allegedly used "the powers of his high office" to obstruct and impede the Watergate investigation. All 21 Democrats on the committee voted to impeach Nixon on this count. They were joined by 6 of the 17 Republicans on the committee.

Article II, adopted by 28 to 10 on July 29, alleged a wide and varied assortment of actions taken by the president in abuse of the constitutional limits of his authority. It charged him with using the Internal Revenue Service, the Central Intelligence Agency, the Federal Bureau of Investigation, and the Secret Service to violate the constitutional rights of citizens.

Article III, adopted by 21 to 17 on July 30, charged Nixon with contempt of Congress for having defied committee subpoenas for White House tapes and documents.

Two other proposed articles of impeachment were rejected 26 to 12. One charged the president with having usurped the powers of Congress by concealing the U.S. bombing of Cambodia. The second charged him with tax fraud and accepting improvements to his private property at government expense.

The committee debate was broadcast on television. Following the deliberations, a poll indicated that 66 per cent of the public wanted to see the full House impeach Nixon, and that 56 per cent wanted him convicted by the Senate.

The Fatal Transcripts. The end came suddenly. On August 5, the president made public transcripts of three conversations between him and former aide H. R. Haldeman on

June 23, 1972—six days after the Watergate break-in. The three conversations were among those in the recordings turned over to Judge John Sirica under the July 24 order of the Supreme Court.

In a statement accompanying the release of the material, Nixon admitted that he had ordered a halt to the FBI investigation of the break-in for political as well as national-security reasons and that he had kept the evidence from his supporters on the House Judiciary Committee. He said, "This was a serious act of commission for which I take full responsibility and which I deeply regret."

The first transcript included the following briefing by Haldeman:

"Now on the investigation, you know the Democratic break-in thing, we're back in the problem area because the FBI is not under control . . . their investigation is now leading into productive areas—because they've been able to trace the money. . . . The way to handle this now is for us to have [Deputy CIA Director Vernon] Walters call [Acting FBI Director] Pat Gray and just say 'stay to hell out of this. . . .' "

After Nixon asked some questions about how the FBI had traced the laundered money used to finance the break-in, Haldeman said, "And you seem to think the thing to do is get them to stop?"

The president replied: "Right, fine." Later in the conversation, he told Haldeman, ". . . these people . . . should call the FBI in and (unintelligible) don't go any further into this case period!"

On numerous occasions, the president had said he had been unaware of the cover-up until John Dean had told him about it on March 21, 1973. The release of the transcripts and the accompanying statement were widely regarded in Congress as an admission of guilt. All 10 Republicans who had supported Nixon in the House Judiciary Committee said they would reverse themselves and vote for impeachment on the House floor.

On August 6, Nixon told the cabinet that he would not resign. But on the following day, Senate Republican leader Hugh Scott of Pennsylvania, House Republican leader John Rhodes of Arizona, and Senator Barry Goldwater of Arizona went to the White House. They reportedly told the president that only 10 representatives would vote against impeachment, and that only 15 senators would vote for acquittal.

The end came the following evening, as Nixon announced on television that he would resign, effective at noon on Friday, August 9. He was the first president of the United States to resign his office.

Senators Hugh Scott and Barry Goldwater, and Representative John Rhodes brought the bad news to the White House that impeachment was inevitable.

Ford's Inner Circle

One of President Ford's first acts was to ask cabinet members to remain in their posts, at least for the early months of the new Administration. Even before he was sworn into office, Ford said he would retain Henry Kissinger as secretary of state. Alexander Haig was to stay on, at least temporarily, as White House chief of staff.

Almost immediately, he named Robert Hartmann and John Marsh as counselors with cabinet rank. Hartmann, a former Washington bureau chief for the Los Angeles *Times*, had been chief of the vice-presidential staff. Earlier, he had been legislative assistant to Ford when Ford was House minority leader. Marsh, a conservative Virginia Democrat who had served in the U.S. House of Representatives, was most recently assistant to the vice president for defense affairs.

A transition team was appointed to ease the new president's first days in office, and make recommendations for staff changes. It consisted of Marsh, former Pennsylvania governor William Scranton, Secretary of the Interior Rogers Morton, and Donald Rumsfeld, ambassador to the North Atlantic Treaty Organization.

Melvin Laird, former secretary of defense and an old colleague of Ford's in the House of Representatives, was expected to be one of the new president's most influential advisers. Laird reportedly had urged Nixon to appoint Ford vice president after the resignation of Spiro Agnew. Some observers expected Laird to trim Kissinger's influence; the former secretary of defense was reported to have felt he had been outmaneuvered by Kissinger and excluded from major policy decisions while serving in the cabinet under Nixon.

Members of Ford's staff expected to join him in the White House were, like Ford, predominantly Midwesterners, middle-aged, conservative, and oriented toward Capitol Hill, where many of them once worked. They included L. William Seidman, Warren Rustand, Richard Burress, William Casselman, Paul Miltich, and Gwen Anderson.

Among other names mentioned as possible influential advisers were John Byrnes, a former Republican U.S. representative from Wisconsin; Bryce Harlow, a former aide to presidents Eisenhower and Nixon; William G. Whyte, assistant vice president of the U.S. Steel Corporation; and Philip Buchen, an old friend of Ford's and his former Grand Rapids law partner.

The Future for Nixon

The departure of President Nixon from office was made without any apparent assurances that he would not be prosecuted on charges of obstruction of justice with regard to the Watergate break-in. He had been named an unindicted co-conspirator by the federal grand jury that indicted six of his aides. The grand jury, still sitting, could issue a superseding indictment that would add the former president's name to those of his former associates.

The Constitution states that impeachment is no bar to criminal prosecution. President Ford could confer a pardon, but the new president's press secretary, J. F. terHorst, said Ford was not likely to do so. Some congressmen spoke of drafting a resolution that would express the sense of Congress as being in favor of immunizing Nixon from prosecution, but such a resolution would have no legal force.

The decision was expected to be made by special prosecutor Leon Jaworski. His office was continuing its investigation of wrongdoing within the Administration; assistants predicted it would take "another year or two" to finish work.

Financially, the former president emerged from the White House with short-term liabilities but long-term assets. His liabilities included more than $300,000 owed in back taxes and mortgage payments. He also faced the likelihood of having to hire legal counsel to defend himself against possible criminal prosecution, disbarment proceedings, or lawsuits by private parties.

Nixon would receive, by law, a $60,000 annual lifetime pension, up to $96,000 yearly in government allowances for staff assistance, and free office space. His wife, should she survive him, would receive an annual $20,000 pension. All these benefits would have been denied had he been impeached and removed from office.

Presidential papers, temporarily stored at the National Archives, apparently belong to Nixon personally, according to a recent report by a joint congressional committee. The White House tapes also apparently are his property—even the subpoenaed ones. This material is probably worth millions of dollars.

In addition, Nixon still owns most of his pre-presidential documents, estimated by an appraiser to be worth $1.5 million. (His vice-presidential papers were donated to the National Archives for the income-tax deduction later declared improper.)

Guards roll up the red carpet as the Nixon family departs from the White House.

Armaments/ 147

Art/ 153

Education/ 169

France/ 176

Middle East/ 200

Race Relations/ 222

Watergate Scandal/ 243

Armaments. In its annual assessment of military power, the Institute for Strategic Studies in London declared that both the United States and the Soviet Union seemed determined to increase their nuclear armories and to engage in a "qualitative" race for improved technology at the same time. "A comparison of Soviet and American outlays," the study declared, "suggests that the equivalent dollar costs of Soviet resources devoted to defense may be comparable to American spending and perhaps well above it."

The arms race continues in spite of two agreements signed in Moscow in May, 1972, by President Nixon and Soviet Communist party chief Leonid Brezhnev. One of the agreements limited the construction of antiballistic missile (ABM) systems. The other froze the number of land-based and submarine-based intercontinental ballistic missiles for five years. (See ARMS CONTROL, second section, 1972.)

The agreements came after seven rounds of the Strategic Arms Limitation Talks (SALT) that began in late 1969. A second series of SALT has sought a permanent agreement on limiting nuclear arms, but little progress has been made. The 1972 agreement left the Soviet Union with an advantage in the number of land-based nuclear missiles—1,618 to 1,054—and submarine-based missiles—710 to 656. Moreover, the Soviet missiles carry bigger payloads. On the other hand, the United States has 465 bombers bearing nuclear weapons to 140 for the Soviet Union. It has a total of 7,940 nuclear warheads on its strategic missiles, as compared to 2,600 for the Soviet Union. U.S. warheads are more accurate than their Soviet counterparts, and many can be independently targeted from a single missile. This capacity is known as MIRV (multiple independently targeted reentry vehicles).

The Russians began developing MIRV capacity in August, 1973, and completed their first full-range tests in January, 1974. They are expected to begin their deployment of MIRV's in 1975.

According to one study, the warheads of merely 220 of the 1,000 U.S. Minuteman missiles could kill 21 per cent of the Soviet population from immediate effects alone and destroy 72 per cent of the industrial capacity. Warheads from 170 of the 656 U.S. submarine-based nuclear missiles, launched from 12 of 41 U.S. nuclear submarines, would cause the same damage. The Soviets have the capability to wreak similar damage.

Both sides, then, have the firepower to destroy each other; the surplus, as Winston Churchill once said, serves only "to make the rubble bounce." Yet both nations continue to expand their nuclear arsenals. President Nixon has insisted that any future arms-limitation agreement must allow both countries roughly equal numbers of strategic missiles, overcoming the Soviet edge.

U.S. negotiators say there is practically no chance that the Russians will make this concession, because they feel threatened by the Chinese. The Institute for Strategic Studies claims that Peking has produced a missile capable of reaching Moscow and is starting work on a missile "capable of reaching most major targets in the United States." China has also tested a hydrogen-bomb warhead and has shorter-range missiles in sites located

Nuclear Delivery Systems. The B-1 bomber, under development for the U.S. Air Force, is expected to be a successor to the aging B-52. Many Soviet and U.S. nuclear submarines are equipped with long-range missiles that carry nuclear warheads and can be fired underwater.

above ground, in silos, and in mountain caves.

New U.S. Nuclear Policy

For 20 years U.S. nuclear strategy has been based on the concept of deterrence that came to be known as mutual assured destruction (MAD); a nuclear strike by either side would be countered by massive retaliation, with vast loss of life and destruction of property. But President Nixon told Congress in his 1973 foreign-policy message that this policy, based on the ability to kill tens of millions of people, was "inconsistent with American values" and that he wanted a strategy with "greater flexibility." Accordingly, Secretary of Defense James Schlesinger's annual report for the fiscal year 1975 seeks an appropriate response to "any kind of nuclear attack."

The argument against MAD is that a limited or accidental nuclear strike could be countered only by an all-out attack on the Soviet Union. Pentagon strategists are now trying to war-game every limited attack the Soviets could make and prepare an equivalent American response. A limited attack on U.S. missile silos, for example, would be countered with a similar assault. An all-out attack would be suicidal as well as inhumane, because the Russians would still retain enough nuclear missiles to obliterate U.S. population centers.

To critics, the strategy of making nuclear war more flexible makes it more thinkable, perhaps more tolerable, and therefore more possible. It would certainly make defense strategy more expensive, they say, since it would require more accurate missiles and perhaps even bigger ones to hit a greater variety of targets.

New Weapons Systems

Pentagon planners have always feared that some day the Soviet Union could strike first and destroy the U.S. nuclear arsenal, thereby leaving the nation at the mercy of the enemy. This fear has led to efforts to reduce the vulnerability of weapons systems to surprise attack. Land-based missiles are dug into underground silos. Nuclear bombers go on airborne alert during political crises. Least vulnerable are nuclear submarines, which cruise the oceans and are difficult to detect.

New delivery systems are intended to add to U.S. striking power and lessen vulnerability to surprise attack. For example, the Administration's defense budget request calls for accelerating the development of the Trident missile-firing submarine. Ten are to be built at a cost of $1.3 billion each. The Navy wants Tridents to start replacing submarines that fire Polaris and Poseidon missiles in 1978.

The budget also calls for $500 million for development of the B-1 bomber. The Air Force hopes to buy 244 of them for $16 billion by 1980 as a successor to the aging B-52's. The B-1 would travel more than twice the speed of sound at cruising altitudes and would be capable of close to the speed of sound at treetop level—low enough to foil Soviet antiaircraft radar systems.

The budget would also permit researchers to begin work on several proposed systems. The Air Force plans to test a Minuteman missile with a larger number of small MIRV's and wants to develop the capability of launching such missiles from aircraft. The Air Force also argues that the Russians have a fully mobile truck-towed intercontinental ballistic missile in advanced development and would like to develop the same system, which would presumably be less vulnerable to attack than missiles in underground silos. Also on the Air Force shopping list are funds for a new nuclear warhead called MaRV (maneuverable reentry vehicle) that could change direction in flight to evade defensive missiles—something no country's missile warheads do now.

Nuclear Testing

In late April, Administration officials confirmed that Secretary of State Henry Kissinger and Soviet Foreign Minister Andrei Gromyko had held talks aimed at a "threshold" test ban, one that would pro-hibit underground nuclear explosions above a particular magnitude. The 1963 treaty banned all tests, except those held underground, by the two nations and Great Britain.

(A threshold test-ban treaty was signed in Moscow July 3. See SOVIET UNION in this section.)

Since the 1963 treaty, the United States has spent more than $3.5 billion to conduct, according to the Atomic Energy Commission's public count, 255 underground tests. The Soviet Union is known to have held at least 90 tests during the same period. Most of these tests are used for weapons development or to test the effects of blast and radiation on equipment ranging from communications satellites to nuclear warheads themselves.

Verification has always been the sticking point to a total test ban, with the United States vainly seeking the privilege of on-site inspection of suspicious activity. The threshold ban would prohibit only those tests large enough to be unambiguously identified by other means, such as seismic detection, satellite photography, and electronic eavesdropping.

A threshold agreement would discourage full-scale nuclear testing and the deployment of large new strategic warheads. It might impede development of a new generation of laser-triggered "pure fusion" weapons under consideration.

France and China maintain nuclear testing in the atmosphere. As of early 1974, 106 nations had signed the 1968 nuclear non-proliferation treaty, agreeing not to manufacture nuclear weapons, and 83 had ratified it. But this left 30 holdouts, including India, which became the world's sixth nuclear power in May. (See INDIA in this section.)

Battlefield Weapons

The United States has 7,000 smaller nuclear warheads in Europe, intended for battlefield use. In the 1950's the Eisenhower Administration came to the conclusion that tactical nuclear weapons (which are equivalent in force to the bombs dropped on Hiroshima and Nagasaki) were an effective way of offsetting Soviet superiority in manpower, aircraft, and tanks in Europe.

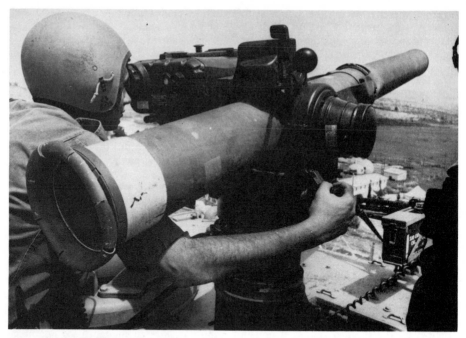

Army Weapons. The TOW antitank missile, *above*, has a warhead capable of penetrating any armor in existence to a maximum range of about two miles. The drawing below is of a proposed new battle tank, the XM-1, that the Pentagon believes will be less vulnerable to antitank weapons than the current M-60.

But Schlesinger argues that large conventional forces are still needed to make an enemy concentrate its forces and thus present a potential target for nuclear weapons. He also believes it has become increasingly unlikely that either side would resort to nuclear warfare in ground combat now that the Soviet Union has reached effective nuclear parity with the United States, because of the possibility of escalation to strategic weapons.

The Yom Kippur war of 1973 showed that tanks—and tracked and wheeled armored fighting vehicles in general—have become more vulnerable to antitank missiles and guns than in the past. But U.S. Army generals say the tank remains the best antitank weapon and is effective both on the offensive and the defensive. Development is continuing of a proposed new battle tank, the XM-1, which will have better fire control and a new type of armor that the Pentagon believes will make it less vulnerable to modern antitank weapons than the present M-60.

The Defense Department, assessing the 1973 Middle East war, has decided to accelerate substantially the production of the TOW (tube-launched, optically tracked, wire-guided) and Dragon anti-tank missiles. The former can be mounted on a vehicle or in a helicopter while the latter can be carried by one man.

Some officers believe the Army is deficient in the field of defense against hostile aircraft because in Vietnam ground forces were comparatively free from attack by enemy planes. The Russians, with a variety of mobile surface-to-air missiles and antiaircraft artillery, appear well ahead in this field. The Pentagon is testing the systems of its NATO allies as a possible answer, and a new system called SAM-D is under development.

Several new airplanes are under development or are being deployed. The Navy plans to buy 300 swing-wing F-14 Tomcat fighters at a cost of $23.3 million each. Its mission is primarily to defend the fleet by destroying bombers that could fire air-to-surface missiles before a ship's surface-to-air missiles could be fired. It is armed with a missile system designed to knock

down six enemy planes simultaneously at ranges well over 50 miles.

The F-15 Eagle fighter is being developed for the Air Force to replace the Phantom F-4, first deployed in 1962. The military says that the Russians have three aircraft whose performance is better than the F-4. The F-15's primary mission will be air-to-air combat.

The Defense Department also plans tentatively to purchase 729 A-10's to support ground forces. These planes will be equipped with Maverick air-to-surface missiles. Also in the works is AWACS (airborne warning and control system), to be embodied in the E-3A aircraft. Schlesinger believes AWACS will provide long-range airborne surveillance and warning and will be capable of supporting ground, naval, and amphibious operations.

The Navy, which once emphasized striking power, is now shifting its emphasis toward defending U.S. ships and merchant vessels on the high seas. Admiral Elmo Zumwalt says "69 of our 72 critical raw materials come to us by sea" and that

New U.S. Fighters. The Navy plans to buy the F-14, *below,* to defend the fleet. The F-15, *bottom,* is being developed for the Air Force to replace the Phantom F-4.

by 1980 "we will be requiring about 50 per cent of our oil from overseas." Norman Polmar, U.S. editor of *Jane's Fighting Ships,* estimates that the Soviets lead the world in antiship missiles, introduction of new technologies to warships, and numbers of attack submarines.

Naval officers reject the argument that aircraft carriers have become dangerously vulnerable to attack. Three projected Nimitz-class carriers are to be built, at a cost, including aircraft, of close to $1 billion each. These carriers will be nuclear-powered, carry 90 aircraft each, and travel at speeds in excess of 30 knots.

The "sea control ship" is probably the most important new vessel. This ship is a carrier accommodating 14 helicopters and three V/TOL (vertical takeoff-and-landing) aircraft. Its mission will be surveillance against submarine and surface threats and defense against limited air attacks. Other escort vehicles include destroyers and frigates, some nuclear-powered. An air-cushion vessel, if successfully developed, could travel at speeds of as much as 80 knots in pursuit of submarines.

Defense Department officials foresee precision-guided "smart bombs" revolutionizing warfare in much the same way as tanks and radar. These bombs are directed to their targets by television cameras or laser beams. Smart bombs were tried successfully late in the Vietnam war and by Israeli forces during the latest Middle East war.

The General Accounting Office, Congress' fiscal watchdog agency, reports that the total eventual cost of 116 weapons systems now being developed is $153 billion, $89 billion of which Congress has not yet appropriated. Moreover, Senator William Proxmire of Wisconsin charged in June that the Pentagon is experiencing "outrageous" cost overruns of 55 major weapons systems, with the difference between original development estimates and current cost estimates of $26.3 billion. One private study holds that the Trident and B-1 programs could be scrapped and three army divisions and eight air wings demobilized without endangering national security. But observers do not expect substantial cuts in the defense budget, which is rapidly approaching $100 billion a year.

Surface Effect Ship. This proposed air-cushion vessel could, if successfully developed for the U.S. Navy, travel at 80 or more knots in pursuit of submarines.

POP ART

In 1964, Pop art suddenly made its impact upon the public consciousness. Perhaps never before has an art movement been so quickly acknowledged, debated, and absorbed.

Ten years later, on April 6, an exhibit entitled "American Pop Art," opened at the Whitney Museum of American Art in New York City. Seventeen artists were represented by 77 works that filled two entire floors of the museum.

After only 10 years, Pop art has come to be taken for granted—even to be considered passé. Most of the movement's major figures, such as Andy Warhol, Roy Lichtenstein, Robert Rauschenberg, James Rosenquist, Claes Oldenburg, Jasper Johns, and Robert Indiana, have been accorded retrospectives at major galleries and museums—some at the Whitney itself. No museum or collector concentrating on contemporary art with any pretense to objectivity can be without several examples of Pop art.

Toward a Definition

Pop art is based on comic strips, common objects, consumer advertising, and the visual culture of the mass media. It is characterized by hard edges and bright, synthetic color. Pop forms and compositions are usually taken from "found" objects.

But even when objects are reproduced faithfully, abstract elements come into play from Pop art's tendency toward magnified size, taut, plain surfaces, and flat colors. Techniques are appropriated directly from commercial art, including silk screening and other stencil methods, airbrush spray-painting, or transferring and enlarging images.

Lawrence Alloway, who organized the exhibit and wrote the catalogue, is credited with having coined the term Pop art in the 1950's. He maintains that Pop is an art style based upon preexistent signs already known to the viewer through the mass media. "The communication system of the 20th century," he says, "is in a special sense, Pop art's subject." He calls Pop "neither abstract nor realistic, though it has contacts in both directions. . . . It is, essentially, an art about signs and signsystems."

The artists themselves, in offering their own interpretations of their work, emphasize that they arrived at their syles independently in the late 1950's. They did not plan a movement, but their styles, subjects, and attitudes converged for a time in revolt against Abstract Expressionism, the dominant form in the 1950's. Since the mid-1960's, the differences as well as the similarities between major Pop artists have grown increasingly evident.

Warhol once called Pop art liking things, and Rauschenberg has said, "There is no reason not to consider the world as one gigantic painting." Roy Lichtenstein, who reproduced in giant form panels from comic strips, says, "I magnify so that you can see . . . that it really is abstract." Oldenburg points out that any ordinary object presents abstract qualities when it is confronted away from its normal environment. Rosenquist came to the same conclusion from painting billboards in Times Square; he once did a 58-foot by 20-foot portrait of actress Joanne Woodward for a Broadway signboard.

There is an aggressiveness about Pop art because it draws on America's relent-

Eat/Die, by Robert Indiana. Oil on canvas, each painting 72 by 60 inches.

less mass-culture images and forms, which beseech the viewer and reader to buy products. Modern mass culture, writes John Perreault in *Art in America,* "is unlike either the high or the folk cultures of the past because its purpose is to incite rather than to satisfy or sublimate desire."

The Pop art movement has had many detractors. They feel that Pop art may be liking things, but the things that are liked are banal and trite, and that by making monuments of Pop objects, the artists are enthroning the trivial. Critic Hilton Kramer, reflecting on Pop art's success, says, "In its synthesis of lowbrow materials and highbrow pretentions, Pop produced the perfect middlebrow amalgam."

Pop art owes much to earlier artists. Early in the 20th century, Marcel Duchamp maintained that everything is art and no subject too lowly for artistic treatment; he hung mass-produced snow shovels and labeled them ready-made art. Later, Dada artists displayed urinals and other objects. (In Pop art, however, the found object is not itself a work.)

The movement also owes much to French Cubism of the World War I period, during which actual or closely imitated consumer items first appeared in works of art. The Cubists incorporated materials such as newspaper clippings and playing cards into collages.

Even if, as Warhol maintains, Pop art is dead, it lives on in Photorealism, with which it shares a fondness for deadpan literalness of image, a choice of preflattened objects (such as photographs), and similar techniques (such as airbrushing). The best works of Photorealism, like those of Pop art, bring about a perceptual "double take" that causes the viewer to ponder what seems to be the obliteration of the fine line that separates the work of art from the real object.

Some Pop Artists

Andy Warhol. Pop's most famous artist made a splash in 1962 with his copies of Campbell's soup cans. In 1964 he turned out faithful copies of Brillo soap-pad shiping-carton designs on more than 100 wooden boxes of the same shape and size.

Another feature of his work has been his tendency to repeat an image over and over in a serial—testimony to his belief in the endless reproducibility of art. Edward Lucie-Smith, an English art critic, says, "With each repetition the image is progressively drained of meaning, and our power to empathize is diminished. This, in a sense, is the point . . ."

Warhol has said he wants to be a machine and to produce objects that make the viewer see and think mechanically. At first he duplicated pictures by hand, but later he clipped photographs out of newspapers and ordered silk screens to be made from them. Then he and his associates ran off any number of prints with intriguing minor variations. (Appropriately,

Marilyn Monroe Diptych, by Andy Warhol. Acrylic and silk screen enamel on canvas, 40 by 40 inches. Warhol's tendency to repeat an image over and over has the effect of draining the image of meaning.

Museum of Contemporary Art

154

Monogram, by Robert Rauschenberg. Four feet high by six feet square, this work combines real objects with silk-screen photo images on canvas.
Leo Castelli

Warhol started out as a commercial artist, and his studio is called the Factory.)

Among his works is *Do It Yourself* (1962), his deadpan version of a partially completed paint-by-number landscape. But much of his work is less amiable, concentrating on images of disaster such as an electric chair in exotic variations of turquoise, yellow, crimson, and green, a car crash printed over and over until the ink grays out, and a grieving Jacqueline Kennedy after the assassination of her husband. Warhol rarely turns out paintings anymore; indeed, he no longer directs the films produced under his own name.

Robert Rauschenberg. One of the earliest Pop works was an abstract painting by Rauschenberg in 1958 in which he inserted four real Coca-Cola bottles. "Art," he says, "is what things become when you use them." His most famous work, *Monogram* (1959), showed a stuffed goat with a tire around the middle. Silk-screened photo images were placed on the canvas on which the goat rested. "Combines" such as these were intended to "fill the gap between art and life," the artist said.

In 1970 Rauschenberg exhibited *Currents,* the largest silk-screen print ever made, 54 feet long, made up of 36 separate panels in two long rows. Each section is covered with collages of pieces of newspapers on a dull gray background. The message is crisis. From above, six purposely tinny loudspeakers drone unintelligibly, occasionally allowing the listener to hear snatches of a politician's speech. More recently Rauschenberg has given up political statements and, indeed, painting, using instead old cardboard boxes as his medium.

Roy Lichtenstein. Lichtenstein scored a sensation in 1962 with his greatly enlarged paintings of comic-strip panels, filling in color with a simulation of the photo-mechanical screen of tiny Ben Day dots that constitute the color shading in comic books. The use of such symbols as balloons for speech, bubbled balloons for thoughts, bolts of lightning, and tears, added, along with the magnification, to the abstract quality. Later he switched to other material, such as landscapes, but continued to use Ben Day dots. He has "reproduced" paintings by Cézanne and Picasso in this manner. His "Monets" are made entirely of stenciled dots.

Jasper Johns. One of the early Pop works was Johns's 1960 *Painted Bronze,* apparently two Ballantine ale cans on a pedestal. Looked at closely, they proved to be two cast-bronze facsimiles of ale cans, one slightly smaller than the other. Moreover, one was punched open and hollow; the other was closed and solid bronze. According to *Time* magazine, the work was inspired by Abstract Expressionist Wiliem de Kooning, who told Johns's dealer, Leo Castelli, "Give that s.o.b. two beer cans

Voomp! by Roy Lichtenstein. Many of the artist's oils on canvas are greatly enlarged paintings of comic-strip panels. He simulates the photo-mechanical screen of Ben Day dots constituting the color shading in comic books.
Museum of Contemporary Art

Flag, by Jasper Johns. Encaustic and collage on canvas, 41¼ by 60¾ inches. His paintings of American flag patterns are visual puns rather than political statements.
Leo Castelli

and he could sell them." (Johns sold *Painted Bronze* for $1,000.)

It was works like this one that inspired critic Leo Steinberg to assert in 1963 that Johns's work had precipitated "a crisis in criticism." "Despite a half century of formalist indoctrination, it proved almost impossible to see the paintings for the subject matter," he wrote.

Johns likes flat images and flat unsensual forms like numerals. He calls numerals a bigger challenge to paint than still-lifes or landscapes, because numerals must be endowed with more eye appeal and meaning than their original human designers gave them.

But Johns is best known for his paintings of American flag patterns. These are visual puns rather than political statements. For example, his canvas showing a green, black, and orange U.S. flag pattern will, if stared at for a while, glow faintly with the red, white, and blue of the stars and stripes when the eye fixes on the gray background below.

Three Flags shows two flag patterns superimposed on a third. The visual irony is that Johns has given a three-dimensional effect to the two-dimensional flag—a reversal of the customary role of painting as a way of representing the three-dimensional in two dimensions.

Claes Oldenburg. In the early 1960's this artist began making giant-sized kapok-filled canvas and vinyl copies of such greasy diner foods as fried eggs and pies. *Giant Fagends* was a work of 13 giant cigarette butts made of canvas and stuffed with polyurethane foam. "I'd like to turn people on to the fact that the world is form, not just function and money," he says.

In his "soft" period Oldenburg made such works as a nine-foot slice of canvas cake stuffed with foam. Traditional sculpture opposes gravity and is rigid, while these soft works actually depend somewhat on gravity for their form. Soft sculptures have other interesting qualities. As Oldenburg says, "Anything that goes into a soft state tends to be humorous," and the works can be slapped, poked, and pushed around. He says, "I want to make it touchable—to translate the eye into the hand."

Oldenburg has sketched proposed Pop sculptures of monumental size, such as a giant toilet-tank float anchored to a bridge on the Thames in London, a giant clothespin for Chicago, and a Good Humor ice-cream bar at the foot of Manhattan's Park Avenue. "Why should a monument commemorate something that happened 100 years ago?" he asks. "It should reflect what's going on today." In 1969 a 24-foot aluminum lipstick was installed on the Yale University campus—the first of his monuments actually to get off the drawing board. But Yale did not accept the gift and it was eventually removed.

Falling Shoestring Potatoes, by Claes Oldenburg. Kapok-filled canvas, 108 by 46 by 42 inches. This work is typical of the artist's copies of greasy diner foods. Unlike traditional sculpture, these "soft" works depend somewhat on gravity for their form.
Courtesy Walker Art Center—Eric Sutherland

Australia. Prime Minister Gough Whitlam's Labour party government was confirmed in power in parliamentary elections held May 18. Labour won 66 seats in the House of Representatives, while the opposition coalition, consisting of the Liberal and Country parties, won 61. Labour had held 67 seats in the outgoing House.

The Labour government took office after winning a majority of seats in the House in December, 1972. During its first 16 months in office, however, six of its bills were rejected by the Senate, where opposition parties held 31 of the 60 seats.

On April 3, Whitlam appointed a longtime Senate foe to be ambassador to Ire-

Gough Whitlam, prime minister of Australia, received congratulations from his wife as his Labour party government retained power in parliamentary elections. Obstruction by the opposition-dominated Senate was his chief issue.

land, calculating that Labour would win the vacant Queensland seat in May, when elections were to be held for half the Senate seats. The appointment created a furor; Bill Snedden, leader of the Liberals, called it "the most shameful act by any government in Australia's history," and the independent Melbourne *Age* denounced it in an editorial as an act of "ratlike cunning." Whitlam's strategy was foiled when the governor of the state of Queensland took advantage of a loophole in the law to fill the seat with a non-Labour nominee.

More ill-feeling followed when the Senate blocked a money-supply bill essential for the day-to-day workings of the government. This action was unprecedented in Australian history and aroused a storm of protest. The bill was approved April 10, but only after Whitlam had called for new elections in both the House and Senate.

The Senate's obstruction was Labour's main issue. Whitlam said the senators had prevented the government from passing a universal health-insurance program, legislation aimed at reducing industrial disputes, and a bill to combat restrictive trade practices and monopolies. He pledged more money for housing and health, modernization of the social-welfare system, a federal government role in reshaping the cities, reconstruction of educational systems, and help for homeowners.

Snedden made inflation—running at an annual rate of 14 per cent—the main issue. He promised fewer restrictions on private enterprise, more aid for rural areas, a pension increase, and abolition of the means test for aged pensioners. He also called for closer ties with Australia's traditional allies, the United States and Britain.

Election returns indicated that the new Senate would be divided equally between government supporters and opponents. However, the constitution provides that bills twice rejected by the Senate can be considered again in a joint session of both houses. The government presumably would have enough votes to pass its legislation in such a session.

Bangladesh. The foreign ministers of Bangladesh, Pakistan, and India signed an agreement in New Delhi, India, on April 9 settling most of the issues arising from the December, 1971, war in which East Pakistan, aided by India, won its independence from Pakistan and became the new nation of Bangladesh. Hundreds of thousands of people were held in detention in the aftermath of the war.

In August, 1973, representatives of India and Pakistan signed an agreement to speed the repatriation of Pakistani prisoners of war from India and the exchange of civilians in Pakistan and Bangladesh. (See INDIA, third section, 1973.) The April 9 accord, signed after five days of negotiations, cleared the way for normalization of diplomatic and economic relations among the three countries of the Indian subcontinent and for Bangladesh's entry into the United Nations, which had previously been vetoed by China at Pakistan's request.

A key step toward reconciliation between Pakistan and Bangladesh was achieved when Bangladesh agreed in the pact to drop its planned trial of 195 Pakistani prisoners of war for war crimes and to allow them to be repatriated. Perhaps a million people died during Pakistan's attempt in 1971 to stamp out rebellion in its eastern wing.

In the text of the agreement, the foreign minister of Bangladesh said that the "manifold crimes committed by those [195] prisoners of war constituted . . . war crimes, crimes against humanity, and genocide," but that his government would not proceed with the trials "as an act of clemency." The foreign minister of Pakistan said that his government "condemned and deeply regretted any crimes that may have been committed."

The document noted that Prime Minister Zulfikar Ali Bhutto of Pakistan had declared that he would visit Bangladesh to "appeal to the people of Bangladesh to forgive and forget the mistakes of the past in order to promote reconciliation." Similarly, it noted that Prime Minister Mujibur Rahman of Bangladesh had declared "that he wanted the people to forget the past and make a fresh start."

By the terms of the August, 1973, agreement, India had agreed to repatriate 76,-000 Pakistani soldiers and 16,000 Pakistani civilians taken prisoner during the 1971 fighting. Almost all of these prisoners and internees had been repatriated by the time of the April agreement. The last ones were returned to Pakistan on April 30.

Pakistan had agreed in 1973 to repatriate the Bengalis—natives of East Pakistan—who had been stranded in West Pakistan

War Refugees. An agreement between Bangladesh, India, and Pakistan provided for the repatriation of hundreds of thousands of people held in detention following the 1971 war in East Pakistan. Still to be decided was the fate of hundreds of thousands of non-Bengalis in Bangladesh being held in emergency camps.

when the war broke out. The April 9 pact said that the repatriation of these 117,000 Bangladesh nationals was approaching completion.

More difficult to resolve was the question of the Biharis—Moslems who were natives of the Indian state of Bihar but who fled to East Pakistan when the Indian subcontinent was partitioned between Pakistan and India in 1947. The Biharis were considered to have sided with the Pakistani occupation army in 1971, and following the war they were shifted to squalid emergency camps in Bangladesh. Their numbers were estimated at from 600,000 to 900,000; most of them expressed a desire to go to Pakistan.

In August, 1973, Pakistan agreed to take a substantial, but unspecified, number of Biharis. During the following months, Pakistan accepted 100,000 but said privately that only 40,000 more would be admitted.

In the April 9 agreement, Pakistan agreed to accept all non-Bengalis in Bangladesh if they had been either domiciled in the former West Pakistan, were employees of that government, or were members of divided families irrespective of their original domicile. In addition to accepting all persons in these categories, Pakistan said it would issue clearance to 25,000 persons who constituted hardship cases and would review the applications of all persons rejected.

Business and Finance. Administration officials were attempting at midyear to cope with a combination of factors which heretofore were thought incompatible. The economy had experienced declining production and rising unemployment, a situation which, if continued, would be called a "recession." At the same time though, the economy was enduring its steepest inflation in almost a quarter of a century. Inflation is usually associated with wars and their immediate economic aftermath, and certainly not with recession.

Nevertheless, analysts were confident that the economic downturn brought about in early 1974 by the Arab oil boycott and the increased price of oil had leveled off, and hoped the economy might begin to recover in the later months of 1974. Inflation, running at an annual rate of 11 per cent during the first five months of 1974, was expected to diminish in intensity. Prices would continue to rise, but not at the breakneck pace of the first half of 1974. Unemployment, which rose from a fall, 1973, level of 4.6 per cent to a spring, 1974, level of 5.1 per cent, had apparently leveled off.

There was widespread belief that total production had stopped its downward trend and would begin to rise in late 1974. By definition, this would mean no depression and, depending on when the upswing occurred, possibly no recession.

Bad Economic News was relayed to the press by a government official. Inflation was running at an annual rate of 11 per cent and production had declined. Administration economists forecast better news for the second half of 1974.

A troubled economy with rising prices is not restricted to any single country. As Federal Reserve Board Chairman Arthur Burns noted, "Inflation now is the dominant economic force in every nation around the world."

Many economists trace inflationary problems in the United States to the economic slogan that prevailed following World War II: "maximum employment, production, and purchasing power." Inflation was seen as a problem, but not as much so as the prospects of returning to the depression of the 1930's, which the war itself relieved. While government policies helped keep production and employment at high levels, many economists believe they also set a bad precedent by making the public believe in a constantly expanding economy. Inflation has eroded this belief.

Paying for Oil

A year of quadrupling oil prices has swelled the coffers of many Middle Eastern countries while sending many oil-consuming nations looking for loans to balance their books. With the cash reserves of the consuming nations dwindling, international economists are finding that existing monetary mechanisms designed to prevent such problems are often not sufficient.

The oil-exporting nations have not yet put their skyrocketing revenues into the marketplace, where consuming nations hope to make back the money they spend on oil. A study by economists at a major New York bank predicted that the gross oil revenues of the Organization of Petroleum Exporting Countries (OPEC), mainly Mideast nations, will rise in 1974 by some $80 billion, to total close to $105 billion. The study estimated that only half of this money would be spent on imported goods, leaving some $55 to $60 billion unspent and recorded as operating deficits by the oil-consuming nations. If recent statements from Arab leaders were any indication, the flow of money would continue its one-way course.

Meeting in June, OPEC members found themselves in disagreement as to how the monetary problems of oil-consuming nations should affect oil prices. Saudi Arabia proposed that prices be adjusted in the interests of the European, African, and Asian countries having budgetary problems. On the other hand, most member nations were considered "hawks," strongly opposed to any price reduction. Furthermore, some countries were ready to restrict the flow of oil from the Mideast to maintain high prices. Said Kuwait's Minister of Finance and Oil Abdel Rahman Salem al-Atiqi, "If consumers don't want to pay our price, we will leave the oil in the ground."

The situation has worsened as interest rates have risen, owing largely to the worldwide inflation aggravated by the oil boycotts and shortages of the winter. Franz Aschinger, economic adviser of the Swiss Bank Corporation, warns that if the trend continues over the next eight years "the accumulated debt [of the industrialized oil-burning nations] would be $400 billion, with annual interest payments of $30 billion." Some European economists fear that if just one country defaulted on its payments several banks might fail and send the continent into a monetary crisis.

International economists see a sort of "recycling" plan, based on the fact that the oil-consumers' deficits are equal to the sellers' surpluses, as the only solution to the situation. European banks have traditionally served as a conduit between oil sellers and buyers, but they are now encountering difficulties in helping countries maintain their monetary reserves. One problem is that most Arab countries will not deposit their money for any longer than a 90-day maturity, while others leave their funds "on call," meaning that they can immediately ask for their money. Such procedures make banks understandably hesitant about lending these deposited sums.

One idea has potential for the future. H. Johannes Witteveen, managing director of the International Monetary Fund, is setting up an "oil facility" which would accept deposits from oil producers and lend the money at the bargain interest rate of 7 per cent to countries having trouble paying for their oil. But, by June, only $3.6 billion had been pledged, which would do little to alleviate the problem.

Many observers believe, that, in the long run, only massive Arab investment can keep some nations from going bankrupt. Financiers all over the world have been waiting for a massive flow of oil money, but thus far the money has been coming slowly.

Nevertheless, a small trickle of Arab oil revenue has begun to flow westward in long-term investment, including $1 billion to the United States. The bulk of this money has been spent on real estate—hotels, apartment houses, and office buildings.

One transaction that gained national attention was the purchase by the Kuwait Investment Company of Kiawah Island, 15 miles south of Charleston, South Carolina, for $17.4 million. A $100-million residential resort is planned.

And, as Arab investors look westward, Western financiers are scurrying to the Mideast to gain footholds in the area where much of the world's wealth lies. American banks are busy opening branches in Mideast countries or acquiring interests in the existing institutions. The First National City Bank has opened the first U.S. bank in Saudi Arabia.

Other Commodities

Bumper crops in the United States, the Soviet Union, and Australia were expected to help alleviate inflation. The price of wheat, for example, dropped from more than $6 a bushel to about $4. If these trends continued, many believed that the inflationary spiral would be greatly lessened over the next two or three years.

What the oil crisis has emphasized though, is that economists must contend with a relatively new concept—true world markets. Raw materials as well as finished goods are desired all over the world, and the flow of such goods is a major factor in a global economy. Consequently, policies that restrict the demand for goods and services in one country, even in the United States, cannot stem inflation. Only a concerted effort through coordinated economic slowdowns by a number of major nations could result in an effective downward trend in prices.

Numerous suggestions have been made as to how such cooperation could be achieved. The most important, for human-itarian as well as economic reasons, is an effort to boost world food production. Many countries in prime food-producing areas lack the technology and funds to exploit the full potential of their natural resources while others, particularly in Europe, have not organized their production capabilities to full potential.

The creation of a world commodities union is also seen by many as an essential step in stabilizing the world economy. Such an organization, composed of both consuming and producing nations, would attempt to stop the frenzied bidding for commodities that often drives prices higher than demand justifies. At the same time, it would prevent the nosedive in prices that often follows a speculative frenzy.

Condominiums

Condominiums are the hottest item on an otherwise lackluster real-estate market. Housing starts were predicted to be off 15 to 20 per cent in 1974 from 1973's 2 million units, but the National Association of Home Builders said condominium starts would increase 4 per cent to 240,000 individual units. People who formerly lived in single-family houses or rented apartments are moving into condominiums so fast that federal officials expect half of the population to live in them within 20 years.

But there are problems. "The condominium concept is no flash in the pan, but so many have been built in the last three years that many inexperienced developers got into the business," says Alan J. Brody, chairman of Heitman Mortgage Company of Chicago. "Consequently, some terrible things have been pushed down buyers throats, and in today's competitive market the selling pressures and abuses are bound to get worse."

A buyer of a condominium usually obtains two things outright. First, he acquires his individual apartment-like unit and secondly, he becomes a part owner with the other residents of common areas like lawns, roof, and heating plant. In addition to paying off the mortgage for the individual unit, the owner must pay his share of the maintenance for the common areas.

Some buyers discover too late that shoddy construction requires additional investment in their unit and major increases in maintenance fees for the common areas. The most costly problem, though, often turns out to be the recreation facilities which are used to lure buyers in the first place. Many condominiums offer such amenities as swimming pools and tennis courts, but often these facilities are kept in the hands of the developer, who in turn leases them back to the condominium owners. Some developers have been known to lease recreational facilities to the apartment dwellers over long terms at costs of as much as $300,000 annually.

Another problem caused by the growth of condominium housing is that, because many such units are converted apartment houses, the availability of rental units is declining in many urban centers. For the landlord, conversion to a condominium is an attractive proposition, for he can quickly rid himself of tenant complaints while divesting himself of ownership of an aging building which may be deteriorating in value.

When the tenant of a rental unit is informed of its conversion, he often has only a month to vacate or decide to purchase the unit. If he holds a lease, he may well be harassed by prospective buyers coming to view the unit or by poor maintenance. Those who decide to purchase their units may find it hard to predict when renovations will be required for older buildings. If in the future major work had to be done to the building, the unit owners would have to share this cost.

Proposals to aid the rent-paying resident include longer periods of warning before conversion would begin and possibly a provision by which the majority of tenants would have to agree before the apartment building could be turned into a condominium.

All 50 states have passed laws concerning condominiums. California and New York are the states with the toughest measures. In New York, long-term lease arrangements under which the builder retains ownership of recreational facilities and charges substantial rent for their use are not permitted. Furthermore, extensive plans, including projected costs, for all proposed projects must be filed with the attorney general.

In most states, however, the buyer must beware. Experts in the field suggest that purchasers check into the background of the developer and inspect some of his other projects. It is also imperative to read and understand all the legal papers as well as to become aware of exactly what services are covered by monthly maintenance fees. Other precautions include finding out who will manage the building and determining whether the builder has set aside funds for any unanticipated building faults.

Condominiums. Point East, *left*, and Century 21 in North Miami, Florida, are among the growing number of condominium apartment buildings.

Alfonso López Michelsen was elected president of Colombia on April 21. His platform was one of moderate social, economic, and political reform.

Colombia. Alfonso López Michelsen was overwhelmingly elected president of Colombia in elections held April 21. His party won control of both houses of Congress.

"What López's victory means," a leader of the victor's Liberal party commented, "is that people want a change but not a revolution." By contrast, many of Colombia's South American neighbors have opted for autocratic regimes to cope with the problems of inflation, poverty, and over-population.

López polled about 2.5 million votes, compared to about 1.5 million for the second-place Conservative candidate, Alvaro Gómez Hurtado. López's platform was one of moderate social, economic, and political reform to combat Colombia's major economic problems, including inflation at an annual rate of 30 per cent and an unemployment rate of 20 per cent.

These economic problems are aggravated by a large gap between rich and poor. The government's latest figures on wealth distribution showed that 40 per cent of the population has 9.42 per cent of the wealth while 6.67 per cent controlled 37.58 per cent. Half the country's 23 million people live by agriculture, and 80 per cent of these are tenant farmers or owners of subsistence plots. One military observer said, "It's the last chance for the Establishment," before Latin America's fourth-largest country endures "a popular explosion."

The elections marked the end of a 16-year agreement between the Liberals and Conservatives under which the two parties alternated four-year terms in the presidency and shared equally the legislature and other government posts. This arrangement, which was enacted by a constitutional amendment in 1958, ended nine years of civil war. Nevertheless, the power-sharing agreement remains in force for cabinet ministers, governors, and mayors, and consequently Colombian political observers saw resistance to López's proposed reforms.

López was born in Bogotá on June 30, 1913, to a political family; his father, Alfonso López Pumarejo, was elected to the presidency twice, in 1934 and 1942, and is thought by many to have been Colombia's finest president. His second term was cut short, though, by a scandal; unproven charges were raised that his son, the current president-elect, was involved in dubious financial dealings.

Educated in both his own country and Europe, López received his law degree at Bogotá National University and began a private practice, mixed with university teaching and political interests. His political career began in earnest when he founded the Liberal Revolutionary Movement and made his first attempt for the presidency in 1962. Although he lost the presidential election, he was elected a senator. He opposed the Liberal-Conservative coalition and called for diplomatic relations with Cuba. In later years he modified his position concerning the coalition and gained prominence in the Liberal party, serving first as a provincial governor and later as foreign minister from August, 1968 until 1970.

Administration Plans

During the campaign, López attempted to downplay his radical past, describing himself as a middle-of-the-road reformer. The large majority of Colombian voters preferred his moderate stance to the Conservative position, which favored a government similar to Brazil's military regime.

Concerning foreign relations, López advocated a more independent course for his country, including the establishment of trade with Cuba and China. This stand was indicative of his criticism of United States–Latin American relations, particularly as they apply to Cuba.

Economically, López planned to fight inflation by introducing a policy by which government, management, and labor would agree on price and wage levels as well as tariffs and taxes. Additionally, he would attempt to unite the different labor federations into a single organization and require companies to reinvest their profits and consequently create new jobs.

Disasters. Among the disasters that occurred during the second quarter of 1974 were the following:

Aviation. A chartered DC-4 carrying gold-mine laborers from South Africa home to Malawi crashed in Francistown, Botswana, on April 4. Seventy-seven of the 82 persons aboard were killed.

All 107 persons aboard a Pan American World Airways Boeing 707 jet were killed April 22 when it crashed on the Indonesian island of Bali. The plane was on a flight from Hong Kong to Los Angeles, with about 70 of the passengers scheduled to vacation in Bali. It was the fourth crash of a Pan Am 707 in nine months, prompting the Federal Aviation Administration to order an emergency inspection of the airline's flight operations.

All 118 persons aboard a Soviet turboprop airliner were killed April 27 when it crashed and burned after taking off from the Leningrad airport, according to Western travelers. The Aeroflot flight was en route to Krasnodar in the northern Caucasus.

Explosion. Twenty-nine persons were killed and 94 injured following the explosion on June 1 of a chemical plant in Flixborough, England, located 180 miles north of London. The plant produced cyclophexane, a gasoline-like substance which is used to make nylon. Fire-fighters fought the subsequent 20-acre blaze for

Explosion of a Chemical Plant in Flixborough, England, killed 29 and injured 94. The $50-million plant was totally destroyed, as were nearby homes.

Xenia, Ohio, was devastated by a tornado that left 35 people dead. Half of the city of 25,000 was destroyed.

24 hours. The $50-million plant was completely destroyed, as were 30 nearby homes.

Fire. Twenty-four persons were killed when a fire swept through a crowded discotheque in Port Chester, New York, on June 30. Police speculated that some died from smoke inhalation while others were trampled as the Saturday-night patrons at Gulliver's—which is literally located on the border between New York and Connecticut—attempted to flee the building. Thirty-two people were treated for injuries. A man was later arrested and charged with setting the fire.

Floods. Brazilian officials reported that at least 1,500 were killed following massive flooding. The rains, which ended on March 29, followed months of drought and caused damage estimated at over $400 million. More than 100,000 people were left homeless.

The hardest hit area was Tubarão, an agricultural community in southern Santa Catarina State, where the waters of the Tabarão River reportedly rose 36 feet within hours, leaving the city completely underwater. As many as 1,000 were reported dead in the city of 70,000. As the floods subsided, there were reports of malaria, yellow fever, and typhoid.

Landslides. The Peruvian government estimated that between 200 and 300 people died in a landslide in early May. The slide was apparently caused by abnormally heavy rains along a fault line on the south side of the Mantaro River. A natural dam was created by the slide and, between the shifting earth and rising waters, 11 small settlements were destroyed along with one government camp.

Colombian officials estimated that at least 200 persons died on June 28 as a landslide covered a section of highway 95 miles east of Bogotá. General José Jaime Rodríguez, Colombia's civil defense director, said, "We'll never know exactly the number of victims of this national tragedy."

Tornadoes. More than 350 people died in the worst U.S. tornado disaster in 49 years as storms ripped from Ontario to Georgia on April 3 and 4. The winds left 1,200 injured, thousands homeless, and caused $1 billion in property damage.

President Nixon declared six states disaster areas: Kentucky, the most devastated state with 72 dead; Tennessee, with 46 dead; Indiana, 39 dead; Georgia, 16 dead; and Ohio, with 37 dead. Xenia, Ohio, was the hardest-hit town, with 35 killed and half the town destroyed.

The large formation of tornadoes was due to an unusually strong spring storm which pulled masses of warm, moist air north from the Gulf of Mexico. When the air met a cool, dry front from the East Coast, a deep low-pressure system was formed.

Education. The Carnegie Commission on Higher Education, headed by Clark Kerr, completed an exhaustive examination of American colleges and universities in October, 1973. The group's final report, *Priorities for Action,* summarized the recommendations of more than 100 documents produced by the group over a six-year period. The research was sponsored by the Carnegie Corporation, at a cost of $6.3 million.

The commission, which included college executives, prominent professors, lawyers, and businessmen, was first organized in 1967 to study the financing of higher education. The scope of its inquiry broadened during the period of campus turmoil which ended the decade. In *Priorities for Action,* however, the commission members emphasized that they had concluded their survey of higher education "with faith in its potential for continued vitality and with a deepened belief in its essential value to American society."

They encouraged colleges and universities to clarify their goals, promote excellence in both research and teaching, and diversify educational opportunities through innovative programs. In addition, the report urged institutions to advance social justice through hiring and admissions policies. It recommended access to post-secondary education for all Americans, with financial support for students from low-income families. The introduction of more flexible enrollment requirements was suggested as another method of enabling more students to earn degrees. At the same time, the report urged that "reluctant attenders" (which it estimated as 12 to 15 per cent of the total) be encouraged to leave.

Clark Kerr, head of the Carnegie Commission on Higher Education, holds one of the more than 100 documents prepared by the group in its comprehensive survey of higher education in the United States.

Colleges in Trouble

A study prepared in 1971 by Earl F. Cheit, a University of California professor of business administration, found that two-thirds of the nation's colleges and universities were either in financial difficulty or headed for difficulty. Cheit's report, *The New Depression in Higher Education,* was based on a sample of 41 schools, ranging from large private universities, like Harvard, to small community and parochial colleges. The financial squeeze had affected a disproportionate number of private colleges, black institutions, and schools in urban areas.

Cheit concluded that the major cause of economic strain in the universities was not an absolute decline in the number of students (although the *rate* of enrollment growth has fallen), but a slowdown in income growth which began in 1968—at the same time that colleges and universities were setting up new academic programs, widening services, and raising standards.

Private institutions have traditionally relied heavily on income from endowments, tuition and fees, grants for research and fellowships, and private gifts from alumni, friends, and corporations. But aid from these sources failed to keep pace with inflation and outlays for campus expansion, faculty salaries, and other long-term commitments.

The federal government, which had heavily subsidized higher education in the 1960's, reduced basic research programs drastically toward the end of the decade, leaving universities with high overhead for expensive facilities. At the same time, government-sponsored fellowships and traineeships for the support of graduate stu-

Parsons College in Fairfield, Iowa, once a haven for drop-outs from other colleges, is now bankrupt, its grounds covered by weeds.

dents were cut back from 51,500 in 1968 to only 6,600 in 1973.

In April, 1973, the Carnegie Commission issued a restudy by Cheit which indicated that most of the colleges and universities in his sample had managed to achieve a fragile financial stability, primarily by cutting costs. But some institutions were less fortunate: in 1972, 44 colleges closed their doors permanently, up from 32 in 1971 and 18 the previous year.

Cheit's finding was corroborated in a survey undertaken by the National Commission on the Financing of Post-Secondary Education. In a report submitted to President Nixon in December, 1973, this group concluded that "between 1968 and 1972, there occurred a severe and widespread slowing down of income growth and, for many key components, a sharp absolute decline. . . The general adjustment in income has been much more severe and has lasted longer than the recent mild recession of the general economy. At present, however, there are general signs of moderate financial improvements and stabilization."

The response of public policy has been insufficient to halt the financial deterioration suffered by institutions of higher education. Although one-third of the states passed legislation directed at the problem, the effect has been insignificant, except in New York State. Administrators in both public and private colleges continued to seek additional support from state legislatures, however, as well as increased federal appropriations.

Traditional rivalries between tax- and privately-supported institutions for money, students, and prestige have been heightened by the educational recession. As the gap between fees at public and private colleges widens, more students are choosing state universities and community colleges, which are less expensive than private schools. (A typical resident undergraduate could expect to pay $4,039 for tuition, room and board, and personal items during 1974-75 at a private college, compared to $2,400 at a public school.)

Legislative proposals to increase tuition fees at state universities are welcomed by officials of private colleges, and by some economists who believe that the educational subsidy of middle- and upper-income families should be reduced. But educators at public colleges argue that raising tuition would exclude many of the students their institutions were created to reach—the children of the lower and middle classes.

The Birth Dirth

Demographic changes in this century are an important factor in the financial difficulties confronting colleges and universities. Total degree-credit enrollments in higher education rose from 3,861,000 in 1961 to 8,116,000 in 1971. But enrollment growth then leveled off to about half the 5 per cent annual increase that educators had predicted.

The post-World War II "baby boom" —an aberration in a pattern of declining birth rates since 1900—led to the tremendous influx of students absorbed by colleges during the 1960's and early 1970's. In 1946, the fertility rate (which had fallen to an average of 19.8 births per 1,000 population during the depression and war years) shot up to 24.1, remaining at that level or higher until 1957. The lower birth rate of the 1960's began to be reflected in lower elementary-school enrollments in 1967. (By 1972, the birth rate had dropped to 15.6.) Accordingly, college and university enrollment should begin falling in the 1980's.

Unlike elementary-school enrollment, however, enrollment in institutions of higher education is affected by variables in addition to population, such as general economic conditions. Intensified competition among colleges and universities for money and students is casting all but the most prestigious institutions into an unaccustomed role as "sellers" of opportunity for learning—in a buyer's market.

Selling Higher Education

Administrative innovations in public relations and aggressive student recruitment are saving some colleges from extinction. The new approach of admissions officers around the country was reflected in a typical recent article in *College Board Review,* entitled "Marketing Admissions: Using Modern Business Techniques in Student Recruiting."

To help colleges locate students, the College Entrance Examination Board has begun offering subscribers lists of the names and addresses of high-school students participating in the Admission Testing Program and the Preliminary Scholastic Aptitude Test. One-fourth of the nation's colleges and universities were reported to have utilized the new service in 1973.

More controversial are the techniques of so-called "admissions entrepreneurs." Admissions management is a new industry which has evolved to advise colleges on advertising and promotion, fund raising, student recruitment, and financial-aid administration. Services range from a few hours of consulting work to the administration of a client's entire admissions budget ("take-over management"). A typical three-day workshop for admissions personnel might cost a school $225 per participant. Under the more extensive operations of take-over management, colleges retain final authority over admissions standards and policies. However, many admissions officials fear the loss of their jobs to outside contractors.

Among the smaller, financially pinched institutions which have benefitted from the services of admissions contracting are Colorado Women's College, Houston Baptist College, and Beaver College in suburban Philadelphia. Public schools such as Southern Illinois University and the prestigious Colorado School of Mines have also hired consulting firms to bolster flagging enrollment.

Under a typical contract, a "goal" is set for the number of students to be recruited. The consulting company (often composed of former college-admissions officers) then surveys the school's strengths and weaknesses and applies industrial recruiting techniques to encourage new applicants.

Promotional media used by recruiters include radio spot commercials, mass telephoning, direct-mail blitzes, and colorful brochures. Direct mailings were formerly scorned by all but vocational institutions. But a mailing of 5,000 pieces at a cost of 25 cents per item may produce 50 freshmen paying $4,000 each—$200,000 in annual income.

One recruitment incentive which has drawn fire from the National Association of College Admissions Counselors involves partial tuition rebates to those students who persuade acquaintances to matriculate. For example, Salem College in West Virginia rebates $100 per new student, while Loretto Heights College in Denver offers $50. Many academic people find the concept of "paying by the head" distaste-

Traveling Offices are increasingly being used by colleges in student recruiting, registration, and alumni relations. This "mobile office" logs more than 8,000 miles annually as an outreach service center.

ful. But the president of Loretto Heights, Ronald D. Hayes, defends the practice, saying, "We're not lowering our admissions standards, and we're not turning the admissions process over to students. What's happening is that the student is communicating as a person who has been here, a peer, his own personal experience."

The circuit-riding admissions officer and the traveling alumnus are being replaced by more efficient spokesmen. Shimer College in Mount Carroll, Illinois, sends a colorful bus to nearby high schools, while the University of Chicago recruits rural students through its Small School Talent Search. Representatives of 150 colleges and universities set up booths at Atlanta's first national college fair in May. About 1,000 enthusiastic students and their parents showed up to do some comparison shopping. Similar fairs, sponsored by the National Association of College Admissions Counselors, are being held in other cities.

Many schools are revamping instructional programs to meet the requirements

A College Fair in Philadelphia provides prospective students with information and interviews. College admissions officers are turning to innovative recruitment techniques as the birth rate drops and student recruitment becomes more competitive.

of a changing job market, as more and more students request vocationally-oriented courses. One example of educational innovation is Lambuth College in Jackson, Tennessee, where a program in hotel and restaurant management was developed in cooperation with Holiday Inns. (Some professors, however, have voiced concern that colleges' preoccupation with increasing enrollments will lead to declining academic standards and the abolition of traditional course requirements, to satisfy student demands.)

Other colleges are experimenting with new types of extended education to attract increasing numbers of older students. At C. W. Post College, a "weekend college" was instituted, offering courses for students who work full-time. The University of Southern California has announced a new evening session which offers 40 different degree programs. "Mornings at Manhattanville," a popular program developed for adults by Manhattanville College, draws almost as many students as the regular undergraduate curriculum.

The Academic Marketplace

During the 1960's, the products of the post-war baby boom were entering graduate school and obtaining doctorates in record numbers. The number of Ph.D.'s awarded tripled in one decade. But, while more young Ph.D.'s were looking for employment in the academic job market than ever before, the colleges—strapped for cash—suddenly stopped hiring. Higher education, which had formerly absorbed about half of all new Ph.D.'s, restricted its hiring to replacements for retiring professors. Graduate students began moving into disciplines oriented toward nonacademic professions—medicine, law, business, and the applied social sciences. Younger teaching Ph.D.'s found their job security jeopardized.

Under the traditional system of academic tenure, assistant professors who successfully complete a probationary period of up to seven years receive virtual lifetime appointments. The system was intended to provide an environment in which professors could not be penalized for freedom of expression and research.

To maintain staffing flexibility, college

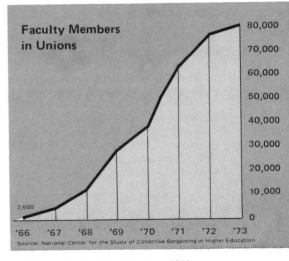

Faculty Members in Unions

Source: National Center for the Study of Collective Bargaining in Higher Education

Rapid Growth of Faculty Unions since 1966 reflects lack of job security among professors as colleges cut back on hiring and stiffen requirements for obtaining tenure. Academic personnel formerly considered unions incompatible with their professional status.

administrators consider 50 per cent (about the national average in 1973) to be the desired proportion of tenured faculty. But because half of present faculty were hired during the 1960's, the decade of rapid expansion, a "tenure bulge" is expected to occur by 1985. At that point, about 85 per cent of faculty members will be "tenured in" if present trends continue.

Some radical, black, and female instructors have charged that the tenure system has been used to exclude qualified members of minority groups from permanent academic positions. Prospects for increased hiring of women and other minority scholars were termed "dismal" by the Carnegie Commission. "Not before the year 2000 and perhaps not even then," Kerr has stated, "will the percentage of women and minority members on faculties be in proportion to their representation in the general labor force." Legal challenges from blacks and women over hiring practices have led to fears by college officials that if tenure regulations are not reformed, the power to make decisions on "excessive tenure" will be taken away from them by the courts or by federal agencies concerned with equal opportunity.

Suggested solutions to the problem of tenure bulge include incentives for early retirement and the hiring of new instructors for terms of from four to six years. Stricter standards could also be applied in the evaluation of candidates for tenure. (According to a study made in 1971 by the American Council on Education, 100 per cent of those considered for tenure at most community colleges received it.) But professional groups and educators' unions oppose changes in the tenure system. Defenders of the traditional system believe that it ensures academic freedom at a time when higher education is becoming increasingly dependent on subsidies from the federal government and other organizations.

The financial crisis in higher education has also accelerated a trend toward faculty unionization that began around 1966. In the past most faculty unions were organized in community colleges, but new rulings by the National Labor Relations Board have encouraged the formation of professional unions at private institutions. In 1973, almost 300 colleges and universities bargained collectively with representatives of 80,000 faculty members—about 15 per cent of the national total.

Most faculty unions are affiliated with one of three prominent professional organizations: The National Education Association, which represents about 47,000 faculty members at 102 colleges and universities, the American Federation of Teachers, which is attached to the AFL-CIO and covers 15,000 instructors on 200 campuses, and the American Association of University Professors, which has 13 contracts including some 12,000 members in higher education.

The growing acceptance of trade unionism is one manifestation of heightened insecurity among academic personnel, who have traditionally considered such groups incompatible with their status as professionals. As the "new depression" in higher education becomes the primary source of campus discontent, student revolution may be replaced by faculty rebellion among the halls of ivy.

Expo '74. Spokane, Washington, was host to a six-month world's fair that opened on May 4, keyed to a theme of improving man's environment. A city of 180,000, Spokane was the smallest ever to win sanction for a world's fair by the Bureau of International Exhibitions. However, it is the hub of a region—commonly called the inland empire—that includes parts of Washington, Idaho, Montana, and Oregon, with a population of 1.2 million.

Because of Spokane's remoteness from major U.S. population centers, the fair was expected to pile up an attendance of only 5 million people—small by comparison, for example, with Montreal's Expo '67, which had an attendance of 50 million. Some reporters dubbed the fair "America's best-kept secret." But 10 foreign nations erected pavilions. There were also 37 domestic exhibits and an amusement park. Many top-name draws were scheduled to provide entertainment.

A Spokane bank official said, "Even if nobody came to see Expo, it would still be a success." A network of dilapidated railway yards, warehouses, and seedy taverns that separated the main shopping center from the Spokane River and its picturesque falls was cleared to make way for the fair, which was located on two islands and the river banks. City fathers attracted $20 million worth of state and federally financed construction for a post-Expo riverfront park and convention center. Local officials said Expo had created 7,200 new jobs and had given a $200-million boost to the economy.

The United States pavilion was a huge tepee-like vinyl tent stretched in the center to the equivalent of 14 stories in height. It featured the history and accomplishment of American Indians and the nation's interest in an unpolluted environment. The largest screen in the world (nine stories wide by six stories high) was used to exhibit a 23-minute film that featured a swooping flight into the Grand Canyon and a raft ride down the Colorado River. One display in the pavilion was an assemblage of old bathtubs and sinks around a fountain to illustrate America's waste of water; another was a pile of junk, to depict the solid-waste disposal problem.

Expo Fairgrounds. *Above,* aerial view of Expo '74, located on 100 acres (half land, half water) on two islands and the banks of the Spokane River. *Right,* U.S. pavilion overlooks river rapids. *Below,* visitors enjoy a ride on the Sky Float as it passes the Soviet pavilion.

The Soviet pavilion featured art montages, three movie theaters, an exhibition of Armenian archeological artifacts, and ingenious models of air- and water-purification systems. Dozens of visiting artists and athletes were to include the Moiseyev Dancers and Olympic gymnasts Olga Korbut and Ludmila Turishcheva. Other international pavilions represented Japan, Mexico, Iran, West Germany, Australia, Canada, South Korea, Taiwan, and the Philippines. General Motors, Ford, General Electric, Boeing, Kodak, and Bell Telephone were among the corporations sponsoring industrial pavilions. There was an Energy pavilion established by oil, coal, and electric companies, an Afro-American pavilion, and a Mormon pavilion.

The Smithsonian Institution displayed such Pacific Northwest highlights as totem-pole carving, salmon fighting their way upstream, and a recounting of 19th-century railway wars and the building of the Grand Coulee Dam. A folk festival featured crafts and dancing by ethnic groups that settled the area, such as Scandinavians, Scots, and Basques, and such attractions as skilled workmen constructing boats and a sluice where children could pan for gold.

The state of Washington built a pavilion that included an auditorium and convention center to be turned over to Spokane after the closing of the fair. Entertainment in the auditorium was to include performances by the Philadelphia Orchestra, the Mormon Tabernacle Choir, Bob Hope, Jack Benny, Ella Fitzgerald, Bill Cosby, Margot Fonteyn, Marcel Marceau, the Royal Shakespeare Theater, Isaac Stern, Van Cliburn, and Lawrence Welk.

Conservationists were upset because there were no exhibits representing national conservation groups, while automakers and other corporations that are significant polluters were represented. An official of the Rocky Mountain chapter of the Sierra Club called Expo "ecophony. This is a trade fair put on by a bunch of merchants to increase profits." Expo officials said conservation groups were welcomed but had been unwilling to pay the fees required of all exhibitors.

France. Finance Minister Valéry Giscard d'Estaing was elected to a seven-year term as president of France on May 19. He polled 50.7 per cent of the vote, narrowly defeating Socialist party leader François Mitterrand, who polled 49.3 per cent. Giscard succeeded Georges Pompidou, who died April 2. With his election, France entered a new and uncertain period of post-Gaullist politics.

Death of Pompidou

Georges Jean Raymond Pompidou, president of France, died April 2 at the age of 64. Pompidou's poor health had become increasingly obvious during his last year in office; he was forced to cancel many appointments and curtail public appearances. Although the nature of his terminal illness was not officially disclosed, it was widely believed that he had suffered from multiple myeloma, an invariably fatal cancer of the bone marrow.

Nearly 70 world leaders, including Britain's Prime Minister Harold Wilson, West German Chancellor Willy Brandt, Japanese Premier Kakuei Tanaka, Soviet President Nikolai Podgorny, and U.S. President Richard Nixon attended a memorial mass in Pompidou's honor at the Cathedral of Notre Dame in Paris on April 6. Pompidou had been buried two days earlier in the graveyard of the parish church in Orvilliers, a small village 31 miles from Paris.

A poor but brilliant schoolboy, Pompidou had gained entrance to the elite École Normale Supérieure, and he graduated at the head of his class. In later years he served as an aide to General Charles de Gaulle and as a director of the Rothschild bank. When de Gaulle appointed him premier in 1962, Pompidou was virtually unknown, but he soon emerged as a popular and effective leader of the Gaullist party, the Union for the Defense of the Republic. After de Gaulle suddenly resigned in the spring of 1969, Pompidou was easily elected to be the second president of the Fifth Republic.

The Campaign

Under the French constitution, a new election must be held 20 to 35 days after a vacancy occurs in the presidency. Alain Poher, president of the French Senate,

Valéry Giscard d'Estaing took office as president of France in a ceremony held in the Élysée Palace. The former minister of finance narrowly defeated Socialist François Mitterrand in the election that followed the death of Georges Pompidou.

automatically became acting president during the interim.

In the first round of voting on May 5, Mitterrand received the most support, 44 per cent, while Giscard, leader of the small Independent Republican party, won 33 per cent. The Gaullist candidate, former premier Jacques Chaban-Delmas, came in third with 15 per cent. Since no candidate received a majority, a run-off between the two leading candidates was scheduled. Most Gaullist voters sided, as expected, with Giscard rather than Mitterrand, the left's unity candidate who was supported by the Communist party as well as the Socialists.

Issues were largely obscured by personalities during the campaign, with Giscard and Mitterrand battling frantically for the support of undecided middle-of-the-road voters. Mitterrand advocated more democracy in government and benefits for the working class. A red rose became his symbol for the flowering of social change. But he was handicapped by his alliance with the Communists. In exchange for their support—Communists regularly deliver about one-fifth of the electorate—he had promised them several ministries in a coalition cabinet.

The 48-year-old Giscard, who capitalized on his youth and handsome family, worked hard to dispel his image as a cold and aristocratic technician. Characterizing himself as a humanistic social reformer, Giscard offered a 12-point program of "reform without risk."

In contrast to the Gaullist sobriety of previous elections, the *campaigne l'Américaine* featured rallies with entertainment, campaign buttons, and chartered planes for barnstorming the country. At Giscard's rallies and in the streets, his younger supporters appeared in T-shirts lettered *Giscard à la barre* (Giscard at the helm).

A record number of voters—87 per

Candidates Debate. Giscard, *left*, and Mitterrand, *right*, sought the support of undecided middle-of-the road voters in a televised debate. The *campaigne l'Américaine* featured rallies with entertainment, campaign buttons and T-shirts, and chartered planes for barnstorming the country.

cent of the electorate—turned out to decide a race so close that the results of last-minute polls were suppressed so as not to influence the outcome. Despite Mitterrand's defeat, his leftist coalition mustered its strongest bid to govern France since the Popular Front lost power in 1938.

In a televised victory speech which he repeated in English for foreign viewers, Giscard promised to carry out political, social, and economic reforms, and proclaimed that "a new era of French politics starts today, an era of renewal and change." The new president would, however, have to negotiate with the Gaullists, who remained the largest parliamentary party, with 181 out of 490 seats; Giscard's Independent Republicans hold only 55. (The National Assembly's term does not expire until 1978, unless Giscard decides to dissolve it before then and call new elections.)

New Cabinet

The first weeks of Giscard's presidency were marked by a continuation of the informal style which had characterized his campaign. At his inauguration May 27, Giscard passed up the traditional pomp and panoply of Gaullist ceremonies. He spoke briefly before officials gathered in the Élysée Palace and accepted—but did not wear—the great necklace of the Legion of Honor customarily presented to French chiefs of state. After the simple indoor proceedings, Giscard walked several blocks down the Champs Élysées with five other officials in business suits to offer flowers at the tomb of France's unknown soldier.

A few hours later, Giscard announced his selection of a Gaullist, Jacques Chirac, the 41-year-old former minister of the interior, as premier. Although he served President Pompidou loyally, Chirac became regarded as a renegade during the electoral campaign by helping to outmaneuver Giscard's Gaullist rival, Chaban-Delmas. Under France's half-parliamentary, half-presidential system, the premier is appointed by the president, but must maintain the confidence of parliament while he is executing the president's legislative program.

The remaining 15 members of Giscard's cabinet were announced the following day. The number of Gaullists was reduced from 10 to 5 (including Chirac). Three new ministers were members of Giscard's party and four belonged to a small centrist reformist group which had been in opposition under Pompidou but which had backed Giscard. Most of the nominees, however, were known for their technical expertise rather than their political affiliations. Only three ministers, including Chirac, were holdovers from the previous cabinet.

The most important of the new cabinet members was clearly Michel Poniatowski, minister of the interior. A long-term political associate and close friend of the new president, he had helped him establish the Independent Republican party in 1966.

Other ministers included centrists Jean Lecanuet and Jean-Jacques Servan-Schreiber for justice and reform, respectively; Mrs. Simone Veil, the only woman cabinet member, for health; and Jean Sauvagnargues, a career diplomat, as foreign minister. Jacques Soufflet, a Gaullist, became defense minister, and Jean Pierre Fourcade, a former civil servant who had worked with Giscard for a number of years, was named minister of economy and finance.

Servan-Schreiber's tenure was short. On June 9, Premier Chirac announced that the president had dismissed Servan-Schreiber for publicly criticizing a government decision to resume nuclear testing in the Pacific. (See FRANCE in the third section, 1973.)

During his first days in office, Giscard decreed several measures intended to "relax" French political life. Among these were an end to government wiretapping (except by the narcotics and counterespionage departments), and a ban on arms sales to unspecified regimes at odds with France's "liberal mission." (It was reported that quick action on government wiretapping—which had become a national scandal—was due in part to Poniatowski's discovery in 1973 that his own phone was among some 5,000 tapped by the interior ministry for years.) Giscard also pledged "the development of France as a country of political and intellectual asylum" and promised that no newspaper would be confiscated even if it attacked the president.

The precise outlines of Giscard's program were unclear. Pressing economic problems, in particular, had received little attention during the campaign. France was suffering from severe inflation (at an annual rate of 16 per cent during the first quarter of 1974), which had led to wildcat strikes by workers whose real wages had fallen. The rising rate of inflation, up from 10.3 per cent in 1973, was partly due to petroleum prices.

The main factor, however, was a stepped-up export program instituted by Pompidou to remedy France's balance-of-payments deficit without reducing employment. Giscard, considered a brilliant economist and administrator, was faced with a dilemma: while he had promised to raise minimum wages and take other actions to increase social welfare, the tougher domestic policies necessary to curb inflation would probably result in more unemployment.

End of an Era

The election of the Fifth Republic's first non-Gaullist president was a turning point in modern French history. Analysts expected the structure of French politics to gradually revert to traditional patterns. The strong presidential regime of the Gaul-

Cabinet Members. Mrs. Simone Veil was appointed minister for health. Jacques Chirac, *glasses*, a Gaullist, was appointed premier.

lists—sometimes known as the "monarchical republic"—had blurred important distinctions between the various parties. Under Giscard, the National Assembly was expected to play a greater role in the political process, with the president acting more as an arbiter of conflicting interests than as a political commander in chief.

Giscard's appointment of Sauvagnargues, the pro-German ambassador to Bonn, as foreign minister suggested that France was ready to embark on a policy of closer cooperation with other members of the European community. Under the Gaullists, France had obstructed British membership in the Common Market, expelled NATO forces from its territory, and weakened the Atlantic alliance by its often-virulent anti-Americanism. Giscard, by contrast, was a close friend of the new German chancellor, Helmut Schmidt, and had criticized the disruptive role played by France at the February energy conference in Washington. (See PETROLEUM in the first section.) The widespread feeling that

a new era in France had begun was accentuated by political upheavals in other western European nations during early 1974.

Germany. In a year of political surprises, the world was again caught off-guard May 6 when West German Chancellor Willy Brandt resigned in the wake of an espionage scandal that revealed one of his closest aides was an East German spy. Brandt accepted full responsibility for negligent security and asked his foreign minister, Walter Scheel, to assume his duties until another chancellor was selected. On May 16, the lower house of the parliament elected Helmut Schmidt to fill the vacancy until the next general election in 1976. Schmidt, who served as defense minister in Brandt's cabinet from 1969 until 1972 and then became finance minister, pledged to continue the policies conceived and initiated by Brandt.

The Scandal

The discovery of a spy within the innermost ranks of his administration was

Spy Scandal. A pensive Willy Brandt, *right,* resigned as chancellor of West Germany in the wake of an espionage scandal. Gunter Guillaume, *far left,* a trusted aide shown on a campaign tour with Brandt, was revealed to be an East German spy. Brandt accepted full responsibility for negligent security and resigned his position.

the final blow of a hard political winter for Brandt. The spy, 47-year-old Gunter Guillaume, served as a top aide to Brandt and was arrested along with his wife and four others on charges that they were spies for Communist East Germany.

Officials reported that Guillaume's career as a spy began in 1956 when he supposedly "fled" from Communist East Germany and immediately joined Brandt's Social Democratic party. Working in its Frankfurt branch, he rose to the rank of secretary, and in 1970 his hard work paid off when he was summoned to Bonn to work in the federal chancellory. In 1973 he became an important political aide to Brandt and, owing to their similar temperaments, became friendly with the chancellor. He even accompanied him on a summer vacation to a fishing retreat in Norway. It was speculated that he saw many of the chancellor's secret papers while on this trip.

Officials knew that before emigrating Guillaume had worked for an East Berlin newspaper known to be a front for Communist intelligence work, but he nevertheless passed security-clearance investigations in both 1969 and early 1970. Bonn officials claimed that they had known for some months that Guillaume was a spy but were keeping a close watch in hopes of discovering more about Communist espionage activity in West Germany. They claimed that Brandt had passed on false information during the fishing trip, but foreign diplomats seemed convinced that during his 15-month association with the chancellor the spy discovered a number of state secrets.

The revelation of a Communist spy in Brandt's ranks was a serious blow particularly because it seemed a contradiction of Brandt's basic political innovation—*Ostpolitik,* a series of actions that led to diplomatic relations with East Germany and other east European governments. A friend of the former chancellor said that Brandt "felt that he had been discredited and deceived in the eyes of the people. It was hard enough to explain *Ostpolitik* to them and get them to go along with it, he felt. Now how could he defend it?"

The scandal seemed to justify the distress many Germans felt about the treaties with the Eastern bloc, fears that such dealings allow the Communists, particularly the Russians, to take advantage of the West. Many of these arguments run parallel to dissident views in the United States concerning the Nixon-Kissinger efforts at détente.

(West Germany is acknowledged to be riddled with Communist agents. By official reckoning there are between 15,000 and 16,000 such spies, more than in any other Western country. Most of them work for East German intelligence, which undoubtedly passes on information to other Soviet-bloc intelligence officials. In 1967, for example, a U.S. Sidewinder missile was stolen from a West German NATO base, dismantled, and shipped in pieces to Moscow by air freight. Gunther Nollau, head of Bonn's principal internal-security agency, conceded in a television interview that other spies of Guillaume's caliber were probably operating at the highest levels of government, and a magazine charged that Nollau was himself an East German agent.)

The Soviet Union expressed regret over Brandt's resignation because he, along with the late French President Georges Pompidou and U.S. President Richard Nixon, formed the basis of the détente policy the Russians hope to advance. Some observers believed relations between the Soviets and East Germany had been strained as a result of the incident.

An Apprehensive Germany

The spy scandal was the final blow to Brandt's administration, whose popularity had been sagging since the elections of 1972. The shift in sentiment was, in large part, due to the energy shortage which, although endured in West Germany with less hardship than in other European nations, was seen by many as the first unfavorable sign in an economy which had been steadily growing since World War II. The automobile, a symbol in West Germany as well as in the United States of economic progress, was suddenly in danger, and the German people seemed to lose their optimism.

Peter von Ortzen, who heads the Social

Democratic party in Lower Saxony, summed up this change of sentiment: "There was always a fundamental sense of optimism in this country. The oil crisis, the four Sunday driving bans last fall and the inflation of the last year have created a general unhappiness, which, of course is being expressed against the party in power. People didn't freeze to death last winter, but they have the feeling they might have if the weather had been colder, and that upset them profoundly."

The energy shortage aggravated Germany's basic economic problem—an inflation rate of 7.8 per cent—which the Brandt government was having a difficult time curbing without alienating his party's main constituency, labor. When the federal employees' union began to negotiate new contracts in February, Brandt opposed their demand for a 15-per-cent pay increase in hopes of slowing the inflationary spiral. Bus drivers, garbage collectors, and postmen responded with a three-day strike that forced the government to up its original offer, giving some employees a 14-per-cent increase and generally establishing an 11-per-cent increase as the norm for labor negotiations.

Brandt's handling of the energy shortage also alienated many of his party's usual supporters. Many Social Democrats, particularly the younger left-wingers known as Jusos, were outraged at a policy which seemed to give the large oil companies what they wanted while the workers were asked to limit their requests for pay increases. Furthermore, many questioned Brandt's failure to fulfill his campaign promises of increasing worker representation on company boards and establishing a government-run profit-sharing plan. Thus the former chancellor found himself caught between the radicals of his own party who said he was not doing enough, and the more conservative political and business interests, which had prevented him from enacting his promised reforms.

Private Life Questioned

The aspect of the scandal which probably hit Brandt the hardest was the unsubstantiated gossip concerning his private life. Opposition newspapers speculated that Guillaume had information on Brandt's private life that he could have used to blackmail the chancellor. Brandt replied to these allegations sharply in his first public statement on his resignation: "No matter what may be written about that [my private life] it is and remains grotesque to maintain that a German chancellor can be blackmailed. I, certainly cannot be." He admitted, however, that he resigned in part because "there were indications that my private life would be drawn into speculation about the case."

Willy Brandt, whose given name was Herbert Ernst Karl Frahm, was born in the Hanseatic trading port of Lübeck on December 18, 1913. He never knew his father and grew up under the care of his mother and grandfather. A bright child, he won a scholarship to high school, where he found himself to be the only student believing in socialism. He followed this path under the guidance of Julius Leber, a Social Democrat who was executed in 1945 for plotting against Hitler.

When Hitler came to power in 1933, Brandt (his party-given name) fled first to Denmark and finally to Norway, where he became a citizen. He returned to Germany after the war and resumed his citizenship in 1947. He served under two post-war mayors of West Berlin and succeeded them in 1957, serving for nine years and gaining world recognition for his cool and pragmatic handling of the tense city during the days when the Berlin wall was erected.

Brandt will be best remembered for his development of the policy of closer relations between East and West. The plan to bring about a relaxation of tensions between the politically opposed factions of Europe won him the Nobel Peace Prize in 1971. The Norwegian parliament cited him as a man who had "stretched out his hand to reconciliation between countries that have long been enemies."

The award committee also cited his accomplishments as foreign minister, a post he held from 1966 until his election to the chancellorship in 1969. Among these accomplishments was the signing of a treaty to prevent the spread of nuclear weapons, the signing of friendship treaties with Poland and the Soviet Union, numerous ef-

Helmut Schmidt, *right,* shown with French President Valéry Giscard d'Estaing, succeeded Brandt as chancellor of West Germany. Schmidt, who had been finance minister, pledged to continue Brandt's policies. He was known to oppose wage and price controls as a means of fighting inflation—West Germany's chief economic problem.

forts to secure the safety of the citizens of West Berlin, and the strengthening of economic and political bonds with other nations in western Europe.

The New Chancellor

Schmidt took over a government in deep political decline. A poll released in mid-May showed that voter preference for his party was at an all-time low: 27 per cent. Only 7 per cent favored the Social Democrats' coalition partners, the Free Democrats, while an overwhelming 62 per cent supported the Christian Democrats. Clearly Schmidt would have to mend his political fences before the next national election.

Schmidt, 55, was born to a conservative family but grew up in a largely Communist section of Hamburg. Resisting these influences, he joined the Hitler Youth and, in World War II, fought on the Russian front and, towards the end of the war, in the Battle of the Bulge on the Western front. He joined the Social Democrats in 1947. Prior to joining Brandt's cabinet, his duties included heading the city-state of Hamburg's Department of Interior and serving as a federal deputy in Bonn.

Almost half of the incumbent ministers retained their portfolios in the new cabinet. But, though pledging to maintain Brandt's policies, Schmidt is known for his independence, and political observers expected a slightly more conservative administration. Economically, Schmidt is an avid supporter of free markets and has chosen to rely on tight-money policies rather than wage and price controls in order to curb inflation.

Concerning Germany's role in the Common Market, Schmidt stated that "we cannot sacrifice the stability of our economy for the sake of a European Community that is unable to act. We cannot place our cash reserves at the disposal of others. Nor can we make our economic policy dependent on the miserable plight of Britain or Italy." Concerning relations with the United States, Schmidt said that "the security of western Europe remains, for the forseeable future, dependent on the presence of the U.S. in Europe."

India Joins Nuclear Club. India became the sixth nation to set off a nuclear device, with an underground test that pushed a round hill of soil above barren desert. India's premier, Mrs. Indira Gandhi, said her nation had no intention of producing nuclear weapons and had detonated the nuclear device for peaceful purposes.

India. On May 18, India carried out what the government called "a peaceful nuclear explosion experiment at a depth of more than 100 meters" (about 330 feet). With the explosion, India became the sixth nation to set off a nuclear device. The others are the United States, the Soviet Union, Great Britain, France, and China.

India initially reported that the blast was about the force of the bomb dropped by the United States on Nagasaki in World War II. Later reports put the explosion in the range of 10 to 15 kilotons (the equivalent of 10,000 to 15,000 tons of TNT), making it somewhat smaller than the Nagasaki blast.

The Indian government said it "has no intention of producing nuclear weapons." Its statement said India's nuclear program was designed for "peaceful uses" such as mining and earth moving, and reiterated the government's "strong opposition to military uses of nuclear devices." The statement was met with skepticism in the United States and elsewhere, especially since the United States has been unable to develop safe and effective uses for nuclear explosives despite repeated tests.

India's Atom-Bomb Potential

India has at least four large nuclear power plants producing plutonium as a by-product. In addition, there is a Canadian-designed plant at Trombay capable of extracting plutonium from the spent fuel elements of the other plants. Plutonium can be used in reactors for power generation—or as the basis of a bomb. The nation's plutonium stockpile is estimated to be at least 200 pounds—roughly enough to make 19 bombs of Nagasaki-force. The step from exploding a nuclear "device" to producing a bomb that could be delivered by plane is not technically difficult.

India signed the 1963 nuclear test-ban treaty that banned explosions on land, in the air, or underwater in the seas. By conducting its test underground, India did not violate the accord.

India has not signed the 1968 Geneva treaty barring the spread of nuclear weapons. Its refusal was based on the argument that the treaty divided the world into nuclear and non-nuclear nations and imposed obligations on the non-nuclear states without making similar restrictions on countries which already had nuclear weapons.

The 1968 treaty prohibits nations already possessing nuclear weapons from helping other countries to obtain or manufacture them. Participating nations are obliged to submit regular accountings of their nuclear materials on hand to the International Atomic Energy Agency and allow regular inspections of their facilities. Spokesmen at the Geneva conference concerning disarmament considered the explosion a major setback for the United States and Russia in their effort to stop the spread of nuclear weapons. The 1968 treaty makes no distinction between nuclear bombs and other devices.

India said the explosion was part of a plan to make the nation self-sufficient in energy. Nuclear explosions could be used to crumble deep-lying beds of lignite, a low-grade coal, so that it could be burned underground and produce a stream of gas that could be used to run a conventional power plant.

India's interest in nuclear development can be traced to the late Prime Minister Jawaharlal Nehru, who encouraged its use for industrial needs but supported a ban on military use. G. K. Reddy, a leading observer of Indian politics, claims, however, that "a qualitative change came about in India's stand after China exploded its first bomb in 1964. India did not consider its policy of unilateral renunciation of nuclear weapons as something that was binding for all times to come irrespective of other international developments."

Political Implications

The nuclear test strengthened India's military posture on the subcontinent and provided firmer leverage over its main rival, Pakistan. Pakistani Prime Minister Zulfikar Ali Bhutto said the explosion was a "fateful development" and a threat to his country. As a result of the test, recent attempts to reestablish good relations between the two countries in the wake of the 1971 war were badly hurt. (See BANGLADESH in this section.)

India drew sharp criticism from Canada, which, since 1956, had given $96.5 million in aid, most of it in long-term loans, to build two nuclear reactors. Upon the news of the test, Canada immediately suspended its atomic aid to India and announced that it would review its other aid programs. Canadian officials believed the plutonium for the nuclear device had come from the research reactor at Trombay built with Canadian help.

"What concerns us about this matter," said Canada's secretary of state for external affairs, Mitchell Sharp, "is that the Indians, not withstanding their great economic difficulties, should have devoted tens or hundreds of millions of dollars to the creation of a nuclear device for a nuclear explosion." (The cost of the five-year effort had been estimated by U.S. experts at about $220 million.)

Other nations, including the United States, voiced similar misgivings about India's judgment and announced plans to review aid to India. Japan, the only nation to sustain a wartime nuclear attack, indicated its displeasure in a statement by a cabinet spokesman: "The government can only express regret because we have been and are still against any nuclear test by any nation for any reason."

The nuclear test threatened to divide the world between those nations that have signed and ratified the nuclear non-proliferation treaty and those that have not. Among those that have not signed the treaty and are thought to possess the know-how to make atom bombs are Israel and South Africa. Furthermore, it was known that Egyptian scientists were working at one Indian atomic-research center. Some diplomatic observers speculated that relations between the Arab world and India might be enhanced by trading atomic expertise for lower oil prices.

Plutonium-producing fast-breeder power reactors may be a major U.S. export during the 1980's. The spread of these reactors would compound the administrative problems in trying to control the components of nuclear weapons.

Rail Strike

A 20-day national railway strike cost India between $1.5 billion and $2 billion in terms of lost production and trade disruption. The end of the walkout came on May 28 and was seen as a major victory for Prime Minister Indira Gandhi, who had been bitterly criticized by the railwaymen's unions and others for her methods of breaking the strike. Among the government's tactics was the jailing of railway leaders and workers, with arrest figures ranging from 20,000 to 50,000.

Mrs. Gandhi said the strike was illegal and that the government would not negotiate until it was over. Behind this tough stance was the fear that India's troubled economy, which in 1973 alone endured a 27-per-cent inflation rate, could not meet the workers' demands. If the government had succumbed to the demands of the rail unions—the largest in India, boasting a membership of almost 2 million—similar pay demands might have come from workers in other nationalized industries.

The unions' strategy was equally simple: to strangle the vital arteries of commerce and food transport by shutting down the rail system. But the arrests added to confusion and divisions already rampant among the railwaymen. The workers demanded a doubling of their present salaries, which range from $26 to $200 a month, as well as an annual bonus of 15 days' salary.

National sentiment, as reflected through the newspapers, was against the strikers but was also critical of the tactics employed by the government. Most observers feared that if pending negotiations between the government and the unions did not yield productive and well-received results, the scene might be set for wildcat strikes that could create further trouble.

Nationwide Rail Strike stranded passengers and cost India close to $2 billion in lost production and trade disruption. The government broke the strike, jailing many railwaymen and their union leaders.

Life in Ulster. Shoppers undergo body searches before being allowed into a Belfast shopping area. A 15-day general strike by Protestant militants further disrupted life in Northern Ireland, which has been repeatedly rocked by bomb blasts and execution-type slayings.

Ireland, Northern. Ulster's executive, composed of moderate Catholics and Protestants, fell May 28. The British government resumed direct rule of the province after a 15-day general strike organized by Protestant militants. The strike cost Northern Ireland $200 million in lost production, sales, and wages.

The chief of the executive body, William Faulkner, resigned with his Protestant colleagues. Faulkner said it had become "apparent to us from the extent of the support for the present stoppage that the degree of consent needed to sustain the Executive does not at present exist." Gerard Fitt, deputy chief of the executive and a Catholic, called the strike leaders "fascist agitators." "I can only envisage complete anarchy," he said.

The Ulster Workers Council, which had organized the strike, called it off on May 29. A few hours later, the British government suspended the Northern Ireland Assembly for four months. Merlyn Rees, secretary of state for Ulster, said the Assembly would remain in existence but that its functions would be assumed by Parliament.

Strike Paralyzes Economy

The strike began May 15, the day after the Assembly approved in principle the establishment of the Council of Ireland. Many Protestants had been opposed to the 1973 agreement by which Ulster was to be made partly self-governing, with power shared by Protestants and Catholics. They also opposed the part of the agreement establishing a council, with limited powers, representing the Republic of Ireland and Northern Ireland. Protestants, who form a 2-to-1 majority over Catholics in Ulster, feared the council would be a prelude to unification of Ireland, with the Catholics a 3-to-1 majority. (See also IRELAND, NORTHERN, fourth section, 1973.)

The UWC vowed to strike until plans to

Dublin Blast Kills 25. The violence in Ulster spread south of the border to the Republic of Ireland. Bombs planted in three cars exploded without warning on May 17 in downtown Dublin at the height of the afternoon rush hour.

set up the Council of Ireland were abandoned and new elections for the Assembly called. Militants opposed to the power-sharing agreement had won only 25 of the 78 assembly seats in 1973, but they won 11 of Ulster's 12 seats in the British Parliament in elections held in February.

The British army, with 16,500 troops in Ulster, could have taken over essential services at the begining of the strike, but the government apparently underrated the effectiveness of the walkout. Although most workers initially ignored the strike call, they were soon forced to leave work, many reportedly after intimidation by the paramilitary Ulster Defense Association. Shopkeepers were also forced to close. Leaders of three Protestant parties added impetus to the strike May 19 by issuing a statement of support. British Prime Minister Harold Wilson stiffened the resolve of the militants by going on television to call them "thugs" and "bullies."

Electricity was cut to about six hours a day, mail service and trucking ceased, all factories were shut, and downtown stores closed in Belfast. Milk and food trucks were often hijacked by street gangs. Nearly 100 barricades set up in Belfast sealed off Protestant areas in order to keep people from going to work—but this measure became unnecessary after the UWC announced on May 21 a cutoff of all deliveries of gas and oil except for "essential services." Many people then had to go to UWC leaders in order to get gasoline or food. Unable to move their produce to the towns, farmers dumped milk and eggs and drowned baby chicks for lack of feed.

On May 27, British troops occupied 21 gasoline stations and two oil-storage depots to assure supplies for essential services. The UWC retaliated by ordering all gas, power-station, and oil-supply workers to cease responsibility for supplying bread, milk, and animal feeds. By evening, gas supplies were cut off in Belfast and nearby towns, blacking out many homes. Grave-diggers were ordered to stop burying the dead. A total power shutoff meant that homes and hospitals were faced with no running water. Raw sewage would have flowed through the streets had the strike continued.

Violence Continues

On April 20, the official death toll reached 1,000 since violence erupted in Ulster between Protestants and Catholics in 1969. At least 18 more people were killed in the next three weeks. Besides the dead, more than 9,000 had been injured and more than 8,000 families had been intimidated into leaving their homes. There had been over 4,000 bomb explosions.

The worst bombing attack since the beginning of the violence struck the Republic of Ireland on May 17. Bombs planted in three cars exploded without warning in downtown Dublin at the height of the afternoon rush hour, killing 25 and wounding about 200. A half-hour later, five more were killed and 20 injured when a bomb exploded in front of a bar in Monaghan, 80 miles north of Dublin. Both the Provisional wing of the Irish Republican Army and the Ulster Defense Association disclaimed responsibility.

The consensus of informed opinion was that eventually there would be a new attempt to work out a form of power-sharing between Protestant and Catholic leaders. This time, however, the Protestant representatives were likely to be hard-liners like the Rev. Ian Paisley, William Craig, and perhaps some of the men who organized the strike. "I'm afraid moderates are a dying breed up here," said one Protestant. "It's getting harder and harder to find them on both sides."

Italy. The government headed by Premier Mariano Rumor resigned on June 10, the 35th Italian government to fall in the last 31 years. More surprising, no other politicians attempted to fill the void, an indication that Italy was experiencing a true political crisis. The fall of the government had been preceded by a surprising result in a recent divorce referendum. A more important factor was the failure to find a solution for Italy's acute economic problems.

President Giovanni Leone beckoned Rumor to return to the task he had abandoned: overcoming the trade deficit of over $1 billion a month and a credit rating which made it difficult for Italy to borrow money. Milan's *Corriere Della Sera* editorialized: "This crisis is different. We are running the risk of a total collapse of the economic system."

Italy ranks seventh among the world's industrial powers, but its economic policies of the past few years—shared with those found in all industrialized nations—have brought it dangerously close to bankruptcy. A series of governments dominated by the Christian Democrats encouraged a speedy recovery from a recession, but in so doing apparently prompted spiraling inflation. Labor unions added fuel to inflation with large wage demands and strikes. And Italian consumers, feeling that the good life had finally arrived, were not to be deterred from spending. Inflation climbed to a level of 20 per cent annually. The final blow came in early 1974 as oil prices quadrupled, adding $10 billion to the expected payments deficit for the year.

The Divorce Issue

Italians voted by a 3-to-2 margin May 12 and 13 to retain a three-year-old divorce law. Probably more important than the vote itself was the heated debate which the issue gave rise to in this heavily Catholic country. The controversy set the scene for the governmental crisis over the economy.

Italy's divorce law—the nation's first ever—was passed on December 21, 1970, and is the least liberal in Europe. It permits a divorce if both partners desire it after a five-year separation or, if the divorce is contested by either party, after seven years apart. The law also allows divorce in cases of incest, when one partner is imprisoned for life, or when a partner has an incurable mental illness.

Opponents of the law predicted that it would bring about a rash of terminated marriages but, since its enactment, only 66,000 couples have obtained divorces. Nevertheless, many persons objected to the law, and over 1.3 million signatures were

Divorce Issue. Italians voted in May to retain the three-year-old divorce law—the nation's first ever. The Christian Democrats, supported by the Catholic clergy, urged a *si* (yes) vote to the referendum, which would have abolished divorce had it passed. Urging a no vote was a married couple who posed for a poster that told voters there was no contradiction between favoring matrimony and supporting the divorce law.

collected supporting its repeal, almost three times the number required by Italian law to bring about a referendum.

The final tally showed that 59.1 per cent voted to retain the law, with 88.1 per cent of the electorate voting on the issue. Many political observers viewed the referendum as a choice between left-wing and right-wing politics.

Premier Rumor and his Christian Democrats—the largest political party, commanding 38.8 per cent of the vote in the last parliamentary elections—came out in support of the referendum, arguing that divorce was an indication of increased permissiveness in Italian society. The only other major political group supporting the law's repeal was the neo-Fascist Italian Social Movement, a right-wing group which has a bad reputation among many Italian voters because of its association with violence and clandestine plotting. Striking out at the Communists, the neo-Fascists stood to gain by posturing themselves on the "respectable" side of the issue.

The Communists, who had commanded 27.2 per cent of the popular vote in the last elections, supported the divorce law. Rumor's coalition partners, including the Socialist party, also urged the voters to reject the challenge to divorce. The outcome was a serious blow to the Christian Democrats and to the influence of the Roman Catholic Church.

Pope Paul VI kept out of the controversy in its early stages but later spoke in

support of the bishops advocating repeal. On the news of the sustaining vote, the pope expressed "amazement and pain." Italian bishops, while saying they would duly respect the law, called for new educational efforts to extol the virtues of family life.

Economic Measures

The Socialists, as expected, exploited the defeat of the referendum by demanding a bigger voice in the government. The cabinet resigned on June 10 when the coalition partners were unable to resolve a stalemate over credit policies.

The Christian Democrats insisted on maintaining existing curbs on borrowing money in order to combat inflation and speculation. Socialist ministers opposed the restrictions on the grounds that it deprived business and industry of operating cash and would consequently force many workers off their jobs.

But, with the credit issue still unresolved, the reinstated Rumor cabinet had to deal with more immediate business. Foreign banks—both private and government institutions—had agreed to help Italy by means of a formula which, in effect, quadrupled the value of the country's gold reserves and made it easier to obtain additional loans. In exchange, Italy was to immediately impose measures to tighten its monetary situation.

Towards this end, the cabinet not only raised taxes but also broadened the tax base by imposing a withholding tax on wages. By this process Italy's tax ranks would climb from 5 million to an estimated 14 million. Gasoline prices were to be raised to $2 a gallon. Furthermore, in defiance of Common Market practices, Italy imposed severe restrictions on imports.

The next few months were expected to be critical in determining Italy's future. All Europe was in economic disarray from widespread inflation and the effect of boosted oil prices but, as Social Democrat Flavio Orlandi observed, "our economic crisis is worse than Britain's economic crisis because in Britain, an authoritarian alternative does not exist. In Italy, an economic crisis on such a scale can become a crisis of the democratic system."

Labor. Wage and price controls expired on April 30, and with them the 5.5-percent guideline for annual pay increases. Workers were seeking larger pay boosts to compensate for inflation, which was running at an annual rate in excess of 10 per cent.

The Bureau of Labor Statistics found that a typical factory worker with three dependents had real spendable earnings of $99.74 a week in April, 1974, compared to $107.93 in April, 1973. AFL-CIO President George Meany, speaking to a union audience, assailed "two-digit inflation that eats away at your members' paychecks like a flash fire."

In early June, federal mediators were trying to resolve 523 strikes involving 308,600 workers, compared to 280 strikes during the same period in 1973. And millions of workers were covered by major collective bargaining agreements due to expire later in 1974, including pacts involving communications, aerospace, railways, coal, and nonferrous metals.

On April 12, negotiators for the United Steelworkers of America and the major steel manufacturers reached agreement on a new three-year contract. Cost of Living Council employees estimated that the new contract would cost the companies close to 11 per cent a year in increased wages and other benefits.

First Industry-Wide Strike since 1921 in the men's-clothing field ended after 10 days. Workers won a one-year wage boost of 13 per cent.

Coalition Government in Laos. Government police and members of the pro-Communist Pathet Lao began joint patrols of Vientiane, the capital, after a new coalition government was sworn into office. A cease-fire agreement ending warfare in Laos had been signed in early 1973.

Laos. The kingdom of Laos moved, in contrast to South Vietnam, closer to peace as a coalition government was sworn into office on April 6. A cease-fire agreement ending warfare between government troops and the pro-Communist Pathet Lao had been signed in early 1973.

Twice, in 1957 and 1962, coalition governments had been formed in this landlocked Indochinese nation, only to collapse, largely because of cold-war tensions and the spillover of the Vietnam war. But, on April 6, cabinet ministers representing the old government and the Pathet Lao, attired in traditional sarongs and high-buttoned tunics, took their oaths of office in a Buddhist ceremony at Vientiane's most sacred pagoda. Earlier, on April 5, King Savang Vatthana formally invested the government at the royal capital of Luang Prabang.

An agreement in September, 1973, had provided for a provisional government headed by Premier Prince Souvanna Phouma, with ministries to be equally divided between the two sides. At the time of the cease-fire, the Pathet Lao controlled three-quarters of the area of Laos, but two-thirds of the people lived in the territory controlled by Souvanna Phouma's government.

The new cabinet consisted of 12 ministers—five representing the old Vientiane government, five from the Pathet Lao, and two agreeable to both sides. Defense, interior, finance, health, and education were allotted to Souvanna Phouma's allies. Public works, economy and planning, information, foreign affairs, and religion went to the Pathet Lao. Telecommunications and justice were allotted to neutralists.

The September agreement also provided for a 42-member National Political Council "independent of" and "equal to" the cabinet. This body had been empowered to advise and "activate" the cabinet on "great problems," while the cabinet "examines and executes rigorously the recommendations of the NPC." The council, like the cabinet, was divided equally between the factions but was to be headed by Prince Souphanouvong, the titular Pathet Lao leader and a half-brother of Souvanna Phouma.

Both the cabinet and the council were to operate on the principle of unanimity on major questions. The council was given extensive powers over the organization of elections expected ultimately to provide the basis for a new, more representative cabinet.

Mixed police forces were patrolling both Vientiane and Luang Prabang. Each side had been officially permitted to station 1,000 soldiers and policemen in each of the two cities.

Foreign Troops

The cease-fire agreement had called for the withdrawal of all foreign troops and advisers from Laos within 60 days of the formation of the new government. But the deadline passed June 5 with a considerable number of North Vietnamese soldiers—allies of the Pathet Lao—reported to be still in the country. Defense Minister Sisouk na Champassak said, "They have withdrawn into the scenery but not back home."

The cease-fire agreement said "foreign military personnel" were to leave the country. The United States and Thailand were named, but not North Vietnam. U.S. and Thai spokesmen said that the last Thai mercenaries in Laos—who in 1972 numbered 21,400—had left on May 22. Thai troops in Laos had been paid by the CIA.

U.S. officials said the number of Americans in Laos had been reduced from 1,100 to 472. The United States assured the government that 140 military men had departed by the deadline; about 30 remained in the office of the defense attaché in the embassy. However, American planes were still believed to be flying reconnaissance missions over Laos in violation of the accord.

Western analysts estimated that 30,000 to 55,000 North Vietnamese troops were still in Laos, most of them stationed along the Ho Chi Minh Trail, which leads through Laos from North Vietnam into South Vietnam. There was general agreement that in other areas North Vietnamese units had been thinned out and, at least in the front lines, replaced by Pathet Lao units. Also remaining in Laos were an uncertain number of Chinese soldiers and workers, who had been building a road system linking the two countries.

The cease-fire agreement did not establish a mechanism for monitoring foreign troop withdrawals, and Western diplomats were convinced the North Vietnamese would not go home as long as fighting continued in South Vietnam. Hanoi has never acknowledged stationing troops in Laos. The situation left the Laotian government with a choice of pretending the North Vietnamese had left or were leaving, or demanding publicly that they leave, which might create a cabinet crisis.

One American, a pilot whose plane crashed in Laos after the cease-fire agreement, was being held by the Pathet Lao. He was the only American known to be in captivity there, although some 1,100 pilots and others are officially counted as missing in action over Laos.

Literature. The National Book Award for fiction was awarded on April 18 to Thomas Pynchon for his novel *Gravity's Rainbow* and to Isaac Bashevis Singer for his short-story collection *A Crown of Feathers*. Other awards were as follows:

Poetry—Allen Ginsberg for *The Fall of America* and Adrienne Rich for *Diving into the Wreck.*

Arts and letters—Pauline Kael, for *Deeper into Movies.*

Contemporary affairs—Murray Kempton, for *The Briar Patch,* dealing with the trial of 21 Black Panthers in New York City.

Science—S. E. Luria, for *Life: The Unfinished Experiment.* Luria received the 1969 Nobel Prize for physiology or medicine.

History—John Clive, for *Macaulay, The Shaping of the Historian.*

Biography—Douglas Day, for *Malcolm Lowry,* an English novelist best known for *Under the Volcano.*

Philosophy—Maurice Natanson, for

Best-Selling Books

FICTION

Watership Down, by Richard Adams
Jaws, by Peter Benchley
The Fan Club, by Irving Wallace
The Snare of the Hunter,
  by Helen MacInnes
Cashelmara, by Susan Howatch
Burr by Gore Vidal

NONFICTION

All the President's Men,
  by Carl Bernstein and Robert Woodward
Times to Remember,
  by Rose Fitzgerald Kennedy
You Can Profit from a Monetary Crisis,
  by Harry Browne
Plain Speaking, by Merle Miller
Alive: The Story of the Andes Survivors,
  by Piers Paul Read
The Gulag Archipelago,
  by Aleksandr Solzhenitsyn

Edward Husserl, Philosopher of Infinite Tasks.

Translation—Karen Brazell for *The Confessions of Lady Nijo,* an autobiographical novel written by a 14th-century Japanese woman; Jackson Mathews, for *Monsieur Teste,* by the French poet Paul Valéry; and Helen R. Lane, for *Alternating Current,* by the Mexican poet and essayist Octavio Paz.

Children's books—Eleanor Cameron, for *The Court of the Stone Children.*

Novelist Vladimir Nabokov was awarded the National Medal of Literature, annually given to a living American writer.

At the presentations in New York City's Lincoln Center, "Professor" Irwin Corey, a stand-up comic, "accepted" for Pynchon, a reclusive figure seldom seen even by his agent. Corey, who bills himself "the world's greatest expert on everything," specializes in obfuscation—a charge sometimes directed at Pynchon. However, the "presentation" was thought by many to be in dubious taste.

Singer, who writes in Yiddish, transmitted an acceptance speech from his apartment in Israel. He said, "I am happy to call myself a Jewish writer, a Yiddish writer, and an American writer."

Ginsberg's acceptance statement was made by his friend and fellow poet, Peter Orlovsky, who, clad in blue jeans and a T-shirt, denounced U.S. government policies and ended, "There is no longer any hope for the salvation of America." Rich said she accepted the award on behalf of herself and two other female nominees, and "in the name of all the women whose voices have gone and still go unheard in a patriarchal world."

A streaker jogged through the hall shouting "Read books! Read books!" He was later seen at a reception, but hardly anyone seemed to recognize him with his clothes on.

Among the books published during the second quarter of 1974 were the following:

Fiction

Cogan's Trade, by George V. Higgins. Another study of small-time mobsters and underworld life by a former prosecutor, the author of *The Friends of Eddie Coyle.* (Knopf—$6.95)

The Dispensable Man, by Wolf Rilla. An Englishman steals a quarter of a million dollars and flies to Mexico, a country from which he cannot be extradited. Nevertheless, he is brought to justice by an investigator sent by the insurance company liable for the theft. (John Day—$6.95)

The Gypsy's Curse, by Harry Crews. Marvin Molar, a deaf-mute who walks on his hands because his legs are undeveloped, has a beautiful girl friend. She fulfills the curse of the title in a grotesque and utterly sick climax. (Knopf—$5.95)

The Hair of Harold Roux, by Thomas Williams. A novel-within-a-novel contrasts the rigid behavior of the 1950's with the cultivated spontaneity of the 1960's. (Random House—$7.95)

Harry and Tonto, by Josh Greenfeld and Paul Mazursky. In a world where the old are often treated like children, many—like the hero of the novel—kick up their heels. The authors indicate that the very old and the very young may be our only remaining leisure class, wholly devoted to doing as they please. (Saturday Review Press/Dutton—$5.95)

Let's Fall in Love, by Carol Hill. A spoof of murder and intrigue, this book also offers erotic passages, a paranoid view of current events, a liberated superwoman, and numerous perverse thrills. (Random House—$6.95)

Mooncranker's Gift, by Barry Unsworth. This novel of an alcoholic Englishman in Istanbul also introduces a number of other bizarre but well-depicted characters. (Houghton Mifflin—$5.95)

Mundome, by A. G. Mojtabai. Richard, an archivist, lives with his schizophrenic sister whom he hopes to nurse back to health in this rich but puzzling first novel. (Simon & Schuster—$6.95)

My Life As a Man, by Philip Roth. In this autobiographical novel the writer seeks to free himself first from a woman, then from her ghost—ultimately from his obsessions. (Holt, Rinehart & Winston—$8.95)

The Wine of Astonishment, by Rachel MacKenzie. Two sisters past 30 carry on love affairs in a small town in New York. (Viking—$5.95)

Nonfiction

Alive: The Story of the Andes Survivors, by Piers Paul Read. The survivors of a 1971 airplane crash in South America endured for 60 days under circumstances that forced them to devour their dead companions to stay alive. Here is the full story of the ordeal that made international headlines. (Lippincott—$10)

All the President's Men, by Carl Bernstein and Robert Woodward. The authors, Washington *Post* reporters, broke the story of the Watergate scandal. Their account is also a primer on the techniques of investigative reporting. (Simon & Schuster—$8.95)

The American People: The Findings of the 1970 Census, by E. J. Kahn, Jr. The 1970 census produced more than 200,000 pages of data, but the author has managed to synthesize the material in surprisingly readable form, with very few charts, graphs, or tables, and a good index. There is documentation for such startling observations as the statement that rural America constitutes "the world's sixth largest underdeveloped nation." Trivia fans will be interested to learn that there were 249 female blacksmiths in 1970, of which six were employed in eating and drinking places and 11 in credit agencies. (Weybright and Talley—$8.95)

Blue-Collar Journal: A College President's Sabbatical, by John R. Coleman. One winter's day, the president of Haverford College left his home to work for two months as a laborer in various Eastern locales. He concluded that there is no getting away from it all and that every job has its "frustrations, joys, pains, and dreams in just about the same mixture." (Lippincott—$6.95)

The Book, the Ring, and the Poet, by William Irvine and Park Honan. This biography

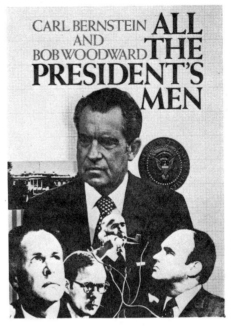

Watergate Best-Seller. The Washington *Post* reporters who broke the story of the Watergate scandal describe the techniques of investigative reporting they employed.

of Robert Browning and Elizabeth Barrett Browning is also an account of intellectual life in Victorian England. (McGraw-Hill—$15)

Cruel and Unusual Justice, by Jack Newfield. The author of such articles as "The 10 Worst Judges in New York" delivers an indictment of what he sees as a corrupt, politicized judicial system in which the poor are herded into squalid jails while rich and influential defendants escape punishment. (Holt, Rinehart & Winston—$7.95)

Democracy and Its Discontents, by Daniel Boorstin. A distinguished professor thinks Americans are straying from their heritage and must make an "effort to see the price tag that history has placed on our civilization." (Random House—$5.95)

The Denial of Death, by Ernest Becker. The unquenchable urge for immortality, says the author, is the life force at work—often perverted or trivialized but not to be denied. Man, with the equipment of an animal, wants to be a god, but must settle for fashioning "something—an object, or ourselves—and drop it into the confusion, make an offering of it. . . " (Free Press—$7.95)

Captain Cook. The renowned navigator of the South Seas accurately charted vast regions of the Pacific and contributed greatly to knowledge of the island peoples and their institutions. His life and voyages are the subject of a biography by J. C. Beaglehole.

The Figure Finaglers, by Robert Reichard. Mathematical and statistical tricks are used by government and business to mislead people. Price indexes, for example, are imperfect means of measuring inflation, auto dealers omit "extras" from their pricing, and chartmakers present distorted graphs to make a case. The book offers a wealth of advice on how to detect the lies, the deceits, and shortcomings of those who juggle figures to gull the public. (McGraw-Hill—$8.95)

A Home for the Heart, by Bruno Bettelheim. The retired director of a school for disturbed children describes how his methods might apply to the treatment of mental patients everywhere. A shortcoming is that his proposals require skilled, sensitive, dedicated therapists who must be willing to confront their own unconscious problems. (Knopf—$12.50)

Ladies and Gentlemen—Lenny Bruce!! by Albert Goldman. Showman, hipster, junkie, genius, and rebel—Lenny Bruce, stand-up comic, was all these things—even, the author believes, a "shaman" bent on purging the evil spirits of America by exposing the hypocrisies of our times. (Random House—$10)

The Life of Captain James Cook, by J. C. Beaglehole. The great explorer of the South Seas gave the world not only a mass of geographical knowledge but also a large body of information on the Pacific island peoples he visited. This massive biography belongs to the indispensable literature on the Pacific area and the history of exploration. (Stanford University Press—$18.50)

Lincoln Steffens, by Justin Kaplan. This biography of the king of the muckrakers is also an intellectual history of the left during the first third of the 20th century and a powerful psychological portrait of a rebel curiously attracted to such authoritarian figures as Stalin and Mussolini. (Simon & Schuster—$10)

Pilgrim at Tinker Creek, by Annie Dillard. More than just another "nature" book, this work reminds readers that the natural world is not only beautiful but also is violent, rapacious, profligate, and ultimately mysterious. (Harper's Magazine Press—$7.95)

Something's Wrong With My Child, by Milton Brutten, Sylvia O. Richardson, and Charles Mangel. Learning disabilities, which affect an estimated 7.5 million American children, can be traced to coordination problems, perceptual disorders, language difficulties, or short attention spans. In calling attention to the problem, the authors list specific resources to which parents can turn for help. They urge that schools gear education to a child's functional level rather than to his age or grade placement. (Harcourt Brace Jovanovich—$7.50)

Thomas Jefferson: An Intimate History, by Fawn Brodie. This psychohistorical portrait focuses on Jefferson's heart rather than his mind. The author argues that he had several offspring by a slave woman, Sally Hemings— a contention rejected by some other scholars. (Norton—$12.50)

The Uneasy Chair, by Wallace Stegner. Bernard DeVoto, influential journalist and historian, and failed novelist, is recalled by one of his friends in this biography of a man who never flinched from controversy. (Doubleday—$12.50)

Zen and the Art of Motorcycle Maintenance, by Robert Pirsig. An autobiographical narrative of a cross-country motorcycle trip, this work is a harrowing account of a man's mentally troubled past, his philosophical quest, and his fears for his son's future. (Morrow—$7.95)

Literature for Children

Picture Books and Easy-to-Read Books

C Is for Cupcake, by Carolyn Haywood. Beginning readers will be delighted when Christie brings her special, living Cupcake to the first grade's Cupcake Day. (Morrow—$4.75)

The Cat and Mouse Who Shared a House, retold with pictures by Ruth Hurlimann. Retold with refreshing humor is this old tale from Grimm of a strange partnership. (Walck —$6.95)

Circus, by Jack Prelutsky, pictures by Arnold Lobel. Lions, tumblers, clowns, seals, and other exciting circus acts prance exuberantly through these verses and pictures. (Macmillan—$5.95)

David's Windows, by Alice Low, pictures by Tomie de Paola. Every child who likes to stop and look will understand David's problem with his busy mother and his happy discovery. (Putnam—$4.69)

Dragon Kite, by Thomas P. Lewis, pictures by Errol Le Cain. The dragon kite leads a boy of Tibet to a strange adventure. (Holt— $4.95)

The Elephant and His Secret, by Doris Dana, illustrated by Antonio Frasconi. Told in Spanish and in English and in bold, beautiful pictures is this tale of the first elephant on earth. (Atheneum—$5.25)

Firerose, by Susan Jeschke. When a baby girl with a dragon tail is left on a fortuneteller's doorstep, it takes no crystal ball to foretell exciting adventures. (Holt—$4.95)

Gray Duck Catches a Friend, by Vicki Kimmel Artis, illustrated by Giulio Maestro. A lonely duck sets a trap to catch a friend— and what does she get? (Putnam—$4.29)

Gregory's Stitches, by Judith Vigna. How did Gregory get his stitches? The story grows and grows in this gay cumulative tale. (Albert Whitman—$3.25)

He's My Brother, by Joe Lasker. Told with warm tenderness is this story of a brother who is "different." (Albert Whitman—$3.95)

I Never Saw, by Judson Jerome, illustrated by Helga Aichinger. Rhythmic verses and evocative pictures challenge children to look and wonder. (Albert Whitman—$3.95)

Merle the High-Flying Squirrel, by Bill Peet. Tired of the noisy city, a squirrel sets out to find trees that are as tall as a building. (Houghton—$5.95)

Mushroom in the Rain, by Mirra Ginsburg, pictures by Jose Aruego and Ariane Dewey. What happens to a mushroom in the rain? Assorted animals find out! (Macmillan —$4.95)

The Nuns Go West, by Jonathan Routh. When seven cheerful nuns borrow an elephant for a western vacation, anything can happen. (Bobbs—$4.95)

Ralph and the Queen's Bathtub, by Kay Chorao. Ralph was frightened of the witch's house until he peeked into the window and began the adventure of his life. (Farrar— $4.95)

The Sesame Street 1, 2, 3 Story Book, by Kingsley, Moss, Stiles, and Wilcox. An amusing collection of stories about numbers from 1 to 10. (Random—$3.95)

Shawn Goes to School, by Petronella Breinburg, illustrations by Errol Lloyd. On a scary and wonderful day, a small boy first goes to nursery school. (Crowell—$4.50)

Speak Up, Edie! by Johanna Johnston, pictures by Paul Galdone. Chatterbox Edie talked too much—until the night of the school play. (Putnam—$4.86)

There Really Was a Dodo, by Esther S. and Bernard L. Gordon, pictures by Lawrence Di Fiori. The simply told story of the strange bird that couldn't fly and how it became extinct will help children understand why we must protect our wildlife. (Walck—$4.95)

Why Noah Chose the Dove, by Isaac Bashevis Singer, pictures by Eric Carle. A lively and amusing account of Noah and the animals on the Ark. (Farrar—$5.95)

Why the Sky Is Far Away, retold by Mary-Joan Gerson, illustrated by Hope Meryman. A warm and humorous folktale from Nigeria of the days when the sky was close enough to touch—and eat! (Harcourt—$4.95)

The Wind Blew, by Pat Hutchins. One day the wind blew and blew and blew away everything it touched. Children will chuckle over this gay, cumulative saga of the wind's mischief. (Macmillan—$5.95)

Fiction (8 to 12 Years Old)

Jason and the Money Tree, by Sonia Levitin. Jason didn't believe in magic, but he had to believe his eyes, and there were ten-dollar bills growing on his tree. Jason was happy until he discovered the complications a money tree can cause. (Harcourt—$5.95)

Luke Was There, by Eleanor Clymer. After his mother went away, Julius trusted nobody until he ran away and made a surprising discovery. (Holt—$4.95)

Mirror of Danger, by Pamela Sykes. Lonely Lucy needed a friend, but was the strange girl from a hundred years ago a friend or an enemy? (Nelson—$4.95)

Nothing Rhymes with April, by Naomi J. Karp. Irrepressible Mollie discovered that entering a poetry contest led to unpredictable adventures in the Depression days of 1936. (Harcourt—$5.95)

Playmaker, by Mike Neigoff. Max was new to the team, a team that was split down the middle by warring factions. Then the coach challenged Max to become playmaker and help lead the team to victory. How Max met the challenge makes a fast-moving basketball tale. (Albert Whitman—$3.50)

Round About and Long Ago, retold by Eileen Colwell. Twenty-eight funny, sad, fantastic, exciting folktales from the counties of England that children will enjoy and remember. (Houghton—$4.95)

Somebody Go and Bang a Drum, by Rebecca Caudill. Based on a real family is this story of a family that grew bigger and bigger as children came from all around the world. (Dutton—$5.95)

Thank You, Jackie Robinson, by Barbara Cohen. Sam was a baseball nut, but he didn't expect that to help him make new friends and lead to an unforgettable summer. (Lothrop—$4.50)

The Truth About Stone Hollow, by Zilpha Keatley Snyder. Weird tales were told about Stone Hollow, but Amy didn't believe them until she and Jason found the place where time did not exist. (Atheneum—$6.25)

With a Deep Sea Smile, selected by Virginia A. Tashjian. Here are stories, poems, riddles, and songs that children can enjoy individually and in story groups. (Little—$5.95)

Nonfiction (8 to 12 Years Old)

Cook Mates, by Betsy Weiss and John

Laskey. Easy-to-make recipes for foods of many kinds for parties, picnics, and just everyday good eating and fun. (Macrae—$4.50)

Famous American Indians of the Plains, by S. Carl Hirsch. Wild riders and brave hunters, the Indians of the plains created their culture as they followed the buffalo herds. Here is their fascinating story. (Rand—$4.95)

Let's Go to the Moon, by Michael Chester. Newly revised is this graphic introduction to moon travel and exploration. (Putnam—$3.29)

Number Ideas Through Pictures, by Mannis Charosh, illustrated by Giulia Maestro. Odd and even numbers, square and triangular numbers are presented entertainingly and will help boys and girls recognize that mathematics can be fun. (Crowell—$3.95)

Fiction (11 to 14 Years Old)

I Tell a Lie Every So Often, by Bruce Clements. One reckless lie catapulted Henry and his brother into a dangerous and exciting trip down the Missouri in 1848. (Farrar—$5.95)

The Keeping Days, by Norma Johnston. A provocative and warmly human tale of the summer Tish began growing up and learning to accept her unpredictable family. (Atheneum—$5.95)

Phoebe's Family, by Pamela Sykes. A writer father, a Shakespearean play, and the agony and rapture of first love made Phoebe's summer exciting and unforgettable. (Nelson—$5.95)

Pool of Swallows, by Martin Cobalt. How can a small pool of water swallow up nine cows at the same time? But Martin saw it happen, and that was the beginning of a fantastic adventure. (Nelson—$5.25)

Tough Chauncey, by Doris Buchanan Smith. Small for his age, Chauncey had to be tough—and he was. That got him into trouble at home and at school, but it also helped him make the toughest decision of all. (Morrow—$5.50)

Nonfiction (11 to 14 Years Old)

The Changing Tools of Science, by Irving Adler. A comprehensive and graphic survey of the continually evolving tools scientists use to explore our modern world, measure an atom, or launch a space satellite. (John Day—$4.68)

A Forest of Pencils, by Winifred Trask Lee. An illuminating account of schools through the ages and how they have changed and developed. (Bobbs—$6.95)

The Incredible Incas, by Carleton Beals. As fascinating as fiction is this story of an

Indian civilization that flourished in Peru, Ecuador, and Bolivia before the coming of the Spaniards. (Abelard—$6.95)

Science Fun, by James and Mildred Hyer. Here are more than 50 experiments to do in the house, back yard, or garden—experiments that will help prove science is fun. (McKay—$4.95)

The Story of Glaciers and the Ice Age, by William H. Matthews III. A tantalizing introduction to the secrets glaciers hold about our past—and future. (Harvey—$7.25)

Why the Chinese Are the Way They Are, by Benjamin Appel. This newly revised edition answers many of the questions young people are asking about China today and its peoples. (Little—$5.95)

Your Insect Pet, by Richard Headstrom. For beginning entomologists and for pet lovers is this clear and detailed explanation of the anatomy and habits of the inhabitants of the insect world. (Walck—$4.95)

Fiction (Teen-age)

Authors' Choice 2, an anthology of stories chosen by 18 distinguished writers. What stories do authors themselves consider their favorites? Here are stories selected by Andre Norton, Joan Aiken, John Christopher, Peter Dickinson, and other authors whose stories boys and girls enjoy. Here are stories that will entertain, enthrall, and make you want to read more. (Crowell—$6.95)

Blue Fin, by Colin Thiele. Snook was a disappointment to his fishing-captain father—and it was Snook who had to save the ship from shipwreck. (Harper—$4.95)

Bright Candles, by Nathaniel Benchley. Jens risked the danger of torture and death when he joined the Danish resistance fighters to defy the power of Nazi Germany. (Harper—$5.50)

Brothers by Choice, by Elfreida Read. To Brett, Rocky was his real brother, adopted or not. But when Rocky ran away, Brett had to fight to prove he was a brother by choice. (Farrar—$5.95)

Burning Star, by Eth Clifford. One Reed, the boy of ancient Mexico, saw the stranger descend from the sky, and believed he was the reincarnation of Quetzalcoatl, the god of peace. Why then did tragedy follow? (Houghton—$4.95)

A Cold Wind Blowing, by Barbara Willard. Piers is drawn into dangerous intrigue when a mysterious girl becomes his charge in the days of Henry VIII. (Dutton—$5.95)

The Drugged Cornet, chosen by Susan Dickinson. A suspense-filled collection of mystery stories that will keep you guessing and breathless. (Dutton—$5.95)

Ghost Plane of Blackwater, by William F. Hallstead. Greg finds a baffling mystery when he takes his first assignment as an agricultural pilot and almost ends up a ghost himself. (Harcourt—$5.95)

The Guns of Darkness, by Ann Schlee. The dramatic story of a girl who lived in the dangerous days when the Emperor Tewodros ruled Ethiopia. (Atheneum—$5.95)

John Come Down the Backstay, by Caroline Tapley. To John, the youngest on the sailing ship, the search for Sir John Franklin and his men who had been lost in the Arctic in 1845 was a thrilling adventure. But he did not know the incredible hardships he would face. (Atheneum—$6.25)

The Perilous Gard, by Elizabeth Marie Pope. Sent as a prisoner to the eerie castle by Bloody Mary, Kate knew she faced danger— but she did not know that a greater danger from another world threatened her, a danger it would take all her courage and wit to overcome. (Houghton—$5.95)

The Son of Someone Famous, by M. E. Kerr. Adam thought he was the nothing son of his famous father, and Brenda Belle thought she was the nothing daughter of her mother—and their search for identity is hilarious and thought-provoking. (Harper— $4.95)

The Stronghold, by Mollie Hunter. Lame Coll could never be the chief of his ancient Scottish people, but he could fight in his own way to protect them from the invading Romans. (Harper—$5.95)

To See the World Afresh, compiled by Lilian Moore and Judith Thurman. As contemporary as tomorrow are these poems for young people, written by blacks, Indians, Chicanos, and others. (Atheneum—$4.95)

Nonfiction (Teen-age)

Animals of Europe, the Ecology of the Wildlife, by Maurice Burton. Vivid text and photographs portray the lives, habitats, and adaptation of wild animals to their environment and our need to protect them. (Holt— $11.95)

Famous Custom & Show Cars, by George Barris and Jack Scagnetti. For car buffs, here is an exciting collection of cars by a variety of designers. (Dutton—$6.95)

Highlights of the Olympics, by John Durant. The pageant of the Olympic Games and the athletes who created their history is presented here. (Hastings—$6.95)

Resistance, by Jules Archer. A challenging appraisal of resistance movements and their role in today's world. (Macrae—$5.95)

Ships Through History, by Ralph T. Ward. A colorful evocation of the sailing ships that made history from the time of the Vikings to the Yankee clippers. (Bobbs—$7.95)

Disengagement Accord provided for a cease-fire and the establishment of a neutral buffer zone between Syrian and Israeli troops in the Golan Heights region. Israeli forces west of Line A and Syrian forces east of Line B were thinned out. The agreement ended the aerial dogfights and intense artillery fire, *right,* exchanged between the two sides. Israel and Egypt had signed a similar agreement in January.

Middle East. A military disengagement agreement signed by Israel and Syria May 31 brought new hope for a negotiated peace settlement in the Middle East. The accord, which followed 32 days of "shuttle diplomacy" by U.S. Secretary of State Henry Kissinger, provided for a cease-fire and the establishment of a neutral buffer zone between Syrian and Israeli forces in the Golan Heights region. (Israel and Egypt had reached a disengagement agreement on the Sinai front in January.)

Under the provisions of the pact, a buffer zone one to four miles wide was to be established approximately along the old demarcation line that was created in June, 1967, when Israel seized the Golan Heights. The deserted Syrian town of El Quneitra and a narrow strip captured by Israel in 1967 were to be included in the UN-patrolled neutral area, but Israel was permitted to keep three strategic hills overlooking the town, and several nearby Israeli settlements. Israel agreed to withdraw from a 300-square-mile salient

northeast of the Golan Heights which was taken from Syria in October, 1973. When precise lines were determined in early June, the buffer area ran from Mount Hermon in the north to the southern end of the Golan Heights, varying in width from 500 yards to six miles.

On either side of the buffer area, a 15-mile zone of reduced military forces was created, in which antiaircraft missiles were to be barred. In the first six miles of the "thinning out" zone, each side would be limited to a force of 6,000 soldiers armed with light weapons (36 artillery pieces of 122-mm. or the equivalent, with a range of 10 to 12 miles) and 75 tanks. In the second six-mile belt, an unlimited number of troops, 450 tanks, and additional medium-range artillery pieces were to be permitted, but no long-range weapons. There were no further restrictions in the remaining three miles of the corridor.

About an hour after the cease-fire was signed by Syrian and Israeli representatives in Geneva, shelling stopped on the

Golan Heights. Fighting had continued sporadically in the area since October, 1973, but exchanges of artillery and tank fire had intensified in the weeks before Kissinger began his marathon mission. The first Israeli air strikes since October took place on April 6, when jets struck at Syrian forces that had crossed the truce line on Mount Hermon, and dogfights had resumed on April 18.

The first official proclamation of the cease-fire agreement was made by President Nixon, who hailed it as "a major diplomatic achievement" and congratulated Israeli Premier Golda Meir and Syrian President Hafez al-Assad for "the statesmanship they have shown." According to disclosures by Golda Meir and by U.S. officials in Cairo on May 30, the United States had underwritten the cease-fire with a number of unpublished "understandings." Among these, it was said that the United States had agreed to conduct aerial reconnaissance to insure implementation of the agreement and had assured Israel of political support if Israel retaliated for commando raids across the demarcation line. It was also reported that Assad had given Israel secret oral assurance that Syria, in what appeared to be a major policy shift, would not allow Palestinian guerrillas to infiltrate into Israel from Syrian territory.

The United Nations buffer zone was to be patrolled by 1,250 troops supplied by non-Security Council member nations. A joint U.S.-Soviet resolution setting up the United Nations Disengagement Observer Force (UNDOF) was approved by the Security Council on May 31. The first units of UNDOF—500 Austrian and Peruvian troops from the 7,000-man United Nations Emergency Force stationed along Egyptian-Israeli lines—began arriving in Quneitra June 5.

An accord outlining practical details of the cease-fire was signed June 5. It was negotiated within the framework of the Israel-Egypt working group established by the Geneva Middle East peace conference in December, 1973. A phased withdrawal of Israeli forces from the salient began two days later. Under the terms of the agreement, the Israeli evacuation was scheduled to be completed by June 26.

Prisoner exchanges between Syria and Israel took place June 1 and 6. Wounded prisoners of war were repatriated first in Red Cross planes—12 to Israel and 26 to Syria, including two Moroccans. Cheering crowds greeted the 68 POW's returned to Israel and the 362 flown to Syria June 6. Most appeared to be in good health, although charges of physical and psychological torture were later made by both sides.

Mideast Looks West

As a result of the prominent role played by the United States in bringing about the Israel-Syria accord, American relations with the Arab world improved dramatically. Strenuous efforts by the Nixon Administration to demonstrate a more "even-handed" foreign policy in the area had also helped to bring about a shift in Arab public opinion and had strengthened the position of more moderate Arab leaders. As American prestige rose in the Middle East, Russian influence was seen to be declining (Syria had formerly been Moscow's chief client in the area). The beginning of a new era in Arab-American relations was symbolized by President Nixon's seven-day visit to Egypt, Saudi Arabia, Syria, Israel, and Jordan on June 12-18.

Egypt. The first stop on Nixon's ceremonial journey was Egypt, where President Anwar Sadat had gambled his political future on the success of American diplomatic efforts in the Middle East. Exuberant crowds greeted the Nixon entourage wherever he went. An estimated 300,000 cheering Egyptians lined the route from the airport to downtown Cairo. Some 2 million more were said to have watched the train pass that carried Nixon and Sadat to Alexandria the following day. In recognition of their efforts for peace, Sadat presented Nixon with Egypt's highest honor, the Collar of the Nile, and Kissinger with the Order of the Republic, the country's second highest award.

For several months before the presidential plane touched down in Cairo, rapid changes had been taking place in Egyptian-American relations. Full diplomatic ties were restored in February. A U.S. naval task force finished a minesweeping operation in the Suez Canal, closed since 1967. In April, Sadat had announced a decision to end nearly two decades of Egyptian dependence on Soviet weapons by negotiating an agreement with Yugoslavia for a joint arms industry. (The "Czech arms deal" of 1955 had marked the introduction of Soviet influence in the Arab world.) Another indication of the new trend was the announcement in Washington June 1 of a joint cooperative committee to improve economic, scientific, and cultural relations between Egypt and the United States.

On June 14, a more far-reaching declaration of friendship and cooperation was signed at Abdin Palace, the presidential mansion in Cairo. Included in this agreement was a provision under which the United States would provide Egypt with a 600-megawatt-capacity nuclear reactor and nuclear fuel for the generation of electricity. (Egypt already had two nuclear reactors obtained from the Soviet Union, but would no longer be dependent on Soviet nuclear fuel.)

The American offer of nuclear technological assistance to Egypt was in line with
previous agreements the United States had
concluded with some 35 countries, including Israel. Safeguards developed by the
United States and the International Atomic Energy Agency were to be placed on
the handling of fissionable materials produced by the reactor, to prevent them from
being used in the development of nuclear
weapons.

Other clauses of the Nixon-Sadat declaration dealt with U.S. economic aid to
Egypt, including the donation of wheat
and other basic commodities (subject to
congressional approval). The United
States pledged to "help strengthen the financial structure of Egypt," to encourage
private investment by Americans, and to
assist in reconstructing the war-damaged
cities along the Suez Canal. (American
business investment in Egypt was soaring;
at the time of Nixon's visit, deals worth
$2 billion were under consideration.)

Saudi Arabia. Nixon was greeted warmly by King Faisal when he arrived in Jidda
on June 14. At a state dinner in the royal
guest palace, the king praised the new role

Arab-American Accords. President Nixon,
shown with President Anwar Sadat of Egypt,
received a warm welcome from crowds in
Cairo. Substantial U.S. economic and
technological aid to Egypt was promised,
including a nuclear reactor. Nixon's visit
to Saudi Arabia followed a wide-ranging
agreement signed in Washington by U.S.
Secretary of State Henry Kissinger.

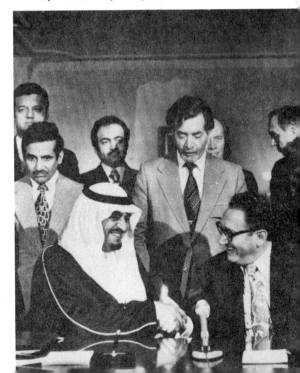

being played by the United States in the Middle East, but he warned that a lasting peace would ultimately depend upon justice for the Palestinians.

Nixon's visit to the desert kingdom followed the conclusion of a wide-ranging U.S.-Saudi pact which was signed in Washington on June 8. Under the terms of the agreement, joint economic and military commissions were to be established. Four working groups were set up to prepare for the first meeting of the joint economic commission, scheduled for October: (1) a group on industrialization and economic development, which was to pay particular attention to the use of flared gas (an oil-well by-product) in the production of fertilizer; (2) a group on manpower and education aimed at increasing Saudi skills in technical areas; (3) a group on research and development to consider cooperative projects in such fields as solar energy and water desalinization; and (4) a group to examine proposals for agricultural development.

The two governments also agreed to consider setting up an economic council to encourage cooperation in the private sector and in the field of finance. (A small but growing amount of Arab oil revenues was flowing back to the West in the form of investments. See BUSINESS AND FINANCE in this section.)

The joint military commission was to "review programs already under way for modernizing Saudi Arabia's armed forces in light of the kingdom's defense requirements, especially as they relate to training." In talks between Prince Fahd Ibn Abdel Aziz (second deputy premier of Saudi Arabia and a half brother of King Faisal) and officials in Washington, the United States had expressed a desire to support cooperative measures among the states of the Arabian peninsula in order to promote orderly development. The United States, which had sold military equipment to Saudi Arabia for some 20 years, was expected to provide a large quantity of fighter aircraft and naval vessels in the future.

Discussions on the expansion of U.S. economic and military aid to Saudi Arabia had been conducted for several months.

Although oil was not mentioned publicly in connection with these conversations, American officials were said to believe that the accord would encourage increased production of Saudi petroleum, possibly lowering the world oil price. The pact signaled the end of a period of strained U.S.-Saudi relations which had begun with the Arab oil embargo in October, 1973. It was also hoped that the agreement would become a model for American cooperation with other Arab nations.

Syria. In Damascus, where American flags flew for the first time since 1967, Nixon received a friendly welcome from President Assad and smiling, if restrained, crowds. On June 16, Nixon and Assad announced the resumption of U.S.-Syrian diplomatic relations, broken off by Syria during the June, 1967, Arab-Israeli war. A flag-raising ceremony was held at the American embassy building the following day.

Israel. More than 100,000 people turned out to watch President Nixon's motorcade travel from the airport to Jerusalem on June 16. Nixon and Kissinger conferred with the new Israeli premier, Yitzhak Rabin, and other officials, briefing them on their discussions with Arab leaders. Nixon also visited former premier Golda Meir and U.S. ambassador Kenneth Keating, and attended a ceremony at Yad Vashem, a memorial to the 6 million Jews who were killed during World War II.

Nixon concluded his visit to Israel with assurances of U.S. economic and military assistance and urged Israel's new government to take risks for peace. A communiqué released June 17 announced that the two nations would negotiate an agreement on "nuclear energy, technology, and the supply of [nuclear] fuel from the United States under agreed safeguards." (Israel obtained a small five-megawatt research reactor from the United States in 1961. A second reactor, which produces plutonium, the fissionable material used in

Nixon in Israel. Speaking at a reception held in Israel's parliament, the president urged the Israeli government to take risks for peace. (Part of Marc Chagall's tapestry, The Exodus, is shown in the background.)

atomic bombs, was provided by France in the late 1950's.)

Jordan. At the last stop on Nixon's tour, the presidential party was met by jet fighters in formation, a military drill team, and thousands of spectators. Jordan's claim to the Israeli-occupied West Bank area, which King Hussein feared would be set aside in a negotiated Middle East settlement, was believed to be the major issue raised during discussions. Like other Arab leaders, Hussein also expressed his concern over the future status of the Israeli-occupied Arab sector of Jerusalem.

Following Nixon's meeting with Hussein, it was announced that the United States and Jordan would set up a commission to review on a regular basis areas of cooperation in trade and investment, military assistance, and scientific, social, and cultural relations. The joint statement also noted that Nixon had sent to Congress proposals which included a substantial increase in economic and military aid to Jordan.

Raids and Reprisals

Despite the cease-fire in the Golan Heights, a murderous pattern of guerrilla raids and Israeli reprisals developed in northern Israel. The worst incident occurred on May 15 at the village of Maalot, where 27 Israelis were killed in the course of an attack by three Arab commandos on a schoolhouse where 90 teenagers on an outing had been sleeping. When the guerrillas broke into the school, 17 children and 3 adults escaped through windows. The remainder were held as hostages by the commandos, who demanded that 20 Arab prisoners in Israel be released and flown to Syria or Cyprus by 6 P.M. the same day.

Israeli officials said that they had agreed to the demands because the guerrillas had threatened to blow up the school and its occupants. But attempts to negotiate with the guerrillas failed, apparently through confusion over the commandos' terms for release of the hostages, and the deadline for release of the prisoners was never met. Instead, Israeli soldiers stormed the building, and the guerrillas and many of the hostages were killed in a shootout. Altogether, 21 students and one Israeli soldier were killed, and 70 persons were wounded. The three guerrillas had also caused the deaths of two Arab women who were riding in a truck that was sprayed with machine-gun fire earlier in the night, and they murdered a family of three in a Maalot apartment before coming upon the school building.

Calling the Maalot massacre "a bitter day for all of us," Premier Golda Meir vowed that "the government—any government of Israel—will do everything in its power to cut off the hands that want to harm a child, a grown-up, a settlement, a town or a village." The next day, Israeli jets struck at Palestinian targets in southern Lebanon from Mount Hermon to the Mediterranean city of Saida, in the heaviest Israeli raids ever inflicted on that country. Official Lebanese casualty figures were 48 persons dead, 20 missing, and 174 wounded. The Israeli defense ministry said that the bombing and strafing had been directed at commando storehouses, workshops, and training camps in the vicinity of Nabatiyah, Saida, and Tyre.

On May 17, 19, and 21, Lebanese targets were again raided by Israeli jets and ships. One person was killed in a bombing attack on the villages of Kfeir and Meimis and near the Mount Hermon town of Rachaya, Lebanon. Palestinian guerrilla leaders said that eight people had been killed and 50 buildings damaged in a naval attack by Israeli gunboats on the Rashidiyah refugee camps south of Tyre. According to the Lebanese defense ministry, the May 21 raids resulted in three children killed and 17 persons wounded.

Responsibility for the Maalot raid was claimed by the Popular Democratic Front for the Liberation of Palestine. Its leader, Nayef Hawatmeh, said in Beirut May 16 that his organization's action had been directed against the negotiations being conducted between Israel and Syria by Kissinger, because a negotiated settlement would "mean the surrender of the Palestinian people and the liquidation of the Palestinian cause."

Major raids by Palestinian guerrillas also occurred in the Israeli towns of Qiryat Shemona and Nahariya and at Kibbutz Shamir. At Qiryat Shemona, a town of

15,000 less than a mile from the Lebanese border, 18 people were killed and 16 wounded when three Arab guerrillas stormed a four-story residential building on April 11. The invaders died in a gun and grenade battle with Israeli troops.

In Beirut, a small splinter organization called the Popular Front for the Liberation of Palestine—General Command claimed credit for the attack. Israel responded with attacks on six towns in Lebanon south and west of Qiryat Shemona on April 12. According to an Israeli communiqué, "the action was intended to harm villages whose residents had given assistance to terrorists." Two Lebanese women died when a house was blown up in Muhebab. At Ett Taibe, 24 houses and a power station were blown up and 13 hostages kidnapped. (On June 7, Israel released 12 Lebanese civilians in exchange for two pilots who had been captured when they bailed out over Lebanon after a raid on Syria April 8.)

Three women were slain by four Arab guerrillas at Kibbutz Shamir on June 13. One of the guerrillas was shot to death by armed members of the kibbutz, while the other three were killed by explosives they were carrying. The Popular Front for the Liberation of Palestine—General Command also claimed responsibility for this assault. The group maintained that in attacks on both Qiryat Shemona and Shamir Kibbutz, its members had struck from "within the depths of Israel" rather than from bases in Lebanon. (The PDFLP, which allegedly carried out the Maalot massacre, also claimed that its three guerrillas had operated out of underground cells in Israel.)

As in the earlier episodes, Israeli reprisals took the form of attacks against Palestinian installations near Mount Hermon and at other sites to the west, including a dozen refugee camps and settlements. According to unconfirmed reports, at least 70 people were killed and 70 wounded in a series of Israeli strikes June 18-20. On June 20, the Israeli government announced that the raids were part of a new preemptive policy designed to pressure the Lebanese government into curbing the activities of Palestinian guerrillas within its jurisdiction. Israel was also constructing

Civilians Die. *Top,* an Israeli mourns on the grave of his wife, one of 18 killed by Arab guerrillas in a raid on an Israeli town. *Above,* a Palestinian refugee camp in Lebanon struck by Israeli jets.

a security fence along the Lebanese border to prevent further infiltration by commandos.

At Nahariya, a resort town on the Israeli coast six miles from Lebanon, a woman and two children were killed when three guerrillas attacked an apartment building during the night of June 24-25. One Israeli soldier was also slain by the guerrillas, who all died in a shootout. It was believed that the commandos had reached Nahariya by boat.

Two Arab guerrillas who had been sentenced to death by Greek authorities for their role in the attack on the Athens airport in August, 1973, were released and deported to Libya on May 5. Shafik Hussein al-Arida and Tallal Khaled Kaddourah were granted full pardons by Greek President Phaidon Gizikis, who had earlier commuted their sentences to life imprisonment. The Athens government had decided to treat the two guerrillas leniently following the February hijacking of a Greek ship in Karachi, Pakistan, and further threats of Arab violence in Greece.

Eight other guerrillas who had murdered two American diplomats and a Belgian in Khartoum in March, 1973, were flown to Cairo on June 25. The guerrillas were understood to have been temporarily transferred to a Cairo prison, following an agreement between Sudanese President Nimeiry and Egyptian President Sadat.

Although the eight confessed murderers had been given life sentences by a Sudanese court, Nimeiry had commuted their terms to seven years, to be served in the custody of the Palestine Liberation Organization. The United States condemned the action and recalled its chief diplomatic representative in the Sudan.

New Israeli Government

The coalition government headed by Golda Meir fell on April 10, a casualty of the October war. The 75-year-old prime minister announced her resignation at a meeting of the Labor party, which had become divided over the question of responsibility for Israeli unpreparedness during the last round of the Arab-Israeli conflict. She was to continue in a caretaker capacity pending the formation of a new government or elections.

Dissatisfaction with the governing party had been increasing in Israel due to economic as well as military consequences of the October battles. The 3,350,000 people of Israel, already the most heavily taxed in the world, were faced with financing the $7-billion estimated cost of the 18-day war. Finance Minister Pinhas Sapir had ordered the end of government subsidies on bread, butter, rice, and milk. Golda Meir's personal popularity had fallen from 65 per cent in polls taken before the war to 21 per cent in February.

The immediate incident that precipi-

Yitzhak Rabin, new premier of Israel, was toasted by his predecessor, Golda Meir. Rabin was the first sabra (native-born Israeli) to head his country's government.

Palestinian Commando Leaders. *Left to right,* George Habash, leader of the Popular Front for the Liberation of Palestine; Nayef Hawatmeh, head of the Popular Democratic Front for the Liberation of Palestine; and Yasir Arafat, chief of Al Fatah and chairman of the Palestine Liberation Organization.

tated Meir's resignation was the release of interim findings by the Agranat Commission, which was investigating culpability for Israel's military shortcomings in October, 1973. In a report issued on April 2, the commission had placed the blame on the military and had recommended that top army officers be dismissed for negligence. The Israeli armed forces chief of staff, David Elazar, promptly resigned, but publicly rejected the commission's findings, arguing that Defense Minister Moshe Dayan had been the "operative authority" over him at the time.

Dayan and Meir were cleared of responsibility by the commission, but public demonstrations and some factions of the Labor party continued to call for Dayan's resignation. Dayan refused, asserting that the government shared collective responsibility for the results of the October conflict. Meir resolved the controversy by quitting and forcing all ministers to resign. Major General Mordechai Gur, Israel's military attaché to the United States and Canada, was selected by the Israeli cabinet April 14 to succeed Elazar as chief of staff.

Labor Minister Yitzhak Rabin was designated by the Labor party's central committee to try to form a new government. On May 28, he announced the formation of a 19-member, three-party coalition cabinet to replace the caretaker government headed by Golda Meir. Besides Labor members, two Independent Liberals and one member of the Civil Rights Movement comprised the new cabinet. It included 15

holdovers from the previous cabinet, but excluded three prominent members: Pinhas Sapir, who was retiring as finance minister; Abba Eban, who had been foreign minister; and Moshe Dayan, who refused to serve in the Rabin cabinet mainly because it included Mrs. Shulamit Aloni of the dovish Civil Rights Movement.

Rabin, 52, had served as armed forces chief of staff from 1963 to 1967 and played a prominent role in the 1967 war. From 1968 to 1973 he was Israel's ambassador to the United States. As the first sabra (native-born Israeli) to head his country's government, Rabin represented a shift in national leadership away from the immigrant "founding fathers" to a younger generation.

Palestinian Convention

The Palestine National Council—the 150-member parliament of the Palestine Liberation Organization—ended a nine-day conference in Cairo on June 9. The PLO is an umbrella group encompassing many factions of the Palestinian nationalist movement.

During the session, the executive committee was enlarged to 14 members by the inclusion of four independent moderates who had recently been expelled from the Israeli-occupied West Bank. This action tended to strengthen the position of the moderates, headed by Yasir Arafat, who was re-elected chairman of the executive committee. But for the first time, a seat on the executive committee was also granted to the extremist Popular Front for the Liberation of Palestine—General Command, which had previously been represented only in the council.

One of the texts adopted by the council in Cairo barred Palestinian leaders from attending any conference based on UN Security Council Resolution 242 of November, 1967, which refers to the Palestinian "refugee problem" but not to the Palestinian people's national rights. (The Middle East conference being held in Geneva was convened on the basis of UN Security Council Resolution 388 of October, 1973, which invoked Resolution 242.)

Moderate Palestinian leaders were expected to begin discussions with Egypt, Syria, and other governments in an effort to get the Palestinian national cause accepted as a topic in Geneva. While the Palestinians did not expect the wording of Resolution 242 to be changed, they sought to have the United States and the Soviet Union, co-chairmen of the Geneva conference, declare that the talks would deal with Palestinian rights.

Future progress at the Geneva conference was expected to depend heavily on several issues directly concerning the Palestinians: formation of a national authority or government-in-exile accepted by most Palestinians, the question of negotiating with Israel, and a decision on relations with King Hussein of Jordan. Hussein had agreed on May 1 to the presence of a separate PLO delegation at the Geneva peace talks. This was considered a major shift of policy, because Jordan had previously insisted that its delegation represent all Palestinians at the conference.

Obituaries. Late March, April, May, and June, 1974.

ABBOTT, BUD, straight man who, with partner Lou Costello, created a mass market for slapstick comedy on radio, television, and in the movies; April 25, age 78.

ALSOP, STEWART, veteran Washington reporter and commentator who wrote syndicated columns with his brother Joseph before joining the *Saturday Evening Post* and, later, *Newsweek;* May 26, age 60.

AYUB KHAN, MOHAMMED, president of Pakistan from 1958 to 1969; April 20, age 66.

BACKER, GEORGE, former publisher of the New York *Post,* philanthropist, and writer; May 1, age 71.

BATES, MARSTON, naturalist distinguished for his research on mosquitoes, malaria, and yellow fever; April 3, age 67.

BOYLE, HAL, widely published columnist for the Associated Press who won a Pulitzer Prize for his reporting during World War II; April 1, age 63.

BROWN, ROBERT W., editor of the Augusta *Chronicle* since 1968. He received the Pulitzer Prize for meritorious public service in 1955 while he was editor of the Columbus (Georgia) *Ledger;* April 1, age 62.

BUSH, VANNEVAR, engineer who organized American technology to aid in World War II. He directed the work of 30,000 men throughout the country in the effort that eventually led to the creation of the atomic bomb; June 28, age 84.

See also BUSH, VANNEVAR, in your encyclopedia.

CLAPP, MARGARET, president of Wellesley College from 1949 to 1966 who received the Pulitzer Prize for biography in 1948 for *Forgotten First Citizen: John Bigelow;* May 3, age 64.

COLLINGE, PATRICIA, British actress and writer who arrived in New York in 1908 and became an important part of the American theater for the next 40 years; April 10, age 81.

CONDON, EDWARD U., one of the leading American physicists of the 20th century and a key figure in the World War II atomic-

Katharine Cornell

Duke Ellington, 1899-1974

"Music is my mistress," mused Duke Ellington, "and she plays second fiddle to no one." Throughout the 56 years of his bandleading career, this artistic passion was responsible for the most distinctive catalog of music in all of jazz and, in many minds, in all of American music.

"Every musical honor this country can bestow is little enough for such a musical giant as this man," wrote noted jazz critic and historian Ralph J. Gleason. "In reality, he has already won them and more by his imprint on the minds of all who have heard him."

On May 24, Ellington's lifelong affair with music ended, as he died at the age of 75 from pneumonia contracted while under care for lung cancer.

Edward Kennedy Ellington, who as a child was dubbed "Duke" owing to his innate elegance, was born on April 29, 1899, in Washington, D.C., and grew up with two main passions: painting and music. Music won the battle though, and by the age of 20 he was heading his own band. His first break came when the band began a five-year date at Harlem's Cotton Club in New York City.

It is said that Ellington's real instrument was his orchestra. Many of his players maintained working relationships with him throughout his long career. The importance of these relationships is evident in his compositions, for while his early work was rooted in his own rhythmic piano style, his later works reflect the textural abilities of his musicians. While absorbing the New Orleans rhythm techniques of players like Louis Armstrong, Ellington developed his own music, using his players as his palette from which he created the colors, dynamics, and emotions he desired. Ellington mixed his own sophisticated sense with his orchestra's raw talent in a blend which never lost touch with the essential component of jazz—spontaneity and emotional vigor.

To say that Duke Ellington was prolific is an understatement. He wrote over 6,000 pieces of varying length, running the gamut from popular tunes ("Solitude," "Sophisticated Lady"), to standard jazz pieces ("Black and Tan Fantasy," "Mood Indigo"), and extended compositions ("Harlem," "Far East Suite"), which led to a series of three Sacred Concerts begun in 1965. Ellington called them "the most important thing I've ever done."

Duke Ellington received many honors throughout his career, including the Presidential Medal of Freedom in 1969, the French Medal of Honor, and countless honorary college degrees, but all seem best summed up in the crowd that attended his funeral in New York City. They were black and white, rich and poor, famous and unknown, gathered to say goodbye as he himself used to sign off his radio program: "We love you madly."

---

bomb and radar programs. Condon also was a consultant to the Senate committee that drafted legislation to place atomic energy under civilian control after the war; March 26, age 72.

CORNELL, KATHARINE, leading Broadway actress in the second quarter of the century who was called by critic Alexander Woollcott, "The First Lady of the Theater." She was known for her expertise in romantic roles and her energy in bringing her productions to cities across the United States; June 9, age 81.

See also CORNELL, KATHARINE, in your encyclopedia.

CROSSMAN, RICHARD, a leader of Britain's Labour party who saw himself as keeper of Britain's socialist conscience; April 5, age 66.

CUTLER, ROBERT, special assistant for national security affairs to President Eisenhower and member of the National Security Council (1953-55, 1957-58); May 8, age 78.

DANIELOU, JEAN CARDINAL, leading French Jesuit theologian and staunch defender of papal authority who, after World War II, became a leader of the Catholic Left; May 20, age 69.

DANIELTAN, N. R., economist and author who played a part in the development of the St. Lawrence Seaway; May 13, age 67.

DAS, DURGA, one of India's most prominent journalists who, as a reporter and editor, recorded events from the beginning of India's struggle against British rule until his death; May 17, age 73.

DATER, HENRY M., historian and principal chronicler of United States Antarctic operations since their beginning in 1947; June 26, age 65.

DAVIS, ADELLE, one of the country's best-known authorities on nutrition whose writings held that almost any disease could be prevented by a proper diet; May 31, age 70.

DUMAINE, ALEXANDRE, one of France's

Chet Huntley

most renowned chefs; April 23, age 78.

DUMBRILLE, DOUGLASS, character actor who played hundreds of roles on stage, screen, and television; April 2, age 84.

DUNN, ALAN, cartoonist who contributed over 2,000 works to *The New Yorker* over 40 years; May 20, age 73.

DUNN, LESLIE C., one of the country's ranking geneticists who achieved a world reputation for his research on heredity and evolution; March 19, age 80.

EWING, MAURICE, noted earth scientist who developed the use of shock waves to study the sea floor and the continents; May 4, age 67.

AL-FASSI, ALLAL, founder of the Moroccan nationalist movement which won independence from France in 1956 and president of the Istiqlal party; May 13, age 65.

FERGUSON, ALFRED R., leading Emerson scholar who was editor in chief for 10 volumes of *The Works of Ralph Waldo Emerson;* May 5, age 58.

FIELDS, DOROTHY, prolific songwriter for stage musicals and films over a period of 50 years; March 28, age 68.

FRAZIER, GEORGE, prose stylist whose work appeared in newspapers and magazines both in the United States and abroad for 40 years; June 13, age 63.

FREED, FRED, winner of seven Emmy awards for his work as writer and producer of documentary news programs for the National Broadcasting Company; March 31, age 53.

FRIESELL, RED, veteran football referee who made the famous "5th-Down" officiating error in the 1940 Cornell-Dartmouth game that enabled Cornell to win; June 23, age 80.

FRYXELL, ROALD, anthropologist who discovered what are believed to be the earliest human remains in the Pacific Northwest; May 18, age 40.

FU TSO-YI, popular Nationalist Chinese general who surrendered Peking to the Communists in January, 1949; reported April 25, age 79.

GAYLORD, E. K., publisher of the *Daily Oklahoman;* May 30, age 101.

GERBER, DANIEL F., businessman who introduced strained baby foods to millions of Americans and made his Gerber Products Company the largest baby-food manufacturer in the world; March 16, age 75.

GIEGENGACK, A. E., public printer of the United States who, during his tenure from 1934 to 1948, greatly increased the Government Printing Office's total output; June 21, age 84.

GLENN, TYREE, trombone and vibraphone player with many of the great jazz players of the big-band era; May 18, age 61.

GLOUCESTER, DUKE OF, uncle of Queen Elizabeth II and last surviving son of King George V; June 10, age 74.

GORDON, KITTY, actress for whom Victor Herbert composed *The Enchantress,* in which she starred in 1911; May 26, age 96.

GRUENING, ERNEST, former senator from Alaska who was an early critic of U.S. involvement in Vietnam; June 26, age 87.

GUGLER, ERIC, architect who specialized in monuments and designed the enlargement and reconstruction of the Executive Office wing of the White House; May 16, age 85.

GUTTMACHER, ALAN F., a pioneer and international leader in family planning who served as president of the Planned Parenthood Federation of America from 1962; May 18, age 75.

HANDWERKER, NATHAN, co-founder with his wife, Ida, of Nathan's Famous, Inc., the hot-dog, fast-food restaurant chain; March 23, age 83.

HASSID, WILLIAM ZEV, a pioneer research scientist in sugar biochemistry; April 28, age 76.

HERSKOVITS, BELA, former chief cantor of Budapest and a concert artist of international reputation; May 8, age 54.

HIRSCH, GEORGES, former administrator of the Paris Opera and the Opera-Comique (1945-49 and 1956-59); May 14, age 79.

HUNTLEY, CHET, former television newscaster who, along with partner David Brinkley, created one of TV's most consistently successful news programs; March 20, age 62.

IVY, JAMES W., editor of *The Crisis* magazine (1950-66), the official publication of the National Association for the Advancement of Colored People; April 11, age 72.

JOHNSON, HOWARD A., the canon theologian of the Cathedral Church of St. John the Divine in New York City from 1954 to 1966 and authority on 19th-century Danish philosopher Sören Kierkegaard; June 12, age 58.

JONAS, FRANZ, Socialist president of Austria from 1965 until his death who was known for his administrative abilities; April 23, age 74.

KEIGHTLEY, Sir CHARLES, British general who was commander in chief of the Anglo-French invasion of Suez in 1956; June 18, age 72.

KELLY, GEORGE, playwright specializing in comedy and satire who won the 1926 Pulitzer Prize for *Craig's Wife;* June 18, age 87.

KING, ALBERTINA CHRISTINE WILLIAMS, mother of civil rights leader Dr. Martin Luther King, Jr.; June 30, age 69.

See also UNITED STATES, subtitle *Dr. King's Mother Slain.*

KLEIN, ANNE, influential American designer credited with inspiring the trend toward casual yet elegant clothes; March 18, age 51.

KUUSINEN, HERTTA ELINA, Finnish Communist leader who served in the parliament for 27 years and was one of her country's most popular politicians; March 19, age 70.

LEWIS, JOHN HENRY, light-heavyweight boxing champion of the world from 1935 to 1939; April 14, age 59.

LOWDERMILK, WALTER C., international authority on forest, land, and water conservation who served as assistant chief of the U.S. Soil Conservation Service between 1933 and 1947; May 6, age 86.

LUNN, Sir ARNOLD, ski expert who invented the slalom; June 2, age 86.

MAESTRI, ROBERT, mayor of New Orleans between 1936 and 1946 and political ally of Huey Long; May 6, age 84.

MARIE, ANDRE, French premier for two months in 1948 and many times a cabinet minister; June 12, age 76.

McGEE, FRANK, veteran newsman with the National Broadcasting Company and host of the "Today" show who won a Peabody Award in 1966 for his running coverage of Pope Paul VI's visit to New York, and an Emmy Award in 1968; April 17, age 52.

MICAUD, CHARLES A., nationally recognized authority on French and North African politics; June 23, age 64.

MILHAUD, DARIUS, prolific composer who helped overturn traditional French music in the 1920's with such works as the jazz-influenced *Création du Monde* and *Le Boeuf sur le Toit;* June 22, age 81.

MIRSKY, ALFRED, a pioneer in molecular biology who in the 1940's developed methods to isolate the genetic material of animal cells for scientific study; June 19, age 73.

MOHR, HAL, cinematographer who won two Oscars and made the first sound film, *The Jazz Singer,* starring Al Jolson; May 11, age 79.

MOLYNEUX, EDWARD H., fashion designer whose conservatively flattering clothes dominated fashion for years; March 22, age 75.

MOOREHEAD, AGNES, stage, screen, and television actress who appeared in almost 100 films; April 30, age 67.

MORTON, ALFRED H., director of the Voice of America in the early 1950's and participant in the formation of the Radio Corporation of America; April 9, age 76.

MUNCK, EBBE, Arctic explorer and Danish journalist and diplomat who was Denmark's chief spokeman in exile during the Nazi occupation; May 2, age 69.

MURRAY, MICHELE, novelist, poet, and critic who was book editor for the *National Observer;* March 14, age 40.

NOURSE, EDWIN, first chairman of the President's Council of Economic Advisers (1946-49); April 7, age 90.

PACKER, Sir FRANK, chairman of the Australian Consolidated Press, yachtsman, publisher, and broadcaster; April 30, age 67.

PAGNOL, MARCEL, French film director and playwright whose classic motion-picture trilogy *Marius* (1929), *Fanny* (1932), and *Cesar* (1946) dealt with the lives of simple people on the Marseilles waterfront; April 18, age 79.

PATE, WALTER, nonplaying captain of three victorious U.S. Davis Cup tennis teams before and after World War II; April 27, age 94.

Georges Pompidou

PINCHERLE, MARC, French music historian who wrote a catalogue of the works of the 18th-century Italian composer Antonio Vivaldi; June 20, age 86.

POMPIDOU, GEORGES, president of France since 1969; April 2, age 62.

See also FRANCE in this section.

PROUTY, CHARLES, Yale University professor and a leading Shakespeare scholar; May 10, age 64.

RAGINSKY, BERNARD, authority in psychosomatic medicine who developed the psychotherapy technique called sensory hypnoplasty; April 26, age 72.

RAPER, JOHN, chairman of the Harvard University biology department and a world authority on the reproduction of fungi; May 21, age 62.

RIEFLER, WINFIELD, member of the Federal Reserve Board (1947-59) who played a major role in the evolution of U.S. monetary policy; April 5, age 77.

RODIN, GIL, arranger for many of the early swing bands and winner of Emmy and Grammy awards; June 17, age 64.

RUBEY, WILLIAM W., noted geologist with the U.S. Geological Survey (1924-60); April 12, age 75.

SADUN, ELVIO H., internationally recognized authority on parasitology, particularly parasite infection of humans; April 24, age 56.

SANTOS, EDUARDO, former. president of Colombia and one of the most famous journalists in Latin America; March 27, age 86.

SCHOENSTEIN, PAUL, winner of the Pulitzer Prize for local reporting in 1946 and managing editor of the now-defunct New York *Journal-American* (1956-66); April 14, age 71.

SECUNDA, SHOLOM, composer of popular and liturgical music; June 3, age 79.

SHUTE, DENNY, last golfer to win the Professional Golfers Association championship two years in a row (1936-37); May 13, age 69.

SIMONDS, GUY G., leading Canadian field commander in World War II; May 15, age 71.

SULLIVAN, ELLIOTT, stage and screen actor who dramatically defied the House Un-American Activities Committee in 1955; June 2, age 66.

THOMPSON, HELEN M., chief staff executive of the American Symphony League (1950-70) and one of the foremost arts lobbyists in the country; June 25, age 66.

TOPPING, DAN, co-owner of the New York Yankees (1945-65) during their heyday, in which they won 15 American League baseball pennants and 10 world championships; May 18, age 61.

TORRES, JAIME, director general of the United Nations Education, Scientific, and Cultural Organization (1948-52) who was called the father of modern Mexican education; May 13, age 72.

TROCHTA, STEPAN CARDINAL, Czechoslovakian cardinal sent to prison in 1954 for "espionage for the Vatican," a charge which was cancelled in 1968, allowing Trochta to return to office; April 6, age 68.

WAHL, JEAN, existential philosopher and poet who counted Jean-Paul Sartre among his students; June 19, age 88.

WINKFIELD, JIMMY, turn-of-the-century black jockey who rode two Kentucky Derby winners in a row; March 23, age 91.

ZHUKOV, GEORGI, Soviet military leader who led the Red Army into Berlin during World War II; June 18, age 77.

See also ZHUKOV, GEORGI KONSTANTINOVICH, in your encyclopedia.

Portugal. Rebel military forces seized control of Portugal on April 25. A seven-man "junta of national salvation" pledged to end 48 years of authoritarian rule and to bring democracy to the nation and peace to its African territories, where guerrillas had been fighting government troops since the early 1960's.

About 60 to 70 young officers reportedly organized and carried out the coup; the revolt by a garrison in March (see PORTUGAL in the first section) had been premature but had no major effect on the progress of plans for the revolt. Rebel forces quickly seized key installations in Lisbon and four other cities. There was little fighting; the London *Times* reported a total of 10 deaths, including policemen who resisted and bystanders inadvertently shot.

Premier Marcello Caetano handed over power to General António de Spínola—who had earlier been dismissed for urging a political settlement in Africa—"so that the government would not fall in the streets." Spínola was given a hero's wel-

Rebel Troops rolled into Lisbon, overthrew the government, and promised to bring democracy to Portugal. General António de Spínola, *below*, earlier dismissed for urging a political settlement in Africa, became provisional president.

Leaders of the Left. A May Day throng greeted white-haired Communist party leader Alvaro Cunhal and (on Cunhal's right) Socialist leader Mario Soares, both of whom were returning from exile. As foreign minister in the new government, Soares sought a negotiated settlement in Africa. Cunhal, appointed minister without portfolio, sought to dampen labor unrest.

come by the populace when he arrived to negotiate the premier's surrender.

The New Government

The junta members promised that within a year there would be free elections for both a national assembly and a new president. Spínola was proclaimed provisional president by the junta on May 15. He announced a 15-man cabinet that included three Socialists, two Communists, and other members of the left and center. He said he would give up the presidency after elections and "withdraw again to the armed forces."

The new premier was Adelino da Palma Carlos, a liberal law professor who had been banned from teaching and public office by the old government. Mario Soares, leader of the Socialist party, became foreign minister. Alvaro Cunhal, Communist party leader, was named minister without portfolio. Lieutenant Col-

onel Mario Firmino Miguel, an organizer of the coup, was named defense minister. The key interior ministry, which controls the police, was given to a centrist, Joaquim Magalhaes Motta.

Freedom of speech was guaranteed by the new government, news censorship was lifted, except for disclosure of military secrets, and freedom of assembly, formation of trade unions, and formation of political associations were allowed for the first time in more than 40 years. Hundreds of political exiles began returning to the country; political prisoners were released and their places in jail taken by members of the political police, which the junta abolished.

Among the first to return were Soares, who had spent five years in exile in Paris, and Cunhal, who had spent 14 years in Moscow and Prague. Both received tumultuous welcomes. The Portuguese Democratic Movement, a coalition of Socialists, Communists, and Christian Democrats, was formed.

According to a New York *Times* article published May 7, the Communists had emerged as the strongest and best-organized political force in the new Portugal. During the long years of dictatorship in which any political activity not sponsored by the government was illegal and dangerous, the Communists had maintained their structure and discipline, with thousands of party activists in factories, offices, and schools. The party said it would work within a parliamentary system and attacked extreme leftist groups as "adventurists."

Most organized political groups were leftist. The centrists were composed mainly of professionals such as lawyers, professors, and editors, who were tolerated by the old regime as a not very aggressive opposition. Several royalist groups declared themselves in favor of the monarchy that was ousted in 1910, but in extremely liberal, even leftist, terms.

The only resistance to the coup was offered by the secret police, widely known by its former acronym, PIDE. There had been about 3,000 members, of which about 900 were arrested. The police had been hated for their activities, which included torture, and many PIDE members had to be rescued from the vengeance of street crowds.

In addition to the regular agents, PIDE employed thousands of informers in schools, factories, and government offices. It also operated abroad; one of its most notorious operations was the murder in 1965 of exiled opposition leader Humberto Delgado, who was kidnapped or lured across the border from Spain.

Caetano and President Americo Thomaz were arrested and sent to the island of Madeira; on May 20 they were flown to exile in Brazil. The decision to exile them was made by the junta over the objections of the leftist members of the cabinet, who wanted them tried for crimes committed by the police.

The African Territories

Portugal, a nation of about 35,000 square miles and 9 million inhabitants, rules African territories comprising 800,-000 square miles and 14 million people. An army of 160,000 troops secures the three territories—Angola, Mozambique, and Portuguese Guinea. The war against

Settling Old Scores. Soldiers rescued members of the old regime's hated political police—PIDE—from the vengeance of street crowds. PIDE's activities included torture, and it employed thousands of informers in schools, factories, and government offices.

guerrillas claims the lives of some 250 Portuguese each year. (See also AFRICA, first section, 1973.)

The officers who organized the coup expressed the view—widespread in the army—that the war in Africa was unwinnable. Many were of the opinion that Portugal would have to recognize the independence of the colonies. Spínola, however, was seeking to keep the African territories in a federation loosely linked with Portugal, and the official position was that the future of the colonies should be determined in referendums.

On May 6, the junta offered a cease-fire in Africa. Five days later, a junta spokesman said the liberation movements had been asked to become legitimate political parties and seek their demands by peaceful and democratic means. Until they laid down their arms, he said, Portuguese troops would continue to be sent to the territories to fight. (On May 2, however, an amnesty was declared for the thousands of men who had deserted the armed forces or evaded the draft to avoid fighting in the colonies, if they reported promptly to the authorities.)

The African colonies are symbols of Portugal's rich past, dating back to the voyages organized by Prince Henry the Navigator in the 15th century and the circumnavigation of Africa by Vasco da Gama. Independence could mean the sudden return of hundreds of thousands of Portuguese settlers, with resulting social

War in Africa. *Above,* Portuguese solders board a troop train in Angola to fight guerrillas in the interior. *Below,* rebels in Portuguese Guinea.

and economic problems. Africa sends cheap raw materials to Portugal at an annual profit to Portugal of well over $100 million. And many Portuguese believe that, without its colonies, the nation would be too weak to stand up to other European nations, particularly neighboring Spain, which once ruled Portugal.

On the other hand, economic and political analysts in Lisbon said no economic catastrophe would befall Portugal as a result of the end of the empire. The nation's trade had become oriented toward other European nations rather than Africa, and membership in the Common Market was considered likely under a democratic government. Military expenditures, 40 per cent of the national budget, could be shifted to schools, hospitals, and public housing. Leftists said that the Portuguese corporations which had made profits in Africa had never contributed much in taxes, and that the dividends were largely confined to the rich.

Portuguese Guinea. This small territory has only 2,000 white settlers. PAIGC, the guerrilla movement, controls 75 per cent of the area, and 84 nations have established diplomatic relations with what is called the nation of Guinea-Bissau. Soares offered a cease-fire, to be followed by self-determination through a referendum leading to independence, but PAIGC demanded recognition of the colony's independence as a precondition to a cease-fire. Also complicating negotiations was the guerrilla organization's claim to the Cape Verde Islands, the site of Portuguese air and naval bases.

Mozambique. This African east-coast colony has 220,000 native whites and about 8 million blacks. Exports of sugar, cotton, and coal to Portugal have not been sufficient in value to match investment by the home country. However, the Cabora Bassa Dam, a $500-million project to be completed in 1974, is the biggest such project in Africa.

Frelimo, the Mozambique Liberation Front, conducts extensive guerrilla warfare in the northern part of the territory. The organization rejected a cease-fire until Portugal accepted the territory's independence in principle. A Portuguese government minister announced May 21 that a referendum would be held within a year and that "There is no doubt that the majority of the people . . . will choose independence."

Angola. This territory on Africa's western coast is Portugal's largest and most prosperous. It contains several hundred thousand whites and perhaps 6 million blacks. A Gulf Oil installation in the Cabinda enclave produces 7.5 million tons of oil annually, most of which is exported to Portugal and more than compensates for the Arab-imposed embargo on Portugal. Angola also exports iron ore, diamonds, and coffee. The territory is considered more secure than Mozambique or Portuguese Guinea because the guerrillas are divided into several factions.

The real goal of negotiations, some Portuguese officials said, was to get the best possible terms for white settlers and to maintain the territories' economic and cultural ties with Portugal. Some officials warned that the troops would not fight indefinitely.

Economic Problems

Portugal is the poorest nation in western Europe—indeed the poorest in all Europe except for Albania. Nearly 2 million people have violated restrictions against emigration to find jobs in other countries or to escape the mandatory four-year tour of service in the army, which usually includes service in Africa. In some villages, almost all the men are absent for long periods—working in France or West Germany. Remittances from workers abroad are the nation's leading source of foreign currency.

Portugal's workers, free to demonstrate and walk off their jobs for the first time in 50 years, demanded a 40-hour work week and pay raises in excess of the rising cost of living. (The inflation rate was 30 per cent in 1973.) More than 60,000 industrial workers were reported on strike May 20.

Officials announced a wage-price freeze on May 25, and union leaders appealed to workers to refrain from strikes pending further talks. Communist leaders were urging workers to support the government and stay on the job.

Pulitzer Prizes. For the second year in a row, Pulitzer Prizes were awarded to national reporters involved in unravelling the Watergate scandal. The 58th annual awards included a national-reporting prize for James R. Polk of the Washington *Star-News* for stories which revealed, among other things, that financier Robert Vesco had secretly contributed $200,000 to the 1972 Nixon campaign. Jack White of the Providence *Journal-Bulletin* also received a national award for his report on President Nixon's 1970 and 1971 tax returns, disclosures which eventually led to back-tax payments by the president.

The awards, which carry a $1,000 prize for each recipient, were announced May 6 by the Board of Trustees of Columbia University and were marked—not for the first time—by dissension between the trustees, the 14-member advisory board, and the award juries. Some trustees were said to have challenged the desirability of giving awards for acts such as disclosing Internal Revenue Service records, which are supposed to be confidential.

Another rift occurred when the advisory board rejected the fiction jury's recommendation that the fiction award be presented to Thomas Pynchon for *Gravity's Rainbow*. As a result, no fiction award was made. No prize was given for drama, either.

The gold medal for meritorious service by a newspaper went to *Newsday* of Long Island, New York, for a six-month study leading to a series tracing heroin traffic from poppies in Turkey through processing in France and finally to addicts in the New York City area. New York *Daily News* reporter William Sherman won the award for investigative local reporting for a series on abuses of the Medicaid program. Hedrick Smith of the New York *Times* was awarded the prize for international reporting for his coverage of the Soviet Union and eastern European nations.

Robert Lowell, whom many consider to be the most important English-language poet since T. S. Eliot, won the poetry prize for his collection *The Dolphin*. It was Lowell's second Pulitzer.

Other prizes included the following:

Letters. History—*The Americans: The Democratic Experience,* by Daniel J. Boorstin, the third volume of a series.

Biography—*O'Neill, Son and Artist,* by Louis Sheaffer, who had worked 16 years on the two-volume life of playwright Eugene O'Neill.

General nonfiction—*The Denial of Death,* by the late anthropologist-author Ernest Becker.

Music. *Nocturno,* by Donald Martino, a member of the New England Conservatory of Music. The piece is for chamber orchestra.

Special citation in music—Roger Sessions, 77, for his distinguished composing career.

Journalism. General local reporting—Arthur M. Petacque and Hugh F. Hough, of the Chicago *Sun-Times,* for their story charging that the 1966 murder of Senator Charles Percy's daughter was committed by a man now serving a penitentiary sentence. Upon publication, the case was reopened.

Editorial writing—F. Gilman Spencer, editor of the Trenton *Trentonian,* for a campaign attacking scandals in New Jersey state government.

Editorial cartooning—Paul Szep of the Boston *Globe,* for all his work in his five-per-week series.

Spot-news photography—Anthony K. Roberts, a free-lance photographer, for his series on a kidnapping attempt in Hollywood, California.

Feature photography—Slava Veder of the Associated Press, for a picture of a reunited Vietnam prisoner of war and his family.

Commentary—Edwin A. Roberts, Jr., for his weekly column in *The National Observer,* "Mainstreams."

Criticism—Emily Genauer, art critic for the Newsday Syndicate.

Pulitzer Prize Recipients. *Clockwise from top left:* Daniel Boorstin, senior historian of the Smithsonian Institution; Louis Sheaffer, chosen for his life of playwright Eugene O'Neill; and Donald Martino, honored for *Nocturno,* a piece for chamber orchestra.

Race Relations. Twenty years after the Supreme Court's landmark ruling against segregated school systems, black civil rights leaders and educators were evaluating the progress of two decades and encountering new obstacles to integration in education.

On May 17, 1954, the Supreme Court concluded the case of Oliver Brown *et al.* v. Board of Education of Topeka, Kansas, by declaring that "separate educational facilities are inherently unequal." Passage of the Civil Rights Act of 1964 enabled the Justice Department to enforce the Brown decision by withholding federal funds from segregated districts. In the meantime, other court cases had helped to close off loopholes and refine the meaning of the original desegregation decision.

Integration in education made striking advances in the South during the following decade. In 1964, the proportion of black children in classes with whites in the 11 states of the Confederacy was only 1 per cent. Eight years later, 46 per cent of the Deep South's black children attended predominantly white schools.

Although violent confrontations between some local school boards and federal officials made national headlines, quiet acceptance of the law was the more common reaction in the South. Integra-

tion was accomplished smoothly in such communities as Tampa, Florida. In Yazoo City, Mississippi, where schools remained segregated as late as 1969, blacks serve on nearly all public boards and agencies and participate in a white-led organization aimed at keeping the city's white students in public schools.

Sometimes integration was encouraged by economic incentives. Jackson, Mississippi, schools were desegregated after a tractor manufacturer said he would locate a 2,000-employee plant in the city if local school difficulties were resolved.

Progress in the South has been uneven, however. Integrated schools are more common in rural areas, where black and white families often live side by side and residential patterns could not be used to justify segregation. In some cities, large numbers of white parents have emigrated to the suburbs; in Atlanta the schools flipped from 70-per-cent white to 80-per-cent black in 20 years.

Other white children—perhaps as many as 10 per cent—have been placed by their parents in private "academies" at an annual cost of $600 or more per pupil. At least 1,000 of these segregated schools were set up after 1954; their precise number and status have been difficult to determine at any one time, since schools are

Racial Integration in Elementary and Secondary Schools

| | | Total | | % of black pupils in schools that were: | | | |
	Total Pupils	Black Pupils	Majority White	50-100% Black	80-100% Black	99-100% Black	All Black
Continental U.S.							
1970	44,910,403	6,712,789	33.1	66.9	49.4	28.0	14.0
1972	44,646,625	6,796,238	36.3	63.7	45.2	25.1	11.2
32 Northern and Western States							
1970	30,131,132	3,188,231	27.6	72.4	56.6	29.2	11.7
1972	29,916,241	3,250,806	28.3	71.7	55.9	29.9	10.9
5 Border States and D.C.							
1970	3,724,867	640,667	28.7	71.3	61.9	45.7	24.1
1972	3,742,703	650,828	31.8	68.2	59.8	42.8	23.6
11 Southern States							
1970	11,054,403	2,883,891	40.3	59.7	38.6	22.7	14.4
1972	10,987,680	2,894,603	46.3	53.7	29.9	15.7	8.7

Source: Office for Civil Rights, Department of Health, Education, and Welfare

School Desegregation since 1954 has been marked by uneven progress. *Top,* one of a limited number of black pupils from Boston bused to white suburban schools. In Chicago, *center, de facto* segregation results in nearly 90 per cent of black children attending black-majority schools. *Bottom,* parents in Mississippi enroll children in a new white private school to avoid the Supreme Court's desegregation orders.

continually opening and closing, and gaining or losing accreditation.

Where integration has succeeded in the South, it is usually accompanied by strong classroom discipline and favorable leadership from the business community, as well as from school officials. "Over all, it's a picture that is at once encouraging, discouraging, and terribly confusing," said Mel Leventhal of Jackson, a civil rights lawyer for the NAACP. "What works great in one place sometimes will fail miserably in another—and for no apparent reason. There just aren't many fixed rules and set formulas. Jackson has one of the most desegregated public school systems anywhere in the country, North or South. It also has one of the strongest private-academy systems."

Gains made in desegregating Southern schools were largely offset by growing *de facto* segregation in the North. In 1972, only 28 per cent of black students in Northern and Western schools attended predominantly white schools, and nationally, nearly two-thirds of black pupils remain in black-majority institutions. In Columbus, Georgia, where the schools system is about one-third black, 75 per cent of the blacks go to white-majority schools. Boston, with the same proportion of black pupils, sends only 18 per cent to white schools. In many other large cities, including Chicago, Philadelphia, Detroit, and Cleveland, there are simply not enough white public-school pupils within the city limits to provide balanced integration. Washington, D.C. has only 5,000 white students in a total school population of 140,000.

Second-Generation Problems

Although *de jure,* or statutory segregation has been eliminated in most places, "second-generation" obstacles to integrated schooling have emerged, based on changing features of demography, new awareness of ethnicity, and other forms of resistance.

The *de facto* school segregation that results from residential patterns is grounded in distinctions of socio-economic class as much as race. The legal status of *de facto* segregation, which is a more ambiguous moral and judicial dilemma than the institutionalized inequality of dual school systems, has never been clarified. In the first test case involving a major Northern city, the Supreme Court ordered Denver to desegregate its entire school system. But a long-standing practice of gerrymandering Denver school districts along racial lines had blurred the distinction between *de jure* and *de facto* segregation.

The use of school busing to promote racial integration in the North has become the most emotional and political issue surrounding desegregation. (See EDUCATION in the second section, 1972.) Fist fights, bus burnings, and other violence occurred during efforts to integrate schools in Pontiac, Michigan, and other communities. In Boston, demonstrators led by former Congresswoman Louise Day Hicks rallied around the statehouse to oppose a Massachusetts law ordering cities to improve the racial balance in their schools. Nationally, 47 per cent of schoolchildren ride buses to school, but only 3 per cent are bused for purposes of desegregation. But opposition to busing is widespread among both whites and blacks, who feel it is a needless inconvenience that disrupts their children's education.

Since many cities cannot be desegregated by any amount of busing within the city limits, a few school systems have proposed plans for integration across a broad metropolitan area including both the central city and its suburbs. But parents (including some blacks) who escaped the inner city for the better schools and safer streets of the suburbs have been reluctant to return their children to the environment they had fled.

The Supreme Court ruled in a 1971 North Carolina case that busing could be used to further the cause of racial integration, but it never directly faced the issue of busing across political boundaries as would occur under the "metropolitan" concept. A Richmond, Virginia, case testing the merger of city and suburban school districts was left unresolved in 1973, when the Court split 4-4. (One judge disqualified himself as a former member of the Richmond and state of Virginia boards of education.) The Supreme Court was expected to rule in the summer of 1974 on a similar metropolitan merger planned for greater Detroit. "There's a kind of moratorium," said Herbert Hill, national labor director of the NAACP. "School districts are waiting on the Detroit decision."

Another factor slowing the drive for school integration has been a heightened awareness of black identity and culture, often accompanied by a desire for racial separatism and neighborhood control of urban schools. Many black leaders have come to believe that the education of black children should be upgraded where they are, in the inner city, rather than by busing them to a hostile white environment. They voice concern over the effects of forced integration on the black neighborhood and community.

Ruby Martin, a black woman who formerly directed HEW's Office for Civil Rights, asserts that school integration has become a low priority for her: "It is easy to put black kids in a white school system. But just to integrate will simply compound the problems we have and polarize the community more. I would not close a black school without going into the community to find out what will be the impact."

Commenting on the changes of the past 20 years, federal judge Constance Baker Motley (who represented James Meredith in his attempt to desegregate the University of Mississippi) remarked, "It seems today Brown has little practical relevance to central-city blacks. Its psychological and legal relevance has already had its

effect. Central-city blacks seem more concerned now with the political and economic power accruing from the new black concentrations than they do with busing to effect school desegregation." (But some black parents, perhaps a majority, welcome the opportunity to send their children to white schools, on the principle that "the green goes where the white goes.")

New forms of racial segregation have emerged in many "integrated" schools. Some black children found themselves "tracked" into ability groups containing no whites and excluded from extracurricular activities. Blacks tended to be suspended for disciplinary reasons far more often than whites, leading to "push-outs." A survey made in Little Rock, Arkansas, showed that 8 of every 10 students suspended were blacks, although they comprised only 40 per cent of the school population. Similarly, in Columbia, South Carolina, blacks made up only half of the student body but accounted for 75 per cent of the suspensions.

Black teachers and administrators were also "pushed out" when school systems were consolidated. Civil rights workers who studied the problem in the South estimated that at least 6,000 black teachers and principals lost their jobs and that 25,-

Busing for purposes of desegregation became the most controversial aspect of school integration. In some cities, such as Denver, *above*, pupils were bused without incident to achieve racial balance. But in other communities, busing orders generated violent resistance.

000 whites had been hired to fill positions that would otherwise have gone to blacks.

Integration and Achievement

Twenty years after Brown, both blacks and whites had become less confident that integration and academic achievement were positively correlated. The Supreme Court decision had been based in part on the belief that segregation affected the "hearts and minds" of black children "in a way unlikely ever to be undone" and that integration would improve both the self-esteem and performance of black pupils. But these assumptions were called into question as social scientists analyzed scholastic achievement and conducted "before and after" studies on the effects of integration.

The Coleman Report, an important and extensive study on equality of educational opportunity issued in 1966, concluded that variations in academic performance were more closely related to children's home backgrounds and the socio-economic status of their classmates than to anything contributed by the schools. The report thus implied that only by mixing black children with middle-class whites were educational gains likely from school integration. But this theory was considered virtually impossible to test, since few middle-class white students remained in urban public schools.

Another major study, undertaken on behalf of the U.S. Office of Education, focused on the desegregation of Southern schools. According to the findings of the "Southern Schools" report, racial makeup in the schools had little impact on achievement, although both races did somewhat less well in schools more than 70-per-cent white or 59-per-cent black. Racial tension accompanying desegregation was found to have hampered the achievement of white high-school students, but tolerant racial attitudes among white pupils were correlated with improved performance by blacks.

Several longitudinal, or before-and-after, studies suggested that modest educational gains had been achieved following school desegregation in some cities. In Evanston, Illinois, a 16-per-cent-black suburb of Chicago, schools were integrated smoothly in 1967. Researchers for the Educational Testing Service who examined students annually over a period of four years found no significant gains or losses, except for improvement in mathematics for both races.

In both Berkeley and Riverside, California, longitudinal studies made in the late 1960's suggested a slight narrowing of the performance gap between black and white students. In Riverside, black and Chicano students desegregated before the second grade advanced as quickly as whites in performance, although the gap was not closed. Whites, who were in the majority, did not appear to have suffered from integration. In Berkeley, where integration was accompanied by curricular innovations in 1968, the normally widening gap between whites and blacks was reported as being slowly reduced, especially in the lower grades.

But other scholars came to different conclusions. David J. Armor, writing in *The Public Interest* (Summer, 1972) asserted that the results of "induced integration" in five Northern cities (Ann Arbor, Riverside, Boston, Hartford, and White Plains) have not been promising. He contended that integration had accentuated racial identity and done little to help academic performance. On the basis of his research, Armor concluded that "massive busing for purposes of improving student achievement and interracial harmony is not effective and should not be adopted at this time." Other observers, such as Professor Thomas F. Pettigrew of Harvard University, take the view that the success or failure of school integration is dependent not merely on academic achievement, but also on the quality of interracial interaction in the schools.

Beyond the moral issue of integration, its social costs and benefits are difficult to evaluate. No one has determined the conditions under which integration "works" best. Yet the legacy of the Brown decision can be measured—not in school examination scores—but in the changed attitudes of whites toward segregation. In the words of NAACP's Roy Wilkins, "The whole thing has been flipped over. It used to be the right thing to do. Now it's wrong. That's no mean accomplishment."

Summit Meeting in Moscow. President Nixon and Secretary of State Kissinger joined Soviet leaders in a toast after signing arms agreements in the Kremlin. The United States and Soviet Union agreed to restrict underground nuclear tests and the deployment of ABM systems.

Soviet Union. President Nixon flew to Moscow on June 27 for a summit meeting with Soviet Communist party leader Leonid Brezhnev—the third annual meeting between the two. Arms control was the main topic of negotiations. Two agreements on armaments and arms testing were announced in the final communiqué, issued July 3.

Nixon and Brezhnev signed a treaty prohibiting underground nuclear tests exceeding the force of 150 kilotons (the equivalent of 150,000 tons of TNT), effective March 31, 1976. This agreement extended the scope of the Moscow Treaty of 1963, in which the United States, the Soviet Union, and Great Britain agreed to halt nuclear arms tests in the atmosphere, in space, and underwater. (See also ARMAMENTS, subtitle *Nuclear Testing,* in this section.) The New York *Times* reported that, in addition, Brezhnev had agreed in principle to permit on-site inspection of explosions intended for peaceful purposes of nuclear energy.

Two published protocols limited each nation to a single deployment area for antiballistic missile (ABM) systems. A 1972 agreement had limited each country to building ABM systems in two areas.

No new agreement was reached, however, concerning the broader question of limiting offensive strategic missiles. In 1972, the two leaders agreed to limit the number of land-based and submarine-based intercontinental ballistic missiles for five years. The agreement left the Soviets in the lead in the total number of long-range missiles and total nuclear payload. But the United States had developed multiple independently targeted reentry vehicles (MIRV's) that could be carried on a single missile and it also enjoyed a long lead in warheads. (See ARMAMENTS in this section.) The Soviet Union has since developed its own MIRV capacity.

In their negotiations, Nixon and Brezhnev were unable to agree on new restrictions on the number of long-range missiles that each country could deploy or on limits to the development or deployment of MIRV technology. The communiqué merely called for a new agreement to replace the five-year one due to expire in 1977. Such an agreement would run until 1985 and would govern quality as well as quantity—the kind of nuclear weaponry as well as the number of missile launchers and warheads to be deployed.

In other accords signed during the summit meeting, the two governments agreed upon the following:

• Opening of additional consulates in two or three cities, with, as a first step, agreement in principle to establish a Soviet consulate in New York City and a U.S. consulate in Kiev. (Currently, the Soviet Union maintains consulates in Washington, D.C., and San Francisco, while the United States has consular offices in Moscow and Leningrad.)

• A 10-year economic agreement. It generally followed the terms of the three-year trade accord signed in 1972 but provided administrative machinery for trade. No new commitments were made concerning specific trade deals under discussion. The issue of lower tariffs for Soviet goods, which had been blocked in Congress by critics of Soviet curbs on emigration, was not mentioned.

• Scientific cooperation in the fields of housing, energy, and research on artificial hearts. There was also an agreement to begin discussions on controlling the use of environment-modification techniques—such as rainmaking and defoliation—as a means of warfare.

President Nixon arrived in Moscow after conferring with European leaders at NATO headquarters in Brussels. After the economic and scientific agreements, Nixon and Brezhnev flew on June 29 to Brezhnev's villa at the Black Sea resort of Yalta. (Yalta had been the site of a World War II Big Three summit conference in 1945 attended by Franklin D. Roosevelt, Winston Churchill, and Josef Stalin.)

On July 1, Brezhnev returned to Moscow while Nixon visited Minsk, capital of the Byelorussian S.S.R. This city of about a million inhabitants, almost totally destroyed in World War II, was celebrating its 30th anniversary of liberation from German occupation.

Nixon delivered a speech over Soviet radio and television on July 2. He said the two countries were weaving a fabric of cooperation that would give both a positive stake in peace. In toasts at a dinner on the eve of Nixon's departure, the president emphasized his intention to invite

Moscow Residents gather inside a department store to watch President Nixon deliver a live television broadcast to the Soviet people. He said the two countries were cooperating to give both a positive stake in peace.

Monaco Grand Prix. Ronnie Peterson won the oldest and most famous of the Grand Prix races, driving the 78 laps through Monte Carlo's streets at an average speed of 80 miles an hour.

Brezhnev to the United States in 1975 to insure the regularity of annual meetings between leaders of the two countries.

Before Nixon's departure, the press revealed that he was suffering from thrombophlebitis—the inflammation of veins and formation of blood clots—in his left leg. This malady carried with it the threat of a blood clot moving from the leg to a lung, with potentially fatal consequences. Dr. Walter Tkach, the president's physician, said after Nixon's return to the United States that the period of danger to the president's health had passed.

News reports by all three U.S. television networks were blocked in transmission one evening by Soviet authorities. Two of the transmissions reported on the hunger strike of physicist Andrei Sakharov in protest against the detention of political prisoners in Russia. The third reported on efforts by the police to prevent Jewish scholars from holding a seminar in Moscow on their attempts to emigrate.

Sports and Athletics. Among the outstanding sporting events during the second quarter of 1974 were the following:

Automobile Racing

Johnny Rutherford, surging from 25th starting position, won the Indianapolis 500 on May 26, covering the 200-lap course in a McLaren at an average speed of 158.-589 miles per hour. A. J. Foyt, who led for much of the way, had to drop out with a damaged engine; Bobby Unser finished second.

The 24-hour endurance race in Le Mans, France, was won in June by the Mantra team for the third straight time. Henri Pescarolo and Gerard Larrousse covered 2,862 miles at an average speed of 119 miles per hour.

In Grand Prix racing during the spring, Austria's Niki Lauda won the Spanish and Dutch events; Jody Scheckter of South Africa the Swedish race; Ronnie Peterson of Sweden the Monaco event; and Emerson Fittipaldi of Brazil the Belgian race.

Baseball

Henry Aaron became the leading home-run hitter in baseball history on April 8, when he blasted his 715th major-league career homer before a hometown crowd in Atlanta Stadium, eclipsing the record set by Babe Ruth.

Basketball

The Boston Celtics won their 12th National Basketball Association championship in 18 years on May 12, defeating the Milwaukee Bucks, 102-87, in the deciding game of the best-of-seven series. Celtic forward John Havlicek, who averaged 26.2 points per game in the series, was selected the most valuable player.

The New York Nets defeated the Utah Stars 111-100 on May 10 to win the American Basketball Association championship, four games to one. Net forward Julius Erving was named the most valuable player of the series.

Boxing

Light Heavyweight. Bob Foster retained his title in June before hometown fans in Albuquerque, New Mexico, fighting Jorge Ahumada of Argentina to a draw in their 15-round bout.

Middleweight. Rodrigo Valdes of Colombia won the World Boxing Council championship in Monte Carlo in May with a seventh-round knockout of Bennie Briscoe of Philadelphia. The council had stripped Carlos Monzon of Argentina of his title for failing to defend it within a stipulated time period.

Lightweight. Suzuki Ishimatsu of Japan knocked out Rudolfo Gonzales of Mexico in the eighth round of their Tokyo bout April 11 to win the World Boxing Council championship.

Flyweight. Chartchai Chionoi of Thailand, the World Boxing Association champion, retained his title April 27 with a 15-round split decision over Fritz Chervet of Switzerland in Zurich, Switzerland. Enraged Swiss fans stormed the ring when the decision was announced, and Chart-

chai was knocked down by a bottle as he was being hustled to the dressing room after his unpopular victory.

Football

Sweeping rules changes were made by the National Football League on April 15 in an effort to enliven the game. One new rule was intended to discourage field goals by returning the goal posts to the end line of the end zone, as in college football; missed field goals were to be returned to the line of scrimmage if beyond the 20-yard line. Forward passing was to be encouraged by restricting blocking of potential receivers. Kickoffs were to be made from the 35-yard line instead of the 40-yard line. Sudden-death overtime periods would be played in an effort to reduce the number of ties.

Golf

Gary Player of South Africa won the Masters tournament on April 14 with a 72-hole score of 278 over the Augusta, Georgia, course. He first won the Masters in 1961 and remains the only foreigner to do so.

Hale Irwin won the U.S. Open on June 16 in Mamaroneck, New York, with a score of 287 over the tough Winged Foot Golf Club course. He finished two strokes ahead of Forrest Fezler.

Curtis Strange of Wake Forest won the individual NCAA title and the team title for his college with an eagle on the par-five 18th hole in Santee, California, in June. The women's titles were won by Mary Budke of Oregon State and by San Diego State.

Trevor Homer of England won the British Amateur tournament in Muirfield, Scotland, in June, defeating Jim Gabrielsen of Atlanta, two-up. Homer had also won the tournament in 1972.

Sandra Haynie won the Ladies Professional Golf Association championship on June 23 in Sutton, Massachusetts. She scored 288 to win the tournament for the second time.

Handball

Steve Sandler regained the national AAU one-wall title that he had won six times previously by defeating Al Torres, 21-11, 21-14, in Brooklyn, New York, in June.

Henry Aaron smashed home run number 715 in Atlanta on April 8, breaking the record for major-league career homers that had been set by Babe Ruth.

Women in Sports

One effect of the women's liberation movement has been to bring about greater participation of women and girls at all levels of American sports. Whereas in 1971, 300,000 high-school girls competed in organized athletics, by 1973 the number had passed 800,000. Women are demanding—and getting—a larger share of funding for athletics by citing Title IX of the U.S. Education Amendments of 1972, which forbids sex discrimination in the programs of any institution receiving federal funds. Judy Wenning, sports coordinator for the National Organization of Women (NOW) says, "Women are free now to express their competitiveness."

In 1973, *Sports Illustrated* said that 50,000 men and probably less than 50 women had college athletic scholarships; it estimated that only 5 per cent of high school and 1 per cent of college athletic funds were spent on women's sports. But the situation is changing rapidly. UCLA, for example—long a sports powerhouse —has upped its annual sports budget for women from $60,000 to $180,000 and is making plans to spend half a million annually by the fall of 1979. The colleges are offering a growing number of athletic scholarships to women, and some are recruiting women athletes vigorously.

On the professional level, television coverage of women's events has increased, and prize money is up. In 1971, Billie Jean King became the first female athlete to earn more than $100,000 in prize money; in 1973, five women tennis players won more than $100,000.

Women are competing in sports previously thought suitable only for men. For example, 80 coeds signed up for women's crew at the University of Washington, and almost as many girls turned out in Dallas to take part in a boxing program. There is a women's professional football league, and women have long taken part in the violent sport of roller derby.

Mixed competition has drawn the most controversy. Girls mature earlier than boys, and a number are playing on Little League baseball teams despite resistance by some coaches and parents. A court in New Jersey has ruled that Little League teams must admit qualified girls.

After puberty, the average boy tends to be stronger than the average girl because of a higher proportion of muscle to fatty tissue. But mixed competition in non-contact sports is now permitted in most high school and collegiate programs. Laurel Brassey, a member of two U.S. women's volleyball teams, won a starting position on San Diego State's men's national championship team. Charlise Brown shattered a 122-year-old Yale sports tradition by joining its previously all-male diving team.

Jockeys Robyn Smith and Mary Bacon are competing successfully with men at leading race tracks. About 60 other female jockeys ride at various smaller tracks.

Hale Irwin won the U.S. Open by two strokes, with a 72-hole total of 287 at the Winged Foot Golf Club in Mamaroneck, New York.

Hockey

The Philadelphia Flyers defeated the Boston Bruins, 1-0, on May 19 to win the Stanley Cup—the National Hockey League's championship series—four games to two. Flyer goalie Bernie Parent was voted the outstanding player in the series.

Philadelphia and Boston had led their respective divisions during the 78-game regular season. Phil Esposito of Boston led the league in goals scored (68) and total points (145). Bobby Orr of Boston led in assists (90).

The Houston Aeros defeated the Chicago Cougars, 6-2, to win the World Hockey Association championship on May 19. Forty-six-year-old Gordie Howe, long-time Detroit Red Wings star who came out of retirement to play for the Aeros, was named the league's most valuable player; a son, Mark Howe, 19, was named rookie of the year.

The Soviet Union won the world amateur championship on April 20 in Helsinki, Finland. Czechoslovakia finished second in the tournament and Sweden was third.

Horse Racing

Cannonade won the Kentucky Derby in Louisville on May 4, pulling out from a record 23-horse field to win U.S. thoroughbred racing's most prestigious event for three-year-olds. But Little Current, who finished fifth, won the Preakness Stakes on May 18, coming from behind to forge to a seven-length victory in near-record time. Little Current also won the Belmont Stakes—the final leg of the Triple Crown —by seven lengths on June 8. Cannonade finished third in both the Preakness and Belmont.

Skiing

Hugo Nindl won a $50,000 bonus for having amassed the most points on the Benson & Hedges pro tour, which ended in April. In addition to the bonus, he earned $89,200 in prize money during the 1973-74 tour.

Tennis

John Newcombe of Australia defeated 17-year-old Bjorn Borg of Sweden, 4-6, 6-3, 6-3, 6-2, to win the $50,000 first prize in the World Championship of Tennis in Dallas, Texas, on May 12.

Stanford University won the NCAA championship in June in Los Angeles. John Whitlinger of Stanford defeated teammate Chico Hagey to win the singles title and then paired with Jim Delaney to win the doubles.

Team tennis made its debut on May 6, with professional teams representing 16 major U.S. and Canadian cities. Each team consisted of three men and three women, with each match consisting of two women's-singles sets, two men's-singles sets, and two mixed-doubles sets. With a few major exceptions—Stan Smith, Ilie Nastase, Bjorn Borg, Arthur Ashe, Virginia Wade, and Chris Evert—all the world-class professional players signed on.

Track and Field

Neil Cusack, a 22-year-old Irishman, won the Boston Marathon on April 15 with the third fastest performance in the 78-year history of the race—2 hours, 13 minutes, and 39 seconds for the 26-mile, 385-yard event.

Tennessee upset defending champion UCLA, 60 to 56, to win the NCAA track-and-field championship in Austin, Texas, in June.

Ivory Crockett ran the 100-yard dash in nine seconds flat to set a new world record in Knoxville, Tennessee, in May.

Faina Melnik of the Soviet Union set a new women's world record for the discus throw with a toss of 229 feet, 4 inches, in Prague, Czechoslovakia, in May.

Rick Wohlhuter broke his own 880-yard world record with a time of 1:44.1 minutes in Eugene, Oregon, in June.

Poland's Irena Szewinska set a new women's world record in Potsdam, East Germany, in June with a time of 22 seconds for the 200-meter dash. A week later, she set a new world record for the 400-meter run with a time of 49.9 seconds in Warsaw.

Steve Williams equaled the world record for the 100 meters on June 21 in Los Angeles with a time of 9.9 seconds.

Theater. *The River Niger,* a drama about a black serviceman returning home from the armed forces, was awarded the Tony as the best Broadway play of the 1973-74 season. (The play, which opened in 1972 in the East Village, moved to Broadway a year later.) *Raisin* was voted the best musical of the season. The 28th annual Antoinette Perry Awards were presented on April 21 at the Shubert Theater.

Tonys for best performances in a drama went to Michael Moriarty in *Find Your Way Home* and Colleen Dewhurst in *A Moon for the Misbegotten.* The top awards for acting in a musical went to Christopher Plummer in *Cyrano* and Virginia Capers in *Raisin.*

José Quintero received a Tony for his direction of *A Moon for the Misbegotten,* and Harold Prince was honored for his direction of *Candide.* Both plays, which were revivals, received special awards. Other special awards went to the one-woman shows given by Bette Midler and Liza Minnelli, and to Peter Cook and Dudley Moore, stars of *Good Evening,* a series of sketches. Cook and Moore were honored for their "unique contribution to the theater of comedy."

Among the plays that appeared in New York City during the 1973-74 season were the following:

Comedies and Dramas

An American Millionaire is a comedy about a rich young man unable to consummate his third marriage because he is subject to fainting fits. The play was written by Murray Schisgal, and Paul Sorvino played the millionaire.

The Au Pair Man, written by Hugh Leonard, is a two-character comedy set in London. Julie Harris and Charles Durning performed.

Bad Habits consisted of two one-act plays by Terrence McNally set in exclusive nursing homes. In one home, for the unhappily married of all sexes, Dr. Jason Pepper profers marital guidance. In the other, Dr. Toynbee, a saint of a man, dispenses dope. Robert Drivas directed.

Boom Boom Room, by David Rabe, portrays a go-go girl seeking a different way of life. Madeline Kahn played the girl

Tony Awards. Best musical actor and actress supporting awards were presented, above, to Janie Sell for her performance in *Over Here,* and Tommy Tune for his performance in *Seesaw.* The best Broadway play of the 1973-74 season was judged to be *The River Niger,* right.

and Joseph Papp directed.

Find Your Way Home, by John Hopkins, depicts a love triangle—a married man, his wife, and his male lover. Lee Richardson played the husband, Jane Alexander his wife, and Michael Moriarty his lover.

The Good Doctor is a Neil Simon comedy with plot and characters based on the short stories of Chekhov. Christopher Plummer starred as the writer. Setting and costumes were by Tony Walton and direction was by A. J. Antoon.

Good Evening is a comedy with music written and performed by Peter Cook and Dudley Moore. They previously starred in *Beyond the Fringe.*

Jumpers, by Tom Stoppard, employs intellectual wit to drive home man's absurdity. Brian Bedford played the pivotal role, a philosopher.

My Fat Friend featured Lynn Redgrave in a comedy about the transformation of a London girl from shapeless loser to slender vamp. Charles Laurence wrote the play.

The Orphan, the last of a trilogy by David Rabe about the Vietnam war, draws on Greek drama and is concerned with

guilt and apathy. Cliff DeYoung played Orestes and Jeff Bleckner directed.

Short Eyes was written by ex-convict Miguel Piñero and was mostly acted by former inmates of a New York jail. The play shows young convicts acting out a violent and ironic parody of straight society, complete with its racism and corruptions. Marvin Felix Camillo directed.

Thieves, by Herb Gardner, concerns the experiences of two New York City schoolteachers, played by Marlo Thomas and Richard Mulligan. Charles Grodin directed.

Veronica's Room is a suspense thriller. Angela Baff played the lead, Eileen Heckert and Arthur Kennedy were her tormentors, and Ellis Rabb directed.

When You Comin' Back, Red Ryder? is concerned with disaffected youth and impotent violence. Kevin Conway starred as a brutal and sadistic lout. Mark Medoff wrote the play and Kenneth Frankel directed.

Musicals and Revues

Cyrano is based upon Anthony Burgess' adaptation of the play by Edmond Rostand. Christopher Plummer played the long-nosed hero. Michael J. Lewis wrote the music and Burgess wrote the lyrics. Michael Kidd directed.

The Faggot, written, composed, and directed by Al Carmines, is a revue dedicated to portraying the homosexual lives of both men and women.

Gigi, based on the novel by Colette, was adapted from the film musical with music by Frederick Loewe and lyrics by Alan Jay Lerner. Karin Wolfe played Gigi, Agnes Moorehead was her aunt, and Alfred Drake was the boulevardier played by Maurice Chevalier in the film. Joseph Hardy directed.

Lorelei is the updated version of the 1949 hit *Gentlemen Prefer Blondes,* and it starred, as in the original, Carol Channing as the mercenary Lorelei Lee. Jules Styne added three new numbers to his score, Betty Comden and Adolph Green contributed lyrics, and Kenny Solms and Gail Parent wrote a new book. Robert Moore directed.

The Magic Show starred Doug Henning, a master illusionist who performs tricks on stage, in a musical with book by Bob Randall and music and lyrics by Stephen Schwartz.

Molly is based on the radio and television series "The Goldbergs." Kay Ballard starred, Alan Arkin was the director, and Grover Dale was the choreographer.

Over Here! is a nostalgic musical, with the two surviving Andrews sisters playing entertainers aboard a troop train and their partner—played by Janie Sell—in reality a German spy named Mitzi. Music and lyrics were by Richard Sherman and Robert B. Sherman. Joseph Klein was the musical director and Tom Moore was the director.

Raisin is an adaption of Lorraine Hansberry's play *Raisin in the Sun* (1959) concerning a Chicago black family's attempt to move into a white suburb. Judd Woldin wrote the music and Robert Brittan the lyrics.

Seesaw was adapted from William Gibson's play *Two for the Seesaw,* about a married Nebraska lawyer who meets a Jewish girl in the Bronx. Ken Howard and Michele Lee were the leads and Tommy Tune played a choreographer. Michael Bennett wrote, directed, and choreographed the production.

Words and Music is a revue starring lyricist Sammy Cahn, who played and sang his hits and told the audience how songs are written.

Revivals

Candide is a comic operetta based on Voltaire's novel. Hugh Wheeler wrote a new book for the work, which was first presented in the 1950's. Leonard Bernstein wrote the music; Stephen Sondheim and John Latouche supplemented the original lyrics by poet Richard Wilbur. Mark Baker played Candide, Lewis J. Stadlen

Raisin, an adaptation of Lorraine Hansberry's play *Raisin in the Sun,* was awarded the Tony as the best Broadway musical of the 1973-74 season.

was Dr. Pangloss, and Maurice Brennan was Cunegonde.

Chemin de Fer is a typical bedroom farce by Georges Feydeau. Rachel Roberts played a wife betrayed into divorce on her first lapse from virtue and John McMartin was the married man who leads her to folly.

Dance of Death is August Strindberg's horrifying picture of a marriage made in hell. Robert Shaw and Zoe Caldwell played the partners and A. J. Antoon directed.

The Iceman Cometh is Eugene O'Neill's drama of a collection of down-and-out people who live on booze, illusions, and false promises. James Earl Jones played Hickey, the salesman who briefly resurrects them. Theodore Mann directed.

A Moon for the Misbegotten is O'Neill's play of two would-be lovers, portrayed by Jason Robards and Colleen Dewhurst, who cannot put aside their fears and thus must part. José Quintero directed.

Noel Coward in Two Keys consisted of two Coward plays. Hume Cronyn, Jessica Tandy, Anne Baxter, and Thom Christopher were the cast in both. Vivian Matalon directed.

The Play's the Thing is Ferenc Molnar's witty play-within-a-play of Pirandellian proportions. The comedy, adapted by P. G. Wodehouse, was directed by Gene Feist.

Scapino is Molière's farce about a wily scamp of a servant who puts two fat, pompous, and moneyed fathers in their places at the behest of two lovelorn sons. The Young Vic actors, including Jim Dale as the servant, performed in the bouncy tradition of British vaudeville.

Ulysses in Nighttown is a new dramatization, by Marjorie Barkentin, of James Joyce's *Ulysses*. Like the version presented 16 years earlier, it starred Zero Mostel as Leopold Bloom and was directed by Burgess Meredith. Fionnuala Flanagan played Molly Bloom.

Uncle Vanya is Anton Chekhov's drama of unfulfilled people in provincial Russia. The cast included George C. Scott, Julie Christie, Nicol Williamson, and Lillian Gish. Mike Nichols directed.

The Visit is Friedrich Durenmatt's tale of a woman, played by Rachel Roberts, who revenges herself upon the lover, played by John McMartin, who seduced her and left her pregnant. Harold Prince directed.

The Women is Clare Boothe Luce's brittle 1936 comedy of the manners and mores of New York society. The cast included Alexis Smith, Rhonda Fleming, Kim Hunter, and Myrna Loy. Morton Da Costa directed.

A Streetcar Named Desire, by Tennessee Williams, featured Rosemary Harris as Blanche DuBois and James Farentino as Stanley Kowalski. Ellis Rabb directed.

Ulysses in Nighttown. Fionnuala Flanagan delivered part of the famous "Molly Bloom Soliloquy" from a brass bed. The play was based on James Joyce's novel *Ulysses.*

United States of AMERICA. Among events of note during the second quarter of 1974 were the following:

Presidency

The Watergate scandal continued to plague President Nixon (see WATERGATE SCANDAL in this section), but foreign affairs was the principal focus of his activities. In June, he traveled to several Middle East countries, visited NATO headquarters in Brussels, then flew to Moscow for a summit meeting with Soviet Communist party leader Leonid Brezhnev. (See MIDDLE EAST and SOVIET UNION in this section.) Earlier, on April 7, he held brief private meetings with world leaders in Paris while attending memorial services for the late French president, Georges Pompidou.

William Simon was named April 17 to succeed George Shultz as secretary of the treasury. Simon, who had been administrator of the Federal Energy Office, was succeeded by his deputy, John Sawhill.

Shultz's role as chairman of the Council on Economic Policy was assumed by the president himself. Deputy Press Secretary Gerald Warren said, "the president intends to play an increasing, expanded role in the formulation of economic policy." On May 25, Nixon appointed Deputy Secretary of State Kenneth Rush as counselor to the president for economic affairs. Rush was to coordinate domestic and international economic policy at the White House, where he would have cabinet rank.

Congress

A new minimum-wage bill was passed by Congress March 28 and signed by Nixon on April 8. It increased the minimum wage in stages from $2 to $2.30 by the end of 1975 and extended coverage to 7 to 8 million workers not previously covered. The workers covered for the first time were employees of federal, state, and local government, farm workers, domestic-service workers, and retail and service employees of chain-store operations.

On June 12, Congress sent to President Nixon a compromise version of a bill setting rules for conversion to coal by oil- and gas-burning plants and extending to the 1977 model year the Environmental Protection Agency's strict standards for auto-exhaust emissions.

Congress passed and sent to the White House on June 21 a bill revising the processing of the federal budget through Congress. In addition, the bill would change the federal fiscal year to begin October 1 instead of July 1, curb spending programs outside the regular budgetary process, and restrict impoundment of congressionally mandated funds by the executive branch. A Budget Office was to be established in Congress to provide expertise, and each chamber would have a budget committee. A budget resolution, considered a tentative alternative budget to the presidential budget, would be devised to set target figures for total appropriations, spending, and tax and debt levels. Nixon signed the bill in July.

Supreme Court

Bank Records. The Supreme Court upheld on April 1 the 1970 Bank Secret Act, which gave the federal government broad access to bank customer records, by a vote of 6 to 3. Under regulations established by the Treasury Department, banks are required to record all customers' checks, keep records of depositors' identities and all loans over $5,000 except mortgages, and report domestic deposits or withdraw-

William Simon, *right,* was named secretary of the treasury, succeeding George Shultz. John Sawhill, *left,* replaced Simon as administrator of the Federal Energy Office.

A Congressional Budget Office was established by the terms of a bill signed by President Nixon. The legislation was designed to give Congress a tighter grip on federal spending.

als larger than $10,000 and foreign financial transactions exceeding $5,000.

Zoning. The Court, over the dissents of justices Thurgood Marshall and William Brennan, upheld April 1 the right of Belle Terre, New York, to pass zoning ordinances restricting land use to one-family dwellings, and thus forbidding six unrelated male and female college students from living in a house.

Kent State. The Supreme Court ruled unanimously on April 17 that the parents of three students allegedly killed by National Guardsmen at Kent State University in 1970 could sue Ohio officials and officials of the National Guard. Chief Justice Warren Burger said the well-established constitutional prohibition against suing a state provided "no shield for a state official confronted by the claim that he has deprived another of a federal right under the color of state law."

Prisoners' Mail. The high court ruled unanimously April 29 that mail censor-

ship in the California prison system was unconstitutional. While the Court did not flatly prohibit mail handlers from reading incoming and outgoing mail, it specified that when a letter was blocked its writer had to be notified and given a means of protest. The Court also upheld the right of California inmates to seek legal advice from law students and legal paraprofessionals.

Wiretaps. The high court ruled unanimously May 13 that former attorney general John Mitchell failed to meet the requirements of a 1968 law when he allowed his executive assistant to approve wiretap applications, rather than doing it himself or designating a specific assistant attorney general to act in his place. The ruling was expected to void indictments in 61 narcotics and gambling cases involving 627 defendants.

Job Benefits. The Supreme Court ruled 6 to 3 on June 17 that states can deny disability benefits to women incapacitated by normal pregnancy without committing unconstitutional discrimination. In a dissent, Justice William Brennan said that "the economic effects caused by pregnancy-related disabilities are functionally indistinguishable from the effects caused by any other disability."

Segregation. The high court voted 8 to 1 on June 17 to prohibit the use of city-owned recreational facilities for games sponsored by racially segregated schools. The case involved, in Montgomery, Alabama, went back to 1958.

Pornography. The Court ruled unanimously on June 24 that the film *Carnal Knowledge* was not obscene, thus reversing the conviction of a theater owner in Georgia, because under the Court's 1973 standards it did not "depict sexual conduct in a patently offensive way." But, in a related case, the Court ruled 5 to 4 that a brochure advertising an illustrated version of the 1970 report of the President's Commission on Obscenity and Pornography was "a form of hard-core pornography" proscribed by the Court's standards. The divergent decisions raised the possibility that the justices would continue to be called upon to decide what is obscene on a case-by-case basis in the future, a course they have tried to avoid.

Convicts' Rights. In two 5-to-4 decisions June 24, the high court ruled that prisons could prohibit news reporters from interviewing specified inmates without violating the prisoners' right of free speech or media rights of freedom of press. In a 6-to-3 decision, the Court ruled that states have the authority to deprive convicted felons of their voting rights.

Right of Reply. The Supreme Court unanimously struck down on June 25 a Florida law requiring newspapers to print replies from political candidates criticized in their columns. The justices held that the law was an unconstitutional restriction on freedom of the press.

Libel. The Supreme Court ruled 5 to 4 on June 25 that an ordinary citizen elevated to sudden prominence by news events can sue any newspaper or radio or television station that circulates a false and defamatory account of his role in those events. The decision restricted the scope of a 1971 ruling that protected the news media from such libel suits as long as the news accounts were not knowingly false or recklessly malicious. It left standing, however, protection against libel suits when news accounts deal with "a public official" or "a public figure."

"Zebra" Killings

Four Black Muslims were indicted by a grand jury in San Francisco May 16 on charges of murdering three white persons and conspiring to murder other whites at random. The three killings cited in the indictment were among 12 so-called Zebra killings in the past six months. (They were so dubbed because police communications regarding them had been handled over the Z police radio band.) According to victims who survived, a young black man shot them in the back without warning.

San Francisco Mayor Joseph Alioto had ordered police to stop, search, and question all young black men who appeared to match the description of a man thought responsible for the shootings. U.S. District Court Judge Alfonso Zirpoli ruled April 25 that police had violated the rights of 600 black men they had stopped and questioned, and he issued a temporary injunction forbidding the practice.

Boyle Convicted

Former United Mine Workers President W. A. (Tony) Boyle was convicted April 11 of three counts of first-degree murder in the 1969 murders of union rival Joseph Yablonski, his wife, and his daughter. The conviction carried a mandatory sentence of life imprisonment. It was the fifth murder conviction obtained in the Yablonski case; in addition, three persons had pleaded guilty. Boyle was serving a three-year federal prison sentence for misuse of union funds.

Patty Hearst Case (Continued)

Six members of the Symbionese Liberation Army died in a gun battle and ensuing fire that erupted after police surrounded their Los Angeles hideout May 17. But Patricia Hearst, who had earlier been kidnapped by the SLA, remained at large. She had told her parents in a tape recording received April 4 that she was staying with the SLA. (See UNITED STATES, subtitle *Kidnappings*, in the first section.)

Los Angeles police, alerted to the hideout by a tip, surrounded the house with 150 heavily armed men. A gun battle erupted, with more than 1,000 rounds of ammunition exchanged. After more than an hour, flames engulfed the house—ignited by a police tear-gas cannister or an SLA gasoline bomb. The charred bodies found in the house were identified as those of Donald DeFreeze, Nancy Ling Perry, William Wolfe, Patricia Soltysik, Angela Atwood, and Camilla Hall. Wolfe, Atwood, and Soltysik died from burns and smoke inhalation, the coroner's office said, while the others died from gunshot wounds.

The FBI said earlier that the armed robbery in April of a San Francisco bank that netted $10,960 was the work of the SLA. DeFreeze, Perry, Soltysik, Hall, and Patricia Hearst were identified through bank surveillance camera photographs. All were armed, and two bystanders were seriously wounded when the robbers began firing wildly as they fled to getaway cars. A bank guard said Patricia Hearst "absolutely was a participant" in the robbery.

Formal charges were filed against Hearst on May 22 and against SLA members William and Emily Harris. The three were charged on various counts of assault with a deadly weapon with intent to commit murder, kidnapping, and robbery. In two tape-recorded messages, Hearst denied that she had been "brainwashed" by

Patty Hearst was identified as the armed bank robber shown in the picture below, which was taken by the bank's surveillance camera. Four others identified in the robbery were among six Symbionese Liberation Army members who died in a gun battle and ensuing fire, *bottom*, after police surrounded their hideout in Los Angeles.

Mrs. King Slain. The Rev. Calvin Morris comforts a girl shortly after the shooting inside Atlanta's Ebenezer Baptist Church that killed the mother of the late Dr. Martin Luther King, Jr. Morris was in the pulpit when an apparently deranged young man opened fire.

the SLA and said her participation in the bank robbery had been voluntary.

Dr. King's Mother Slain

Mrs. Martin Luther King, Sr., mother of the slain civil rights leader Dr. Martin Luther King, Jr., was shot and killed June 30 by a young black man while she was playing the organ in Atlanta's Ebenezer Baptist Church. A church deacon was also killed by gunfire, and a member of the congregation was wounded.

Witnesses said the gunman, who was identified as Marcus Wayne Chenault, Jr., 23, of Dayton, Ohio, cursed and shouted before firing: "I'm tired of all this. I'm taking over." Members of the congregation wrestled him to the floor.

Investigators said Chenault had declared that he had received orders from his god to come to Atlanta and kill Rev. Martin Luther King, Sr., pastor of the church and the husband of Mrs. King. Rev. King was entering the church when the shooting broke out.

Chenault, arraigned in court on July 1, referred to himself as "a Hebrew" and gave his name to the court as "Servant Jacob." U.S. Deputy Assistant Attorney General K. William O'Connor said July 4 that there was no conspiracy involved and that a preliminary FBI investigation of the case had been halted.

Campaign Reform

Common Cause, a self-styled citizens' lobby, reported that since the beginning of 1973, 40 state legislatures had passed as many as 67 reform measures dealing with campaign finances, ethical standards for officeholders, and requirements for open meetings by governmental units. Twenty-five states had enacted new laws requiring disclosure of, or limits on, campaign contributions, while also imposing some curbs on spending by candidates. Eight of these states had authorized experiments with public financing of campaigns. Many states had established independent commissions to enforce the new laws.

In June, the nation's governors, at their annual conference, called on "all levels of government" to enact comprehensive "clean government" measures. The governors endorsed broad campaign finance reforms, including experiments with public financing; open meetings of all public bodies; registration of lobbyists, coupled with "full disclosure" of their activities; and ethical codes for public officials, including disclosure of their personal finances.

California voters, by a more than 2-to-1 margin, approved a proposal that provided for strict campaign finance disclosure, limited campaign spending, and strict regulation of lobbying activity. It also barred state and local officials from voting on matters involving personal financial conflicts of interest and created a commission with broad enforcement powers.

Budget Surpluses

After years of financial crisis, many state and local governments were in mid-1974 experiencing budget surpluses—the result of revenue-sharing funds and rising tax receipts. The Tax Foundation, a research organization, estimated that tax reductions totaling $1.2 billion a year were being considered in 15 states.

Budgetmakers were reported to have often failed to make adequate allowance for price and wage boosts. As prices soared, sales-tax receipts rose; higher wages meant more income taxes collected; and higher profits meant more corporate-tax collections.

New York, with a surplus of $127 million, increased aid for education and doubled its tax credit for business investments. Connecticut cut its sales tax from 6½ per cent to 6 per cent, and Pennsylvania cut corporate and personal income taxes. Florida boosted the homestead-tax exemption to $10,000 for the elderly and disabled. Iowa boosted pay for teachers and state employees, doubled the standard income-tax deduction, and removed the sales tax from food and prescription drugs. Colorado cut property taxes. California gave residents a one-time income-tax credit and repaid localities for giving tax relief to homeowners and renters.

See also ARMAMENTS; ART; BUSINESS AND FINANCE; DISASTERS; EDUCATION; EXPO '74; LABOR; LAOS; LITERATURE; OBITUARIES; RACE RELATIONS; SPORTS AND ATHLETICS; and THEATER, in this section.

Watergate Scandal. On April 30, President Nixon turned over to the House Judiciary Committee and publicly released 200,000 words of edited transcripts from tapes of White House conversations relating to the Watergate break-in and cover-up and related matters. He said in a televised address April 29 that the transcripts included "all the relevant portions of all the subpoenaed conversations that were recorded."

The transcripts comprised Nixon's answer to a House committee subpoena on April 11 for 42 taped conversations believed to bear on Watergate. But the White House reported that 11 of the 42 conversations were nonexistent or missing. And the typescript record had nearly 2,000 omissions marked "inaudible," "unintelligible," "expletive deleted," or "material unrelated to presidential action." Also not supplied were supplementary notes, memoranda, and Dictabelts that had been subpoenaed. On May 1, the Judiciary Committee, which was conducting an impeachment inquiry, voted 20 to 18 to send Nixon a letter informing him that he had "failed to comply" with the subpoena.

In his address the president offered to allow the two senior committee members to come to the White House and listen to the actual tapes of the conversations so that they could determine "beyond question that those transcripts are accurate." However, Committee Chairman Peter Rodino said it would be impossible for him to "responsibly authenticate" the transcript without professional help. Committee special counsel John Doar said that, after comparison with some overlapping material obtained previously, the committee staff had determined the White House transcripts were "not accurate." He said the staff's own tape experts had been able to pick up parts of conversations marked "unintelligible" in the transcripts.

The president said the transcripts "show clearly" that, contrary to former White House counsel John Dean's charge that he was fully aware of the cover-up in September, 1972, "I first learned of it" from Dean on March 21, 1973. He conceded that in the course of the day's conversa-

(Continued on page 252)

NIXON'S TRANSCRIPTS

Deletions have been made for the sake of conciseness. Whole sequences of dialogue have been dropped for reasons of space; deletions within a single conversation by one person are indicated by ellipse points (. . .). Explanatory identifications are indicated by brackets.

P. represents President Nixon; D., White House counsel John Dean; H. and E., presidential aides H.R. Haldeman and John Ehrlichman; M., former attorney general John Mitchell; K., Attorney General Richard Kleindienst; and HP., Assistant Attorney General Henry Petersen.

The first selection is from the White House tape of September 15, 1972, during a meeting between Nixon, Haldeman, and Dean. They discussed the indictment that day of Liddy, Hunt, and the five men arrested during the Watergate break-in. After a phone call from Mitchell in which Nixon tells the former attorney general and campaign chief to "Get a good night's sleep. And don't bug anybody without asking me," the president and Dean continue their conversation:

D. Three months ago I would have had trouble predicting there would be a day when this would be forgotten, but I think I can say that 54 days from now [election day] nothing is going to come crashing down to our surprise.

P. That what?

D. Nothing is going to come crashing down to our surprise.

P. Oh well, this is a can of worms as you know a lot of this stuff that went on. And the people who worked this way are awfully embarrassed. But the way you have handled all this seems to me has been very skillful putting your fingers in the leaks that have sprung there . . . We are all in it together. This is a war. We take a few shots and it will be over. We will give them a few shots and it will be over . . . Don't worry. I wouldn't want to be on the other side right now. Would you?

D. Along that line, one of the things I've tried to do, I have begun to keep notes on a lot of people who are emerging as less than our friends because this will be over some day and we shouldn't

forget the way some of them have treated us.

P. I want the most comprehensive notes on all those who tried to do us in. They didn't have to do it. If we had had a very close election and they were playing the other side I would understand this. No —they were doing this quite deliberately and they are asking for it and they are going to get it. We have not used the power in this first four years as you know. We have never used it. We have not used the Bureau and we have not used the Justice Department but things are going to change now. And they are either going to do it right or go.

D. What an exciting prospect.

February 28, 1973. Nixon and Dean discuss the planned hearings by the Senate Watergate Committee, a conversation in the course of which Nixon observes that "no civilized (characterization deleted) informs" and Dean assures him "There has never been a leak out of my office. There will never be a leak out of my office." The conversation continues:

P. . . . I feel for those poor guys in jail, particularly for Hunt with his wife dead.

D. Well there is every indication they are hanging in tough right now.

P. What the hell do they expect though? Do they expect clemency in a reasonable time? What would you advise on that?

D. I think it is one of those things we will have to watch very closely. For example,—

P. You couldn't do it, say, in six months.

D. No, you couldn't. This thing may become so political as a result of these hearings that it is a vendetta. This judge [John Sirica] may go off the deep end in sentencing, and make it so absurd that it's clearly injustice that they have been heavily—

P. Is there any kind of appeal left?

D. Right. Liddy and [former CRP security chief James] McCord, who sat through the trial, will both be on appeal and there is no telling how long that will last. It is one of these things we will just have to watch.

P. . . . . But the President should

not become involved in any part of this case. Do you agree with that?

D. I agree totally, sir. Absolutely. That doesn't mean that quietly we are not going to be working around the office. You can rest assured that we are not going to be sitting quietly.

P. It will be somewhat serious but the main thing, of course, is also the isolation of the President.

D. Absolutely! Totally true!

P. Because that, fortunately, is totally true.

D. I know that sir!

P. (expletive deleted) Of course, I am not dumb and I will never forget when I heard about this (adjective deleted) forced entry and bugging. I thought, what in the hell is this? What is the matter with these people? Are they crazy? I thought they were nuts! A prank! But it wasn't! It wasn't very funny. I think that our Democratic friends know that, too. They know what the hell it was. They don't think we'd be involved in such.

D. I think they do too.

March 13, 1973. Nixon and Dean again confer on Watergate strategy in the Oval Office. The discussion turns to targets of the Senate investigation:

P. Let's face it, I think they are really after Haldeman.

D. Haldeman and Mitchell.

P. Colson is not a big enough name for them. He really isn't. He is, you know, he is on the government side, but Colson's name doesn't bother them so much. They are after Haldeman and after Mitchell. Don't you think so?

D. Sure . . .

P. In any event, Haldeman's problem is [Presidential appointments secretary Dwight] Chapin isn't it?

D. Bob's problem is circumstantial.

P. Why is that? Let's look at the circumstantial. I don't know, Bob didn't know any of those people like the Hunts and all that bunch. Colson did, but Bob didn't. OK?

D. That's right.

P. Now where the hell, or how much Chapin knew I will be (expletive deleted) if I know.

D. Chapin didn't know anything about the Watergate.

P. Don't you think so?

D. Absolutely not.

On April 30, President Nixon turned over to the House Judiciary Committee and publicly released 200,000 words of edited transcripts from tapes of White House conversations relating to the Watergate break-in and cover-up.

P. [Haldeman aide Gordon] Strachan?
D. Yes.
P. He knew?
D. Yes.
P. About the Watergate?
D. Yes.
P. Well, then, he probably told Bob. He may not have.
D. He was judicious in what he relayed, but Strachan is as tough as nails. He can go in and stonewall, and say, "I don't know anything about what you are talking about." He has already done it twice you know, in interviews.
P. I guess he should, shouldn't he? I suppose we can't call that justice, can we?
D. Well, it is a personal loyalty to him. He doesn't want it any other way. He didn't have to be told. He didn't have to be asked. It just is something that he found was the way he wanted to handle the situation.
P. But he knew? He knew about Watergate? Strachan did?
D. Yes.
P. I will be damned! Well that is the problem in Bob's case. Not Chapin then, but Strachan. Strachan worked for him, didn't he?

D. Yes. They would have one hell of a time proving that Strachan had knowledge of it, though.
P. Who knew better? Magruder?
D. Magruder and Liddy.
P. Oh, I see. The other weak link for Bob is Magruder. He hired him et cetera.
D. That applies to Mitchell, too.
P. Mitchell—Magruder. Where do you see Colson coming into it?
D. . . . . I think that Chuck had knowledge that something was going on over there, but he didn't have any knowledge of the details of the specifics of the whole thing.
P. There must have been an indication of the fact that we we had poor pickings. Because naturally anybody, either Chuck or Bob, were always reporting to me about what was going on. If they ever got any information they would certainly have told me that we got some information, but they never had a thing to report. What was the matter? Did they never get anything out of the damn thing?
D. I don't think they ever got anything, sir.
P. A dry hole?
D. That's right.
P. (Expletive deleted)

D. Well, they were just really getting started.
P. Yeah. Bob one time said something to me about something, this or that or something, but I think it was something about the Convention, I think it was about the convention problems they were planning something. I assume that must have been [Clark] MacGregor —not MacGregor, but Segretti.
D. No, Segretti wasn't involved in the intelligence gathering piece of it at all.
P. Oh, he wasn't? Who the hell was gathering intelligence?
D. That was Liddy and his outfit.
P. Apart from Watergate?
D. That's right. Well you see Watergate was part of intelligence gathering, and this was their first thing. What happened is—
P. That was such a stupid thing!
D. It was incredible—that's right. That was Hunt.
P. To think of Mitchell and Bob would have allowed—would have allowed—this kind of operation to be in the campaign committee!
D. I don't think he knew it was there.
P. I don't think that Mitchell knew about this sort of thing.

D. Oh, no, no! Don't misunderstand me. I don't think that he knew the people. I think he knew that Liddy was out intelligence gathering. I don't think he knew that Liddy would use a fellow like [James] McCord, (expletive removed), who worked for the Committee. I can't believe that.

P. Hunt?

D. I don't think Mitchell knew about Hunt either.

P. Well Mitchell thought, well, gee, and I hired this fellow and I told him to gather intelligence. Maybe Magruder says the same thing.

D. Magruder says—as he did in the trial—well, of course, my name has been dragged in as the guy who sent Liddy over there, which is an interesting thing. Well what happened they said is that Magruder asked—he wanted to hire my deputy over there as Deputy Counsel and I said, "No way. I can't give him up."

P. Was Liddy your deputy?

D. No Liddy never worked for me . . .

P. How the hell does Liddy stand up so well?

D. He's a strange man . . .

P. Strange or strong?

D. Strange and strong. His loyalty is—I think it is just beyond the pale . . .

P. He hates the other side too, doesn't he?

D. Oh, absolutely! He is strong. He really is.

P. Is it too late to go the hang-out road?

D. Yes, I think it is. The hang-out road—

P. Ehrlichman always felt it should be hang-out.

D. Well, I think I convinced him why he would not want to hang-out either. There is a certain domino situation here . . . and there can be a lot of problems if everything starts falling . . . There is a reason for not everyone going up and testify.

P. I see. Oh no, no, no! I didn't mean to have everyone go up and testify.

March 17, 1973. At this session, Dean and Nixon discuss Donald Segretti's "dirty tricks" and the break-in of the office of Daniel Ellsberg's psychiatrist. Dean mentions Ehrlichman's "potential problem":

P. In connection with Hunt?

D. In connection with Hunt and Liddy both.

P. They worked for him?

D. They—these fellows had to be some idiots as we've learned after the fact. They went out and went into Dr. Ellsberg's doctor's office and they had, they were geared up with all this CIA equipment—

cameras and the like. Well they turned the stuff back in to the CIA some point in time and left film in the camera. CIA has not put this together, and they don't know what it all means right now. But it wouldn't take a very sharp investigator very long because you've got pictures in the CIA files that they had to turn over to (unintelligible).

P. What in the world—what in the name of God was Ehrlichman having something (unintelligible) in the Ellsberg (unintelligible)?

D. They were trying to—this was a part of an operation that—in connection with the Pentagon papers. They were—the whole thing—they wanted to get Ellsberg's psychiatric records for some reason. I don't know.

P. This is the first I ever heard of this. I, I (unintelligible) care about Ellsberg was not our problem.

D. That's right.

P. (Expletive deleted) . . .

March 21, 1973. This meeting between the president and Dean was the one in which Dean warned of a "cancer . . . close to the presidency." Haldeman joined them later.

D. The reason that I thought we ought to talk this morning is because in our conversations, I have the impression that you don't know everything I know and it makes it very difficult for you to make judgments that only you can make on some of these things and I thought that—

P. In other words, I have to know why you feel that we shouldn't unravel something?

D. Let me give you my overall first.

P. In other words, your judgment as to where it stands, and where we will go.

D. I think that there is no doubt about the seriousness of the problem we've got. We have a cancer within, close to the Presidency, that is growing. It is growing daily. It's compounded, growing geometrically now, because it compounds itself. That will be clear if I, you know, explain some of the details of why it is. Basically, it is because (1) we are being blackmailed; (2) People are going to start perjuring themselves very quickly that have not had to perjure themselves to protect other people in the line. And there is no assurance—

P. That that won't bust?

D. That that won't bust.

Dean then gives a description of how Liddy's plan—"the most incredible thing I have ever laid my eyes on"—led to the Watergate break-in. He continues:

D. . . . Apparently after they had initially broken in and bugged the DNC they were getting information. The information was coming over here to [Gordon] Strachan and some of it was given to Haldeman, there is no doubt about it.

P. Did he know where it was coming from?

D. I don't really know if he would.

P. Not necessarily?

D. Not necessarily. Strachan knew it. There is no doubt about it, and whether Strachan—I have never come to press these people on these points because it hurts them to give up that next inch, so I had to piece things together. Strachan was aware of receiving information, reporting to Bob. At one point Bob even gave instructions to change their capabilities from Muskie to McGovern, and passed this back through Strachan to [Jeb] Magruder and apparently to Liddy. And Liddy was starting to make arrangements to go in and bug . . . McGovern . . .

P. Magruder is (unintelligible).

D. Yeah. Magruder is totally knowledgeable on the whole thing.

P. Yeah.

D. Alright now, we have gone through the trial. I don't know if Mitchell has perjured himself in the Grand Jury or not.

P. Who?

D. Mitchell. I don't know how much knowledge he actually had. I know that Magruder has perjured himself in the Grand Jury. I know that Porter has perjured himself in the Grand Jury.

P. Who is Porter? (unintelligible)

D. He is one of Magruder's deputies. They set up this scenario which they ran by me. They said, "How about this?" I said, "I don't know. If this is what you are going to hang on, fine."

Further on, Dean discusses demands by the convicted burglars for money and says that Hunt has threatened to talk. He then sums up:

D. So that is it. That is the extent of the knowledge. So where are the soft spots on this? Well, first of all, there is the problem of the continued blackmail which will not only go on now, but it will go on while these people are in prison, and it will compound the obstruction of justice situation. It will cost money. It is dangerous. People around here are not pros at this sort of thing. This is the sort of thing Mafia people can do: washing money, getting clean money, and things like that. We just don't know about those things . . .

P. That's right.

D. It is a tough thing to know how to do.

P. Maybe it takes a gang to do

Principals who conversed with Nixon in the released transcripts were, clockwise from top left: H. R. Haldeman, John Ehrlichman, Henry Petersen, Richard Kleindienst, John Mitchell, and John Dean.

that . . . How much money do you need?

D. I would say these people are going to cost a million dollars over the next two years.

P. We could get that. On the money, if you need the money you could get it. You could get a million dollars. You could get it in cash. I know where it could be gotten. It is not easy, but it could be done. But the question is who the hell would handle it? Any ideas on that?

D. That's right. Well, I think that is something that Mitchell ought to be charged with.

P. I would think so too.

D. And get some pros to help him . . .

P. Just looking at the immediate problem, don't you think you have to handle Hunt's financial situation damn soon?

D. I think that is—I talked with Mitchell about that last night and—

P. It seems to me we have to keep the cap on the bottle that much, or we don't have any options.

D. That's right.

P. Either that or it all blows right now?

D. That's the question . . . What really bothers me is this growing situation. As I say, it is growing because of the continued need to provide support for the Watergate people who are going to hold us up for everything we've got, and the need for some people to perjure themselves as they go down the road here. If this thing ever blows, then we are in a cover up situation. I think it would be extremely damaging to you and the—

P. Sure. The whole concept of Administration justice. Which we cannot have!

D. That is what really troubles me. For example, what happens if it starts breaking, and they do find a criminal case against a Haldeman, a Dean, a Mitchell, an Ehrlichman? That is—

P. If it really comes down to that, we would have to (unintelligible) some of the men.

D. That's right. I am coming down to what I really think, is that Bob and John and John Mitchell and I can sit down and spend a day, or

however long, to figure out one, how this can be carved away from you, so that it does not damage you or the Presidency. It just can't! You are not involved in it and it is something you shouldn't—

P. That is true!

D. I know, sir. I can just tell from our conversation that these are things that you have no knowledge of.

P. You certainly can! Buggings, etc! Let me say I am keenly aware of the fact Colson, et al., were doing their best to get information as we went along. But they all knew very well they were supposed to comply with the law. There was no question about that! You feel that really the trigger man was really Colson on this then?

D. No. He was one of us. He was just in the chain. He helped push the thing . . .

P. So what you really come to is what we do. Let's suppose that you and Haldeman and Ehrlichman and Mitchell say we can't hold this? What then are you going to say? What are you going to put out after it. Complete disclosure,

isn't that the best way to do it?
D. Well, one way to do it is—
P. That would be my view—
D. One way to do it is for you to tell the Attorney General that you finally know. Really, this is the first time you are getting all the pieces together.
P. Ask for another Grand Jury?
D. Ask for another Grand Jury. The way it should be done though, is a way—for example, I think that we could avoid criminal liability for countless people and the ones that did get it could be minimal.
P. How?
D. Well . . . You know, some people could be granted immunity.
P. Like Magruder?
D. Yeah. To come forward. But some people are going to have to go to jail. That is the long and short of it, also.
P. Who? Let's talk about—
D. Alright. I think I could. For one.
P. You go to jail?
D. That's right.
P. Oh, hell no! I can't see how you can.
D. Well, because—
P. I can't see how. Let me say I can't see how a legal case could be made against you, John.
D. It would be tough but, you know, I can see people pointing fingers. You know, to get it out of their own, put me in an impossible position. Just really give me a (unintelligible).
P. Oh, no! Let me say I got the impression here—but just looking at it from a cold legal standpoint: you are a lawyer, you were a counsel—doing what you did as counsel. You were not—What would you go to jail for?
D. The obstruction of justice.
P. The obstruction of justice?
D. That is the only one that bothers me.
P. Well, I don't know. I think that one. I feel it could be cut off at the pass, maybe, the obstruction of justice . . . Let me put it this way: let us suppose that you get the million bucks, and you get the proper way to handle it. You could hold that side?
D. Uh, huh.
P. It would seem to me that would be worthwhile.
D. Well, that's one problem.
P. I know you have a problem here. You have the problem with Hunt and his clemency.
D. That's right. And you are going to have a clemency problem with the others. They all are going to expect to be out and that may put you in a position that is just untenable at some point. You know, the Watergate Hearings just over, Hunt now demanding clemency or he is going to blow. And politically, it's impossible for you to do it. You know, after everybody—

P. That's right!
D. I am not sure that you will ever be able to deliver on the clemency. It may be just too hot.
P. You can't do it politically until after the '74 elections, that's for sure. Your point is that even then you couldn't do it.
D. That's right. It may further involve you in a way you should not be involved in this.
P. No—it is wrong that's for sure.

Turning to the Ellsberg burglary, the two and Haldeman, who has joined them, search for a way to explain the incident.

D. You might put it on a national security grounds basis.
H. It absolutely was.
D. And say that this was—
H. (unintelligible)—CIA—
D. Ah—
H. Seriously,
P. National Security. We had to get information for national security . . .
D. Then the question is, why didn't the CIA do it or why didn't the FBI do it?
P. Because we had to do it on a confidential basis.
H. Because we were checking them.
P. Neither could be trusted.
H. It has basically never been proven. There was reason to question their position.
P. With the bombing thing coming out and everything coming out, the whole thing was national security.
D. I think we could get by on that.
P. On that one I think we should simply say this was a national security investigation that was conducted.

The three next consider calling another grand jury:

P. . . . And that gives you a reason not to have to go before the Ervin and Baker committee . . .
H. . . . You can refuse to talk.
D. You can take the 5th Amendment.
H. You can say you have forgotten, too, can't you?
D. Sure but you are chancing a very high risk for perjury situation.
P. But you can say I don't remember. You can say I can't recall. I can't give any answer to that that I can recall.

The discussion returns to the Watergate break-in.

D. [The others are] going to stonewall it, as it now stands. Excepting Hunt. That's why his threat.
H. It's Hunt opportunity.
P. That's why for your immediate things you have no choice but to come up with the $120,000, or whatever it is. Right?
D. That's right.

P. Would you agree that that's the prime thing you damn well better get that done?
D. Obviously he ought to be given some signal anyway . . .
P. (Expletive deleted), get it . . .
D. Well, Colson doesn't have any money though . . .
P. Well look, what it is you need on that? When—I am not familiar with the money situation . . .
D. . . . . You have to wash the money. You can get a $100,000 out of a bank, and it all comes in serialized bills.
P. I understand.
D. And that means you have to go to Vegas with it or a bookmaker in New York City. I have learned all these things after the fact. I will be in great shape for the next time around.
H. (Expletive deleted)

(The grand jury that indicted seven Nixon aides on cover-up charges and named Nixon as an unindicted co-conspirator charged that a hush-money payment of $75,000 was made to Hunt's lawyer on the evening of March 21.)

April 14, 1973. By this time the full dimensions of the cover-up were emerging. McCord had told Judge Sirica that perjury had been committed. Magruder went to federal prosecutors on April 14 and implicated Mitchell and Dean. Dean himself had opened negotiations with the prosecutors. In the following conversation, Nixon, Haldeman, and Ehrlichman turn to Dean's problems after discussing Mitchell's liability:

P. Dean is not like Mitchell in the sense that Dean only tried to do what he could to pick up the pieces and everybody else around here knew it had to be done.
E. Certainly.
P. Let's face it. I'm not blaming anybody else—
E. No, I understand that. I have great trouble in (unintelligible) in the light of the known involvement that he had in the
P. Aftermath?
E. Right, but—
H. But the known involvement he had in that was for what was understood here to be the proper system.
P. The question is motive. That's right.
E. That number one. Number two, there is nothing new about that. As I have developed this thing—I want you to read this—
P. Yeah.
E. There were 8 or 10 people around here who knew about this, knew it was going on. Bob knew, I knew, all kinds of people knew.
P. Well, I knew it. I knew it.
E. And it was not a question of

whether—

P. I must say though, I didn't know it but I must have assumed it though you know, fortunately —I thank you both for arranging it that way and it does show the isolation of the President, and here it's not so bad—But the first time that I knew that they had to have the money was the time when Dean told me that they needed forty thousand dollars. I had been, frankly, (unintelligible) papers on those little envelopes. I didn't know about the envelopes (unintelligible) and all that stuff.

E. The point is that if Dean's, if the wrongdoing which justifies Dean's dismissal is his knowledge that the operation was going on, then you can't stop with him. You've got to go through a whole place wholesale.

P. Fire the whole staff.

E. That's right. It's a question of motive. It's a question of role and I don't think Dean's role in the aftermath, at least from the facts that I know now, achieves a level of wrongdoing that requires that you terminate him.

P. I think he made a very powerful point to me that of course, you can be pragmatic and say, (unintelligible) cut your losses and get rid of 'em. Give 'em an hors d'oeuvre and maybe they won't come back for the main course. Well, out, John Dean. On the other hand, it is true that others did know.

E. . . . . The history of this thing has to be though that you did not tuck this under the rug yesterday or today, and hope it would go away . . . When somebody comes to (unintelligible) what the hell was the White House doing all this time? Then you're in a position to say, well, we began to investigate personally the external circumstances and we came to some conclusions—we acted on those conclusions.

P. John Erhlichman conducted an investigation for the President.

April 15, 1973. The president meets with Attorney General Kleindienst in the Executive Office Building across from the White House and asks him about obstruction of justice:

P. Explain that legal point please.

K. Well, I inquired into it personally.

P. Of course I was thinking of the Berrigans and all the funds that have been raised through the years, Scottsboro, etc. Nobody ever raised any question about it. If you raise money for the defense and it's for support—and Ellsberg —(expletive removed) in Ellsberg, the defense—

K. And likewise in this case. If I

had committed a crime and you know about it and you say, "Kleindienst, you go in the Court and plead guilty to the commission of that crime and here is ten thousand dollars, you know, to tide you over and so forth."

P. That's isn't a crime?

K. No. On the other hand, if you know that I committed a crime.

P. Right.

K. And you say, "you go in there and plead guilty, and here is twenty-five thousand dollars on the condition that thereafter you'll say nothing. You just make the plea, take the Fifth Amendment, the judge cites you for contempt, you've got to continue to testify you don't. You do not take it." Then you are now in a position of obstructing justice.

P. Excuse me. If you'd explain that again. If you tell 'em—if you tell 'em—if you raise the money for the purpose of telling them *not* to talk.

K. After he's pleaded guilty. Let's take the—

P. Well, they were all before the Grand Jury at this point, Right?

K. And the judge says, "I'm going to give you immunity—I have ordered you to testify to what you know." He refuses, takes the Fifth Amendment and he's punished for contempt. And you give him twenty five thousand dollars. (unintelligible)

P. There was some thought that— that was all after the election that that happened, huh?

K. I don't know but that happened after the conviction—after Liddy's conviction.

P. Oh, in other words, the obstruction they are talking about is what happened after the conviction?

K. Yes sir.

P. Rather than before the conviction?

K. Yes sir.

P. Well, who the hell would—you mean—but I can't see Haldeman or Ehrlichman or anybody in that (unintelligible)

K. Well.

P. No—I'm just asking. Or Dean, ah, you mean that after that that they raised—they gave money for that purpose?

K. For whatever they gave—let's say that money was given to Liddy in connection with—and.

P. Let me say this—there isn't any question that money that they have had on that or whatever— Mitchell's defense frankly—it would be—you know—these people had worked for the Committee and they were provided with money for their legal fees and for their support. That is—this is before their conviction. Now comes the point of after their conviction.

That's when the case may be, that's when you get the jeopardy.

K. Or if people are up for trial, Mr. President, you say.

P. NO — no — no I'm sorry — not conviction—but after their indictment.

K. Yes. After the indictment "here's fifty thousand dollars. You plead guilty and thereafter take the Fifth Amendment. If they offer you immunity, you know, not testify about anything." If that's.—

P. And then you give 'em money?

K. Yes.

P. That's—I agree.

K. Yes—obstruction of justice.

April 16, 1973. The president summons Dean to the Oval Office. They discuss the possibility of Dean resigning or taking a leave of absence. The president then takes up once more the question of legal liability for White House staffers:

P. . . . . But you remember when you came in, I asked you the specific question "Is anybody on the White House staff involved in it?" You told me, "No."

D. That's right. And I have no knowledge—

P. You still believe that—

D. Yes sir, I do.

P. But you did tell me that in the aftermath there were serious problems.

D. That's right.

P. Right. And, I said, "Well, let's see what they are."

D. And now you are beginning to see what they are. They are potential, technical, obstruction of justice problems.

P. I talked to Petersen last night and he made exactly the same point. He said the obstruction was morally wrong. No, not morally. He said it may not have been morally wrong and it may not have been legally wrong, but he said from the standpoint of the Presidency you can't have it. So, he seems to think that the obstruction of justice thing is a (expletive omitted) hard thing to prove in court.

D. That's right.

P. Which I think should be some comfort to you.

D. Well, my lawyer tells me, you know, that, "legally you are in damn good shape."

P. Is that right? Because you're not—You were simple helping the defendants get their fees and their—What does he say?

D. In that position, I am merely a conduit. It is very technical, very technical. I am a conduit to other people. That is the problem.

P. What was the situation, John? The only time I ever heard any discussion of support for the defense fund was (inaudible). I guess I should have assumed somebody was helping them. I must have assumed it. But I must say people were good in a way because I was busy. Was when you mentioned to me something about hard-hitting problem. But that was handled by Mitchell. Was that true or what?

D. The last time we had a request was the week before sentencing.

P. In other words, that was done at the Mitchell level?

D. That's right.

P. But you had knowledge; Haldeman had knowledge; Ehrlichman had knowledge and I suppose I did that night. That assumes culpability on that, doesn't it?

D. I don't think so.

P. Why not? I plan to be tough on myself so I can handle the other thing. I must say I did not even give it a thought at the time.

D. No one gave it a thought at the time.

P. You don't think the thing is likely to break today?

D. No, I don't.

P. I wonder what Ziegler's got. He must, he seems to think something is going to break. He hasn't been in to see me and I will have to get him in later. Well, I will ask Petersen. Don't you agree with me that it is better that we make the first announcement and not the Justice Department.

D. Yes I do. On your own staff.

P. Oh hell, I am going to make the announcement on Magruder too. (expletive omitted) It was our campaign. I am not going to have the Justice Department—we triggered this whole thing. Don't you agree? You helped to trigger it. You know what I mean.

D. When history is written and you put the pieces back together, you will see why it happened. Because I triggered it. I put everybody's feet to the fire because it just had to stop.

P. That's right.

D. And I still continue to feel that.

P. You put Magruder's feet to the fire. Where did you see Magruder?

D. I didn't. In fact, I refused to see him. That was one of the problems.

P. Oh, and that's why—

D. I started to talk with—I met with him in one of these outer offices at a meeting.

P. What got Magruder to talk? I would like to take the credit.

D. Well.

P. I was hoping that you had seen him because—

D. He was told, one, that there was no chance.

P. As a matter of fact, he made a statement about (inaudible) around the White House. I guess this was pre-primaries — it was all committed. But on Magruder, come again.

D. The situation there is that he and Mitchell were continuing to talk. Proceeding along the same course they had been proceeding to locking their story, but my story did not fit with their story. And I just told them I refused to change, to alter my testimony. But would repeat it just as I had given it. This had to do with a number of meetings in the Department of Justice.

P. Oh yes, I remember. You told me that. I guess everybody told me that. Dean said, "I am not going down there and lie," because your hand will shake and your emotions. Remember you told me that.

D. Yes, I said that. I am incapable of it.

P. Thank God. Don't ever do it John. Tell the truth. That is the thing I have told everybody around here. (expletive omitted) tell the truth! All they do John is compound it . . .

D. The truth always emerges. It always does.

P. Also there is a question of right and wrong too.

D. That's right.

P. Whether it is right and whether it is wrong. Perhaps there are some gray areas, but you are right to get it out now.

D. I am sure.

P. I could have told you to go to Camp David and concoct a story couldn't I? And you have never heard that said, have you?

D. No Sir.

P. In fact, I think I covered a little of that (inaudible). But on the other hand, it was your job to tell me, wasn't it?

D. Uh, huh.

P. And you have. Basically what you have done—no, you told me the truth though. You've told me the truth. It was your job to work for the President, the White House staff and they were not involved in the pre-thing. But then you thought the post-thing. You thought about it and that is why you decided, as you said,

D. I thought we should cut the cancer right off because to keep this whole thing—

P. Look, one thing I want to be sure. When you testify, I don't want you to be in a position, and and I don't want the President to be in a position, that his Counsel did not level with him. See my point?

D. There is no point that I have not leveled . . . as you should know . . .

P. I would like for you to say—and you are free to talk. You are to say, "I told the President about this. I told the President first there was no involvement in the White House. Afterwards, I told the Pres-

ident that I—" And the President said, "Look, I want to get to the bottom of this thing, period." See what I am driving at—not just the White House. You continued your investigation, et cetera, and the President went out and investigated on his own. Which I have done, believe me. I put a little pressure on Magruder and a few of

D. Uh, huh.

P. And as a result of the President's actions this thing has been broken.

D. That's right . . .

April 16, 1973, and April 17, 1973. In two conversations with Haldeman and Ehrlichman, the president discusses how to deal with Dean, who is talking to federal prosecutors. On the second day, Nixon talks to Assistant Attorney General Petersen:

P. Good, good, how has the scenario worked out? May I ask you?

H. Well, it works out very good. You became aware sometime ago that this thing did not parse out the way it was supposed to and that there were some discrepancies beween what you had been told by Dean in the report that there was nobody in the White House involved, which may still be true.

P. Incidentally, I don't think it will gain us anything by dumping on the Dean Report as such.

E. No.

P. What I mean is I would say I was not satisfied that the Dean Report was complete and also I thought it was my obligation to go beyond that to people other than the White House.

E. Ron [Ziegler] has an interesting point. Remember you had John Dean go to Camp David to write it up. He came down and said, "I can't."

P. Right.

E. That is the tip off and right then you started to move.

P. That's right. He said he could not write it.

H. Then you realized that there was more to this than you had been led to believe. (unintelligible)

P. How do I get credit for getting Magruder to the stand?

E. Well it is very simple. You took Dean off the case right then.

P. Now, look, I don't want to get into the position of—

H. Hanging someone else? Well, but he is going to have hung himself at that point in time . . .

P. . . . Colson's recommendation is to get him out by firing him—

E. Colson would like to discredit him.

P. Well I know. But the question is what he could do to discredit us.

E. Well.

P. That's a problem.

H. Yeah. But I think at some point, like you do on anything else, you gotta face up to the fact that the guy is either a friend or a neutral. If he's a neutral you don't have to worry about him; if he's a friend you rely on him, if he's a foe you fight him, and this guy—it seems at that point—is a foe.

P. When I talked to him I said, "Now John, any conversations are (unintelligible)." I said, "Anything (unintelligible) National Security are (unintelligible) you understand?" He said, "Yes (unintelligible) testified to it (unintelligible)."

H. O.K. He said it and it was no problem for him to say it. But it was no problem for him to say a lot of things to us over the last couple of weeks too.

P. The point is, if you break it off with him, then he could go out and say, "Screw the (unintelligible)."

H. No he can't. It's not his privilege. It's yours.

P. I know it's mine, but—

H. If he screws the privilege—

P. Well, I think you have to charge Henry Petersen or whoever is in charge here . . . not to go into matters of national security importance. Any matters involving a conversation with the President —or national security, anything like that, they can ask me.

E. Now, the question comes up—I don't know how far this will run—but this caper in California for instance . . . I said, "Well Chuck, if I were asked that—I would say that was a national security project and I'm not in the position to answer a question on that, because I would have to refer to the President for a waiver of executive privilege on that if he desired to do so." And he said, "Well, can I say the same thing?" And I said, "Well, I don't know whether you can or not." He said, "Well what would the President say if it's referred to him?" I said, "I don't know. I'll go ahead and ask him."

P. That's what we'd say.

E. Can I tell him that for you?

P. Yep. Anything on the (unintelligible) thing, the plumbing thing was national security, the ITT thing.

In meeting with Petersen, the question arises whether Dean should be granted immunity from prosecution in return for testimony before the Watergate grand jury:

P. I don't care what you do on immunity to Strachan or any other second people but you can't give immunity to any top people—not Dean—needless to say you don't want to to Haldeman or Ehrlich-

man . . .

HP. The thing that scares the hell out of me is this—suppose Dean is the only key to Haldeman and Ehrlichman and the refusal to immunize Dean means that Haldeman and Ehrlichman go free. That is the decision that we are going to ultimately come down to . . .

P. . . . I cannot, for example, in good conscience and, you can't in good conscience say that you are going to send Haldeman and Ehrlichman—or anybody for that matter — or Colson — down the tube on the uncorroborated evidence of John Dean. You see—so basically what your problem is and the problem of the prosecutors is to find some corroboration for Dean.

HP. If I could only put your mind at ease—I have been arguing with those prosecutors for three days on this issue . . . if I sound like a devil's advocate—I am. I have been saying the same to the prosecutors—how in the hell can I immunize John Dean?

P. That's the point. Well, I feel it strongly—I mean—just understand I am not trying to protect anybody —I want the damn facts if you can get the facts from Dean and I don't care whether—

HP. Mr. President, if I thought you were trying to protect somebody, I would have walked out . . .

April 27, 1973. Petersen reports to the president in the Oval Office:

P. Sit down, sit down. I was down in Mississippi today. We have gotten a report that, ah, that really we've got to head them off at the pass. Because it's so damned—so damn dangerous to the Presidency, in a sense. There's a reporter by the name of [Seymour] Hersh of the *New York Times* you probably know . . . Hersh has information . . . indicating that Dean has made statements to the prosecuting team implicating the President. And . . . the [Washington] *Post* has heard similar rumors. Now, Henry, this I've got to know. Now, understand —I have told you everything I know about this thing.

HP. . . . you know, I've said to [Federal prosecutor] Titus, "We have to draw the line. We have no mandate to investigate the President. We investigate Watergate." And I don't know where that line draws, but we have to draw that all the time.

P. Good . . .

HP. Yeah. My understanding of law is—my understanding of our responsibilities, is that if it came to that I would have to come to you and say, "We can't do that." The only people who have jurisdiction to do that is the House of Representatives, as far as I'm concerned.

P. That's right . . .

P. . . . Now for—who is going to believe John Dean? We relied on the damned so—Dean, Dean was the one who told us throughout the summer that nobody in the White House was involved when he, himself apparently, was involved, particularly on the critical angle of subornation of perjury. That's the one that—I will never, never understand John . . . Dean. You will get Dean in there. Suppose he starts trying to impeach the President, the word of the President of the United States and says, "Well, I have information to the effect that I once discussed with the President the question of how the possibility, of the problem" . . . Henry, it won't stand up for five minutes because nothing was done, and fortunately I had Haldeman at that conversation and he was there and I said, "Look, I tried to give you this, this, this, this, this and this." And I said, "When you finally get it out, it won't work." Because, I said, "First, you can't get clemency to Hunt."

HP. I agree . . .

P. . . . I said, "The second point to remember is 'How are you going to get the money for them?' If you could do it, I mean you are talking about a million dollars." I asked him—well, I gave him several ways. I said, "You couldn't put it through a Cuban Committee could you?" I asked him, because to me he was sounding so damned ridiculous. I said, "Well under the circumstances," I said, "There isn't a damn thing we can do" . . . Mitchell came down the next day and we talked about executive privilege. Nothing else. Now, that's the total story . . .

HP. But you see that's what I see has to get out to the public. But Mr. President, my wife is not a politically sophisticated woman.

P. That's right—

HP. She knows I'm upset about this and you know, I'm working hard and she sees it. But she asked me at breakfast—She, now I don't want you to hold this against her if you ever meet her . . .

P. Of course.

HP. She said, "Doesn't all this upset you?" And I said, "Of course it does."

P. "Why the hell doesn't the President do something?"

HP. She said, "Do you think the President knows?" And I looked at her and said, "If I thought the President knew, I would have to resign" . . . Well, when that type of question comes through in my home—

P. We've got to get it out.

HP. We've got a problem.

tion he suggested that meeting convicted Watergate defendant E. Howard Hunt's demands for money "might be necessary" but noted that he concluded "It is wrong, that's for sure." A related brief written by the president's special counsel, James St. Clair, indicated that Dean had repeatedly perjured himself in sworn testimony. St. Clair accused Dean of trying to blackmail the president in an effort to gain immunity from prosecution.

Some of the material on the transcripts appeared to be damaging to the president, however. Although he said he did not learn of the cover-up until March 21, the March 13 transcript revealed that Dean told him others had known of the bugging besides the seven convicted men. Dean told him, for example, that H. R. Haldeman's assistant, Gordon Strachan, had lied twice to federal investigators in denying knowledge of the bugging.

Also damaging was the transcript of the March 21 conversation, in which the president several times discussed the possibility of offering executive clemency and hush money to the convicted defendants. At one point Nixon asked Dean if it were not essential to come up with $120,000 for Hunt; after Dean agreed, the president, according to the transcript, said "(expletive deleted), get it."

In his address, the president stated that after March 21 "my actions were directed toward finding the facts and seeing that justice was done." The transcripts of presidential conversations over the next 37 days indicated to many readers, however, frantic efforts to keep the cover-up from unraveling as Dean and others began talking to federal prosecutors.

Nixon Named Co-conspirator

The White House acknowledged June 6 that a Watergate grand jury had voted in February to name President Nixon an unindicted co-conspirator in the Watergate cover-up. Seven men, including former presidential aides H. R. Haldeman and John Ehrlichman, were indicted for their alleged roles in the cover-up. (See WATERGATE SCANDAL in the first section.)

The grand jury's vote, reported to be unanimous, had been kept secret under an order by U.S. District Court Judge John Sirica. But, after a report of the jury's action appeared in the Los Angeles *Times*, St. Clair requested that Sirica unseal the records citing Nixon.

According to news reports, the grand jury had been inclined to indict Nixon but had been dissuaded by special prosecutor Leon Jaworski, who had contended such an action could not be taken against a president in office. A secret report by the grand jury had been turned over to the House Judiciary Committee.

Judge John Sirica ordered President Nixon to surrender to him tapes and other records covering 64 White House conversations that special prosecutor Leon Jaworski had subpoenaed as relating to the Watergate cover-up. Sirica said he would examine the material and submit relevant portions to Jaworski.

House Judiciary Committee was holding hearings relating to the possible impeachment of President Nixon. The president declined to comply with eight subpoenas issued by the committee for the tapes of 147 White House conversations.

More Tapes Sought

On May 20, Judge Sirica ordered the president to surrender to him tapes and other records covering 64 conversations that Jaworski had subpoenaed as relating to the Watergate cover-up. Sirica said he would examine the material and submit relevant portions to Jaworski. The White House requested an appeals court to overturn the order, but on May 31 the Supreme Court voted to take up the matter, bypassing the appeals court, in an effort to resolve the issue.

On June 15, the high court agreed to decide whether the Watergate grand jury that had indicted Haldeman and Ehrlichman had the right to name Nixon a co-conspirator; White House attorneys had argued that the action infringed upon the House of Representatives' "sole power of impeachment." In agreeing to decide the issue, the high court included it in the dispute over the 64 subpoenaed conversations that the president had refused to

surrender. Oral arguments were to begin on July 8.

Nixon informed the House Judiciary Committee May 22 that he would not comply with two subpoenas for Watergate-related tapes and documents that the panel had issued a week earlier. He also said he would reject any future subpoenas "allegedly dealing with Watergate."

Earlier in the day, St. Clair informed the committee that its request for 66 conversations material to the International Telephone & Telegraph Corporation (ITT) antitrust controversy and campaign contributions by the dairy industry would not be met, with the possible exception of an edited transcript of one conversation on the ITT case. Committee counsel Doar said the panel would issue a subpoena if the material were not forthcoming.

The two subpoenas sought 11 conversations relating to Watergate on three dates, and diaries of Nixon's White House meetings over four periods considered by com-

253

mittee staff members to be crucial to the affair. On May 30, the committee issued a third subpoena for the tapes of 45 more conversations alleged to relate to Watergate.

Another subpoena issued May 15 by the committee for 45 White House conversations allegedly dealing with Watergate was rejected by the president June 10.

On June 24, the committee issued what were described as its final four subpoenas, for White House tape recordings of 49 conversations. The four new subpoenas brought to 147 the total number of taped conversations sought in the committee's impeachment inquiry.

Sirica on May 30 rejected the House committee's request for access to the complete tapes of four White House conversations in his custody, one of which had an 18½-minute "gap." Sirica had released portions to a grand jury and had withheld others as unrelated to Watergate. He said committee requests "should be directed to the president."

The U.S. Court of Appeals for the District of Columbia ruled 7 to 0 on May 23 that the Senate Watergate Committee had not shown a compelling enough need for tapes of five presidential conversations to require enforcement of its subpoena for the tapes. The decision upheld and expanded upon a lower-court decision.

Mitchell, Stans Acquitted

Former attorney general John Mitchell and former secretary of commerce Maurice Stans were acquitted by a federal jury in New York City April 28 of all charges stemming from a secret cash contribution made to the Nixon reelection campaign committee by Robert Vesco, a financier accused of looting $224 million in mutual funds. Government prosecutors had charged the two former cabinet members with conspiracy, obstruction of justice, and perjury in attempting to block a federal investigation of Vesco, and with later lying to a grand jury about their roles. (See also Feature Article in the second section, 1973.) The verdict came after 42 days of testimony from 59 witnesses.

A principal witness was former White House counsel John Dean. He said that Mitchell had called and asked him to seek a postponement until after the 1972 presidential election from the Securities and Exchange Commission (SEC) in taking depositions from Vesco associates, and said Mitchell feared the disclosure of Vesco's secret $200,000 campaign contribution. Another prosecution witness was former SEC Chairman G. Bradford Cook, who testified that Stans had on four occasions asked him to limit the investigation of Vesco's contribution or to conceal circumstances surrounding the giving of the cash. Mitchell and Stans denied any wrongdoing.

Interviewed after the verdict, the jurors said the basic issue in their 26 hours of deliberation had been the credibility of government witnesses as opposed to that of

Acquitted. Former secretary of commerce Maurice Stans, *left,* and former attorney general John Mitchell were acquitted by a federal jury of all charges, including conspiracy, obstruction of justice, and perjury, stemming from a secret cash contribution made to the Nixon reelection campaign committee by Robert Vesco.

the defendants. A factor in the jury's consideration of Dean's testimony, said the forewoman, was the fact that he had already pleaded guilty to Watergate charges and therefore had something to gain—leniency in sentencing—for cooperating with the prosecution. Another juror said Cook was not credible because he had admitted previous perjury.

Kissinger Threatens to Quit

Henry Kissinger said at a press conference held on June 11 in Salzburg, Austria, that he would resign as secretary of state unless he was cleared of allegations that he had participated in "illegal or shady activity" in the government wiretapping of individuals. He requested the Senate Foreign Relations Committee to review his testimony of September, 1973, during hearings that led to his confirmation as secretary of state. At that time two members of the committee reviewed FBI summaries of the wiretaps of 17 individuals and concluded that Kissinger's role "was not such as to bar him from confirmation."

Kissinger's threat to quit came after allegations in news stories that he had instigated the wiretaps of 13 government officials and four newsmen between 1969 and 1971 and that he had foreknowledge of the creation of the "plumbers" unit in 1971. The taps on the telephones of the 17 men were later ruled to be illegal, and two of Kissinger's former aides have sued him, charging violation of their civil rights. Members of the plumbers unit broke into the office of the psychiatrist of Pentagon Papers defendant Daniel Ellsberg.

In his press conference, Kissinger conceded that early in 1969, when he was director of the National Security Council, he had expressed concern to the president over leaks of classified information to the news media. The president, he said, then ordered "the institution of a system of national-security wiretaps" while he himself provided the FBI with the names of individuals with access to sensitive information. Kissinger denied receiving any "verbatim transcript" from the wiretaps and said he received only short summaries bearing on national security. He denied

Demands Vindication. A grim Henry Kissinger said he would resign as secretary of state unless cleared by the Senate Foreign Relations Committee of allegations that he had participated in "illegal or shady activity" in the government wiretapping of 17 individuals.

that his office received any reports from the taps concerning "extramarital affairs or pornographic descriptions."

(According to the New York *Times,* an FBI report dated May 12, 1973, said that the "original requests" for wiretaps were either from Kissinger or Alexander Haig, who was then his deputy. According to *Newsweek,* House Judiciary Committee members who had seen the FBI files said that in one case the summaries reportedly noted that one official visited a porno shop, while another was said to have been "seen" with a woman when his wife was away. *Time* said an FBI report stated that Kissinger had made a trip to bureau headquarters to examine the raw logs.)

Concerning the plumbers unit, Kissinger reiterated his testimony before the Foreign Relations Committee that he had known nothing about it although one of his staff members, David Young, was detached in 1971 to become a co-director of the unit. In early 1974, reports in the

Charles Colson, former White House aide, left court with his wife after pleading guilty to a felony charge that he had unlawfully influenced, obstructed, and impeded the trial of Daniel Ellsberg. He was sentenced to one to three years in prison.

press said that Kissinger had listened in late 1971 to a tape of Young interrogating Rear Admiral Robert Welander about the alleged leaking of NSC documents. In a January 22 news conference, Kissinger acknowledged that he heard the tape but reiterated that he had not known Young's function.

The other point in dispute concerned an affidavit filed by John Ehrlichman in May that charged Kissinger had been told on July 15, 1971, that Young was being reassigned to the plumbers unit. In another affidavit, Charles Colson said that this meeting took place aboard a helicopter. Kissinger said in the Salzburg press conference that, if he was told anything about the plumbers unit on that flight, the craft's engine noise apparently drowned out the words.

Court Action on Nixon Aides

Charles Colson, former special counsel to President Nixon, pleaded guilty in federal court June 3 to a felony charge that he had unlawfully influenced, obstructed, and impeded the trial of Daniel Ellsberg after Ellsberg was indicted for leaking the

Pentagon Papers. A statement of confession read in court said Colson wanted Ellsberg to "be tried in the newspapers" even though this would have an "adverse effect on his right to a fair trial."

Colson was sentenced to one to three years in prison on June 21. He told the court that Nixon "on numerous occasions" had urged him to "disseminate damaging information" about Ellsberg.

In return, the Watergate special prosecutor's office agreed to drop all other charges pending against Colson. (He had been indicted for his alleged role in both the break-in of the office of Ellsberg's psychiatrist and the Watergate cover-up. As part of the understanding with the prosecutor's office, Colson consented to give sworn testimony and provide relevant documents in his possession concerning Watergate and related cases.

Jeb Stuart Magruder, former deputy director of the Committee to Re-elect the President, was sentenced May 21 to a prison term of 10 months to 4 years for his role in the Watergate break-in and cover-up. Magruder had pleaded guilty in

Jeb Magruder, former deputy director of the Nixon reelection campaign committee, left court with his wife after being sentenced to from 10 months to 4 years for his role in the Watergate cover-up and break-in.

August, 1973, to a one-count indictment covering a variety of charges, and had been cooperating with the prosecution.

Herbert Kalmbach, formerly the president's personal lawyer, was sentenced June 17 to 6 to 18 months in prison and fined $10,000 for illegal fund-raising activities on behalf of the White House. He had pleaded guilty February 25 to a two-count charge and had promised to cooperate with the Watergate investigation.

Former attorney general Richard Kleindienst pleaded guilty May 16 to a misdemeanor charge that he had refused to testify "accurately and fully" before a congressional committee investigating the controversial ITT antitrust settlement. On June 7, he received a suspended 30-day sentence and a $100 fine.

Dwight Chapin, former appointments secretary to President Nixon, was sentenced to a prison term of 10 to 30 months May 15 for lying to a grand jury about his involvement in political sabotage operations during the 1972 campaign. He had been convicted on two perjury counts April 5.

Herbert Porter, former scheduling director for the Committee to Re-elect the President, was sentenced to 30 days in prison April 11 on a charge of making false statements to the FBI about campaign funds. Porter had pleaded guilty January 28.

Nixon Tax Inquiry

A White House announcement April 3 said President Nixon would pay back taxes plus interest on the basis of a report from the Internal Revenue Service that he owed $432,787.13. With interest, the total amount came to about $465,000. A joint congressional committee found his income-tax delinquency totaled $476,431 during his first term then concluded its inquiry, commending the president for his "prompt decision" to pay the tax deficiencies.

The largest item involved in both the IRS and congressional reports was the deduction of $482,018 taken for Nixon's gift of his vice-presidential papers to the National Archives. The gift was ruled illegal because it was made after July 25, 1969— the effective date of the 1969 Tax Reform

1040 US Department of the Treasury / Internal Revenue Service
Individual Income Tax Return 1970
For the year January 1–December 31, 1970, or other taxable year beginning
Richard M. and Patricia R. Nixon 567 68 0515
The White House
Washington D. C. 20500 Occupation: President, United States
Filing Status—check only one: 2 ✗ Married filing jointly
Exemptions: 7 Yourself ✗ 8 Spouse ✗
9 First names of your dependent children who lived with you PATRICIA 1
11 Total exemptions claimed 3
12 Wages, salaries, tips, etc. (Attach Forms W-2 to back. If unavailable, attach explanation) 250 000 00
13a Dividends $ 180.00 13b Less exclusion $ 200.00 Balance -0-
14 Interest. Enter total here (also list in Part II of Schedule B, if total is over $100) 10 250 56
15 Income other than wages, dividends, and interest (from line 40) 2692 00
16 Total (add lines 12, 13c, 14 and 15) 262 942 56
17 Adjustments to income (such as "sick pay," moving expense, etc. from line 45)
18 Adjusted gross income (subtract line 17 from line 16) 262 942 56
19 Tax -0-
20 Tax surcharge. See Tax Surcharge Tables A, B and C in instructions. -0-
21 Total (add lines 19 and 20) -0-
22 Total credits (from line 55)
23 Income tax (subtract line 22 from line 21) -0-
24 Other taxes (from line 61) 792 81
25 Total (add lines 23 and 24) 792 81
26 Total Federal income tax withheld (attach Forms W-2 to back) 73 407 24
27 1970 Estimated tax payments (include 1969 overpayment allowed as a credit) 100 00
28 Other payments (from line 65)
29 Total (add lines 26, 27, and 28) 73 507 24
30 If line 25 is larger than line 29, enter BALANCE DUE.
31 If line 29 is larger than line 25, enter OVERPAYMENT 72 714 43
32 Line 31 to be: (a) Credited on 1971 estimated tax $ 100 00 (b) Refunded $ 72 614 43
Sign here: Richard Nixon / Patricia Nixon
Arthur Blech, C. P. A.
5900 Wilshire Blvd

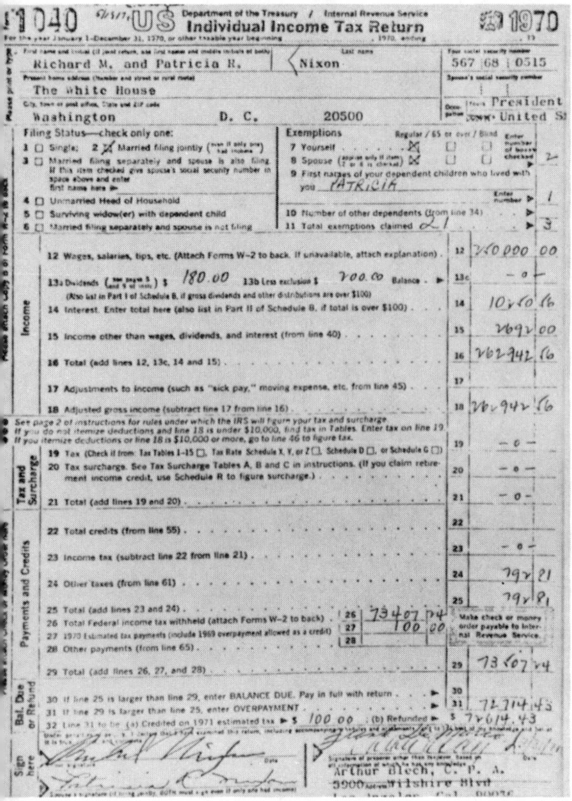

Act eliminating such deductions. The congressional staff report said the deed of the gift, dated March 27, 1969, was not signed, as claimed, on April 21, 1969 (at least by all parties) but rather on April 10, 1970.

A White House spokesman said April 4 that the back-tax assessment had "almost virtually wiped out" Nixon's personal savings and that he would have to borrow a substantial amount in order to meet his obligation. Nixon's net worth, according to his financial statement in December, 1973, was $988,000, of which $432,000 was in cash and most of the rest in real estate. (See also WATERGATE SCANDAL, fourth section, 1973.)

President's Tax Return. The page at left from Nixon's 1970 tax form states that $73,407.24 was withheld in federal income tax on gross income of $262,942.56. The president claimed and received a refund of $72,614.43 for overpayment. In April, however, the White House said Nixon would pay back taxes plus interest on the basis of a report from the Internal Revenue Service that he owed about $465,000 on income earned during his first term in office. A deduction of $482,018 for his gift of his vice-presidential papers was disallowed.

Picture Credits

Ambassade de France—214
Bell Aerospace—152
Chicago Public Library—196
Eric Pollitzer—154
Expo '74 World's Fair—175 (all)
Fairfield *Daily Ledger*—170
Howard Atlee—235 (right)
Keystone Press Agency—160, 167, 179, 186, 188, 205, 229, 259
Leo Castelli—156, 158
Max Eisen—236
Museum of Contemporary Art—155, 157
National Association of College Admissions Counselors—172 (bottom)
National Broadcasting Company—212
Ollie Atkins—144 (top)
Pictorial Parade—150 (top) 180 (right), 183, 215 (both), 218 (bottom), 241 (top), 253
Saint Augustine's College—172 (top)
Simon and Schuster—195
Sygma—cover, 136-137, 138 (bottom), 139, 140, 141, 145, 177, 178, 180 (left), 190 (both), 201, 207 (bottom), 216, 217, 218 (top)
UPI—148 (bottom) 191, 223 (all), 225 (both), 227, 233, 237, 242, 255, 261, 264
U.S. Air Force—148 (top), 151 (bottom)
U.S. Army—150 (bottom)
U.S. Navy—151 (top)
Walker Art Center—159
Wide World—138 (top), 142, 143, 144 (bottom), 161, 162, 165, 166, 168, 169, 184 (both), 187, 192, 200, 203 (both), 207 (top), 208, 209, 210, 221 (all), 226, 230, 232, 235 (left), 238, 239, 241 (bottom), 247 (all), 252, 254, 256, 257, 258, 260, 262, 263
Willis Proudfoot—198, 199

NEWS in brief

NATO Declaration

En route to the Moscow summit, President Nixon joined leaders of the 15-nation North Atlantic Alliance on June 26 at NATO headquarters in Brussels in signing a new Atlantic Charter. The signing came on the occasion of the 25th anniversary of NATO. The reaffirmed alliance insures close consultations among member nations while restating the basic security interests of the North American and European allies.

Agnew Disbarred

On May 2, the Maryland Court of Appeals ruled that former Vice President Spiro Agnew could no longer practice law, as a result of his no-contest plea to a tax-evasion charge in 1973. The court held unanimously that disbarment follows automatically from a lawyer's conviction on a charge involving moral turpitude unless he makes a "compelling exculpatory explanation." In holding that Agnew's lawyers had failed to make such an explanation, Associate Judge J. Dudley Digges maintained that "it is difficult to feel compassion for an attorney who is so morally obtuse that he consciously cheats for his own pecuniary gain that government he has sworn to serve."

Beerball

The 1974 baseball season was marked by some ugly surprises as teams around the country noticed an upsurge in violence directed towards players. The trend hit a peak in Cleveland, where fans were enticed to a game against Texas by the lure of 10-cent beer. Some of the 25,000 in attendance found the atmosphere intoxicating, venting their energy in streaking across the field or attempting to kiss the umpires. Towards the ninth inning though, the energy turned more destructive, as hundreds of fans flooded the field and began fighting with players of both teams. The game was stopped and forfeited to the Rangers.

Record Sale

A 16¼-inch-high early Ming Dynasty blue-and-white bottle, dating from about 1400, set a new world auction record for a piece of porcelain. At Sotheby's in London, the piece brought £420,000, or the equivalent of $1,003,800.

Suspended Animation

Two California scientists reported that they had discovered the oldest living creatures—bacteria frozen in the depths of Antarctica which had been able to survive for between 10,000 and 1 million years. The bacteria were found on a routine drilling project aimed at studying Antarctica's geological history. When the samples were cultured in the lab, the bacteria were revived, and some of them even reproduced. Scientists reported that they were unlike any bacteria yet known. Another drilling site 60 miles away yielded still more unidentifiable bacteria, different even from the first group.

The discovery offered scientists important new clues with which to study the evolution of life on earth and also gave more credence to the possibility of life on other planets. Mars, for example, which is now arid and frozen, might have in an earlier age supported strains of life that now lie buried.

Bad Vibrations

Weather conditions play a role in mental health, according to a report by a research team at the University of Pennsylvania. A study of 879 people in Philadelphia found that high barometric pressure was associated with more people seeking help for depression, while days of low pressure resulted in more cases of intoxication. There were fewer homicides on days with sunshine. The study also found that rising levels of air pollution were associated with increased drug use, psychiatric emergencies concerning children, violence and violent deaths, and neuroses.

Disarming Competition

A total of 150 male and female contestants converged on Las Vegas in May to take part in national tournaments for arm-wrestling—or wrist-wrestling, as the contestants called it. About 500 persons watched the matches, which were held in the grand ballroom of the new MGM Grand Hotel.

As he awaited the final of the heavyweight division, George Ludwigsen of Brooklyn, New York, explained that arm-wrestling calls for not only strength, but also quickness, strategy, and mental concentration. He said he had been working out with pulleys five days a week for a year. In the finals, he succumbed to a former world champion, Jim Dosini of Petaluma, California.

Weather Study

Scientists from more than 70 countries were to participate in the summer of 1974 in what U.S. government officials called "the largest and most complex international scientific experiment ever undertaken." The experiment was a detailed study, from space to the ocean floor, of a 20-million-square-mile land and sea area centered in the South Atlantic.

The main purpose of the study is to observe the origin and development of tropical storms. Additionally, scientists intend to gather all relevant data which might help determine the cause of the disastrous drought that has struck parts of Africa. One scientist described the area under study as "the boiler of the giant heat engine that runs our atmosphere." He and his colleagues expect the expedition to yield data which could help man to understand global climate trends.

Rent-A-Tree

To combat the 25-cent price tag on a single apple and also offer a bit of pastoral pleasure to the city dweller, two Californians have begun providing a rent-a-tree service. Their orchard, located 60 miles north of San Francisco, leases trees for $25 to $150 a year and guarantees the customer a yield of at least two boxes of apples. Renters of large trees may cart off up to a ton of apples. Additionally, renters have full sitting, picnicking and climbing rights.

Singing Telegram Falls Flat

On June 2, the last singing telegram was delivered. California, the last bastion of musical messages, discontinued the service which was inaugurated, Western Union officials say, in 1934 by a greeting sent to actor-singer Rudy Vallee. While interest in the musical telegram ran at a high pitch for many years, the company now admits that its other services have eclipsed the singing telegram on the corporate hit parade.

Money Depletion

In what may have been the biggest swindle of its kind, more than 2,000 rich and not-so-rich persons lost a total of approximately $100 million. The scheme, which reportedly bilked its victims under the guise of an oil-drilling operation, involved such characters as a persuasive Oklahoma oil lawyer and an Oxford-accented salesman who wined and dined prospective investors at Manhattan's 21 Club. Pictures that purported to show the drilling operation apparently were taken on a California vegetable farm, with the irrigation pipes painted oil-field orange.

The "sting" worked on the premise that one investor would attract others. The fact that many of them had Wall Street reputations certainly didn't hurt matters. Among those who invested were Walter B. Wriston, chairman of the nation's second largest bank, First National City of New York, and George J. W. Goodman, the Wall Street maverick who writes books on how to become wealthy under the name "Adam Smith." Also included in the long list of losers were lawyers, politicians, and show-business personalities such as Barbara Streisand, Jack Benny, Liza Minnelli, and Bob Dylan.

"Good Evening"

"The most exquisite murders have been domestic, performed with tenderness in simple, homey places like the kitchen table or the bathtub. Nothing is more revolting to my sense of decency than the underworld thug who is able to murder anyone—even people to whom he has not been properly introduced." Tongue-in-cheek, master filmmaker Alfred Hitchcock delivered these remarks on his conception of psychological horror to a star-studded benefit gathering at New York's Lincoln Center attending a retrospective honoring of his work. Among those in attendance were Hitchcock heroine Grace Kelly and an unabashedly admiring master of ceremonies, French director Francois Truffaut. Those who paid $100 or more also attended a reception, where they received champagne and "just desserts."

Motel Blues

Three out of four Holiday Inns have chaplains on call as part of a unique ministry to the lonely and possibly suicidal traveler. The giant motel chain plans to extend the service to all its facilities, providing the counseling that has already been credited with saving almost 1,000 lives.

A Shattering Experience

The tallest building in New England, Boston's 60-story unoccupied John Hancock Tower, will be getting a facelift as workmen begin replacing the 10,344 windows which comprise the building's outer shell. Plagued by problems since its inception, the skyscraper became a standing joke because of its window breakage—5,160 broken panes—replaced with plywood patches over the past two years.

Architects and engineers, struggling to solve the mystery of the breaking glass, finally recommended the installation of high-strength, tempered glass a half an inch thick. Hancock officials have yet to reveal the nature of the window problem but the building, which has achieved worldwide notoriety because of its architectural flaw, hopes to open its doors in late 1974, three years behind schedule. Meanwhile, the courts are handling $3.1 million in unresolved damage suits against the building's owners.

President for Life

Eighty-two-year-old Marshal Tito of Yugoslavia signed a document May 16 making him president of the nation for life. At the same time officials representing the country's eight republics and provinces were elected to the collective federal presidency that Tito heads. All are old World War II comrades of the president.

Significantly seated at Tito's right was Edvard Kardelj, 64, chief theoretician of Yugoslavia's Communist party, which controls the government. Tito has never named a potential successor, but Kardelj, who was elected as representative of Slovenia in the collective presidency, is generally viewed as Tito's favorite in line for the succession.

League Votes To Expand

By a margin of better than 2 to 1, the League of Women Voters agreed May 7 to end its long-standing policy of barring full membership to men. The decision by the 54-year-old group was seen as historic in its possible effect on other exclusive-sex organizations. Many members opposed the action, arguing that some women did not have enough self-assurance to participate equally with men. But the majority felt that unless the organization began reflecting the confidence the women's-liberation movement has given many women, it would quickly lose its effectiveness. Lucy Wilson Benson, president of the league, put it simply: "If we're ready for the Equal Rights Amendment, then we darn well ought to be ready for men."

Gay Rights Defeated

The New York City Council defeated a bill May 23 that was meant to ban discrimination in housing, jobs, or public accommodation because of "sexual orientation." The proposal's narrow defeat did not end the battle over the issue of homosexual rights in New York, but it was disheartening news for supporters of similar measures in smaller, less-liberal areas of the country. Proponents of the bill plan to reintroduce the measure, hoping to break the resistance of opposition groups like the Uniformed Fire Officers Association and the New York Archdiocese of the Catholic Church, which labeled the measure a threat to family life.

Introduction to Utopia

Having studied the utopian ideas of Plato, Huxley, and B. F. Skinner, 275 students in Boston University's College of Basic Studies are leaving the classroom to search for their own utopias by participating in simulated societies in order to test their ideas. According to one of the program's founders, the exercise is meant "to foster an integrated and imaginative approach to general education."

Fulbright Loses to Bumpers

On May 27, Governor Dale Bumpers of Arkansas, defeated Senator J. William Fulbright in the Democratic party primary, foiling Fulbright's bid for a sixth term. Fulbright, chairman of the Senate Foreign Relations Committee, has been a long-time critic of American foreign policy.

One effect of Fulbright's defeat would be the shuffling of two major Senate posts. Senator John Sparkman of Alabama was expected to succeed Fulbright as foreign-relations chairman. Senator William Proxmire of Wisconsin would then replace Sparkman as chairman of the Banking Committee, which has jurisdiction over much major domestic legislation.

New Belgian Government

A 96-day government crisis was ended April 26 when a minority cabinet composed of members of the moderate Christian Social party and the conservative Party of Progress, or Liberals, was sworn into office by King Baudouin. Leo Tindemans, leader of the Social Christians' Flemish wing, became premier.

Elections on March 10 gave the Social Christians and Liberals 102 of the 212 seats in the Chamber of Deputies—five short of a majority. The new administration won a confidence vote May 4 because 47 members representing French- and Dutch-speaking federalist parties abstained. The abstentions reflected political rifts in Belgium arising from the desire of the federalists to transform the centralized government into a federation split along language lines.

On June 10, however, the French-language federalist party, the Walloon Union, agreed to join the government—the first time one of Belgium's three federalist parties had done so. The newly enlarged cabinet won a vote of confidence on June 14, by a vote of 108 to 79.

For All You Disaster Buffs

Californians have been warned for years of the perils of earthquakes, but it appears that they'll get their first taste at the movie theater. Venturing into the "catastrophe" genre legitimized by the shock-technique box-office success of *The Poseidon Adventure,* Hollywood filmmakers recently simulated the effect of an earthquake registering 10.0 on the Richter scale. (The Richter scale is a logarithmic scale which is used to measure the energy released by an earthquake. The Alaskan earthquake of 1964, one of the most powerful on record, had a Richter measure of 8.4.)

Earthquake, a film chronicling the natural destruction of Los Angeles, is just one of several disaster films currently in production. Others offer such attractions as swarms of giant bees, burning skyscrapers, and threatening cockroaches.

Penniless

Although the U.S. Bureau of the Mint is turning out 12 billion pennies in 1974, twice as many as in 1973, the nation is still caught in a coin shortage. Bank officials estimate that hoarders have packed away more than 30 billion pennies over the past 10 years, some to lighten their wallets, and others in the hopes that rising copper prices will make the coins worth more than one cent each. (A new ruling by the Treasury Department makes this unlikely, as it is now illegal to melt down or export pennies.)

In an attempt to bolster their supplies, many banks have staged collection drives. One bank in Akron, Ohio, offered $1.10 for every 100 pennies brought to the bank, and city residents responded by turning in a total of 1.4 million coins. A grocery-store chain in northern California resorted to issuing credit coupons in place of pennies.

South African Elections

Prime Minister John Vorster's National party gained four seats in South Africa's April 24 general elections, giving it 122 of the House of Assembly's 169 seats. Vorster called the vote "a clear indication that the people have once again chosen the policy of separate development," which would ultimately lead to independence for the new semi-autonomous black enclaves, or Bantustans. The country's black and Asian peoples were not franchised to vote in the national elections with the country's 2.2 million white electorate.

Colin Eglin, leader of South Africa's most liberal official political party, the Progressive party, which won six seats, thought the election results significant because, "for the first time, a significant number of white South Africans have shown that they are prepared to come to terms with modern multiracial South Africa." Others speculated that the results documented a polarization between conservative and reformist factions in the United party, the National party's official opposition which now holds 41 seats in the House of Assembly. It was this split in United party ranks which reportedly prompted Vorster to call for the elections, a year before necessary.

Japanese Roulette

The thrill of danger accompanies the experience of eating fugu—a Japanese fish delicacy. Fugu is among the most poisonous of all marine creatures, and no antidote or cure has ever been found. Each year scores of Japanese suffer paralysis or death from eating the fish, yet it is more popular than ever before and is sold in some 1,500 restaurants in Tokyo alone. Many Japanese still sing a folk song that goes, "I want to eat fugu, but I don't want to die."

In order to lessen the annual body count, Tokyo's Board of Health requires chefs to pass a test before they are licensed to prepare fugu in the city's restaurants. They must classify and label five different species of the fish and then prepare it safely. At the traditional post-exam party, they feast upon the fugu they have certified as safe. In 1972, only 26 per cent of 878 applicants passed the test.

Fugu poisoning spreads from the lips and mouth to the fingers, arms, and tongue. Next the veins swell and blood pressure drops. As the abdomen contracts, it becomes difficult to breathe. The mind remains lucid, but the paralysis spreads. Death puts an end to suffering in about two hours.

Cumulative Index
first and second sections

INDEX

Understanding
the
Brain

A bio-feedback instructor covers his eyes with a sawed-in-half Ping-Pong ball to block out distractions and reach a state of "clear consciousness." *Above,* inside an inflatable plastic environment, he leads a dozen trainees who are tuning in to their alpha brain waves.

The Brain Changers

by MAYA PINES

Scientists and the new mind control

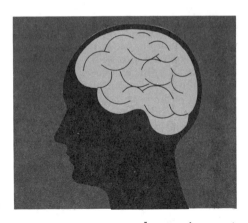

THE MOST EXCITING and mysterious part of the universe is not some primitive jungle or the ocean's floor or even a distant planet. It is the magical three and a half pounds of pinkish-gray jelly we carry around inside our skulls—the human brain. This mechanism, the source of all our thoughts and actions, is at the center of a scientific explosion. Biologists, chemists, psychologists, surgeons, even engineers, are converging on it from every point on the scientific spectrum, and what these brain researchers may tell us about its workings will have a profound effect on the future of human life. We will have the power to use our brains more effectively, to control our own brain waves, to improve our memories, to shape babies' brains, and to sharpen or suppress various emotions—in ourselves and in others. One can only guess what this power may mean in the future, or how it might be used, but now the major directions of research are clear.

It is all extremely new. The brain itself has been studied for less than a century. Encased in its thick armor of skull, this convoluted mass defied analysis. For thousands of years, few tried, and those who did attempt to explore it sometimes took one look and gave up in despair. Aristotle, the "father of psychology," taught that the

Maya Pines is a journalist who specializes in education and science. This article is excerpted from THE BRAIN CHANGERS, copyright© 1973 by Maya Pines. Reprinted by permission of Harcourt Brace Jovanovich, Inc.

brain was merely a cooling mechanism for the blood, while all the real thinking went on in the heart. Even after Galen corrected this error, there were no adequate tools with which to investigate the brain. When the invention of the microscope and the discovery of electricity at last made it possible for research to begin, generations of Western scientists refrained from violating the human brain, out of respect for it as the seat of man's immortal soul.

Even today, despite broad progress, researchers remain totally ignorant about how the brain performs its basic job: how it transforms 10 watts of electricity and some chemicals into our thoughts, feelings, dreams, memories—our awareness of being ourselves. It is beyond understanding. But despite their ignorance, scientists have identified several sensitive triggers or control points in the brain, largely through trial and error, and in the past twenty years, they have made astonishing practical progress in controlling various brain functions. They are now approaching the point, for the first time, where they will know how to change not only our moods, but also our abilities and to some extent our behavior. . . .

Controlling One's Own Brain Waves

. . . A movement to teach people how to control their own brains has been gathering speed in recent years. Some of the nation's most imaginative researchers are now involved in it, as well as thousands of students, volunteers, and camp followers of all kinds. Together they are soaring off into a beautiful world where everything seems possible—the world of bio-feedback.

It is not necessary to drill a hole in the skull to control the brain, they say. Nor is it necessary to take drugs. All one needs is concentration, coupled with precise information on what's going on in one's brain *at the time it occurs*. Then, with training, one can achieve the kind of self-control that people have always dreamed of but seldom attained. One can become oblivious to pain, exceptionally alert, or fall into a creative reverie, at will.

Of course yogis and Zen masters have known such skills for years, but they learn them the hard way, through a lifetime of meditation and study. In the West, we want speed as well as hard evidence. Today both have become available through bio-feedback, a technique that depends on electronic gadgets which measure and amplify physiological changes so small that until recently they were almost totally ignored.

By now hundreds of volunteers have learned to produce small changes in their blood pressure, lower their heart rates, alter their brain rhythms, or stop the activity of a single cell in their spinal cord—functions previously believed to be "involuntary," or beyond human control.

They have done all this without drugs, and without black magic. For bio-feedback simply extends normal ways of learning. Everything we learn depends on some sort of feedback—from eyes, ears, hands, feet, other people, or other sources—that shows us whether we are succeeding or failing in what we are trying to do. But under normal circumstances, we are limited in the kind of feedback we can get from our body. We don't have words to say what's going on inside us. Very often we can't even identify it. Small increases or decreases in blood pressure remain hidden from consciousness. So do changes in the rhythm of our brain waves. With the aid of sensitive bio-feedback equipment, however, such internal fluctuations can be measured, displayed, and evaluated instantly to tell the learner whether he is improving or not.

. . . A number of patients whose hearts skipped a beat succeeded in training their hearts to beat in a normal manner through bio-feedback—at least in the laboratory. Others, who suffered from hypertension, learned to lower their blood pressure, though the changes were too small to be very useful. Migraine patients cured themselves of headaches by increasing the blood flow in their hands, which relieved their heads. . . .

Very fittingly, the first person to offer evidence of Zen-like control over the brain through bio-feedback was a serene psychologist of Japanese descent, Dr. Joe Kamiya, of San Francisco's Langley Porter Neuropsychiatric Institute . . . He had long been interested in states of consciousness—the inner states that change so radically during dreams, under drugs, and at other times. However, his training as a behaviorist

A bio-feedback subject attempts to control the temperature of his hands. Hundreds have learned to produce small changes in their blood pressure, lower their heart rates, or alter their brain rhythms—functions previously believed to be beyond voluntary human control.

Mesmerism. This drawing by the 19th-century artist Honoré Daumier illustrates the mysterious power of suggestion under hypnosis.

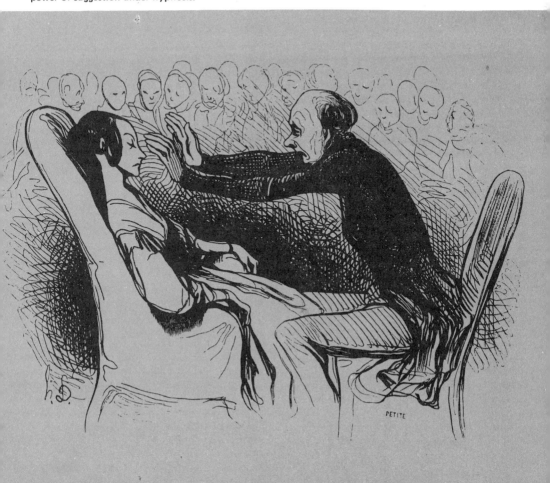

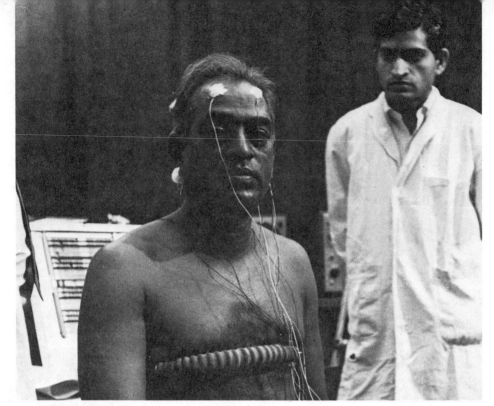

At right, drawing of a
mental patient placed
in a "tranquilizing chair"
recommended in 1810
by the noted physician
Benjamin Rush.
Above, the true tran-
quility of a yogi wired
in order to monitor his
physiological responses.

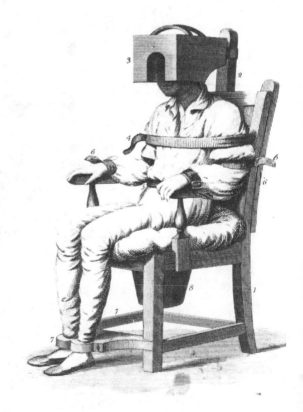

made such vague concepts as "mind" or "consciousness" taboo as subjects for research. Behaviorists were supposed to study only what could be measured—specific stimuli and responses. So, while doing conventional research on EEG [electroencephalogram] changes during sleep and dreams in Chicago in 1958, Kamiya "bootlegged" some work on the EEGs of people who were wide-awake. He wanted to see whether he could train them to recognize the comings and goings of various rhythms in their brains, starting with the most prominent rhythm of all, the alpha rhythm . . . He pasted electrodes on their scalp, watched the pattern of their brain waves on an EEG, and rang a bell sometimes when the alpha rhythm was present, sometimes when it was absent, asking the volunteers to guess which state they were in. Every time he rang the bell they had to reply, and each time he told them whether they were right or wrong. During the first hour they usually guessed right only half the time, which suggests that nothing more than chance was operating. But by the second hour of training they could guess right 60 percent of the time, by the third hour they were right 75 to 80 percent of the time, and after a while some of the volunteers could actually guess right every single time—as often as four hundred times in a row!

"The subject had learned to read his own brain, or his mind," Kamiya announced. "He had become aware of an internal state."

Even more exciting was something Kamiya discovered by accident: having learned to recognize his alpha waves, one of the volunteers also knew how to turn them on or off at will. And when Kamiya tested the others, he found that all his subjects were able to do so, at least to some extent. . . .

What's so good about being in alpha? I asked Kamiya. "Here are the words that subjects use to describe it," he replied. "Calm; alert; relaxed; open to experiences of all kinds; pleasant, in the sense that to be serene is pleasant, as opposed to the hassle of American life. It's akin to the good feeling that comes from taking a massage or sauna bath—a relaxed, put-together sort of feeling. It's receptive, as

opposed to a getting, forcing frame of mind. You have to let it occur spontaneously, then be happy you have it." . . .

But as fast as the legitimate research grows, the quacks proliferate even faster. They moved in as soon as alpha training hit the nation's campuses, and publicity in the mass-circulation magazines helped them along. California attracts the most vociferous hawkers, who promise people anything—lose weight! find the man or woman of your choice! learn intuition!—through expensive alpha training. . . .

There is some question, too, whether bio-feedback training can change people quickly and profoundly enough to be of real therapeutic value outside the laboratory. Can a person who is seriously ill with heart disease or hypertension actually rely on his new powers of self-control? Or will they desert him in time of crisis? . . . Bio-feedback's major contribution to medicine may be in the early prevention of disease, in re-educating people before they cause permanent damage to their internal organs.

It might also lead to a healthier way of life. At the University of Colorado Medical Center, Thomas H. Budzynski, a psychologist, has started re-educating insomniacs by training them to produce slow brain waves. Before giving them EEG feedback, he trains them to relax their forehead muscles through feedback from a different instrument, the electromyograph (EMG). Learning to relax these muscles produces a general relaxation, which he considers a prerequisite for slow-alpha and theta rhythms. Two of his three pilot patients learned to fall asleep readily in this way. Budzynski hopes that millions of people will give up barbiturates and tranquilizers, replacing them with feedback training. . . .

Changing The Baby's Brain

Ever since Freud it has been known that a human being's character is pretty well set by the experiences he has had before the age of five. Intelligence, however, was supposed to be fixed by heredity. There was no evidence that early experiences could in any way change the anatomy or chemistry of the brain.

The man most responsible for proving that such changes do in fact occur is Professor David Krech, an ebullient, witty, gray-bearded psychologist at the University of California at Berkeley. . . .

If one wants to make an animal more intelligent, concluded Krech after a long series of experiments, love is not enough; physical exercise is not enough; visual stimulation is neither necessary nor sufficient; the presence of other young animals is not enough; and deliberate teaching helps, but not much. The only experience that really stretches a rat's brain is the opportunity to explore a large number of different objects, or a large variety of mazes. According to Krech, this is a species-specific requirement, since rats need to have good "space-brains." Human beings have different requirements, he believes, mostly connected with language, although he cannot prove it. However, he did prove that by manipulating the environment of the young, one can truly create a "lame brain." Or one can create a better brain and a smarter animal at will. . . .

Meanwhile, the other members of the team are continuing to study the effects of enriched environments on the brains of rats, mice, and gerbils at various times after birth. . . . These experiments tend to support psychologist Benjamin Bloom's theory that the easiest time to make a profound change in a child's intelligence is while that intelligence is growing most rapidly, before the age of four. Bloom, a professor of education at the University of Chicago, analyzed over a thousand longitudinal studies of growth and noted that there is a specific growth curve for each human characteristic. Half of a child's future height, for instance, is reached by the age of two-and-a-half. By the age of four, his IQ becomes so stable that it is a fairly accurate indicator of his intelligence and maturity. Bloom then formulated a general rule: the environment will have maximum impact on a specific trait during that trait's period of most rapid growth. As time goes by, more and more powerful forces are required to produce a given amount of change, if it can be produced at all. This rule now appears to apply equally well to the structure of the brain, since brain changes can be brought about most easily and dramatically shortly after birth, at a time when the brain is growing at top speed. . . .

The best explanation of why rats, like children, "learn by doing" comes from some recent work by scientists at MIT. The key to it is feedback—the information that the brain receives both about its own efforts and about their results. An animal cannot learn a new motor skill just by looking, because this involves no feedback. It must try out certain movements, and it must try them out *voluntarily*. This enormous difference between voluntary and passive movement is an exciting concept. . . .

Everything the newborn does or fails to do shapes its brain, sometimes irreversibly. For in all animals, and presumably man, there are critical periods of development, during which certain things *must* happen or it will be too late.

It takes only four days to kill off the marvelous "feature detectors" in the brains of kittens, for instance. These "feature detectors" are cells in the visual cortex that specialize in identifying patterns and shapes. If a kitten's eye is kept closed for four days during the critical period (which for cats is the fourth week of life, according to recent work by Harvard's David Hubel and Thorsten Wiesel), it loses its connections to the cortex and its retina atrophies, so that the other eye becomes permanently dominant. If both eyes are kept covered during those four days, the cat will be functionally blind. . . .

Most of what is known about critical periods in the development of the human brain is tragic. At certain stages during the first three months of pregnancy, for instance, the German measles virus can irreparably damage the fetus's brain, though later in pregnancy it may do no harm. The brains of millions of babies are being stunted every day as a result of poor nutrition at critical times. It has become utterly clear, from studies by pediatricians such as the late Herbert Birch, of the Albert Einstein College of Medicine, and Myron Winick, of Columbia University's Institute of Human Nutrition, that low-protein diets damage children's brains, and that if this occurs before six months of age the damage may be irreversible. . . .

Slowly, then, we are beginning to learn how to make a superior brain. It is a matter of programming, of providing the most

Young children learn by
doing. The key is feed-
back—the information
that the brain receives
both about its own
efforts and about
the results.

favorable environment for specific needs at
various critical times both before and after
birth. Of course the genes set limits beyond which one cannot go, but these are
so broad that nobody ever reaches them,
and they leave room for infinite variations
according to circumstances. Man's intelligence, for instance, may vary up to 40
IQ points, depending on his environment,
says the University of Arizona's Professor
Samuel A. Kirk. More conservatively, Benjamin Bloom estimates that a child's environment is responsible for roughly 20 IQ
points—still a formidable span, notes Bloom,
one that could mean the difference between life in an institution for the feeble-
minded and a productive life in society, or
between a professional career and an occupation at the semiskilled or unskilled
level. By the age of four, the direction is
usually quite clear. . . .

Prenatal programing of the brain could
include chemical intervention—special
foods, hormones, perhaps drugs if necessary; physical intervention, possibly along
the lines of the "decompression" treatments pioneered by a South African physician, Dr. O. S. Heyns, which reduce
pressure on the mother's womb and increase the amount of oxygen available to
the fetus during the last ten days of
pregnancy (the babies born after these
treatments are said to be exceptionally intelligent and well developed); and psychological intervention, which may be the
most difficult to develop. It is well known
that babies born of mothers who live near
airports or in the path of jet planes have
different reactions to sound than do other
infants. The old wives' tales about maternal
impressions—the stories about children
marked forever by some event in their
mothers' lives just before they were born—
may yet turn out to have more than a
grain of truth. . . .

Within a few decades, it should be in
our power—as it is only partly today—to
produce the kinds of brains we want. We
will know how nutrition, chemistry, activity, environmental variety, and other factors interact to shape the baby's brain. . . .

Which Half of Your Brain Is Dominant?

Linked together like Siamese twins right
down the middle of our brains, two very

275

Brain injury. **The man above has suffered a head wound affecting the area of the brain that helps in understanding spatial relationships; he therefore is confused about such concepts as "above" and "beneath."**

Severe epilepsy sometimes requires a brain operation in which the two halves of the brain are "disconnected." A patient who underwent the operation was shown a composite photograph flashed briefly on a screen, with her eyes fixed upon a red dot in the center of the composite so that the half-face in her left visual field could be projected only to the right hemisphere of her brain, and vice versa. Asked to "point to the face you saw" from a collection of photos, she chose the face on the left side of the composite, indicating that the right hemisphere recognizes faces better than the left.

different persons inhabit our heads. One of them is verbal, analytical, dominant. The other is artistic but mute, and still almost totally mysterious.

These are the left and right hemispheres of our brains, the twin shells that cover the central brain stem. In normal people, they are connected by millions of nerve fibers which form a thick cable called the corpus callosum. If this cable is cut, as must be done in certain cases of severe epilepsy, a curious set of circumstances occurs. The left side of the brain—the speaking half—no longer knows what the right side is doing, yet it insists on finding excuses for whatever the mute half has done, and still operates under the illusion that they are one person. . . .

In animals, a split brain may prove relatively unimportant. After all, both hemispheres are enclosed in a single head, attached to a single body, and normally exposed to identical experiences. Furthermore, the left and right halves of their brains do exactly the same job. But this is not the case for human beings.

Alone among the mammals, man has developed different uses for each half of his brain. This asymmetry, which we all recognize when we say whether we're right- or left-handed, is the glorious mechanism through which man is enabled to speak. It is what separates us from the apes. There are various theories about how it developed and whether it is present right from birth, but it is quite clear that by the time a child reaches the age of ten, one hemisphere—usually the left—has taken over the task of language.

For simpler operations, such as receiving sensations from one's hand or ordering movements to one's foot, the human brain remains generally symmetrical. The nerve impulses that carry messages from one side of the body travel up the spinal column and cross over into the opposite side of the brain, there to form a sort of mirror image of the parts they represent. The nerve connections involved are set at birth in an incredibly precise fashion that allows the brain to know instantly where certain sensations come from and where to aim specific instructions.

When tasks become more complex, however, this mirrorlike representation is aban-doned. Then the association areas of the brain come into play and each one develops in its own way, according to experience. Since we have only one mouth (unlike the dolphin, which has separate phonation mechanisms on the right and left sides of its body), there is no need for right and left speech centers in the brain. On the contrary, these might conflict with each other and compete for control of the speech mechanisms. In most people, therefore, the speech centers are limited to one side of the brain, usually the left, though about 15 percent of left-handed people have speech on both sides.

Even among the left-handed, the left hemisphere generally controls speech. This near monopoly of the left hemisphere was recognized in the early eighteenth century, when surgeons examined the brains of people who had lost the power of speech and found severe damage on the left side. Why this should be so preordained is not clear. The left hemisphere tends to become dominant in other ways as well. For example, it controls the right hand, which does most of man's skilled work with tools. . . .

In spatial abilities, the right hemisphere is clearly tops. It also recognizes faces better than the dominant left. . . . In general, the right hemisphere seems better at grasping the total picture, the Gestalt, of a scene. And this talent cannot be limited to people whose brains have been split. It must be a form of specialization in all people, resulting from a division of labor much like that which gave language to the left hemisphere.

How many other special skills or talents are the province of the right hemisphere? Nobody knows. But many of man's more poetic or imaginative aspects may stem from there. A few years ago the Russian psychologist A. R. Luria described a composer who became speechless after a stroke, yet went on to compose better music than ever before. He could no longer *write* the notes, but he could play and remember them. Other people who lost the use of their right hemisphere remained able to speak, but could no longer remember melodies. So musical talent, too, appears to be located in the right hemisphere. . . .

Above, a headset plays one melody to one ear and a different melody simultaneously to the other ear; since melodies are processed mainly on the right side of the brain, most subjects are able to pick out the melody presented to the left ear better than the one presented to the right ear.

Much mystery surrounds the behavior of the two half-brains in normal people. Nobody knows whether these twin halves also ignore each other, actively inhibit each other, co-operate, compete, or take turns at the controls. [Dr. Roger] Sperry [a California Institute of Technology professor of psychobiology] believes that they mostly co-operate, because of the 200 million fibers connecting them. But there are other opinions.

The best clues come from children and adults who have had terrible accidents. If a child's left hemisphere is destroyed by a head injury or tumor before he is five or maybe even ten years old, he can learn to speak again—sometimes after a year of silence. His right half-brain will slowly take over the job. Not so for adults, who regain some speech after a stroke only if they have enough uninjured tissue remaining near the injury, on the left side. They cannot use their right half-brain for speaking. If a young child is injured in the right hemisphere, however, he will also experience difficulty with speech, though an adult would not. . . .

By the age of ten, dominance for speech —and probably for other skills as well—is fixed. Tasks of synthesis, spatial perception, and music apparently go to the right side. The left side gets all the sequential, verbal, analytical, computerlike activities. And, strangely, "excellence in one tends to interfere with top-level performance in the

other," Sperry notes. To avoid bottlenecks, eventually most of the traffic flows in one direction, while few opportunities arise for the other hemisphere to develop its own skills. The "traffic cop" in this case may well be the corpus callosum. The speech learned by the right hemisphere in early childhood is thus functionally suppressed. In time, it may be lost or perhaps erased....

Ideally we should be able to turn on the appropriate hemisphere and turn off the other, whenever the task requires it. But in fact we cannot always do so. "Most people are dominated by one mode or the other," observes Dr. Robert Ornstein, a neurologist. "They either have difficulty in dealing with crafts and body movements, or difficulty with language." Culture apparently has a lot to do with this. Children from poor black neighborhoods generally learn to use their right hemisphere far more than their left—and later do badly on verbal tasks. Other children, who have

learned to verbalize everything, find this approach a hindrance when it comes to copying a tennis serve or learning a dance step. Analyzing these movements verbally just slows them down and interferes with direct learning through the right hemisphere.

"We don't have the flexibility we could have," says Ornstein. "We are under the illusion of having more control than we really do." Early in life, it seems, we become shaped either as a "left-hemisphere type," who functions in a largely verbal world, or as a "right-hemisphere type," who relies more on nonverbal means of expression. These are two basically different approaches to the world....

Some training ... may prove particularly useful for children who suffer from what is generally called dyslexia, or specific learning disabilities—a variety of subtle perceptual difficulties that interfere with reading, writing, or spelling. About 10 percent of the nation's children cannot process the information received from their eyes or ears with sufficient accuracy. Despite normal vision and hearing, and normal or even superior intelligence, they may confuse left and right or up and down, or give other evidence of poor coordination. Their symptoms have baffled doctors for years. At a National Academy of Sciences conference in 1969, Dr. Sperry suggested that their problem may be "an overly strong, or extensive, perhaps bilateral, development of the verbal, major-hemisphere type of organization that tends to interfere with an adequate development of spatial gnosis [knowledge] in the minor hemisphere." If there is verbal development on both sides of the brain, the right hemisphere's special skills cannot fully emerge. At the same time, the verbal, analytic skills may suffer from what Gazzaniga calls a problem in decision-making —"Like a husband and wife trying to decide what to have for breakfast; one of them's got to take the lead." If these children don't have a well-established decision system, and then receive two different interpretations of the world, they may be confused or slowed down. Through practice, they might learn to rely on one hemisphere more than the other, thus straightening out their lines of command.

ART/ 283

FOOD/ 309

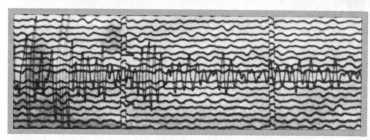

GEOLOGY/ 318

INTERNATIONAL TRADE/ 325

MUSIC/ 341

WOMEN/ 382

Argentina. Juan Perón, president of Argentina, died on July 1 at the age of 78. He was succeeded by his widow and the nation's vice president, Maria Estela (Isabel) Martínez de Perón. She became the first female chief of state in the history of the Americas. Mrs. Perón said she would follow her husband's policies "without an iota of change."

Illness had forced Perón to curtail his activities several times since his return to the presidency in September, 1973. Just before his death, doctors said they were treating him for infectious bronchitis with heart complications.

Perón, president from 1946 to 1955, was ousted in a military coup but retained widespread popularity among the masses through 17 years of exile. After returning from Spain in 1973, he was easily elected president. During nine months in office, he managed to slow inflation, opened diplomatic and trade ties with many Communist countries, and largely removed military influence from politics. He was unable, however, to heal deep rifts within the Peronist movement or to stop terrorism by extremist groups.

Hundreds of thousands of citizens lined the five-mile route on July 2 as Perón's body was transported from the presidential palace to the Metropolitan Cathedral in Buenos Aires for a requiem mass. It was then borne to the Capitol building to lie in state for three days. A crowd lined up eight abreast in the rain outside the Capitol, and many people waited up to 24 hours for the opportunity to pass by the bier and pay their final respects to their leader.

Cuba's Communist regime and Brazil's military government declared three days of mourning—testimony to Perón's standing among both the left and right in Latin America. Cuba had become Argentina's leading trade partner in Latin America during Perón's last presidency.

Argentina's Problems

The new president's term of office was not due to expire until 1977, and she could then run to succeed herself. Isabel Perón,

Isabel Martínez Perón became president of Argentina on July 1, following the death of her husband, Juan Perón. She was the first female chief of state in the history of the Americas.

281

43, her late husband's third wife, had met him in 1956 while performing in a Panama night club. She became not only his wife but also his confidante, political emissary, nurse, and, occasionally, chauffeur. News correspondents reported that she assumed her new duties with confidence despite a lack of formal training in government affairs.

Reportedly closest to Mrs. Perón was José López Rega, minister of social welfare, the late president's personal secretary, and a practicing astrologer. Argentine politicians called him "Rasputin" and said he held an almost hypnotic power over the new president. He was known to side with the conservative wing of the Peronist movement, and the left wing had sworn to kill him.

The death of Perón brought only a scant respite to the political violence that had plagued Argentina for years. Arturo Mor Roig, minister of the interior under the previous military regime, was assassinated in suburban Buenos Aires on July 15. During the following five days, at least six suspects were killed by police and 28 were arrested, all allegedly members of left-wing extremist groups.

More than two dozen people were killed for political reasons between July 31 and August 12, including a left-wing Peronist congressman. The violence included assaults by the People's Revolutionary Army on army installations and arms factories.

By September, political violence was claiming a victim every 48 hours. In mid-September, there were more than 100 bombings during two days alone.

Montoneros, the largest left-wing Peronist group, had declared open opposition to Mrs. Perón's regime. There were half a dozen other leftist terrorist groups in operation and an undetermined number of right-wing terrorist groups, usually described as "death squads," that specialized in eliminating leftists. All, except the most extreme leftist groups, such as the People's Revolutionary Army, described themselves as Peronists. One legislator said, "There could never be a civil war. Nobody knows what the sides are."

But the major concern for most Argentinians was the cost of living. In 1973, inflation was reduced from an annual rate of about 80 per cent to 20 per cent by a "social pact" between labor and management negotiated by Perón that set restraints on prices and wages. But price-controlled foodstuffs such as eggs, milk, and sugar became scarce. "The real inflation is hidden in the black market and the scarcities," said one economist, who blamed large government deficits and inefficient state-owned enterprises for the economic troubles. Mrs. Perón was awarding periodic bonuses to workers, pensioners, and retired persons in order to compensate for inflation and the government's prohibition of strikes.

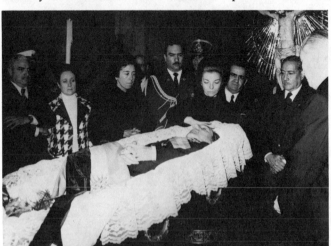

Funeral of Perón. Hundreds of thousands of Argentinians passed by the bier to pay their final respects to their leader. During his most recent term in office, Perón was unable to heal deep rifts within his movement or to stop terrorism by extremist groups.

Hirshhorn Museum, set on Washington's Mall, holds the largest public bequest of art ever made by a single American. The Sculpture Garden is shown below.

Art. On October 1, the Joseph H. Hirshhorn Museum and Sculpture Garden —by far the largest public bequest of art ever made by a single American—was formally unveiled in Washington, D.C. The collection of 6,000 modern paintings and sculptures was valued at close to $100 million in 1966, when it was donated to the federal government. It approaches the collection of New York City's Museum of Modern Art in scope and for the first time gives the nation's capital the status of a major modern art center.

Congress had passed legislation in 1938 authorizing a modern gallery to supplement the National Gallery of Art, which is oriented toward old masters. Construction of the $16-million museum was financed mainly by the government, but Hirshhorn spent about a million dollars of his own money on it.

Hirshhorn, 75, came to the United States from Latvia as a boy. He worked his way up from a $12-a-week office boy to a Wall Street broker, made a fortune buying and selling stocks, and later be-

Galleries Devoted to Late 19th-Century American Painting include works by John Singer Sargent, Thomas Eakins, and Mary Cassatt.

came a uranium magnate. He began buying art in 1917. In addition to his large donation, he holds thousands of other works in his warehouses and homes.

The museum, which from above resembles a giant doughnut, was built on the section of the Mall that runs from the Capitol to the Washington Monument. The building, designed by Gordon Bunshaft of Skidmore, Owings and Merrill, met with little favor from critics. Piers suspend the structure 14 feet above ground level. Because of its mass and the almost total lack of exterior windows, it has a fortresslike appearance.

Interior windows, however, face a central courtyard with sculptures and a large fountain which can spray water as high as the building—82 feet. The courtyard flows under and out the building into a sunken sculpture garden.

About 850 of the 6,000 works were put on exhibit for the museum's first year of operation. The collection is considered strongest in sculpture, and among the works on display were ones by Pablo Picasso, Henri Matisse, Jacques Lipchitz, Henry Moore, Alexander Calder, David Smith, and Alberto Giacometti. Rodin was represented by *The Burghers of Calais* and

20th-Century Art includes a variety of paintings, sculptures, and graphics. The museum's collection is considered strongest in sculpture.

Monument to Balzac.

The exhibits of paintings, graphics, and mixed media, though considered less even in quality and scope than the sculptures, included many fine works from the 19th century to the present. Among the 19th-century Americans represented were John Singer Sargent, Winslow Homer, Mary Cassatt, and Thomas Eakins. There were works by Expressionists Oskar Kokoschka and Edvard Munch, Abstract Expressionists Mark Rothko and Franz Kline, and Surrealists René Magritte and Salvador Dali.

Among the graphics shown were works by Willem De Kooning, Piet Mondrian, Josef Albers, and David Siqueiros. More recent works included ones by Robert Rauschenberg, Andy Warhol, Larry Rivers, and Robert Motherwell.

The museum is administered as a branch of the Smithsonian Institution. Abram Lerner, previously employed by Hirshhorn as his private curator, was appointed director. Art critics, while expressing their admiration for the collection, pointed out that some gaps would have to be filled if the museum were not to remain a static monument to one man's taste.

Automobiles. Detroit automakers emphasized small cars for the 1975 model year. Eight new compact and subcompact models were introduced, with small engines and light weight to conserve gasoline, but also an array of "luxury" options.

Consumers were faced with sharply escalating prices. The average price of a new car had risen nearly $1,000 in a year —about $500 during the 1974-model year and between $400 and $450 for the 1975's. Ford Motor Company president Lee Iacocca conceded that customers would "be in shock" when they saw the 1975 price tags. The auto manufacturers blamed skyrocketing costs of labor, parts, and materials.

The $2,000 subcompact had become a thing of the past. Indeed, only three domestic models bore a sticker price under $3,000—the Chevrolet Vega, Ford Pinto, and American Motors Gremlin. The Vega basic price was $2,799—an increase of 34 per cent in little more than 12 months.

Production schedules for 1975-model cars were set at 6 per cent below 1974, indicating that the automakers felt high prices and the stagnant economy would hurt sales. They predicted sales of 10 to 10.5 million 1975 cars, far below the 1973 record total of 11.8 million. Otto Eckstein, president of Data Resources, Inc., an economic-forecasting concern, was more pessimistic. He predicted that sales would amount to 9.7 million new cars for the 1975 model year.

The initial outlook was that small cars —compacts and subcompacts—would account for more than half the sales in 1975 and an increasing proportion in future years, not only because they are cheaper and use less gas, but also because of the trend toward smaller families and because small autos are useful as second cars. One survey found that in U.S. suburbs, 88 per cent of all households own at least one car, and almost 40 per cent have more than one.

To accommodate consumers concerned with fuel economy, the automakers offered the following:

• Greater availability of small cars and small engines.

• Wider use of radial tires as standard equipment. They improve gas mileage by 5 per cent or more.

• Improved combinations of transmissions and axles, along with better tuned engines for increased efficiency.

• Concentrated efforts to reduce auto weight.

Auto dealers were cheered to find that buyers of small cars were avid for options. Four out of five were ordering automatic transmission, and two out of five were buying air conditioning. The profit margin on accessories is far greater than on the basic vehicle itself.

On the other hand, some auto executives believed that the trend toward small cars had been halted. The gasoline shortage of the 1973-74 winter prompted all the manufacturers to slash output of their big cars in favor of stepped-up assembly of compacts and subcompacts. With fuel supplies plentiful, many buyers showed renewed interest in gas guzzlers, and big cars were in short supply by midsummer.

Most new cars came equipped with a device called a catalytic converter to meet 1975 federal antipollution rules intended to combat two types of pollutants: hydrocarbons and carbon monoxide. The device, which requires the use of unleaded gas, added more than $100 to the price of a new car. Automakers said, however, that it would boost gasoline mileage by up to 15 per cent.

Ford

About half of Ford's production were small cars. Introduced for the first time were the Ford Granada and a slightly higher-priced cousin, the Mercury Monarch. They were touted as small cars with a luxury image and bore sticker prices in the area of $4,000.

The Granada is eight inches narrower, 20 inches longer, and 800 pounds lighter than the intermediate Torino, but is virtually as roomy inside. Its boxy look was designed to bear a resemblance to the Mercedes-Benz. Options include leather upholstery, V-8 engines, and power assists for almost everything.

Aside from the Monarch and Granada, Ford limited its changes for 1975 to a new window design here and there. The Mustang, for example, offered a sliding glass

New 1975 Models. *Top to bottom:* Ford Granada, a subcompact designed to bear a resemblance to the Mercedes-Benz; Chevrolet Monza, a sporty subcompact with dual rectangular headlights; Chrysler Cordoba, an attractive intermediate-size entry.

"moonroof." For the first time, three engine choices were made available for the Mustang—a standard four-cylinder, V-6, and a new V-8.

General Motors

Pontiac offered its first subcompact, the Astre, which was earlier introduced in Canada. This car is the same as the Chevrolet Vega except for differences in the grilles and taillights, plus additional antinoise insulations.

Three sporty subcompacts were added to the GM line—the Chevrolet Monza, Oldsmobile Starfire, and Buick Skyhawk. These models share many components with the Vega and Astre, but prices start much higher, at $4,000.

Chevrolet Nova was given a new body shell. This model and Pontiac Ventura, Buick Apollo, and Oldsmobile Omega, all compacts, show more individuality in grilles, lights, and side ornamentation, and have more glass area.

General Motors planned to offer its first small Cadillac, just slightly larger than its compacts. The tentative name was La-Salle, a brand made by Cadillac before World War II.

GM raised prices of its 1975 models by an average of $434 per car, or 8.5 per cent—the biggest single-year hike in the history of the auto industry. The company planned an even larger increase, but backed down by an average of $70 per car in the face of an admonition by President Ford.

Chrysler

Chrysler spent its styling budget on a line of intermediate-size cars—Chrysler Cordoba, Plymouth Fury, Dodge Charger SE, and Dodge Coronet. Top-line models of the Cordoba, which was a new entry, come equipped with a battery and spark plugs designed for 50,000 miles before replacement. All four share a common body, with the Dodge Coronet and Plymouth Fury less expensive, less fancy versions of the other two. No subcompacts were introduced.

American Motors

AMC, which was not introducing its 1975 models until November, dropped two model lines—the Javelin and Ambassador. With the standard-size Ambassador gone, the largest car in its lineup was the Matador, an intermediate. The Pacer, a new subcompact, was scheduled to be introduced in early 1975. An offshoot of the Gremlin, which American Motors was selling as fast as supply problems permitted, the Pacer would be distinguished by a sharply sloping front hood.

Business and Finance. While Watergate hogged the headlines, inflation had become the No. 1 political concern for most Americans—and for most people abroad as well. The leading non-Communist industrialized nations were suffering from stagflation—stagnant economic activity at the same time as rapidly increasing prices.

In the United States, the cost of living was increasing at an average annual rate of 11 per cent while economists were conceding that the nation was in its sixth postwar recession. Overseas, inflation was much worse, with prices soaring at an annual rate of 19 per cent in France, 20 per cent in Britain, and 26 per cent in Japan. And economic growth in 1974 for 24 leading countries was expected to average only 1.5 per cent.

Ford Weighs Alternatives

In Washington, President Ford initiated a series of meetings that began on September 5 and culminated in an "economic summit" conference on September 27 and 28. He met with economists, businessmen, labor leaders, and state and local officials in seeking to identify the causes of inflation and to develop a consensus on basic policies. The sessions covered different sectors of the economy, including agriculture, transportation, housing, manufacturing, medical care, welfare, finance, and natural resources.

The president had ruled out wage and price controls. A new Council on Wage and Price Stability was created, however, and observers speculated that it might issue industry-by-industry guidelines and hold public hearings when price hikes seemed excessive.

Ford announced his intention to pare the federal budget below $300 billion in expenditures for fiscal 1975—$5 billion below the spending estimate that had been made by the Nixon Administration in Jan-

Economic Summit. President Ford presided over a two-day meeting of economists, businessmen, labor leaders, and government officials that discussed means of fighting inflation. No quick relief was seen.

uary. He reaffirmed Nixon's intention of reducing the federal payroll by 40,000 workers, and he deferred for three months a scheduled 5.5-per-cent pay increase for civil servants. He also asked Congress to cut $20 billion in long-range spending.

Tight Money

One effect of the high rate of inflation was high interest rates. The Federal Reserve Board had been seeking to curb inflation by holding down the supply of money through a high rediscount rate—the rate at which banks can borrow from the Federal Reserve System. As a result, banks were charging their customers high rates for loans; the lowest rate, for preferred customers such as large corporations, was 12 per cent annually. Rates abroad were even higher.

The high cost of borrowing was having numerous effects on the economy. With the stock market in a long-term slump, companies were raising money not by floating new stock issues but by issuing commercial paper—types of promissory notes that pay 11.5 to 13 per cent in annual interest. Attracted by these offerings, investors were abandoning stocks, which led to a further decline of the market.

One study found that since the end of 1968, the average share of stock on the New York Stock Exchange, adjusted for inflation, had dropped 79 per cent—the worst slump since the Great Depression. In September, the Dow Jones index dropped to its lowest level since 1962. About 106 million Americans have at least an indirect interest in the stock market

Alan Greenspan, chairman of the Council of Economic Advisers, warned Congress that there would be no quick, easy cures for inflation and recession. He opposed any significant easing of credit.

Debate on Policy

Many economists maintained that the Federal Reserve Board's tight-money policy must be eased or U.S. industry would be unable to raise the $4.7 trillion of new capital that one study estimates will be needed through 1985 to expand production, clean up pollution, and develop new technology. Tight money, they argued, would send the nation into a severe recession with rising unemployment, and yet would not curb inflation. Restricting the supply of money would not cut wage demands, they said, or bring down oil and food costs, which had been responsible recently for about half the increase in the cost of living. Many think the government should eliminate protectionist regulations that raise prices in such fields as shipping, construction, and steel.

The orthodox view, however, remained that a restrictive monetary policy must be continued to curb inflation. The painful effects on business were necessary, according to this view. Advocates of a restrictive monetary policy argued that there was no indication of a severe economic downturn, since basic industries were operating at more than 90 per cent of productive capacity—high compared to earlier years.

Unemployment increased from 4.6 per cent of the working force in October, 1973, to 5.8 per cent in September, 1974. Many economists believe that the measures they consider necessary to control inflation would entail an unemployment rate of 6 per cent or more. Some policymakers recommended that the federal government create 500,000 to 800,000 public-service jobs at a cost of $4 to $6 billion to hire the unemployed. Others advocated a tax cut for those in low-income brackets, offset by higher taxes on oil companies and the rich.

Cutting the federal budget to $298 billion for fiscal 1975, as recommended by Secretary of the Treasury William Simon, would be an anti-inflation measure, paring the estimated deficit from $11 billion to $4 billion. In just eight years, total federal spending has nearly doubled. But 90 per cent of the annual increase in spending is accounted for by federal programs commonly described as uncontrollable, such

through holdings in trusts, mutual funds, policies issued by insurance companies that invest in stocks, and pension funds.

The Treasury was competing for available money by issuing bills yielding 9 per cent or more in interest. The Treasury issues these bills to finance the national debt; interest on the public debt currently runs $31.5 billion a year.

Savings and loan associations, prime sources of mortgage money, had lost deposits as savers withdrew their funds to seek higher interest than the associations are allowed by law to pay. As a result, home building was in its most drastic decline since World War II.

The commercial banks had stretched their own resources to the limit. At the end of July, the money the nation's banks had out on loan amounted to more than $3 out of every $4 on deposit—unprecedented since the days before the Great Depression. Many large banks actually had more money out on loan than on deposit. They were making up the difference by borrowing from other banks.

as Social Security, Medicare, unemployment benefits, veterans' benefits, retirement pay for civil servants, disaster aid for farmers, and welfare for the elderly and disabled. Since one out of every four Americans benefits from one or more of such programs, budget cutting becomes politically difficult.

World Inflation

In Europe, as in the United States, the central banks were carrying the burden of fighting inflation virtually alone, by restricting credit. Increasing affluence had raised expectations among all groups, not only for material benefits but also for an improved environment and other manifestations of a better "quality of life." European governments, mostly holding power precariously in recent years, mollify all groups by deficit spending.

An additional problem was the $100 billion annually being shifted from oil consumers to producers. Nearly all industrialized countries were running payments deficits because of the sharply increased price of oil imports. Deflationary measures that would reduce demand for oil and other imported goods were seen as politically unacceptable.

In mid-1974, most of the oil producers' income was in dollars on short-term deposit in a handful of institutions, chiefly the London branches of giant U.S. banks. The hope was that since the oil-producing lands, most of them with small populations, can only utilize part of the money for their own development, the rest would be "recycled"—put back in the marketplace and channeled to the nations that need it. However, a "liquidity" problem had developed because the deposits were for extremely short terms—often just overnight. The banks were therefore leery of extending credit for industrial projects, which require long-term loans.

Some banks were restricting their loans to corporate customers of the very highest credit quality. Even European governments found it difficult to borrow money in order to pay their oil bills. Government and business leaders, haunted by fears of a depression, felt they were facing an economic challenge greater than any since the 1930's.

Petrodollar Deposits. Most of the oil producers' income—estimated at $100 billion annually—was being held in dollars on short-term deposit in a handful of banks. The hope was that the bulk of this money would be "recycled"—put back in the marketplace and channeled to the nations that need it the most.

291

Prime Minister Trudeau was congratulated by his wife after election returns showed the Liberal party capturing a majority in Canada's House of Commons. During the campaign Trudeau argued that the best remedy for inflation was to increase supplies and subsidize consumers.

Canada. Prime Minister Pierre Elliott Trudeau won a stunning victory July 8 when his Liberal party captured 141 seats in Canada's 264-member House of Commons. Thus, at a time when the leaders of most Western nations were holding power precariously, Trudeau returned to office with a parliamentary majority.

The Liberals secured 32 more seats than in 1972, when they won 109 seats to 107 for the Conservatives. Their biggest gain was in Ontario, where they won 55 of 88 seats, compared to 36 in 1972. Combined with the usual overwhelming Liberal support in Quebec, the party was able to secure its majority despite being badly beaten, as usual, in the Western provinces.

The socialist New Democratic party suffered a worse setback than the Conservatives, who won 95 seats, a loss of 12. In 1972 the New Democrats won 31 seats, giving the party a vital swing role in Trudeau's maintenance of power. The July elections came about because the New Democrats refused to support Trudeau's budget, forcing the prime minister to call for a new vote in which the New Democrats fell in strength to 16 seats. Apparently, the voters blamed the New Democrats and decided, in an atmosphere of general economic and social uncertainty, that a Trudeau administration offered the best chance for political stability.

The Campaign

The campaign's prime issue was the cost of living, increasing at an annual rate of 11 per cent. Robert Stanfield, the Conservative party leader who had lost to Trudeau in both 1968 and 1972, claimed the Liberals' budgetary and economic policies were not coping with the problem. His own anti-inflation proposal was a 90-day wage and price freeze to be followed by sliding controls and measures to cool the economy.

Many voters found these proposals distasteful. Trudeau fanned their apprehensions by calling Stanfield's program "a proven disaster looking for someplace to happen," referring to the failure of wage and price controls in both Britain and the United States. Trudeau put forward the argument that because Canada's inflationary problems were less critical than those of other industrialized nations, the best remedy was to increase supplies and use tax benefits and consumer subsidies as protection against rising prices. And Trudeau claimed that, even with inflation, the Canadian economy was growing at a 5-percent rate in 1974, very close to its real growth potential.

The emotional language issue was defused by an agreement between party leaders not to emphasize it. Many English-speaking Canadians feel alienated by concessions made to French-speaking citizens during the six years of Trudeau's administration. (Trudeau himself is a fluently bilingual Canadian.) His government had elevated the status of French by making both languages official for government and legal business throughout Canada, by requiring many civil servants to learn French or face demotion, and by placing more French-Canadians in government posts.

(Three weeks after the federal elections, the Quebec legislature passed a bill making French the sole official language of the province. Eighty per cent of the population is French-speaking.)

During the campaign, Trudeau managed to shake off the elitist and snobbish image he had suffered from as his initial charisma wore off following the 1968 elections. His 1972 campaign, which netted him little more than the ability to hold onto his office, was thought by many to have been marred by the intellectual discourses he called "Conversations with Canadians."

As he approached the July elections, Trudeau remarked that "nine-tenths of politics appeals to emotions rather than reason. I'm a bit sorry about that, but this is their world we are living in and therefore I've had to change." This time he was often accompanied on the hustings by his young wife, whom he had heretofore sheltered from public life. She and their two children turned out to be political assets, helping Trudeau shed the swinging-bachelor image he had once sported.

Future Prospects

Trudeau's first major project was expected to be a restructuring of Canadian trade with the United States, which totals $40 billion a year. Each nation is the leading trade partner of the other.

One of Trudeau's campaign promises was that his government would insist that all major new natural-resource projects, such as pipelines and mines, be owned at least 50 per cent by Canadians. Many have been completely owned by foreign companies, principally American.

In a related action, the government planned to shift export emphasis to finished goods instead of raw materials, thereby providing more jobs for Canadi-

ans. Trade Minister Alastair Gillespie explained the importance of such a change: "Americans sensitive to the current Canadian climate must be aware that we are no longer interested in simply supplying rocks, logs, and brains to more highly industrialized nations. Canadians want to make greater use of our own economic skills and potential."

In the area of foreign affairs, Trudeau's government had expressed concern over the spread of nuclear weapons. Its recent sharp criticism of India's nuclear test (see INDIA in the second section) and its decision to review aid to that country because of the test were indications of a more assertive Canadian role in world affairs.

Chile. One year after the overthrow of the Marxist government of President Salvador Allende, Chile remained in the iron grip of military rule. President Arturo Pinochet Ugarte, leader of the ruling junta, told a press conference the military might well remain in power for "10, 15, 20, or even 25 years."

Pinochet marked the first anniversary of Allende's overthrow on September 11, 1973, by declaring that the state of internal war would be reduced to a state of siege. However, Congress remained closed and political parties dissolved, a nightly curfew remained in effect, and military courts were to continue to administer justice "for a considerable time to come."

The number of political prisoners ranged from the official figure of 2,200 to unofficial estimates of 8,000. Military commanders had assumed police powers, and civilians were being tried in secret by military courts-martial. Numerous human-rights groups charged that the torture of prisoners was widespread. In addition to the thousands held in detention, many others had been rounded up in massive dragnets and held for hours or days as part of a "law-and-order" campaign.

Semi-official statistics indicated 15,000 Chileans had left the country by air alone since the coup, some for political, others for economic, reasons. Thousands of professors and university students had been suspended or expelled after the coup.

Although many people felt the politicians had brought Chile to the brink of

Chile's Ruling Junta. One year after the overthrow of the Allende government, Chile's Congress remained closed and political parties dissolved. President Arturo Pinochet Ugarte, *left,* said the military might remain in power for 25 years.

ruin, discontent with the military's handling of the economy was reported to have spread to the retailers and small businessmen who helped bring down the Allende government. The poor were even worse off; cheese, eggs, milk, and meat had become expensive and were replaced as staples by bread, noodles, beans, and tea without sugar. "Under the old government," said one Chilean, "there was plenty of money but nothing to buy. Now the stores are full, but there's no money."

The regime's economic measures were intended to bring inflation under control. Prices had increased eightfold during the last year of Allende's rule, and many goods were available only on the black market. The inflation rate was expected to be "only" about 200 per cent for 1974, with quarterly raises compensating for increases in the cost of living.

During Allende's rule, agricultural production decreased almost 30 per cent annually, industrial output dropped 5 per cent, and copper-mining output—the country's chief earner of foreign exchange —fell slightly after years of steady growth. Under the military regime, the trend had been reversed and economic production had increased. Expropriated concerns were being returned to private hands. Agreements were being made to compensate U.S. copper companies for expropriation by Allende's government, in order to improve the business climate for foreign investment.

CIA Role Revealed

The New York *Times* reported September 8 that CIA Director William Colby had told a House subcommittee meeting in closed session on April 22 that the Nixon Administration authorized more than $8 million for covert activities by the Central Intelligence Agency between 1970 and 1973 in order to make it impossible for Allende to govern. More than $7 million of the $8 million authorized reportedly was spent.

Questioned about the story and similar allegations, President Ford told reporters

William Colby, director of the CIA, reportedly told congressmen in closed session that the Nixon Administration had authorized more than $8 million for covert activities by the CIA in order to make it impossible for Allende to govern.

at a news conference September 16 that the CIA activities had been authorized because "there was an effort being made by the Allende government to destroy opposition news media . . . and to destroy political parties." He said the CIA operations were "in the best interests of the people of Chile" and denied U.S. involvement "in any way whatsoever" with the military coup that overthrew Allende.

The New York *Times* reported September 15 that "well-informed government sources" said Henry Kissinger, while chief of the National Security Council, had directed an economic campaign against the previous Chilean government as head of a secret high-level intelligence panel called the 40 Committee. Kissinger, testifying before the Senate Foreign Relations Committee on September 19, took the same position as Ford, saying CIA activities were designed to prevent a minority president from imposing one-party rule and not to "destroy or subvert" the government. (Allende was elected president in

1970 after receiving 36 per cent of the popular vote.)

U.S. officials had declared there was no overall Administration program to deny Chile economic aid, but during Allende's term in power there were reductions in U.S. foreign-aid grants and credit from commercial banks. Chile was also denied dozens of loans by the World Bank and the Export-Import Bank, the latter a U.S. government-owned institution. Administration spokesmen had said the reason was because Chile was a poor credit risk, but a number of sources told reporters the decision was political.

Colby was reported to have testified to the House subcommittee that $1 million was authorized for anti-Allende forces in Chile before his election in 1970. Another $350,000 was authorized in an unsuccessful effort to bribe members of the Chilean Congress not to elect Allende. (Allende was elected by the Congress after he received a plurality, but not a majority, of votes in the popular election.) Another $5 million was reportedly authorized for "destabilization" of the government during 1971-73, and $1.5 million more to aid anti-Allende candidates in the 1973 municipal elections.

In 1973, a Senate subcommittee held hearings in which officials of the International Telephone & Telegraph Company (ITT) acknowledged they had offered $1 million to the CIA and had discussed plans with government officials to bring about "economic collapse in Chile." (See CHILE, first section, 1973.)

Staff members of the Foreign Relations Committee recommended that contempt charges be brought against four former government figures who had testified in 1973, including Charles Meyer and Edward Korry. Meyer, former assistant secretary of state for Latin America, had told a Senate Foreign Relations subcommittee, "We bought no votes, we funded no candidates, we promoted no coups." Edward Korry, ambassador to Chile from 1967 to 1971, told the senators, "The United States did not seek to pressure, subvert, or influence a single member of the Chilean Congress at any time in the entire four years of my stay."

Turks Invade Cyprus. Shaded area shows the part of the Mediterranean island of Cyprus occupied by Turkey after Archbishop Makarios, *right,* the nation's president, was overthrown by elements favoring union of the island with Greece.

Cyprus. Declaring its right to protect the Turkish community on Cyprus, Turkey invaded the eastern Mediterranean island on July 20. In spite of a number of declared cease-fires, the Turkish forces continued to advance until mid-August. By that time they had occupied about 40 per cent of the island.

Greek Cypriots outnumbered Turkish Cypriots by more than 4 to 1, but Greece was not militarily strong enough to come to the aid of its compatriots. The humiliated Greek military regime turned over control of the government to civilians on July 23. (See GREECE in this section.) Greeks blamed the United States for not stopping Turkey, and the new Greek government announced it was withdrawing from the military aspects of NATO.

Background

Cyprus, which is about half the size of New Jersey and has a population of about 600,000, was under British rule between 1878 and 1960, when it became independent. Before independence, Britain, Greece, and Turkey agreed that Cyprus would not be united with Greece, that the rights and safety of the Turkish minority would be guaranteed, and that Britain would retain two air bases on the island.

In late 1963, however, Archbishop Makarios, an Orthodox priest serving as president of Cyprus, sought to abolish provisions of the constitution that gave the Turkish Cypriot vice president veto power over legislation. Fighting between Greek and Turkish Cypriots broke out, and a United Nations force was sent to the island in 1964 to keep the peace. By then Turkish Cypriots had taken refuge in villages surrounded by heavily fortified barricades; they found themselves virtually blockaded in these enclaves.

The political situation became more complicated in 1967, when a military junta overthrew the Greek government. The new regime was hostile to Makarios because of his close ties to the Communist party on the island and his friendly relations with Communist nations. It favored Greek Cypriots who supported the goal of *enosis*—union of Greece and Cyprus.

Makarios Overthrown

In early July, Makarios accused the Greek government of conspiring to assassinate him and seize power in Cyprus. He demanded the removal of 650 Greek army officers on Cyprus, charging that they supported EOKA-B, a terrorist organization that had been seeking *enosis* through armed struggle for years.

On July 15, Makarios was overthrown in a coup staged by the Cypriot National Guard. The 10,000-man body, commanded by the Greek officers Makarios had wanted to expel, overwhelmed the lightly armed pro-Makarios police force in Nicosia, the capital, and in other cities. Makarios escaped from the besieged presidential palace and flew to London, where he attempted to rally foreign support.

Nikos Giorgiades Sampson, 38, a former terrorist who had once been sentenced to death by British colonial authorities, was named the new president. Sampson was a fervent supporter of EOKA-B.

Turkish Premier Bulent Ecevit charged that the coup constituted intervention in Cyprus by the Greek government. He sent a note to Britain, asking it to consider joint intervention under the treaty guaranteeing Cypriot independence.

After two days of talks in London, Ecevit warned that Turkey was losing patience and hinted at possible military action. By July 18, about 50,000 troops with landing craft were reported assembled on the southern coast of Turkey, only 40 miles from Cyprus.

Turkey Invades

At dawn on July 20, Turkish jets attacked the port of Kyrenia while, simultaneously, assault troops landed by sea and paratroopers dropped near Nicosia. About 6,000 men were involved in the initial action. The Turks claimed control of a 10-mile corridor stretching from Kyrenia to Nicosia after the first two days of battle.

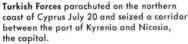

Turkish Forces parachuted on the northern coast of Cyprus July 20 and seized a corridor between the port of Kyrenia and Nicosia, the capital.

Fighting also broke out between the Turkish and Greek Cypriot communities in several cities and along Nicosia's UN-supervised "Green Line" separating the two sectors. A cease-fire arranged by UN peacekeeping troops was ignored, and a second one remained in effect only long enough for foreigners, mostly British and American tourists, to be evacuated. Throughout the fighting, the 4,000-man UN force was able to do little; it was expelled from certain areas by the Turkish army, and its supply convoys were frequently blocked.

International Reaction

A UN Security Council resolution unanimously adopted on July 20 called for "an immediate end to foreign intervention," the start of peace negotiations, and the withdrawal of "foreign military personnel present otherwise than under the authority of international agreements." The resolution specifically cited only Makarios' call for the withdrawal of the Greek officers. Greece and Turkey accepted the cease-fire aspects of the resolution on July 21.

On July 23, the Greek government fell

Resuming Their Advance, Turkish troops captured Famagusta, the island's leading port. They were greeted by Turkish Cypriots, *below,* but Greek Cypriots fled south, leaving their part of the city deserted. More than a third of the population was left homeless by the fighting.

and Sampson resigned as president of Cyprus. He was replaced by a moderate Greek Cypriot, Glafkos Clerides, speaker of the island's House of Representatives. Clerides said he considered himself a temporary president whose task was to carry out the cease-fire, ease tensions between the Greek and Turkish communities, and prepare for elections.

Greece was unable to come to the aid of the Greek Cypriots because the island is 500 miles from mainland Greece (compared to only 40 miles from Turkey) and because its armed forces are outnumbered 3 to 1 by Turkey's. The United States was widely criticized in Greece for not using its influence on Turkey to halt the invasion. (President Johnson reportedly stopped an impending 1964 Turkish invasion of Cyprus by threatening to withdraw military aid and treaty support, but during the July crisis U.S. policymakers clearly were anxious not to alienate Turkey, which is more important to the NATO alliance geographically and militarily than Greece.)

Advance Continues

Despite the UN cease-fire resolution, Turkey continued to expand its hold on the Kyrenia-Nicosia corridor and sent more troops to the island. Greek Cypriots, with no air force and few tanks, were unable to halt the advance.

On July 30, Turkey, Greece, and Britain signed an agreement in Geneva that ordered a standstill cease-fire. The agreement gave Turkey the right to keep military forces on Cyprus at least temporarily and scheduled further negotiations to discuss the island's political problems. Among the issues cited was full restoration of the powers that the Turkish Cypriot vice president, Rauf Denktash, was supposed to share with the Greek Cypriot president under the constitution.

Peace talks resumed on August 8 in Geneva, but broke down August 14 when Turkey refused to recess the talks for 36 to 48 hours in order to allow the Greek and Greek Cypriot representatives to consult with their governments on a Turkish proposal for the creation of six separate and autonomous cantons on Cyprus for the Turkish minority. According to this proposal, Greek and Turkish Cypriots

Demonstrators in Washington, Athens, and Nicosia demanded that the United States cut off aid to Turkey. Rodger Davies, U.S. ambassador to Cyprus, was killed by a sniper during an anti-American demonstration by Greek Cypriots.

would have their own administration, language, and police force under a single national confederation.

Within a few hours after the breakdown of the talks, the Turks renewed fighting with a strong air attack on Nicosia. Simultaneously, ground forces pushed across the Green Line and armored columns advanced on the port of Famagusta, which was subjected to a heavy air strike and a naval bombardment that set port installations afire.

By August 16, Turkey controlled the northeast third of Cyprus—from Famagusta west as far as Lefka. Although the Turks unilaterally announced a cease-fire, soldiers kept advancing and took control of every main access road but one linking Nicosia to the south.

Refugees and Casualties

Large numbers of Greek Cypriots fled before the Turkish forces. Clerides' government estimated that Greek Cypriot refugees numbered 190,000—more than a third of the total Greek Cypriot population. About 38,000 Turkish Cypriot refugees fled to the Turkish-occupied zone or the British bases in order to escape the feared vengeance of Greek Cypriots.

Each side accused the other of atrocities. Denktash, the Turkish Cypriot vice president, said that on August 14 Greek Cypriot soldiers apparently killed 90 Turkish Cypriot civilians near the city of Limassol, where about 1,750 Turkish Cypriots were being held in a soccer stadium. A Turkish official said that on the same day about 70 Turkish Cypriots from Maratha had been murdered and buried in a mass grave. Meanwhile, Greek Cypriots charged that hundreds of their people had been killed in cold blood.

Each side was holding people from the opposing community as hostages. In late September, the first of 3,366 Turkish Cypriots and 2,327 Greek Cypriots were released from detention.

Rodger Davies, the U.S. ambassador to Cyprus, was shot and killed at the embassy in Nicosia on August 19 during an anti-American demonstration by Greek Cypriots. An embassy secretary who rushed to his aid was also shot to death. The gunfire apparently came from a neighboring building and penetrated the window of the ambassador's office.

Situation in September

The Greek Cypriot government estimated that the Turks had taken control of an area that accounted for two-thirds of the island's wealth—assets that had been 80 per cent in the hands of Greek Cypriots. In this zone were the leading port, Famagusta; the lemon groves that gave the country substantial export income; and half of the grain belt that feeds the island. Also occupied were the northern coast beaches that had constituted most of the Greek-controlled tourist trade, which had brought in even more foreign exchange than the citrus crop.

Substantial wealth remained in the unoccupied part, including the ports of Limassol and Larnaca; the only two electricity generating systems on the island; the only petroleum refinery; the fruit orchards, vineyards, and wineries of the south; and light industry. Also in the unoccupied area were the two British bases; soldiers and their dependents spend about $60 million a year on Cyprus.

The Greek Cypriots refused to return to the bargaining table until the Turks first pulled back to their positions of August 9, when cease-fire lines were jointly fixed. Clerides warned of guerrilla warfare unless the Turks pulled back. UN Secretary General Kurt Waldheim arranged, however, for weekly meetings between Clerides and Denktash to discuss humanitarian problems, such as the exchange of prisoners.

The general assumption was that Cyprus would eventually be divided, as Turkey was insisting, into two autonomous parts of a federated state, with the federal government responsible for finance, defense, and foreign affairs. Turkish forces were preparing for an extended occupation unless the Greeks agreed to these terms.

Disasters. Among the disasters that occurred in July, August, and September, 1974, were the following:

Aviation. A Trans World Airlines jet bound for the United States crashed on September 8 in the Ionian Sea off Greece, killing all 88 persons aboard, including 17 Americans. TWA said that the Boeing 707 fell from the sky after the pilot reported an engine failure, but a Palestine youth organization claimed it had placed a bomb-carrying guerrilla aboard the flight, which had originated in Tel Aviv. Airline officials called this "highly unlikely" due to airport precautions but instituted a full investigation.

Sixty-nine persons were killed September 12 when an Eastern Airlines DC-9 bound for Chicago crashed into a wooded area as it was preparing to make a scheduled landing in Charlotte, North Carolina. Thirteen survived the unexplained accident because they were thrown clear when the plane cracked apart and burst into flames on impact.

All 70 persons died September 15 when an Air Vietnam Boeing 727, allegedly hi-

Food Relief. Camel caravans financed by the UN Food and Agriculture Organization carry food to remote areas of the sub-Saharan drought zone. Torrential rains in August washed away roads but held out the hope that normal life might soon resume in the stricken area.

jacked by a man demanding passage to Hanoi, exploded near a provincial airfield 175 miles northeast of Saigon. Several accounts of the crash claimed the plane exploded 1,000 feet above the ground when the hijacker detonated two powerful M-26 hand grenades. Air Vietnam is known to have a hard-line policy on dealing with hijackers, though what actually transpired in the plane was unknown except for the fact that the pilot reportedly told the abductor that a refueling stop would be necessary before they could fly to Hanoi.

Forty-nine of the 50 passengers aboard a Venezuelan plane were killed when torrential rains and hurricane-force winds caused it to crash into a hill on the Caribbean island of Margarita on August 14.

It was reported on August 13 that an Air Mali airliner, while making an unexplained detour, ran out of gas and crashed on a highway in the Upper Volta, killing 47 passengers.

Drought. Heavy rains in late August swept parts of the sub-Saharan region of Africa, which had been suffering from a catastrophic drought since 1968. While the rains brought some areas to their normal levels of rainfall, it was feared that if the rains subsided, even wider crop failures would result. Furthermore, the rains washed away many of the region's dirt roads and desert passages, making delivery of relief food and medicine more difficult. Although poor communications made accurate estimates impossible, deaths from the prolonged drought were thought to number in the tens of thousands.

Epidemic. Knowledgeable epidemiologists estimated in August that between 800 and 900 people had died during the year due to an epidemic of meningitis in the São Paulo, Brazil, metropolitan area, Latin America's largest and fastest-growing. Eleven thousand cases of the disease had been reported in the metropolitan area. Officials established a vaccination program, although the vaccine has never received wide use because it requires sophisticated biochemical techniques developed only in the past few years. Meningitis attacks the victim's cerebrospinal system and may cause death or disability.

Floods. More than 2,500 persons were killed in the aftermath of floods that devastated Bangladesh during the early weeks of August and aggravated the country's two most acute problems—hunger and disease. The disaster occurred as the three mighty Himalayan rivers, the Ganges, the

Maghna, and the Brahmaputra, which flow into the Bay of Bengal, rose simultaneously and destroyed 80 per cent of the country's summer crop. The government estimated that at least 40 per cent of the annual crop was also lost in the floods, a heavy burden for a nation which already imports 2 million tons of grain a year.

Making matters worse was the threat of cholera and typhoid epidemics, aggravated by the fact that most of the country's 2,000 relief camps lack pure drinking water. Official figures report that 100 people die every day in the camps.

Indian officials estimated that 260 people died during a six-week period of incessant rains which ended August 11, leaving millions homeless and a reported 4 million on the brink of starvation.

A week of monsoon rains battered the main island of Luzon in the Philippines during mid-August, leaving 78 people dead and nearly a million homeless.

Rail. More than 150 people were killed on August 31 when an express train ignored a red signal and jumped the track, ramming into the main station in Zagreb, Yugoslavia. More than 150 were injured.

Storms. At least 1,000 people were killed when hurricane Fifi ravaged the Central American nation of Honduras on September 20. The storm, which caused particularly devastating floods and landslides along the country's northeastern coast, was propelled by 130-mile-an-hour winds which wrought destruction throughout Central America before finally dying out over southeastern Mexico.

Major international relief efforts were begun to bring aid to the many thousands of people left homeless in Honduras or unaccounted for. Health officials were fearful that polluted waters would provoke an epidemic, particularly cholera, that would be aggravated by the lack of proper food and clothing for the homeless. Estimates of crop and property damage resulting from the storm ran as high as $500 million, with officials reporting that three-quarters of the country's banana crop—its chief export—had been destroyed.

Typhoon Gilda swept through all Japan and part of South Korea in early July, causing at least 108 deaths and $334 million in property damage.

Hurricane Fifi struck the northern coast of Honduras in September, taking at least 1,000 lives and destroying most of the nation's banana crop—its chief export.

Deposed. Emperor Haile Selassie of Ethiopia, *left*, was removed from office on September 12, ending his 58-year rule. Lieutenant Aman Michael Andom, *right*, chief of staff of the armed forces, was named to act as head of the cabinet until elections were held.

Ethiopia. The military decree signaling the end of his 58-year rule of Ethiopia simply read: "As from today, September 12, His Imperial Majesty Haile Selassie has been deposed from office." With these words, the emperor was taken from his palace in Addis Ababa, Ethiopia's capital, to military headquarters and then to a palace 19 miles outside the city for his "personal safety."

There was little pomp as Haile Selassie left the palace for the last time. He was driven not in the customary limousine but in a blue police Volkswagen. Hundreds of youths shouted insults at him as he was driven away. "Thief, thief," many of them cried, referring to the widespread accusations that he had secreted vast sums of money in foreign banks and had refused to return the funds to Ethiopia.

The finale of the monarch's long career had been building since February, when the military began stripping him of his absolute powers. (See ETHIOPIA in the first section.) Surprisingly, in deposing Haile Selassie, the Armed Forces Coordinating Committee did not proclaim an immediate end to the monarchy but called on the emperor's only son, the 57-year-old Crown Prince Asfa Wossen, to return from Geneva and assume the crown as a figurehead without any powers.

Provisional Government

The military committee announced the dissolution of the parliament and the formation of a provisional government which would rule until elections were held. Lieutenant General Aman Michael Andom, chief of staff of the armed forces, was to act as the head of the cabinet.

The committee's immediate governmental plans were announced over the radio the day before the emperor's removal, a precaution designed to prepare the populace for the action. In foreign policy, Ethiopia was to continue its nonalignment policy and strive for peaceful relations with its neighbors, including Somalia, with which Ethiopia has had long-standing territorial disputes.

Domestically, the committee pledged to work towards broader equality for all Ethiopians, pledging an end to all ethnic, religious, and age discrimination. Land reform would be a top priority, the statement said, adding that "land to the people" would be a slogan for the movement. (Most Ethiopians are tenant farmers.)

Although the move to depose Haile Selassie was widely backed, there was some question about continued support for the military leaders who overthrew him. Criticism was mainly directed at their failure to set a definite date for elections. Furthermore, the military had imposed press censorship and had withdrawn the right to strike and hold public demonstrations. These rights did not exist in Ethiopia until the military established them during the

summer, and Ethiopians were unwilling to see them disappear again. Unions, student groups, journalists, and other professionals joined in calling for immediate creation of a popular civilian government and the restoration of civil rights.

The fact that the military government remained faceless, aside from General Andom, did not help to calm the dissenters. It was believed that the coordinating committee numbered 80 officers, mostly majors and captains, but their anonymity unnerved many citizens. Nobody was even sure whether Andom was the real leader or merely a spokesman for others.

It was not known whether Haile Selassie would be sent into foreign or domestic exile or face trial for the corruption in his government. Over the past months, the military had brought charges against 160 former ministers and officials, including Haile Selassie's daughter, Princess Tenagne Woro.

Victims of Drought. A British nurse distributes food and medicine to Ethiopian villagers suffering from a long-term drought and resulting famine. One reason for the emperor's fall was his government's failure to abate, or even to admit, the extent of the tragedy.

The Monarch's Downfall

The military chipped away at Haile Selassie's grip on the government over a six-month period, assessing its public support after each action. But the process of eroding the emperor's mystique had begun long before, as other African nations started to modernize while Ethiopia remained largely undeveloped, plagued by poverty and disease. A long-term drought and resulting famine had wracked Ethiopia, but, while living in regal splendor, the emperor failed to work to abate, or even to admit, the tragedy which was killing hundreds of thousands of his countrymen.

The contrast between the poverty of 90 per cent of the population and the wealth of their leader was exploited to the full by Ethiopia's new rulers. Whereas newspapers and broadcast news reports had been formerly forbidden to criticize the emperor, a film shown on television the night before his deposition showed starving children and their diseased parents begging for food, and then quickly cut to pictures of cakes which had been flown in from Europe for one of the emperor's banquets.

The actual shifting of power began in February when, after a series of demonstrations demanding higher pay, the military forced Haile Selassie to replace the existing rubber-stamp government. He chose a younger cabinet headed by a new premier, aristocrat Endalkachew Makonnen.

With the new government in place, the Armed Forces Coordinating Committee surfaced and, on April 27, arrested the entire pre-February cabinet. But the initiative then shifted to the National Security Commission, which brutally halted strikes in May and June. It became clear that even within the military there was no united front for change. Some charged that Endalkachew had bribed generals in order to divide the government's opponents.

In June, these conflicts came to a head, and there was a coup within a coup. A new group, the Coordinating Committee of the Ethiopian Armed and Police Forces and the Territorial Army, took over radio stations, airports, and other communications. A new roundup of the former governmental establishment began, with hundreds jailed. Millionaire landholders were locked up along with judges and former cabinet members and eventually, Endalkachew himself.

Finally, on August 16, the military committee abolished the emperor's crown council, court of justice, and military committee, leaving him powerless. With the media reporting on the reality of the drought and the other hardships facing Ethiopia, the public began to perceive that many of these problems had been aggravated by their once-exalted leader. And so, with public trust lost, Emperor Haile Selassie had little choice but to succumb to the orders that reached him on September 12.

The Emperor's Career

Haile Selassie, whose name means "Power of the Trinity," was considered the 225th emperor of Ethiopia in a line traced back to King Solomon and the queen of Sheba. He was crowned emperor in 1930, although he had essentially ruled Ethiopia since a 1916 palace coup in which he asserted his dominance over other influential aristocrats and paved the way for his assumption of the crown.

He rose to world prominence in 1935 when Mussolini's Italian legions invaded Ethiopia. Appealing to the League of Nations for help, he prophesized that "It is us today, it will be you tomorrow." His pleas were in vain though, and in 1936 he fled into exile, returning in triumph after the Allied victory over the Axis.

During his early years in power, he strove to modernize the archaic African nation. He built schools and hospitals, but failed in the most meaningful task of lifting Ethiopia from its feudal ways. A handful of aristocrats and other wealthy landowners continued to extract riches from the peasants.

An African representative at the United Nations reflected upon Haile Selassie's removal by saying, "He was one of the world's great men. He did a lot for his country, and early became a respected voice for Africa and the Third World. It's a pity he proved unable to adjust himself to the winds of change."

Fashion. The return of "casual elegance" for both men and women was predicted for fall and winter by observers of the fashion scene. Quieter, more classic designs continued to replace the colorful "hippie" dress of the early 1970's. Stanley Marcus, chairman of the Neiman Marcus stores, declared: "We are emerging from the 'anything goes' period when the bizarre and outlandish became chic and fashionable." "Men are looking more like men, women more like women," added a well-known fashion director.

Many commentators noted a relationship between economic conditions and the new emphasis on classic styles that can be worn for many seasons. Even wealthy women are spending less on clothes than they used to, according to designers. But, in the interpretation of one Chicago expert, "A few new things used creatively are great mood lifters. . . . American women are discovering that fashion can make you feel good in bad times."

The Big Look

The longer, looser silhouette (pioneered by designer Kenzo Takada in 1973) was evident in sportswear as well as dresses. Skirts—dirndl, circle, bias-cut, or gored—appeared in below-the-knee lengths in nearly every fall collection.

Longer skirts in flower prints on a black or navy background had already replaced jeans during the summer for many young women, especially in Europe. The longer skirts were usually worn with a softly tailored shirt or a skinny knitted tank top.

But, while there was universal agreement among American retailers that the micromini skirt was passé, uncertainty reigned over what would sell in its place. One consultant for a chain of specialty shops remarked: "Women didn't want longer lengths four years ago and they don't want them now. They're not flattering." But the longer skirts seemed to be selling well in many cities.

American designers whose fall ready-to-wear collections appeared in June showed tentlike dresses, mid-calf skirts, swirling capes, and loose, flowing jackets and coats —all in contrast to the close-fitting "body" clothes of the 1960's. Besides the French influence, the Western look was reflected

The Big Look featured tentlike dresses, chemises, mid-calf skirts, swirling capes, loose, flowing, jackets and coats, and longer, bulkier sweaters. *Above,* a Halston cape with asymmetrical hem.

in many styles. Ralph Lauren, for example, included frontier-style maxiskirts and vests.

One of the most versatile offshoots of the looser look for fall and winter was longer, bulkier sweaters, often with fur trim at the collar and cuffs. Sweaters and sweater-jackets of wool, mohair, or acrylic, in many shapes and textures, were enjoying continued popularity from last winter. Some were combined with matching knitted vests as sweater-sets. Pockets, front zippers, leather trimming, and hoods were among the innovative variations which made the new sweaters practical as well as pretty.

Russian Dressing

The pre-revolutionary Russian peasant and the booted Cossack of the steppes inspired many French, Italian, and American designers in 1974. The Russian influence began with St. Laurent's high-necked tunics, suits, and Cossack dresses in March. More tunic blouses, belted and worn outside pants or dirndl skirts (with yokes to control the gathers) appeared in the fall couture shows.

Italian designers such as Valentino, Mila Schön, and Princess Irene Galitzine turned out many variations on the Russian theme, including evening dresses. A fur toque and knee-high boots crushed at the ankles added to the Cossack look. (Other popular hats included berets and knitted or crocheted caps with long matching scarves.)

Over the tunics, pants, and boots, Galitzine threw a dashing fur-bordered cape. In fact, capes were everywhere—over dresses, flared skirts, straight-leg pants. They came in long or short lengths, solids or plaids (some were reversible), mohair, cashmere, jersey, or water-repellent poplin. Some were fur-trimmed, others had hoods. And, for the first time, people actually seemed to be buying them.

Shirtwaist Is Old Hat

The biggest news in women's fashion in 1974 was the return of the chemise, a loose, beltless dress which was first introduced by Balenciaga and Givenchy in the early 1960's. Yves St. Laurent launched the 1974 version at his Paris haute couture showing in July. His "Naive Chemise"

The Russian Look. Adolfo showed a white crepe blouse over a black velvet skirt. Other designers turned out variations on the Russian theme, including baggy pants, fur hats, and knee-high boots.

Leisure Suits, designed for weekend and casual wear, were proving popular. Less dressy versions than the one above were generally unconstructed, with shirt-style jackets sporting two flapped chest pockets.

featured a high neckline, long sleeves with buttoned cuffs, and generally flowing lines.

Galanos, the most prestigious American designer, included an assortment of chemise styles in his fall collection, which was presented in August. Many featured tucks over the bosom, while another design was square-necked, with long, full sleeves. The fabrics were light and airy silks, crepe de chine, and similar materials which skimmed the wearer's body. Some of the dresses were two-piece styles with loose tops and full skirts.

More chemises appeared in September

showings of clothes for resort wear. Chemises in Bill Blass's collection were mostly in pastel colors, with long sleeves. The loose, easy-fitting chemises were considered especially appropriate for warm weather.

Leisure Suits

In men's business wear, a quiet, conservative look appeared to be gaining ground, with a return to the traditional and understated in color and fabric. Demand increased for solid-colored shirts and shirts with white-on-white designs.

But in sportswear, the "leisure suit," designed for weekend and casual wear, was making news. The suits have a Western flavor, with shirt-style jackets sporting two flapped chest pockets, buttoned cuffs, and, frequently, epaulettes. The fancier models might have a little shoulder padding, but generally the style is unconstructed, and therefore cheaper than tailored suits. The pants which accompany the shirt-jackets were straight or slightly flared, in such fabrics as corduroy or wool melton.

Another type of casual suit which had enjoyed wide popularity for several seasons was the "safari suit." The original version evolved from the poplin tropical uniforms worn by British officers in the 19th century. Later, the style was immortalized in Hollywood "jungle" films. Photographers and others picked up the style because the jackets come with at least four flapped patch pockets with bellows, useful for carrying equipment.

Like the leisure suits, safari suits are generally unconstructed, although dressier versions with some tailoring are becoming available. These can be worn with a shirt and tie. The jackets (known as "bush jackets") are longer than those of the leisure suits and are given shape by a belt. The outfits are available in a wide variety of fabrics, for both summer and winter.

Internationally known designers such as Yves St. Laurent and Bill Blass, who offered safari suits for years, have come to regard the style as a classic. As a spokesman for Pierre Cardin explained: "What the safari suit is, is another aspect of occasional clothing for today's liberated male."

Midwest Wheat Field. The United States is the breadbasket for a hungry world, earning $21 billion a year for its agricultural products. In spite of good harvests in the world's major grain-producing areas, there is a continuing excess of demand over supply.

Food. The international food crisis which began in 1972-73 worsened in 1974, despite good harvests in the world's major producing areas. Analysts attributed the shortage and accompanying higher prices mainly to a continuing excess of demand over supply. In developing countries, production growth was hurt by the fertilizer shortage which began in 1973. At the same time, developed nations were reducing food aid and development assistance to other countries, due to their own diminished reserves.

World Crop Summary

World grain production in the marketing year 1974-75 was expected to be slightly lower than the 1973-74 record harvest of 1,276.4 million tons (including rice), due to less favorable weather conditions. Grain production (excluding rice) in the 1974-75 marketing year was expected to reach 942 million tons—27 million less than the world consumed in the year ending June 30, 1974. Because of a carryover of 106 million tons, the world would be able to continue consuming more grain than it produces, but it was expected to use about 25 million tons less in 1975-76 than in the previous marketing year.

The world's hungriest nations remained unable to feed themselves. In India, a potentially good harvest was destroyed by drought. An uneven monsoon brought heavy rain in eastern sections of the country, but left the interior, especially the north, parched. In Rajasthan, for example, up to 85 per cent of the autumn harvest was lost to the worst drought in its history. India's total wheat crop was expected to fall about 2.5 million tons below 1973's 24.9 million, while rice declined 2 million tons below 1973's 65 million. The coarse-grain and peanut crops also suffered from the drought.

Millions of hungry people were reported moving to Bombay, Calcutta, and other Indian cities in search of food. Violence erupted in some areas, including Agra, where food shops were looted. An official estimated that 15 million people in West Bengal were starving or living on one meal a day, and thousands in that state were expected to die from malnutrition.

The Indian government was attempting to force wealthy farmers to "dehoard" food supplies, but observers agreed that sizable imports would be necessary to avert mass starvation. India's food gap for the agricultural year July, 1974, to June, 1975, was estimated at 20 million tons, based on a harvest of about 100 million tons and minimum needs of 115 to 120 million tons. Since most of its food reserves had been consumed during the previous two years, India was expected to begin purchasing large amounts of grain on the world market.

In early October, India reversed its independent food policy of recent years and officially appealed to the United States for assistance through the Food for Peace program. Secretary of State Henry Kissinger was expected to take details of a limited American aid plan to New Delhi later in the month.

Extensive flooding damaged rice and other crops in neighboring Bangladesh. About 15 million people who lost their homes and jobs were in need of food. Meager rations were being distributed by government-run gruel kitchens.

In the Sahel region of sub-Saharan Africa and the East African drought zone, plentiful rain began falling in June, for the first time in six years. Fields of millet were flourishing, and nomads who had migrated south to villages to escape starvation were beginning to trickle northward to rebuild their herds of cattle. The rain also brought floods, however, which washed out roads being used to carry emergency supplies into the interior.

Good harvests in the Soviet Union's European section were offset by droughts in the eastern grain-growing region, lowering the total expected grain output to 205 million tons, compared with a record 220 million tons in 1973.

Famine is a grim reality in many African lands, such as Ethiopia, *below,* and in such Asian countries as India and Bangladesh. An estimated 15 million children under age five die each year from the combined effects of malnourishment and infection.

Knowledge of agricultural conditions in China is imprecise. Although a big producer of grain, China is still the world's largest importer of food, with a net import of more than 8 million tons of wheat expected for 1974. China reported a total output of 250 million tons of grain for 1973.

Western plant scientists who traveled to China in September found that the country had made impressive gains in disseminating new agricultural techniques. The scientists (who included Norman Borlaug, winner of the Nobel Peace Prize in 1970) brought back samples of new varieties of dwarf rice developed in China, similar to the "miracle rice" grown at the International Rice Research Institute in Los Banos, the Philippines. According to the Chinese, the Philippine rice had required a growing season too long for Chinese conditions.

U.S. Harvest

Spring flooding, a dry summer, and early frosts reduced the corn and soybean

Summer Drought, preceded by spring floods and followed by early frosts, reduced the corn and soybean harvests in the United States.

harvests in the United States below 1973's record crops. Production of wheat, however, reached a record high of nearly 50 million tons (1.8 billion bushels), 70 million bushels more than in 1973. The corn crop was estimated at 4.7 billion bushels, 16 per cent lower than the previous year, and soybeans were down 19 per cent, based on October 1 figures released by the Department of Agriculture.

As a result of the high price of wheat and soybeans, demand for grain to be used as livestock feed began to decline. The use of corn as a feed grain was expected to fall by up to half a billion bushels in the 1974-75 season, from a projected consumption of 4.5 billion bushels. Some ranchers began sending their cattle from the range directly to market, rather than to feedlots for fattening. Normally, about 1 per cent of U.S. cattle coming to market are grass-fed only, but this figure was expected to rise to between 10 and 20 per cent by the end of the year.

Smaller U.S. exports of corn, wheat, and soybeans were predicted for 1974-75. But the effect of future exports on domestic food prices remained uncertain, since the government's policy on exports was vaguely defined. Fewer exports would mean more food available for domestic use and less pressure on prices, but farmers were opposed to export controls that would lower their profits.

Observers expected that the United States would enact some form of broader controls on exports, because carryover grain stocks were low. In anticipation of such a move, Japan and other countries had been placing orders far in advance to avoid having their food supplies cut off by an embargo (as Japan experienced when the United States temporarily stopped exporting soybeans in 1973).

On October 6, a limited system of controls over large sales of grain for export was announced by the Ford Administration. The announcement followed by two days the forced cancellation of orders placed by the Soviet Union for U.S. wheat and corn worth a total of $500 million. (In 1972, Russia bought one-fourth of the U.S. wheat crop for $1 billion, sending the price of the remaining wheat soaring.)

311

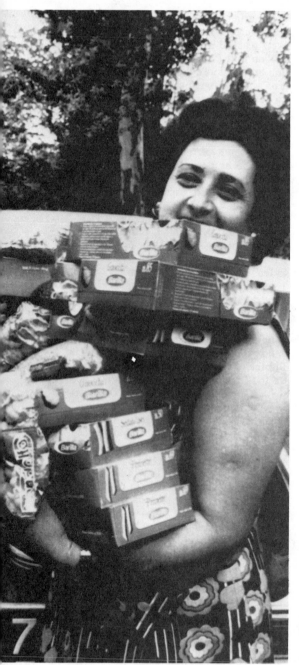

Italian Housewives stocked up on pasta in anticipation of a new price ceiling by the government that upped the price of a pound by more than 25 per cent. Consumers around the world were paying more for food because of a sharp rise in grain commodity prices.

The new program called for voluntary reporting by grain-exporting companies of sales above 50,000 tons of wheat, corn, sorghum, soybeans, or soybean meal. Such sales were made subject to advance approval by the government. If the voluntary export controls did not work, according to Agriculture Secretary Earl L. Butz, mandatory controls might be imposed.

Food Supply and Demand

The first world food conference in history was to be convened in Rome November 5-16 by the United Nations, to evaluate international trends in food production and consumption. A special report prepared for a conference preparatory session by the UN Food and Agriculture Organization estimated that food demand in the 1970's and 1980's (making no allowance for improved nutrition or greater income equality) would grow at a rate of 1.6 per cent in the developed nations, and 3.7 per cent in the developing countries. The overall estimated increase in food demand was expected to grow at a rate of 2.5 per cent per annum, of which 2 per cent represents increased population, and 0.5 per cent, increased purchasing power.

Food production has also been increasing: projections based on the period 1961-63 to 1973 show a growth rate of 2.4 per cent for developed market-economy countries, 2.6 for developing countries, and 3.5 per cent for eastern Europe and the Soviet Union.

But projected trends suggest that, while food supply and demand may be balanced overall, most developing countries would be faced with food deficits in coming years. During the last two decades, agricultural output expanded at about the same rate in both the industrialized and developing countries. But the rate of growth of demand remained much higher in the latter—3.5 per cent vs. 2.5 per cent per annum—due primarily to faster population growth.

One consequence for developing countries has been little progress in combating widespread malnutrition. In some areas, including Guatemala, Barbados, Bangladesh, Thailand, and India, the incidence of malnutrition was found to be up sharply since early 1974. While no reliable statistics exist, some experts estimate that 1 billion people suffer from a lack of essential nutrients at least part of the year. (See also FOOD in the fourth section, 1973.)

Malnutrition, which stunts both physical and mental growth, strikes young children hardest. An estimated 15 million children under age five die each year from the combined effects of malnourishment and infection. (This figure represents one quarter of all deaths in the world.) In many countries, an increasing tendency for mothers to abandon breast-feeding—either in imitation of upper-class practices or to look for work—contributes to the toll of malnutrition. Formula given to the child as a substitute is frequently watered down and of little nutritive value.

Yet remarkable advances were made in agricultural production in the developing countries between 1953-71, although the rate of growth of agricultural production appears to have slowed in recent years. In 32 of the 72 developing nations for which data have been available, food output grew faster than demand during this period.

Objectives established by FAO's Indicative World Plan for Agricultural Development (IWP) for 1970-85 include expansion of land area, improving productivity of land already under cultivation, increased fertilizer consumption, and mechanization. Except in Africa, cultivated land area had been increasing faster than the IWP goal of 0.7 per cent per annum.

But, since most of the world's land area suitable for agriculture is already being utilized, further gains in productivity must come from increased yields per acre, through such inputs as better seeds, livestock improved by selective breeding and animal nutrition, more fertilizer, and the use of pesticides.

Fertilizer Shortage

Consumption of nitrogen, phosphate, and potash fertilizers was increasing at a yearly rate of almost 14 per cent—close to the IWP goal—when further expansion was checked by the beginning of a worldwide shortage in 1973. The causes of this shortage included the high price of petroleum (the main raw material for nitrogen fertilizers) and an increase in demand

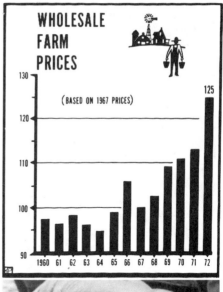

Rising Farm Prices. The graph shows that farm products which cost $100 in 1967 cost $125 at the end of 1972. Wisconsin farmers killed their calves to support their claim that high feed-grain prices had made it unprofitable to raise cattle for dairy products and beef.

313

Fertilizer Production. *Left,* a Florida chemical plant receives wet phosphate rock for processing into fertilizer; *below,* an Israeli facility at Sodom on the Dead Sea mines potash for fertilizer. Higher fertilizer production is needed to increase world crop yields.

that outstripped manufacturing capacity and reserves.

Fertilizer plant construction for years had followed a cycle of boom-and-bust; when the advent of the "Green Revolution" of the late 1960's greatly increased demand for chemical fertilizer, manufacturing capacity expanded too rapidly, eventually threatening the industry with bankruptcy. New mines and plants are being constructed in many parts of the world, but they will not be productive in time to alleviate the present shortage. Another difficulty hindering rapid expansion of fertilizer production is a shortage of chemical engineers trained in this type of technology.

Although the fertilizer shortage affects both rich and poor nations, it hurts developing countries most. This is because the same amount of fertilizer will produce a larger increase in yield if applied to the poorer soils of Asia, Africa, or Latin America, than if it is added to the already heavily fertilized cropland of Europe or the United States. (American farmers use at least seven times as much fertilizer per acre as do Indian farmers.) According to James Grant and Lester Brown of the Overseas Development Council, scarce fertilizer should preferably be allocated to developing countries, because, while the extra yield from one pound of fertilizer would be at least 10 pounds of grain in India or Bangladesh, only two to five extra pounds would be produced in the United States or Europe.

Maldistribution of fertilizer is such that India suffered half of the 2-million-ton shortfall in the developing countries. Indian consumption fell from 3 million to 2 million tons in the last year, resulting in an estimated loss of 10 million tons of grain. This lost production has international effects: for lack of one pound of fertilizer (cost, 15 cents), 10 extra pounds of wheat must be purchased on world markets (cost, $1 or more). These pressures help to drive up the price of wheat in the United States, since U.S. food prices are increasingly determined by international markets and price levels.

Several nations have made official responses to the question of fertilizer distribution and scarcity. Sri Lanka proposed the establishment of a world fertilizer "pool" through which nations could share available supplies. FAO created a special fertilizer commission which met for the first time in July. In the United States, both houses of Congress introduced resolutions calling for a reduction in "non-critical, non-food-producing uses of fertilizer." (The 3 million tons of fertilizer applied to flower gardens and lawns in the United States each year is approximately equal to the total annual amount used by farmers in India before the shortage.)

But U.S. farmers oppose any action which might reduce their supplies, leading to what one critic termed a "quasi-embargo" on U.S. fertilizer exports. In the fall of 1973, the Cost of Living Council acted to decontrol the price of fertilizer, in exchange for a promise by the industry that an additional 1.5 million tons would be reserved for domestic use. (World fertilizer prices were 50 per cent above U.S. levels, generating fears by American farmers that the industry would increase exports.)

Many countries stepped up efforts toward self-sufficiency in fertilizer production in the wake of the sudden increase in the cost of petroleum and fertilizer. In Southeast Asia, Indonesia (rich in petroleum and natural gas) dedicated one large fertilizer plant at Palembang on Sumatra, and signed a contract for another, twice as big. Some of the ammonia to be produced at these plants was to be shipped to the Philippines, where it would be combined with sulfuric acid (a by-product of the Philippine copper industry) to make ammonium sulfate fertilizer, or with imported phosphate rock to make ammonium phosphate.

The discovery of natural-gas reserves 100 miles north of Dacca, the capital of Bangladesh, has led to plans for several nitrogen fertilizer plants which would supply the needs of Bangladesh and part of India. India has little petroleum or natural gas, but wants to develop deposits of lignite (brown coal) which could also be used to make nitrogen fertilizer. The World Bank is assisting India in the construction of two plants for this purpose.

Fertilizer plants already operating in developing countries tend to produce at only about 60 per cent of capacity, due to such factors as poor management, lack of spare parts, and interruptions in power supply. In other places, resources which could be used in the production of fertilizer are wasted for lack of markets. In Venezuela,

New Type of Grain, a wheat-rye hybrid called triticale, is inspected by scientists at the International Maize and Wheat Improvement Center. The researchers say this new grain can out-produce wheat by hundreds of pounds per acre in soil with very little fertilizer.

Nigeria, North Africa, and the Persian Gulf region, it is estimated that enough natural gas is "flared off" into the atmosphere to produce twice the world's annual consumption of nitrogen fertilizer.

(In a speech before the United Nations on April 15, U.S. Secretary of State Henry Kissinger pledged American technical assistance to help improve the operations of fertilizer factories abroad, to help make more effective use of fertilizer, and to help build new fertilizer plants in areas such as the Persian Gulf, where the raw materials for nitrogen fertilizer are plentiful.)

Attention is also being given to ways in which farmers can achieve larger yields by using fertilizer more effectively. Research is in progress at the International Rice Research Institute and other laboratories to determine simple methods of applying fertilizer at precisely the times when the plants need it most.

The National Fertilizer Development Center is working on a sulfur-coated form of urea fertilizer (the kind most widely used in Asia) which will release nitrogen slowly. The objective is a fertilizer which can be applied in one dose to intermittantly flooded rice paddies at the beginning of the growing season.

At North Carolina State University, scientists are attempting to develop a hybrid soybean that would increase yields per acre. The soybean is a protein-rich plant which supplies most of its own nitrogen needs through nitrogen-fixing bacteria in nodules on its roots. But, until a successful hybrid can be developed, the only way to increase yields will be to plant more acres. Researchers would also like to extend the range of the soybean, which grows best in temperate regions in the United States and China.

In the future, it may be possible to increase the amount of nitrogen in the soil by increasing the number of types of nitrogen-fixing bacteria. A new technique using bacterial "plasmids," rings of genetic material around the main rings of genes, may eventually be used to transfer the genes for nitrogen-fixing protein (nitrogenase) into many microorganisms now lacking them.

Food and Development Aid

Countries stricken by crop failures in recent years have looked to the United States and other "breadbasket" nations to alleviate food shortages with free food shipments or easy credit. Much of this assistance was supplied by the Food for Peace program from surplus stocks held by the American government.

But American food assistance has been shrinking. Beginning in 1973, farmers were released from acreage restrictions and all U.S. farmland was returned to production to meet growing demand. (See also AGRICULTURE in the first section, 1974.) Government grain stocks were depleted in 1973, and the new agricultural policy made the accumulation of more surpluses unlikely. Thus, grain for the Food for Peace program will in the future have to be purchased with cash, further accelerating the tendency to wide fluctuations on world commodity markets.

The federal government has budgeted about $1 billion annually for food aid in the last few years, but inflation has reduced the quantity which can be purchased with that amount. Church groups and other associations have campaigned for increased food aid on humanitarian grounds. But there is also opposition, especially from government planners, who see the $21 billion that commercial exports of agricultural products annually bring into the United States as an important factor in alleviating payments problems.

(However, James Grant of the Overseas Development Council noted in testimony before the House Foreign Affairs Committee that a $1-billion increase in food and fertilizer aid by the United States would still "be less than half of the more than $2 billion we will receive in 1974 from the developing countries as a result of our higher food prices.")

Consumers, questioning the effect of food assistance on their grocery bills, may become another source of opposition. But as yet, there is no organized resistance to food aid, according to Senator Hubert Humphrey, who sponsored a unanimously-supported Senate resolution calling for an increase in such programs.

Meanwhile, the cereal "gap" of the developing countries is growing, and growing faster than their capacity to pay for food on commercial terms. It is estimated that, by 1985, the gap might amount to as much as 85 million tons per year—perhaps 100 million in a bad crop year. At 1973-74 prices, 80 to 90 million tons of grain would cost developing countries $16 billion, on top of other necessities they would normally import.

The World Food Conference to be held in Rome was to discuss formation of a world food-reserve system through which the needs of importing countries could be met, especially in emergencies, without the destabilizing effects on international trade experienced since 1972. (International grain reserves amount to less than a 26-day supply—the lowest level since 1949.)

At the conference, the United States was expected to suggest larger food stockpiles in major consuming nations, such as Japan (which normally keeps only a six-week reserve of grain), a broader exchange of information on harvests and import needs, and an increase in farm-production assistance.

However, the U.S. delegation, headed by Agriculture Secretary Butz, was not expected to play a leading role at the conference, which was to be attended by 130 nations. While the United States has no clearly defined food policy, Butz and most of his colleagues are known to oppose the creation of a world food-reserve system, fearing that stockpiling will depress prices and production for American farmers.

There is also a controversy over domestic grain reserves—whether stockpiles should be maintained by the government, or be held by the industry. Senator Humphrey and some food experts take the position that a program of public food reserves should be established, and aid increased abroad.

Others side with Butz, who opposes publicly held domestic reserves and believes other countries should take over a larger share of the responsibility for food aid. In his view, the best insurance against world food shortages is the transfer of technology and capital investment to underdeveloped countries to enable them, in the future, to feed themselves.

San Francisco Earthquake of 1906 was responsible for more than 500 deaths. U.S. Geological Survey scientists believe they will soon be able to predict where an earthquake will strike, its magnitude, and roughly when to expect it.

Geology. During the past 1,000 years, more than 3 million people have died from the effects of earthquakes. A quake of major magnitude can be expected somewhere on earth at least once a year on the average.

U.S. Geological Survey scientists think they will soon be able to predict where an earthquake will strike, its magnitude, and roughly when to expect it. Authorities believe a functioning network making regular public predictions could be in service by 1980. Such an early-warning system might save thousands of lives in the United States and billions in property damage.

The Earthquake Zones

Most earthquakes occur along two long, narrow belts. One is the Pacific "Ring of Fire," an area of volcanoes and frequent earth tremors that encircles the Pacific from New Zealand northward to Japan, across to Alaska, and south through California, Mexico, Central America, and the west coast of South America. The other major zone runs from Portugal east through Italy, Turkey, Iran, and India, to the East Indies.

Most earthquakes occur at the boundaries between the earth's plates—irregular chunks of the earth's crust, constantly in motion, that are slowly sliding above a heavier mantle of rock. Although these giant plates move only a few centimeters a year, their motion causes great stresses. An earthquake releases pressures built up for years or even centuries.

A *fault* is a fracture in the earth's crust along which two plates have slipped with respect to each other. One plate may move horizontally while the plate facing it moves in the opposite direction, or one may move upward while the other moves downward. Sometimes the movement is both horizontal and vertical. Geologists have found that earthquakes tend to recur along faults.

Geologists believe that several million earth tremors occur each year. More than one million of these can be detected by today's instruments; 700 are strong enough to cause at least some damage, and a few rank as catastrophic.

California, the country's earthquake state, has a broad fault system. The major one is the San Andreas Fault, varying from a few feet to a mile in width. It extends north from the Gulf of California, running east of Los Angeles, and falling into the Pacific just south and west of San Francisco.

Other parts of the country are not immune from earthquakes. Boston, Charleston, South Carolina, and St. Louis lie in major-risk areas. Southern Missouri was struck in late 1811 and early 1812 by three of the most powerful earthquakes ever to hit North America. Fortunately the tremors, which were powerful enough to bring down chimneys in Cincinnati, 400 miles

away, occurred in an area which was then sparsely settled. In 1964, the most powerful North American earthquake ever recorded struck Alaska, resulting in more than 100 deaths.

The magnitude of earthquakes is expressed by the Richter scale, a mathematical formula that measures ground motion as recorded on seismographs. A quake with a rating of two is the smallest that can be felt. One with a rating of eight is 33 times as powerful in energy released as one rated seven, and is about 1,000 times as powerful as one rated six. The earthquake that struck Alaska in 1964 was 8.4 in magnitude; 8.9 is the most powerful ever registered.

Chandler's Wobble

In 1891, an American astronomer found that the earth wobbles in a circular pattern over a 14-month span as it rotates on its axis. Later, another wobble over a 12-month span was discovered. The combined effect of what is known as Chandler's Wobble causes the North and South poles to wander within a circle some 50 feet in radius.

Once every seven years, the two mo-

Earthquake-Risk Map. Most earthquakes occur along a fault—a fracture in the earth's crust. The West Coast is in an area of frequent earth tremors that encircles the Pacific. (Map measures severity, not frequency, of earthquakes.)

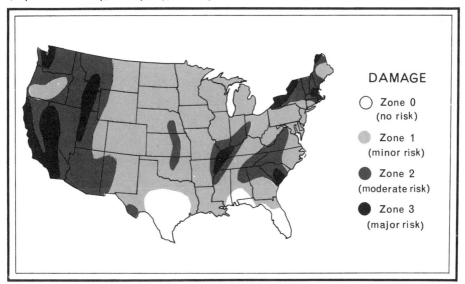

DAMAGE

○ Zone 0 (no risk)

Zone 1 (minor risk)

● Zone 2 (moderate risk)

● Zone 3 (major risk)

Seismograph records vibrations in the earth. The vertical lines in the left-hand part of the graph at bottom deviate from the near-normal pattern at right and indicate that an earth tremor has taken place.

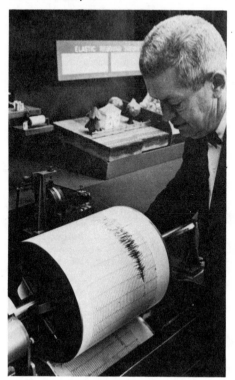

tions are in phase, working to produce a rapid shift in the spin axis. In 1968, two Canadian geophysicists suggested that the incidence of large earthquakes around the world correlates closely with this cycle. The year 1971 was, as they predicted, a peak year for earthquakes, with three major ones. Charles A. Whitten, chief geodesist of the National Ocean Survey, says Chandler's Wobble seems to determine the total amount of energy released by earthquakes during a given period.

While some scientists think the wobble causes earthquakes, others think earthquakes cause the wobble. Still others think both phenomena are caused by other powerful forces, such as the tidal effects of the sun and the moon. Two astronomers fear a cataclysm in 1982, at a time when all nine planets will be more or less aligned in a row on one side of the sun, the other planets presumably exerting unusual gravitational force on the earth.

Predicting Earthquakes

Geologists now believe they have a theoretical tool not only for predicting in which years earthquakes are likely to occur, but for predicting an earthquake at a specific time and place. The theory, called the dilatancy-diffusion model, is, while not universally accepted, the most convincing explanation ever advanced about what

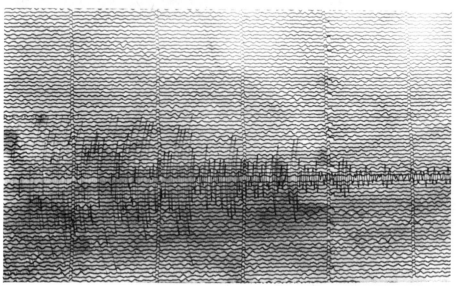

San Andreas Fault. The hillside above, sliced through to make way for a southern California freeway, reveals old slippage along the San Andreas Fault. One geologist predicts at least 10 damaging earthquakes along this fault in the next 25 years.

happens miles beneath the earth's surface when tremendous stresses build toward earthquakes.

The theory states that, as stresses on rocks in a fault increase, the rocks begin to develop tiny cracks and fissures. As this happens, the rocks dilate—that is, their volume increases.

Ordinarily, the rocks and the spaces around them are saturated with underground water, but the new cracks and fissures open faster than water can seep into them. The speed of pressure waves—vibrations that travel along the earth's surface and through the crust—slows because these waves travel faster through liquid-filled spaces than through dry ones. As water seeps into the new cracks, however, . the wave speed picks up again. Soon after, weakened by the additional pressure and the lubricating effect of the water, the

rocks break, and an earthquake results.

The dilatancy-diffusion model explains findings first made by Soviet scientists in the mid-1960's, when it was discovered that a quake followed the slowing down and speeding up of pressure waves. The Soviets claim to have predicted three earthquakes since then by studying pressure waves. An American scientist successfully predicted an earthquake in New York's Adirondack Mountains on August 3, 1973.

The theory also offers plausible explanations for other phenomena that have been noted before earthquakes. For example, the earth above the center of a coming earthquake often begins slowly rising before the shock. The theory explains that the increase in the volume of the underground rocks tends to push up the crush of the earth from beneath. Also, the water level in wells near the site of a quake may change. This may be because the well is partially drained off as the underground water that supplies it is diverted to fill all the new openings in the dilating underground rocks.

The earthquakes successfully predicted have all been small ones. It appears that the longer the cycle of abnormal pressure-wave speed, the heavier the ensuing shock. A moderate earthquake, like the one in the Los Angeles area in 1971 that measured 6.4 on the Richter scale, would be preceded by a cycle three to four years long. For great earthquakes, the process of cracking, filling, and pressure-wave abnormality would last for decades before a quake.

Wide-scale forecasting of earthquakes would involve thousands of earth sensors hooked into a computer. The only extensive existing network in the United States is located in central California, but the U.S. Geological Survey plans similar ones for Alaska, Hawaii, Washington, and the northeast Rockies. Barry Raleigh of the USGS says, "Our strategy is to predict as many moderate or small earthquakes as possible before we are forced to predict a big one."

Preventive Measures

USGS geologists even believe they may be able to modify earthquakes, taming potentially damaging ones by reducing them to harmless size. The possibility originated from unexpected tremors near Denver in the 1960's that followed the injection of liquid waste into a 12,000-foot-deep disposal well at an army base. In order to test the hypothesis that the injections had somehow triggered the quakes, scientists set up equipment at four water-injection wells in a Colorado oilfield. They found that when water from the wells was withdrawn, the quakes stopped. When water was pumped in again, the tremors started again.

The USGS researchers believe that the accumulating stress in a fault could be relieved by deliberately releasing it in a series of small quakes triggered by pumping water into drilled holes at selected points along the fault. John Healy, one of the researchers, has enough confidence in the technique to advocate drilling into the San Andreas Fault.

In 1969, thousands of Californians were sufficiently panicked by the warnings of soothsayers that an earthquake would topple the entire western portion of the state into the Pacific on April 4 to speed out of the state. The panic became a national joke, but the earthquake threat in crowded California is deadly serious. One geologist predicts at least 10 damaging earthquakes along the San Andreas Fault within the next 25 years, one of which, like the famous 1906 San Francisco earthquake, "is likely to be a really bad one." And a structural engineer says a major earthquake in California today would result in large losses of life and over $30 billion in property damage.

The 1971 earthquake centered at Sylmar, California, killed 64 and caused $500 million in property damage. Much of the death and destruction occurred at two hospitals and a freeway interchange built over an undetected fault. An earthen dam collapsed to within one foot of the reservoir's water level, threatening to flood the San Fernando Valley below and its 80,000 inhabitants.

Stringent building codes in California have resulted in flexible, steel-framed high-rise buildings resistant to earthquakes —unlike the highly rigid, heavy-walled buildings that collapsed in San Francisco in 1906. Steel frames, engineers agree, are best for tall buildings and wooden frames for dwellings; both materials are far more elastic than concrete or brick.

Yet California officials estimate that 250,000 children in the state attend schools too hazardous to meet earthquake safety standards. Forty-six schools, four hospitals, and a football stadium are within 1,000 feet of the Hayward Fault east of San Francisco Bay.

If scientists could predict a major earthquake well in advance, all construction could be halted in the areas most vulnerable to destruction. Unsafe structures could be condemned and torn down, reservoirs drained, and unsafe schools closed. Part of the population might be evacuated. But, at present, Californians face the possibility of very bad vibrations indeed.

Greece. The leaders of the Greek military regime that assumed rule in 1967 ceded power to civilians on July 23, in the wake of Turkey's invasion of Cyprus. (See CYPRUS in this section.) President Phaidon Gizikis immediately summoned former premier Constantine Caramanlis back to Athens from his self-imposed exile in Paris. He returned the next day and was sworn in as premier.

Gizikis said that the military would return to their barracks and would not interfere in the formation or functioning of the new government. The junta strongman, Brigadier General Demetrios Ioannides, was put under "comfortable house arrest." Ioannides and 26 other generals were placed on compulsory retirement in late August as the new government began purging the armed forces.

Ioannides had owed his power to his control of the military police, which had almost unlimited authority to pursue and punish political dissenters, and from junior officers loyal to him who informed him regularly on the actions of their superiors. Reportedly, it was a "coup of generals" that overthrew the junta and demanded the return to civilian rule.

The New Government

Caramanlis, founder of a conservative political party named the National Radical Union, was premier from 1955 until 1963, when he left Greece shortly after his party was defeated in parliamentary elections by the Center Union party. On his return from Paris, he named an essentially right-of-center cabinet. Center Union leader George Mavros was appointed deputy premier and foreign minister. On July 26, however, Caramanlis appointed a number of leftist leaders to the cabinet in response to criticism that he had not formed, as promised, a government of national unity.

The first order of business was a "full and unreserved amnesty" for political crimes. Caramanlis said all political prisoners jailed since 1967 would be released and every decree violating the rights of citizens would be abolished. The military police were stripped of their power to arrest and interrogate civilians.

The exiled king, Constantine, who fled Greece after an abortive attempt in 1968

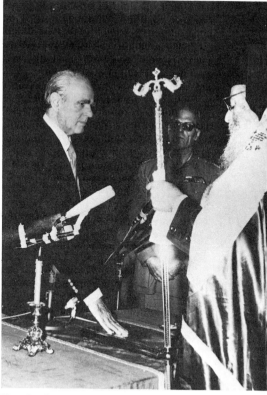

New Greek Government. Constantine Caramanlis was sworn in as premier by Archbishop Seraphim as President Phaidon Gizikis looked on. After six years of rule, the military regime had summoned civilians to power July 23. Elections were scheduled for November.

to overthrow the junta, expressed his "deep satisfaction" at the ouster of "the dictatorial regime." Constantine described the members of the new government as "old friends of ours" and said he hoped to return to Greece. He was reportedly willing to shun any political function and to accept a symbolic role instead of the considerable powers the monarchy had formerly held.

On August 1, the new government reinstated the 1952 constitution abolished in 1968 by the junta. It said, however, that until a constitutional assembly was convened, legislative power would be vested in the cabinet and the government would retain the right to rule by decree. Consti-

Political Prisoners Released. The first order of business was a full amnesty for political crimes. Caramanlis said all political prisoners jailed since 1967 would be released and every decree violating the rights of citizens would be abolished.

tutional provisions relating to the monarchy were suppressed pending a decision as to whether the king would be recalled from exile.

Among those returning from abroad were leftist leaders Andreas Papandreou and the popular composer Mikis Theodorakis. Both announced intentions to form parties that would take part in the assembly elections scheduled for November 17. Also expected to take part were the Communists. The party had been illegal since 1947.

Withdrawal from NATO

On August 14, the government issued a directive withdrawing its troops from the NATO alliance and calling for the phasing out of NATO bases in Greece over a three-year period. The action came in response to the continuing advance by Turkey—also a NATO member—on Cyprus, and to anti-American feeling in Greece, which blamed the United States for the Turkish invasion.

American officials were uncertain whether Greece was demanding the withdrawal only of NATO forces and installations or, additionally, American forces under a bilateral treaty. Seven U.S. military bases and five communications sites were in Greece under a treaty not directly related to NATO; these included army, air, and naval bases on the mainland, naval

home-port facilities near Athens for six destroyers, and a naval installation on Crete. Two NATO facilities were also on Crete. In all, about 4,500 U.S. military personnel, plus 5,000 to 6,000 dependents, were stationed in Greece.

Loss of the Greek bases would deprive the Western alliance of the antisubmarine-warfare and U.S. Sixth Fleet resupply facilities at Suda Bay, Crete, described as one of the best natural harbors in the world. It would weaken the U.S. position in the volatile eastern Mediterranean, because the next closest facilities available were in Italy, 1,000 miles to the west. NATO's southern rim would also be weakened by giving up bases near the Bulgarian border, where tactical nuclear warheads had been stockpiled, and by a resulting gap in NATO's southern-rim early-warning radar system.

Anti-American feeling was also fanned by the widespread belief, echoed publicly by Foreign Minister Mavros and other politicians, that the CIA had installed the military junta in power in 1967. According to a New York *Times* article that cited "well-placed officials," many Greek political and military figures, both rightists and leftists, had received personal subsidies over many years from the CIA. Reportedly, votes had been bought in the Greek parliament.

International Trade. A special session of the UN General Assembly, held in New York City from April 9 to May 2, highlighted important changes taking place in patterns of world trade and investment. The conference agenda reflected increasing discontent among many of the less-developed countries over their deteriorating terms of trade with the industrial nations, and their desire to emulate the success of the Organization of Petroleum Exporting Countries (OPEC) in securing higher prices for their exports. (See Feature Article in the first section.)

The April meeting—initiated by Algerian President Houari Boumédienne—was seen by some observers as a diversionary tactic by OPEC in reaction to the U.S.-sponsored conference of energy-consuming nations held in Washington two months earlier. (See PETROLEUM in the first section.) But the presence of an unusual number of high-ranking European and "Third World" officials, including four African heads of state and Chinese Deputy Premier Teng Hsiao-ping, suggested a new recognition by the less-developed countries of their influence in world economic affairs.

Two documents drafted by the developing countries were adopted during the session, following negotiations with the European nations. A "Declaration of Principles on the Establishment of a New International Economic Order" included provisions upholding the right of countries to nationalize foreign-owned industries and demanding that former colonies be compensated for past exploitation. It also called for the development of cartel-like associations among poor nations, and a closer link between the price of manufactured goods and the cost of raw materials produced by the less-developed countries.

Also approved by the Assembly was an "Action Program" in two parts: an emergency-aid operation designed to help the world's poorest countries maintain essential imports over the next 12 months, and the establishment of a special fund under

UN General Assembly met in a special economic session to discuss international trade relations. A "Declaration of Principles on the Establishment of a New International Economic Order" and an "Action Program" drafted by developing nations were adopted.

UN auspices to provide relief and development assistance starting in January, 1975. The program would be funded by contributions from industrial and other nations. The nine members of the European Economic Community, Iran, and some other nations promptly pledged funds, but most of the oil-producing countries indicated that they wished to organize their own aid programs.

On May 3, UN Secretary General Kurt Waldheim called the heads of the World Bank and the International Monetary Fund to a meeting on emergency aid for countries hardest hit by world economic problems. (In April, the World Bank had listed these as Bangladesh, Bolivia, Ethiopia, India, Kenya, Mali, Pakistan, Sri Lanka, Sudan, Tanzania, Uganda, and Zaïre.)

The United States reacted nervously to the prospect of a conference of "have-not" nations calling for a redistribution of the wealth which the "haves" had accumulated in part through the importation of cheap raw materials. U.S. officials were also said to fear that the Assembly session would undercut the efforts of a planned series of conferences in Washington to coordinate activities among the petroleum-producing and -importing nations.

U.S. Secretary of State Henry Kissinger addressed the Assembly on April 15, warning that "large price increases coupled with production restrictions" would lead to "global inflation followed by global recession from which no nation could escape." He cautioned the developing countries against use of "the politics of pressure and threats."

Toward the end of the special session, the United States came forward with a plan for an 18-month, $4-billion development assistance program, but by then most of the conference participants were indifferent or hostile to the proposal, and it was later withdrawn.

World Commodity Inflation

The April conference was called in the midst of a worldwide economic boom which had sent the cost of commodities skyrocketing due to shortages of many basic materials. After decades of relative stability, prices had begun to climb sharp-

Floor of the Chicago Board of Trade, the world's oldest and largest commodity exchange, is shown in its normal state of hubbub. Brokers on the floor buy and sell contracts to deliver certain commodities—mainly meat and grains—later at a given date and price. Position of broker's hand and fingers, *left,* indicate quantity to be traded and price offered. After decades of relative stability, commodity prices have climbed sharply, benefiting the rich nations more that the poor ones.

ly. Between 1968 and 1973 the price of nickel, for example, rose from 94¢ a pound to $1.53 in the United States. Copper went from 42¢ to 59¢ in the same period. The cost of petroleum nearly quadrupled in 1973.

Participants in the UN economic session agreed that inflation is an international process, exported "in the pipelines and grain tankers of world trade." But, while the conference generated fears among the industrialized nations of further price hikes, a report presented to the Assembly showed that it was actually these nations which had profited most from the inflationary trend of the past two years. The

study, prepared by UNCTAD (the United Nations Conference on Trade and Development), demonstrated that the 1973 commodities boom had "resulted in much greater benefits to developed than to developing countries" because the cost of food, fertilizer, and manufactured goods imported by the less-developed countries had risen faster than that of the raw materials which these countries export.

The industrialized nations also export many important commodities, and they gained more income during recent inflation from these sources than the poorer countries. Sales of raw materials other than petroleum earned an additional $29

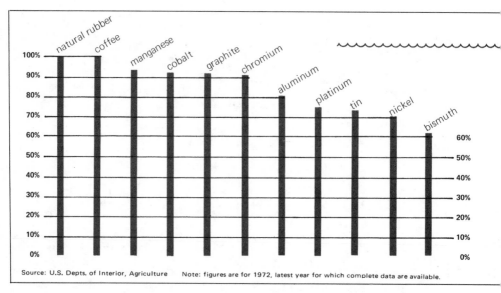

Source: U.S. Depts. of Interior, Agriculture   Note: figures are for 1972, latest year for which complete data are available.

billion for developed countries in 1973 over 1972, compared with an extra $11 billion for developing countries.

(The price of petroleum played a relatively small part in the hardships of the poorer countries: oil imports by the less-developed countries cost them an additional $1.2 billion in 1973, compared with additional food and fertilizer import costs of $5 billion. For 1974, food and fertilizer imports were expected to increase by $5 billion and petroleum by $7 billion. Oil is used in the production of fertilizer, but fertilizer costs began rising in 1972, before the price of petroleum jumped.)

Another report, presented to the special session by Waldheim, considered the evolution of prices of 64 basic commodities between 1950 and 1973. It concluded that "on the whole, the prices of commodities that are exported mainly by the developing countries apparently rose less than those of primary commodities [exported mainly by] developed countries. This is especially striking in the case of foodstuffs. . . ."

Unlike many industrialized countries, the United States is largely self-sufficient in raw materials. Japan and western Europe, which depend heavily on food imported from the United States, have been struck much harder by commodity inflation. Thus the United States was able to

pay for the increased cost of its petroleum imports in 1973 with expanded agricultural exports. The price of food products sold by the United States went up 55 per cent that year, while the price of its food imports (many of them from other industrial nations) increased only 22 per cent.

The secretary general's report showed clearly how recent trends in commodity inflation favor the rich nations at the expense of the poor. Of the 20 world commodities whose prices increased the most between 1970 and the end of 1973, the United States was the leading world exporter of eight, Canada of three, and other developed countries, of five more. The four other commodities were exported primarily by developing countries, but of these, petroleum was worth 12 times as much as the other three (cocoa, sisal, and copra) combined. Tea and jute, exported by poverty-stricken India and Bangladesh, were among those commodities whose prices fell the most.

The less-developed countries are especially dependent on the United States for supplies of agricultural products—a trend which is expected to continue. Large quantities of wheat, soybean oil, cottonseed oil, and rice—among the food items with the highest rates of inflation—are imported from the United States by developing

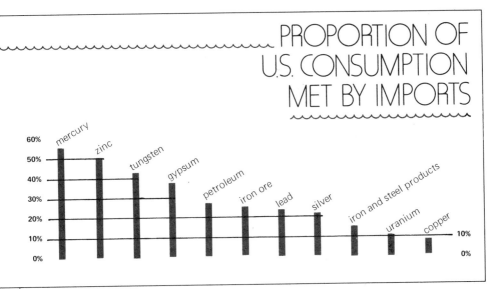

PROPORTION OF U.S. CONSUMPTION MET BY IMPORTS

countries. A U.S. government international economic report noted that, since 1950, food production per capita had increased three times as fast in developed countries as in the rest of the world.

In much of Africa, food production has actually declined. Drought and poor harvests struck many countries in 1972-73. In others, such as Zaïre (a major copper exporter) agricultural production was allowed to decline in favor of investment in mining and manufacturing. (See also FOOD in this section.)

Commodity Producers' Cartels

Calls for the formation of international associations on the model of OPEC have raised concern among American businessmen and officials over future sources of imported commodities. Although the United States meets most of its needs for copper, uranium, oil, iron ore, potash, lead, and some other minerals from domestic sources, it is becoming increasingly dependent on imports for these and other materials. Metals which are mainly imported include zinc (53 per cent of total U.S. consumption), tungsten (56), tin (83), nickel (80), bauxite (89), manganese (97), and chromium (100). Interior Department officials have estimated that, by 1985, more than half of U.S. iron ore and lead supplies may also come from

abroad. (See also METALS in the third section, 1973.)

Although the producers of most raw materials lack the geographical and ethnic unity of most of the petroleum exporters, the formation of cartels among some mineral producers is encouraged by the natural concentration of deposits. For example, Australia, Guinea, and Jamaica control 60 per cent of the world's bauxite reserves, while Chile, Peru, Zambia, and Zaïre have 80 per cent of the copper. Malaysia and Bolivia account for 70 per cent of the tin that moves in international trade.

In January, President Mobuto Sese Seko of Zaïre called on African countries to band together and demand higher prices for copper, potash, diamonds, gold, and cocoa "to put an end to the deteriorating terms of trade." Copper-exporting countries have been seeking advice from OPEC on the control of supplies and prices, and Zaïre and Zambia were reported to be coordinating copper production to keep prices high.

For the bauxite-producing nations, cartelization has become a reality. Seven nations which export 63 per cent of the world's bauxite (the ore used in the manufacture of aluminum) met in Conakry, Guinea, in early March and set up the In-

Copper Smelting in Zambia. Vernon J. Mwaanga, foreign minister of the African nation of Zambia, was among the speakers at the UN who called for a closer link between the prices of manufactured goods and the cost of raw materials produced by the less-developed countries. One of the four nations that account for 80 per cent of the world's copper production, Zambia was reported to be seeking the formation of a cartel that would coordinate production in order to keep copper prices high.

ternational Association of Producers of Bauxite. Australia was regarded as a moderate force in the organization. The other founding members were Guinea, Guyana, Jamaica, Sierra Leone, Surinam, and Yugoslavia.

The group's final accord stated that the organization would seek to "secure fair and reasonable profits for member countries in the processing and marketing of bauxite, bearing in mind the interests of the consumer nations." The association also called on bauxite producers to develop domestic aluminum-processing industries, and to "secure maximum national ownership of their national resources."

Jamaica (where the United States obtains two-thirds of its semi-refined alumina) announced several steps toward nationalization of its huge bauxite industry in June. Following a breakdown in talks between the government of the island and the six firms (five American, one Canadian) that control Jamaican bauxite production, Jamaica raised export taxes on bauxite by more than 500 per cent. The export levy per ton of bauxite went from $2.50 to $11.72, and the royalties to be paid to the government increased from 28¢ to 56¢ per ton. Income from the new taxes was expected to increase the country's revenue from bauxite fivefold, to about $200 million annually.

In response to criticism from the foreign corporations and the U.S. government, Jamaican Prime Minister Michael Manley said May 30 that the tax and royalty were raised because of the higher ingot price realized in the United States. Earlier in May he had emphasized that "the underdeveloped nations can no longer continue to supply raw materials to developed countries on the old basis, and in an inflationary world it is important to link the value of raw materials to the value of finished products."

(Bauxite was among the few commodities whose prices fell between 1970 and 1973. Meanwhile, the prices of major Jamaican imports were spiraling. Wheat, for example, rose from $78 a ton in December, 1972, to $243 a year later, and oil imports cost the country $24 million more in 1973 than in 1972.)

The governments of Jamaica, Guyana, and Trinidad and Tobago announced plans on June 10 for the construction of two $500-million aluminum smelters, one to be built in Trinidad and the other in Guyana. The new plants—the first aluminum refineries in these countries—would make possible the local processing of bauxite into aluminum. The government of Jamaica also revealed plans to negotiate the repurchase of bauxite lands from the aluminum companies by the end of 1974.

Aluminum Ore. Jamaica is the world's leading producer of bauxite (aluminum ore). The government has increased its revenue from bauxite production fivefold and plans to repurchase bauxite lands from the six North American firms that currently dominate mining on the island.

For producers of most other commodities, cartels will not be easy to establish or maintain. Such forces as falling demand or a glutted market can break a cartel, and high prices encourage "cheating" on export quotas by cartel members. Importing nations can replace many raw materials with substitute products. Alternative sources of supply, such as lower-grade domestic ores, may be profitably exploited if imports become expensive. The recycling of scrap and the stockpiling of essential commodities could provide additional short-term reserves against "artificial shortages."

No nation, however, can achieve autarky—total economic independence—without great cost to its industry and consumers. Its goods would be priced out of world markets, and its standard of living would fall.

A better solution to the problem of regulating trade in raw materials may be provided by commodity-stabilization agreements. Accords of this type, between consuming and producing nations, have worked well in the past for some commodities, such as tin, but less well for others, such as cocoa. Stabilization agreements, which could take years to negotiate, might benefit the exporting countries by preventing the typical boom-or-bust cycles of commodity prices, while protecting the importers against embargoes or production cutbacks.

The present trend toward higher prices for raw materials, which was generated by an economic upturn in the industrialized nations, may not be permanent. But as long as the "have-nots" have what the "haves" need, the less-developed countries can expect to receive a better deal in their trade relations with the commodity consumers.

Korea. President Chung Hee Park was delivering his Korean Liberation Day address in Seoul August 15 when a young man in the audience rushed towards the lectern, pistol blazing. As the shots rang out, the president hit the floor. His security men captured the gunman, but caught squarely in the temple by one of his bullets was the president's wife. She died that evening.

The assassin was later identified as Mun Se Kwang, a 22-year-old Korean radical born and raised in Japan. He used a forged passport to enter South Korea, smuggled in a disassembled gun stolen from a Japanese police station, and passed through the heavy security cordon by arriving at the ceremony in a rented limousine.

Many wondered what effect the killing would have on the president, who had been tightening his authoritarian rule to alarming proportions. One churchman involved in the Protestant and Catholic resistance to the regime's repression said, "The president is a man with a rage. With Madame Park gone, he will become more vindictive. But the harder he hits us, the harder we will hit back. There will be many martyrs."

President **Chung Hee Park** survived an assassination attempt while he was delivering an address, but his wife, *left*, was killed. Christian clergymen, opposition politicians, and students had denounced a new constitution that gave Park almost absolute powers.

Political Background

American reporters described Seoul, the capital, as tense. President Park had stamped his authority on every aspect of life, even dictating the acceptable length of men's hair and women's skirts.

In late 1972, Park imposed a new constitution whose main design was to maintain him in office indefinitely with almost absolute powers. In 1973, student demonstrations began in Seoul against the new constitution. Intellectuals, politicians, and the clergy quickly joined the students in opposition. Initially, Park made some modest concessions, but he later issued a series of harsh emergency measures aimed primarily at students.

The most severe restriction was announced on April 3, 1974: all dissident activists could be punished by death. Furthermore, they could be arrested without warrant and tried by secret court-martial. The final and harshest decree stated that "any person who defames the present emergency measures shall be punished by death, life imprisonment, or imprisonment for not less than five years."

As of August 14, 194 people had been convicted of conspiring to overthrow the government. As the arrests increased, world attention was awakened, particularly in reaction to the death penalty imposed on South Korea's best-known poet, Kim Chi Ha. (His sentence was later commuted to life imprisonment.) Bishop Daniel Chi Hak Soun, a liberal Roman Catholic cleric, was sentenced to 15 years in jail for giving the young poet money.

South Korean Premier Kim Ching Pil said that opponents of the government were "only a handful of disgruntled dissidents," and that the government would weed them out "like a cancer." He termed criticism in the United States over the government's actions irrational, assuring reporters that South Korea "will never betray your expectations for us to become a democratic and prosperous country."

Relations with Japan

One effect of the assassination of Madame Park was a deterioration of relations

Anti-Japanese Demonstration. Police in Seoul tear-gas demonstrators near the Japanese embassy protesting the assassination attempt. The man who intended to kill Park was a Korean radical born and raised in Japan. Park's government blamed Japanese negligence for the incident.

between Japan and South Korea. Park's government blamed Japanese negligence for the incident and demanded that Tokyo ban a large pro-Communist Korean organization in Japan. To back up the government's demand, Koreans staged 29 days of demonstrations, some of them violent, in front of the Japanese embassy. (Anti-Japanese feeling is easily fanned in Korea, which was under Japanese rule between 1910 and 1945.)

The diplomatic dispute ended September 19 when a special Japanese envoy handed Park a letter from Japanese Premier Kakuei Tanaka, with no address, date, or signature, expressing regret over the shooting. The envoy also orally conveyed the message that Japan "feels duly responsible" for the incident, would punish offenders, and would do its utmost to forestall future incidents.

Another breach in Japanese-South Korean relations had been precipitated in 1973, when Kim Dae Jung, Park's opponent in the 1971 presidential election, was kidnapped from Tokyo, reportedly by South Korean agents. To quell Japanese protests, South Korea agreed to free Kim, but instead put him on trial for alleged election-law violations. Japanese officials indicated that Park had reneged on an agreement to allow Kim to return to Tokyo and to try his kidnappers.

American Support

During the Korean War, the United States defended South Korea's independence at a cost of 33,000 dead. Since that time, Washington has provided $12 billion in economic and military aid. More than 20 years after the war's end, there remain 38,000 American soldiers in South Korea, including an infantry division. Under the United Nations Command structure, U.S. General Richard Stilwell commands both American and South Korean forces.

American aid to South Korea in 1973 totaled $142 million for the economy and $177 million in military assistance. The largest share of American aid falls within a $1.5-billion commitment to modernize South Korea's military, made in 1970 when a U.S. infantry division was withdrawn. This modernization program has been slowed by congressional budget cuts, and objections to the increasingly repressive nature of President Park's government were likely to result in a further slowdown.

In military strength, North and South Korea appear to be about equal. The armed forces of South Korea (army, air force, and navy) total 633,600 men, while North Korea's forces number 470,000. In the air North Korea holds an advantage, with an air force estimated at 45,000 men and 600 combat planes.

South Korea has 25,000 trained airmen using 200 combat aircraft. The United States maintains 60 fighting planes and additional air-warfare machinery. South Korea's trump card is the American presence, with its troops and tactical nuclear weapons.

Secretary of State Henry Kissinger has stated the official U.S. position remains that "the stability and security of South Korea is crucial to the security of the East Asian area," and that this concern has "led us to continue economic aid and military assistance when we would not have recommended many of the actions that were taken by the Government of South Korea." Arthur W. Hummell, acting assistant secretary for East Asian affairs, elaborated, saying that "the prevention of war on the Korean peninsula is the first and most important step toward the maintenance of human liberties."

But Edwin Reischauer, a Harvard University East Asian expert and former U.S. ambassador to Japan, believes that continued support of the Park regime might well hasten a war in Korea. He argues that governmental repression will eventually alienate many Koreans as well as their American allies, allowing North Korea to become bolder and possibly attack the weakened government. At this point the United States would have to decide whether it could actively support the repressive South Korean government in a war effort, and the bitter legacy of the Vietnam war might make Washington hesitate. But if the United States did not actively aid South Korea, other Southeast Asian allies might interpret its decision as abandonment.

Reischauer suggested that U.S. aid should be gradually withdrawn in order to apply pressure on Park to restore civil liberties and, if these changes were not made, a complete pullout should follow. The Senate Foreign Relations Committee had voted to reduce proposed military aid to South Korea, adding that such aid should be completely phased out by 1977. And in 1973, the House of Representatives passed a resolution that stated "the President should deny any economic or military assistance to the government of any foreign country which practices the internment or imprisonment of that country's citizens for political purposes."

Troubled Border. A South Korean soldier stands guard along a fence south of the demilitarized zone between North and South Korea. The United States maintains 38,000 soldiers in South Korea and contributes $300 million annually in economic and military assistance.

Labor. See WOMEN.

Literature. Among the books published during July, August, and September, 1974, were the following:

Fiction

The Black House, by Paul Theroux. An English anthropologist and his wife return home after 10 years in the African bush, only to find in this Gothic novel that the natives of Dorset are even more aloof, hostile, and superstitious than the tribe he had been studying. (Houghton Mifflin—$6.95)

Centennial, by James Michener. Another epic treatment by the author of *Hawaii* and *The Source* traces the site of a small fictional town in Colorado from its geological origins 3.6 billion years ago to the present day. After the first human—an Arapaho Indian—makes his appearance in 1747, trappers, miners, ranchers, businessmen, and ecologists follow. (Random House—$12.50)

The Connoisseur, by Evan S. Connell, Jr. A middle-aged insurance executive who finds a pre-Columbian figurine in a knicknack shop is soon gripped by the passions and moral ambiguities of the compulsive collector. Something new has entered his life, combining greed, love of beauty, and the challenge of detective work. (Knopf—$6.95)

The Dogs of War, by Frederick Forsyth. This thriller by the author of *The Day of the Jackal* is set in a West African kingdom, where the discovery of a vast fortune in platinum deposits arouses the cupidity of European capitalists and their hired army of mercenary soldiers. (Viking—$7.95)

Ending, by Hilma Wolitzer. Jay Kaufman is dying of bone cancer at the age of 32. The impact on his children, parents, and most of all, on his wife, is the subject of this moving, though emotionally draining work. (William Morrow—$6.95)

The Secret Glass, by Beryl Bainbridge. An American soldier enters the lives of three working-class women in Liverpool during World War II, with unfortunate consequences, in this brooding psychological novel. (George Braziller—$5.95)

The Silver Bears, by Paul Erdman. Financiers tamper with the world silver market in a novel whose familiar message is that big organizations are the crooks but little guys go to jail. (Scribners—$6.95)

The War Between the Tates, by Alison Lurie. A middle-aged professor, his vacuous student mistress, resentful wife, and ill-mannered children, offer abundant satirical material in this novel of domestic warfare. (Random House—$6.95)

Best-Selling Books

FICTION

Centennial, by James Michener
Tinker, Tailor, Soldier, Spy, by John le Carré
The Dogs of War, by Frederick Forsyth
Jaws, by Peter Benchley
The War Between the Tates, by Alison Lurie
The House of a Thousand Lanterns, by Victoria Holt

NONFICTION

All the President's Men, by Carl Bernstein and Bob Woodward
The Memory Book, by Harry Lorayne and Jerry Lucas
The Woman He Loved, by Ralph G. Martin
Alive: The Story of the Andes Survivors, by Piers Paul Read
You Can Profit from a Monetary Crisis, by Harry Browne
More Joy, Edited by Alex Comfort

Nonfiction

American Odyssey, by Robert Conot. This ambitious history of Detroit also serves as a case study of the industrial society in which cities were built to serve corporations and then abandoned to decay. The author offers a number of suggestions for easing the plight of contemporary Detroit. (William Morrow—$14.95)

Arnold Bennett, by Margaret Drabble. In a number of realistic novels no longer in fashion, Bennett chronicled everyday life in the "Five Towns" of industrial northern England from where he came. His biographer champions him as "a great writer from a stony land. He was also one of the kindest and most unselfish of men," and an effective popularizer of high culture. (Knopf—$10)

Chief! by Albert A. Seedman and Peter Hellman. The man who was for many years chief of detectives for the New York Police Department recalls such well-known cases as the murder of Kitty Genovese, the gangland shootings of Joe Colombo and Joey Gallo, and the Weatherman bomb factory in a Greenwich Village townhouse. Seedman indicates that most crimes are solved by legwork and dogged attention to the smallest details. (Arthur Field Books, Inc.—$10)

A Documentary History of the Italian Americans, edited by Wayne Moquin with Charles Van Doren. Brought to America to fill the demand for cheap labor, ostracized as Mafia criminals, anarchists, or Fascists, Italian-Americans have understandably been defensive about their origins. This work tells not only of the contributions to America by Columbus, La Guardia, Fermi, and Mother Cabrini, but also of lesser-known Italian-American soldiers, pioneers, farmers, and financiers. (Praeger—$15)

Emperor of China: Self-Portrait of K'ang-hsi, by Jonathan D. Spence. Delving through a vast body of historical materials, Professor Spence constructed a self-portrait of the man who ruled China from 1661 to 1722 as the second emperor of the Manchu dynasty. A remarkable figure emerges from scattered and fragmentary sources—crafty politician, indefatigable traveler, vigorous searcher for knowledge, and avid hunter. (Knopf—$8.95)

Khrushchev Remembers: The Last Testament, by Nikita Khrushchev, translated and edited by Strobe Talbott. In the second and concluding volume of the late Soviet leader's tape-recorded memoirs, Khrushchev endorses more freedom for writers and artists and more goods for the Soviet consumer. (Little, Brown—$12.95)

Kissinger, by Marvin Kalb and Bernard Kalb. Two CBS correspondents have written a biography that tells essentially what Kissinger has chosen to reveal to them about his secret diplomacy among the mighty. (Little, Brown—$12.50)

The Life and Death of Yukio Mishima, by Henry Scott-Stokes. The death by hara-kiri of Japan's most famous postwar author was the appropriate end of a complex personality dominated by morbid romanticism, obsessions with the samurai code and the mystique of body building, exhibitionist and masochistic tendencies, and a tenuous belief in reincarnation. (Farrar Straus & Giroux—$10)

The Lives of a Cell, by Lewis Thomas. Essays by a former medical-school dean cover such subjects as insect behavior, the evolution of language, man and his environment, but, most of all, the universe within the cells that reminds the scientist that "man is embodied in nature." (Viking—$6.95)

One Sunset a Week, by George Vecsey. Dan Sizemore, once a company man, now a radical, has little to show for 36 years in the coal mines except a chronic hacking cough. The hard and dangerous life of a coal miner and the fierce enmities of mining country are described in this depressing overview of Appalachia and its wreckage, both human and ecological. (Saturday Review Press—$7.95)

The Power Broker, by Robert A. Caro. Robert Moses, the most powerful nonelected public official in American history, built bridges, highways, parks, and housing projects while holding as many as a dozen New York state and local jobs at one time. But this exhaustive biography concludes that human values were buried under concrete. (Knopf—$17.95)

Literature for Children

Picture Books and Easy-to-Read Books

Arthur's Honey Bear, by Lillian Hoban. When are you old enough to give your favorite toys away? Arthur finds out in this warm and funny easy-to-read book. (Harper—$2.95)

Camels, Ships of the Desert, by John F. Waters, illustrated by Reynold Fuffins. Bold pictures and simple, clear text will help young scientists understand how the camel survives in the desert. (Crowell—$3.95)

Come Away, by Myra Cohn Livingston, pictures by Irene Haas. Rich in imagination is this story of two city children who discover the magic of the woods. (Atheneum—$5.95)

Dinosaur Time, by Peggy Parish, pictures by Arnold Lobel. Which dinosaur was the biggest? The fiercest? Beginning readers will enjoy finding the answers for themselves. (Harper—$2.50)

Harry Is a Scaredy-Cat, by Byron Barton. A wild ride on a balloon transforms timid Harry into a daredevil in this rollicking tale. (Macmillan—$5.95)

I Was So Mad! by Norma Simon, pictures by Dora Leder. Warm and humorous pictures

Things to Make and Do, by Douglas W. Downey and Karin Wisiol, design by Yvonne Beckwith, drawings by Dick Fickle. A 192-page arts-and-crafts book for children, from pre-school through the fourth grade, illustrated with 73 photographs and 440 step-by-step drawings. Contains information about basic techniques and crafts materials as well as more than 70 individual projects. (Standard Educational Corporation—$8.95)

and simple text help children understand that everybody gets mad sometimes! (Albert Whitman—$3.95)

Kim's Place and Other Poems, by Lee Bennett Hopkins, drawings by Di Fiori. Rhythmic poems evoke a little girl's special feelings for her special world. (Holt—$4.95)

Marko the Rich and Vasily the Unlucky, translated from the Russian by Thomas P. Whitney, illustrated by Igor Galanin. A dragon king, a whale bridge, and a talking oak tree help Vasily find fortune in this colorful folk tale. (Macmillan—$5.95)

Omoteji's Baby Brother, by Mary-Joan Gerson, illustrated by Elzia Moon. A boy of Nigeria finds the perfect gift for his new baby brother. (Walck—$5.95)

The Runaway Roller Skate, by John Vernon Lord. Gay verses and pictures tell the misadventures that were created by the runaway roller skate. (Houghton—$5.95)

The Secret Box Mystery, by Joan Lowery Nixon, illustrated by Leigh Grant. What was the something in the box that gurgled, hissed, cooed—and suddenly disappeared? (Putnam —$3.96)

The Third Gift, by Jan Carew, illustrated by Leo and Diane Dillon. From black Africa is this rich and beautiful tale of the Jubas who gave the world the most important gift of all. What was it? (Little—$5.95)

Well Done, by Barbara Morrow. A wise and hilarious tale of how the women of a medieval castle stopped a war. (Holt—$5.95)

What Can She Be? An Architect, by Gloria and Esther Goldreich, photographs by Robert Ipcar. Vivid photographs and text describe an architect's role in construction. (Lothrop —$4.50)

Where Does the Garbage Go? by Paul Showers, illustrated by Loretta Lustig. How much garbage do we accumulate each day? How do we dispose of it? Here are lively answers. (Crowell—$3.95)

Fiction (8 to 12 Years Old)

Alvin Fernald, Superweasel, by Clifford B. Hicks. When Alvin, the superbrain, becomes the Superweasel, fighter against pollution, hilarious adventures follow. (Holt—$5.95)

Cinnamon and Nutmeg, by Anne de Roo. The mystery of the orphan calf helps bring Tessa and her father together again. (Nelson —$5.95)

Greedy Mariani, by Dorothy Sharp Carter. A fascinating collection of folk tales from Puerto Rico, Jamaica, Haiti, and other countries of the Antilles. (Atheneum—$5.50)

Greenwitch, by Susan Cooper. The search for a stolen treasure involves three children in an eerie battle against the forces of darkness. Will the Greenwitch aid them? (Atheneum—$5.50)

The Last of the Really Great Whangdoodles, by Julie Edwards. Lindy, Tom, and Ben make a fantastic journey to find the last Whangdoodle and grant his heart's desire. (Harper—$5.95)

The Ostrich Chase, by Moses L. Howard. Khuana, a girl of the Bushmen tribe, defies tradition to prove her skill as a hunter, and then faces a greater challenge. (Holt—$5.95)

Katzimo, Mysterious Mesa, by Bobette Gugliotta. Half-Jewish, Half-Indian Carl finds challenge and new friends on an Indian reservation. (Dodd—$4.50)

Rod-and-Reel Trouble, by Bobbi Katz. Lori is delighted to find that this year the fishing contest is open to girls as well as boys —but can she win? (Albert Whitman— $3.25)

Terror on the Ice, by Mike Neigoff. Josh played the oboe, and he had to fight to prove that he was tough enough to be a terror on the ice in this fast-moving hockey story. (Albert Whitman—$3.95)

The Vandals of Treason House, by Nancy Veglahn. The boys and girls had been caught vandalizing an old house—but they didn't expect that to lead them into a strange mystery. (Houghton—$4.95)

The Winds of Time, by Barbara Corcoran. When rebellious Gail ran away from an uncle she did not trust, she found refuge with a strange family and a surprising new way of life. (Atheneum—$5.95)

Nonfiction (8 to 12 Years Old)

A Ball of Clay, by John Hawkinson. Here, in easy-to-follow text and photographs, are the ways you can shape clay into bowls, figures, anything you choose. (Albert Whitman —$3.95)

Hang in at the Plate, by Fred Bachman. What is it really like to play Junior League baseball? A boy tells his own story. (Walck —$5.50)

Jamestown, the Beginning, by Elizabeth A. Campbell. A fascinating description of the brave men and women who dared to found a colony in a new and unexplored world. (Little —$5.95)

Kids Are Natural Cooks, by Parents' Nursery School. These child-tested recipes will inspire children (and their parents and teachers) to try cooking ventures of their own. (Houghton—$5.95)

Sahara Trail, by Kelman D. Frost. A vivid account of an actual caravan journey across the Sahara desert with fascinating glimpses of fakirs, sheiks, mirages, sandstorms, and oases. (Nelson—$5.50)

Shadowplay, by George Mendoza, with Prasanna Rao. Prasanna Rao, the Indian Prince of Shadows, and George Mendoza have created a magical parade of shadow figures—and also present the hand positions so that others can create them, too. (Holt—$5.95)

The Story of Sea Otters, by William Weber Johnson. Are the sea otters just clever clowns or a valuable asset to ecology? Here are illuminating answers. (Random—$4.50)

Fiction (11 to 14 Years Old)

Duffy's Rocks, by Edward Fenton. Timothy knew there was a mystery about his long-vanished father, so he set out on a search that led to a surprising discovery. (Dutton—$5.95)

Mama's Ghosts, by Carol Lee Lorenzo. Ellie loved her grandmother's stories of the past, but would they hinder or help her to take a giant step into the future? (Harper—$4.95)

The Mural Master, by Adrienne Jones. Trapped in a magic picture, a girl and three boys find themselves in another world where they must fight the powers of evil. (Houghton—$5.95)

My Black Me, edited by Arnold Adoff. An evocative collection of poetry by 25 black poets. (Dutton—$5.50)

The Nargun and the Stars, by Patricia Wrightson. The lonely Australian sheep run was strange to orphaned Simon, but stranger still and more frightening was the ancient stone monster that crawled closer and closer. (Atheneum—$5.50)

The Rat-Catcher's Daughter, by Laurence Housman, edited by Ellin Greene. An enthralling collection of tales of magic and sorcery, brave princes and princesses, wicked ogres, and enchantments of many kinds. (Atheneum—$5.95)

Septimus and the Minster Ghost Mystery, by Stephen Chance. Did the clue to strange happenings lie in the ancient past? An unusual detective finds the answer to the puzzle. (Nelson—$4.95)

Sister, by Eloise Greenfield. A poignant and warm story of a girl who found the strength and wisdom to be herself. (Crowell—$4.95)

Sunset in a Spider Web, adapted by Virginia Olsen Baron. Lovely, haunting, and imaginative are these sijo poems of ancient Korea. (Holt—$4.95)

Nonfiction (11 to 14 Years Old)

Demons, Devils, and Djinn, by Olga Hoyt. As fascinating as fiction is this exploration of the supernatural. (Abelard-Schuman—$5.95)

Gods and Heroes of War, by C. A. Burland. What is a god? What is a hero? Here are comparisons of gods and heroes of a variety of cultures and the ways they still influence our own experience. (Putnam—$4.49)

Latin American Crafts and Their Cultural Backgrounds, by Jeremy Comins. How craftsmen express their own cultures through their crafts is demonstrated in this book. The clear and direct instructions will also help young craftsmen create handicrafts of their own. (Lothrop—$5.50)

More Puzzles for Pleasure and Leisure, by Thomas L. Hirsch. An unusual and challenging collection of puzzles of many kinds that will delight puzzle fans of any age. (Abelard-Schuman—$4.95)

Paintbox on the Frontier, by Alberta Wilson Constant. An exciting biography of George Caleb Bingham, who painted an unforgettable chronicle of the early America he lived in. (Crowell—$7.50)

Pollution Lab, by Melvin Berger. A behind-the-scenes look at the laboratories where scientists work for pollution-free air, water, and land. (John Day—$5.95)

Waves, Wheels and Wings, Museums of Transportation, by Robert B. Jackson. This is an irresistible invitation to step back into the days of the sailing ships, steam locomotives, and old cars and planes by visiting the museums that celebrate their glories. (Walck—$4.95)

Fiction (Teen-age)

A Chill in the Lane, by Mabel Esther Allan. What was the eerie terror in the lane, and why could only Lyd, the stranger, feel it? Lyd must travel backward into time to find the answer that leads her to happiness and love. (Nelson—$5.50)

The Emperor's Winding Sheet, by Jill Paton Walsh. A young English seaman becomes a slave of the last Byzantine emperor in the 15th century and fights fiercely to defend Constantinople. (Farrar—$6.95)

Glory in the Flower, by Norma Johnston. A baby in a blizzard, a school scandal, and playing Juliet in the school play all help Tish make growing-up discoveries. (Atheneum—$6.25)

House of Stairs, by William Sleator. A chilling story of a fantastic psychological experiment and a boy and girl who fought to keep their minds free. (Dutton—$5.95)

Mollie Make-Believe, by Alice Bach. All her life Mollie has relied on others; now she must choose between the future and the past. (Harper—$4.95)

Sidewalk Indian, by Mel Ellis. Charley Nightwind was a city Indian, but the reservation was his only refuge when he fled from the police. Could Charley survive alone in the wilderness? (Holt—$5.95)

Nonfiction (Teen-age)

Automotive Tune-Ups for Beginners, by I. G. Edmonds. To save gas in these days of the energy crisis and keep your car running in top condition, here is an easy-to-follow, step-by-step guide to tuning up your own car. (Macrae Smith—$6.95)

The Birth of the United States, 1763-1816, by Isaac Asimov. A fresh and illuminating recreation of the beginnings of our nation and of the men and events that influenced its growth. (Houghton—$5.95)

A Carnival of Sports, by Bill Severn. Subtitled "Spectacles, Stunts, Crazes, and Unusual Sports Events," this book rollicks through the funny, picturesque, and bizarre. Here, too, are the exciting daredevils who walked over Niagara on a tightrope, rolled down the falls in barrels, and risked their lives in a variety of other thrills and spills. An entertaining and factual treasure for the sports library. (McKay—$9.95)

Faith Has Need of All the Truth, by Charlie May Simon. A warm and perceptive biography of Pierre Teilhard de Chardin, scientist, writer, co-discoverer of Peking Man, and, above all, a man whose home was in the spiritual as well as the material world. (Dutton—$5.95)

The First American Revolution, by Milton Lomask. According to John Adams, the American Revolution began long before the war "in the minds and hearts" of the American people. Here is a vivid account of that revolution and what it may mean for us today. (Farrar—$6.95)

The Mystery of Emily Dickinson, by Laura Benet. A sparkling biography of the elusive poet whose poems have delighted many readers, but whose life still holds many mysteries for us all. (Dodd—$4.25)

On the Move, by D. S. Halacy, Jr. A penetrating exploration of man and his drive to move swiftly across the land, seas, and skies, and space itself. Travel and transportation are traced from their beginnings to the latest technological triumphs, in vivid text and graphic illustrations. (Macrae Smith—$5.95)

The Perfect Life, by Doris Faber. A fascinating and comprehensive description of the Shakers in America and the communities they founded in order to live a "perfect life." (Farrar—$6.95)

What a Funny Thing to Say! by Bernice Kohn. A witty and provocative search into how words originated and changed, secret languages, and codes—plus word games that are fun to play. (Dial—$4.95)

Music: The Pop Scene

It's been ten years since the Beatles, four English kids with unusually long hair, made their first impression on the popular music charts in the United States. But after their initial acceptance, their impact was fast and furious, helping to create a music industry to tap the economic potential of post-war babies turned adolescents and, almost on the side, making rock music the basis for that generation's counter-culture.

The pop-music scene was a blend of politics, rebellion, and a large part hedonism but, if nothing else, the economic boom in the industry allowed more music to be recorded than at any time in history. The pop-music market has grown with its audience, and its diversity and sheer variety reflect the fact that 30-year-olds buy records as they did when they were 20, and as their younger brothers and sisters do today. Americans spend $2 billion annually on recorded music, in addition to billions more spent on concerts, clubs, and movies involving music. More than three-quarters of all records bought fall into the category of pop music: rock, folk, country, and jazz.

The Founding Fathers

When the Beatles finally disbanded, critics wondered if as individuals they could sustain the caliber of their music. John Lennon and Paul McCartney had written a veritable compendium of pop music for the group. As their solo careers evolved, it became evident that each was seeking his own unique expressions.

John Lennon's first solo recording was produced after he underwent primal therapy with his wife, Yoko Ono, and the music produced set a precedent for unveiled personal statements through rock. The music was brittle with lyrics conveying the pain Lennon felt in realizing the Beatle myth and his efforts at finding his true self within the trappings of stardom. The album ended with the simple statement, "The dream is over."

Paul McCartney produced albums which, if not critically successful, made the best-seller charts. For many, his full solo potential was realized in his 1974 release, *Band on the Run*. Using the metaphor of escaping desperados for a rock and roll band, McCartney wove his melodic technique through songs reflecting his musical and lyrical playfulness, characteristics which were effective foils to Lennon's artistic seriousness in the Beatles' heyday.

If the Beatles were the group of the sixties, Bob Dylan was certainly the individual. Embodying influences as varied as William Blake and Woody Guthrie, his poetics, coupled with his folk-rock flair, knew no true bounds. Choosing for many years to avoid the spotlight which had killed either the body or spirit of many of his rock contemporaries, Dylan set out in early 1974 on a nationwide tour, his first in eight years. What emerged from these concerts and his new recordings was a new Dylan, not as revolutionary as his earlier persona, but surely as important artistically.

His new songs are domestic and inspirational, dealing with his wife and home and the importance of such loving institutions in the face of the darker visions he expressed in earlier years. His new material does not refute his earlier work, which remains frighteningly valid to this day, but

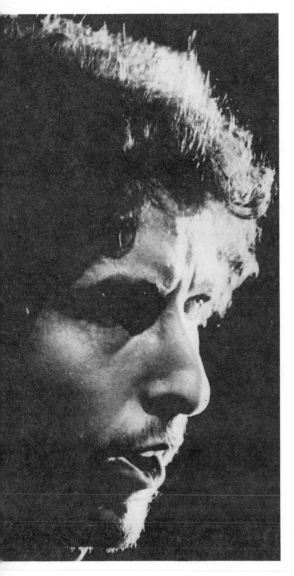

Bob Dylan: "I've been walking the road, I've been living on the ledge, now I've just got to go before I get to the edge." From "Going Going Gone."

calls on his listeners to find strength and solace by realizing their powers as well as their limitations.

Joni Mitchell stands as a feminine reflection of Dylan's concerns and is seen by many as the finest woman songwriter working today. Her works are finely wrought melodies graced with the sensibilities of a vulnerable and very warm woman. Her lyrics are extremely personal, dealing usually with her search for a secure relationship with a man, often a difficult goal in the face of her own instinctual need for freedom. Within her songs there is a spirit in which the listener can sense that she will never abandon her search.

Both Mitchell and Dylan established themselves in the sixties and paved the way for other singer-songwriters, such as James Taylor, Carly Simon (Taylor's wife), and Carole King. All deal from varying perspectives with their own lives and their upper-middle-class and white backgrounds. They have drawn huge audiences of young people with similar upbringings.

New Wave

Among the new singer-songwriters, Jackson Browne stands out as unique to the seventies. His music is a blend of California groups like the Byrds and the Beach Boys with the individual consciousness of a Dylan. His songs hover between childlike romanticism and adult rationality, digesting the traumas of the times within his own personality and concluding that the search for higher meaning within himself is more important than gut reactions of fear towards the outside world.

Other new writers, most notably Randy

Joni Mitchell: "But I know my needs, my sweet tumbleweeds; I need more quiet times, by a river flowing, you and me, deep kisses and the sun going down." From "Lesson in Survival."

Newman and Loudon Wainwright III, have taken more novel approaches. Both use disarmingly simple music and words to create black-humor landscapes which reveal very personal and often dark views of the world. Their sheer originality, though, supplies the sunshine.

Another breed of American musicians has looked to the native musical heritage of jazz, rhythm and blues, and pop tunes, for their material. Critical success has come to artists like Ry Cooder and Maria Muldaur who, employing the techniques of indigenous American musical forms, have created their own personal statements. Rolling Stone music critic Jon Landau puts this creative process simply in talking about Cooder: "By embodying traditions with such grace, he becomes one with them."

The Band, a rock group, also seeks to explore the American past, though its approach is more literary than musical. Guitarist Robbie Robertson writes much of the group's material, dealing with the American past in an almost hauntingly true voice. (The Band also serves as Dylan's back-up group.)

A different view of America comes from British pop star Elton John, enormously successful in producing hit singles. His lyricist, Bernie Taupin, revels in America's mystique, conjuring images ranging from the western frontier to Marilyn Monroe. John's tunes are sometimes inspired, sometimes insipid, but he must certainly be considered a major pop voice of the seventies. He is also one of the best paid; his latest contract reportedly guarantees him $8 million in royalties for his next six albums.

343

Mick Jagger of the Rolling Stones: "But what can a poor boy do but to sing in a rock and roll band, cause in sleepy London town there just no place for street fightin' man." From "Street Fighting Man."

The Rolling Stones

The Rolling Stones were the dark side of the Beatle myth, cultivating a profitable rebel image in presenting their aggressively brash music. Brimming with a youthful bravado that struck a responsive chord among their fans, the Rolling Stones became superstars—a role which ultimately could only undermine their mystique. As rock music moved into the seventies, the Stones became the touchstone where the avant-garde of art and letters found compatriots in the new world of pop music.

From a base of rhythm and blues, and particularly the rock and roll of Chuck Berry, the Stones moved into more adventurous terrain. Often their images were dark, like Jagger's persona in "Sympathy for the Devil," and the desperation evoked in "Gimme Shelter." When they played a free concert in California following their 1969 tour, similar feelings of cynicism pervaded the crowd, and Hell's Angels, hired to patrol the stage area for a bounty of beer, killed a man within feet of "the greatest rock and roll band in the world." The Stones no longer perform "Sympathy for the Devil."

Today, one is likely to find Mick Jagger in the pages of *Women's Wear Daily*. He is a chic star, and yet at the same time he heads one of the most creative and long-standing rock and roll bands ever. Whether the two roles can co-exist remains to be seen, but one must wonder how Jagger deals with the contradictions of his rebellious image and his jet-set acceptance. It's a long way from the cries of distraught parents in 1965: Would you want your daughter to marry a Rolling Stone?

344

Lou Reed: "I don't know just where I'm going. But I'm going to try for the Kingdom if I can, cause it makes me feel like such a man to put a spike into my vein and I tell you, things ain't quite the same." From "Heroin."

Rockin' Decadence

Rock and roll has always had its roots in sex, but just as the Ed Sullivan Show would not allow Elvis Presley's swinging hips to be shown as he performed on television, the mass audience of the sixties was not ready for the often-ugly view of life portrayed by bands like the Velvet Underground. But in the seventies, as sex became more open and mass magazines casually wrote about bisexuality, rock responded with a flurry of theatrical bands which exploited what remained of the old taboos.

Alice Cooper, both the name of a band and its fitfully inspired male singer, mixed both sex and violence into its stage act, a multimedia event which included ripping apart toy dolls and a mock beheading of Alice. It sold records and filled concert halls. Even more amazingly, Alice Cooper himself has been accepted into the celebrity mainstream: he occasionally appears on the TV quiz show Hollywood Squares.

Pop-artist Andy Warhol formed the Velvet Underground in 1966 as part of his traveling show, the Exploding Plastic Inevitable. Quickly breaking away from the Warhol clique, the Velvet Underground, led by vocalist Lou Reed and violinist John Cale, pictured the dark underside of life in New York City. (The band's name was lifted from a trashy novel.) The Velvets disbanded with little popular recognition but, along with the Doors, a West Coast band led by singer-poet Jim Morrison, they left a literate and uncompromising approach to rock which would be emulated in the seventies.

Bisexual David Bowie was the most important artist to rise amid the seventies'

David Bowie: "You're too old to lose it, too young to choose it, and the clock waits patiently on your song. You walk past the cafe but you don't eat when you've lived too long, you're a rock'n'roll suicide." From "Rock'n'Roll Suicide."

new permissiveness. Bowie's appeal falls within the term "glitter rock," meaning music which, often with disastrous results, uses sexual ambiguity to establish an image. Bowie, who uses his last name as a full signature—like Garbo or Brando—embodies the extremes of modern rock, its best artistic intentions as well as its decadent self-destructive tendencies. While he has sometimes fallen prey to the fads he helped create, Bowie has shown himself to be a creator of intelligent rock and roll, with lyrics often dealing with the unreality of being a pop star. Inherent in much of his writing is a fear of impending holocaust and the ever-present threat of violence. Like Jagger, Bowie is afraid for his own safety, as his notoriety exposes him to the same danger of assassination as that of a charismatic politician.

Bowie's approach to recording is indicative of the new craftsmanship involved in modern pop music. Up until the late fifties, recording was done in monophonic, meaning that all volume and tone levels were set before the final recorded performance. As stereo records became the norm, four-track equipment was used, allowing musicians to add instruments on one of four synced tracks, with the various parts mixed into the final product. The Beatles' "Sgt. Pepper," considered a masterpiece of studio technique when it was released in 1967, was recorded on a four-track machine. By 1970, most rock bands were using 16-track machines, allowing every instrument and vocal its own track, and resulting in a highly polished sound. The advent of new equipment also elevated the role of producers and engineers in the new music.

The Who, a British band together since before the Beatles hit the American shores, provides a ready example of the use of both studio and dramatic technique to present very high-powered rock and roll. While continuing to identify with the British teen culture from which this group emerged, the Who's writer-guitarist Peter Townshend applied operatic concepts to his often-thematic songs. The Who scored a big success with their rock-opera *Tommy,* and are currently collaborating with film-maker Ken Russell on a star-laden non-dialog adaptation.

Heavy Metal

"There was the sound of mountains crashing in this holocaust of decibels, hearts bursting, as if this were the sound of death by explosion within . . . electric crescendo screaming as if at the electromechanical climax of the age." Such was Norman Mailer's description of the MC5 as they performed at the 1968 Chicago demonstrations. The genre is called "heavy metal," a phrase lifted from author William Burroughs.

The musical components of heavy metal are extraordinary volume, distortion, repetition of musical phrases ("riffing"), and often a disregard for swing, punctuated by leaden drum work. The sound is thick with guitars; an occasional keyboard is mixed in with the rhythm section, but rarely are horns heard. Heavy metal has

The Who: "People try to put us down, just because we get around. Things I see look oh so cold, hope I die before I get old." From "My Generation."

changed the sound of hard rock from the crisp chordal music of a Chuck Berry to the distorted sonic-sound of a Led Zeppelin.

The birth of heavy metal can be traced to the British bands of the mid-sixties, most notably the Yardbirds. The Yardbirds' main asset was their various lead guitarists: Eric Clapton, Jimmy Page, and Jeff Beck all displayed their prowess with the Yardbirds, experimenting with techniques of guitar distortion and fuzz tones which they would apply to their later successes.

Clapton established himself as a superstar with the first power trio, Cream, which spawned countless other guitar, drums, and bass bands. His Yardbirds replacement, Jimmy Page, heads probably the world's most popular heavy-metal group, Led Zeppelin. American bands were not long in establishing their own heavy-metal

sound, and Grand Funk Railroad led the pack with a ragged Cream sound.

As the seventies progressed, though, the heavy-metal scene diverged, with the two poles indicated by two current exponents of the genre. The Blue Oyster Cult mix a staged demeanor of violence with science-fiction images and highly-crafted, ear-thudding material. The New York Dolls, on the other hand, are a primitive mix of Velvet Underground sleaze and high-powered amplification. Whereas the Cult apply dynamics and tongue-in-cheek subtlety, the Dolls display high-tension punk bravado. In the arena of heavy metal, both approaches carry equal power.

To many minds though, the most innovative musician to develop out of metal music was Jimi Hendrix. "Jimi Hendrix changed rock more than the Beatles," claims Peter Townshend, referring to his use of feedback and other distortion tech-

Miles Davis, who for the beat generation provided "the sound of the night," helped create the jazz/rock synthesis of the seventies.

niques which expanded the guitar's scope and truly made it "electric." Observers saw him coming into his prime when he died in 1970. He left rock audiences with an increased respect for musicianship and broader musical forms.

The New Jazz

For many years, jazz music was the property of an intellectual and largely white audience. The music of the "beat" generation of the fifties, Jack Kerouac described it in his novel *On the Road* as "the sound of the night."

As rock audiences matured in their tastes, many found new life in jazz, which itself was being transformed by the electronics and economics of the rock explosion. Miles Davis, who had played with such jazz giants as Thelonius Monk, Charlie Parker, and John Coltrane during the fifties and had himself become a legend on the trumpet, initiated a new era of jazz with his albums *In a Silent Way* and *Bitches Brew*.

Davis' approach to the new music, influenced by such diverse talents as Parker and psychedelic soul-man Sly Stone, depended heavily on his chosen accompanists. Chick Corea, who played piano in these sessions, reveals that Davis wrote out very little of what he wanted played but rather "put the musicians together and nudged them with comments in such a way that he would in effect be structuring the music." One motif which Davis helped to establish was the repetition of melodic patterns throughout a composition, a stylistic device now common among many new jazzmen. Among the players in these sessions who later established their own names in jazz and rock were John Mc-

349

John McLaughlin of the Mahavishnu Orchestra attracted rock devotees with his guitar style, which combined the sonics of heavy metal and the inventiveness of "out" jazz.

Laughlin, Keith Jarrett, Billy Cobham, Josef Zawinul, and Herbie Hancock.

Zawinul, who plays keyboards and composes for Weather Report, explains that through the influence of rock, the new jazz is a contemporary hybrid. "We're coming from jazz," he explains, "and there is still a lot of improvisations, but the music is more powerful rhythmically. But actually, that's what jazz is all about: motion, emotion, improvisation."

The first jazz-rock outfit to make a major stir among the rock audience was the Mahavishnu Orchestra, led by British guitarist John McLaughlin, whose first sessions in the States were with Davis. His original five-piece band, including a violin and synthesizer, combined the sonic fury of heavy metal with the manic energy of "out" jazz. ("Out" is a term used in jazz music to refer to a player who can improvise in a pattern which is itself not predictable, but at the same time can communicate logically and inventively through his instrument.)

Herbie Hancock, whose album *Head Hunters* was the first record of advanced instrumental improvisation to make the top-ten list of pop records, explains that his new music does not compromise his abilities to play "outside." "I'm still able to go outside," says Hancock, "but I'm also able to play the plain funky truth, which I really wasn't able to do before. There's a simplicity to my new band's approach which people can easily identify with, yet it doesn't sound like anybody else." Hancock used to play almost completely to white audiences, but he now finds himself playing music "the general black public can relate to."

Stevie Wonder: "I'm so darn glad he let me try it again, cause my last time on earth I lived a whole world of sin. I'm so glad that I know more than I knew then, gonna keep on tryin' till I reach the highest ground." From "Higher Ground."

Soul

For most blacks, though, soul music is still king, and recent trends towards more experimentation have helped the form maintain its popularity. The important innovators have altered the total sound of their music. Two artists in particular, Stevie Wonder and Al Green, reflect two approaches to modern soul music.

Stevie Wonder became a star with Motown Records in his early teens. As he grew older, Wonder demanded complete artistic control and, when it was obtained, he proceeded to produce what some see as the perfect union of rock technology and soul music's integrity. His music unites flowing pop-jazz with spiraling rock guitars and synthesizers, always anchored by Wonder's own deliberate and straightforward vocalizing.

Al Green, on the other hand, has looked backwards for his inspiration. While most young black musicians view the soul music of past masters like Otis Redding and Sam and Dave as dated, Green has breathed new life into the style they developed. Within the framework of a simple drum-oriented band, Green's primary instrument is his urbane voice, full-bodied in the mid-range and prone to flights into a quivering falsetto. More than hitting a note precisely, Green attempts to surround it. As in most traditional soul music, his lyrics deal with love, both won and lost.

Country Music

Country music has always had an audience, but recent years saw the market blossom, as rock musicians incorporated country into their own style and consequently introduced the originators to a wider audience. Radio has also contrib-

351

Pop music simultaneously satisfies and perpetuates the public's thirst for new sounds and stars.

uted to the boom: in 1961 there were only 80 pure country-music stations, while today there are over 1,000. The Grand Ole Opry, which over the past decades has been the home of country music in downtown Nashville, has moved into an opulent $15-million Disneylike suburban home called Opryland, U.S.A.

As its appeal has broadened—it now accounts for one-fifth of the record market—country music has diversified. The traditionalists are still strong, singing of loyalty to their mates as well as to their country, but younger performers have introduced a broader approach to the music which has aided its acceptance outside the South.

Like the music they play, today's country-music stars run the gamut from traditionalist Merle Haggard, whose records grossed $44.5 million over the past decade, to Tanya Tucker, a 15-year-old whose first three albums all landed in the top ten. Kris Kristofferson, a former Rhodes Scholar, has been embraced by both rock and country fans and is considered the most important artist bridging the two.

The South Rises

While the South has always been an important force in rock music, its impact came from its black heritage of blues and rhythm and blues and not from any particular post-Beatle style. The Allman Brothers Band, from Macon, Georgia, changed all that.

Duane Allman played slide guitar on many rhythm and blues albums during the sixties and, at the urging of promoter Phil Walden, formed a band with his brother Gregg. Using their blues roots as a base, the Allman Brothers Band has developed a style integrating aspects of rock, blues, and country into a flowing and completely original sound. Even the death of Duane in a motorcycle accident couldn't deter the band's rise to stardom as it singlehandedly created a booming music industry in Macon. Capricorn Records, formed by Walden to promote the Allmans, now boasts 24 acts and grossed $43 million in 1973.

The Yellow Brick Road

"Rock and roll has reached the peak of its zenith," says rock promoter Bill Graham in talking about the 1974 summer season, during which some bands were paid over $125,000 for an evening's work. "The Golden Age of rock was yesterday," he adds, possibly reflecting on the years in which he operated the country's rock showcases, Fillmore East and West.

Rock and roll, on an economic and social scale, is unlike any entertainment phenomenon that preceded it. It has enabled British working-class kids like the Rolling Stones to become bohemian aristocrats, mingling with the jet set and playing to enormous crowds. It has also created a world in which frail artists like Janis Joplin are at once adored and lonely, and finally dead.

John Lennon sang that the dream was over, but the Beatles and all the other rockers have created an industry which serves and perpetuates the public's thirst for new sounds and stars. And while there is a lot of good and a lot of bad in the music, it still boils down to what Lou Reed sang with the Velvet Underground: "Despite all the amputations, you know you can just dance to the rock and roll station and baby, it's all right!"

Obituaries. July, August, and September, 1974.

ABRAMS, CREIGHTON W., who President Ford described as "an American hero in the best tradition," was commander of U.S. forces in Vietnam, 1968-72, overseeing the gradual American withdrawal from the war. He then became army chief of staff. During World War II, he commanded tank forces in Europe with great effectiveness; September 3, age 59.

ACHARD, MARCEL, member of the French Academy whose plays, particularly his comedies, enjoyed an international reputation; September 4, age 75.

ADLERBLUM, NINA, writer known for her works on Jewish philosophy, American history, and the philosophy of history. She was also important in disseminating the teachings of John Dewey; July 25, age 92.

ALLEN, FORREST C. (Phog), basketball coach at the University of Kansas for nearly four decades who fought to have the sport added to the Olympic Games; September 16, age 88.

AMMONS, EUGENE (Jug), distinctive tenor-saxophone stylist who played with such jazz greats as Charlie Parker and Dizzy Gillespie; August 6, age 49.

ANTONIUTTI, ILDEBRANDO CARDINAL, prominent Vatican diplomat and writer who served in Spain, China, Canada, and Portugal; August 1, age 75.

APGAR, VIRGINIA, physician who developed the "Apgar Score," a test to quickly determine the health of a newborn infant; August 7, age 65.

ARQUETTE, CLIFF, comedian who created the character of Charlie Weaver, a regular on TV's "Hollywood Squares"; September 23, age 68.

BEIRNE, JOSEPH A., president of the 500,-000-member Communications Workers of America from the time he helped found it in 1947 until his retirement in June, 1974; September 2, age 63.

BENTHALL, MICHAEL, British stage director and producer who, during his nine years at the Old Vic, gained an international reputation for excellence in the classical theater; September 6, age 55.

BLACKETT, PATRICK M. S., one of Britain's leading and most versatile scientists who won the Nobel Prize for physics in 1948 for his studies of cosmic rays; July 13, age 76.

BLAU, AMRAM, Jerusalem rabbi who was leader of the Neturei Karta, an orthodox Jewish sect which refused to recognize the state of Israel, believing the sovereignty of the Promised Land was in the hands of God; July 5, age 81.

Patrick M. S. Blackett

BRAUN, OTTO, German revolutionary who was a key military adviser to the Chinese Communists in the 1930's and was the only foreigner to participate in the Long March; August 15, age 73.

BRENNAN, WALTER, veteran actor who won three Oscars while working in more than 100 films and television shows, including "The Real McCoys"; September 21, age 80.

BRODE, WALLACE, president of the American Chemical Society and pioneer of modern methods for using light to analyze elements and compounds; August 10, age 74.

BRONOWSKI, JACOB, leading popularizer of science research whose last work, a British television series called "The Ascent of Man," described the place of science in human history; August 22, age 66.

CANNON, JAMES P., Trotskyite who helped found the Socialist Workers party in 1938 and later became its national chairman; August 21, age 84.

CHADWICK, Sir JAMES, English physicist who won the Nobel Prize for physics in 1935 for his discovery in 1932 of the neutron; July 24, age 82.

CHENERY, WILLIAM L., journalist who, for 25 years, first as editor and then as publisher, headed *Collier's* magazine; August 18, age 90.

COLDWELL, M. J., Canadian political leader who served in the House of Commons and headed the socialist-oriented Cooperative Commonwealth Federation between 1942 and 1958; August 25, age 85.

COLWELL, ERNEST, leading New Testament scholar and president of the University of Chicago from 1945 to 1951; September 13, age 73.

CRAIG, LYMAN C., chemist whose research revolutionized techniques for purifying drugs, penicillins, proteins, and hormones; July 7, age 68.

DARVAS, LILI, leading European and Broadway actress whose career spanned more than 50 years; July 22, age 72.

DEAN, DIZZY, folk hero of baseball whose career was cut short by injury, but whose exploits won him election to the Baseball Hall of Fame as one of the game's finest pitchers; July 17, age 63.

DE SEVERSKY, ALEXANDER P., proponent of strategic air power whose inventions were major contributions to military and commercial flying; August 24, age 80.

DUNOYER DE SEGONZAC, ANDRE, France's most respected naturalist painter whose specialized in landscapes, nudes, and still lifes; September 17, age 90.

ELLIOT, CASS, rotund contralto vocalist who gained fame with the folk-rock group the Mamas and the Papas; July 29, age 33.

FOUCHET, CHRISTIAN, French Gaullist who served in the cabinet from 1962 until 1968, when he was forced to resign for dispatching large numbers of riot troops to quell student demonstrations; August 12, age 63.

GAISMAN, HENRY J., inventor of 84 products in such fields as photography and cutlery; August 6, age 104.

GAMBRELL, MARY L., educator who served as president of Hunter College from 1966 to 1967, the first woman president of a major coeducational college; August 19, age 76.

GAUDIN, ANTOINE, mineral expert who led the development of the techniques that made uranium available for the first atomic bombs; August 23, age 74.

GOLDSMITH, ALFRED N., electronics scientist and engineer who developed the first commercial radio-phonograph and early radios, and contributed to the first commercial color-television tube; July 2, age 85.

GRIFFIS, STANTON, ambassador to Poland, Egypt, Argentina, and Spain (1951-52), where he helped open a new era of cooperation between Washington and Madrid; August 29, age 87.

HATHAWAY, SIBYL, dame of Sark, who in 1927 became the feudal ruler of the tiny island in the English Channel; July 14, age 90.

HEYER, GEORGETTE, British novelist who wrote more than 50 books, most of them historical pieces set in early 19th-century England; July 4, age 71.

HULL, WARREN, radio and television master of ceremonies best-known for the "Strike It Rich" quiz show; September 14, age 71.

EL-HUSSEINI, HAJ AMIN, grand mufti of Jerusalem and powerful Arab leader during the 1940's and early 1950's. He was a fervent anti-Zionist who opposed the founding of Israel and was a Nazi collaborator during World War II; July 4, age 80.

INNES-KER, GEORGE, ninth duke of Roxburghe and one of Scotland's richest men; September 26, age 61.

JENKINS, ALLEN, character actor in more than 175 movies, usually as an amiable roughneck beside heavies like Humphrey Bogart and James Cagney; July 20, age 74.

KAESTNER, ERICH, satirist, social critic, and author who spoke out against the Nazi movement while living in Germany in the 1930s; July 29, age 75.

KARTVELI, ALEXANDER, aircraft designer who gave American fighter pilots a series of planes from the P-47, used in World War II, to the F-105, used in Vietnam; July 20, age 77.

KELLY, LAWRENCE, opera impresario who was co-founder of the Lyric Opera of Chicago in 1952; September 16, age 46.

KIRK, NORMAN E., prime minister and foreign minister of New Zealand who rose from humble origins to lead his Labour party to victory in 1972; August 31, age 51.

KRUGER, OTTO, versatile actor on stage and screen whose career stretched from 1905 until his death; September 6, age 89.

LAGERKVIST, PAR, one of Sweden's most prolific literary figures who won the Nobel Prize for literature in 1951; July 11, age 83.

LINDBERGH, CHARLES A., aviator who became an instant hero in 1927 when he completed the first solo airplane flight across the Atlantic, flying from New York to Paris, where he was greeted by thousands of ecstatic Parisians. He was hailed for his valor and presented with decorations by the United States, France, Britain, and Belgium.

In 1932 his fame turned against him as his infant son was kidnapped, creating world

Lindbergh Over the Years. After his solo flight across the Atlantic in 1927, he made other flying trips, worked on an artificial heart, opposed U.S. intervention in World War II, and, in his later years, devoted much time to the cause of conservation.

wide headlines. His child was later found dead and Bruno Hauptmann was subsequently apprehended and convicted of the crime. Always an avid supporter of aviation development, he later became interested in the conservation movement; August 26, age 72.

See also LINDBERGH, CHARLES A., in your encyclopedia.

LONG, LOIS, one of the original staff writers for the *New Yorker* who established standards for the relatively new field of fashion writing; July 29, age 73.

MCCAFFERTY, DON, head coach of the Detroit Lions since 1973. While coach of the Baltimore Colts in 1970, he led the team to a Super Bowl victory; July 28, age 53.

MCCARTEN, JOHN, acerbic writer and critic for the *New Yorker* for 40 years, specializing in movie and drama criticism; September 25, age 63.

MASSEY, ILONA, actress who achieved stardom in Hollywood as a blond temptress, best remembered for her role in *Balalaika* (1939); August 20, age 62.

MOORE, ARTHUR, bishop and noted orator for the United Methodist Church who converted thousands as a missionary in China, Japan, Czechoslovakia, Belgium, Poland, and Korea; June 30, age 85.

MORGAN, CLAUDIA, actress in more than three dozen Broadway plays who was best known for her radio role of Nora Charles in "The Thin Man," popular in the 1940's; September 17, age 62.

MORSE, WAYNE, long-time liberal who served as a senator from Oregon from 1945 until 1969. Morse was best known for his early opposition to the Vietnam war, being one of the two senators to vote against the

1964 Gulf of Tonkin resolution later used to justify U.S. intervention in Vietnam; July 22, age 73.

MUNDT, KARL E., former Republican congressman and senator from South Dakota who was a staunch anti-Communist and figured prominently in the Alger Hiss and Army-McCarthy hearings. Mundt served in the House of Representatives from 1938 until 1948, when he was elected to the Senate, where he remained until 1973; August 16, age 74.

NEWHALL, NANCY, photographic critic and editor credited with developing the photography book into an art form; July 7, age 66.

O'BRIEN, KATE, Irish novelist and playwright whose most successful book, *That Lady,* was a historical romance set in 16th-century Spain; August 13, age 76.

PARTCH, HARRY, avant-garde composer who invented his own musical scales and instruments; September 3, age 73.

PERON, JUAN DOMINGO, president of Argentina from 1946 until 1955 who returned from exile in 1973 to resume his rule; July 1, age 78.

See also ARGENTINA in this section and PERON, JUAN DOMINGO, in your encyclopedia.

PUSSER, BUFORD, Tennessee sheriff who was characterized in the movie *Walking Tall;* August 21, age 36.

RADCLIFFE, GEORGE, Democratic senator from Maryland from 1935 until 1947 who supported most of Franklin D. Roosevelt's social legislation and worked to organize the Works Progress Administration during the the Depression; July 29, age 96.

RANSOM, JOHN CROWE, poet and critic who founded the Kenyon Review in 1939. He led a school of Southern writers, called the Fugitives, which included Allen Tate and Robert Penn Warren. Their poetry rebelled against the binds of the machine age and extolled the virtues of the rural South, though not in a romantic vein; July 3, age 86.

ROTH, SAMUEL, poet, translator, and publisher whose dissemination of allegedly obscene material, including works by James Joyce and D. H. Lawrence, led to a landmark Supreme Court decision defining obscenity in 1957. Though the court sustained Roth's conviction, it ruled that material was obscene if, "to the average person, applying contemporary community standards, the dominant theme of the material taken as a whole appeals to prurient interest"; July 3, age 79.

SHAW, CLAY, New Orleans businessman who was acquitted in 1969 of plotting to assassinate President Kennedy; August 15, age 60.

SHELLEY, JOHN F., San Francisco labor leader and Democratic politician who served as U.S. representative (1949-62) and mayor of San Francisco (1964-67); September 1, age 68.

SOYER, MOSES, Russian-born artist who became an outstanding representational American painter; September 2, age 74.

SPAATZ, CARL A., first Air Force chief of staff (1947-48) and commander of U.S. strategic bombing forces in Europe and the Pacific in World War II; July 14, age 83.

SPAULDING, JOHN P., president of Scholastic Magazines, Inc.; September 4, age 51.

STOUFFER, VERNON B., founder of the Stouffer restaurant chain and former owner of the Cleveland Indians; July 26, age 72.

STRASSER, OTTO, early prominent Nazi spokesman who later broke with Hitler over party ideology; August 27, age 76.

SUSANN, JACQUELINE, popular novelist whose *Valley of the Dolls* (1966) was recognized by the *Guinness Book of World Records* as the best-selling novel of all time, with over 17 million sold in hardcover and paperback; September 21, age 53.

VANDERBILT, CORNELIUS, JR., author and former newspaperman who founded and published three tabloid dailies, and later wrote books "exposing" high society; July 7, age 76.

VOORHEES, TRACY S., government official and lawyer who served as President Eisenhower's director of relief and rehabilitation

Carl A. Spaatz

Earl Warren

Portugal Moves Left. General Francisco da Costa Gomes, *left*, became president following the resignation of General António de Spínola, *right*. Spínola had vainly tried to trim the influence of radical officers and cabinet members.

for Hungarian refugees in 1956; September 25, age 84.

WARREN, EARL, governor of California (1942-53) and chief justice of the United States from his appointment by President Eisenhower in 1953 until his retirement in 1969. This period, characterized by his successor, Warren Burger, as "one of the most dynamic in our history," saw the Court make profound constitutional decisions. Warren became known as a vigorous protector of individual rights and equality.

The Warren Court's most momentous decision was the ruling that segregated schools were unconstitutional, thus overturning the 60-year-old separate-but-equal doctrine; this precedent was used to break down similar racial barriers. Reflecting the dynamics of America's changing institutions, as well as affecting them, Warren led the Court to reinterpret the Constitution in such areas as criminal justice, voting rights, legislative districting, employment, housing, and education; July 9, age 83.

See also WARREN, EARL, in your encyclopedia.

WATSON, ARTHUR K., executive who built International Business Machines into an international enterprise and was U.S. ambassador to France (1970-72); July 26, age 55.

WILLIAMSON, JOHN B., one of the 11 members of the Communist party's national board convicted in 1949 of advocating the violent overthrow of the Government; July 8, age 70.

WOLFSON, HARRY, philosopher and one of the world's leading scholars on comparative religion; September 19, age 86.

Portugal. General António de Spínola resigned as president of Portugal on September 30 and warned the nation, over radio and television, of chaos and "new forms of slavery." General Francisco da Costa Gomes was appointed to replace him. Costa Gomes also continued to direct the armed forces as chief of the defense staff.

The resignation clearly indicated that conservatives had failed in their efforts to put a brake on the leftward drift that had followed the overthrow of the dictatorship on April 29. (See PORTUGAL in the second section.) Spínola had planned to address a rally against "extremist totalitarianism" September 28, but leftists halted buses bringing people to Lisbon for the rally, and Spínola, fearing bloodshed, called it off.

Spínola had vainly tried to trim the influence of radical members of the Armed Forces Movement and the cabinet. Against his wishes, about 200 army officers and 130 naval officers had been retired. About 100 persons were imprisoned on charges of planning an extreme-rightist plot. After Spínola's resignation, four conservative members of the military junta were dismissed.

New Cabinet

The revolutionary government experienced its first cabinet crisis when Premier

Pro-Government Rally voiced approval for Costa Gomes. Among leftist groups, Portugal's Communist party was the best organized and had a strongly committed membership. The government was planning to hold elections in early 1975.

Adelino da Palma Carlos and four centrist ministers resigned July 9. Palma Carlos quit after the Council of State had rejected several of his requests for additional powers to cope with economic and social unrest sweeping the country since rebellious officers seized the government in April.

Provisional president Spínola dismissed the remaining cabinet members July 11 and named Colonel Vasco dos Santos Gonçalves to be the new premier two days later. Gonçalves, a leftist, had been the senior theoretician of the Armed Forces Movement—the military group which conducted the revolt against Marcello Caetano's dictatorship.

A new cabinet dominated by the military was appointed by Gonçalves and sworn in by Spínola on July 17. Military officers (most of them members of the Armed Forces Movement) took 6 of the 16 posts, including the key ministries of defense, interior, labor, and information. In an apparent reference to the country's deteriorating economic situation, Gonçalves emphasized: "We all have to live

now in a true period of austerity." Without "hard work by all the Portuguese at all levels, the development of the nation will never be accomplished."

Portugal's new cabinet was seen as further to the left than its predecessor, a center-left coalition, and potentially more decisive. The military's decision to appropriate the interior and labor ministries was interpreted as signaling its intention to curb strikes and other civil disturbances which had plagued Portugal since the coup. Socialist party leader Mario Soares remained foreign minister in the new cabinet, and Communist party chief Alvaro Cunhal retained his post as minister without portfolio. The first woman to serve in a Portuguese cabinet, Maria de Lourdes Pintassilgo, was appointed minister for social affairs.

A program of economic and social measures to remedy Portugal's financial crisis was decreed July 6. The nation was facing a growing balance-of-payments deficit due to the increased costs of imports and reduced income from tourism (due to an outbreak of cholera and economic setbacks in other European countries) and remittances from Portuguese workers abroad. Rising unemployment in Portugal since April was aggravated by a 1973 West German decision to cut off the immigration of foreign workers, many of whom were Portuguese.

Economic Coordination Minister Vasco Vieira de Almeida warned at a news conference July 5 that citizens would have to exercise discipline, as the country was suffering from an inflation rate of more than 30 per cent annually while trying simultaneously to expand its economy. But when salary increases for government employees under the new economic program were announced, thousands of civil servants in the lowest-paid categories demonstrated in Lisbon, forcing the government to increase wages further.

Political Institutions

At the installation of the new cabinet, President Spínola had remarked: "This climate of anarchy cannot continue. We did not stage the revolution to allow the situation to go from one extreme to the other." With no legislature in session (elections were scheduled for March, 1975), a number of bodies were vying for political power, particularly the following:

• *The Armed Forces Movement,* a group of captains and majors who carried out the revolution, encompasses young officers with a spectrum of political orientations. Three of the new cabinet ministers were drawn from the Movement's elite 12-man coordinating committee. Many Movement officers were said to look to Peru, which is ruled by leftist military officers, as a possible model for Portuguese development.

• *The Junta of National Salvation,* a group of senior officers led by General Spínola, was supposed to provide constitutional guidance, but had increasingly come into conflict with the Movement over questions of national policy.

• *The Council of State* included seven members of the Junta, seven liberal officers from the Armed Forces Movement's coordinating committee, and seven distinguished citizens, appointed by Spínola, who also headed the Council.

• *The Presidency,* a vaguely defined office, was the focus of Spínola's power, which rested heavily on his popular charismatic appeal and his support from the Junta. But Spínola appeared to lose much of his power to the Armed Forces Movement during the cabinet shuffle, and was left playing a largely figurehead role.

A large number of political parties was also emerging in the wake of the coup. By September, more than 70 such groups were reported to have been organized, most of them with a centrist orientation. One of the most prominent was the moderate Partido Popular Democrático (PPD). Two of its members resigned with former premier Palma Carlos.

Among leftist parties, the Partido Comunista Português, Portugal's Communist party, was the best organized and had a strongly committed membership. The party was cooperating with the moderates in the cabinet to maintain order, curb strikes, and restrict the press. Other leftist groups included the Partido Socialista, founded in 1972 by Mario Soares while he was in exile. Organizationally, it was a weak rival of the Communists. The Catholic Movimento de Esquerda Socialista (MES) was the heart of the country's young intellectual left and had been organizing workers in the government-controlled labor syndicates.

On the right, the Centro Democrático Social was beginning to gather support for Spínola among conservatives. The ultrarightist Portuguese National party, organized by former members of the dictatorship's Portuguese Legion and former agents of its secret police, became the first political party to be banned by the military government, on September 18.

Independence for Guinea

The new government moved quickly to promulgate a law permitting decolonization in the African territories of Guinea, Mozambique, and Angola, which have been legally part of metropolitan Portugal since 1933. On July 23, President Spínola announced that transfers of power to the people of "overseas territories considered suitable for this development" would begin immediately. The decree was interpreted as a policy victory for the Armed

African Leaders. Luis Cabral, *left*, became president of the new nation of Guinea-Bissau, formerly Portuguese Guinea. Samora Machel, *right*, signed the cease-fire that ended 10 years of guerrilla war in Mozambique by providing for independence in 1975.

Forces Movement, which had advocated speedy decolonization. Spínola had suggested limited autonomy for the African territories under the Portuguese flag—a proposal which had been rejected by the liberation movements in all three of Portugal's African possessions.

An agreement granting independence to Portuguese Guinea was signed August 26 in Algiers, where Foreign Minister Soares and António de Almeida Santos (minister for inter-territorial coordination) had been conducting negotiations with the African Party for the Independence of Guinea and the Cape Verde Islands.

The future of the Cape Verde Islands, which were not included in the new nation, had been a major obstacle in the negotiations. The islands are located in the Atlantic Ocean some 400 miles off the African coast, but some Guinea nationalist leaders insisted that they were an integral part of the Portuguese territory on the mainland. Portugal agreed to grant self-determination to the people of the islands in a future referendum. (They did not participate in the guerrilla war against Portugal which the nationalists had been waging since 1959.)

In a ceremony in Lisbon on September 10, Portugal formally recognized the independence of the Republic of Guinea-Bissau. A document was signed by Spínola, who then handed it to Major Pedro Pires, head of the nationalist movement's delegation. No speeches were made. The occasion marked the end of five centuries of Portuguese rule in Guinea, which was "discovered" by a Portuguese explorer in 1446.

No public notice was taken of the Portuguese action in Guinea-Bissau, because its independence had been declared unilaterally a year earlier. September 12, birthday of slain nationalist leader Amilcar Cabral, is celebrated as Guinea-Bissau's national holiday. Cabral founded the independence party in 1966. His brother, Luis Cabral, became president of the provisional government created by the nationalists in 1973. In September, the government shifted the capital from Bissau to the rural village of Madina do Boe.

The new government's political, legal,

economic, and educational institutions were developed by the independence movement in guerrilla camps hidden in the jungle. The legislative body is the 48-member Popular National Assembly, elected by popular vote for a three-year term. Its members appoint a 15-man council of state. There is also a network of regional councils, and appointed commissioners who head national agencies.

Guinea-Bissau was the poorest, as well as the oldest, of Portugal's African colonies. Unlike Angola and Mozambique, the country never attracted large numbers of European settlers, because of its malaria-infested swamps. The population of about 500,000 inhabits an area of 14,000 square miles (about twice the size of New Jersey) and is engaged primarily in growing rice and peanuts. Independence was expected to encourage the development of other resources, including bauxite (found in the eastern region), offshore oil, fisheries, and ranches.

Mozambique Accord Reached

Portugal and Frelimo, the Mozambique Liberation Front, signed an agreement September 7 setting June 25, 1975, the 13th anniversary of the movement's founding, as the date for the country's independence. The accord was signed by Soares and Frelimo leader Samora Machel, who had been meeting in Lusaka, Zambia, to work out a settlement. A cease-fire ending the 10-year guerrilla war between Frelimo and Portuguese forces was to take effect beginning midnight September 7.

Carrying out the terms of the agreement, President Spínola appointed Admiral Victor Crespo to be the high commissioner for Mozambique during the transition period. A provisional government and joint military committee were to be established between Portugal and the liberation front. The administration was to have nine cabinet members, of which Portugal was to appoint three, and Frelimo, six. Portugal was to retain foreign affairs and defense functions temporarily. The joint military committee, composed of an equal number of representatives from the Portuguese armed forces and the liberation front, was to implement the terms of the cease-fire.

Arrangements were being made to transfer the assets and liabilities of the Mozambique department of the National Overseas Bank so that Mozambique would have a central bank to issue currency and could pursue an independent financial policy. In an apparent reference to the Cabora Bassa Dam project (under construction with South African funds), the agreement stated that Frelimo would take responsibility for financial obligations incurred by Portugal in the interest of Mozambique.

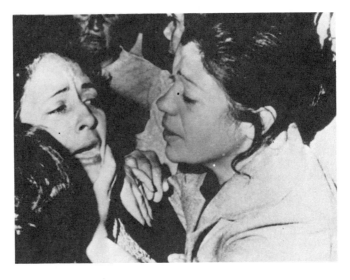

Refugees fled Mozambique for South Africa after sporadic fighting between blacks and anti-independence whites. Other white settlers planned to try living under Frelimo, which had pledged the establishment of a multiracial society.

Violence erupted in Lourenço Marques and Beira, Mozambique's two largest cities, the day the accord was announced. White settlers rioted and seized radio stations, angrily protesting the decision to grant Mozambique rapid independence. Looting and arson then broke out in black neighborhoods in Lourenço Marques. The revolt collapsed in a few days when dissident whites realized that troop reinforcements sent to restore order were not going to support them. But before the mélée was over, 100 people, mostly blacks, had been killed, and 250 injured.

Of Mozambique's estimated population of 8.7 million, fewer than 200,000 are whites, and fewer than 100,000 of the remainder are of Chinese or Indian origin. Some 20,000 to 30,000 Europeans were reported to have left the country within a three-week period after Portugal began talks with Frelimo on June 5, and the exodus picked up again after the September agreement, with perhaps 1,500 leaving each day for South Africa. But many—perhaps most—white settlers were ready to stay and try living under Frelimo, which had pledged the establishment of a multiracial society and protection for white interests. One of the six appointed Frelimo ministers was white and another was of Indian origin.

Frelimo's president and chief theoretician, Samora Machel, remained in neighboring Tanzania but made it clear that, as in Marxist nations, the government would be subordinate to the party. Frelimo's leaders neither denied nor affirmed that they were Marxists, but the party's ideology has a recognizable Chinese flavor. China had in recent years given Frelimo forces the bulk of the weapons and military training they received at their bases in Tanzania.

The white-ruled countries of southern Africa—Ian Smith's white minority regime in Rhodesia and the Republic of South Africa—were further isolated by the impending independence of Mozambique. The Mozambique ports had been Rhodesia's chief link to the outside world, but Frelimo was expected to enforce United Nations economic sanctions against Rhodesia.

Sports and Athletics. Among the notable sporting events in July, August, and September were the following:

Archery

Darrell Pace and Doreen Wilber successfully defended their national titles in Oxford, Ohio, in August.

Asian Games

Japanese athletes won the most gold medals, 75, at the Asian Games, held in Teheran, Iran, in September. Iran won 36 gold medals and China, 33. It was the first time that mainland China had taken part in the games.

Automobile Racing

During summer Formula I racing, Ronnie Peterson won the French and Italian Grand Prix races, Jody Scheckter won the British Grand Prix, Clay Regazzoni won the West German event, Carlos Reutemann the Austrian event, and Emerson Fittipaldi the Canadian race.

Baseball

The Oakland Athletics and Baltimore Orioles won division titles in the American League, while the Los Angeles Dodgers and Pittsburgh Pirates finished first in the National League.

Rod Carew of the Minnesota Twins led the American League in hitting with an average of .364. Ralph Garr of the Atlanta Braves led the National League with an average of .353. Dick Allen of the Chicago White Sox led the AL in home runs with 32, while Mike Schmidt of the Philadelphia Phillies led the NL with 36. Jeff Burroughs of the Texas Rangers had the most runs batted in in the AL, 118, while Johnny Bench of the Cincinnati Reds led the NL with 129.

Catfish Hunter of Oakland and Ferguson Jenkins of Texas led the AL in most wins with 25. Andy Messersmith of Los Angeles and Phil Niekro of Atlanta led the NL with 20. Hunter had the lowest AL earned-run average, 2.49. Buzz Capra of Atlanta led the NL with an earned-run average of 2.28.

Among the landmarks of the 1974 season, in addition to Henry Aaron's career home-run record, were Lou Brock's record 118 stolen bases for the year, relief pitcher Mike Marshall's 106 appearances (also a record), Al Kaline's 3,000th career

Lou Brock set a new major-league baseball record on September 10 by stealing his 105th base in a single season. He ended the season with 118 steals.

hit, and Bob Gibson's 3,000th career strikeout.

Basketball

The Soviet Union won the world amateur championship on July 14 in San Juan, Puerto Rico. Yugoslavia finished second and the United States third.

Bicycling

Eddy Merckx of Belgium won his fifth Tour de France championship July 21 with a cumulative time of 116 hours, 16 minutes, and 58 seconds for the 21-day classic.

John Allis won the men's National Road Race in Pontiac, Michigan, on July 28, covering the 115-mile course in 4 hours, 29 minutes. The women's 35-mile event was won by Jane Robinson in 1 hour, 53½ minutes.

Billiards

Jean Balukas defeated Mieko Harada of Japan, 100 to 99, on August 11 to take her third straight U.S. women's open pocket-billiards championship in Chicago. Joe Balsis won the men's title.

Boating

Averaging 72 miles per hour in his 36-foot craft, *Slap Shot,* Art Norris won the 180-mile Hennessy Grand Prix off Atlantic City, New Jersey, on July 17, assuring him of the 1974 national championship.

Courageous won the America's Cup off Newport, Rhode Island, on September 17, defeating the Australian challenger *Southern Cross* in four straight races. It was the 22nd successful defense by a U.S. yacht in the 123-year-old event, which is held once every four years.

Boxing

Welterweight. José Napoles of Mexico retained his title with a ninth-round technical knockout of Hedgemon Lewis in Mexico City on August 3.

Lightweight. Gattu Ishimatsu of Japan retained his WBC title in September by fighting a 15-round draw with Arturo Pineda of Mexico in Nagoya, Japan.

Featherweight. Ruben Olivares of Mexico knocked out Zensuke Utagawa of Japan in the seventh round of their bout in Inglewood, California, July 9 to win the vacant World Boxing Association title.

Bobby Chacon of Los Angeles won the World Boxing Council title by knocking out Venezuela's Alfredo Marcano in the ninth round of their bout, held in Los Angeles in September.

Bantamweight. Soo Hwan Hong of South Korea won the WBA title on July 3, defeating defending champion Arnold Taylor of South Africa in a 15-round decision in Durban, South Africa.

Golf Champions. Only one month after winning the Ladies Professional Golf Association championship, Sandra Haynie won the U.S. Women's Open. Gary Player won his third British Open title with a score of 282.

Flyweight. Betulio Gonzales of Venezuela retained his title with a 10th-round technical knockout of Italy's Franco Udella. The fight was held in Lignano Sabbiadoro, Italy, on July 20.

Cuba dominated the first world amateur boxing championships, held in Havana in August, winning 5 of the 11 gold medals. Howard Davis of the United States won in the 125-pound classification.

Diving

Keith Russell won both the 10-meter platform and three-meter springboard events at the AAU outdoor championships in Decatur, Alabama. Tim Moore won the one-meter springboard. In the women's competition, Cynthia Potter won the one-meter, Christine Loock the three-meter, and Terri York the platform.

Fencing

The Soviet Union won the team title at the Grand Prix des Nations in Grenoble, France, in July. Sweden's Rolf Edling retained the men's individual épée title. Ildiko Bobis of Hungary won the women's foil.

Golf

Gary Player of South Africa won the British Open with a 72-hole total of 282 in Lytham St. Annes, England, on July 13. It was his third British Open title.

Sandra Haynie won the U.S. Women's Open on July 21 in La Grange, Illinois, with a score of 295.

Bobby Nichols won the Canadian Open in Port Credit, Ontario, July 28 with a score of 270.

Lee Trevino won the Professional Golf Association championship on August 11 in Clemmons, North Carolina, with a 72-hole score of 276.

Jerry Pate won the U.S. men's amateur title at Paramus, New Jersey, on August 31, defeating John Graco 2 and 1.

Cynthia Hill won the U.S. women's amateur title in Seattle, Washington, in August, defeating defending champion Carol Semple 5 and 4.

Johnny Miller won the $60,000 first prize in the World Open in Pinehurst, North Carolina, in September, in a four-way sudden-death playoff.

Lee Trevino won the $50,000 first prize in the World Series of Golf, held in Akron,

Professional Sports:
Too Much of a Good Thing?

In 1959, there were 42 professional sports teams in five major leagues of baseball, basketball, football, and hockey. In 1974, the same sports had 120 teams in eight leagues. In addition, track and field athletes were competing for money, a professional soccer league was in operation, and a team-tennis league had been organized. Promoters had even established professional lacrosse competition and were talking about starting a volleyball league. The National Football League announced it would create a "satellite" league of six teams in Europe, stretching from Barcelona to Istanbul.

But oversaturation threatens. While attendance figures for the four major professional sports have doubled, the number of games played has also doubled. While sports now takes up 10 per cent of home-television time—more than 1,100 hours in 1974—ratings have fallen for four straight years.

Playing seasons increasingly overlap. The World Series now takes place a month after the first NFL openers and three months after the World Football League begins play. By the time the football season ends, basketball and hockey have been going for two months and will continue until May.

Not a single team in three expansion leagues —the American Basketball Association, the World Hockey Association, and the World Football League—has yet shown a profit. Fifteen of the 24 major-league baseball teams ended the 1974 season behind their 1973 attendance. On the whole, only the NFL and the National Hockey League are operating in the black, and some of their teams are losing money.

Expansion has boosted player salaries sharply as rival leagues compete for talent. The average major-league professional basketball player earns an estimated $85,000 a year; the equivalent figure for hockey is $55,000, and for football, $42,000.

Yet, in spite of the figures, owning a team can be highly profitable because professional sports teams qualify for tax advantages that render their occasionally published "book" profit or loss figures virtually meaningless. The owners benefit from tax practices which permit a new owner to declare and then depreciate almost the entire purchase price of player contracts and to apply that—with other debits—

against profits from his other businesses. The tax structure thus encourages the establishment of new teams and leagues, a heavy turnover in ownership, and control by entrepreneurs with a broad range of business interests.

Under baseball's reserve clause, and the slightly modified version called the option system used in football, hockey, and basketball, teams trade players at will and prevent them from playing anywhere else within a league. Team owners arbitrarily shift franchises from city to city and charge fat fees for new franchises. And a recent study found that local governments, which often build and operate sports arenas, subsidize pro sports by $23 million a year in operating losses and uncollected property taxes.

The Brookings Institution, an independent Washington research organization, has published a 428-page study entitled "Government and the Sports Business." It suggests that monopolistic practices—especially the creation and shifting of franchises—and unrealistic tax benefits for owners have encouraged expansion so excessive that the whole structure of professional sports is threatened. It suggests that all sports and leagues and teams should be subject to the same tax and monopoly laws governing other businesses. It also advocates measures that would encourage the return of civic-minded sportsmen in place of the wealthy businessmen who now dominate the game.

Gary Davidson played a leading part in the founding of expansion leagues in basketball, football, and hockey. Although the teams in all three leagues operate in the red, tax benefits can make owning a team surprisingly attractive.

Ohio, in September. Tied at 139 with Player after the regulation 36 holes, he won on the seventh hole of a sudden-death playoff.

Harness Racing

The richest trotting race ever, the $200,000 International Trot at Westbury, Long Island, went to Delmonica Hanover for the second straight year on July 13.

Christopher T. won the Hambletonian, the most prestigious race for three-year-old trotters, in August at Du Quoin, Illinois.

Boyden Hanover won the Cane Pace, the first leg of the Triple Crown for three-year-old pacers, in Yonkers, New York, in August. Spitfire Hanover won the second leg—the Yonkers Trot. Another pacing classic, the Little Brown Jug in Delaware, Ohio, went to Armbro Omaha in September.

Soccer

Before home fans in Munich, the West German team defeated favored Netherlands, 2-1, to win the World Cup on July 7. The winning goal was scored by Gerd Müller.

The Los Angeles Aztecs defeated the Miami Toros, 4-3 in overtime, to win the North American Soccer League championship in Miami on August 25.

Tennis

Jimmy Connors reigned supreme in world tennis after winning the English championship at Wimbledon and the U.S. Open in Forest Hills, New York. Connors defeated Ken Rosewall of Australia in the Wimbledon final on July 6, 6-1, 6-1, 6-4. He crushed Rosewall in the final at Forest Hills, 6-1, 6-0, 6-1, on September 9.

Chris Evert won the women's title at Wimbledon on July 5, defeating Russia's Olga Morozova, 6-0, 6-4. Billie Jean King won the U.S. Open women's title, defeating Evonne Goolagong of Australia, 3-6, 6-3, 7-5, on September 9.

Bjorn Borg of Sweden defeated Tom Okker of the Netherlands, 7-6, 6-1, 6-1, at Brookline, Massachusetts, on August 26, to win the U.S. professional championship.

The World Team Tennis championship was won by the Denver Racquets on August 26. The Racquets defeated the Philadelphia Freedoms, 27-21, 28-24.

Track and Field

Lyudmilla Bragina of the Soviet Union broke her own 3,000-meter women's world record with a time of 8:52.7 minutes in Durham, North Carolina, in July.

Reinhard Theimer of East Germany set a new hammer-throw record of 251 feet,

Gerd Müller, *left,* scored the winning goal as West Germany defeated the Netherlands, 2-1, to win the World Cup—soccer's world championship, held once every four years.

Wimbledon Champs. Jimmy Connors and Chris Evert, engaged to be married, won English singles championships at Wimbledon. Connors later won the U.S. Open at Forest Hills. Each earned more than $200,000 in prize money during the year.

4 inches, in Leipzig, East Germany, in July. Alexei Spiridonov of the Soviet Union broke this record in Munich, West Germany, in September with a toss of 251 feet, 6 inches.

Jim Bolding set a new 440-yard hurdles record of 48.7 seconds in Turin, Italy, in July.

Rich Wohlhuter set a new 1,000-meter record on July 30 in Oslo, Norway, with a time of 2:13.9 minutes.

Brendan Foster of England set a new 3,000-meter record August 3 in Gateshead, England, with a time of 7:35.2 minutes.

Three women's records fell during the European championships, held in Rome in September. Ruth Fuchs of East Germany bettered her javelin world record with a throw of 220 feet, 6 inches. Teammate Rosemarie Witschas set a new world

high-jump record of 6 feet, 4¾ inches. The East German women's 400-meter relay team turned in a new mark of 42.5 seconds.

Helena Fibingerova of Czechoslovakia set a new women's shotput record at Gottwaldov, Czechoslovakia, with a toss of 70 feet, 8¼ inches.

United States of AMERICA. Gerald R. Ford became president of the United States on August 9, following the resignation of Richard Nixon. (See the Feature Article in the second section for Ford's assumption of office and the events leading to Nixon's resignation.) In an unexpected and controversial action, Ford on September 8 granted Nixon a full pardon for any federal crimes he might have committed during his term in office. (See WATERGATE SCANDAL in this section.)

Ford told a joint session of Congress

The Rockefeller Hearings

President Ford's nomination of Nelson Rockefeller to succeed him as vice president quickly ran into difficulty. Although some liberals and conservatives opposed Rockefeller's confirmation by Congress because of the positions he had taken on political issues, or because they disliked his record as governor of New York between 1959 and 1973, the opposition gained impetus because of disclosures indicating that Rockefeller's wealth might give him undue power.

The sheer extent of Rockefeller's personal fortune was enough to invite antagonism. He disclosed that he was worth $62.5 million, not counting the income from two family trusts valued at $116.5 million. This amount was only part of the holdings of the entire Rockefeller family. His six children receive earnings from trusts worth $35.7 million, and his wife from a trust valued at $3.8 million. When the holdings and trusts benefiting his sister, three brothers, and the heirs of a fourth brother were taken into account, the total for the family reached perhaps $1.3 billion.

Because of his vast fortune, there was no

Nelson Rockefeller, nominated to become vice president, was under scrutiny by a Senate committee.

serious suggestion that Rockefeller be forced to sell his holdings in order to avoid a conflict of interest between his public position and his personal wealth; the extent of such a sale could easily have an adverse effect on the stock market. Instead, he offered to place all the common stocks he personally owned—$12 million worth—in a blind trust administered by the Morgan Guaranty Company.

Rockefeller's disclosure of his wealth showed that nearly 29 per cent of his money in trusts was tied up in the stocks of the Exxon Corporation—largest corporation in the world in terms of net annual income—and Standard Oil of California. Another 12.8 per cent was invested in state and municipal bonds. Large sums—in the tens of millions of dollars—were invested in IBM, the Chase Manhattan Bank, and Rockefeller Center.

Soon after, in response to newspaper stories, Rockefeller made public a list of 20 current and former public officials and staff aides to whom he had given about $2 million since 1957. While the gifts were not illegal, and Rockefeller had paid federal and state gift taxes, they indicated to many observers that he had unduly used his wealth to influence public policy and advance his own political fortunes.

The disclosure showed that Henry Kissinger had received a gift of $50,000 in early 1969, before leaving Rockefeller's staff to join the Nixon Administration; Rockefeller's press secretary said the gift was out of gratitude for Kissinger's long-time service. William J. Ronan, chairman of the Port Authority of New York and New Jersey, received a total of $625,000, mostly in the form of a debt cancellation before he assumed his post, which is unsalaried. L. Judson Morhouse got a gift of $86,000; later Morhouse, New York Republican party chairman, was convicted of bribery stemming from a state liquor-authority scandal, but Rockefeller commuted his sentence.

Rockefeller was also linked to a derogatory biography of his 1970 election opponent, Arthur Goldberg. A book written by Victor Lasky and published during the campaign was largely subsidized by a $60,000 investment made by Rockefeller's brother Laurance. Rockefeller apologized for what he called "the whole regrettable episode," which he said he had been unaware of at the time.

Men Near Ford. Donald Rumsfeld, *left*, replaced White House chief of staff Alexander M. Haig, Jr. L. William Seidman, *center*, was named executive director of a new economic-policy board, and Robert Hartmann, *right*, became a counselor to the president.

August 12 that his top priority would be to bring inflation under control. Concerning foreign policy, he pledged "continuity" in all areas of "the outstanding foreign policy" of his predecessor. He also pledged protection of individual privacy, declaring, "There will be no illegal tappings, eavesdropping, buggings, or break-ins by my Administration."

On September 16, President Ford signed a proclamation offering clemency to Vietnam-war-era draft evaders and military deserters. (See subhead *Conditional Amnesty Declared* in this article.)

Appointments. Ford announced August 30 that Nelson Rockefeller, former governor of New York, was his choice to succeed him as vice president. The nomination was sent to Congress for confirmation, which would require a majority vote in each house.

Donald Rumsfeld, ambassador to NATO headquarters, was chosen in September to replace White House chief of staff Alexander M. Haig, Jr. Haig, who had resigned his commission as a four-star general in 1973 to serve under Nixon, was appointed September 16 as supreme commander of NATO forces in Europe. He was also named commander of U.S. forces in Europe.

Robert Hartmann, formerly chief of Ford's vice-presidential staff, was named a counselor to the president on August 9. Philip Buchen, Ford's former law partner, was appointed presidential counsel on August 15. Ron Nessen, an NBC television newsman, became White House press secretary, succeeding Ford's first choice, Jerald terHorst, who resigned in protest against Ford's pardon for Nixon.

George Bush, chairman of the Republican National Committee, was named U.S. envoy to China with ambassadorial rank on September 4. He succeeded David K. E. Bruce, who later was named to succeed Rumsfeld as ambassador to NATO. Mary Louise Smith replaced Bush as Republican national chairman. Economic counselor Kenneth Rush was appointed ambassador to France, replacing John N. Irwin 2nd.

Economics. A series of 12 meetings were held between Administration officials and businessmen, economists, labor leaders, and state and local officials in order to map anti-inflation policy. (See BUSINESS AND FINANCE in this section.) These preliminary conferences led to an "economic summit" conference in Washington in late September, presided over by Ford.

At the close of the two-day conference, Ford announced September 28 the creation of an economic-policy board to coordinate the government's economic efforts, both domestic and international. The board was to be headed by Secretary of the Treasury William Simon, who Ford declared would be his principal spokesman on economic policy. L. William Seidman, a friend of the president, was named executive director of the board.

The president also created a labor-management committee to advise him on major economic policies. It was to be headed by John T. Dunlop, who had been head of the former Cost of Living Council. Albert Rees, a Princeton University economics professor, was named to head the pre-

viously created Council of Wage and Price Stability.

In a press conference held August 28, Ford reaffirmed his intention to cut the federal budget for fiscal 1975 and reasserted that "wage and price controls are out, period." A specific economic program was to be announced in early October.

Foreign Policy. In an address to the United Nations General Assembly on September 18, Ford said that Secretary of State Henry Kissinger had his "full support and the unquestioned backing of the American people," and that Kissinger would continue his efforts "to build a world of peace" both as secretary of state and as the president's national-security adviser. He pledged increased U.S. food assistance to needy countries (See FOOD in this section) and challenged oil-exporting nations to "define their policies" without "imposing unacceptable burdens on the international monetary and trade system."

Presidential Press Conference. Holding his first news conference as president on August 29, Ford fielded 27 questions from newsmen. The White House said Ford planned to hold press conferences about every two weeks.

Speaking September 23 before the annual World Energy Conference in Detroit, Ford deplored "the pulverizing impact of energy price increases" and added that "throughout history, nations have gone to war over natural advantages such as water or food or convenient passages on land or sea." Although Secretary of Defense James Schlesinger denied that the Pentagon was contemplating any military action against the oil producers, the president's speeches, his defense of CIA activities in Chile (See CHILE in this section), and his opposition to proposed cuts in the defense budget suggested a hard-line foreign policy.

Congress

Poverty Legal Aid. Congress passed legislation July 18 establishing an independent legal-services corporation for the poor, and removing legal-services functions from the moribund Office of Economic Opportunity. The bill authorized

Pension Reform. On Labor Day, the president signed a bill establishing federal standards for private pension plans.

funding of $90 million for fiscal 1975, $100 million for 1976, and open-ended funding for 1977.

School Aid. Congress on July 31 authorized $25.2 billion over four years in aid to elementary and secondary schools. The bill contained a provision prohibiting busing for desegregation purposes beyond the school next closest to a student's home except when courts determined that more extensive busing was necessary to protect students' constitutional rights. It also prohibited implementation of integration orders after the beginning of a school year and prohibited busing across district lines unless boundaries were found to have been deliberately drawn to foster segregation.

Housing. On August 15, Congress approved an $11.1-billion housing and community-development bill containing broad revisions in the formulas for distribution of federal aid. Most of the money ($8.6 billion over three years) lay in provisions authorizing locally administered block grants for community development to replace categorical-aid plans such as Model Cities and urban renewal. The funds would be allocated on the basis of population, degree of overcrowding, and poverty (weighted double in the formula). But during the three-year period, no community would receive less than the total previously granted under the categorical programs.

A separate provision established a $1.2-billion rent-subsidy program for low-income families and extended through fiscal 1976 two home-ownership and rental-assistance programs suspended in 1973, but with authorizations of only $75 million in new funds.

Pension Reform. A bill establishing federal standards for private pension plans was passed on August 22. Standards were set for eligibility, vesting, and funding of benefits for the more than 300,000 private pension plans, which have assets of more than $160 billion and cover an estimated 25 to 35 million workers. A federal reinsurance system was to be established to prevent loss of benefits from financial failure of pension plans.

Return to Standard Time. Congress passed a bill on September 30 restoring standard time for four months of the year —from October 27, 1974, to February 23, 1975. The nation had been placed on year-round daylight saving time in January in order to conserve fuel, but many parents objected to sending their children to school in the predawn darkness of winter mornings.

Supreme Court

The Supreme Court on July 25 struck down a plan to desegregate the predominately black Detroit school system by merging it with mostly white, neighboring suburban districts. The 5-to-4 decision all but banned desegregation through the busing of children across school-district lines.

Chief Justice Warren Burger, who wrote the majority opinion, argued that school boundary lines could not be casually ignored and treated as mere administrative conveniences. In a dissent, Justice Thurgood Marshall argued that the state, not simply the Detroit board of education, bore the responsibility for curing the condition of segregation in Detroit schools and charged that the Court's answer to this problem was to "provide no remedy at all."

Conditional Amnesty Declared

On September 16, President Ford announced a general amnesty for Vietnam-era draft evaders and deserters who agreed to work for up to 24 months at public-service occupations contributing to "maintenance of the national health, safety, or interest." The program was to take effect immediately, through the presidential proclamation and two executive orders signed in the White House. (Ford's declaration followed in a tradition of previous amnesties granted by American presidents, beginning with George Washington's 1795 amnesty for participants in the Whiskey Rebellion.)

While Ford cautioned that desertion or draft evasion in time of war was a "serious offense," he added that "reconciliation calls for an act of mercy to bind the nation's wounds and to heal the scars of divisiveness." Under his proposal, draft evaders and deserters at large would turn themselves in to authorities by January 31,

Amnesty Accepted. Among the Vietnam war-era deserters who accepted the government's amnesty offer were the five men shown below. Federal officials estimated that 15,500 draft evaders and 13,000 deserters would be eligible for the program, which called for them to work for up to 24 months in public-service jobs such as hospital orderly.

1975, reaffirm their allegiance to the United States, and agree to spend up to two years in a public-service field such as medicine (for example, as hospital orderlies) or conservation.

Placement of persons in these jobs was to be supervised by the head of the Selective Service, who was expected to apply the same guidelines which governed the employment of conscientious objectors during the war. Applicants were also encouraged to find their own jobs. The 24-month period was set as a maximum; the actual amount of time to be served could be reduced by "mitigating circumstances."

For deserters and draft evaders who had been previously convicted, a nine-member clemency review board was to consider cases on an individual basis. Shortly after Ford's announcement, 95 convicted draft evaders were released from jail on furloughs pending review of their cases. About 600 imprisoned deserters were expected to be released within a few days.

Deserters who applied for amnesty

... And Rejected. Gerry Condon, a former Green Beret living in Canada, was among those rejecting amnesty. Only about 8 per cent of the eligible deserters and 1 per cent of the draft evaders turned themselves in during the first month of the program.

would be given "undesirable" discharges until they had performed alternative service, at which point their discharges would be changed to a new "clemency" classification. As observers quickly pointed out, this regulation created the possibility that a deserter willing to live with an undesirable discharge could receive amnesty without alternative service—unlike a draft evader, who could be prosecuted. But the Defense Department later said deserters who turned themselves in and refused alternative service could be court-martialed.

Reactions to Ford's approach to the amnesty question were mixed. Most congressional leaders expressed support for the plan. Veterans' associations were hostile to the idea of any amnesty, taking the position that, in the words of Arizona Senator Barry Goldwater, amnesty was "throwing mud in the faces of millions of men who have served this country." But the Safe Return Amnesty Committee and other antiwar groups considered the measure vindictive, punishing men whose only crime was resisting participation in an immoral war.

Federal officials estimated that 15,500 draft evaders and 13,000 deserters would be eligible for amnesty. The program covered only offenses which took place between August 4, 1964 (the date of the Tonkin Gulf Resolution) and March 28, 1973, when the last U.S. combat soldier left Vietnam.

It was uncertain how many of those eligible would seek to take advantage of the conditional amnesty. Among the estimated 15,500 draft evaders, 8,700 were listed as convicted, 4,350 under indictment, and at least 100 serving prison sentences. The rest were fugitives, mainly in Canada. Confusion and suspicion were initial reactions by draft evaders, and relatively few inquired about amnesty during the first weeks of the program. For some of the men, the terms of the amnesty were no better than alternatives they had been given earlier; others, in hiding, were not sure they were actually being sought and were reluctant to expose themselves to possible prosecution.

Most deserters also adopted a wait-and-see attitude. Deserters living overseas generally expressed opposition to conditional amnesty on principle and had already established strong ties to their new homes, on the assumption that they would never receive amnesty. For those who had acquired good jobs, families, and even Canadian or Swedish citizenship, the opportunity to visit the United States seemed more important than repatriation.

Wounded Knee Trial

Charges against militant Indian leaders Dennis Banks and Russell Means were dismissed by U.S. District Court Judge Fred J. Nichol September 16 after he strongly criticized government conduct of the case. The charges against the two men—assault on government officers, conspiracy, and larceny—stemmed from the 71-day 1973 occupation of Wounded Knee, South Dakota, by members of the American Indian Movement (AIM) and their supporters.

Leading directly to the dismissal was the illness of a juror September 13, the day after the jury had begun deliberations. In an action which Nichol termed "incredible," the Justice Department refused to allow the case to be decided by the 11 remaining jurors. (A number of jurors later told reporters they had planned to vote for acquittal.)

In ending the lengthy eight-month trial, which was marked by delays and courtroom outbursts, the judge charged that the FBI "stooped to a new low" in dealing with witnesses and evidence. During the trial the FBI was found to have suppressed documents showing that testimony by a prosecution witness was false. Testimony by FBI agents about wiretaps during the Wounded Knee siege was also shown to be false.

See also ART; AUTOMOBILES; CYPRUS; DISASTERS; FASHION; GEOLOGY; GREECE; INTERNATIONAL TRADE; KOREA; LITERATURE; MUSIC; OBITUARIES; SPORTS AND ATHLETICS; VIETNAM; and WOMEN, in this section.)

Charges Dismissed. American Indian Movement leaders Russell Means, *left,* and Dennis Banks raised their arms in victory after all charges against them arising from the Wounded Knee occupation were dismissed. The judge strongly criticized government conduct of the case.

Communist Offensive. Refugees flee fighting in the Queson district of South Vietnam, 30 miles south of Danang. During the summer North Vietnamese forces seized a number of outposts.

Vietnam. President Nguyen Van Thieu's government was challenged in September by demands for an eradication of corruption and the establishment of democratic liberties. Meanwhile, Communist forces made gains against an army weakened by cutbacks in American aid.

The Fighting

Fighting between the South Vietnamese army and Communist forces since the January, 1973, cease-fire agreement took some 80,000 lives in the next 18 months. An American official said, "Neither side has gained anything that comes close to justifying the bloodshed." Fighting was well below the level of a general offensive, but well above the tolerable level of violence that the cease-fire pact was supposed to produce.

During the summer Communists seized a number of outposts in some of the heaviest fighting since the cease-fire agreement. U.S. analysts said North Vietnamese forces had built up their strength, with more than 200,000 combat soldiers in South Vietnam and another 100,000 to 150,000 support troops and guerrillas. They were being supplied by a network of all-weather roads and fuel pipelines leading from North Vietnam.

The Washington *Post* reported August 25 that Saigon, in a major policy shift, had decided to abandon military outposts it no longer had the resources to defend. President Thieu had previously said not one inch should be given up to the Communists, but this policy was being changed to save fuel and ammunition.

Diminishing U.S. assistance had hurt the armed forces. The Administration's request of $1.45 billion in military aid for fiscal 1975 had been cut by Congress to $700 million. Inflation made the situation more serious, since the price of fuel in South Vietnam had almost doubled in a year, and the price of ammunition had risen at least 20 per cent.

According to the *Post*, the government had recently abandoned 120 of the nearly 3,000 government-held outposts in the Mekong River delta. The New York *Times* reported September 3 that some large-unit operations had been replaced by smaller infantry patrols, and the harassing artillery fire that once peppered Communist territory had been halted. While some observers thought a leaner South Vietnamese army might be more efficient, the short-term effect was to lower morale.

Government outposts in the Central

Highlands also fell to the Communists. The fall of Gia Vuc on September 20 meant that the Communists were close to cutting South Vietnam in half, with only a narrow sliver along the coast in the north remaining in government hands.

Politics and Economy

In August, the long-moribund political opposition to Thieu showed signs of revival. An alliance of Catholics, Buddhists, and newspapermen staged demonstrations. Thieu responded by promising to ease the tough censorship laws and to open the political process to "serious-minded" parties. (Thieu's own Democracy party is the only legal political grouping.)

Demonstrators led by Buddhist nuns marched through downtown Saigon, calling for the resignation of President Thieu. The antigovernment alliance included Catholics, Buddhists, newspapermen, and disabled veterans.

On September 8, a Catholic priest, the Rev. Tran Huu Thanh, led a demonstration in Hue and distributed copies of a pamphlet accusing Thieu, his wife, and several relatives of various acts of embezzlement and corruption. Several Saigon newspapers printed it in modified and abbreviated form. The press had been attacking the government for its censorship policies and its frequent confiscation of publications. The antigovernment campaign was joined by a faction of Buddhists and by the Association of Disabled Veterans.

A series of articles by the *Times* reported that, according to lawyers, policemen, and judicial officials, military courts in South Vietnam handle virtually every case of pro-Communist or anti-government activities, plus many purely criminal matters, even though the Supreme Court declared these courts unconstitutional in 1970. Martial law was declared in South Vietnam in 1965, and government decrees in effect outlaw organizations, associations, and political parties not approved by the government. In addition, decrees prohibit strikes and demonstrations, allow police to search homes without warrants, and authorize detention of anyone considered dangerous.

In addition to cutting military aid, the U.S. Congress had slashed South Vietnam's request of $750 million in economic aid for fiscal 1975 to about $400 million. Prices in South Vietnam had risen 70 per cent in a year, real per-capita income had dropped 20 per cent in two years, and the payments deficit was about $750 million. The U.S. pullout from South Vietnam had resulted in the loss of about 300,000 jobs, and the cost to the nation of maintaining a million-man army was proving a crushing burden.

South Vietnam's main natural resources, timber and rubber, are in contested or Communist-controlled territory. The only economic bright spots are rice production, which has increased steadily since the late 1960's, and the possibility of sizable offshore oil deposits. While no major deposits have yet been found, a dozen foreign oil companies have paid Saigon for exploration rights.

Watergate Scandal. President Ford granted Richard Nixon an unconditional pardon on September 8 for all federal crimes that he "committed or may have committed or taken part in" while in office. The presidential power to grant pardons for federal crimes is stated in Article II, Section 2, of the Constitution.

On signing the pardon, Ford read a 10-minute statement in the White House Oval Office. He said he had concluded that there remained "many months and perhaps more years before Richard Nixon could obtain a fair trial by jury in any jurisdiction of the United States under governing decisions of the Supreme Court. . . . During this long period of delay and potential litigation, ugly passions would again be aroused, our people would again be polarized in their opinions, and the credibility of our free institutions of government would again be challenged at home and abroad." He concluded, "Finally I feel that Richard Nixon and his loved ones have suffered enough."

Ford had reportedly been told that Nixon would be indicted as a co-conspirator in the Watergate cover-up by the federal grand jury that earlier had indicted H. R. Haldeman, John Ehrlichman, and other

Pardon for Nixon. On September 8, President Ford signed a document granting Richard Nixon a "full, free, and absolute pardon" for all "offenses against the United States" during the period of his presidency. The unexpected action aroused a storm of criticism; telegrams received at the White House ran 6 to 1 against the pardon.

high White House aides and had named Nixon an unindicted co-conspirator. There were also reports that Ford had been told that the former president's physical and mental health were precarious. In reading his statement, Ford interpolated the remark that the ordeal of facing criminal charges was "threatening his [Nixon's] health."

The former president issued a statement from his home in San Clemente, California, immediately after the pardon. He said he could now see he was "wrong in not acting more decisively and more forthrightly in dealing with Watergate. . . . That the way I tried to deal with Watergate was the wrong way is a burden I shall bear for every day of the life that is left in me."

The pardon aroused a storm of criticism that ended the traditional "honeymoon" accorded to a new president by the public, press, and Congress. White House aides said that telegrams and mail received concerning the pardon were running 6 to 1 against the action. A nationwide poll indicated that the public disapproved by a margin of 2 to 1, and a number of polls indicated that Ford's popularity had dropped sharply.

During Senate committee hearings in 1973 on his confirmation to be vice president, asked whether if he became president he would have the power to prevent prosecution of Nixon, Ford replied, "I don't think the public would stand for it." At his first presidential press conference, on August 28, Ford said he was not ruling out a pardon, but "until any legal process has been undertaken, I think it is unwise and untimely for me to make any commitment."

Press Secretary Jerald F. terHorst resigned in protest against Ford's decision. TerHorst had denied to reporters that a pardon was imminent. He indicated later that he felt he had been misled by Ford's advisers.

At the same time that Ford pardoned Nixon, the White House announced that an agreement had been reached with Nixon providing that all of Nixon's presidential papers and tapes would be preserved for three years for possible use in court cases arising from the Watergate scandal. In general, however, the agreement upheld Nixon's title to the documents—a right reiterated in an accompanying legal opinion from Attorney General William Saxbe. It also stipulated that both Nixon and the federal government had the right to challenge subpoenas and orders to produce the documents.

The agreement provided that the documents would be kept at a government fa-

Treatment for Phlebitis. The former president spent 12 days in a California hospital for tests and treatment of the phlebitis condition in his left leg; later, he had to return for surgery. His condition made it unlikely he would appear in court for the Watergate cover-up trial.

cility not far from San Clemente, with access available only by joint agreement. Nixon agreed not to withdraw any original materials from the files for three years unless subpoenaed, with the exception of the tapes, which he promised to leave intact until September 1, 1979. After that date, the federal government would be obligated to destroy any tapes that Nixon asked it to destroy. All remaining tapes would be destroyed at the time of his death or on September 1, 1984, whichever event occurred first.

Spokesmen for Ford said September 11 that he was not giving consideration to blanket amnesty or pardons for the Watergate defendants. (Forty-eight persons, as of September, had been charged with or convicted of Watergate-related crimes.) The subject had arisen the previous day, when John Hushen, deputy White House press secretary, said he had been authorized by Ford to say that the "entire matter" of pardons for the defendants "is now under study." After a barrage of congressional criticism, White House aides made it clear that the president would consider requests for pardons only on a case-by-case basis and through normal channels.

Nixon Subpoenaed

The federal pardon left Nixon still liable to civil lawsuits, and possibly to some future state prosecution, with regard to matters arising from the Watergate scandal. In addition, he was subpoenaed in August by former White House aide John Ehrlichman to appear as a defense witness at the forthcoming cover-up trial. The pardon made it unlikely he would be able to decline to testify under the Fifth Amendment, which protects citizens against self-incrimination.

On September 19, Nixon was served with a subpoena obtained by special prosecutor Leon Jaworski. Defense lawyers in the cover-up case reportedly had insisted on Nixon being called for exact identification of 33 White House tape recordings assembled for use at the trial. It was expected, therefore, that Nixon would be asked by the prosecution to testify that the recordings were genuine and had not been altered.

The former president entered Memorial Hospital Medical Center in Long Beach, California, on September 23 for extensive tests and treatment of the phlebitis condition in his left leg. His physician reported September 25 that a piece of a blood clot from his leg had lodged in his right lung, a potentially dangerous situation. It was considered likely that he would decline to appear at the cover-up trial because of his illness.

Impeachment Inquiry Report

A 528-page report by the House Judiciary Committee on its impeachment inquiry was accepted by the House of Representatives on August 20 by a vote of 412 to 3. The report included the evidence, which it called "clear and convincing," on which the committee recommended impeachment of Nixon under three articles. (See Feature Article in the second section.) Majority and minority opinions were expressed on each article after the listing of evidence.

The committee's presentation of evidence cited 19 occasions on which Nixon was said to have made false or misleading statements "as part of a deliberate, contrived, continued deception of the American people" on the Watergate scandal. The majority report on Article I, which charged Nixon with obstruction of justice, cited 36 specific items that it said formed "a pattern of undisputed acts" by Nixon that "cannot otherwise be rationally explained" except as part of a conspiracy to obstruct justice.

The 11 Republicans who voted against this article reversed their position on the basis of the transcripts released by Nixon on August 5. "We know," they said, "that it has been said, and perhaps some will continue to say, that Richard Nixon was 'hounded from office' by his political opponents and media critics." But, they concluded, Nixon's Watergate troubles were of a "self-inflicted nature."

Senate Watergate Report

The Senate Select Committee on Presidential Campaign Activities, better known as the "Watergate committee" or "Ervin committee," released its final report July 13 on its investigation of the Watergate and other scandals related to the 1972 presidential campaign. In an introduction to the 2,250-page report, the committee said its investigation had not been conducted, nor its report prepared, "to determine the legal guilt or innocence of any person or whether the president should be impeached." However, the report presented a detailed account of the intricacies of political-intelligence operations, campaign fund raising, and the use of government agencies for campaign purposes. It also presented 35 recommendations for election-campaign reform.

John Ehrlichman, shown with his wife, was convicted and sentenced to 20 months to five years for conspiracy and perjury in connection with the break-in of the office of Daniel Ellsberg's psychiatrist. He appealed the conviction.

Ehrlichman Convicted

Former presidential aide John Ehrlichman was convicted by a federal jury July 12 in Washington, D.C., of conspiring to violate the civil rights of Dr. Lewis J. Fielding, a psychiatrist who was treating Pentagon Papers defendant Daniel Ellsberg. (Members of the White House plumbers unit had broken into Fielding's office to seek information on Ellsberg.) G. Gordon Liddy, Bernard Barker, and Eugenio Martinez were convicted of the same charge. Ehrlichman was also found guilty of three counts of making false statements.

The trial, which began June 28, featured testimony by David Young and Egil Krogh, co-directors of the plumbers unit. Young testified that he and Krogh recommended a "covert operation" to examine Fielding's files. The prosecution introduced a copy of a memorandum on which Ehrlichman had initialed his approval of a "covert operation," and had added in handwriting, "If done under your assurance that it is not traceable."

The defense maintained that Ehrlichman had not authorized an illegal break-in but a legal "covert operation." Krogh and Young conceded under questioning that Ehrlichman had never used the term "break-in." However, U.S. District Court Judge Gerhard Gesell, instructing the jury on the conspiracy charge, said the law had been broken regardless of whether or not there was a break-in, if the government attempted to acquire private information without a search warrant.

Ehrlichman was sentenced on July 31 to 20 months to five years for conspiracy and perjury. Liddy received one to three years, to run concurrently with his sentence for participation in the Watergate break-in. Barker and Martinez were placed on probation for three years.

Dean Sentenced

Former White House counsel John Dean, who became Nixon's principal accuser in the Watergate scandal, was sentenced on August 2 to one to four years in prison by Judge John Sirica for his role in the Watergate cover-up. He had pleaded guilty in 1973 to one count of conspiracy to obstruct justice. He was ordered to begin serving the sentence September 3 in a minimum-security institution.

Milk-Fund Developments

The Associated Milk Producers, Inc. (AMPI), a farmers' cooperative with 37,-000 members, was fined $35,000 on August 1 after pleading guilty to a six-count charge of conspiracy and illegal campaign donations. According to special prosecutor Leon Jaworski's office, AMPI made illegal contributions totaling $330,000 in cash between 1968 and 1972.

The most notable figure accused of wrongdoing with regard to the AMPI funds was John Connally, who was indicted July 29 by a federal grand jury on five counts of accepting a bribe, conspiring to obstruct justice, and perjury. He was accused of accepting $10,000 in two cash payments in 1971 from Jack Jacobsen, a lawyer for the milk producers, while serving as secretary of the treasury. The payment, according to the indictment, was in return for his recommendations concerning an increase in the federal milk price-support level to be fixed by the secretary of agriculture. Jacobsen, who was indicted on one count of bribery, pleaded guilty on August 7.

Harold S. Nelson, former general manager for AMPI, pleaded guilty July 31 to a charge that he conspired to bribe Connally. He also admitted that he had conspired to make illegal campaign contributions to a number of Republicans and Democrats. According to the special prosecutor's office, the $330,000 in illegal AMPI contributions included a $100,000 cash payment in 1969 to Herbert Kalmbach, Nixon's personal lawyer and his chief campaign fund raiser at that time. Another $63,500 had been contributed in 1968 to the Democratic National Committee for Hubert Humphrey's presidential campaign.

Norman Sherman, Humphrey's former press secretary, pleaded guilty August 12 to charges of "aiding and abetting" the illegal donation of $82,000 from AMPI to Humphrey, Senator James Abourezk of South Dakota, and unidentified Democratic candidates in Iowa. Humphrey and Abourezk denied knowing that the contributions were illegal.

John Dean, who became Nixon's principal accuser in the Watergate scandal, surrendered to U.S. marshals September 3 to begin a one- to four-year prison term for his role in the cover-up.

Kissinger Cleared

The Senate Foreign Relations Committee reaffirmed on August 6 its support for Secretary of State Henry Kissinger after probing his role in the wiretapping of 17 officials and newsmen from 1969 to 1971. In June, Kissinger had threatened to resign unless cleared of allegations concerning his role. (See WATERGATE SCANDAL, subtitle *Kissinger Threatens to Quit,* in the second section.)

In a unanimous report, the committee reaffirmed its 1973 finding that Kissinger's role in the wiretapping did not constitute grounds to bar confirmation as secretary of state. It said Kissinger's role "was essentially as he described it in testimony last year."

Women in the
Labor Movement

Working women have begun forming groups to promote their interests as women within the ranks of organized labor. The creation of CLUW (the Coalition of Labor Union Women), Union WAGE (Women's Alliance to Gain Equality), and other associations follows a trend toward the organization of special-interest lobbies in the labor community by blacks and other minorities. Equal job opportunities for women and more representation for women on trade-union executive boards are among the objectives of the new groups.

Labor Women Unite

The weekend of March 23-24, 3,000 women (more than twice the expected number) from at least 58 international trade unions attended a meeting in Chicago held to focus attention on the problems of women in the labor-union movement. Unions represented included the United Auto Workers (the largest delegation, with 400 members present), the American Federation of Teachers, the Amalgamated Clothing Workers, the American Federation of State, County, and Municipal Employees, and the Amalgamated Meat Cutters and Butcher Workmen.

Speakers noted that one in five union members is a woman, and that 4.3 million women are trade unionists. But, although women make up more than half the membership of 26 unions, very few women sit on international executive boards or hold other high union offices. The AFL-CIO, for example, has no women on its executive council, although positions are reserved for blacks. Women auto workers, teachers, and garment workers stated a

belief that they were disadvantaged economically in relation to male workers, and that change could and should be brought about through the unions.

At the conclusion of the convention, Olga Madar, a vice president of the United Auto Workers, was elected to head the newly founded Coalition of Labor Union Women. Addie Wyatt, director of the women's division of the Butcher Workmen, became vice president. No resolutions were passed, but a statement of goals was issued affirming the purpose of CLUW to "unify union women . . . to determine our common problems and concerns and to develop action programs within the framework of our unions to deal effectively with our objectives."

Specific goals of CLUW involve fighting job discrimination through the unions, higher wages and child care for women workers, "truly protective" legislation for all workers, and the encouragement of participation and leadership by women in the labor movement.

Left unresolved at the Chicago meeting was the question of whether membership in the new organization should be open to all women employees, or only to those in unions. The issue was left under study by a 200-member national coordinating committee and a smaller steering committee.

About the same time as the Chicago meeting, the first conference of trade-union women ever held in New York City took place at Martin Luther King Labor Center. The 600 participants included black and white, young and old, cabdrivers, nurses, teachers, and welders—most of them conservatively dressed and

Labor Women's Convention in Chicago is addressed by President Olga Madar, *right,* and Vice President Addie Wyatt, *below.* Working women have begun forming their own organizations within the ranks of organized labor.

not the type usually associated with "women's lib." However, economic issues raised by the women's movement had created a new awareness among them of the unmet needs of women workers. Judy Berek, legislative director of Local 1199 of the Drug and Hospital Union, remarked: "For the first time, labor women in New York are meeting to discuss their problems as women. It's a real breakthrough!"

Like their counterparts in Chicago, the New York women stressed that their actions were not directed against male unionists, but rather were intended to correct past abuses and promote equal opportunity by working through the system. Sponsors of the New York meeting had in fact included 30 local unions, the Central Labor Councils of both New York City and Long Island, Cornell University's School of Industrial and Labor Relations, and nearly all women influential in the New York labor scene.

The large Chicago and New York conventions had been preceded by smaller meetings, many of which were sponsored by regular union organizations. An AFL-CIO women's convention was held in Wisconsin in March, 1970. Between 1970 and 1972, similar conferences were held in Illinois, Arkansas, California, and Iowa by several international unions, including the Auto Workers, Communications Workers of America, Electrical Workers (IUE),

American Federation of Teachers, and American Newspaper Guild.

Reaction to the new women's groups by the traditionally male-dominated union establishment was mixed. While no union specifically endorsed CLUW, some had aided in its founding. The United Auto Workers, especially, had subsidized the administrative costs involved in organizing the Chicago meeting and the travel expenses of its large delegation. Leonard Woodcock, president of the UAW, hailed the meeting as "a giant step" in union organization, but most other union leaders reserved comment. There was believed to be concern in labor circles that the creation of new groups such as CLUW might tend to weaken the labor movement by dividing it into several special-interest blocs.

Legislative Issues

Among the prominent concerns of CLUW is the enactment of legislation to supersede the state "protective" laws regulating the labor of women and children. These laws restrict the number of hours women may work, weights they may lift, and their availability for night work, frequently with the effect of preventing women's advancement to jobs which may, for instance, require overtime.

The Equal Employment Opportunity Commission has held that such laws are discriminatory because they do not take into consideration the abilities and ambitions of women as individuals. The National Safety Council and some other organizations have also described certain statutory limitations and other unfair employment practices as a deliberate effort to keep women as a group from competing with men already in a trade.

Other state sex-oriented employment laws which have been declared invalid by the EEOC require special rest or meal periods or physical facilities only for women. These benefits were held to be discriminatory under Title VII (unless, of course, the employer provides the same benefits for male employees).

In the past, special provisions for women were frequently written into union contracts with employers. This tended to prevent many jobs from going to women for whom the employer would have had to provide extra benefits. As a result, some unions have become co-defendants with employers in discrimination suits filed by women. The unions have sided with management in each of these cases.

Union women have generally turned to the EEOC rather than to the unions to rectify these inequalities. Of some 400 discrimination cases before the commission in 1970, a majority concerned such issues as seniority and layoffs, rates of pay, demotions, and transfers.

Some union women anxious to preserve the gains of the labor movement see, however, a danger in the legal actions being brought against employers and unions. They fear that the principle of collective bargaining between employers and employees may be invalidated by the courts, along with the discriminatory practices. They see more representation for women at the higher levels of union leadership as a better means of bringing about needed reforms.

The trade unions have also been slow to promote passage of the Equal Rights Amendment, another goal of the labor women's groups. The AFL-CIO did not decide to support the amendment until

A New Militancy is being displayed by women in many occupations. But there is also concern in labor circles that the creation of many special-interest associations may weaken the trade-union movement.

FLIGHT ATTENDANTS

New Jobs for Women include patrolling the streets as policewomen and mining coal.

October, 1973, more than a year after Congress presented it to the states for ratification. (As of September, 1974, 33 of the 38 states needed for passage had ratified the ERA, although two later rescinded their ratification.)

The UAW has been more progressive than most unions in its pursuit of women's rights. While the organization has a predominantly male membership, its women members number 200,000—more than the total membership of many international unions. The UAW women's department has actively supported the legal channels available to women through U.S. government offices and has campaigned for removal of the state protective laws for women. The International Union of Electrical Workers (IUE) has also established a department to promote women's interests.

Union Membership Trends

The proportion of both men and women workers who were union members decreased between 1966 and 1970, but the decline was greater among women workers, few of whom have ever been unionized. According to U.S. Labor Department statistics, 33 million American women were wage earners in 1970. Of these, only 13 per cent belonged to labor organizations, as contrasted with 28 per cent of male workers.

Nationally, pay for women workers is about 60 per cent of that received by men with similar skills and education. Those women who belong to unions tend to earn more than those who do not. This advantage is not due to union membership in itself, but to the fact that occupations dominated by men tend to pay more, and

such occupations are also more likely to be unionized.

Women are more likely to belong to unions if they work in industries with predominately male employees. This trend varies somewhat with the type of industry and the nature of the job, but is generally true for white-collar, blue-collar, and service occupations.

However, unionization does not always mean greater income equality. A recent government survey shows that "in 1970, the earnings gap between men and women was narrower among union members who are white-collar or service workers, but wider among union members who are blue-collar workers. . . . Among blue-collar workers, income disparities between men and women were higher for union members than for nonmembers." The same government statistics suggested that a decline in labor-union membership among blue-collar women was associated with increasing disparities in wages between male and female workers in these occupations.

The reasons behind the drop-off in female union participation are not entirely clear. Perhaps, as Marge Albert of the Distributive Workers suggested in New York, the trade unions have been perceived by many women workers as male-dominated hierarchies unsympathetic to their interests.

One reason why so few women belong to unions is that, in the past, unions run by men concentrated on organizing predominately male occupations. Predominately female occupations such as clerical work are virtually unorganized, and also tend to be low-paying. Other low-pay-

Occupations dominated by women
tend to be low paying and unorganized.

Clothing Workers involved in a unionizing drive at a Texas factory were illegally discharged.

ing fields which tend to be staffed by women are hospital and service industries (only 8 per cent organized in 1970) and sales (10 per cent).

Changes in the structure of the national economy may be related to the decline in union membership for both sexes. New white-collar and human-services jobs are increasingly replacing the blue-collar occupations. Many of these newer jobs tend to be low-paying and held primarily by women.

But "organizing the unorganized" is not a high priority for the Coalition of Labor Union Women at present. The group intends to concentrate on legislative issues first, because, as one member explained, "If we got into organizing at the moment, there would be many jurisdictional disputes."

Obstacles to Participation

Labor-women activists have estimated that women hold only 4.7 per cent of all union leadership positions, with about 35 women in major elective or appointive posts in 1970. They also note that, among the rank-and-file, women comprise less than 1 per cent of the enrollment in apprentice-training classes and hold only 4 per cent of all craftsman and foreman positions.

Several major obstacles confront women who seek to become involved in union activities, especially in leadership positions. The dual responsibilities of home and work prevent many blue-collar women from having the time and mobility to participate in union meetings, which are often held at night. Often, they can't afford the household help which would free them to travel or to take on the responsibilities of a union office. Jane O'Grady, legislative representative for the Clothing Workers, cited this problem as one reason her union is pushing for the creation of day-care centers.

The husbands of blue-collar women, frequently regretting that their wives must work at all, sometimes prevent them from becoming members or officers in unions. "Even a decade ago," Leonard Woodcock explained, "it was a badge of dishonor— a reflection on his manhood—for a workingman if his wife worked." But the increasing number of working wives is gradually changing these attitudes. (Half of all women between age 18 and 64 have jobs.)

When women do come to union meetings, they usually elect men to represent them in dealing with male employers. The view that women do not support each other is widely held. Emil Mazey, secretary-treasurer of the UAW, cited a recent election at a Flint, Michigan, plant where 60 per cent of the employees are women. Of eight members elected to bargaining-committee posts, seven were men. He believes that "women in labor unions . . . who claim they have been frustrated in their quest for political office within the union have only members of their own sex to blame."

Fear—whether of failure, of loss of male protection, or of reprisals by employers—undoubtedly lies behind much of the passivity women have displayed toward exercising leadership within the unions, as elsewhere in society. Some union women also charge that men in leadership posts have been reluctant to share policy-making positions with them.

Leadership Training at a shop steward summer school. In the past, women usually elected men to represent them in dealing with employers. But new educational programs, some conducted by unions, are helping women to gain confidence in themselves and in one another.

Child-Care Facilities provide new opportunities for working mothers. This one is operated by the Amalgamated Clothing Workers.

But there are indications that women are beginning to take a larger role in the affairs of unions which encourage their participation. Within the Communications Workers, a union that is 52-per-cent female, women hold 28 per cent of local-union offices and nearly half of the places in the union's shop-steward school. Valerie Howard, director of women's activities for the CWA, explained that the union is publicizing the work of women labor activists in the local unions. Within the IUE, there are women's social-action programs, women's committees in the locals, and women's district conferences.

In pursuing their goals as trade unionists, labor women usually dissociate themselves from the rhetoric and activities of women's-liberation groups, stressing that they wish to act in cooperation with men to achieve their goals. Other observers believe that the women's movement called attention to many of the injustices which the labor women are now fighting. They see the concerns of women's-rights activists and those of trade-union women as similar in the workplace—child care, equal pay, hiring practices, and opportunities for advancement. Although many union women see their needs as different from those of the predominately middle-class members of the women's movement, it is likely that "women's lib" helped create the political and social climate in which the bread-and-butter changes sought by working women could be achieved.

NEWS

Spirit in the Seat Belt

He is usually clad in white, sports long hair and a beard and, when picked up while hitchhiking on the New York State Thruway, likes to sit in the back seat and talk about the Second Coming of Christ. Drivers who pick up the youth report that he disappears out of his buckled seat belt. A couple who reported this mysterious incident to a toll collector in 1971 was told that at least a dozen people had passed through the gate that day with the same story.

Lydia M. Fish, a young folklorist at Buffalo State College, has collected 60 such accounts for a research paper titled, "Jesus on the Thruway: The Vanishing Hitchhiker Strikes Again." The vanishing hitchhiker is a familiar figure in American folklore, and she suspects the legend has become modernized under the influence of *Jesus Christ Superstar*.

Toad You So

In 1935, *Bufo mariunus,* a South American toad, was imported by Australia to help get rid of the cane beetle, which was threatening the sugar fields. Years later, the Aussies have found they got more than they bargained for, not the least of which is the fact that the first generation of Australian toads are only just now dying of old age. Besides living up to 40 years, the toads grow to be eight inches long, weigh three pounds, produce up to 40,000 eggs a year, eat almost anything, and can kill cats and dogs with a glandular poison they secrete. All in all, the toads present a threat to the natural balance of nature in some areas.

For many years the toads were only in Queensland, isolated from the rest of Australia by a belt of dry land, but recent reports have them cropping up in other locales, prompting toad hunts with bounties as high as $37.50 a Bufo.

Record Breakers

A party on Capitol Hill honored Senator Mike Mansfield, the Montana Democrat who set an all-time record August 15 for tenure as the majority leader of the Senate. He has held the post since 1961.

Fastball hurler Nolan Ryan of the California Angels set a new record for the fastest-timed pitch: 100.8 mph from the mound to home plate. Ryan, who was timed during practice and then during a regular game, surpassed the old mark of 98.6 mph held by Bob Feller.

Flying at speeds up to 2,000 mph, a Lockheed SR-271, called the "Blackbird," *above,* set a new record for a trans-Atlantic crossing by making the trip from New York to London in less than two hours, the amount of time many people spend getting to the airport.

Jim Randi put his name in the *Guinness Book of World Records* by spending 44 minutes in a cake of ice. Besides instant fame, the chilled New Jersey stuntman received $300 from a local television show.

Loser Wins Big

Evel Knievel, to some minds a man of daring and to others an obnoxious huckster, was beaten by Idaho's Snake River Canyon on September 8 as a tail parachute on his steam-driven sky cycle opened seconds after the vehicle was launched from its ramp. The rocket, which never came close to gaining its proper speed and altitude, momentarily appeared as if it would crash into the crowd watching from the canyon rim, but the wind guided it down into the canyon. It dropped onto a boulder-strewn ledge overlooking the river.

Minutes later, Knievel was helicoptered up to the launch site, reportedly millions of dollars richer, with but few minor cuts and, presumably, his last stunt behind him.

For Art's Sake

Despite officialdom's rigid concepts of Socialist Realism, Soviet artists have had success selling their ventures into abstract art to discreet collectors. In an attempt to gain a wider audience, a group of artists in September organized an open-air exhibit in a Moscow suburb. As the 20 artists began setting up the show among an entourage of 200 friends and supporters, a group of burly men began grabbing the paintings and destroying them. Within minutes, bulldozers and dump trucks appeared, churning the art works into the mud. While this was happening, uniformed police looked on and the KGB (secret police) engaged in picture taking.

Said one disgruntled artist, "Now you know what they mean by Socialist Realism in art." All was not lost though, as world opinion persuaded the Soviets to permit another exhibit two weeks later. Although most of the artists participating felt it was a one-time affair, they were encouraged because it was the first outdoor exhibit of art not approved by the state since the relatively liberal days following the 1917 revolution.

Planetary News

Analyzing measurements and pictures radioed back to earth by the *Pioneer 10* spacecraft, which flew within 81,000 miles of Jupiter on December 5, 1973, scientists have described the planet as a spinning ball of liquid hydrogen with a turbulent interior and raging atmospheric storms. Further, they have come to believe that the Great Red Spot on the planet is the vortex of a 25,000-mile-long tornado that has been hovering above the cloud belt for hundreds of years.

A report released by the National Aeronautics and Space Administration concluded that, "at best, Jupiter has only a small rocky core, thousands of miles below the heavily clouded atmosphere." The planet's interior is too hot to solidify, the report continued. Scientists estimate the temperature of Jupiter's center at 54,000 degrees, or six times the temperature on the surface of the sun.

In a surprise announcement on September 21, the Hale Observatories in California said that a research assistant, Charles T. Kowal, had discovered what appears to be Jupiter's 13th moon.

Civilization Corrupts

The intrusion of Western civilization on the hunting and fishing society of the Far North has been followed by a sharp rise of mental illness, suicides, and murders among Eskimos. Speaking at the Third International Symposium on Circumpolar Health, scientists working with Eskimos from Greenland to Alaska claimed that increased contact with white civilization since World War II has hurt native people everywhere.

In Alaska, the suicide rate among Eskimos has tripled in the last 15 years, while the homicide rate has doubled in the same period. Similar figures are reported by scientists studying Eskimos in other regions, and all concur that these problems are related to the pervasive use of alcohol.

Scientists have also noted that the cultural gap between Eskimos and whites is such that modern psychiatric methods have failed to help abate these problems. Consequently, there is hope that the use of the natives' own methods, including native healers, or shamans, will relieve the ills wrought by contact with civilization.

Enemies List

Lori Paton, a New Jersey teen-ager who was investigated by the FBI as the result of a school assignment, won her fight to force the agency to destroy all records pertaining to the incident when a federal judge ruled in her favor August 29. An American Civil Liberties Union official said the ruling appeared to be the first of its kind in the country. However, her claim for $65,000 in damages was disallowed.

A "subversive" file on the girl was begun because she wrote to the Socialist Workers party to gather information for a high-school political-science class. Former FBI director L. Patrick Gray had ordered a mail surveillance of the party, which was listed on the now-defunct attorney general's list of subversive organizations. An FBI agent following up the lead ran a credit check on the girl's father and interviewed the local police chief. Although the agent recommended that the case be closed, Miss Paton sued on the ground that the existence of the file could hurt her if it surfaced during a background check by a prospective employer.

Kennedy Bows Out

"There is absolutely no circumstance or event that will alter the decision," said Massachusetts Senator Edward M. Kennedy at a September 24 news conference. "I will not accept the nomination. I will not accept a draft," he added, saying that his decision not to seek or accept the Democratic party nomination for president in 1976 was "firm, final, unconditional, and unequivocal." With those words, the Democratic nomination, till that moment assumed to be Kennedy's for the asking, became a free-for-all.

Kennedy, who did not count himself out of any presidential race beyond 1976, stated that family commitments were instrumental in his decision. His 12-year-old son was receiving treatment for a cancer which has already required a leg amputation and his wife, Joan, has been under treatment for emotional stress. Fears of another Kennedy assassination as well as the lingering Chappaquiddick scandal may have also played a part in the decision.

A New Alaskan Capital

Sixty per cent of Alaska's voters decided August 27 that the state's capital should be moved from Juneau, a coastal city of 6,000, to a location not closer than 30 miles of Alaska's two largest cities, Anchorage and Fairbanks. The next step, expected to take 10 years, will be to whittle down the list of possible locations and then present Alaskan voters with three finalists from which the new capital will be chosen.

The decision to leave Juneau was based largely on the crowded condition of the city, which is bordered on three sides by water and on the fourth by a glacier. Originally a boom town founded early this century as settlers mined for gold, Juneau is located in the state's panhandle and is two time zones away from two-thirds of the state's population. The city is only accessible by air and sea.

The new capital is expected to be located somewhere between Anchorage and Fairbanks, with Nenana, Willow, Wasilla, Palmer, and Talkeetna leading the list of possibilities.

Women Denied Priesthood

On July 29, a bitter flap which has boiled within the Episcopal Church in recent years broke into the news as four bishops ordained 11 women priests. By Anglican tradition and the canons of the Episcopal Church, women are not allowed to be ordained, but, impatient for a reform they thought inevitable, the four bishops went ahead with the ceremony. The women were all deacons, the highest feminine ecclesiastical position permitted under church law.

In late August, 140 members of the Episcopal House of Bishops overwhelmingly invalidated the ordinations and also passed a mild resolution rebuking the bishops for ignoring the church's canons. Nevertheless, it was expected that at the Episcopals' next general convention in 1976 a change would be made to permit woman priests. Carter Heyward, one of the women ordained in the controversial ceremony, declared that the three considered themselves bona-fide priests and that "each must make her own decision as to how and when to affirm the priesthood she knows to be hers."

Dog Days

For $15 a day, a resort offers fresh meat and vegetables and a beauty treatment with an egg shampoo. But first comes an interview and a written reference from the veterinarian. Only then can your dog be a guest at Petti Paws, located in the Manhattan apartment of Patricia Peil, who calls herself the "Elizabeth Arden of the dog world."

If your dog's anxious to get out of the city, he might be interested in Camp Lindo in Margaretsville, New York, where, for $40 a week, campers participate in treasure hunts for bones and hootenany around the campfire with their guitar-strumming counselors.

The pet boom has created more than a market for extravagance, however. In a poll by Nation's Cities magazine, 60.6 per cent of U.S. mayors reported that animal problems lead the list of urban complaints, with street crime running a slow eighth. The past decade has shown dramatic increases in the keeping of large-breed dogs and a similar rise in what is becoming a very real problem —dog bites. Urban ecologist Alan Beck of Washington University estimates the number of dog bites at one million a year, with the annual cost of managing the problem at $50 million.

Is the Stake Missing Too?

The Rumanian government, as well as archeologists, historians, and horror fans, is hoping that a fresh excavation of the floor beneath the chapel on Snagov Island will locate the missing headless skeleton of Dracula. Dracula, whose real name was Prince Vlad of Walachia, was also known as Vlad the Impaler owing to 16th-century accounts of how he had thousands of the citizens of his territory along the Danube slaughtered by slow impalement on upright stakes. His more contemporary bloodthirsty image stems from the 1897 novel by Bram Stoker.

A major excavation of the area in 1931 revealed only ox bones where Dracula was supposed to be buried, but new theories hold that these remains were meant to discourage graverobbers and that, in fact, his real skeleton is farther below. The government interest in the project is easily explained: the alleged grave site has become a major tourist attraction.

Elementary

Nature only required 92 elements to fill the earth, but since World War II, man has created 13 more elements, called transuranic because they are heavier than the heaviest element to occur naturally on earth, uranium. Recently element 106 has been created, although research teams in both the United States and the Soviet Union claim to have synthesized it first.

A new element is made by taking nuclei of a known heavy element and bombarding it with nuclei of another element in hopes that the two will fuse to create the desired new element. Because the transuranic elements are all radioactive, scientists must work quickly so the new substance can be identified before it decays. The half-life—that is, the time it takes for half of the element's atoms to decay—is 0.9 seconds for element 106.

To produce their element 106, scientists at the Lawrence Berkeley Laboratory of the University of California bombarded a target of californium-249 with oxygen-18 in hopes of producing the isotope of 106 with an atomic weight of 263. Their success was verified by studying the pattern of the new element's half-life.

Forests for Iceland

After centuries of denudation and erosion, almost treeless Iceland is beginning to grow forests again. When the Vikings came to the island in the ninth century A.D., 80 per cent of the land was covered with native birches, but they were largely cut down for fuel or lumber. Later, baby trees were destroyed by grazing when sheep were given free run of the island. Since then, half of the topsoil has been swept away by wind erosion.

In recent years, however, small tree plantations, amounting to some 6,000 acres in all, have taken hold. The search for suitable trees has focused on areas with similar climates, including northern Russia, Scandinavia, and Canada. Apparently the closest match to the climate, however, is in southern Alaska. Hence there is heavy dependence on Alaska's Sitka spruce and the hardiest strains of Colorado blue spruce. Sitka spruce have grown 33 feet in the first 21 years since being planted on Iceland.

Because It's There

"If I see three oranges, I have to juggle. And if I see two towers, I have to walk," explained French high-wire artist Philippe Petit after he was arrested on August 7 for sneaking past guards at the World Trade Center in lower Manhattan, running a cable between the tops of the two towers, and dazzling early-morning commuters with a 45-minute performance 1,350 feet above the pavement. The authorities dropped charges in exchange for a command performance over a lake in Central Park for the children of New York. Petit considered these heroics as preliminaries for his high-wire dream: a stroll across Niagara Falls.

Blue Friday

A television station in Toronto that consistently rated last, behind 11 other stations in the area, now attracts 56 per cent of all area viewers for its Friday late-night attraction, "Baby Blue Movie." The attraction is sex, and while station spokesmen say they screen porno films which wouldn't satisfy the hardcore fan, "they satisfy 95 per cent of the viewers." The Canadian Radio-Television Commission has received surprisingly few objections to the movies and has thus far done nothing to stop the program. There is little chance that such programming will spread south of the border, though, since the U.S. networks have received a flood of complaints over even their most tentative efforts to air a little spice.

Feudalism: Alive and Well

Dame Sybil Hathaway died in July at the age of 90 after ruling the island of Sark as a "benevolent dictator" for 47 years. Michael Beaumont, the grandson who assumed the hereditary title of seigneur, promised to maintain the island's medieval ways, which have changed little in 500 years.

Sark is one of the Channel Islands that were once part of the duchy of Normandy and passed to the English crown at the time of the Norman conquest. The seigneur retains many feudal rights; he can claim the eleventh child of each family, one-thirteenth of the selling price of each house, and every tenth sheaf of corn. Sark has no income taxes, capital-gains taxes, estate taxes, or sales taxes. The new seigneur pledged, "I will strive with all my being to keep such so-called advantages as motor cars, helicopters, aircraft, and what-have-you out." Residents travel by foot, bicycle, horse cart, or on the tractors that are supposed to be employed only in agriculture. The island can only be reached by boat.

Police Blotter

A series of tests in New York City found that the public is less honest than the police. The tests, which involved the planting of 50 wallets containing $9 each, were first conducted by the Police Department on its own men. Thirty per cent of those who found wallets failed to return them.

The patrolmen objected to this testing of their integrity and, in an attempt to bring public attention to their grievances and also possibly to downplay their own poor showing, they conducted a similar test on civilians. Using a camera hidden inside an unmarked panel truck for surveillance, the police found that, out of 50 wallets, only eight were returned to either their "owner" or the police, giving the public an integrity-failure rating of 84 per cent. Patrolmen representatives have announced that they will conduct similar tests on the public, publishing the names of those who fail in local newspapers to "encourage better performance on the part of the public."

Meanwhile, 42 suspected burglars were arrested on September 28 in New York City when they arrived at a party thrown by two men who, in the past four months, had collected some $700,000 worth of stolen property, ranging from jewelry to a cardiograph machine. Upon arriving, the guests were surprised to learn that their hosts were detectives who had used their fencing operation to study the stolen-goods racket in New York. Eight uniformed policemen who were also invited to the party dampened everyone's spirits by taking the guests into custody.

"Did you have to invite these people?" one guest asked his host as the party broke up.

Gold Rush?

Congress passed a bill July 31 which, beginning in 1975, will permit Americans to buy and sell gold for the first time since 1933. The question now is whether Americans will respond as Europeans have and hoard gold as a hedge against inflation.

Gold bullion comes in the form of bars weighing from one to forty ounces. The current free-market price is about $157 an ounce as opposed to the officially set price of $42.22, and some gold experts predicted the price could rise to $400 an ounce if Americans anxiously seek the available supply. If they do, the United States may be up against another tricky problem. American mines are already working to capacity, and if demand forces the importation of the substance, the most likely source would be the world's leading gold producer—South Africa, a controversial and thus unlikely trading partner.

Mass Murderer Sentenced

Elmer Wayne Henley, an 18-year-old, was found guilty on July 15 of all charges for his part in the nation's largest mass-murder case of the century. He had been charged with the killing of six of the at least 26 Houston teenage boys who were sexually assaulted and tortured before they were killed. On August 8, Henley was sentenced to 594 years in prison; his lawyers immediately announced that they would appeal the case.

Dean Arnold Corll, the 33-year-old electrician who was the alleged mastermind of the brutal slayings, was killed by Henley during an argument on August 8, 1973. This shooting, which was ruled self-defense by the court, led to the discovery of the murder victims. Another accomplice, 19-year-old David Owen, reportedly had made two written confessions but had not yet come to trial.

Cumulative Index
first, second, and third sections

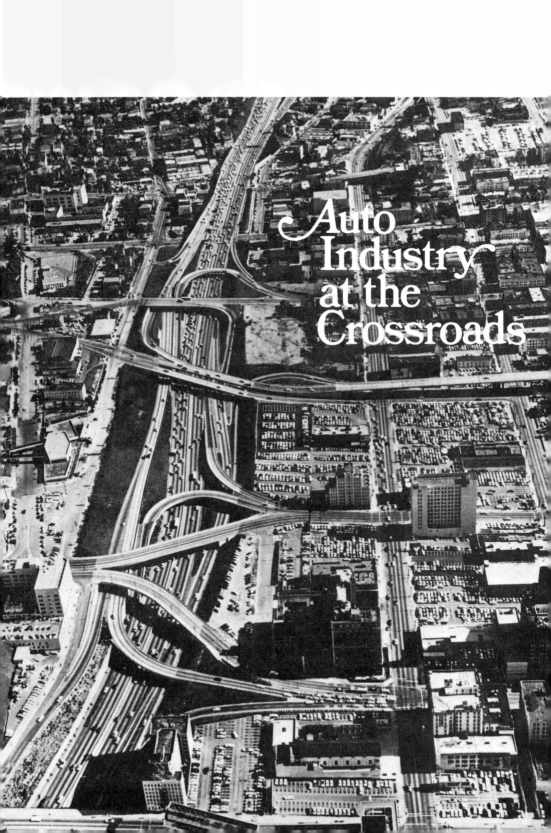

Auto Industry at the Crossroads

Detroit
Shifts
Gears

By William Greider
Washington Post Staff Writer

The stumbling giant of Motor City is like an aging prize-fighter, getting clobbered, dimly conscious that nothing in his future will be quite so glorious as the past.

Right now, it hurts so much, it's hard to think that far ahead. The new cars are stacking up, unsold, all over town, at the city airport and the state fairgrounds. In the morning fog, workers form dreary lines in the company parking lots to pick up their last paychecks.

Right now, according to industry officials, about 225,000 men and women are out of work across the industry and another 100,000 will join them by March. Some of these people won't be called back for a long time, some perhaps never.

At Chrysler, the weakest of the Big Three, a 125-day supply of new cars is backed up and, unless sales pick up dramatically and soon, Chrysler could keep most of its plants shut for the rest of the model year. Executive gossip inside the other companies wonders whether Chrysler might join Studebaker and Packard in automotive heaven.

The governor of Michigan launched his own "buy-a-car" campaign. General Motors, the behemoth, ran a series of "buyer confidence" ads which inadvertently revealed how scared GM is. Do something, Detroit tells Washington almost every day, or our illness will become a national disease.

In the rest of America, where the love-hate for Detroit is so strong, this melancholy spectacle might seem mildly compelling, even satisfying, to some. Except, like it or not, what happens to the automobile happens eventually to all of us. The long-term change that confronts Detroit really means hard choices for the nation.

Big or Small Cars?

Sooner or later, the businessmen assume their industry will recover from its pneumonias. It always has. Even now, there are false signals around town which perversely suggest that the "good old days" will be back, just like before. The new cars that aren't selling are the small ones, the Vegas and Pintos, which are unloved stepchildren in a town that made its fortune selling heavy horsepower in big boats.

"If we're so great at cramming big cars down people's throats," a Chrysler vice presi-

dent asked with bitter satisfaction, "how come we've got these small cars all over the lot?"

On Clark Street, the Cadillac assembly line is running at full schedule, nine-hour shifts and no layoffs, an elegant reassurance to the past as the big cars roll off the line like mammoth tinker toys, 54 new ones an hour, 2½ tons each, Cotillion White and Roxena Red and Jennifer Blue. "I got a Chevy myself," said Leon Kozemchak, 20 years at work on the Cadillac line. "If I had the money, I'd buy one of these. Ten thousand dollars is a lot to put in the automobile for a working man. I guess we're a luxury, but people keep buying them."

The future got turned around this fall, an aberration that has ready reasons. The people who generally buy the smaller cars are the same folks hurt first and scared most by the nation's economic trauma. The faithful Cadillac customers, the doctors and bankers and undertakers, are still buying. Further, when the auto industry prepared for a further surge toward small cars, it jacked up the small-car prices proportionately higher, a move that made the intermediates seem like a better buy this season.

In any case, the gossip along the Cadillac assembly line is about the new "small" Cadillac that is coming out in early spring.

"It's supposed to be two feet shorter," Kozemchak said.

"They say it's going to have good gas

"We like to think of it as competing with the Mercedes," said the Cadillac Public Relations man.

Competing with the Mercedes? A "small" Cadillac? It sounds like advertising flummery, a ludicrous contradiction in terms. Still, the evolving Cadillac will be much smaller and lighter and, if GM can sell that to people who want Cadillacs, why it can sell it to anyone.

What does the future look like? Listen to these voices from the town where the giant lives:

"What we'd like to do," said Pete Estes, the hearty-voiced engineer who is president of GM, "is get more weight out than the other guys. We can do it. Instead of having cars from 2,400 to 6,000 pounds, we expect our line to come down to 2,000 to 4,500 pounds. In the process, we probably won't need as many different models as we do today."

Estes exudes the muscular optimism that made GM the gorilla of the auto industry. GM can sit anywhere it wants to. "They said in Washington, 'GM, just because you sell all those big cars, you're not going to get off easy on fuel economy—you've got to do more,'" Estes related. "We accept that. Hell, we'll carry two buckets of sand and still win the 100-yard dash anytime."

Roy D. Chapin Jr., chairman of plucky little

the rest of the industry will find itself adopting similar habits, where ingenuity displaces bulk as the premium in the marketplace.

"It's a return to some of the fundamentals," Chapin said, speculating on the nation's lifestyle. "We've been a very materialistic society, as we all recognize. I don't say we're going back to a more puritanical life overnight, but I think it's very healthy. We're seeing a more simple way of life, more simple ways of dress and manner. We lost sight of a lot of the fundamentals that we ought to live by. That sounds moralistic, but it's true."

But Detroit also can envision a much darker future. At Solidarity House, headquarters of the United Auto Workers, the top people are beginning to think about a future that includes diminishing membership. The spectacular sales year of 1973, high point for the industry and the union, might never return again for the UAW.

"We're suffering reductions right now," said Irving Bluestone, the UAW vice president who served in the late Walter Reuther's brain trust. "I think we have to envision within the auto industry either a stabilization of our membership or a decline. If the growth of the industry is going to be slow, technology will no doubt outpace growth and that means fewer jobs. How quickly it will be, no one can say."

The optimists, like GM's recently installed

IACOCCA   SPERLICH

chairman, Thomas A. Murphy, speak grandly about a 17 million-car-sale year by 1980. The pessimists say, forget it. The industry will be years working back to 1973 when Americans bought 11.5 million, years full of uncertainty and change, as design evolves toward the "new car" that is more efficient and also sells.

Antipollution Devices

In nearby Dearborn, the public relations folks at Ford have published a potent broadside about the future—a booklet that describes the "Federal Pinto" of 1978, saddled down by new regulatory gadgets, heavier bumpers and additional emission-control gizmos and other things, a car that costs more and weighs more and consumes more gasoline.

That horse won't run according to Lee A. Iacocca, Ford's president, or it certainly won't sell. What started in 1971 as a 2,000-pound economy car, priced at $2,000, will evolve into a 3,000-pound sloth which costs $5,000. The message to Washington: get off our backs, you are endangering the species.

Franklin M. Kreml, president of the Motor Vehicle Manufacturers Association, puts it more bluntly:

"This low-priced economy car which was supposed to be so popular is going to be a high-priced son-of-a-bitch that nobody's going to buy. We're on a course that in the long run isn't in the public interest. If we pursue all these things, it's not going to be a question of when the industry recovers, but whether we recover. And this is the key industry for the United States and the Western world. Whether that's right or wrong is beside the point, that's the way it is."

So the U.S. industry is staging a winter counteroffensive against federal regulation. For 10 years, dating from the lucid essays of Daniel Patrick Moynihan and the harsh consumer analysis by Ralph Nader, the critique of the American auto has triumphed in the political arena, adding successive legal requirements for safety, air-pollution control, damage reduction. Now, in the season of economic despair and armed with the new priority of fuel economy, Detroit hopes to reverse the field or at least win a moratorium, postponing the new standards scheduled for 1977-78 and rescinding other debatable ones already on cars.

The economic pressures have already produced some grudging converts in Michigan. Sen. Philip A. Hart, the Democrat whose criticism of his homestate industry has been consistently tough over the years, now thinks these competing claims on the automobile should at least be given careful study, to see if the industry is right this time. The UAW, which used to ravage the companies for their lack of social consciousness, now agrees that a moratorium on new regulations is justified.

Back in Washington, however, the regulators and a lot of congressmen and senators are not only skeptical of these new claims of disaster ahead, a lot of them also believe the government must enact a new regulatory imperative for automobile performance—legisla-

tion which would force Detroit to improve the fuel economy of its cars, to as much as an average of 21 miles per gallon by 1980.

Eric Stork, the "iron duke" of EPA, a regulatory bureaucrat who zestfully challenges the automotive giants, looked over Ford's booklet on the "Federal Pinto" and dismissed it as blatant propaganda.

"Mr. Iacocca came up on the sales side of Ford and he is a superb salesman," Stork said. "But I have more respect for Ford's engineers than he does. In any case, I fully expect that some sneaky foreigners will come on the market and do all of these things—with a car that is much cheaper and more efficient than the 'Federal Pinto,' and they will sell a lot of them."

Indeed, Detroit has been repeatedly embarrassed by the way foreign designers have incorporated new safety and air-pollution devices, requiring much less weight. Volvo, for instance, increased its weight by about 5 per cent while Chevy Nova in the same weight class was going up 17 per cent, according to UAW President Leonard Woodcock. No one outside the companies has ever developed definitive statistics, but the general understanding is that Detroit has always made its biggest profit percentage on its biggest cars, including mark-ups on the added devices for safety and pollution control.

Nader, who thinks Congress ought to set a 30 mile-per-gallon fuel standard, sees Detroit talking out of both sides of its mouth.

"In the last two months," Nader observed, "every important automobile executive has said higher prices have not caused the lower sales this year. They won't cut prices now. On the other hand, they are saying that life-saving devices and pollution controls are pricing the car out of the market. Not only is this a contradiction, but it exposes the strategy of the industry—to divert attention from their own mismanagement and make safety and environmental controls the scapegoats."

Irv Bluestone concedes that the American auto companies have claimed so many times that they couldn't do something—like meeting the current air-quality standards—only to do it under firm regulatory pressure. "They sound very much to the public like the boy who cried wolf," he said. "My own feeling is that in the situation today their cry is very legitimate."

Is the wolf really there? The new Congress will have to decide, wading into a forest of conflicting claims and dense technical arguments. The subject will test the wisdom of the political process because, in this case, every decision imposes a price that someone must pay.

If you step back from the particulars of that approaching debate, the automobile with its troubles is an appropriate symbol of what's

happening all across American society. The long postwar era of unmatched growth and opulence, the generation of tailfins and fancy hood ornaments and the so-called "muscle cars," is gone, replaced by new definitions of what society needs or wants. New words have crept into the conversation, words like "functional" and "ingenuity" and "efficient." GM is offering optional fuel-mileage gauges on all its '75 cars.

"Except for the fact that they've taken all our money and kept it," said Hal Sperlich, Ford's group vice president for automobiles, "we might thank the Arabs 50 years from now for forcing us into conservation measures we had to adopt. We're coming down to the narrow end of the funnel on the globe and we've got to start doing things differently."

Doing things differently, however, forces Detroit and Washington to go back to the first question: What does America want from the automobile?

Competing Objectives

For millions of us, it is an expression of social status and even personality, including the reverse snobbery of owning a small import. For many, it is an important element of individual freedom ("the only place where a man can be alone," as one auto exec quipped). It is a livelihood, directly or indirectly, for millions of

workers and 800,000 businesses not to mention the stockholders. It is, likewise, a social miscreant which fouls the air, maims and kills. It gobbles up enormous resources, steel and rubber and especially oil, a good thing in times of abundance, but not so good now. It is also how most Americans get from one place to another. Over time, a very long time, that might change, but mass transit notwithstanding, not very soon.

Tim Nulty, the young economist who is research director for the UAW, says: "It took 60 years to build this nation's physical plant around the automobile. It will take at least 60 years to un-build it, maybe longer."

America, in other words, has built its homes, its cities and suburbs, its highways, in a way which can only function if nearly everyone owns cars. It will take long years of building mass transit systems and high-rise apartment buildings to reverse that reality.

In part, the political debate is between what might happen and what must happen to this animal. Does Detroit sincerely want to make more efficient automobiles or does it simply want more breathing space, free of government regulation? Will the American car buyers accept these new lighter, smaller cars in the national interest of fuel economy or must the government require the manufacturers to make them? Does the price for tighter regulation and

less monstrous autos have to be paid by unemployed auto workers?

Each of those volatile questions implies a simple trade-off between competing objectives, the four imperatives that now face the automobile—safer design, cleaner exhaust, better gas mileage and economic prosperity. Safety adds weight, fuel economy takes it off. One demands a higher price, another holds it down. But the problem is even more complex—like that marvelous assembly line where they put the cars together. If you interrupt the fellow bolting on bumpers, it affects the woman who is fastening gas tanks.

For example: one sure way to save gasoline is to build lighter cars, more efficient though not necessarily cheaper or less comfortable. But smaller cars, generally, are less safe. But they can be made safer (which usually adds weight back on). But small cars would be much safer if we could get the big monsters off the road (which also saves gasoline). But if big cars vanish, what happens to sales and profits and jobs? Detroit has never been through that sort of equation.

Or take another example: airbags, according to the safety advocates, would save tens of thousands of lives (a claim still disputed by the industry). But airbags would also add $150 to $300 to the price of each car (and even more to replace one that's activated in an accident).

Airbags also take up space, just when designers are trying to find more passenger space inside small outer frames (in order to save gasoline).

It is difficult to trace these effects and countereffects to absolute conclusions. The regulators argue, for instance, that adding a little bit to the price of new cars for safety or emissions control or fuel economy is still a net gain to the American public, saving billions in accident prevention and reduced health bills and gasoline.

"Having a 30 mile-per-gallon standard by the end of the decade," Nader asserted, "is like giving a pay raise to everyone in America who drives a car. It's just the opposite of taxation. Give the industry four years and tell them, if they don't do it, they can't sell cars. They'll do it."

But, suppose they can't, what happens then? The industry claims it will voluntarily increase average gas mileage on its new-car fleets by 40 per cent over 1974 (a bad year) by the end of the decade, if it is left alone and if it is relieved of the fuel penalties it expects from new safety and pollution devices. Their voluntary goal is 18.7 miles per gallon—way below what the congressional critics think is possible.

If Congress insists on more, GM's Estes warns, it will be legislating the larger cars off the market.

"We took a look at what we could sell," he said, "and based on today's technology, we'd be selling only Vegas and a few compacts, only six-cylinder compacts. We told them, to heck with you guys, to heck with the government, the customer isn't going to buy that."

While it is widely argued that depressed car sales would be a healthy thing for American society over the long run, fewer automobiles and less economic dependence on them, it im-

AIRBAG SAFETY TEST

407

plies plenty of pain in the short run. The industry comes back with another argument: if new car sales are dampened, the net effect on safety and health is negative—because it means people hang on longer to their old cars which have neither safety nor pollution-control equipment.

As General Motors figures it, safety and damage-reduction items have added $400 to its average car price thus far and promise to add another $150 plus. Air-pollution control improvements have cost $215 so far and will add another $260 to meet the 1978 standards —plus a substantial loss of fuel economy, not to mention the technical arguments over whether the '78 standards can be met at all. In sum, these imperatives would cost its customers another $614 on the sticker price, plus lost ground in gas mileage, according to GM.

The regulatory advocates are skeptical of those statistics but, more important, they insist that GM and Ford and the others are making arbitrary choices about what that new car should be like—imposing the old values of bigness and luxury on the new car which is supposed to be more utilitarian.

"Do we really need six-way power seats and power windows?" asked EPA's Eric Stork. "Is the American life-style really in danger if we have to crank down the window by hand?

"Is petroleum to make vinyl for the roof of a car really an essential use? Since air conditioning also adds weight and takes fuel and costs much more than emission controls, is it more important to have cool air or clean air?"

Detroit, citing a variety of government and academic studies, argues that it is being pushed in different directions simultaneously. Meeting the '78 emissions standards for hydrocarbons and carbon monoxide (even if the disputed requirement for controlling nitrogen oxides is lifted) will still impose a fuel-economy loss of 10 to 15 per cent, according to a joint study by the EPA and the Federal Energy Administration.

But the report still calculates that the industry can reach the 1980 goal of a 40 per cent improvement in fuel economy by adopting a wide array of new technology, from sleek auto designs that reduce air resistance to electronic fuel injection. Yet, the EPA-FEA report also acknowledges that the sales price of this more economical car would go up about 10 per cent.

"When we point out to the industry that gas savings, together with emission controls, would offset the price increase of $200 to $400 in a couple of years," Stork recalled, "they say to us, 'Ah, but the average car buyer looks at the sticker price. He doesn't think like an insurance actuary.' That's why something has to be done to implement fuel economy—you can't sell it in the showroom if your competition is selling something for $200 to $400 less."

The government has other methods by which it could force auto buyers and auto makers toward a more rational future. One approach, favored by the industry, would be to jack up the price of gasoline through a stiff federal tax—which would conserve energy and, no doubt, push customers toward all those small cars which aren't selling right now.

Another indirect approach would be a steep excise tax, levied on automobiles by weight, which presumably would hasten the shift toward smaller cars and at least make people pay dearly for the privilege of driving a big gas guzzler. Neither idea is very palatable in political terms, but some believe the government should have the courage to try one of them anyway.

"If we had put the 55-mile-per-hour speed limit to a referendum, it would have lost so badly we wouldn't have believed it," said Robert Sansom, former EPA executive. "Now that we did it, you go out and ask people about it and everybody says we ought to keep it. That's

the threshold we've got to penetrate on the automobile.''

What Will Americans Buy?

As these arguments suggest, the major element of uncertainty, beyond the blue-sky questions of technology, is really: What will Americans buy? We, the people, have been schizoid about the automobile, telling politicians to harness its ill effects, telling Detroit that people will still put the big sales dollars on luxury and size, if they can afford it. The small car, including imports, has been marching relentlessly in on the American taste and is now roughly half the market (though today's ''compacts'' are approximately what most Americans thought of as ''standard'' size in 1947).

But if Detroit pushes its production ahead of the trend—as it did with the '75 models—it gets burned. ''If you're making dog food,'' as GM's president explained, ''you have to make something the dogs will eat.''

Stork, the EPA regulator, agrees that Detroit's insecurity about the marketplace is what produces so much of its resistance to change:

''Detroit's mind-set is best characterized by the old joke, 'Turn on the green light, the customer wants a green suit.' Now the auto industry is certainly trying to build smaller cars. They're smart people and they believe the energy crisis is permanent. But I have a lot of skepticism because in a completely free market, the industry is clearly going to build whatever people want to buy and most people still like big cars.''

Hal Sperlich of Ford: ''We can go out there and build this efficient car that's good for America—and lose . . . Because the public won't buy it.''

For a generation, Detroit served its own profit objectives and what it perceived as American taste by repeatedly weaning buyers from small to big, from simple to more luxuriant, power steering and air conditioning and vinyl roofs. Now it is stuck between competing values. Can the industry successfully lead buyers back in the other direction toward smaller and less wasteful vehicles without insulting those habits of comfort which it worked so hard to establish?

While most political and industrial leaders agree that this evolution would be a healthy thing for the nation, it is at least debatable whether it will be such a good thing for Detroit. Cars, more or less, have been sold by the pound plus the expensive electrical gadgets added on, but the industrial executives have been assuring Wall Street that auto profits can prosper in a world of smaller vehicles (something they used to deny).

''Smaller cars doesn't mean we have to move around the streets in square tin cars,''

said Roy Chapin of American Motors, a company that found profit and stable growth in small cars. He sees the trend in Gremlin sales —40 per cent of the buyers opt for the more expensive model which has fancy hub caps, a sportier steering wheel and bucket seats. "The car doesn't run a damn bit better," Chapin said. "It just looks snappier."

GM President Estes says: "There's a philosophy that small is cheap and austere. Big is luxury and has a lot of options. So what you got now is small cars with luxury trim in them. We did that because of our experience last year. A guy wants small cars because of the energy crisis, but he wants comfort. Now I'm in business as far as profitability is concerned."

Retooling for the Future

But, if Detroit truly builds a better car, even a more expensive one, what does that do to future car sales? On the average, a new car owner keeps his auto for five or six years now, before it starts down the used-car chain and winds up in a junkyard somewhere at the age of 11. If technological improvements or higher prices added one year to the life of that animal, this could shrink new-car sales as much as 10 per cent. The industry optimists reply that, never mind, the three-car family is just around the corner and, besides, there are campers and recreational vehicles and all of the other specialty cars coming on strong. Others are not so sure.

What about parts and repairs? Critics like Nader have always insisted that industry profits were based on the steep mark-ups charged for replacement parts. Would a more efficient automobile trim that income?

The industry might find new sources of profit, however, in a different life-style. If Detroit offers a smaller choice of models, as everyone says it will, then it can also reduce the incredible diversity of parts that it has to design and manufacture. Worldwide, said Sperlich, Ford makes about 30 different heaters. Yet it could get along with three or four, he said, if all of its production, foreign and domestic, was brought closer in design.

That may be the clue to the future. The major American companies already know how to make a "European" car, smaller and more fuel efficient. Why? Because they are already making them in Europe. In the past, they have struggled to keep one market's tastes from contaminating the other's. Now, their long-range welfare may be served by melding the two.

That, in short, is what's happened to us. The economic pressures that forced European companies to build smaller, more ingenious cars, have now entered the American market— mainly in the form of higher fuel prices.

"Our cars were all pretty much designed in the wide-open days of 35 cents a gallon," Sperlich observed. "It would have been inefficient to design those cars differently when there was abundance. The Europeans had to serve different goods because they always paid a lot more for gas. They went for efficiency, now we have to go for it."

Tim Nulty, the UAW economist, has withering criticism for the corporate decision-makers in his town, but he agrees with Sperlich's long view of the U.S. auto. "I don't contend that the American automobile is a stupid idea," Nulty said. "Under the circumstances, it made sense. In Europe, they built cars under different constraints. They couldn't just build it bigger, so they had to get real clever. You couldn't just make bigger engines because gas was so expensive. That situation is coming to be our situation."

Will the giant of Motor City adjust to this brave new world which faces him?

"I'm thoroughly convinced," said GM's Pete Estes with utter confidence in the voice, "that functionality is what we got to put out there. I think you can impress your neighbor now with the functionality of your car the way you used to impress your neighbor with your new Corvette."

Hal Sperlich of Ford, who spends a lot of time with marketing studies, sees the future in slightly different terms. He looks at the under-30 car buyers who are coming along with somewhat different values for the marketplace. They love cars, they love driving, they buy lots of cars (one-third of new ones). But three-fourths of what they buy are small models, 25 per cent are foreign-made. Perhaps, as these young people get older, with families and more income, they will move up to larger and more luxurious models, just as their parents did. But Sperlich is doubtful.

"We spend a lot of time talking to young people about what they want in cars," Sperlich said. "As I read it, they want a little less bull."

■

Brazil. November elections in Brazil indicated that the military dictatorship ruling the country for a decade might be easing its grip on national politics. Nevertheless, the Brazilian Democratic Movement's joy over its gains at the expense of the government party was tempered by fears of a backlash. General Ernesto Geisel, who became president in March, had said he favored a gradual return to the democratic process, but his three military predecessors had said the same thing.

Ulysses Guimaraes, president of the opposition party, said that when Congress reconvened in March, his Democratic Movement would begin to institute its campaign pledges. Among these were an end to legislation which gives the president arbitrary powers, restoration of legislative and judicial authority, and correction of "cruel and unequal distribution of wealth."

The Democratic Movement defeated ARENA, the government party, by a margin of 2 to 1, but, because most seats were not up for election, emerged with only one-third of the Senate seats and fewer than half of the Chamber of Deputies places. But the party planned to use its right to form congressional investigations, question government officials, and introduce constitutional amendments.

Officials of the military regime claimed the lackluster showing of the government party was a result of Brazil's troubled economy. "You can't win an election with a 30-per-cent inflation rate," said one high official. While both the military and the opposition were congratulating each other on the orderly and free elections, observers on both sides feared that radical elements could spoil matters by either pushing too quickly for reforms or prompting military hard-liners simply to annul the election results, as occurred in 1968, when Congress was dissolved.

The Economy

Since assuming power in 1964, the military had claimed that by limiting social and political freedoms, Brazil could be the site of an economic revolution which would make it a world power by the end of the century. From 1968 to 1973, it appeared that Brazil was on its way, with an annual growth rate of more than 10 per cent. Construction boomed and investment capital flowed in from the United States, Japan, and the European Common Market. Exports also increased, with shoes, motor vehicles, and computers added to the traditional staples of coffee and sugar. But then the price of oil began to skyrocket, and in 1974, Brazil, which imports 80 per cent of its oil, spent three times what it spent in 1973 for oil.

With a payments deficit of more than $4 billion and slackening foreign investment, Brazil was forced to dip into its foreign reserves. If the trend were to continue, the government would have to sharply limit imports and thereby cut down on industrial expansion.

Continued economic problems could spell disaster for the military regime, since its power had been based on a climate of continuous advancement. Though citizens had grumbled about a decline in workers' purchasing power and the curtailment of public liberties, the high growth rate insured the regime basic support. But if the promised Brazilian economic miracle were to prove an illusion,

Brazil's "Death Squads." More than 2,000 people, most of them alleged to be petty crooks or big-time gangsters, have been executed by lawmen dispensing "instant justice." Usually a note with a skull and crossbones is left next to the corpses. These actions, and the practice of torturing political prisoners, have been denounced by citizens' groups demanding a return to the rule of law.

people would be less willing to accept military rule.

Domestically, the government has dealt with the problems of inflation through a process called indexing. The method involves adjusting income to the rising cost of living so that the poorest-paid wage-earner, and presumably everyone else, can buy as much with his salary as he did the previous year. Additionally, authorities attempt to stabilize the economy by discouraging businesses from commodity speculation while encouraging savings and further business investment. With the assurance of indexing, investors can, in theory, attempt new ventures without fear that inflation will destroy their potential profitability.

Some economists, most notably Professor Milton Friedman of the University of Chicago, believe that the United States should consider some form of indexing. (Social Security pensioners, as well as some union members already enjoy cost-of-living escalator benefits.) But, although the indexing process ideally spreads the ill-effects of inflation evenly, some see it as contributing to the problem, and nobody believes that indexing alone can solve the problem of spiraling prices.

Even with the widespread use of indexing in Brazil, it is estimated that working people lost as much as 30 per cent of their buying power in 1974 due to inflation. Problems arise for businessmen when buying foreign goods; since domestic indexing cannot solve the problems of inflation in the international marketplace. And the biggest question concerning indexing involves its application to an economy plagued with escalating inflation. Until 1974, Brazil's rate of inflation had been dropping, but rising oil prices and other pressures drove the rate up from 14 per cent in 1973 to 35 per cent in 1974.

Domestic Horrors

The continuing practice of torturing political prisoners and the persistent activities of infamous "Death Squads" seemingly reflected dissatisfactions which could only multiply if an economic upturn were not imminent. Though unrelated, the two phenomena have brutality as a common denominator.

During the past decade, more than 2,000 people, most of them alleged to be petty crooks or big-time gangsters, were executed by lawmen. The first squad came into existence in Rio de Janeiro to avenge the slaying of a policeman, but as the practice of killing criminals spread to other cities, some policemen began to use it as a means of circumventing the judicial, penal, and police establishments, which they felt could not deal with the problems of crime. The Fifth Institutional Act, a 1968 decree which gave the president dictatorial powers and outlawed habeas corpus, also gave the vigilante groups new ways to avoid the rule of law.

Until recently, many Brazilians viewed the squads tolerantly. In a 1970 public-opinion poll, 46 per cent—including 60 per cent questioned in São Paulo, South America's largest city—said they favored the Death Squads' activities. But the tide began to turn after President Geisel spoke out against the squads and newspapers extensively reported on their activities. A São Paulo lawyer expressed the change in public mood simply: "They started out killing people everybody knew to be gangsters, then they began to go after petty criminals, now they're as bad as the outlaws themselves."

Of greater political importance was the continued furor over the torturing of political prisoners. According to legal sources, physical torture has been pervasive in Brazil since 1968, when the Fifth Institutional

Act was decreed. A 96-page report on these activities, including the organization of Brazil's national-security apparatus, methods of torture, and the names of people who have died under torture, was smuggled out of Brazil and circulated among human-rights organizations in late 1974. The report, compiled by a large group of Roman Catholic militants, lawyers, relatives of political prisoners, and former prisoners, was authenticated by independent sources, including journalists and professors.

According to the report, the principal organization for anti-subversive activities is the Operations Center for Internal Defense, which is directly under the army's intelligence service. Since 1965, the operation allegedly killed 79 people for political reasons, with all but one death occurring after 1969. Furthermore, the list indicated only a small decline in the number of deaths since 1971, when all revolutionary organizations were virtually crushed.

Among the 13 methods of torture described in the report was the administration of electric shocks by sophisticated electronic equipment. The "electric microphone" dispenses shocks of varying intensity and duration in proportion to the sounds around the prisoner, including his own screams. The "refrigerator" is a small cubicle in which powerful loudspeakers play continuously deafening sounds, including screams and screeching automobiles.

Brazilian opposition to the practice of torture has grown in recent months, with the Catholic Church and the Brazilian Bar Association among those calling for a return to the rule of law. The torture issue has become the principal cause of strain between church and state in this largely Catholic country of 104 million.

Even though President Geisel entered office pledging to end torture and other such abuses, reports of continued atrocities continue to be heard. Reportedly under pressure from right-wing factions in the military, Geisel announced in August that the security services would continue "the rigorous combat to safeguard public order and institutions without useless violence."

Business and Finance. On October 8, President Ford presented an anti-inflation program to Congress that included a 5-percent income-tax surcharge for corporations, families with incomes of $15,000 or more, and individuals earning $7,500 or more. But at the end of the year, with the nation bogged down in a recession, the surcharge proposal was scrapped. Indeed, presidential advisers were openly discussing the possibility of asking Congress to enact a tax cut in an effort to stimulate the economy.

On December 11, Ford told members of the Business Council that the "economy is in difficult straits" and indicated the Administration was shifting its economic policies to focus on the new reality of recession. He said there would be no "180 degree turn" with recession replacing inflation as "public enemy number one." But he said the Administration would seek a "balanced program" aimed at combating the nation's three domestic "devils"—inflation, recession, and the energy crisis.

As an indication of hard times, industrial output declined 2.3 per cent during November, the largest one-month drop since October, 1970, bringing the index to a point 4.3 per cent below the peak reached in November, 1973. The unemployment rate reached a 13-year high of 6.5 per cent in November; the number of unemployed increased by 482,000 during the month to a total of 5,975,000. In December, the unemployment rate reached 7.1 per cent.

The Department of Commerce announced December 17 that the number of new housing starts declined in November to a seasonally adjusted annual rate of 990,000 units, the lowest since December, 1966. It was the fifth consecutive monthly drop in new housing construction.

The auto industry was particularly hard hit as car sales slowed and inventories mounted. On December 18, General Mo-

tors announced plans to idle 59,000 workers during the first quarter of 1975, bringing the total number of GM workers on indefinite layoffs to 91,000—a quarter of the company's hourly work force. For the whole industry, 142,000 workers were on permanent layoff and another 76,000 were temporarily without work. Auto-industry officials said December 8 that inventory supplies of unsold cars were large enough to last 86 days even if all assembly plants in the nation were shut down.

The slump in auto sales was affecting other sectors of the economy. The heaviest impact was on iron and steel manufacturing, fabricated metal products, nonelectrical machinery, business services (including advertising), transport and warehousing, rubber, and glass.

Recession in Europe

Europe was also in an economic slump. The European Economic Community (Common Market) predicted that production in the member nations would rise only 2.5 per cent in 1974 against a 5.6-per-cent increase in 1973. The Organization for Economic Cooperation and Development was even more pessimistic, predicting no increase in goods and services at all.

The increased cost of oil was draining European nations of their foreign-exchange reserves. Business bankruptcies were up sharply in Great Britain, West Germany, and Italy. Even more ominously, small banks were reported to be in trouble because they had relied on short-term deposits to finance long-term lending in recent years, and cash was running short.

Role of Oil Earnings

The massive increase in the price of oil led in 1974 to the largest transfer of wealth the world had ever known. For all of 1974, exports from the 13-nation Organization of Petroleum Exporting Countries (OPEC) were estimated at $100 billion in value, more than double the amount earned in 1973. Imports to the OPEC countries rose from $25 billion to $40 billion.

This left $60 billion in surplus earnings available for worldwide investment. But most of the money was in short-term,

Unemployment. Laid-off workers scoured want ads as the unemployment rate reached 7.1 per cent at the end of 1974. With the economy bogged down in a recession, Administration officials decided a tax cut was needed.

usually three-month, deposits. The banks, which were endeavoring to meet the longer-term loan needs of businesses and governments, were fearful of a breakdown in the worldwide monetary system.

Information on the location of the $60-billion surplus was difficult to obtain because some of the funds had moved through secret government-to-government deals, while private investments were often made under the names of banks in Lebanon, Switzerland, Hong Kong, and Singapore. Two large deals that surfaced, however, were the purchase by Kuwait of 14 per cent of Daimler-Benz AG, the West German producer of Mercedes cars and trucks, and the purchase by Iran of a one-fourth interest in the West German Krupp works.

At the end of November, about $10.5 billion of the surplus oil earnings was reported to be in the United States, much of it in short-term deposits and some $5 billion in U.S. government securities. About $18 billion was in the Eurocurrency market, mostly in dollar deposits outside the United States. About $12.5 billion more had been placed, mostly in

bank deposits and government securities, in industrialized countries other than the United States, much of it in Great Britain. An estimated $8 billion had gone to underdeveloped countries, including $3 billion in loans to the International Monetary Fund and the World Bank, $2 billion in direct aid, and $3 billion described as "private or unknown."

Some OPEC countries, such as Indonesia, Nigeria, Algeria, and Ecuador, had little or no surplus funds because their oil earnings were being spent on imports to develop their economies, build armed forces, and improve the standard of living. But other members with small populations —particularly Saudi Arabia and the small Persian Gulf states—were earning more money than their economies could absorb productively. The World Bank forecast a $650-billion accumulation by OPEC countries of excess revenues over imports by 1980. The Organization for Economic Cooperation and Development made a more conservative forecast of $300 billion.

Prosperous Businesses

Despite the growing effects of recession in the United States, some business sectors were doing well. In the drug, chemical, farm-equipment, plastics, and domestic-oil industries, companies continued to enjoy strong demand. Food processors and fertilizer producers were also reporting good business.

Other business sectors doing well in late 1974 included the following:

• Factory-outlet stores specializing in irregular and out-of-season apparel.

• Seed suppliers and home-canning equipment manufacturers, because 20 million American families are growing some of their own vegetables.

• Used-car dealers, spare-parts suppliers, and auto repairmen, because people were seeking to postpone buying new cars. Suppliers of hardware, fasteners, and electrical parts were also profiting from the desire to make do.

• Businesses that help customers deal with various recent shortages and cutbacks, such as bathroom-plumbing fixtures.

• Small-plane manufacturers, because of cutbacks in commercial flights. At 20

Sugar Prices quadrupled in 1974 because of rising world consumption and bad weather in many producing areas.

miles to the gallon, some single-engine planes are more economical on fuel than many cars.

• Courier services, because of discontent with the U.S. Postal Service.

• Bill-collection agencies.

• Moviemakers. Receipts were up 35 per cent for the first half of 1974.

• Makers of swimming pools, sporting goods, and hobby kits, because more people were staying close to home instead of taking expensive vacations.

The Sugar Spurt

The price of sugar soared from 17 cents a pound in December, 1973, to more than 70 cents in November, 1974, before dropping to about 50 cents at the end of the year. Two days of federal hearings in Washington ended with the conclusion that prices would not be coming down in the near future.

The typical American consumes 100 pounds of sugar a year, but less than a quarter of the total in the form of granulated sugar. Bakers, candymakers, soft-drink bottlers, and other food processors use large quantities of sugar for consumer goods.

World consumption of sugar outstripped production for the first time during the period from 1970 to 1972. World stocks have continued to fall ever since. The Department of Agriculture estimated world sugar consumption in 1974 at 81.5 million metric tons, while bad weather in many producing areas would hold production to 81.1 million tons. The United States imports more than half of its sugar needs.

The reasons for the sugar shortage appeared to be complex. One reason was crop limitations set by many producing nations in the late 1960's because of a glut that had caused prices to fall. Adverse weather conditions in 1974 sharply reduced the beet-sugar crop in Europe; the Soviet Union and its eastern European allies had switched from exporter to importer status for this reason. Some observers also believed Arab oil producers had driven up the price of sugar by speculating heavily on commodity markets.

The spread between raw and refined sugar—that is, the difference between what refiners pay and what they get for their product—more than doubled in 1974, but refiners said much of their profit had been dissipated by inflationary cost increases in labor, fuel, transportation, packaging, and interest rates. The chief beneficiaries appeared to be cane and beet-sugar growers, both domestic and foreign. (See also CUBA in this section.)

Coal Miners' Strike

United Mine Workers President Arnold Miller signed a new national coal contract December 5, officially ending a 24-day strike by coal miners. Miller announced that 56 per cent of the 79,495 miners voting on the new pact had approved it. It was the first contract in the union's history to be subject to rank-and-file ratification.

The contract with the Bituminous Coal Operators Association provided a 54-per-cent increase over three years in the $8.11 average hourly compensation. The increase included wages and fringe benefits and assumed an 8-per-cent annual rate of inflation—the maximum written into the cost-of-living escalator clause in the contract.

The strike had begun November 12. An accord was reached November 13, but Miller and other union negotiators encountered resistance to the pact from the UMW's 38-member bargaining council, the first step in the ratification process.

Agreement on a revised contract was reached November 24 after Secretary of the Treasury William Simon intervened because of the "very serious economic implications" of the strike. The major revision concerned a vacation provision; instead of splitting two basic weeks of vacation as proposed in the original agreement —one in the summer and one at Christmas, when absenteeism traditionally is high—the revised contract permitted the miners to take the two weeks in the summer, as in the past.

Aside from the union's 120,000 miners, more than 23,000 workers in affected industries, notably the railways and steel, were idled by the strike. Soft-coal production the week before the end of the strike dropped to 4,310,000 tons nationwide; a year earlier it had been 11,525,000 tons during the same week.

Cheers for Castro. Cubans wave flags and flowers at a rally addressed by Premier Fidel Castro. Sharply rising sugar prices, generous Soviet economic aid, and the Cuban government's own efforts have led to a marked improvement in the country's economic picture.

Cuba. Cuba's supporters in the Organization of American States failed November 12 to obtain the necessary two-thirds vote to end the economic and political blockade imposed on that country a decade earlier. But seven member nations—Argentina, Peru, Panama, Mexico, Trinidad and Tobago, Jamaica, and Barbados—had already established relations with the Castro regime, and more countries were expected to follow suit. Consequently, some diplomatic observers saw the potential effectiveness of the hemispheric organization eroding.

During the five-day meeting in Quito, Ecuador, the United States remained neutral on the Cuban question. The U.S. delegation—notable for the absence of Secretary of State Henry Kissinger—took the position that any movement towards support or rejection of the proposal would be interpreted as an attempt to influence the decision. Undersecretary of State Robert S. Ingersoll, who headed the delegation, said that the United States originally opposed even discussing the Cuban question but was convinced by other OAS nations that the issue should be resolved. Ingersoll described the basic problem concerning Cuba as its tendency to deal with some nations with hostility while maintaining normal relations with others. Nevertheless, he seemed to leave the door open for a possible shift in Washington's position by saying that "the United States has voted in accordance with its own perception of this question at this time."

The OAS decision concerning the blockade came on the heels of a late September trip to Cuba by two senators, Claiborne Pell of Rhode Island and Jacob Javits of New York. Though Kissinger had feared their visit might hurt the future bargaining power he might have with Havana concerning the resumption of trade, the senators contended that the time was ripe to begin movement towards reconciliation. Pell explained: "It seems ridiculous to improve relations with centers of Communist power thousands of miles away while maintaining a quarantine on a tiny satellite just a few miles offshore."

The Cuban position, which Washington

deems unacceptable, is that the U.S. trade embargo must be lifted before negotiations can begin between the two countries. A number of other barriers stand in the way of normal relations—principally the claim by U.S. companies and individuals for compensation for $1.8 billion in property expropriated by the Cuban government, and the U.S. base at Guantánamo, which Havana wants returned.

Sharply rising sugar prices, generous Soviet economic aid, and the Cuban government's own efforts have led to a marked improvement in the country's economic picture. Pat M. Holt, chief of the staff of the Senate Foreign Relations Committee, returned from a 10-day visit in July and said, "The Cubans are on the verge of making their system work—that is to say, of constructing a Socialist showcase in the Western Hemisphere."

From Spanish colonial days, Cuba inherited an economy largely based on sugar; about 7,000 square miles of the 44,000-square-mile area are devoted to growing sugar cane. Because of the high price of sugar on world commodity markets, Cuba was expected to earn an unprecedented $2 billion in hard currency for its exports in 1974, double its earnings in 1973. Of the six million tons of sugar produced in 1974, about half was pre-sold

to the Soviet Union and other Communist countries at fixed prices. The remaining 2.7 million tons were sold at world-market prices, with Japan ranking as Cuba's best customer by purchasing 1 million tons.

According to Cuban figures, which Western analysts consider realistic, the economy grew 26 per cent between 1970 and 1973. Cuba's per-capita output of goods has tripled to nearly $1,000 a year, the highest in Latin America with the possible exception of oil-rich Venezuela.

A major effort is under way to increase nickel production. Cuba has 24 per cent of the world's known deposits of the metal.

Economically, the country is tied to the Soviet Union for at least another 10 years. At the end of 1972, the Russians agreed to postpone repayment of Cuba's $5-billion debt until 1986. Also in 1972, Cuba became a full member of the Soviet-bloc Council for Mutual Economic Assistance. The Russians supply Cuba with oil at $5 a barrel, compared to the $11 world-market price.

Cuba is spending its cash eagerly, buying trucks and cars from the Argentine subsidiaries of U.S. companies, sophisticated medical gear from Sweden, flatbed trucks from Czechoslovakia, and sugarcane harvesters from East Germany.

Harvesting Sugar Cane. Modern combines are being purchased from abroad so that the industry can be mechanized and field workers put to other employment.

Archbishop Makarios, deposed president of Cyprus, returned to the troubled island in December. Makarios and other Greek Cypriots were resisting any settlement that would divide the island into two zones, with full Turkish Cypriot control over the north.

Cyprus. At year's end, the northern 40 per cent of the Mediterranean island of Cyprus remained under occupation by the Turkish army. Turkey had invaded the island on July 20, asserting its intention to protect the Turkish minority there. (See CYPRUS in the third section.)

No formal talks had been convened to negotiate the future status of the island. A conference presumably would include representatives of Turkey, Greece, and the ethnic Greek and Turkish communities on Cyprus.

While politicians and diplomats discussed the situation behind closed doors, the people of Cyprus faced an uncertain future. More than 140,000 Greek Cypriots had fled before the Turkish forces to the unoccupied south; more than 15,000 Turkish Cypriots had fled north to the Turkish-occupied zone or to two British military bases in order to avoid vengeance by Greek Cypriots. About 20,000 more Turkish Cypriots in the south reportedly were seeking to move north but were being held as virtual hostages.

The northern part of Cyprus had become a de facto Turkish colony. Turkish money was being used for currency, the Turkish Cypriot administration had issued its own postage stamps, and all residents were required to obtain identity cards issued by the "Autonomous Cypriot Turkish Administration." Thousands of Greek Cypriot-owned houses, farms, and businesses had been expropriated and given over to Turkish Cypriots who had moved into the area from the south.

On November 1, by a vote of 117 to 0, the United Nations General Assembly urged "speedy withdrawal" of all foreign troops from Cyprus, safe return of all refugees to their homes, and continued negotiations between the Turkish and Greek communities for a "mutually acceptable political settlement." The resolution called for respect for Cyprus' sovereignty and territorial integrity and maintenance of its nonaligned status. A 4,000-man UN force was helping to keep the peace.

Negotiating Positions

Turkey and the Turkish Cypriots were insisting on the division of Cyprus into two separately administered zones within a federation. Rauf Denktash, leader of the ethnic Turkish community on the island, said that the Republic of Cyprus existed as an entity only in international relations. He insisted that there could be no discussion of a return of ethnic Greeks to their homes or compensation for their property losses until the Greek Cypriots accepted the principle of a federal Cyprus divided into two zones, with full Turkish Cypriot control over the north.

Greek Premier Constantine Caramanlis, deposed Cyprus President Archbishop Makarios, and Acting President Glafkos Clerides completed two days of talks in Athens on December 1. Reportedly, they agreed that they would accept a federated Cyprus only under the following conditions:

• The right of the Greek Cypriot refugees to return to their homes in Turkish-occupied parts of the island.

• Turkish withdrawal to a territorial salient approximating the proportion of ethnic Turks in the total population—about 20 per cent.

• No forcible population movements by either side.

• A strong central government for Cyprus, with well-defined powers.

• Complete demilitarization of the island.

Reportedly, the Greeks and Greek Cyp-riots were proposing, instead of a two-zone federated Cyprus, an arrangement of Swiss-style cantons that would give ethnic Turks control over several scattered areas rather than one large compact zone.

Makarios Returns

Archbishop Makarios returned to Cyprus from exile December 7 and was greeted by tens of thousands of Greek Cypriots. He declared, "We shall not accept any solution involving transfer of populations and amounting to partition of Cyprus."

The only conciliatory note struck by the archbishop was toward the Greek Cypriot EOKA-B guerrillas who overthrew him in July and tried to assassinate him. Declaring, "People not of our faith have raped our island," he offered his ethnic Greek rivals forgiveness and amnesty.

Turkish officials said they would negotiate only with Clerides, not with Makarios, but the archbishop reportedly had told U.S. Secretary of State Henry Kissinger that he had the power to destroy any settlement made over his head. Also complicating efforts toward a settlement was the instability of the Turkish government. The cabinet headed by Premier Bulent Ecevit had resigned September 18; after a 61-day crisis, a caretaker government was appointed November 13 to serve until elections to be held in the spring of 1975.

The Refugee Problem. Almost one-third of the population had fled from their homes during the fighting, and many were left to shift for themselves until a settlement would clarify their future status.

Air Crash Kills 59. A Boeing 747 crashed in Kenya November 20, shortly after take-off from Nairobi. It was the first crash ever of a 747 jumbo jet.

Disasters. Among the disasters that occurred in October, November, and December, 1974, were the following:

Aviation. Ninety-two people died in the worst U.S. aviation disaster of 1974 when their Trans World Airlines Boeing 727 jet, en route from Columbus, Ohio, to Washington's Dulles Airport, crashed into the Blue Ridge Mountains of Virginia on December 1. The flight, which had originated in Indianapolis, had been scheduled to land at Washington's National Airport, but heavy winds caused the rerouting. The tape of the pilot's conversation prior to the crash, recovered from the wreckage, showed no sign of concern. Three other pilots who had taken jets over the same area earlier in the morning had reported poor visibility and mild turbulence.

This crash, along with the crash of a Northwest Orient Airlines jet the same day 30 miles north of New York City, killing its three crew members, raised the total number of fatalities in U.S. airline flights to 461 for 1974. This figure was more than twice that of any of the five previous years and was the second highest total in history, surpassed only by the 499 deaths in 1960.

A total of 191 people, including 182 Indonesian Moslems en route to Mecca, died when their Dutch DC-8 chartered jet crashed December 4 while approaching the airport at Colombo, Sri Lanka. The craft burst into flames as it hit a hilltop 60 miles outside Sri Lanka's capital, resulting in the second worst disaster in aviation history.

Fifty-nine people died when a Lufthansa Boeing 747 jumbo jet crashed during take-off from Nairobi International Airport in Kenya on November 20. The airplane failed to gain the proper altitude and was forced to make an emergency landing; 98 people survived, 73 of them virtually unharmed. The crash was the first for a 747 since the jet was introduced in 1970. The accident was attributed to wing flaps being in an improper position even though the pilot claimed lights indicating their proper placement registered positive.

Twenty-one American tourists and the three-man crew of a Lockheed Lodestar aircraft were killed when the plane crashed following take-off in northern Guatemala on December 28. The cause of the crash was not known.

Thirty-two of a total of 34 oil executives and flight crew died on October 29 as their Panarctic Oil Ltd. Lockheed Electra transport aircraft crashed through the Canadian Arctic icecap, short of an airstrip on Melville Island.

Bridge. The Nepal Foreign Ministry reported on November 26 that 142 people

Devastating Cyclone. Darwin, Australia, was struck on Christmas Day by a cyclone that destroyed 90 per cent of the city of 43,000 and killed 48 people.

were believed to have drowned when a suspension bridge collapsed on the Nepal-Indian border.

Earthquake. An estimated 5,200 people died in an earthquake that hit northern Pakistan on the last weekend of 1974. Aid to the estimated 15,000 injured was hampered by the inaccessibility of the hard-hit mountain region, which is located 200 miles north of the capital of Islamabad among the peaks of the Karakoram Mountains. The region's main roadway was rendered useless by the earthquake.

Prime Minister Zulfikar Ali Bhutto appealed for international aid, claiming that "all we can do is draw the world's attention to what has happened." The earthquake was the most destructive since the Chirstmas, 1972, quake in Nicaragua, which killed 8,000 to 10,000 people.

Seventy-three people died and more than 2,000 sustained injuries October 3 when a minute-long earthquake struck Lima and the surrounding coastal area of Peru. The quake destroyed 60 per cent of Canete, 120 miles south of Lima.

Fire. Eighty-eight people died in a hotel fire in Seoul, South Korea, which police blamed on a careless smoker. Most of those who died were in a discotheque in the hotel which had been locked by the employees to make sure all the customers settled their bills before leaving.

Marine. More than 200 persons were believed to have drowned on October 25 when a ferryboat capsized about 90 miles southwest of Dacca, Bangladesh.

Mine. Forty-one coal miners died and six more were badly burned December 27, when an explosion and fire tore through a 2,100-foot-deep mine in Lievin, France. The mine disaster, France's worst since World War II, was caused by accumulations of either methane gas or coal dust.

Storms. A cyclone devastated the Australian port city of Darwin on Christmas Day, killing 48 people and leaving nearly half of the city's 43,000 people homeless. The cyclone, a rotating wind system that would be called a hurricane in the United States, destroyed 90 per cent of the city, with damage estimated at around $1 billion. One pilot who flew over the ravaged city likened it to "Hiroshima after the atom bomb."

The Australian government responded with a massive airlift that brought food and medical supplies to the city while evacuating the homeless. Prime Minister Gough Whitlam pledged "a determined and unremitting effort to rebuild Darwin."

Philippine officials estimated November 1 that 52 people had been killed and more than $5-million worth of crop damage sustained as a result of four typhoons that hit the country during October.

425

President Ford campaigned on behalf of Republican candidates in 20 states, but the Democrats piled up their biggest majority in both houses of Congress since 1964. Inflation, recession, and the Watergate scandal all worked against the GOP.

Elections in the UNITED STATES. Democrats made sizable gains in elections held on November 5, piling up the biggest Democratic majority in both houses of Congress since the landslide of 1964. They picked up 43 House of Representative seats to give them 291, compared to 144 for the Republicans. They gained at least three Senate seats for a total of 61 Democrats, compared to 38 Republicans. One seat was in doubt.

Democrats also scored a net increase of four governorships for a total of 36, including California and New York. Democrats won control of eight additional state legislatures, upping their total to 36 —the party's highest since 1936.

President Ford campaigned on behalf of Republican candidates in 20 states, but was unable to turn the tide. The GOP lost ground in every region of the country. Inflation, the recession, the Watergate scandal, Ford's pardon of Nixon, and his unpopular proposal of an income-tax surcharge all worked against the Republican party. Political observers agreed that a disillusioned electorate had turned to the Democrats by default. Only 38 per cent of voting-age Americans turned out at the polls—the lowest percentage since 1946.

The state of the economy was the main campaign issue, but most candidates were reluctant to offer detailed remedies for inflation, and a few conceded that they had no answers. Republicans generally urged cuts in government spending. Democrats generally emphasized cutting defense spending, closing tax loopholes, and imposing heavier taxes on oil companies.

Women made gains. A total of 18 were elected to the House of Representatives, an increase of two. According to one compilation, the number of women state legislators rose from 305 in 1969 to 587 after the November election. Ella Grasso, a Democrat, was elected governor of Connecticut, the first woman to make it on her own. (The previous three women governors were the wives or widows of governors.) Janet Gray Hayes of San Jose, California, became the first woman mayor of a U.S. city of more than 500,000.

Harold Ford was elected from a district in Memphis, Tennessee, to raise the black membership in the House to 16. Another black, Melvin Dymelly, was elected lieutenant governor of California. There were other minority "firsts": Raul Castro was elected the first Mexican-American governor of Arizona, and George Ariyoshi, elected governor of Hawaii, became the first American of Japanese ancestry to become a governor.

Environmental issues were important in many states. Environmental Action, which every two years labels 12 House incumbents the "Dirty Dozen," saw eight of them go down to defeat in 1974.

Republicans who were critical of Watergate fared better than those who defended Nixon. Of the 10 Republican House Judiciary Committee members who voted in the televised hearings against impeachment on all counts, four lost their bids for reelection.

Senate

All 15 Democratic incumbents seeking another term were reelected. Birch Bayh of Indiana and George McGovern of South Dakota survived stiff challenges, but most were easy victors, including Abraham Ribicoff, Daniel Inouye, Adlai Stevenson 3rd, Thomas Eagleton, Alan Cranston, Frank Church, Ernest Hollings, and Herman Talmadge. The only seat lost to the Republicans was in Nevada, where

The Senators-Elect

(Name is in italics where a seat changed party)

Alabama—*James B. Allen (D)
Alaska—*Mike Gravel (D)
Arizona—*Barry Goldwater (R)
Arkansas—Dale Bumpers (D)
California—*Alan Cranston (D)
Colorado—*Gary Hart* (D)
Connecticut—*Abraham Ribicoff (D)
Florida—*Richard Stone* (D)
Georgia—*Herman Talmadge (D)
Hawaii—*Daniel Inouye (D)
Idaho—*Frank Church (D)
Illinois—*Adlai Stevenson 3rd (D)
Indiana—*Birch Bayh (D)
Iowa—John Culver (D)
Kansas—*Robert Dole (R)
Kentucky—*Wendell Ford* (D)
Maryland—*Charles McC. Mathias, Jr. (R)

Missouri—*Thomas Eagleton (D)
Nevada—*Paul Laxalt* (R)
New Hampshire—Louis Wyman (R) or
                        John Durkin (D)
New York—*Jacob Javits (R)
North Carolina—Robert Morgan (D)
North Dakota—*Milton Young (R)
Ohio—John Glenn (D)
Pennsylvania—*Richard Schweiker (R)
South Carolina—*Ernest Hollings (D)
South Dakota—*George McGovern (D)
Utah—Jake Garn (R)
Vermont—*Patrick Leahy* (D)
Washington—*Warren Magnuson (D)
Wisconsin—*Gaylord Nelson (D)

* Denotes incumbent

The Governors-Elect

(Name is in italics where a seat changed party)

Alabama—*George Wallace (D)
Alaska—*Jay Hammond* (R)
Arizona—*Raul Castro* (D)
Arkansas—David Pryor (D)
California—*Edmund G. Brown, Jr.* (D)
Colorado—*Richard Lamm* (D)
Connecticut—*Ella Grasso* (D)
Florida—*Reubin Askew (D)
Georgia—George Busbee (D)
Hawaii—George Ariyashi (D)
Idaho—*Cecil Andrus (D)
Iowa—*Robert Ray (R)
Kansas—*Robert Bennett* (R)
Maine—*James Longley* (I)
Maryland—*Marvin Mandel (D)
Massachusetts—*Michael Dukakis* (D)
Michigan—*William Milliken (R)
Minnesota—*Wendell Anderson (D)

Nebraska—*J. J. Exon (D)
Nevada—*Mike O'Callaghan (D)
New Hampshire—*Meldrim Thomson, Jr. (R)
New Mexico—Jerry Apodaca (D)
New York—*Hugh Carey* (D)
Ohio—*James Rhodes* (R)
Oklahoma—David Boren (D)
Oregon—*Robert Straub* (D)
Pennsylvania—*Milton Shapp (D)
Rhode Island—*Philip Noel (D)
South Carolina—*James Edwards* (R)
South Dakota—*Richard Kneip (D)
Tennessee—*Ray Blanton* (D)
Texas—*Dolph Briscoe (D)
Vermont—*Thomas Salmon (D)
Wisconsin—*Patrick Lucey (D)
Wyoming—*Ed Herschler* (D)

* Denotes incumbent

New Governors. *From left,* Robert Bennett, James Longley, James Edwards.

New Senators. *From left,* Jake Garn, John Glenn, Gary Hart.

Elected to House of Representatives. *From left,*
Martha Keys, Abner Mikva, Helen Stevenson Meyner.

former governor Paul Laxalt narrowly defeated Lieutenant Governor Harry Reid to pick up the seat held by Alan Bible, who was retiring.

Seven Republicans were reelected, including Jacob Javits of New York and Barry Goldwater of Arizona. Henry Bellmon of Oklahoma and Robert Dole of Kansas won close races over their Democratic challengers, and Milton Young of North Dakota won another term with a 177-vote margin. But Democrats picked up four Republican seats, two from incumbents: in Kentucky, Marlow Cook was defeated by Governor Wendell Ford, and in Colorado, Peter Dominick lost his seat to Gary Hart, McGovern's presidential campaign manager in 1972. The biggest upset was in Vermont, where Patrick Leahy won a vacated seat to become the first Democratic senator from the state since the Republican party was organized in 1854. In New Hampshire, Republican Louis Wyman led John Durkin for a vacated seat by two votes out of more than 220,000 cast.

In one of the country's most closely watched races, former astronaut John Glenn was elected to the Senate from Ohio, defeating his Republican opponent by a margin of more than 2 to 1.

House of Representatives

Democrats picked up five seats in New York and Indiana, four each in California and New Jersey, three in Illinois, and two each in Iowa, Michigan, North Carolina, Oregon, Tennessee, Virginia, and Wisconsin. They gained one additional seat in each of 14 other states and polled 58 per cent of the nationwide congressional vote. The Republicans took Democratic seats in Florida, Louisiana, Ohio, Pennsylvania, South Dakota, and Maine.

In one closely watched race, former congressman Abner Mikva, a Democrat, edged incumbent Samuel Young in a Chicago-area district. In another, Helen Stevenson Meyner won a New Jersey seat from Republican incumbent Joseph Maraziti, a strong supporter of Nixon. Thomas Downey upset Republican incumbent James R. Grover to win a Long Island seat and become, at 25, the nation's youngest congressman.

Governorships

The elections left Republicans in charge of the statehouses in only Michigan and Ohio among the 10 most populous states. In New York, Brooklyn congressman Hugh Carey crushed incumbent Malcolm Wilson, who had succeeded Nelson Rockefeller as governor. In California, Edmund G. (Jerry) Brown, Jr., son of a former governor, defeated Houston Flournoy to succeed Ronald Reagan. In Massachusetts, incumbent Republican Francis Sargent was defeated by Michael Dukakis, a former state legislator who had sponsored the nation's first no-fault auto-insurance law and had been moderator of the television show *The Advocates*.

In a major upset, Democratic incumbent John Gilligan lost a close race in Ohio to former governor James Rhodes. Republican Governor William Milliken of Michigan overcame the national trend to win another term of office.

In Oklahoma, David Boren, a 33-year-old Democrat, became the nation's youngest governor after a campaign in which he promised to clean up the scandal-plagued state administration. James Edwards became the first Republican governor in South Carolina since 1876 after the Democratic primary winner, Charles Ravenel, was ruled ineligible by the courts, creating confusion and rancor among state Democrats.

Richard Lamm, emphasizing environmental questions—especially limiting population growth—was elected governor of Colorado, replacing incumbent John Vanderhoof. Jay Hammond, campaigning against "malignant growth," won in Alaska, defeating Democratic incumbent William Egan by 287 votes.

James Longley bucked the odds in Maine to become the first independent elected a governor since 1936. Longley, an insurance executive, promised to cut the state budget through efficient business-type management.

George Wallace was reelected governor of Alabama with 85 per cent of the vote. Democratic incumbents Reubin Askew, Milton Shapp, and Dolph Briscoe were returned in Florida, Pennsylvania, and Texas, respectively.

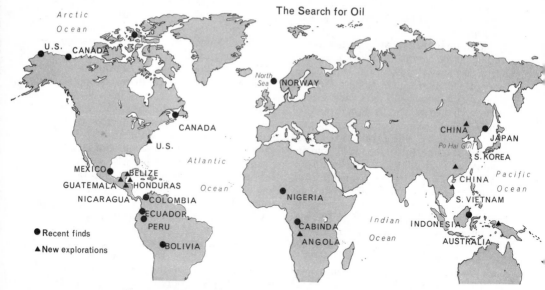

The Search for Oil

● Recent finds
▲ New explorations

New Sources of Oil. The greatest search for oil in history is under way as a direct result of quadrupled oil prices; every available drilling rig is being employed. But two-thirds of present proven world reserves are located in the Middle East.

Energy. The American Petroleum Institute announced November 10 that U.S. consumption of petroleum products during the first 10 months of 1974 averaged 16.5 million barrels a day, down 3.7 per cent from the same period in 1973. Gasoline use declined by 2.4 per cent. Most of the falloff in consumption was during the first quarter, while the Arab oil embargo was in effect.

Domestic oil production during the same 10-month period also declined. Production, at a rate of 8.5 million barrels a day, was off 3.5 per cent from the same period in the previous year.

In his economic address of October 8, President Ford said imports of foreign oil were to be reduced by 1 million barrels a day by the end of 1975, either by saving fuel or by increasing domestic production. In order to increase available domestic supplies of fuel, Ford asked Congress to deregulate natural-gas prices.

On November 14, Secretary of State Henry Kissinger made a major policy declaration in Chicago, calling for stern en-

ergy-conservation efforts, and exceptional cooperation among the major non-Communist oil-importing nations. He outlined a plan with two essential ingredients: a proposed $25-billion mutual-aid fund, financed by the industrial nations themselves, to provide emergency loans to any participating nation in financial distress; and a major oil-conserving push designed to cut imports by 3 million barrels a day or about $11 billion a year. Only those nations that pledged to cut oil imports would be eligible for the loans.

The reasoning behind Kissinger's proposal was that a cutback in oil consumption might be able to break the cartel of the Organization of Petroleum Exporting Countries (OPEC) and cause prices to fall. Kissinger declared, "Today the producers are able to manipulate prices at will and with apparent impunity. They are not persuaded by our protestations of damage to our societies and economies because we have taken scant action to defend them ourselves. They are not moved by our alarms about the health of the Western world, which never included and sometimes exploited them."

(World oil consumption, had, in fact, fallen in 1974 by about 2 per cent. A surplus of output over demand reached nearly a million barrels a day during the summer, but disappeared when several OPEC members cut their production, and panicked consumers stepped up buying in order to fill their storage tanks.)

The International Energy Agency was established a week after Kissinger's speech. An outgrowth of the February energy conference held in Washington, it consisted of 11 oil-importing nations committed to seek solidarity on all aspects of the energy problem. France declined to participate, and Norway declined full membership because it had become an oil-producing country, but the 11 participants consume four-fifths of the world's petroleum. (While remaining outside the agency, France had taken dramatic steps to reduce oil consumption, setting a $10-billion ceiling on spending for oil imports in 1974 and ordering cutbacks in industrial and home-heating oil consumption.)

World Oil Prices Raised

OPEC, the organization of major oil exporters, decided at a meeting in Vienna December 13 to raise the price of oil and adopt a new uniform pricing system. Petroleum prices were to be increased by about 38 cents a barrel, or almost 4 per cent, on January 1, 1975, and they were to continue at that level until October 1, 1975.

Under the new pricing system, OPEC for the first time based actual prices on government revenue per barrel of oil instead of the posted price, the traditional artificial price upon which tax and royalties were estimated. An official communiqué indicated that the action was aimed at reducing the profits of the major international oil companies.

Secretary of the Interior Morton said that the OPEC price increase would add an additional $4 billion to world oil costs "and further depress economic activity." Morton said "the OPEC governments' take has now risen over fivefold since last year—$1.70 then [a barrel] compared to $10.12 now."

FEA Study

A $5-million study that drew upon the thinking of some 750 government officials and private consultants was released by the Federal Energy Administration on November 13. It urged a strong conservation effort, including mandatory federal standards for energy requirements of automobiles, appliances, and buildings.

The 1,000-page analysis made no recommendations as such, but suggested the imposition of a ceiling on oil imports. The report calculated that energy conservation could reduce the growth of demand to about 2.2 per cent as an annual average for the period from 1972 to 1985. One major requirement would be increasing average automobile gas mileage to 21 miles per gallon by 1985, compared to 13.5 miles for 1975 models.

The report favored a major effort to shift toward reliance on electric power plants fueled by coal or uranium rather than by oil. But it concluded that synthetic fuels made from shale oil and coal would not play a major role by 1985, nor would geothermal heat nor solar radiation.

The report said domestic U.S. production of oil, which peaked in 1970, would continue to decline for several years because of the time needed to explore or develop new fields. Natural-gas supplies would not increase unless federally regulated prices were raised.

The coal industry, the study said, had the capacity "to satisfy almost any foreseeable demand" at prices near 1972-73 levels. It advocated shifting energy demand from oil to coal by bolstering the demand for electricity and suggested that the federal government might prohibit the use of oil and natural gas to heat homes and other buildings, forcing builders to install electric heating instead.

The report hinted that the $11-a-barrel price of imported oil would be good for energy independence, in that it would be easier to cut demand substantially and would spur domestic oil production, while a lower price would widen U.S. dependence on imported oil. It concluded that retarding the growth of energy consumption and expanding domestic energy supplies "are cheaper in economic terms

New Energy Lineup. Secretary of the Interior Rogers Morton, *left,* was appointed chairman of a newly created Energy Resources Council, and Frank Zarb, *right,* replaced John Sawhill as director of the Federal Energy Administration.

than imported oil or any other emergency option," even if the price of imported oil dropped to $7 a barrel.

FEA Shakeup

John Sawhill, FEA director, was fired on October 29. Administration sources said he had irked President Ford by openly recommending specific measures, such as an increased tax on gasoline and perhaps a general surtax on excessive energy use, that the president opposed.

Andrew Gibson was nominated to replace Sawhill, but the nomination was withdrawn November 12 after the disclosure that Gibson's former employer, Interstate Oil Transport Company, had agreed to pay him $1 million over 10 years under a financial agreement that led members of Congress to charge a conflict of interest. Frank Zarb, associate director of the Office of Management and Budget, was nominated in his place. Secretary of the Interior Rogers Morton was appointed chairman of a newly created Energy Resources Council.

While the president made it plain that he was opposed to higher taxes on gasoline, he hinted at a news conference that he would seek to limit oil imports if voluntary measures failed to cut oil imports by 1 million barrels a day. Some Administration spokesmen predicted a return soon to measures in effect during the Arab oil embargo, such as alternate-day gasoline fill-ups and a ban on Sunday sales of gas.

Coal Production

"The United States is the Saudi Arabia of coal," says Carl E. Begge, the chief lobbyist for the industry, to dramatize the country's huge coal reserves. Yet, although coal prices in late 1974 had risen sharply from late 1973, coal production was running only 5 per cent ahead of 1973.

Roughly 25 per cent of U.S. production is metallurgical coal, which goes to steelmakers. The other basic kind is steam coal, burned by utilities to generate electricity. Quality and price depend largely on sulfur content and heating power. The highest price hikes were mainly in metallurgical and small-scale contracts, since the utilities have long-term contracts for steam coal. According to the Federal Power Commission, the average price of coal burned by electric utilities rose 22 per cent between February and November.

Coal-company executives say that recent price increases still leave them with a low ratio of profit to invested capital. And production cannot be expanded significantly overnight; it takes 18 months to open a strip mine and three to five years to develop an underground mine.

Half of all U.S. coal now comes from strip mines. Strip-mining is free of the health and safety problems of deep-mining, the demands of the United Mine Workers, and the problems of meeting air-quality standards (since surface coal is relatively clean).

Western coal, most of it strip-mined, now accounts for more than 10 per cent of the 600 million tons of coal the United States produces annually. Costs are lower in the West because many strip miners belong to no union and ownership of the land is less fragmented and thus easier to acquire. The result is that coal can be strip-mined in the West for $3 to $5 a ton, compared with $9 to $14 in the Eastern deep mines.

But strip-mining has scarred 2 million acres—roughly the size of Delaware and Rhode Island. Western ranchers and farmers worry that it will ruin their land and oppose the efforts of coal companies to acquire water supplies needed to mine and process the coal. And Congress passed a bill—vetoed by President Ford in December—restricting strip-mining on all private land for which the federal government owns the mineral rights—roughly 35 per cent of Western surface reserves.

Water is needed for dust control, coal washing, reclamation of the land, and, in some cases, for creating a coal-and-water slurry that is to be transported by pipeline to electric power plants. But coal-rich Western states also need water for irrigation and fear that the coal companies will cause water tables to drop. Montana has imposed a three-year moratorium on the use of its water for energy development so that it can study the situation.

For shale mining, the extraction of oil or coal from shale would leave huge residues of loose waste; water would be needed for compacting it and for revegetating the ravaged land. It is estimated that shale mining would require almost three barrels of water for each barrel of oil brought forth.

Natural Gas

Natural gas furnishes one-third of all U.S. energy needs, but supplies were expected to fall 13 per cent below contracted deliveries during the 1974-75 winter. Moreover, gas reaching homeowners was expected to average 16 per cent more in cost than during the previous winter and 37 per cent more than in 1970. The major impact of the gas shortage was falling on industrial users, and the result was expected to be the layoff of thousands of workers.

U.S. Coal Reserves. The United States has lots of recoverable coal reserves—an estimated 428 billion tons—but coal production in 1974 ran only 5 per cent ahead of 1973. Western coal, most of it strip-mined, is cheap, but farmers and ranchers fear their land will be ruined.

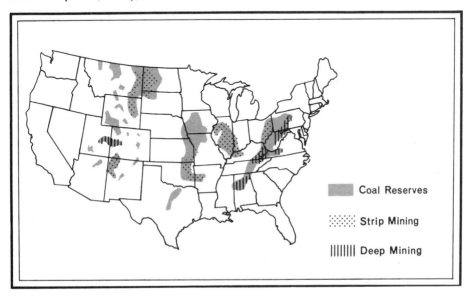

Transamerica Building in San Francisco saves energy because warm air generated by fluorescent ceiling lights is used for heating. Moreover, because of its pyramid shape, the building has more employees on lower levels and therefore needs fewer elevators than most high-rises, thus saving electricity.

Producers say the gas shortage results from setting the controlled price of gas sold to interstate pipelines so low that it has discouraged new drilling. Also, demand for natural gas has soared because it is nonpolluting and cheap in comparison to other fuels.

Industry officials say recent price increases allowed by the federal regulatory authorities are not sufficient to spur exploration. The only long-range answer, they say, is to remove all price regulations on newly discovered gas. Secretary of the Interior Morton has said the wellhead price of deregulated gas could rise as high as $2 per thousand cubic feet, compared to 50 cents in late 1974.

Even if Congress decides to deregulate gas prices, it takes about five years to secure leases, drill new wells, and build gather facilities. Industry officials anticipate no sizable increase in gas output before 1980 at the earliest.

Energy-Saving Buildings

Experts say about a third of all the energy consumed in the United States goes for operating buildings. Two design changes, they say, would be instrumental in conserving energy:

• Cutting back sharply on the amount of glass, which is a poor insulator that lets out too much heat in winter and lets in too much heat in summer.

• Fewer skyscrapers, since tall buildings tend to use more elevators, more electric lights, and more power for heating and cooling than lower buildings with comparable space.

Glass-faced, tightly sealed skyscrapers are extremely wasteful of energy. For example, the 110-story twin towers of Manhattan's World Trade Center, with a daytime population of about 50,000, use as much electricity as Schenectady, New York, which has 100,000 people.

The Transamerica Corporation Building in San Francisco is estimated to use 29 per cent less energy than a conventionally designed building with comparable space. Because of its pyramid shape, it has more employees on the lower levels and therefore needs fewer elevators, saving electricity. In addition, heat from fluorescent lighting fixtures is mixed with outside air and circulated through the building, usually making other heating unnecessary.

The Denver headquarters of Financial Programs, Inc., has vertical bronze louvers on each window that can be opened and shut to minimize heat loss in winter and cut down on solar heat in summer. Cooling water flows through the louvers in summer.

For homeowners, extra insulating in walls and ceilings is suggested. The Federal Housing Authority has changed its criteria for housing it insures, requiring more and better insulation. It estimates that implementation of its new standards will cut heat loss by 35 per cent.

Ethiopia. Up until mid-November, the military coup which had deposed Emperor Haile Selassie on September 12 had remained bloodless. But on November 23, the military regime announced that 60 aristocrats and former officials, among them Lieutenant General Aman Andom, the chairman of the 120-man military council until a week earlier, had been executed. (Junta leaders later claimed that Aman had died while resisting arrest.)

Most of those executed had been arrested during the seven-month anti-corruption drive which culminated in Haile Selassie's ouster in September. (See ETHIOPIA in the third section .) Radio Ethiopia announced that the executions had taken place because of crimes committed against the Ethiopian people, including the disruption of the reform movement and the covering up of the famine in Wallo Province, where more than 100,000 people reportedly had died.

"Those executed have been found guilty of trying to sow dissension and division within the armed forces," the official explanation said, "of putting their own personalities above the general welfare of the state and of grossly abusing authority." Concerning the execution of Aman, the former head of the military council, it was known that he had advocated a negotiated settlement to the 10-year secessionist guerrilla war being waged by the Eritrean Liberation Front in the northern province of Eritrea, while others in the council favored increased military action against the dissidents.

Tank Attack left the home of interim Ethiopian head of state General Aman Andom in ruins. Aman was killed while resisting the attack, and 59 aristocrats and former officials were executed by the military regime, which later declared it would make Ethiopia a socialist country.

On November 28, the military junta elected a new chairman, Brigadier General Tafari Banti, though it was not clear whether he would act as both chairman of the civilian cabinet and chief of state, as had Aman. What became clear around the time of the executions, though, was the importance of Major Mengistu Haile Miriam within the junta. The 36-year-old Mengistu was credited with masterminding the "creeping coup" which deposed the emperor and eventually led to the bloody killings. General Tafari was also known as a hard-liner and supporter of Mengistu, a description borne out by his order to deploy 7,000 troops to reinforce the army's Second Division, possibly for a showdown in the north.

The new military government also announced that the deposed emperor had signed a letter authorizing the transfer of "all his personal and family fortune," most of which was believed to be in Swiss banks, to aid drought and famine victims in his country. But legal scholars questioned whether the agreement was legally binding, and Swiss bankers insist that transfer of assets must not be made under duress.

Although Ethiopians enjoyed long-denied freedoms immediately after Haile Selassie was deposed, the possibility of maintaining these freedoms seemingly vanished. Strikes and agitation by labor prompted the government to ban such activities and jail union leaders who defied the new laws. Student demonstrations were similarly repressed, and a plan evolved by which schools would be closed for a year while students were sent to the countryside to teach the peasants. And the press, which when it gained its freedom claimed it would never again be a tool of an autocratic master, succumbed to government pressure.

On December 20, the governing military council announced that it would turn Ethiopia into a socialist country with a one-party system, collective farms, and direct government control over all property useful for economic progress.

Violence Spreads

The insurgency in the northern province of Eritrea had boiled at a low level since 1962, but the death of Aman and a decision to send more troops north prompted predictions that the situation would get bloodier. In late December, Asmara, the provincial capital, was shaken by grenade attacks, clashes between army units and secessionist groups, and a wave of stranglings.

On December 29, the government announced it had agreed to hold negotiations with two rebel groups. But observers in Asmara believed neither group would agree to anything less than full independence, which the government was not likely to accept.

The threat of violence was not confined to Eritrea. Many feared the failure of promised reforms could agitate peasants throughout the nation to violence. Observers agreed that in this land, where more than half the population are impoverished peasants, the most important reforms must deal with land distribution. Although the military junta had pledged such reforms, it was feared that violence might ensue when landlords attempted to collect rent from peasant farmers. Incidents of murder and arson had already been reported on a small scale in the central highlands where, as throughout rural Ethiopia, firearms are widely owned.

General Tafari Banti was elected chairman of the military junta, replacing Aman.

Great Britain. British voters gave Harold Wilson's Labour party a narrow victory in general elections held October 10, but the margin was too slim to be considered a mandate for broad economic or social reforms. Voter apathy was widespread —only 72 per cent of the electorate cast ballots, as compared with 79 per cent in the February, 1974, elections which ousted Conservative Prime Minister Edward Heath and brought Wilson to power. (See GREAT BRITAIN in the first section.) In the period between elections, the country's economic crisis had continued to deepen, increasing social tensions and contributing to a mood of national uncertainty.

Wilson's retention in office made him the first British prime minister in the 20th century to lead his party to victory in four nationwide elections. The Labour party gained 18 seats, for a total of 319 of the 635 seats in Parliament's House of Commons—a majority of two. The Conservatives lost 20 seats, for a total of 276. The remaining seats went to the Liberals (13), Northern Ireland's (Protestant) Unionist party (10), the Scottish Nationalists (11), Welsh Nationalists (3), and Ulster's (Catholic) Social Democratic and Labour party (1). The remaining two seats were held by an independent Roman Catholic from Northern Ireland and by the speaker of the House, who is a Conservative but has no vote.

The Conservatives, discouraged by their showing, were expected to dump party leader Edward Heath after a decent interval. Heath was hampered during the campaign by popular identification of his government with the miner's strike and three-day work weeks endured by the country the previous winter.

Economic Crisis

The major campaign issue was Britain's spiraling cost of living, rising at the rate of 17 per cent annually. Wilson had claimed that his government could control inflation by means of its "social contract," a voluntary agreement under which labor unions would restrain wage demands. Conservatives, led by Heath, argued that this informal arrangement would be unworkable.

Prime Minister Harold Wilson and his wife received a new lease on 10 Downing Street— the official residence of Britain's head of government—after Wilson's Labour party won a narrow victory in general elections. Wilson became the first British prime minister in the 20th century to lead his party to victory in four nationwide elections.

British companies' gross profits declined by more than a third between the second half of 1973 and the first half of 1974, after stock appreciation due to inflation was deducted. In addition, business was caught in a liquidity squeeze. Inflation and price controls contributed to the difficulty many firms were having obtaining credit and bank loans. Ferranti Ltd., a large electrical and electronics group which is a major military contractor and employs 17,000 workers, was reported in financial straits for these reasons. News of Ferranti's problems helped drive down the British stock market, which hit a 16-year low on September 25.

Another large British enterprise, Court Line Ltd., had declared bankruptcy on August 15. The company was Britain's biggest package-tour agency, and 40,000 tourists stranded around the world had to be brought back to Britain in an emergency airlift. On June 26, the government had announced that it would nationalize Court Line's shipbuilding interests, as requested by the corporation.

Britain's large trade deficit was also a matter of concern. While the country usually runs the equivalent of a $247-million monthly surplus in "invisibles," (the sale of services such as financial transactions, tourism, and shipping), "visible" trade in goods showed a record monthly deficit in November of $1.23 billion.

The quadrupling of petroleum prices since October, 1973, contributed to the deficit, but a major trade gap had existed previously. In September, exports rose to a record high of $3.33 billion, while imports rose to $4.22 billion—the third highest figure ever. Oil accounted for $707 million of the imports.

The severity of inflation, the trade deficit, and other economic problems have aggravated preexisting tensions in British society. The middle class feels trapped between inflation, on one hand, and the militancy of the trade unions, on the other. The working class feels disadvantaged by the rigid class structure and by its inability to protect itself against inflation as successfully as the property-owning middle and upper classes. Conservatives worry about the political power of Communist-dominated or -influenced unions, and the inability of the government to cope with labor unrest.

All Britons have been touched by the

A Baker's Strike forced shoppers to scramble for diminishing supplies of bread. Workers feel disadvantaged by inflation and the rigid class structure, while all Britons have been touched by the country's fall in living standards relative to other Western nations.

country's fall in living standards relative to other Western nations. Once ranked behind only the United States and Sweden in terms of standard of living, Britain has fallen to "somewhat ahead of Italy and Greece," in the words of one prominent economist, and now relies on money from places like Iran and Kuwait to support the value of the pound sterling.

Labour's Legislative Program

On October 14, Prime Minister Wilson, in a television address to the nation, appealed for unity in the face of national economic crisis. He pledged that his government would not undertake any anti-inflation measures that would increase unemployment, already estimated at around 700,000.

At the same time, he announced that the government was reviewing the possibility of financial aid for corporations caught in the liquidity squeeze.

It was uncertain whether Wilson would be able to fulfill all of his party's campaign promises. Labour moderates were hoping that Wilson would cite his narrow parliamentary majority to avoid granting all the demands of the party's left wing, which included nationalization of several industries and a referendum on Common Market membership which could result in Britain's withdrawal from the EEC. But more pressing than these issues was maintenance of the voluntary agreement with labor that Wilson had stressed during the campaign as the only alternative to a "wages explosion."

At the opening of the new Parliament on October 29, Queen Elizabeth presented Labour's 26-bill package of legislative proposals. The new program included extension of nationalization to the shipbuilding and aircraft industries, formation of a new national oil corporation to insure a larger share for the government of profits from the North Sea oil fields being developed, and the establishment of a new board to oversee nationalization projects. Since members of some of the smaller parties were considered likely to vote with Labour, the Wilson program was expected to obtain approval.

The new agency for nationalization, the National Enterprise Board, would have authority to take a controlling interest in any company, following "agreement," and to provide advice and funds for businesses in trouble. It would also have power to start new businesses, either independently or in partnership with private industry. All major shipbuilding concerns were to be nationalized, pending negotiations on "fair compensation," but plans for government control of the aircraft industry were incomplete.

Scottish Nationalism

The Scottish National party's enlargement of its representation from 7 to 11 seats in the October election suggested that the development of North Sea oil fields off the Scottish coast was politicizing this economically depressed section of Great Britain. As in the past, most of Scotland's 71 elected members of Parliament adhered to the Conservative, Labour, or Liberal parties, but the new government's narrow majority gave the claims of smaller political groups more status.

Local autonomy, if not independence, is the goal of the SNP, which campaigned on the slogan "It's Scotland's Oil." The effectiveness of the SNP's challenge to the government in London was reflected in new planks in both the Conservative and Labour platforms, calling for a vaguely defined Scottish Assembly. The Conservatives also proposed a Scottish development fund, to be financed with oil revenues, and transfer of the oil division of the Department of Energy from London to Aberdeen.

In addition to a development agency for Scotland, Labour called for nationalization of the drilling platform sites, a British national oil corporation, and transfer of the oil-supplies office from London to Glasgow. (The Scots have long resented the concentration of government offices in remote London, feeling that their country's interests are being neglected.)

Other Scottish concerns include the formulation of a coherent, long-range oil production policy (the SNP models its proposals along the lines of Norway's successful precedent); the economic development of the region through the creation of petrochemical plants and other "land-based oil-related activities"; mitigating the harmful effects of future oil spills, and coping with a potential "Texanization" of Scotland resulting from the influx of U.S. technicians and oil capital.

IRA Outlawed

On November 25, the British government asked Parliament to approve emergency legislation outlawing the Irish Republican Army, giving the police sweeping powers of arrest and detention, and imposing new controls over travel between Great Britain and Ireland. Parliamentary support for the measure, which Home Secretary Roy Jenkins called "unprecedented in peacetime," was virtually unanimous.

The action followed the explosion, on November 21, of bombs in two crowded Birmingham pubs. Nineteen persons were killed and 184 were injured, the worst toll in a series of bombings that had struck Britain in the previous two years. Although the Irish Republican Army disclaimed responsibility for the Birmingham bombings, an IRA official had warned only two days earlier that bombings would be stepped up unless Britain agreed to withdraw its troops from Northern Ireland. Moreover, Birmingham police had angered IRA supporters by forbidding them to stage a funeral cortege for a man who blew himself up in a bomb attack on Coventry.

The IRA had been outlawed in the Republic of Ireland and Northern Ireland, but British officials had argued that banning the organization in Britain would merely drive its members underground and hamper the work of police. But the Birmingham bombings outraged public opinion and impelled the government to reverse its stand.

The legislation, which had a six-month time limit, empowered the government to declare other organizations illegal as well as the IRA. Members or persons supporting the outlawed organizations financially or "in other ways" could be sentenced to up to five years in jail. Police were given the authority to arrest suspected IRA terrorists or accomplices without a warrant and to hold them without charge for up to seven days. The home secretary was given the power to expel suspected IRA terrorists or refuse them entry into Britain. Immigration officers as well as the police would have the power to arrest, detain, and search suspects at airports and docks.

Bombs killed 19 people in two crowded Birmingham pubs on November 21—the worst toll in a series of bombings that had struck Britain during the previous two years. Parliament, in reaction, passed emergency legislation outlawing the Irish Republican Army.

Premier Constantine Caramanlis led his party to an overwhelming victory as Greece held its first free elections in more than a decade.

Greece. Premier Constantine Caramanlis won an overwhelming victory on November 17 as Greece held its first free elections in over a decade. Caramanlis had been acting premier since July 23, when the military government relinquished power to civilians following its disastrous handling of the Cyprus crisis (see GREECE in the third section.) His New Democratic party won an impressive 54 per cent of the vote and gained 220 of the 300 seats in the single-chamber parliament.

"Without bloodshed, without upheavals, and finally with the free expression of the will of the people," said the victorious Caramanlis, "democracy has returned to its birthplace."

Second place was garnered by the Center Union, a traditionally liberal antimonarchist party headed by George Mavros, the former foreign minister and deputy premier in Caramanlis' national-unity government. The Center Union party won 60 seats, with 20 per cent of the vote. Andreas Papandreou's Panhellenic Socialist Movement finished a weak third, with 14 per cent of the vote and only 12 seats.

The Communist party was allowed to campaign legally for the first time in three decades, but its strength proved minimal. Garnering only 9 per cent of the vote, the Communists won only 8 seats. The relatively poor showing for the left was seen as the result of internal policy squabbling and the fear of many voters that the election of a leftist government would precipitate another round of repression or possibly another military coup.

The campaign's two sticky issues were whether the monarchy would be reinstated, and what the government would do, if anything, to punish the Greek military leaders who ruled the country by fiat from 1967 to 1974. To defuse the emotional issue of King Constantine, who lives in exile in London, Caramanlis announced that a plebiscite would be held on December 8 on whether the monarch should return to his throne. Although Caramanlis was reported to oppose a restoration of the monarchy, he kept his thoughts to himself during the campaign.

Concerning retribution towards the military, Caramanlis had former president George Papadopoulos and four top aides arrested in an October dawn raid and exiled them to the Greek isle of Kea. To appease the military, though, Caramanlis was careful only to depose the top leaders and leave the officers' corps intact.

Monarchy Rejected

On December 8, Greeks voted by a decisive 2 to 1 margin to establish a republic and thereby end the monarchy which was installed 142 years ago. The commanding vote for what was called an "uncrowned democracy," ended both the transition period for the Greek government and the long debate on the emotion-charged issue, which had long plagued the country.

Calling on all Greeks to respect the decision of the referendum, Caramanlis said, "All must recognize that the uncertainty of the form of the government has been decisively eliminated." Speaking from London, the defeated Constantine said he prayed "that future developments may justify the outcome" of the vote.

Political observers had predicted that King Constantine, who had inherited the throne in 1964, 101 years after the House of Glucksburg was selected by the powers of Europe to rule Greece, would retain support in the provinces. But the final results revealed that the king had no major pockets of strength, a pattern which indicated that the traditional differences between rural and urban Greeks are diminishing in the age of television. In deciding to end the monarchy, voters expressed a belief that the institution was outdated, occasionally troublesome, and a vestige of the past which most would prefer abandoned.

Caramanlis' Plans

Premier Caramanlis' aides reported that he intended to propose reforms which would strengthen the premier's office and limit the president to a ceremonial role. A new constitution was expected to be adopted in spring of 1975, at which time a permanent president would be chosen.

On December 11, Caramanlis told the Greek people that they faced a year of austerity and sacrifice as his government battled the problems of inflation and stagnant industrial growth. Inflation had been cut to an annual rate of 15 per cent, but there would be no economic growth for 1974, and production would possibly fall even below the 1973 level.

The premier said his government's measures would require "pain and sacrifice from all Greeks and mostly from the well-to-do classes," who faced an increase in tax rates, primarily to finance a modernization of the armed forces. He said the government was examining technicalities involved in withdrawing Greek troops from NATO and was reviewing the status of U.S. military installations in the country. Caramanlis expressed the hope that Greece would receive full membership in the European Economic Community, making the country less dependent on the United States.

No to Monarchy. Exiled King Constantine lost his bid to return to his throne when Greek voters decisively rejected the monarchy in a plebiscite. Constantine, shown in London with former queen Anne-Marie, expressed the royal family's desire to return to Greece as private citizens.

HOUSE PLANTS

The windows of houses, apartments, and stores all bear testimony to the increasing popularity of house plants. Most windows do not have just a single pot in the center of the window sill, but a whole row of pots, with more hanging from the top. Plants are used as decorations in the lobbies of banks, apartment houses, and office buildings, and they serve as status symbols inside the private offices of the highest corporation executives.

Plant "boutiques" are opening. Corporations are acquiring seed companies and adding plants and garden equipment to their lists of diversified enterprises. Books about plants are earning more money for their publishers than ever before. There are television programs about plants, plant-of-the-month clubs, and studies on the psychology of plant buying.

San Francisco police report that there are even "plantnappers"—people who steal plants to add to their own collections at home. Any type of plant may be the victim, from a 10-foot-high palm to a tiny succulent. Plants have been taken from such diverse places as botanical gardens, highway medians, corner parks, and bars.

Reasons for Growing

It seems to be important to many people to have something that is growing and living in a time when there is great attention paid to death and dying. Green plants provide an antidote to the urban world of concrete and exhaust fumes. This is literally true, since plants give off oxygen as a product of the chemical changes that go on in their cells, and figuratively true, since their green color contrasts with the prevalent gray of the city.

One owner of a plant store in New York City, who was not worried by the competition of all the other plant stores around,

pointed to the street choked with traffic and said, "Look, you see that out there? There's enough business out there for everybody."

The ecology movement and the "back to the land and the simple life" philosophy is certainly a stimulus to the great interest shown in plants. Not everyone can leave the city, but everyone can have a philodendron. Of course, some people do not want what everyone can have. One storeowner says that with professional people, "Kentia plants are hot right now, because they are scarce and expensive at $100 to $300 apiece. That lends prestige."

The question of how people choose which plants to buy has intrigued both plant sellers and psychologists. They say that, consciously or subconsciously, people choose plants to match their personalities. According to the storeowner quoted above, while professional people like tall plants with strong lines, hippies go for offbeat plants like jades and 12-leafed flowering apostles. Little old ladies, predictably, like traditionally romantic plants such as lilies of the valley or African violets. Jet-setters want elegant plants like orchids. Middle-class homeowners choose spider plants, grape ivy, and asparagus ferns, all solid, inexpensive plants—"the frozen food of the plant world."

Plant Boutiques

Since the early 1970's, many small plant stores have opened for business. They often have catchy names, for example, Fancy Plants, Happy Plants, The Plant Palace, Bloomin' Jungle, and Horticulture Holiday. The Plant Orphanage puts an "adoption certificate" on each of its plants, with a message like: "My name is Chester. I am a foundling. Please take care of me."

Mother Earth, in Hollywood, is said to have been the first plant "boutique." It features a "jungle"—a miniature rain forest with the fragrance of 1,000 tropical plants, rock music, and incense. The owners, Lynn and Joel Rapp, publish a weekly newsletter on their customers and their plants, offer classes on plant care, and have a plant-of-the-month club. They say they won't sell a plant to a customer who they feel will not take care of it. "If the customer is a hysterical type and her kids

are climbing all over your legs," says Lynn, "you can tell she isn't going to take care of a plant." The Rapps have also written *Mother Earth's Hassle-Free Indoor Plant Book,* one of the large number of books on the market with advice for plant growers.

Other stores have added plants to their original stock. A store in Cambridge, Massachusetts, has a sign saying "Beer & Wine" in large letters, with "Potted Plants" below as an afterthought. Beer and wine are in the back, and the plants have taken over the display window and the front half of the store.

Many storeowners are concerned with advising their customers on what types of plants to choose. They ask what the customer wants, what direction his or her windows face, and whether the plants will be in a draft or near potentially harmful heaters.

Others tell their customers to "read a book" for advice. One plant seller says that his customers "know more than us anyway. They come in here, they look under the leaves—I don't even know what they think they're looking for."

Corporations Move In

Forbes magazine reports that the profit-making potential of the plant industry, with markups of 50 to 300 per cent, has attracted several large corporations, including International Telephone & Telegraph, General Foods, Upjohn, Pillsbury, and United Brands. Six billion dollars are spent each year in the United States on plants, seeds, fertilizer, tools, and garden furniture. The annual growth rate of the industry is 6.5 per cent. Backyard gardeners make up a market estimated at 31 million households, nearly half the households in the country.

House Plants. Shown on the opposite page, left to right, top to bottom, are the following: rubber plant; lady palm; wandering jew; Peruvian cereus cactus; dragon tree; pineapple plant; tobira, or Japanese Pittosporum; jade plant; Norfolk Island pine; Boston fern; and peperomia. Plant sellers and psychologists say that, consciously or subconsciously, people choose plants to match their personalities.

The corporations figure they can make big profits by concentrating on the fastest-growing segments of the industry and by using their size and power to push aside smaller competitors. Currently, the plant industry is characterized by small businesses; in the corporations' language, the industry is "fragmented." Thousands of local garden clubs sell plants, and of the 20,000 florists in the United States, 12,000 gross only $500 a week or less.

Corporate ventures into the plant-selling business are on a much larger scale. For example, Green Giant, the food-processing company, had plans for a chain of 200 "garden centers" when it opened its first one in Minneapolis in 1972. But big plans were not enough; business suffered because the salespeople did not have the necessary training to inspire the confidence of the plant buyers.

The "garden center" chain stores are like supermarkets, selling everything from house plants to bird feeders. Campbell Soup's Lexington Garden Centers even have little red wagons for the customers to load their purchases.

Frank's Nursery Sales is a publicly owned retailer that has already proven itself successful. The main problem this chain has is seasonal sales—people don't buy garden equipment in the winter. The solution was to shift to Christmas decorations, but the energy crisis in 1973 meant that people didn't buy many lights either. Frank's lost $93,000 in the fourth quarter of 1973, but it still showed an overall profit of $1.1 million on sales of $37 million. The company is buying five of Green Giant's six stores.

Pillsbury is doing well with its flower-selling kiosks in supermarkets, shopping malls, and airports. Pillsbury runs the kiosks, and the owner of the space collects a percentage of the sales. The only problem is getting growers to supply all the plants and flowers that are needed.

Stratford of Texas, a public-owned agribusiness company, entered the business at the growing level. It grows stock in Guatemala and delivers it to the shopkeeper's door. Executive vice president Peter Knudtzon says, "Our bread and butter is a little philodendron in a three-inch pot

Plant Supermarket. This Chicago-area store offers an array of house plants and garden equipment. The profit-making potential of the plant industry has attracted several large corporations.

Windows of a "Plant Freak." Some people favor certain types, such as cacti or ferns; others want to grow a little of everything.

that we sell for 35 cents. The chain store sells it for 69 cents; the florist sells it for $1."

General Foods, Purex, Upjohn, and IT&T have acquired seed companies. Although the total size of the market for garden seeds is a relatively small $100 million, the annual growth rate is 20 per cent.

Then there are the bigger projects, such as Bill Cagle's "condo-garden" concept. Cagle, an established condominium builder, invested $200,000 in the first condo-garden, near Mobile, Alabama. The land cost him $2,000 an acre. For a price of $1,300 to $2,000, the purchaser gets a lot for a garden, the services of a professional caretaker, and the use of the condominium's tools, wells, canning kitchen, and roadside stand for selling vegetables. Cagle advertizes the condo-garden as a "real money-saver."

Garden Way Associates plans to develop 100-acre housing projects that feature large community gardens instead of the usual golf course or tennis courts. The self-sufficient "Garden Way" of life is its sales slogan. The company already markets everything that could be needed for this lifestyle, including windmills selling for $5,000.

Plant Societies

Another section of the fragmented plant industry is made up of local and national plant societies. The names of some of the groups show the wide variety represented: The American Gloxinia and Gesneriad Society, The Bonsai Society of Greater New York, The Cactus & Succulent Society, The Indoor Light Gardening Society of America, The National Fuschia Society, and The American Orchid Society.

Such groups exist for almost every type of plant, especially the exotic varieties. Very popular plants have more than one society; for example, there are at least three societies in the Untied States devoted to the culture of the African violet and its relatives.

The societies offer, for an annual fee between $5 and $10, monthly or bi-monthly publications with advice for both new growers and experts, discounts on horticultural books, tickets to plant shows, and the opportunity to buy unusual plant seeds at low prices. The meetings also give growers a chance to meet other plant fanciers and exchange tips.

"The whole idea of plant societies," writes Charles M. Fitch in a journal called *Plants Alive*, "is to help people get more pleasure from growing plants by introducing them to new plants, helpful techniques, and other enthusiastic growers."

Sometimes meetings feature speakers with plant travelogues, slide shows of trips to countries, or gardens with unusual plants. Exposure to new varieties stimulates growers to want to try them out. Nurseries often work with plant societies, bringing seedlings to sell at meetings, with a percentage going to the society.

In many cities, garden clubs combine forces to hold annual public sales, thereby attracting more potential members as well as earning money. The annual two-day Garden Mart in Erie, Pennsylvania, held just before Memorial Day, earns between $200 and $500 for each participating club.

Best-Selling Books

The craze for plants is also reflected in the book-publishing industry. Almost every publisher has at least one book out on how to grow plants. This has become a major trend in the past two years; before that, says *Publisher's Weekly,* a publisher would have laughed at the idea of a book on house plants being a best-seller.

The most successful book has been *The Secret Life of Plants,* by Peter Tompkins and Christopher Bird. This book reports on many experiments designed to show that plants respond to stimuli in the world around them; it attempts to demonstrate

Thalassa Cruso, TV authority on plants

a mystical interconnection among all life. It appeals not only to plant lovers but also to those caught up in the current interest in psychic phenomena.

Sales of more mundane books, like the *Woman's Day Book of House Plants,* first published in 1965, have also thrived recently. In 1973, 57,830 copies of the book were sold, almost equalling the total sales for the years between 1965 and 1973.

Thalassa Cruso has a regular television program with tips on caring for plants. Her book, *Making Things Grow Indoors,* was an alternate selection for the Book-of-the-Month Club. (The sequel, *Making Things Grow Outdoors,* has not sold as well.)

Jack Kramer, author of *1000 Beautiful House Plants,* has written dozens of books on growing specific kinds of plants. He wrote his first book, *Growing Orchids at Your Windows,* in 1961 because he had been unable to find any advice when he began to grow the flowers.

Plants Are Like People, by Jerry Baker, advocates talking to plants to help them grow. Many plant owners seem to enjoy doing just that. One plant seller says people "used to buy plants because they looked pretty. Now they want genuine involvement with them." A woman, asked why she had taken up indoor gardening, says now that her sons are grown up and have moved away, the plants "give me something to mother. They make me feel needed."

Caring for Plants

Most people agree that caring for plants is basically a matter of common sense. The most important factors are how much light and water the particular plant needs.

But if the plants become sick, help can be found. Plant doctors, many of whom have degrees in horticulture or agriculture, make house calls for an average of $15 and will "plant sit" for about $10 a day. In Hartford, Connecticut, ailing plants can recover at the Mother Earth Hospital. In Boston, Plant Parenthood offers a version of health insurance for plants.

Often the trouble turns out to be a simple matter of too much water and fertilizer lavished on the plant by its devoted owner.

Israel. See MIDDLE EAST.

Japan. Takeo Miki, a surprise compromise choice, was designated to be premier of Japan on December 2 by the ruling Liberal-Democratic party, which commands majorities in both houses of the Diet, or parliament. He succeeded Kakuei Tanaka, who resigned November 26 after only 28 months in office.

The popularity of Tanaka, a self-made millionaire, had sunk from a record 62 per cent when he took office to a record low of 16 per cent. Japan was suffering from a recession, and from a 25-per-cent annual rate of inflation.

The final blow for Tanaka was a 61-page exposé published by a monthly magazine that revealed he had accumulated $10-million worth of homes and villas while a public servant. It exposed his financial dealings through dummy corporations, secret bank accounts, incomplete tax statements, and the use of vast amounts of money to buy support within the Liberal-Democratic party. He clung to office just long enough to welcome President Ford to Japan during Ford's Far Eastern tour. (See UNITED STATES in this section.)

Takeo Miki, a surprise compromise choice, was designated premier of Japan. Miki pledged to make reform of the ruling Liberal-Democratic party a priority item.

The New Premier

The 67-year-old Miki was a last-minute compromise selection, chosen behind closed doors by party leaders who concluded that the designation of either of the leading candidates, Masayoshi Ohira and Takeo Fukuda, could split the party. Miki's selection was ratified the next day by the Liberal-Democratic members of the Diet, and he was formally elected by the Diet on December 9.

Miki, who had served in the parliament for 37 years, had long called for party reform—open election of premiers, control over gathering and spending political funds, revision of the electoral system, and the elimination of highly organized factions within the Liberal-Democratic party. The party is in fact a loose coalition of factions amply funded by business interests.

Miki opposed the war with the United States and thus escaped the post-World War II occupation purge, which sent many Japanese politicians into oblivion.

He had held nine cabinet posts, including foreign minister, at various times, but had broken with the last four premiers over one issue or another. He had the advantage of a clean reputation and had pledged to make party reform a priority item, but was not considered a man of action. *Newsweek* called him "the Gerald Ford of Japan."

The new premier hardly benefited from a newspaper interview with his wife, who called him "that man" and portrayed him as clumsy and absent-minded. "That man hardly knows how to wash his own face properly," she said. "He'll stand upright over the wash basin and splash water all over while fully dressed."

Miki's first act was to allot cabinet posts among the various rival party factions. Ohira kept his post as finance minister, while Fukuda was named deputy premier and head of the Economic Planning Agency.

Economic Woes

The Japanese economy was being squeezed by the fourfold increase in oil

prices imposed in late 1973 by the Organization of Petroleum Exporting Countries (OPEC). Japan, the world's leading oil importer, imports all its petroleum and gets a large proportion from the Middle East. Fearful of offending the oil producers, the government had adopted a pro-Arab foreign policy, and Japanese officials said publicly that the government would not join the U.S. effort to restrict oil consumption and thus bring down the OPEC-set price level. (See ENERGY in this section.)

The Japanese also feared that, despite U.S. assurances, President Ford might impose export controls on foodstuffs in order to keep food prices from rising at home. (Nixon had restricted soybean exports for a brief period in 1973.) The threat of food export controls was of serious concern since Japan does not feed itself and imports about $2.6-billion worth of foodstuffs a year from the United States. Another irritant to U.S.-Japanese relations was the cancellation, under pressure from U.S. environmental groups, of plans by a Japanese firm to purchase coal from Montana strip mines.

Consumer prices in Japan rose 25 per cent between October, 1973, and October, 1974—the highest inflation rate of the world's major nations. Tokyo, Osaka, and Kobe are the world's three costliest cities for foreign residents, based on international living standards.

The economic growth rate had dropped from 11 per cent in 1972 to an estimated near-zero figure for 1974. Business bankruptcies reached a new high in October. The new premier was on record as saying that the economy would have to be adjusted from high growth and reliance on exports to improvement of the quality of life. (Congested traffic, substandard housing, and air and water pollution are major problems in Japan's crowded cities.)

A new feature of Japanese life was the increased frequency, length, and seriousness of strikes by a newly aroused labor force. Lifetime employment is the custom

among Japan's paternalistic businesses, but unemployment, previously below 1 per cent, had reached 1.7 per cent. (The figure is deceptively low because labor statistics do not count the self-employed, employees of family businesses, seasonal workers, or day laborers.)

Nuclear-Arms Controversy

Testimony before Congress by a retired U.S. admiral to the effect that American warships were routinely entering Japanese ports with nuclear weapons aboard raised a storm of controversy in Japan during October. Rear Admiral Gene La Rocque had testified: "Any ship that is capable of carrying nuclear weapons carries nuclear weapons . . . . they normally keep them on board ship at all times."

As the only nation to suffer nuclear attack, Japan has pledged not to manufacture nuclear weapons and opposes the introduction of such weapons to its territory. Under the bilateral security treaty, the United States is allowed to maintain bases and other facilities in Japan, but many Japanese charged that the entry of U.S. vessels bearing nuclear weapons would be a violation of the treaty.

A U.S. government statement did not deny that American nuclear weapons had been brought into Japan but merely restated the terms of a 1960 joint agreement, to the effect that the temporary entry into Japan of U.S. nuclear weapons would not constitute a "major change" of forces and equipment and thus would not be subject to prior consultation, as provided for under the security treaty. The New York *Times* reported that a secret 1969 U.S. government memorandum had stated there was a U.S.-Japanese agreement permitting the United States to bring nuclear weapons into Japan temporarily but not to deploy them there. However, Foreign Minister Toshio Kimura denied the existence of such an agreement.

The nuclear issue played a large part in rallies organized by the Communist and Socialist parties and major labor unions to protest Ford's visit and the U.S.-Japanese alliance. More than 2 million people were said to have participated in 465 rallies held throughout the country on October 21.

Tokyo's Main Street, the Ginza, welcomed President Ford with a flag display. Economic questions dominate U.S.-Japanese relations.

Best-Selling Books

FICTION

Centennial, by James Michener
Something Happened, by Joseph Heller
The Seven-Per-Cent Solution,
  by Nicholas Meyer
The Pirate, by Harold Robbins
Tinker, Tailor, Soldier, Spy
  by John le Carre
The Ebony Tower, by John Fowles

NONFICTION

All Things Bright and Beautiful,
  by James Herriot
The Palace Guard, by Dan Rather and
  Gary Paul Gates
The Bermuda Triangle,
  by Charles Berlitz
Strictly Speaking, by Edwin Newman
A Bridge Too Far, by Cornelius Ryan
Tales of Power, by Carlos Castaneda

Literature. Among the books published during the last quarter of 1974 were the following:

Fiction

Dog Soldiers, by Robert Stone. Greed and corruption are the themes of this talented novelist's tale of heroin smuggled to the States by Americans in Vietnam. The three kilograms of "scag" become a metaphor for the evil effects of American involvement in the war. (Houghton Mifflin—$8.95)

The Ebony Tower, by John Fowles. Five stories by the author of *The French Lieutenant's Woman* bring to mind recurrent themes from his earlier works. (Little, Brown—$7.95)

Guilty Pleasures, by Donald Barthelme. This collection of parodies and other satirical pieces exposes absurdity in literature, politics, and other aspects of contemporary life. (Farrar, Straus & Giroux—$7.95)

Hot to Trot, by John Lahr. George Melish, a TV producer, is the "nicest guy" his wife knows, so why has she left him to sleep with a rock star he himself developed? Sexism, liberation, open marriage, and "the good life" are themes of this comic novel, and the author successfully maintains a light touch. (Knopf—$6.95)

Something Happened, by Joseph Heller. After 13 years, the author of *Catch-22* comes through with a new work, a despairing account of a man's worries, pain, vulnerability, guilt, and bad memories. (Knopf—$10)

Tattoo, by Earl Thompson. A poor Kansas boy grows to troubled manhood in this powerfully told autobiographical novel. (Putnam—$8.95)

Winter in the Blood, by James Welch. Indians in Montana are portrayed without sentimentality (and without much hope for the future) by the author, who is himself an Indian. (Harper & Row—$6.95)

Nonfiction

All God's Dangers: The life of Nate Shaw, edited by Theodore Rosengarten. Hailed as one of the greatest of American autobiographies, this work is the story of Nate Shaw, an illiterate black tenant cotton farmer in Alabama who died in 1973 at the age of 88. Recorded on tape were his recollections of former slaves and slaveholders, his fight to organize sharecroppers, and his 12 years in jail for resisting an assault by white deputy sheriffs. (Knopf—$10)

Babe: The Legend Comes to Life, by Robert W. Creamer. Anecdotes about the mighty Babe Ruth bring this man of gargantuan appetites back to life as a human being rather than as an "inspiration" to the boys of America. (Simon & Schuster—$9.95)

Badmen of the West, by Robert Elman. Hollywood to the contrary, the fastest guns in the West were often "fast" only in the sense that their owners drew them before the idea even occurred to the other fellow. "Heroes" like Wyatt Earp, Doc Holliday, and Wild Bill Hickok were in fact the vicious products of the lawless frontier—where lives were typically nasty, short, and brutish. (Ridge Press/Pound—$14.95)

Billion Dollar Baby, by Bob Greene. A newspaper columnist who went on tour with Alice Cooper and his rock'n'roll group tells what it was like in an account that suggests the audiences Out There are far sicker than the performers. (Atheneum—$10)

A Bridge Too Far, by Cornelius Ryan. The chronicler of D-Day this time describes the complicated, tragic Battle of Arnhem, an Allied failure that, if it had succeeded, could have ended the war in Europe six months earlier. (Simon & Schuster—$12.50)

Comanches: The Destruction of a People by T. R. Fehrenbach. The Comanches proficiently exploited the horse once the Spaniards introduced it to America, became the most successful Plains hunters, and ferociously resisted the territorial expansion of the white man; in the minds of many settlers they represented the untamable savagery of the American Indian. Eventually they fell victim to Ranald S. Mackenzie—now forgotten but perhaps the best Indian fighter in the West—

Babe Ruth, the sultan of swat, is recalled in *Babe: The Legend Comes to Life*, by Robert W. Creamer.

and his Negro "buffalo" soldiers. (Knopf—$12.50)

Great Times, by J. C. Furnas. The events and personalities—both large and small—that filled the 15 years between the outbreak of the Great War and the start of the Great Depression are recorded in an informal, witty, and absorbing narrative. The account is a worthy continuation of the story begun in the author's *The Americans*, which described the years from the Lost Colony of Roanoke to 1914. (Putnam—$15)

Helter Skelter: The True Story of the Manson Murders, by Curt Gentry. Every gory detail of the depredations of the Manson "family" is told (or retold) in this account by the prosecutor, who scores what he regards as the incompetence of the Los Angeles Police Department. (Norton—$10)

Notes on the Old System, by Marcus Raskin. Raskin, who once served on the staff of the National Security Council, argues that Watergate was the result of America's 20th century imperial expansion. He urges the establishment of congressional grand juries functioning on the community level to bring people into closer contact with the system. (McKay—$6.95)

Supership, by Noël Mostert. This account of a journey on a supertanker warns that their hasty design and deployment almost guaran-tee frequent breakups and massive oil spillages which could soon lead to ecological disaster for marine life. (Knopf—$8.95)

Surviving the Long Night, by Sir Geoffrey Jackson. The former British ambassador to Uruguay, captured and held for ransom by revolutionary guerrillas, describes how he kept himself from going crazy while living for eight months under conditions of sensory deprivation in a cell no bigger than a modest-sized bathroom. (Vanguard Press—$7.95)

The Workhouse, by Norman Longmate. The Victorian workhouse was a house of horrors in an age that treated poverty as a kind of damnation and lumped together as "paupers" infants, children, the elderly, the infirm, the insane, and the delinquent. Its abuses, though combated by a small number of dedicated men and women, were defeated only by a change in society's thinking. (St. Martin's Press—$8.95)

Literature for Children

Picture Books and Easy-to-Read Books

Can You Find the Animal? by Wilda Ross, pictures by John Hamberger. As children hunt for the wild creatures hiding in these realistic illustrations, they will discover how animals use camouflage for survival. (Coward—$4.49)

City of Gold, by Fiona French. Two brothers set out to fight the demon who threatens the wonderful golden city. Magnificent, colorful illustrations highlight their exciting adventures. (Walck—$7.95)

Dawn, by Uri Shulevitz. Evocative text and pictures portray the mysteries of the night and the coming of an everyday miracle to an old man and his grandson. (Farrar—$5.95)

Hulda, by Carol Svendsen, pictures by Julius Svendsen. Even the bold Vikings were terrified by Hulda's terrible tantrums. It took a troll to tame her! (Houghton—$5.95)

In a Forest of Flowers, by Iris Schweitzer. Lost in towering flowers, two tiny creatures watch funny, scary, exciting happenings before they find their way home. (Putnam—$5.29)

Lyle Finds His Mother, by Bernard Waber. When lovable Lyle sets out to find his crocodile mother, rollicking adventures follow. (Houghton—$5.95)

Merry-Go-Riddle, by Ann Bishop, pictures by Jerry Warshaw. For all young puzzle fans is this amusing collection of riddles old and new. (Albert Whitman—$3.25)

Owlet, The Great Horned Owl, by Irene

Brady. One shivery morning, a baby owl was born. His exciting, funny, and dangerous adventures as he grows into an adult great horned owl will fascinate young scientists. (Houghton—$4.95)

Sunlight, by Sally Cartwright, illustrated by Marylin Hafner. A sparkling invitation to young readers to make their own discoveries about sunlight. (Coward—$4.97)

A Toad for Tuesday, by Russell E. Erickson, pictures by Lawrence Di Fiori. When Warton the toad skis out to visit his old aunt, he meets a dangerous enemy and defeats him with a surprising and heart-warming weapon. (Lothrop—$4.25)

What's Good for a Three-Year-Old? by William Cole, illustrated by Lillian Hoban. Flashlights, pillow fights, jumping on beds, sliding on sleds, and many other delightful things are presented in joyous text and pictures. (Holt—$4.95)

Where Are You, Jason? by Greta Matus. Every child who sometimes wants a private place will enjoy Jason's ingenious hiding places. (Lothrop—$4.50)

Willis, by James Marshall. An unusual bird, snake, and lobster help Willis solve his problem in hilarious fashion. (Houghton—$5.95)

Fiction (8 to 12 Years Old)

Coyote Tales, adapted by Hettie Jones. Coyote, the trickster, is both villain and hero in these fascinating American Indian folk tales. (Holt—$4.95)

Hey-How for Halloween! selected by Lee Bennett Hopkins. Ghosts, goblins, and witches on broomsticks weave an eerie, enchanting spell in this delightful collection of poems. (Harcourt—$4.75)

A Home with Aunt Florry, by Charlene Joy Talbot. Wendy and Jason make startling discoveries when they come to live with a stranger aunt in an old warehouse. (Atheneum—$7.25)

The Hunting Trail, by Ester Wier. A young coyote learns how to survive in the wilderness in this authentically detailed story. (Walck—$5.95)

Libby Shadows a Lady, by Catherine Woolley. Impulsive Libby rushes headlong into danger when a mysterious phone call leads her to a kidnapping. (Morrow—$5.50)

The Liberation of Clementine Tipton, by Jane Flory. In 1876, the country was celebrating its hundredth birthday in Philadelphia with a splendid International Centennial Exposition—but nobody expected Clementine to celebrate her independence at the same time. (Houghton—$5.95)

Mystery of the Melting Snowman, by Florence Parry Heide and Roxanne Heide. Why would anybody hide an iron dog inside a snowman? Jay, Dexter, and Cindy find themselves in humorous predicaments as they try to solve the mystery. (Albert Whitman—$3.95)

Penalty Killer, by Sheldon Ilowite. Mark from Canada fights to prove himself to his American teammates in this swifty paced hockey story. (Hastings—$4.95)

The Return of the Great Brain, by John D. Fitzgerald. Can the Great Brain reform from his swindling ways? Here are hilarious misadventures to answer the doubters. (Dial—$5.95)

Sailing to Cythera, by Nancy Willard. Anatole journeys to a land where the merry-go-rounds never stop playing, to the house of the sun, and into a magical country through the wallpaper in these fantastical adventures. (Harcourt—$5.95)

Sore Loser, by Genevieve Gray. When a new boy in town gets a reputation as a sore loser, he needs all his courage to meet the challenge. (Houghton—$4.95)

Stiff Ears, by Alex Whitney. Entertaining legends from the Hopi, Pawnee, Chippewa, and other tribes of American Indians. (Walck—$4.95)

The Toothpaste Millionaire, by Jean Merrill. Though Rufus was a genius who had strange ideas of how to run a business, he didn't expect to become a millionaire at 12 years of age. But he did! (Houghton—$5.95)

Trouble on Treat Street, by Anne Alexander. Chicano Manolo and Black Clem hated each other from their first meeting—but when they had to face danger together, they made a surprising discovery. (Atheneum—$5.95)

Walk Together Children, by Ashley Bryan. A rich collection of black spirituals that are part of the heritage of all Americans. (Atheneum—$6.95)

The Yellow Airplane, by William Mayne. Where did the mysterious yellow airplane come from and where did it go? As English Rodney finds the answers, he also finds new friends. (Nelson—$4.95)

Nonfiction (8 to 12 Years Old)

Be a Smart Shopper, by Kathlyn Gay. A lively and clear introduction to wise consumerism for young readers. (Messner—$5.95)

Between the Devil and the Sea, the Life of James Forten, by Brenda A. Johnston. The inspiring biography of a free black man who fought for freedom for all blacks in the days of the American Revolution. (Harcourt—$6.75)

Nine True Dolphin Stories, by Margaret Davidson. Entertaining and factual adventures of clever and unpredictable dolphins. (Hastings—$4.95)

The Special World of the Artisan, by Frederick J. Pratson. Dramatic photographs and vivid text will help young readers gain insight into the world of the potter, glass blower, weaver, and other artisans. (Houghton—$5.95)

Fiction (10 to 14 Years Old)

A *Billion for Boris,* by Mary Rodgers. When Annabel and Boris come into possession of a TV set that can project the future, they are on their way to making a million—or are they? (Harper—$4.95)

A Dance to Still Music, by Barbara Corcoran. Runaway Margaret had been deaf for a year, and she still could not reconcile herself to a world of silence. Then she met Josie and discovered a new world. (Atheneum—$6.95)

The Devil's Storybook, by Natalie Babbitt. A tantalizing collection of stories about the devil, who sometimes wins—and sometimes loses—his battle with humankind. (Farrar—$4.95)

The Edge of Next Year, by Mary Stolz. A sensitive growing-up story of a boy who had to deal with a death in his family and the changes it caused. (Harper—$6.95)

My Pretty Girl, by Bianca Bradbury. All Shannon knew about horses was that they had four legs, but that didn't stop her from acquiring a jumper and trying to keep it in her housing development. (Houghton—$4.95)

Ruth Crane, by Alison Morgan. Rebellious Ruth resented the new responsibilities thrust upon her when her mother was hurt, but but when her young brother ran away, she knew that she must follow him. (Harper—$5.95)

Songs of the Chippewa, adapted by John Bierhorst. A rhythmic collection of dream songs, medicine charms, and lullabies of the American Indian that both soloists and group singers will enjoy. (Farrar—$6.95)

The Way Things Are and Other Poems, by Myra Cohn Livingston. Thought-provoking poems that reflect the doubts, the questions, and the laughter of today's young people. (Atheneum—$4.95)

Witch of the Cumberlands, by Mary Jo Stephens. An eerie tale of a prophecy that came true and helped solve an ancient mystery. (Houghton—$4.95)

Nonfiction (10 to 14 Years Old)

Black Women of Valor, by Olive Burt. Swiftly paced biographies of Juliette Derricotte, social worker; Maggie Mitchell Walker, banker; Ida Wells Barnett, journalist; Septima Poinsette Clark, educator; and other black women who have made their mark on history. (Messner—$6.25)

Model Cars and Trucks and How to Build

Them, by Harvey Weiss. Clear and specific text, diagrams, and photographs initiate young craftsmen in making model cars of their own. (Crowell—$5.50)

Ride Your Pony Right, by Frederick L. Devereux, Jr. Beginning riders will welcome this step-by-step introduction into pony care and horsemanship. The explicit photographs are invaluable learning aids. (Dodd—$4.95)

The Town of Hercules, by Joseph Jay Deiss. As fascinating as fiction is this account of the rediscovery of a buried city and what it revealed of the way people lived centuries ago. (Houghton—$5.95)

Treasure Hunting, by Arnold Madison. Did you ever find buried treasure? Here is an invitation to go hunting for treasure of many kinds and find fun—and maybe fortune. (Hawthorn—$6.95)

You've Come a Long Way, Sybil Macintosh, by Charlotte Herman. An outrageously funny, but informative book on how to act in every kind of situation. Boys and girls will enjoy this very different kind of book on manners. (O'Hara—$3.95)

Zooming In, by Barbara J. Wolberg, photographs by Dr. Lewis R. Wolberg. The startling world revealed by the microscope is dramatized in astonishing photographs and vivid captions. (Harcourt—$7.75)

Fiction (Teen-age)

Cross-Country Runner, by Leon McClinton. When Vern, a football star, turns his back on the sport and goes out for cross-country running, his father, his girl, the whole school, and even the cross-country coach think he is a quitter. (Dutton—$6.95)

The Forgotten Beasts of Eld, by Patricia A. McKillip. Sybel, daughter of a wizard, had strange powers over fantastic beasts, and this led her into a strange danger, a danger that threatened more than life itself. (Atheneum—$7.25)

Gentle Like a Cyclone, Stories of Horses and Their Riders, selected by Phyllis R. Fenner. Eight stories of horses—and their riders—that will be difficult for any reader to forget. (Morrow—$5.95)

The Girl in the Grove, by David Severn. A girl ghost from the past almost ruins the future for a modern girl and boy. (Harper—$5.95)

Guarneri, by Leonard Wibberley. Based on fact is this tale of the tortured genius and master violin maker. (Farrar—$5.95)

Hot & Cold Running Cities, compiled by Georgess McHargue. A provocative collection of science-fiction stories that challenge our views of an urban future. (Holt—$6.50)

The Jargoon Pard, by Andre Norton. The belt with the strange stone had magical powers that led Kethan on a strange trail, a trail he walked on four paws! (Atheneum—$6.95)

Of Nightingales That Weep, by Katherine Paterson. Takiko was a daughter of a samurai of old Japan, and her heritage was courage. Would it help her meet the challenge of war and disaster? (Crowell—$5.95)

Pennington's Heir, by K. M. Peyton. A wry and perceptive story of a young genius who had to make a career, a new wife, and a new son all work in harness. (Crowell—$5.50)

The Rare One, by Pamela Rogers. Toby had family trouble and school trouble and no escape route until he met a remarkable old man. (Nelson—$4.95)

Stone of Terror, by Margaret Greaves. Did black magic rule the island? Philip of the 17th century fought to find out and save a girl witch. (Harper—$4.95)

Nonfiction (Teen-age)

Green Treasures, Adventures in the Discovery of Edible Plants, by Charles Morrow Wilson. A provocative and timely book that celebrates the plants that supply much of our food and other needs, and the lives of the plant hunters who discovered these plants. But it also warns us to preserve our plant heritage. (Macrae Smith—$5.50)

Metric Power, by Richard Deming. A comprehensive introduction into the history of the metric system, how it works, and the part it will play in our measuring future. (Nelson—$5.95)

Presenting the Marching Band, by Vincent Scuro. With a roll of drums and a clash of cymbals, the band marches by—and you'd like to be part of it. Here is a graphic guide to help you do just that! (Dodd—$4.95)

Six Days to Saturday, by Jack Newcombe. With the active participation of Joe Paterno and Penn State, here in lively text and on-the-scene photos is the authentic record of the six-days planning and work that precede each Saturday's university football game. (Farrar—$6.95)

Street Gangs, Yesterday and Today, by James Haskins. A realistic, hard-hitting survey of the growth and passing of street gangs throughout our country's history—and an appraisal of gangs of today. (Hastings—$6.95)

The Teenage Chess Book, by Reuben Fine. A clear and lively introduction to chess by a chess grandmaster at playing—and teaching. (McKay—$5.95)

You and the Metric System, by Allan C. Stover. How measurement developed, how the metric system evolved, and how to use the metric system are presented entertainingly and graphically in this book. (Dodd—$4.50)

MEDICINE

One of the fastest-growing specialties in medicine in the 1970's is the identification and treatment of genetic diseases. In the past 10 years, a great amount of information about hereditary ailments has been discovered. Genetics has been a part of the medical-school curriculum for about the same length of time. Progress is being made so rapidly that many doctors are not aware of the latest research and methods of treatment available for genetic diseases.

Genetic diseases occur more often than is generally realized. In the United States, about one baby in 14 is born with some type of genetic disorder. According to the National Foundation-March of Dimes, about 6 million Americans have imperfect organ systems due to genetic errors. Genetic mistakes afflict 2.9 million with mental retardation, 1 million with congenital bone, muscle, or joint diseases, 750,000 with impaired hearing, and 500,000 with complete or partial blindness.

About 2,000 ailments have been traced to mistakes in the genes or chromosomes. Some are extremely rare, some are fatal, and some are common and present no great problems to those afflicted. Among the less serious genetic errors are those that cause color-blindness, myopia, premature white hair, and early baldness.

Heredity is suspected of playing a part in some kinds of heart disease, mental illness, ulcers, and diabetes. Medical researchers think there is a genetic predisposition to these ailments; that is, the diseases do not occur solely because of heredity, but they have a tendency to develop, if certain environmental factors are also present. The reason that some people get lung cancer from smoking while most do not may lie in the genes. There is evidence that some severe physical and emotional problems of old age may be of genetic origin.

Genetic Counseling

Genetic-counseling services, staffed by doctors with extensive training in genetics, have been set up in most states. The National Foundation-March of Dimes has compiled a list of about 200 such facilities in 44 states. The National Genetics Foundation, with headquarters in New York City, coordinates a network of 46 genetic counseling centers. About three-fourths of these services have come into existence since the late 1960's.

Genetic counselors have identified certain people with a high risk of passing on genetic diseases. These include women over 35 and women who have had several miscarriages or stillborn babies; people who already have deformed children or have a family history of genetic trouble; those who have diabetes, hyperthyroidism, or other metabolic diseases; and those who belong to ethnic groups among which particular genetic diseases are common.

Detecting Diseases. Genetic counselors have available sophisticated equipment for biochemical analysis of cells from blood or skin samples of prospective parents. Many tests require the culturing of cells, with large numbers of similar cells grown from the samples. Biochemical analysis then reveals irregularities, such as the absence or ineffectiveness of enzymes, that would not be evident from the examination of a single cell.

Amniocentesis is a technique that can be used to detect genetic disease before a baby is born. It is a relatively painless procedure, usually performed only after the 14th week of pregnancy. It is not completely risk-free to the unborn child and

Karotype, a photographic analysis of the chromosomes, used to detect abnormalities, is shown and explained to prospective parents by a genetic counselor. Making an accurate chromosomal analysis requires much time and skill.

is not done routinely, but it is useful in cases where there is reason to suspect trouble either because the parents fall into the high-risk category or because the pregnant woman has been exposed to radiation, German measles, or some types of drugs.

In amniocentesis, a hollow needle is inserted through the abdomen into the uterus, and a small amount of amniotic fluid is drawn out. Cells of the fetus are present in the fluid. The fluid can be scanned for chromosomal irregularities, or the cells can be cultured and analyzed. The cell study takes from four to six weeks.

The Karotype, a photographic analysis of the chromosomes, is used to detect chromosomal abnormalities. Dividing cells are photographed, and the silhouettes of the chromosomes are examined with a fluorescent microscope or by staining techniques. Making an accurate chromosomal analysis requires great time and skill. Computers with pattern-recognition devices are being developed to do this work more quickly and cheaply, perhaps leading ultimately to routine screening of fetuses.

Advising the Parents. Genetic counselors ask for complete family medical records before meeting with the prospective parents. The counselor examines the records for evidence of recurring illness, which may indicate hereditary diseases, and then, with the parents, draws up a medical geneology to trace inheritance patterns. If the parents have any children with an ailment suspected of being genetic in origin, the child is given a thorough physical examination.

Then the counselor discusses the case with specialists to decide whether additional tests are needed. When the counselor feels that he has enough information, he advises the parents of the risk. He may say, for example, that any child they may have has a 50-per-cent chance of being the victim of a serious disease, or a 25-percent chance, or no chance. Then it is up to the parents to decide what to do—continue with the pregnancy or choose abortion.

Parents react differently to the information. Some insist on having the child even though the risk is high, and some are unwilling to risk even the slightest chance of disease. Some geneticists believe that couples should be encouraged to avoid giving birth to children with a high risk of inheriting genetic disease. The availability of the means of detecting such diseases raises questions that society will ultimately have to deal with, the major one

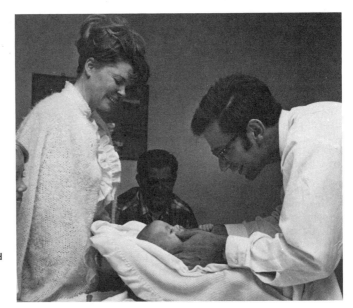

Advising Parents. Genetic counselors ask for complete family medical records in order to trace inheritance patterns. If the parents have a child with an ailment suspected of being genetic in origin, the child is given a thorough physical examination.

being whether society can or should limit the right to procreation.

An Effective Screening Program

A simple blood test can detect whether a person carries the gene that causes certain ailments. Tay-Sachs disease, which is found among Jews whose forebears came from central and eastern Europe, is one such disease. Tay-Sachs victims appear normal, and often extremely beautiful, until about the age of six months, after which they deteriorate physically and mentally, go blind, become helpless, and die.

The abnormality that causes this disease was not discovered until 1969. A very effective screening program was set up in the Baltimore-Washington area by Michael Kaback, who was at the time a research physician at Johns Hopkins University Medical School.

Kaback and his associates spent a year explaining the program and then tested 10,000 people over the next two years. They found 11 couples with both husband and wife carrying the particular defective gene that causes Tay-Sachs disease. According to the inheritance pattern, the risk of their having a child who would be a victim was one in four. Among the 11 couples, there were five pregnancies. All five chose to undergo amniocentesis, which

resulted in the detection of the disease in one fetus. That fetus was aborted, and the other four babies were born normal.

The success of Kaback's program rests to a great degree on his well-thought-out approach. He says, "On the surface, it appears very simple. You go out, do a blood test, tell people if they are carriers. But there are lots of very delicate issues involved in this kind of a program. Unlike an experiment with a thousand mice, or a million bacteria, when you experiment with 5,000 or 10,000 human beings, you have to be able to deal with 5,000 or 10,000 individual problems, because every person perceives this information in a slightly different way."

Defects within the Chromosomes

In the nucleus of every normal human body cell are 46 chromosomes, dark rod-like bodies that contain DNA (deoxyribonucleic acid). A gene—the basic unit that determines a hereditary human trait—is a segment of the DNA molecule.

The structure of genetic materials in the embryo sets the pattern of future cell growth and determines the inherited traits of the offspring, such as skin and eye color. The genetic material also produces enzymes, which cause chemical reactions that are necessary for normal growth and health. In a healthy body, tens of thousands of genes are functioning properly. If even one gene is absent or does not function properly, the body chemistry may be severely altered.

In the case of many genetic diseases, one of the inherited genes is defective. The gene is always one which is responsible for producing a vital enzyme.

Most genetic diseases are transmitted in one of three ways: dominant, recessive, and X-linked inheritance. The patterns follow the basic principles discovered by Gregor Mendel in the 19th century.

Dominant. More than 900 diseases are known to follow a pattern of dominant inheritance, in which a single dominant but defective gene from one parent causes abnormalities in certain cells of the child. Each child has a one-in-two chance of inheriting the bad gene. Among the ailments transmitted this way are several forms of dwarfism and deafness, polydactyly (too many fingers or toes), congenital heart ailments, a number of blood disorders, and almost a dozen types of eye cataracts.

Recessive. Recessive inheritance accounts for more than 780 known ailments, including sickle-cell anemia, Tay-Sachs disease, cystic fibrosis, galactosemia, and albinism. A person unaffected by cystic fibrosis, for example, may nevertheless have a defective gene; since he also carries a normal gene and the disease is recessive rather than dominant, he does not suffer from the disease but is a carrier. If he marries a woman who is also a carrier, however, any child has a one-in-four chance of being afflicted by inheriting the defective gene from each parent. The child has a two-in-four chance of being a healthy carrier (by inheriting a normal gene and a defective one), and a one-in-four chance of being neither a victim nor a carrier (by inheriting the healthy gene from each).

X-Linked. There are some 150 ailments that are recessive and are caused by a defective gene within the X chromosome. Females have two X chromosomes in each cell and males only one (instead of a matching X chromosome, males have a Y chromosome). Female carriers of a de-

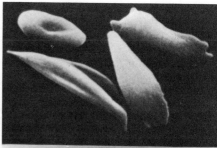
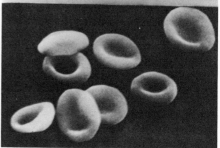

Sickle-Cell Anemia is a recessive genetic disease that chiefly afflicts black people. An inherited defect in the molecular structure of hemoglobin results in sickle-shaped red blood cells instead of the normal doughnut shape.

fective X-linked gene have a normal gene on their second X chromosome to offset the defect; not having this second X chromosome, male inheritors contract the ailment.

The classic example is hemophilia, which was passed on by Queen Victoria to several sons and grandsons. Certain forms of muscular dystrophy are also X-linked, as is color-blindness and agammaglobulinemia (lack of normal defense against disease). Each son of a female carrier has a one-in-two chance of inheriting the disease, and each daughter has a one-in-two chance of being a carrier. Men with the disease produce only carrier daughters; sons are not affected because they inherit the father's Y chromosome, not the X chromosome.

Treatment. No diseases arising from inborn errors of metabolism are curable, but the symptoms of about 40 of them can be minimized if proper treatment is begun in time. The treatments are generally simple and inexpensive, involving a special diet or

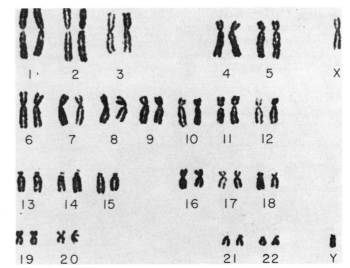

Chromosomal Pattern of a Human Male is shown at right. Females have matching X chromosomes, while males have an XY pattern. Sex-linked genetic ailments result from a defective gene within an X chromosome.

drugs to compensate for the imbalance of the enzymes. The number of diseases for which treatment is available is increasing rapidly.

The time when an enzyme-deficiency disease shows its effects depends on the enzyme involved. Some enzyme reactions are not needed until the individual reaches a particular point in development. If the faulty enzyme is needed for fetal development, the fetus will be stillborn or will be born with a physical or neural defect. If the enzyme is needed for mental development, its lack will become apparent in the first year or two of a child's life. If the enzyme is involved in producing sex hormones, the child will appear normal until the age of puberty.

Phenylketonuria, or PKU, is a well-studied genetic disease that causes severe mental retardation, hyperactivity, and difficulty in walking. Its frequency is about one in 10,000 births. Its cause is the lack of the mechanism required to make the enzyme phenylalanine hydrozylase, which oxidizes phenylalanine, an essential ingredient of food protein. Abnormal concentrations of phenylalanine build up in the blood and spinal fluid. With a protein-free diet, the damage to the central nervous system is averted or sharply reduced. The diet can be ended at about age seven or eight, when the nervous system is fully developed. Testing of newborn babies for PKU is mandatory in most states.

In Wilson's disease, too much copper, which is present in most foods, is retained in the body and causes progressive deterioration of the brain and liver. The victims of this disease are normal at birth. The symptoms may appear any time from about age 5 to 40. If the disease is detected at birth and treated with a diet low in copper and a drug that promotes the excretion of copper, the neurological degeneration can be avoided or slowed.

Galactosemia strikes children in whom galactase, an enzyme essential for the digestion of milk sugar, is defective. If a child with defective galactase drinks milk, he will develop the disease, which causes cataracts, cirrhosis of the liver, mental retardation, and even death, within the first month. Testing of blood samples reveals whether a person is a carrier of galactosemia. Some states require testing of newborn infants to see if they are victims of the disease. If the test is positive, milk can be withheld from the child before damage is done.

Chromosomal Defects

Twenty-two matching pairs of chromosomes are present in every normal body cell of the human body, plus two sex chromosomes (XX in females, XY in males). Each pair has a distinctive shape and size. If any one of the chromosomes is missing, duplicated, broken, or wrongly attached, the cell is abnormal. Because the resulting body disorders are so serious, most embryos and fetuses with chromosomal abnormalities are aborted spontaneously; nevertheless about one baby in 200 is born with a chromosomal abnormality.

The causes of chromosomal defects are uncertain. It is suspected that some drugs and overdoses of radiation can cause changes in the chromosomes. The errors occur either in the egg or sperm before conception or in the embryo afterwards, and they are passed on to many or all of the subsequent cell divisions.

The most common chromosomal disease is Down's syndrome or mongolism, which occurs when there is an extra chromosome No. 21. The frequency is about one in 600 births. Some 65 symptoms are connected with this disease, all caused by the one extra chromosome. Most children with Down's syndrome are born to normal and healthy parents; the extra chromosome No. 21 apparently is found originally in the egg cell of the mother.

The chances of producing such a baby increase as a woman becomes older. Before age 30, the risk is about one in 3,000. From age 30 to 34, it is one in 600; from 35 to 39, one in 280; from 40 to 44, one in 100; and after 45, one in 50. The explanation for the age factor is unknown, but one theory is that, since the egg cells in every woman are present at birth, the mere passage of time increases the chance of "over-ripeness" or environmental damage to the cells.

The symptoms of the disease in any one child may be mild, but in most cases mental retardation is so severe that the victims require lifetime care, usually in an institution. Half die before the age of five, but advances in heart surgery and the use of antibiotics make it possible for many victims of Down's syndrome to live into adulthood.

The disease can be detected before birth by amniocentesis. Many scientists urge that free amniocentesis and abortion be made available to all women over the age of 35. James F. Bonner, a biologist with the California Institute of Technology, believes that the procedure "will ultimately become standard practice in the developed countries."

Detecting Down's Syndrome. An indication of Down's syndrome, or mongolism, is hands with short, stubby fingers and unusual fingertip markings and palm creases. Down's syndrome, the most common chromosomal disease, occurs where there is an extra chromosome No. 21. Normal hand is shown directly below; mongoloid hand at bottom.

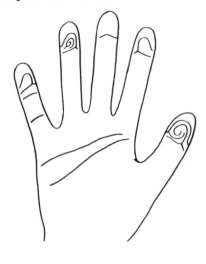

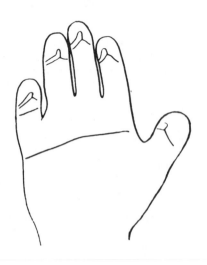

Middle East. A summit meeting of 20 Arab heads of state in Rabat, Morocco, unanimously approved a resolution recognizing the Palestine Liberation Organization as "the sole legitimate representative of the Palestinian people." The resolution, adopted on October 28 at the end of the three-day meeting, called for the creation of an independent Palestinian state "on any Palestinian land that is liberated" from Israeli occupation.

The summit conference, which was the seventh such meeting of the Arab League since 1964, was called to map a coordinated Arab strategy for the immediate future with respect to Israel. According to conference sources, Saudi Arabia, Kuwait, and other major Arab oil producers—excluding Iraq and Libya—agreed to donate $1 billion annually over a four-year period to Egypt and Syria, $300 million a year to Jordan, and $50 million a year to the PLO. Southern Yemen was to receive $150 million for a 99-year Arab League lease of strategic Perim Island in the Bab al Mandeb, the strait at the southern end of the

Red Sea which could be mined to blockade the Israeli port of Eilat.

Yasir Arafat, head of the PLO, called the summit conference "the turning point in the history of the Palestinian people and Arab nation." As a result of the summit decisions, U.S. Secretary of State Henry Kissinger's "policy is in ruins," Arafat said.

King Hussein of Jordan had been at odds with the PLO as to who would administer any relinquished territory on the West Bank of the Jordan. (The West Bank region had been governed by Jordan between 1949 and 1967, when it was occupied by Israel during the Six Day War.) But, in a broadcast October 30, Hussein hailed the Arab summit decision as "a triumph of the Arab nation's will." He said in a New York *Times* interview that Jordan planned to rewrite its constitution and to reorganize its cabinet and parliament in order to remove Palestinians from the government. "The West Bank is no longer Jordan," he said, "and we have no place in the negotiations over its future."

Arab Summit. King Hussein of Jordan, *wearing suit,* accepted a decision by Arab heads of state to turn over any territory relinquished by Israel on the West Bank of the Jordan to the Palestine Liberation Organization. The PLO, headed by Yasir Arafat, *checkered headdress,* was recognized as "the sole legitimate representative of the Palestinian people."

Arafat, speaking before the UN General Assembly, said his group sought to replace Israel with a Palestinian state including Moslems, Christians, and Jews. He said he had come to the United Nations "bearing an olive branch and a freedom fighter's gun."

Israeli Premier Yitzhak Rabin reiterated his government's decision "not to negotiate with terrorist organizations whose avowed aim is Israel's destruction." He denounced the Arab summit for supporting the aim of a group "that would negate our existence as a state and resorts to violence and terror to destroy our state." If the Arabs barred Jordan from participation in peace talks, he said, there would be no one to talk to about Israel's eastern frontier.

The Soviet Union called November 6 for Palestinian statehood as part of a Middle East settlement. In an evident rebuff to Kissinger's peacemaking mission, Foreign Minister Andrei Gromyko called for immediate resumption of the Geneva conference on the Middle East, which met only for a few days in December, 1973, to ratify the cease-fire following the October war.

By the end of 1974, Kissinger's efforts toward a Middle East settlement appeared stalled, and war within a year was freely predicted by both sides. The only channel immediately available to stave off war appeared to be an Israeli withdrawal from territory in Egypt's Sinai Peninsula, but in exchange Israel was demanding major steps by Egypt toward formal peace, which would go against the spirit of the Rabat meeting.

Arafat Speaks at UN

The United Nations General Assembly opened debate November 13 on the Palestine question with an opening address by Arafat, who said his group's goal remained the creation of a Palestinian state which would include Moslems, Christians, and Jews. Concluding his address, the PLO chief said, "I have come bearing an olive branch and a freedom fighter's gun. Do not let the olive branch fall from my hand." (Arafat made his appearance on the rostrum wearing a holster that a UN guard said contained a gun.)

Israeli delegate Yosef Tekoah denounced Arafat's speech in rebuttal, asserting that his proposal would mean the destruction of Israel and its replacement by an Arab state. He reiterated his government's policy of refusing to permit the PLO to take over any territory relinquished by Israel.

On the instruction of Assembly President Abdelaziz Bouteflika of Algeria, Arafat was accorded the honor of chief of state. After his address and Tekoah's rebuttal, the General Assembly voted to limit each nation to one major speech in the debate. The restriction was believed to be the first of its kind in UN history and allowed a number of delegates from Arab nations to speak without rebuttal by Tekoah.

The General Assembly concluded its Palestine debate November 22 by approving two resolutions declaring that the Palestinian people had the right to independence and sovereignty, by a vote of 89 to 8 with 37 abstentions, and granting the PLO observer status in UN affairs, by a vote of 95 to 17 with 19 abstentions. The first resolution also affirmed "the inalienable rights of the Palestinians to return to their homes and property from which they have been displaced and uprooted."

Palestinian Refugees

Palestinian demonstrations were held on the Israeli-occupied West Bank in support of Arafat and the PLO and to coincide with Arafat's UN appearance. The largest show of support occurred in Nablus, where Arabs staged a general strike, closing their shops. Violent demonstrations between November 16 and 19 spread to East Jerusalem for the first time. Dozens of protestors and Israeli riot police were injured, and one Arab schoolgirl was killed in Jenin. Arafat urged West Bank Arabs November 18 to "continue and escalate your resistance and sacrifices."

There are about 3 million Palestinian Arabs and 3 million Israeli Jews. Nearly half those who are Arab Palestinians by birth or ethnic origin live in Israel proper (where they are citizens), or under Israeli occupation on the West Bank or in the Gaza Strip. Another 1 million live in Jordan, east of the Jordan River, while the remainder live in Lebanon, Syria, Kuwait, or other Arab countries. More than half of Israel's Jewish population consists of Jews who left Arab countries to come to Israel, and their descendants.

Mideast Turmoil. *Above,* angry Israelis tossed and burned the bodies of three Arab terrorists killed after murdering four civilians. *Below,* Israeli troops patrol the streets of East Jerusalem, where Arab demonstrations took place.

New Products. Thousands of new products and services reach the marketplace each year, despite increasing costs and a high risk of failure. Special emphasis is being placed on home renovation and repair jobs, energy-saving devices, and low-cost leisure activities and vacation trips.

Transportation

"Dale," a three-wheeled compact car, is due on the market for 1975. It will sell for less than $2,000, weigh about 1,000 pounds, and go 70 miles on a gallon of gas.

An adult-sized, five-speed tricycle is available for $190. A steel basket behind the seat carries up to 150 pounds.

"Electra Ride" is an electrical device attached to a bicycle or tricycle. A standard storage battery which can be recharged overnight provides enough power with one charge for a ride of 15 miles. The price is $109.95.

The Mars Electra is a lightweight, battery-powered bike popular in fuel-pinched Europe. It travels 25 miles on a single charge, will reach a speed of 16 miles per hour, and can also be pedaled like an ordinary bicycle. The power unit can be recharged from any wall outlet.

For a battery that loses its charge, a portable generator that runs on gasoline is available. It weighs only 28 pounds and will recharge the battery in less than 10 minutes.

"Rescue," a chemical fuel that substitutes for gasoline in an emergency, can be carried safely in an automobile trunk. The liquid comes in a one-gallon container that will carry a moderate-sized car 12 to 15 miles.

"Accelerite," a device mounted on the dashboard of a car, tells the driver when he is bearing down too heavily on the gas pedal and thus wasting fuel. It sells for $14.95.

"Start-O-Matic" is a device that will start an auto engine up to 500 feet away by remote control on cold winter mornings with the press of a button on a shirt-pocket-sized transmitter. The engine will run for seven minutes, then shut off automatically. It is available from auto dealers and supply stores for $249.

Home

"Mowtron" is a computerized gasoline-driven lawnmower that automatically mows a lawn. Wires buried a few inches under the ground "program" the mower to follow a prescribed path. The machine returns to the shed or garage after completing the job and parks itself. The price is $895 for the machine plus about one cent per square foot for wire installation.

An aluminum-truss geodesic dome, developed as a result of NASA space research, can be applied to year-round swimming-pool use. The frame supports a high-strength vinyl membrane which can be removed in warm weather. The cost is about $6 per square foot of floor surface area.

"Sonic Raider" eliminates rats, mice, and similar rodents without poisons. It emits high-frequency ultrasonic waves inaudible to humans but devastating to rats, covering inaccessible areas where chemicals can't reach.

A battery-powered smoke detector senses small fires up to 22 feet away within seconds and sounds an alarm.

Viterra hydrogel, a soil additive, acts as a plant baby-sitter, releasing moisture gradually into the root zone so that watering need be done only about once a week.

"Unigroom" contains a retractable three-inch comb and a container to hold either aerosol hair spray or flavored breath spray. Some units have glass make-up mirrors on the side.

A hand saw with a tungsten carbide blade cuts and trims bricks, and slices through glass, cement blocks, slate, marble, and rubber.

Business

"Talkatron," an ultrasonic device, can monitor the location of anyone wearing a fountain-pen-sized transponder. The press of a button on a central console shows the location of the person called, by room and phone extension. The device then switches calls to the nearest telephone.

"Little Yeller," a portable electronic megaphone, could prove useful for football coaches. It runs on four transistor batteries and has a range of more than 300 yards. The price is $89.95, not including batteries.

Viterra Hydrogel increases the water-holding capacity of soil; chrysanthemums are shown wilting at left after six days without water but still flourishing in soil to which the product has been added.

Electric-Powered Bicycle has been converted by the addition of a motor, battery, and other parts. A typically modified bike will travel up to 15 miles per hour on level terrain and should be able to travel about 10 miles on a battery charge.

Battery Charger. The portable generator above weighs only 28 pounds and will recharge a battery in less than 10 minutes.

Long-Distance Life Saver. Left, a walkie-talkie, coupled with an antenna built upon the frame of a golfer's umbrella, enables persons in distress to summon help— via space satellite if necessary.

Robert Altman

Yasir Arafat

Newsmakers. Among the personalities prominently mentioned in the news media during 1974 were the following:

Robert Altman. One of America's most artistically innovative and passionately personal motion-picture directors, Robert Altman, learned the basics of his craft making industrial films in St. Louis. After moving to the West Coast, he began directing such television shows as "Bonanza" and "The Millionaire." Altman describes his television experience as "guerrilla warfare": "I was making films under a system and trying to sneak my own personal message through all that veneer."

Eventually, Altman created his own veneer, which has become one of the most recognizable styles in modern film. His trademarks are overlapping dialogue, an abundance of throwaway humor, a veritable tapestry of visual detail, and a company of actors who often seem indistinguishable from their roles. With these tools, he set to work creating his own interpretations of different film genres: the war comedy (*M*A*S*H*), the frontier western (*McCabe and Mrs. Miller*), the private-eye yarn (*The Long Goodbye*), the Depression melodrama (*Thieves Like Us*), and the depiction of compulsive drives, in this case gambling (*California Split*). By concentrating more on the characters themselves than on their parts in the evolving plot, Altman hints at emotions with a broader palette than most filmmakers and, at the same time, revitalizes overworked cinema motifs.

Yasir Arafat. The head of the Palestine Liberation Organization once told a journalist he was married to "a woman called Palestine," and in late 1974, while tensions increased in the Middle East, Arafat was installed as the head of his household. In November, the Arab summit meeting in Rabat, Morocco, unanimously endorsed the PLO as "sole legitimate" spokesman for the Palestinians, including the 640,000 who live under Israeli occupation on the West Bank of the Jordan River. (See MIDDLE EAST in this section.) The Israelis maintain that they will only negotiate the complex Palestinian question with Jordan's King Hussein, and never with the leader of the PLO, which has been responsible for many anti-Israel terrorist attacks.

Arafat's star rose higher later in the

same month when the United Nations General Assembly voted to allow him to present the Palestinian position. While the Israeli delegate walked out in protest, Arafat, speaking with an unloaded pistol on his belt, said, "I have come bearing an olive branch and a freedom fighter's gun. Do not let the olive branch fall from my hands." His speech opened no doors toward a Middle East settlement as he called for a unified Arab/Jewish state, a notion Israel rejected.

Having gained, experience from his training with the Egyptian army and university studies in engineering, Arafat dedicated himself in the early 1950's to the militant Palestinian group Al Fatah. After the Six Day War in 1967, Al Fatah gained respect from the Arab community since it was not tarnished by the humiliating defeat. By February, 1969, Al Fatah had gained control of the PLO, and Arafat was named its executive chairman. The PLO's strategy, implemented through the tactics of terrorist activities, has been to make a political settlement in the Middle East impossible without its participation.

Edmund G. Brown, Jr. "Jerry" Brown, an unconventional candidate in a year that found voters disillusioned with politics as usual, was elected governor of California. Described as a tense and introverted intellectual, Brown has been influenced by his four years in a Jesuit seminary and by his father Edmund G. ("Pat") Brown, who was governor of California from 1959 to 1967. Though his father's reputation certainly didn't hurt Brown, it didn't elect him; the youthful Democrat established his own image.

To be elected governor of the most populous state at the age of 36 was an auspicious leap after only five years in state politics (his last post was secretary of state). Brown, who dryly described his new job as "a learning experience," may someday seek postgraduate education in the White House.

Earl Butz. Named secretary of agriculture by President Nixon in November, 1971, Earl Butz replaced Clifford Hardin. Having taught agricultural economics and served as dean of continuing education for 10 years at Purdue University, Butz

Earl Butz

came to the Administration with an established philosophy. He maintains a fundamental belief in the free-market system and also believes that technological and social changes must invariably change the structure of agriculture, with small farms giving way to larger and more efficient units.

Fearing a loss of farm support, Nixon had brought Butz into the Administration with a mandate to reverse the downward trend in farm prices. To accomplish this, Butz used federal funds, including funds previously frozen by the Administration, in such a way as to boost farm prices. Unfortunately, this practice caused food prices to rise, and the already inflated economy worsened. The Soviet grain deal, which Butz helped negotiate, sent prices still higher. Butz concedes, "We have learned that we cannot run an incentive economy from Washington."

Food is more than a national issue, though, as the escalating world food crisis has tragically shown. Speaking at the UN Food and Agriculture Organization conference in Rome, Butz pointed out that the United States had given 46 per cent of all food aid that developing countries had

469

Hugh Carey

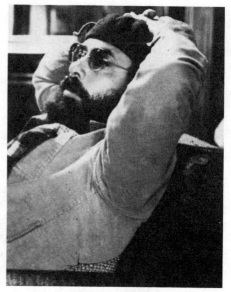

Francis Ford Coppola

received since 1962. He added that the United States could not be expected to carry so heavy a burden in solving the food crisis.

Hugh Carey. Democrats were pleased to capture the statehouse of the second largest state, New York, where Hugh Carey beat the incumbent Governor Malcolm Wilson, who assumed the post when Nelson Rockefeller resigned.

Carey, a 55-year-old moderate liberal, had been a member of Congress from Brooklyn since 1960. He served on the powerful House Ways and Means Committee, where he came to be regarded as a protégé of Chairman Wilbur Mills, and on the Education and Labor Committee.

Once Carey beat Howard Samuels, the official party choice, in the September primary, the major hurdle of his campaign was passed. Carey is a widower with 12 children.

Jimmy Connors. Some stories put the beginning of Jimmy Connors' tennis career back some 19 years ago, when he was two years old and somebody threw him a tennis ball. With the tutoring of his mother, a regional tennis champion in her own right, his playing improved steadily until,

in 1974, he won both the Wimbledon and U.S. Open men's singles championships.

Connors is also the enfant terrible of tennis, the cocky kid who shunned the Davis Cup competition and the World Cup tour, which featured most of the best players. Connors answers his critics by saying the USLTA schedule was better for his game's pace and development, and anyway, "my definition of best is Wimbledon and Forest Hills. Play there and see who wins and he's the champion."

There was no arguing that logic in 1974, as Connors devastated Australian Ken Rosewall in the finals of both tournaments. Describing his play at Forest Hills, Connors said, "From the moment I took the court and hit the first ball, I felt I was gliding. I was on a cloud." At his age, he'll probably be feeling that way for a while.

Francis Ford Coppola. With the movie industry seemingly bursting with young directing and writing talent, Francis Ford Coppola is among the best on both counts and stands a good chance of revolutionizing the art and industry of filmmaking. Artistically, Coppola is able to make a blockbuster box-office success which at

Ella Grasso

the same time amply displays his crafts-manship and sensibilities. *The Godfather,* both the original and sequel, confirmed his unique talents, while *The Conversation* showed Coppola's skills within a more limited scope, yet with a more potent emotional punch.

Graduating from UCLA's film school, Coppola made a distribution deal for his master's thesis, the film *You're a Big Boy Now,* and, over the next few years, he made films which put him $300,000 in debt. He also established himself as a top-notch script writer, earning an Oscar for co-writing *Patton.* His big break was *The Godfather,* which by late 1974 had grossed an astounding $285 million, es-tablishing his reputation and allowing him to set up his own production and distribu-tion companies. With the expected success of *Godfather II* supplying the financial cushion, Coppola's immediate plans are to direct two films and produce two others under the Coppola Company banner, dis-tributing them world-wide and thus avoid-ing the domination of marketing by major production companies.

Though realistically nervous about his ambitious plans, Coppola feels they are

necessary for both his own art and the continued creativity of the industry. "I want to keep rocking the boat," he ad-mits. "Taking chances is what makes you strong, makes you wise."

Ella Grasso. In Connecticut, Ella Grasso became the first woman governor to be elected without benefit of a hus-band's previous incumbency. But she is not an ardent feminist and, owing to her quiet but firm opposition to abortion and her absence during a child-care vote, the Washington-based Women's Lobby ranked her in the bottom third of their congressional list.

Grasso's political career began in 1952, when she was elected to the state legisla-ture. She served there two years, and then served three terms as secretary of state. In 1970, she was elected to the first of two terms in the U.S. House of Repre-sentatives. Although this experience taught her the ins and outs of Connecticut's Dem-ocratic party, she had to struggle for the gubernatorial nomination, which she se-cured only after winning a key local pri-mary by 2,000 votes.

In the November election. Grasso hand-ily defeated U.S. Representative Robert Steele, and her party regained control of the state's General Assembly. The cam-paign revolved around state spending, with Steele charging that Grasso's poli-cies would force the enactment of a state income tax.

The issue of sex was adroitly avoided by both candidates. Concerning being a woman in politics, Grasso has said, "I don't give any quarter and I don't ex-pect any as a woman. I expect to be treated as a person, and I usually am."

Joseph Heller. With the publication of his first novel, *Catch-22,* Joseph Heller es-tablished himself as a major figure in con-temporary fiction. Published in 1961, the novel drew upon Heller's World War II experiences in the Air Force for technical details and used black humor to portray an insane and immoral society through its most blatant cruelty—war. The book's moral stance is centered around "Catch 22," an Air Force rule which states that a man is considered insane if he continues to fly combat missions but, if he makes a

Joseph Heller

Mary Tyler Moore

formal request to be relieved of these duties, that act shows that he is sane and therefore not eligible to be relieved.

After the publication of *Catch-22,* Heller abandoned his career in magazine advertising and devoted himself to his second novel, various theater projects, and university teaching. His play, *We Bombed in New Haven,* brought some of the themes from *Catch-22* up to date and, though it received mixed critical reviews, ranked as one of the theater's most telling indictments of the Vietnam war. However, most of Heller's time and energy went to his second novel, *Something Happened.*

Published in 1974, *Something Happened* is largely an interior monologue of corporate man Robert Slocum. In the view of novelist Kurt Vonnegut, Jr., the book is "the most permanent variation on a familiar theme . . . . that many lives, judged by the standards of the people who live them, are simply not worth living."

Johnny Miller. It's hard to believe that Johnny Miller once had a reputation as a golfer who choked up at crucial moments, because ever since he jolted the sporting

world by winning the U.S. Open in 1973, he's been the hottest player in golf. And, at just 27, he enjoyed his best year in 1974, taking home more earnings than any player before him.

Miller started the 1974 circuit with a bang, winning the tour's first three tournaments. As of mid-October, Miller had entered 21 tournaments and won an astounding eight of them. His strategy was a consistent game highlighted by one knockout round. For instance, at the Kaiser International Open, in the space of three holes, Miller shot two birdies and a hole-in-one. Such play has earned him the record-breaking amount of $353,021 in 1974.

Mary Tyler Moore. Television has always been a highly derivative medium, with the hit of one season reappearing in at least three different guises the next year. "The Mary Tyler Moore Show," along with the actress and the production company that bears her name, have updated the mold and currently comprise the hottest property on prime-time television.

Mary Tyler Moore first gained prominence from her five-year stint on the popular "Dick Van Dyke Show," during which she won two Emmies and an additional nomination for television's highest honor. After Van Dyke decided to leave the series, she found only sporadic success in movie and theater projects. In 1969, however, she teamed up with Van Dyke for a successful TV special, and all three networks lined up to offer her a weekly series. Working with writers James Brooks and Allan Burns, she created Mary Richards, who works in Minnesota producing a television news program. "But the really subversive thing about the show," noted one critic, "is that she's over 30 without being either a widow or a nurse."

The trademark of MTM Enterprises programs (now numbering four: the MTM Show, "Rhoda," "The Bob Newhart Show," "Friends and Lovers") is an interesting premise, such as Mary's occupation, and a strong group of supporting characters. Valerie Harper, who for four years played Mary's neighbor Rhoda, proved so successful in the role that it evolved into her own series, which in late 1974 was racking up number-one ratings.

Frank Robinson

Jack Nicholson. One of Hollywood's newest stars, Jack Nicholson has risen to the top with a carefully honed anti-hero image, one which often seems indistinguishable from his real self. After years of hustling bit parts in "B" movies, Nicholson's break came with a comic role in *Easy Rider* (1967) that earned him an Oscar nomination.

In the roles that followed—in *Five Easy Pieces, Carnal Knowledge, The Last Detail*—his image became one of controlled fury, a usually intelligent man feeling constant pressure from his surroundings and the demands they make of him. It is his scenes of anger, when this friction breaks into an open wound, which pack Nicholson's hardest punch. Ironically, their drama is largely derived from the feeling that even as he tries to expel the demon, he never lets everything go and thus there is always something left simmering and unrevealed.

Nicholson's star soared with the 1974 release of Roman Polanski's *Chinatown*, a slick private-eye yarn set in 1930's Los Angeles in which he plays less an individual character than the persona of the Humphrey Bogart-Sam Spade macho detective. Unlike his predecessors, though, Nicholson's J. J. Gittes is over his head in a case which reveals corruption at every level of society. Where Bogart's personality wouldn't tolerate defeat, even by ever-present and untouchable evil, Nicholson is battered into acquiescence. But like Bogart, Nicholson has become the most distinctive male lead of his time.

Frank Robinson. With the announcement on October 3 that Frank Robinson would become manager of the Cleveland Indians, major-league baseball gained its first black manager. In 1947, Jackie Robinson (no relation) broke baseball's color line by becoming the first black major league player.

Frank Robinson broke into the majors with the Cincinnati Reds in 1956 after spending three years in the minors. Wasting no time, he racked up 38 home runs (the highest ever for a rookie) and was voted the National League's rookie of the year. Robinson became the NL's most valuable player in 1961 and, five years later, following his trade to the Baltimore Orioles of the American League, he became the first player to achieve that honor in both leagues. Following his five years with the Orioles, Robinson played briefly with the Los Angeles Dodgers and the California Angels before moving to the Indians. His major-league career statistics show a batting average of .298, 1,778 runs batted in, and 574 home runs clouted. Aside from his managerial duties, he will also be a designated hitter for the Indians.

Robinson has gained managing experience through five seasons with Santurce, a club in the Puerto Rican Winter League, and through studying the managers he has played for. On the sociological implications of his new post, Robinson says, "The only reason I'm the first black manager is that I was born black." Nevertheless, he is understandably proud of his achievement and adds, "The only wish I could have is that Jackie Robinson could be here today to see this happen."

Donald Rumsfeld. Although recently named as assistant to President Ford, Donald Rumsfeld is no newcomer to Republican politics. After graduating from Princeton University in 1954, he served as aide to U.S. Representative Robert Griffin of Michigan and, in 1962, ran successfully for the House of Representatives from his home district in the wealthy northern suburbs of Chicago. Reelected four times, he gained a reputation as a moderate Republican, an image conjured from a combination of his conservative voting record and his efforts to modernize the Republican party in the House.

In 1968, Rumsfeld served as one of Richard Nixon's 10 surrogate speakers. After Nixon moved into the White House, Rumsfeld assumed the dual capacity of assistant to the president and director of the poverty program. Later, though, he began to have difficulty working with Nixon staffers, H. R. Haldeman and John Ehrlichman in particular, and eventually he requested a foreign assignment. In December, 1972, he was named the Administration's envoy to NATO headquarters in Belgium.

Rumsfeld returned to Washington to help with the transition to the Ford Administration. Rather reluctantly, owing to the relative political obscurity of the job,

Kurt Vonnegut

he accepted an assignment on the Ford White House staff. Though replacing General Alexander Haig, Rumsfeld will not hold the power of his predecessor, as Ford desires a more open administration and exposure to more advisers.

Kurt Vonnegut. By his own definition of a writer as "a person who makes his living with his mental disease," it would seem that Kurt Vonnegut, one of America's most popular novelists, is one very sick man. Yet, given the often absurd view of the world projected in his novels, Vonnegut's disease strikes one as a healthy alternative.

Vonnegut began writing in earnest in 1950 when he started contributing short fiction to various magazines, many of the stories being in the science-fiction genre. His first two novels, beginning with *Player Piano* in 1952, stayed within the realm of science fiction, though they contained the germs of Vonnegut's further promise, which came to fruition in 1962 with the publication of *Cat's Cradle*, the novel which established Vonnegut as a literary force. *Cat's Cradle*, like the novels that followed (*God Bless You, Mr. Rosewater; Slaughterhouse Five;* and *Break-*

fast of Champions) entered into the realm of absurdist fiction, dealing with man's compulsion to find factors which set people apart from one another rather than to search for the common thread of humanity. Further, Vonnegut deals with man's rationalization, and thereby acceptance, of the evils that he finds around him.

Notwithstanding, humor plays a major part in Vonnegut's work. As a character in *Cat's Cradle* explains: "Maturity is a bitter disappointment for which no remedy exists, unless laughter can be said to remedy anything."

Ahmed Yaki Yamani. The energy crisis has created new centers of power in the Middle East, and Ahmed Yaki Yamani, minister of petroleum and mineral resources of Saudi Arabia, is one of the kingpins in creating and executing Arab energy policies. During the winter of 1973-74, while the United States was experiencing the effects of the Arab oil embargo, Yamani became a familiar face in the news, explaining to American officials the reality behind the embargo as well as the Arabs' rationale for the action.

After having studied in both Egypt and the United States, Yamani entered into government service in Saudi Arabia, and in 1962 he was named minister of oil. Yamani was the prime Arab agent responsible for arranging the 1972 "participation" agreements which permitted Arab nations to purchase 25-per-cent interest in foreign oil companies. A year later, he warned the United States that oil might become a weapon to modify U.S. support of Israel, but the State Department dismissed his warnings as a bluff.

Yamani is aware of the strain the oil crisis has put on the world monetary system and acknowledges that "we in Saudi Arabia cannot stand isolated if the economies of other nations collapse around us." Nevertheless, the mixing of economic necessities with political and nationalistic factors makes the oil question a particularly difficult problem. Yamani, with an understanding of the world of oil from both the Arab and American perspectives, will remain an important voice in devising a possible solution.

Nobel Prizes. The 1974 Nobel Prizes for literature, physics, chemistry, physiology or medicine, and economics were presented by King Karl Gustav of Sweden on December 10 in Stockholm. The peace prize was presented in Oslo, Norway, on the same day. Each prize was worth approximately $124,000.

Aleksandr Solzhenitsyn attended the Stockholm ceremony, accepting the 1970 Nobel literature award. The Russian novelist, who was expelled from the Soviet Union earlier in 1974, had not previously come to Sweden to accept the prize for fear he would not be allowed by Soviet officials to return home.

Peace

The Nobel Committee of the Norwegian parliament awarded the peace prize on October 8 to former Japanese premier Eisaku Sato and to Sean MacBride, United Nations commissioner for South-West Africa. Sato, premier from 1964 to 1972, was cited for policies that led Japan to pledge, through signing the nuclear nonproliferation treaty, never to acquire nuclear arms of its own. MacBride, Ireland's foreign minister from 1948 to 1951, was honored for work on behalf of human rights. He was secretary general of the International Commission of Jurists from 1963 to 1970, and is chairman of Amnesty International, an organization that works on behalf of political prisoners. As UN commissioner, he is charged with supervising the UN's efforts to gain independence for South-West Africa, which is currently ruled by the Republic of South Africa.

Literature

On October 3, the Swedish Academy awarded the literature prize to two native sons—Eyvind Johnson and Harry Edmund Martinson, both members of the Academy. Few of their works have been published in English, and none were in print in the United States at the time of the award.

Johnson, 74, was cited for "a narrative art, far-seeing in lands and ages, in the service of freedom." Many of his novels and short stories are based on his early hard life in the north of Sweden. His best-known work in English translation is *Re-*

Nobel Awards. Exiled Soviet author Aleksandr Solzhenitsyn received his 1970 literature prize during award ceremonies in Stockholm. Recipients for 1974, shown in the front row applauding Solzhenitsyn, included, *left to right:* Albert Claude, Christian de Duve, and Emil Palade, physiology or medicine; Eyvind Johnson and Harry Martinson, literature; and Gunnar Myrdal and Friedrich von Hayek, economics.

turn to Ithaca, a novel that explores Greek culture simultaneously in its early, semi-barbaric stage and in the mid-20th century.

Martinson, 70, a poet, novelist, essayist, and dramatist, was praised for "writings that catch the dewdrop and reflect the cosmos." His most widely published work is *The Road,* a sympathetic study of the lives of tramps and other social outcasts in an age of growing industrialization. Also well known is a long narrative poem called *Aniara,* the tale of a spaceship on a journey into the void. But Martinson called the English translation of this work "a scandal."

Physics

For the first time the physics prize, awarded October 15 by the Royal Swedish Academy of Sciences, went to astronomers—Martin Ryle and Antony Hewish, both of the Cavendish Laboratory of Cambridge University. Ryle is best known for devising the technique called aperture synthesis, by which several small radio telescopes, rather than one big dish, can be used to locate objects several billion light-years away. Hewish, also a radio astronomer, headed the group that discov-ered pulsars in 1967. (See also the Feature Article in the third section, 1972.)

Chemistry

Paul Flory of Stanford University was awarded the chemistry prize on October 15 by the Royal Swedish Academy of Sciences. Flory put the study of synthetic polymers on a firm quantitative basis in studying the properties and molecular architecture of long-chain molecules. (A polymer is a giant molecule made of many smaller molecules strung in a long chain.)

Flory was a member of the team that created nylon, one of the earliest synthetic polymers to receive wide application. His work has made possible the wide range of plastics and other polymer compounds used in clothing, tires, paints, films, machine parts, lubricants, and other products.

Physiology or Medicine

On October 10, the Royal Caroline Institute awarded the prize for physiology or medicine to Albert Claude, George Emil Palade, and Christian de Duve for their research into the physiology of cells. Claude, the senior member, was born in Luxembourg and is a naturalized American, although he works at the Institut

Jules Bordet in Brussels. He pioneered in the use of the electron microscope to study cells and the use of high-speed centrifuges to separate the various components of the cell for examination.

In 1945, Claude published the first detailed picture of the anatomy of a cell. Palade, a Rumanian-born researcher who teaches at Yale University, and de Duve, a Belgian who holds positions at Rockefeller University and the University of Louvain, advanced and refined Claude's work with sophisticated biochemical analyses of the components of cells. Palade discovered the ribosome, the cell's protein "factory," while de Duve discovered lysosomes—the "stomachs" of the cell.

As a result of their research in cell physiology, scientists are working on more selective ways to treat disease. If a disease is found to be a defect or ailment of only one cell part, a more precise treatment may be devised than the use of drugs that have a far wider effect than necessary.

Economics

Gunnar Myrdal and Friedrich von Hayek were awarded the economics prize on October 19 by the Royal Swedish Academy of Sciences. In announcing the joint award to men with very different convictions, the Academy cited them for putting forward "new ideas on causes and politics."

The Austrian-born Hayek has taught at universities in England, the United States, Germany, and Austria; he was a professor at the University of Chicago from 1950 to 1962. *The Road to Serfdom* (1944) spells out his laissez-faire views on economics and politics. He opposes big government, deficit spending, and the creation of money by central banks, and argues that there cannot be rational allocation of economic resources under socialism.

By contrast, Myrdal, who is Swedish, supports his country's widespread welfare measures and the government's large-scale intervention in the economy. Among his works is the classic *An American Dilemma* (1944), concerning race relations in the United States. He is working on a sequel with psychologist Kenneth Clark.

Obituaries. October, November, and December, 1974.

ACE, JANE, radio comedian who delighted audiences with her malapropisms in the 1930's and 1940's, when, with her husband Goodman Ace, she starred in the program "Easy Aces"; November 11, age 74.

BEARD, M. G. (Dan), engineer who contributed to the development of commercial aircraft over a period of more than 40 years; December 25, age 78.

BENNY, JACK, (Benjamin Kubelsky), one of America's most popular comedians, noted for his meticulous sense of timing. His radio show, broadcast nationwide from 1932 to 1955, portrayed him as stingy and vain, and he was often the butt of jokes by his valet, Rochester, and other characters on the show. He also appeared occasionally in movies, most notably in *To Be or Not To Be;* December 26, age 80.

BICKEL, ALEXANDER M., Yale University professor of law and one of the nation's leading authorities on the Constitution. He was best known for his participation in the successful suit by the New York *Times* to block the federal government from barring the publication of the Pentagon Papers in 1971; November 7, age 49.

Jack Benny

Paul Hoffman

BRANZELL, KAREN, leading contralto for 21 seasons at New York City's Metropolitan Opera; December 15, age 83.

BROOK, CLIVE, British actor who starred on stage and screen in roles that epitomized suavity and elegance; November 17, age 87.

BROWN, JOHNNY MACK, star in hundreds of Western movies of the 1930's and 1940's after an outstanding college-football career for the University of Alabama that saw him become the hero of the 1926 Rose Bowl; November 14, age 70.

BRYAN, JULIEN, documentary film-maker who photographed people and cultures around the world and produced more than 30 documentaries for the State Department; October 20, age 75.

CADBURY, HENRY J., Biblical scholar and founder of the American Friends Service Committee who accepted the 1947 Nobel Peace Prize, which was awarded to his organization and the British branch for humanitarian work; October 7, age 90.

CARNEY, HARRY HOWELL, jazz saxophonist who was a long-time associate of Duke Ellington; October 8, age 64.

CHILDERS, ERSKINE HAMILTON, president of Ireland since 1973; November 17, age 68.

CONNOLLY, CYRIL, English literary critic, author, and editor noted for his wit and urbanity; November 26, age 71.

COUNTS, GEORGE S., educator who was professor at Columbia University's Teachers College from 1927 to 1959 and the author of 29 books on educational philosophy; November 10, age 84.

DE SICA, VITTORIO, Italian film actor and director who received five Oscars for films ranging from the neo-realist *The Bicycle Thief* (1949) to *The Garden of the Finzi-Continis* (1972). Earlier, he gained a passionate army of women admirers as a matinee idol of the Italian cinema; November 13, age 73.

DEWEY, BRADLEY, engineer and industrialist who helped develop such products as synthetic rubber, sealant for metal cans, and plastic film for packaging food; October 14, age 87.

DRAPER, WILLIAM H., JR., investment banker, diplomat, and high-ranking army officer who helped administer the economic recovery of post-World War II Europe and later held several positions dealing with the world population problem; December 26, age 80.

DUTT, R. PALME, a founder and for many years the leading theoretician of the British Communist party; December 20, age 79.

EARLE, GEORGE H. 3RD, Democratic governor of Pennsylvania, 1935-39, and diplomat who served in the Balkans during World War II; December 30, age 84.

FARRAR, JOHN C., poet, playwright, and founder of two publishing houses; November 5, age 78.

FLYNN, F. M., president and publisher of the New York *Daily News*—the largest general circulation newspaper in the country— from 1946 to 1973; November 15, age 71.

FURTSEVA, YEKATERINA A., only woman in Soviet history to be admitted to the ruling inner circle (as a member of the Communist party's Presidium, 1957-61), and minister of culture since 1960; October 25, age 63.

GERAUD, ANDRE, French editorial writer who under the pseudonym "Pertinax" was one of the most influential political commentators in France between the two world wars; December 11, age 92.

HARRIS, SEYMOUR A., economist who was a Harvard professor for more than 40 years, a supporter of the theories of John Maynard Keynes, and an influential adviser to presidents Kennedy and Johnson; October 27, age 77.

HERSHFIELD, HARRY, cartoonist, toastmaster, raconteur, and humorous columnist who appeared weekly on the radio show "Can You Top This?" during the 1940's; December 15, age 89.

HODGES, LUTHER H., textile executive who served as governor of North Carolina, 1954-60, and secretary of commerce, 1961-64, under presidents Kennedy and Johnson; October 6, age 76.

HOFFMAN, PAUL G., auto executive who was the first administrator of the Marshall Plan, drafted to rebuild post-World War II Europe. After serving as president of Studebaker, 1935-48, Hoffman supervised $10 billion in aid to Europe during a 2½-year period. From 1959 to 1972 he served as president of the UN Development Program and its predecessor, the Special Fund, which channeled large sums from prosperous nations to underdeveloped countries; October 9, age 83.

HOLT, L. EMMETT, JR., internationally acclaimed pediatrician who expanded the pediatrics department of the New York University School of Medicine into a major research center and whose *Holt's Care and Feeding of Children* was a perennial bestseller; November 30, age 79.

HUNT, H. L., oilman who was one of the world's richest men, his worth estimated at between $1 billion and $2 billion. A wildcatter who made his first big stake in Arkansas during the 1920's, Hunt struck it even richer in the east Texas fields. Later the Hunt interests, exploring in Libya, brought in one of the biggest oil finds of the century.

Hunt's style of life was modest, even miserly, in proportion to his resources; he often carried his lunch to his office in a brown paper bag, and his clothes were apt to be shabby. He espoused right-wing political causes, but his influence was limited by his reluctance to provide substantial financial support; November 29, age 85.

ISMAIL, AHMED, Egypt's minister of war and commander in chief of its armed forces during the 1973 Yom Kippur War against Israel; December 25, age 57.

JONES, DAVID, Welsh poet and painter whose reputation rested chiefly on his long poem "In Parenthesis" (1937), an account of his experiences in France during World War I; October 28, age 78.

KALVEN, HARRY, JR., professor of law at the University of Chicago whose *The American Jury* (1966), co-authored by Hans Zeisel, was a landmark study on how juries deliberate; October 29, age 60.

KLEBERG, ROBERT, JR., president of the King Ranch, Inc., which owns 960,000 acres of cattle and oil lands—about the size of Rhode Island—in Texas, operates an addi-

Walter Lippmann

tional 11.5 million acres of ranches abroad, and is the largest single U.S. producer of beef cattle. Kleberg developed the Santa Gertrudis breed of cattle and also bred thoroughbred horses, two of which won the Kentucky Derby; October 13, age 78.

KRIPS, JOSEF, Austrian conductor whose career spanned 53 years with various symphony orchestras, including the Buffalo and San Francisco ensembles; October 12, age 72.

KRISHNA MENON, V. K., diplomat who as India's representative to the United Nations during the 1950's was a scathing critic of U.S. policies. He also served as India's defense minister, 1957-62; October 6, age 77.

LENGYEL, MELCHIOR, Hungarian playwright whose plays were staged by Max Reinhardt in Berlin and Vienna and filmed by Ernst Lubitsch in Hollywood (including *Ninotchka* and *To Be or Not to Be*). He also wrote the libretto for Béla Bartók's opera *The Miraculous Mandarin;* October 25, age 95.

LIPPMANN, WALTER, dean of American political journalism whose views on national and international affairs were read and respected by millions during a career that spanned six decades. An independent thinker, he supported what he defined as "liberal democ-

David Oistrakh

U Thant

racy"—an open society governed by law. A socialist in his youth, he later turned conservative and was critical of the New Deal; an interventionist during both world wars, he opposed U.S. intervention in Vietnam and Cold War policies, and was an advocate of Soviet-American détente; December 14, age 85.

LITVAK, ANATOLE, Russian-American film director whose pictures included *Sorry, Wrong Number* and *The Snake Pit;* December 15, age 72.

MARINATOS, SPYRIDON, Greek archeologist who in 1967 discovered a port city on the island of Thera that had been destroyed 3,500 years ago by a volcanic explosion and was identified as the legendary Atlantis; October 3, age 73.

MARTIN, FRANK, Swiss composer who was regarded as one of his country's outstanding creative figures; November 21, age 84.

MELNIKOV, KONSTANTIN, Russian avant-garde architect whose Soviet Pavilion was one of the highlights of the 1925 Paris Exposition; November 28, age 84.

OISTRAKH, DAVID, the Soviet Union's premier violinist. Hailed by audiences the world over, he played with most of the leading orchestras; October 24, age 65.

PIERCE, BILLIE GOODSON, pianist who with her husband, De De Pierce, led the Preservation Hall Jazz Band in the 1960's; October 1, age 67.

RYAN, CORNELIUS, Irish-American author of three best-sellers about World War II: *The Longest Day, The Last Battle,* and *A Bridge Too Far;* November 23, age 54.

SAILLANT, LOUIS, French union leader who for 24 years headed the Communist-run World Federation of Trade Unions; October 28, age 73.

SAQQAF, OMAR, Saudi Arabia's minister of state for foreign affairs who was active in carrying Arab views to Latin America; November 14, age 51.

SCHINDLER, OSKAR, wartime Nazi intelligence officer who saved more than 1,200 Jews from the gas chambers; October 12, age 66.

SEXTON, ANNE, "confessional" poet who received the 1967 Pulitzer poetry prize for her volume *Live or Die;* October 4, age 45.

SHAZAR, ZALMAN, president of Israel from 1963 to 1973; October 5, age 84.

SPOTTSWOOD, STEPHEN GILL, bishop of the African Methodist Episcopal Zion Church and chairman of the board of the National Association for the Advancement of Colored People since 1961; December 1, age 77.

STANLEY, FRANK L., civil rights leader and owner and publisher of the Louisville *Defender* who drafted legislation that led to the integration of Kentucky's public universities; October 19, age 69.

STARK, PAUL C., nurseryman credited with finding and developing the Golden Delicious apple; October 28, age 83.

SULLIVAN, EDWARD VINCENT, host and producer of "The Ed Sullivan Show," televised between 1948 and 1971. At its peak, the Sunday evening show with a vaudeville-like format attracted as many as 50 million viewers and featured the American television debuts of the Beatles, Elvis Presley, and many other entertainers and artists. Sullivan was also long a Broadway columnist for New York City newspapers, starting in 1929; October 13, age 73.

THANT, U, Burmese diplomat who served as secretary general of the United Nations from 1961 to 1971. During this strife-filled period he emerged as a quiet, patient negotiator who sought to reconcile the power blocs. Originally a schoolteacher, Thant became Burma's chief representative at the UN in 1957; November 25, age 65.

TROISGROS, JEAN-BAPTISTE, French restaurateur whose restaurant in Roanne was often acclaimed as the greatest in the world; October 23, age 77.

VANDERBILT, AMY, syndicated columnist and authority on etiquette whose 700-page book of customs, mores, and manners, *Amy Vanderbilt's Complete Book of Etiquette,* sold millions of copies; December 27, age 66.

WELLESZ, EGON, Austrian-British composer and music historian who was a disciple of Arnold Schoenberg and an authority on Byzantine music; November 9, age 89.

WHITNEY, RICHARD, stockbroker who became a hero on Wall Street when he temporarily halted the market crash in 1929 by placing generous orders, later president of the New York Stock Exchange for five years —and embezzler sent to Sing Sing Prison in 1938 for stealing hundreds of thousands of dollars entrusted to him by the stock exchange, the New York Yacht Club, and his father-in-law's estate; December 5, age 86.

WIGHTMAN, HAZEL HOTCHKISS, queen mother of American tennis who won 45 national titles and donated the Wightman Cup, which is presented to the winners of an annual competition between U.S. and British women players; December 5, age 87.

Petroleum. See BUSINESS AND FINANCE and ENERGY.

Physics. On November 16, two teams of researchers working independently at the Brookhaven National Laboratory in Upton, Long Island, and the Stanford Linear Accelerator Center in Palo Alto, California, announced that they had both discovered a new type of subnuclear particle. Within days of the announcement, researchers in Frascati, Italy, confirmed the discovery, and a few days later, the Stanford team discovered another similar particle.

Many physicists believed the discoveries might open a whole new dimension to the study of elementary, subnuclear particles. But there were differing views as to how the discoveries might fit into current theories on elementary particles.

The Stanford team named the first particle psi 3100, with the number representing the mass in millions of electron volts (MEV's) if completely converted to energy. The second, more massive particle, was called psi 3700. The particles were from three to four times heavier than the proton, which is one of the heaviest subnuclear particles.

Subnuclear Particles

At one time the atom was thought to be a fundamental, indivisible particle of matter, but by 1961 close to 100 smaller particles had been discovered. Theory could not explain the existence of so many, most of them short-lived and having a perplexing diversity of characteristics. (See also the Feature Article in the third section, 1971.)

One way of classifying subnuclear particles is by their mass. Baryons are particles that are heavier than neutrons or protons. Mesons are intermediate in mass between protons and electrons. Leptons are lightweight particles.

Another way of classifying them is according to how they respond to the four basic forces, or interactions, affecting matter. The two best known are electromagnetism and gravity. The two others, which operate only within the atom, are the strong and weak forces. The strong force binds neutrons and protons together within the nucleus of the atom. The weak force

—which some physicists believe is actually only a manifestation of electromagnetism —is known to delay the decay of some elementary particles.

Almost every kind of elementary particle has a counterpart called an antiparticle, which is identical to the particle except for having an opposite electrical charge or spin.

The most distinguishing characteristic of the new particles is that they are at the same time very massive and relatively long-lived. As a rule, massive particles are short-lived, but the two new particles lasted much longer before decaying than the most similar particles known, surviving a full one-hundred-billionth of one-billionth of a second. (Some physicists believe the heavier of the two particles is simply an energized or "excited" state of the other.)

One popular theory was that the new particle (or particles) possesses a combination of mathematical properties known as "charm," a term proposed in 1964 to explain an apparent lack of symmetry between the behavior of particles whose interactions are in some cases controlled by the strong force relative to those that are affected only by the weak force.

The Quark Theory

Nobel prizewinner Murray Gell-Mann, a professor at the California Institute of Technology, has theorized the existence of a trio of truly fundamental particles named "quarks" from which (along with three antiquarks) all known particles could be constructed. No quark has ever been found, but the theory continues to fascinate physicists. One variant of the theory is that a fourth type of quark—one bearing the quality of charm—should combine with each of the three other types of quark (and their respective antiquarks) to produce a variety of heavy particles.

Another idea that excites physicists is the possibility that the new particle might help in devising a unified field theory that would explain the relationship between the four basic forces. (Albert Einstein was only one of many theoretical physicists who sought in vain to devise an acceptable unified field theory.) Dr. Benjamin Lee of the Fermi National Accelerator Laboratory remarked that confirmation of charm could lead physics "close to a unified picture" of three of the forces: strong, weak, and electromagnetic.

New Particle. The Stanford University physicists at left directed a team of researchers that discovered a new type of subnuclear particle. A Long Island group, working independently of Stanford, also discovered the particle, and researchers in Italy confirmed the discovery.

World Population Conference. Delegates from 135 nations debated the nature of the population problem and the range of possible remedies. The global total of nearly 4 billion people is expected to double by the year 2000 if the present rate of increase continues.

Population. The United Nations designated 1974 as World Population Year, to draw attention to the problems of the overcrowded planet. Every year, 80 million people are added to the global total of nearly 4 billion. This figure is expected to double by the year 2000, if the present rate of increase (1.9 per cent annually) continues.

World Population Parley

To consider these trends, the first World Population Conference, sponsored by the UN, was convened in Bucharest, Rumania, August 19 to 30. Delegates from 135 governments debated the nature of the population problem and the range of possible remedies, but there was little agreement between the representatives of the developed and underdeveloped countries. While industrialized nations sought restrictions on population growth to reduce hunger and shortages of raw materials, many other nations saw advantages for economic development in a larger population and urged greater sharing of

the world's wealth by the major resource consumers.

At the end of the conference, a Plan of Action drafted at earlier symposia was adopted by acclamation. The first two sections of the document provided background and "principles and objectives," while the third part contained recommendations on population goals and policies, information and implementation, and social and economic policies affecting birthrates, including economic and political equality for women.

No specific national or international population goals were set, but the plan suggested that the world growth rate could be substantially reduced by 1985, if the necessary policies were implemented. The plan avoided the most controversial issues surrounding population growth, including its relationship to world resources and the development of the less economically advanced nations.

Still, the international ramifications of population expansion were cited: "The

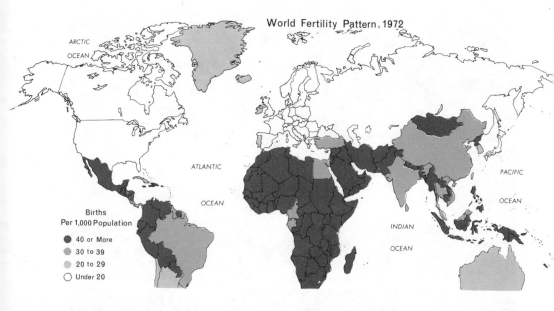

World Fertility Pattern, 1972

Births
Per 1,000 Population

- 40 or More
- 30 to 39
- 20 to 29
- Under 20

Birth Rates are highest in the countries of Asia, Africa, and Latin America. But the social attitudes that determine birth-rate trends can change rapidly and are not well understood by demographers.

effect of national action or inaction may . . . extend beyond national boundaries. Such international implications are particularly evident with regard to aspects of morbidity, population concentrations, and international migration, but they may also apply to other aspects of population concern." The plan called for international cooperation to play a "supportive role" in the form of technical and financial assistance in addition to economic development aid, such as monitoring and information sharing.

The Action Plan also declared that individuals have a basic human right to determine freely and responsibly the number of their children and to have information, education, and means to do so. It called on governments to provide such information and means before 1985, and invited countries with very high birth rates to consider reducing them by 5 to 10 births (per 1,000 population) by that year. At the same time, the plan advocated measures to reduce infant mortality and extend average life expectancy.

Birth and Death Rates

Although the developed nations have generally succeeded in reducing population growth rates to under 1 per cent a year, in the developing countries, the average annual rate remains around 2.6 per cent. Latin America has the most rapid regional growth, at a 2.9-per-cent overall rate yearly, with Ecuador, El Salvador, Paraguay, Mexico, and Belize increasing in population at an annual rate of 3.4 per cent or more. At the rate of 2.5 to 3.5 per cent per year, population doubles in only 20 to 28 years.

The current high rates of population growth worldwide represent a deviation from the historical norm. It is believed that, from the time of the first cities some 5,000 years ago to the late 17th century, the annual rate of increase in human numbers probably never reached as high as .1 per cent. But from about 1800 on, a decline in death rates in Europe and lands settled by Europeans overseas began to accelerate the rate of population expansion.

A decline in birthrates followed later, as fewer children were needed per family to ensure the survival of several to maturity. Children also became more of an economic liability in urban society, contributing less to family income than in agricultural communities.

In the developing countries today, the same process is being repeated, as better sanitation and medical care increase longevity. But there is a time lag between the dropping of death rates and the parallel decline in fertility. It is expected that, eventually, growth rates will be slowed everywhere to the replacement level (at which the average family includes parents and two children), restoring the historical pattern which prevailed before the industrial revolution.

However, even in countries where the population-growth rate has approached the replacement level, the population will continue to expand until the age structure of the society shifts from predominantly young to predominantly older people. This shift is expected to take about 60 more years in the developed nations.

In the most industrialized countries, a new pattern is appearing in the age structure of the population, in which there are roughly equal numbers of people in every age group up to the sixth decade. This is very different from the pyramid-shaped age structure of most underdeveloped nations, which have large numbers of young adults and children. (More than half the world's population is under age 25.)

There is no assurance that the present trend toward near-zero rates of growth in the most developed countries will continue. The uncertainties of population projection can be seen in the events of recent decades in the United States.

During the low-birth period of the 1930's, demographers predicted that the country's population would reach 150 million about the middle of the century and then decline. But, by the late 1950's, the total population had already passed 170 million, and the postwar "baby boom" showed no signs of ending. Fears of an imminent "population explosion" which would lead to "standing room only" became widespread.

But in the 1960's, the fertility rate (the number of births per 1,000 females aged 15 to 44) suddenly declined. In the early 1970's, when the postwar babies had been expected to be marrying and starting families of their own, the birthrate mysteriously continued to fall, defying all predictions of the Census Bureau. The fertility rate, which had been forecast at between 84.6 and 119.1 in 1970 and between 84.1 and 127.6 in 1975, had already dropped to 69 in early 1973 and is still declining.

Social attitudes regulating these trends —such as the number of children most desired by young women—can change rapidly, and are not well understood. Economic influences on birthrates are also difficult to predict. But if the long-range downward trend in births continues, the United States is expected to achieve a stable population soon after the year 2000.

Economic Effects

In the 1960's, it was generally taken for granted that high population growth rates retarded economic and social modernization in the less advanced nations by consuming too much of their limited human and material resources. High rates of population growth absorbed one-half to two-thirds of the annual increase in national product in these countries, and limited opportunities for education and employment. Pressure on food prices increased the danger of malnutrition and famine. These conditions were seen as contributing to social unrest, political instability, and sometimes, violence.

But population growth is not seen by all current analysts as an obstacle to development. A preparatory symposium to the 1974 World Population Conference declared: "A preoccupation with population should not divert attention from critical issues in the world development process. . . . Population growth is not always an obstacle to development [although] very high rates of population growth are usually an obstacle. . . ."

Some observers see certain advantages in population growth, even in low-income countries, such as increased savings for capital investment, larger markets, and other stimuli to innovation in agriculture and industry. Others argue that the real issue is not population growth, but the proper organization of society (for example, socialist as opposed to nonsocialist forms of government), the redistribution of income and resources, and the rectification of social injustice.

In the transition from predominantly rural, traditional society to predominantly urban, modern life, new values and behavioral patterns emerge. Different religious and social attitudes toward the family; the migration of people and the movement of ideas; the education and employment of women—all of these features of modernization may have an influence on fertility levels. Thus modernization is a cause, as well as an effect, of lower birthrates. Although the view that rapid population growth is a serious hindrance to development is widely held, experts are found on both sides of the question.

Food and Population. Authorities fear that population growth is outstripping world food supplies. *Below,* a delegate to the World Food Conference, held in Rome in November, checks his weight on the "Scale of Justice." Overweight delegates were invited to pay a tax for the benefit of those facing starvation.

Family Planning

Most governments, including more than 40 in the developing world with 80 per cent of its people, conduct family planning programs. But the explicit goal of these programs is not always to reduce birthrates. Some thinly populated nations wish to increase their workforce or military manpower. In many, there is a political "backlash" toward population-control policies, which are seen as a form of neocolonialism.

In developed countries, government policy toward fertility tends to be pronatalist, whether or not a written population policy exists. This is because government tax and welfare laws usually provide incentives for marriage and the birth of children. Yet, in most of these nations, the birthrate continues to fall.

In developing countries which are attempting to limit population growth, there are several means by which a lower birthrate can be encouraged. Government services and social institutions can manipulate reproductive behavior by means short of outright coercion. In Singapore, for example, no paid maternity leaves are granted after the first two children, and income-tax deductions and obstetrical fees are similarly scaled to promote smaller families. In China, where the birthrate is reported to be declining, birth control (and a high minimum age for marriage) are supported by community pressure and the political apparatus of the one-party state.

A number of internationally financed agencies assist nations wishing to limit their population growth. Funds for such efforts, which totaled $180 million in fiscal 1973, come from the United Nations Fund for Population Activities (supported by more than 60 countries), the World Health Organization and other UN agencies, the World Bank, the Organization for Economic Development, and individual governments.

Private associations working in this field include the International Planned Parenthood Federation, the Population Council, the Pathfinder Fund, Family Planning International Assistance, and many other groups. Planned Parenthood,

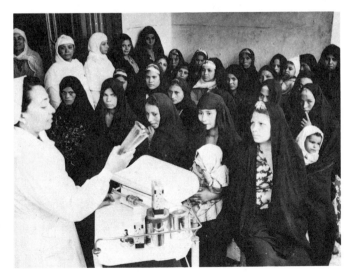

Family Planning. Expectant Egyptian mothers attend a prenatal-health lecture. A number of internationally financed agencies assist nations wishing to lower their birth rates and thus limit population growth.

which is 40-per-cent financed by the United States, assists in the operation of family-planning associations in more than 80 countries.

Although most of these programs are less than a decade old, they already seem to be having an impact on population growth. For 65 countries of the 79 for which data are available, there was a decrease in growth rates between 1960 and 1972. Most of those countries showing increases were very small or developed.

U.S. Population Policy

The United States has long supported population-control activities conducted by the United Nations. About 60 per cent of the estimated $180 million made available to the UN from external sources for population programs in developing nations was contributed by the United States, although contributions from other donors are rising.

At the UN, the United States has supported resolutions affirming family-planning information as a basic human right. Beyond the Action Plan adopted by the World Population Conference, the United States has proposed medium-range goals for fertility reduction by both developing and developed nations, with an ultimate goal of reducing global population growth to 1.7 per cent by 1985.

Family-planning services and facilities are increasingly becoming available to Americans wishing to space their children. Laws in some states which formerly restricted the sale of contraceptives have been declared unconstitutional. A nationwide family-services program enacted by Congress is administered by the federal government, and some form of government-subsidized family-planning service exists in 85 per cent of U.S. counties. A national Center for Population Research supports a large biomedical and social-service program of research in human fertility and its control. Other research is conducted by the U.S. Agency for International Development.

Three alternative approaches to the issue of continued growth are found among population scientists today. The 1972 report of the U.S. Commission on Population Growth took the position that, while increased population is not the only cause of social and economic difficulties, it is a "multiplier factor" which intensifies other kinds of social ills. Another viewpoint holds that population expansion constitutes an international crisis leading to global catastrophe if steps are not taken immediately to reduce birthrates. A third body of opinion, widely represented at the World Population Conference, regards population as a nonproblem, which will disappear as other economic, social, and political goals are attained by the developing nations.

Religion

With 530 million adherents, Islam is the world's second largest and most rapidly expanding faith. Although the religion is usually associated with the Arabs by Westerners, fewer than one-fourth of the world's Moslems are Arabs. The largest national Islamic community is in Indonesia (105 million), followed by Bangladesh (65 million) and India (61 million). It is estimated that from 25 to 40 million Moslems remain in the Soviet Union, and 10 million in mainland China.

A de-Arabized style of Islam flourishes in Southeast Asia, its theology blended with local beliefs. In Africa south of the Sahara, Islam is making inroads in both animist and Christian areas, from Guinea-Bissau on the West Coast eastward to Nigeria, Zaïre, and Mozambique.

The essential simplicity of Islam, which literally means "submission" (to God's will) in Arabic, is a major factor in its dynamism. The core of the religion is the "five pillars": the *shahadah,* or declaration of faith—"There is no god but Allah, and Mohammed is His messenger"; prayer, five times daily; fasting, during daylight hours in the lunar month of Ramadan; almsgiving; and the hajj, or pilgrimage to Mecca (the birthplace of the Prophet, in Saudi Arabia) once during one's lifetime, if physically and financially possible.

Theology does not occupy as central a position in Islam as in Christianity. There is no religious hierarchy, no sacraments such as baptism, and no concept of original sin. In the words of Ahmed Fathy al-Zayat, vice rector of al-Azhar University in Cairo: "We believe that the universe is controlled by something, and we call it Allah."

But Islam is a social and ethical system as well as a transcendent faith. The *Sharia* ("way")—the body of Moslem law (comparable to the Jewish Talmud) prescribes behavior for nearly every aspect of life. Most of the four major schools of legal interpretation in Islam accept as the "roots" of the Sharia the *Koran* (literally: "reciting"), the book of divine revelation given to Mohammed in the Arabic language; the *Hadith* ("tradition") based on the behavior of the Prophet and his earliest followers; *Ijma* ("consensus"), variously interpreted as the collective agreement of the community or of the ulama, or religious scholars; and *Qiyas* (deduction by analogy).

Ethically and politically, Islam is a flexible religion which is well suited to its proselytizing tradition. Travelers, soldiers, and the sick are excused from the performance of most religious obligations. Clifford Geertz, an anthropologist and authority on Islam, has commented. "There is very little that is ambiguous. It's built to travel."

In the Middle East, a religious revival has taken place since the defeat of Arab forces in the June, 1967, war with Israel. A widespread sense of frustration and loss inspired increased devotion among some Moslems; others interpreted the defeat as a divine punishment for their religious laxity. The successful Egyptian crossing of the Suez Canal in October, 1973, was seen by many Moslems as divine recognition of their increased piety.

One element of the religious awakening

Moslem Oil Workers in Saudi Arabia face Mecca during one of their five-times-daily prayer sessions. The oil tanks symbolize the growing power and prestige of Islam resulting from the Arab nations' successful "oil diplomacy."

Moslem Judges in Nigeria. The *Sharia*, or body of Islamic law, prescribes behavior for nearly every aspect of life.

has been a resurgence of traditional Islamic values. In Libya, Colonel Muammar el-Qaddafi has instituted a puritanical domestic code and has attempted to ban Western influences. His foreign policy is based on Pan-Islamism, which affirms the political potential of Moslem unity. King Faisal, the fundamentalist ruler of Saudi Arabia, a country whose constitution is the Koran and whose legislation is based on the Sharia, has gained new status as a symbol of fidelity to the faith as a result of his successful "oil diplomacy."

The Moslem Brotherhood, a secretive organization suppressed in Egypt in 1954, is reported to be making a comeback. A right-wing political force, the Moslem Brotherhood seeks to reconstruct society along traditional lines.

Even in socialist revolutionary governments such as those of Iraq or Syria, political leaders refrain from attacks on Islamic institutions, and direct criticism of Islam is rarely published anywhere. Throughout the Arab world, Islam contributes to a sense of pride and unity.

But, although in most Moslem countries there is no formal separation between religion and the state, the religious codes usually function only in matters involving personal status, such as marriage and inheritance. Commercial and criminal law are based on borrowed European codes.

Islam in Africa

One out of three Africans is a Moslem, including one of five black Africans. The estimated 70 million African Moslems are one-eighth of the world total. Although the precise rate of expansion is difficult to determine, Islam is the fastest-growing religion in Africa and continues to make converts among both animists and Christians.

The success of Islam in sub-Saharan Africa is attributed in part to its compatibility with native religion, and in part to its acceptance by Africans as an indigenous faith—in contrast to Christianity, which they identify with French and British imperialism. In an era of nationalism, Islam has often played a role in African struggles against both old and "neo" colonialism. But in some countries, it has also created new divisions.

Islam was first brought to black Africa centuries ago by nomadic traders such as the Tuaregs of the Sahara, who carried salt, leather, sugar, and cloth to ancient desert crossroads like Kano and Timbuktu. Syrian and Indian Moslems imported Islam to the commercial cities of the East and West African coasts. Along with their religion, the Moslem migrants brought the Arabic language and Islamic art and architecture. (Swahili, widely spoken in East Africa, is one-quarter Arabic in vocabulary.)

Today, the frontier of Islamic penetration extends diagonally across the continent, from Guinea and Senegal in the West, through the sub-Saharan Sudan to northern Zaïre and Ethiopia, and south as far as Mozambique. (There are also many Moslems in the Republic of South Africa.) Besides Senegal and Guinea, Islam is the dominant religion in seven sub-Saharan countries, including Mauritania, Gambia, Mali, Niger, Chad, and Sudan. In six others, Moslems are a substantial minority (over 25 per cent): Nigeria, Ivory Coast, Ethiopia, Guinea-Bissau, Sierra Leone, and Cameroon.

Political ties between African and Arab Moslems are strengthened by the thousands of black Africans who annually make the hajj, or pilgrimage to Mecca, and through economic-assistance programs. Saudi Arabia, for instance, pro- vided $4 million for an Islamic center in Senegal and agreed to build a $12-million mosque in Chad. Former African colonies regard Arab nations as "Third World" countries like themselves, and tend to support them in the Arab-Israeli dispute. In turn, the Arab nations promoted African independence.

As an ethical system, Islam was congenial to most African cultures it encountered. Some Islamic practices, such as polygamy and emphasis on the extended family, were already elements of many African tribal societies. But in other places, Islam was adopted despite conflicts with native traditions. As a result, Islam in Africa acquired many variations, differing widely from the austere, formal, doctrine promulgated by Arab scholars.

Mahdism and religious brotherhoods are prominent features in African Islam. Mahdism is a heretical concept based on belief in the coming of a Mahdi, or Chosen One, who will lead the Moslem community to salvation politically and spiritually. Several Mahdist uprisings occurred in the Sudan and Somalia around the turn of the

Pilgrims pitch tents, preparing for a day of meditation on a hill outside Mecca—one of the three traditional observances. The pilgrimage to Mecca is an obligation once during one's lifetime for every Moslem physically and financially able to make the journey.

century; later the idea appeared in Nigeria and elsewhere.

Religious brotherhoods (which are also found in the Middle East and South and Southeast Asia) are widespread in tropical Africa. Some are mystical, while others emphasize moral reform. The Qadariyya and Tijaniyya are two of the best known West African brotherhoods. The Ahmadiyya is a leading East African group which is active in the field of education and social reform, teaching that study and science are encouraged by the Koran.

Islam has united diverse ethnic groups and communities in some parts of Africa, thereby assisting in nation-building. But in others, it reinforced existing tribal or ethnic interests, leading to tension and, sometimes, warfare. Conflict between predominantly Moslem northerners and Christian or animist southerners is especially common along the sub-Saharan belt.

In Chad, Moslems rebels in the north and east, aided by Libya, have been conducting a guerrilla war against the French-backed government in Fort Lamy since 1968. Although the population is slightly over one-half Moslem, President François Tombalbaye's regime is dominated by the better-educated animist and Christian south. A long period of warfare in neighboring Sudan between southern dissidents and the Moslem-controlled government in the north ended officially in 1972.

In West Africa, Nigeria has been a battleground between Moslem and non-Moslem ethnic groups. The Hausa northern half of the country is a Moslem stronghold, and Islam is spreading among the Yorubas in the Western section. But a massacre in 1966 of thousands of Catholic Ibos by Moslem Hausas led to a civil war that continued until 1970.

Cameroon is also an area of many racial, tribal, and religious divisions. Although a north-south schism exists, the government of President Ahmadou Ahidjo (a Moslem northerner) has managed to maintain stability.

Ethiopia, where the Coptic Christian government of Haile Selassie excluded the Moslem half of the population from power, illustrates the difficulties involved in obtaining accurate statistics on religious groups in Africa. For many years, the number of Moslems in the population was systematically underestimated. Today, Moslems are agitating for greater representation, and a rebellion is simmering in the Red Sea province of Eritrea, which is predominantly Moslem. (See also ETHIOPIA in this section.)

Islam in Asia

As in Africa, the simple message of Mohammed became overlaid in India and other parts of Asia with elements of local tradition. In India, where Islam was politically dominant from about 1200 A.D. until the final collapse of the Mogul Empire in the 19th century, the majority of the people remained Hindu, and Hindu rituals and festivals remained popular among converts to Islam. Sufism (Islamic mysticism) became especially widespread in India, in part because its emphasis on love and personal communion with God were themes familiar to Hindus.

The prevalence of Moslem shrines in India, mostly to local saints, is a prominent reflection of the influence of Hinduism. Despite the Islamic precept that no one may come between the individual believer and Allah, such shrines are regarded as holy places, perhaps even more important to most Indian Moslems than the mosques. One of the most famous Indian shrines is the Nizamuddine Mosque in Delhi, named after a 13th-century saint, Hazrat Nizamuddine. Each year about 100,000 people, including many non-Moslems, visit the shrine on the anniversary of the saint's death.

Other practices borrowed from Hinduism are the cracking open of a coconut at the start of a ceremony (for good luck), and a ritual commemorating a child's first haircut which involves the slaughter of goats and distribution of the meat to the poor. Moslem weddings, which in the Middle East are simple affairs, in India are elaborate celebrations which may last a month.

Unfortunately, religious borrowings on both sides have not prevented communal strife between Moslems and Hindus in India. In most nations, Islam either became the dominant faith or was expelled. In India, the two religions coexist, but in a

Indian Moslems pay homage to a saint at a shrine in Delhi. Such shrines are regarded as holy places, perhaps even more important to most Indian Moslems than the mosques.

state of hostility and mutual distrust which breeds social and intellectual isolation.

Many Hindus regard the Moslem population (one-tenth of the nation) as a potential fifth column in the event of war with Moslem Pakistan—although Moslem soldiers have served India well in several confrontations. Their fears are fanned by radio broadcasts from Pakistan on the condition of Moslems in India. Hundreds of people, most of them Moslems, have been killed in communal riots in recent years.

Moslems in India face economic and political isolation as well. Fewer than 2 per cent of civil servants are Moslems, and Moslems are discriminated against in education, other forms of employment, and political representation.

Like other minorities in India, Moslems abide by the codes of their religious community in matters affecting personal status. Because Indian Moslems are citizens of a democratic, secular, state, some Western observers have hoped that they would be able to set precedents for other Moslem communities in adapting Islamic law to the requirements of a modern society.

(Sharia law differs from the laws affecting Hindus, which were modernized in 1956. Among these differences are the Sharia's tolerance of polygamy and divorce by repudiation, and its ban on the charging of interest.)

But legal reform has been stalemated by the reluctance of the Moslem community to permit non-Moslems, in this case the Indian government, to participate in changing Islamic law. India may be a secular state, but it is not a secular society. Thus, it is difficult to separate political from religious actions in terms of their effect on the Moslem minority. But change is favored by liberal Moslems, who know that Pakistan and some other Moslem countries have modified their legal systems.

East of India, Moslem Malays comprise 45 per cent of the population of Malaysia. (The remainder are mostly Chinese, with a few Indians, Eurasians, and others.) Malaysia's easternmost extension, the province of Sabah on the island of Borneo, is reported to be the fastest-growing Moslem region in the world. Since 1971, an estimated 75,000 of Sabah's 650,000 people have converted to Islam.

National Mosque of Malaysia serves as a focus for the government's efforts to unify its population through the establishment of Islam as the religion of the federation.

This trend is due largely to a concerted effort by Malaysia's central government to unify its population through the establishment of Islam as the religion of the federation. In Malaysia, the Chinese ethnic group carries on most economic activity, while the Malays control the government through Prime Minister Abdul Razak's Malay-dominated National Front coalition. But tension between the two groups divides the society. In 1969, hundreds of people, mostly Chinese, died in riots in Kuala Lumpur, the capital. One response to the disturbances was the policy of *bumiputra* ("sons of the soil"), under which preference in jobs and education was to be given to the poor among the Malay majority.

Another consequence was the "Meccanization" campaign being conducted throughout the 13-state federation. Although officials deny the use of coercion, economic incentives for conversion were created. (This policy is in keeping with the historical tradition of Islam, which, rather than create converts at swordpoint, usually seized political power and arranged social and economic affairs in a way which made conversion attractive.)

Nevertheless, the Islamization drive has stirred considerable resentment among non-Moslems, who assert that being a Moslem is necessary for promotion in the civil service or for obtaining business permits or development rights on the rich timber lands. Other critics say that non-Moslems are being paid to accept Islam and that local leaders have convened whole villages for mass conversion ceremonies.

The version of Islam which is practiced in Malaysia and other parts of southeast Asia is diluted by Buddhist, Hindu, and animistic traditions and rituals. Alcohol is served at state functions, and women are unveiled and enjoy a generally higher status than their Middle Eastern counterparts.

In Indonesia, the largest Moslem country in population, "pure" Islamic practice is more likely to be found in the outlying islands such as Sumatra and south Sulawesi (Celebes) than on the central island of Java, where the core of popular religion is a blend of Buddhism, Hinduism, and animism. Animosity between the *santri* (strong Islamic believer) and *abangan* (traditional Javanese peasant) sectors of the population dates from the 16th century, and was exploited by the Dutch to divide and rule the archipelago. Religious hostilities are mixed with resentment of Javanese control of commerce and the government.

Since independence in 1955, the growth of political parties has exacerbated traditional religious rivalries in Indonesia. The largest Islamic political party, Masjumi, was banned in 1960 for participating in revolts on Sumatra and Sulawesi during 1958-59. Islamic organizations later worked with the army to destroy support for the Communist party in Indonesia; however, the ruling military and non-Islamic groups have frustrated the desire of Moslems for political representation comparable to the Islamic community's strength in civil society.

Secularization and Islam

Like other religions, Islam in the modern world is facing pressures which challenge the validity of traditional values and institutions. But in the Middle East and Moslem Africa and Asia, the question of secularism and of science as an alternative world view is only beginning to be confronted.

In the 19th century, an Islamic modernist movement arose from the teachings of Muhammad Abduh, who called for a return to "pure" Islam, based on the Koran and the Hadith and devoid of later foreign influences. Abduh and many of his followers rejected the unthinking acceptance of *takdir* (fate) and believed that there would be no conflict between the tenets of Islam, properly restated, and modern economic and scientific development. Other, more conservative, religious scholars rejected Abduh's interpretation, denying the need for reform of Islamic regulations affecting personal and communal life. Many feared that opening the door to reform would bring about what in their view was the moral decay and social breakdown they had observed in the West.

Yet, there is little public debate in the Middle East over Islam's compatibility with scientific attitudes. In part, this may be due to the absence in Islam of a tradi-

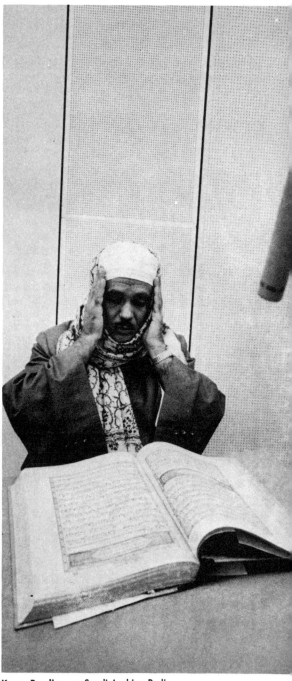

Koran Reading, on Saudi Arabian Radio. Moslem countries seek the benefits of science and technology while preserving their social, cultural, and religious institutions.

495

tion of Koranic criticism comparable to Biblical criticism in Christianity. (Unlike the Bible, the Koran is not regarded as the work of divinely inspired writers; rather, it is seen as the words of Allah, directly transmitted to Mohammed.) Perhaps the simplicity of Islam's demands upon the faithful has reduced public awareness of potential conflicts. Also, in a society where religion, culture, and social institutions are so closely related, any attack upon religion becomes politically dangerous.

Religious leaders continue to wield strong political influence in most Moslem countries. There is no tradition of separation of "church" and state, and political change has rarely been anti-clerical in form. The ulama of Egypt's al-Azhar still issue hundreds of traditional *fatwas*—religious judgments and opinions—to heads of state in other Moslem countries.

But the replacement of the Islamic *umma* (community) by a series of secularized nation-states is a problem of political development which Islam has never resolved, at least in theory. The Islamic ideal is one religious community governed according to the Sharia. But the rise of nationalism in 19th-century Europe, and its gradual transfer to the Middle East, helped put an end to the last great Islamic empire, that of the Ottomans, and with it, all hope for Islamic unity. Today, Pan-Islam survives as a spiritual, but not political, aspiration.

Liberal Islamic modernists are reinterpreting the Sharia and other traditional ideals to accommodate the imported concepts of nationalism and parliamentary government. Islam is not by its nature incompatible with a democratic political system, although most Moslem nations are governed by military or monarchical rulers. Popular sovereignty is widely accepted, in principle.

Despite legal reform and the pressures of secularization, Islam remains a vital force in both cities and more traditional villages. Moslem societies are changing, but they will not follow the same path taken by Western nations. They will have the advantage of alternative models of development from which to choose, while building upon their Islamic heritage.

South Africa. On November 12, the president of the United Nations General Assembly, Algerian Foreign Minister Abdelaziz Bouteflika, suspended the Republic of South Africa from participating in the remainder of the session, which ended December 17. His ruling was upheld by a vote of 91 to 22, with 19 abstentions. The action barred South Africa from appearing, speaking, making proposals, or voting during the session. The South African government recalled its delegate and froze its $1-million annual contribution to the UN.

The decision was without precedent in United Nations history. It was based on widespread feeling against South Africa, particularly by other African nations, because of its racial policies, its refusal to relinquish control over South-West Africa, and its military and economic support for Rhodesia's white-minority government.

Earlier, on October 30, a Security Council resolution to expel South Africa from the UN was vetoed by the United States, Great Britain, and France. Ten of the 15 Council members voted for expulsion and two abstained.

During the Council debate, all 15 members condemned South Africa's racial policies. The government was accused of constantly violating the UN Charter and the Universal Declaration of Human Rights. U.S. Ambassador to the UN John Scali argued, however, that it would be "a major strategic mistake" to expel South Africa "at a time when we have been hearing what may be new voices of conciliation." He warned, "The pariah is an outlaw, free of restraint."

Separate Development

The South African government distinguishes between the 4 million whites, 16 million blacks, 2 million coloreds, and 600,000 Asians (almost all descendants of immigrants from India) who live within the nation's borders. It maintains that its policy of "separate development" is not discrimination based on race but differentiation based on nationality. The government contends that blacks make up distinct "nations" outside white society, and its policy aims at eventual independence for nine tribally based so-called Bantustans, or homelands, which now have varying degrees of limited self-government.

About half the black population live in these homelands, which comprise 14 per cent of South Africa's area. The other half live and work in the remaining area, which includes all major cities and industrial complexes and most sources of minerals. All these blacks are regarded by the government as migrants who must hold passes to remain, even those who have been born in urban areas and lived there all their lives.

The leaders of one of the homelands, Transkei, have indicated they will accept independence, but the leaders of the other eight said in November that they would not accept independence unless their fragmented territories were consolidated, with a viable economic infrastructure. Transkei is divided into two noncontiguous parts; the other homelands are split into a total of more than 50 fragments.

Political rights in the remaining 86 per cent of South Africa belong exclusively to whites. The ruling National party won 122 of 171 seats in parliamentary elections held in April, 1974. The opposition parties think that gradual, limited reforms could defuse black grievances but do not advocate integration in the foreseeable future.

Black Homelands. The South African government maintains that blacks make up distinct nations and has given limited self-government to nine tribally based Bantustans split into a total of more than 50 fragments. About half of the black population live in these homelands; the others live in segregated townships in what the government considers white South Africa, since the economy requires a large pool of black labor.

Segregation. In recent years, the government has desegregated some facilities, including public parks and libraries. Integrated sporting teams have been sent abroad and admitted from abroad.

The coloreds and Asians have no homelands. The government's policy of separate but parallel development calls, in theory, for them to evolve distinct political institutions, but these are undefined.

The coloreds are persons of mixed European, African, and Asian origin. Most live in Cape Province and are gradually being moved into segregated areas by the government. Until 1968, six white members of Parliament were elected by those coloreds who qualified to vote, but in that year the government abolished even this indirect representation. A Coloured People's Representative Council was created in 1969. The Labor party, which won most of the elected seats, rejects separate development and demands full civil rights and direct representation in Parliament.

Restrictions on Blacks

Perhaps 2 million blacks have been moved to the Bantustans since 1948 and several hundred thousand more are to be moved as unproductive. But, since the economy requires a large pool of black labor, millions of blacks continue to live and work in what the government considers white South Africa, even though the blacks in theory comprise distinct "nations" outside white society.

In order to square theory with practice, eventually only those blacks born in urban areas will qualify for permanent residence in the black residential townships. The additional demand for black labor will be met by workers taking employment under one-year renewable labor contracts. Blacks in the residential townships must provide proof that they are qualified to be there in order to remain more than 72 hours, and there is an almost total embargo on the introduction of black women into urban areas.

There is a measure of desegregation; for example, the Pretoria public parks have been desegregated and blacks are now permitted unsegregated use of the Johannesburg Library reading rooms. Integrated sporting teams have been sent abroad and admitted from abroad, though integration is forbidden in local and national sporting events.

(Black leaders have been jailed and black-nationalist organizations have been suppressed, but, unlike the purely racial laws, security and control measures also affect the whites. Laws permit widespread police searches without a warrant and can even prevent someone from appearing in court in his own defense if this is deemed not in the public interest. Laws also authorize detention without trial. The minister of justice can restrict persons to what amounts to house arrest, and it is a crime for such persons to speak for publication. The courts do not have the power to overturn laws as unconstitutional. Censorship is widespread, although some South African newspapers are outspokenly critical of the government.)

Foreign Policy

Forthcoming independence for two large Portuguese possessions in southern Africa, Mozambique and Angola, means that white-ruled Africa is shrinking. South African Prime Minister John Vorster favors a conciliatory foreign policy. He is the first South African prime minister to meet with black African leaders and has even conferred periodically with selected South African blacks.

In November, Vorster promised non-interference in the affairs of the former Portuguese colonies and pleaded for the continuation of established economic ties. He also urged Rhodesian Prime Minister Ian Smith to come to terms with neighboring nations and with Rhodesia's blacks, who outnumber whites 20 to 1.

On December 11, Smith announced an immediate cease-fire between his government and black nationalists. He said all detained black leaders and followers of the various nationalist movements would be released at once and that a constitutional conference would be held on the nation's political future.

Vorster was reported to have directed a program of secret diplomacy over several months aimed at marshaling the cooperation of black African nations in bringing an end to hostilities in southern Africa. After Smith's announcement, Vorster said that South Africa would withdraw its paramilitary police forces, numbering several hundred men, from Rhodesia as soon as confirmation was received that hostilities had ended.

Rhodesian Blacks Released. Joshua Nkomo, *left,* and the Rev. Ndabaniugi Sithole, detained black leaders, were freed in December as part of a cease-fire agreement. South Africa has urged the Rhodesian white-minority regime to come to terms with its blacks and neighboring nations.

World Series. Bill Buckner of Los Angeles was thrown out at third base as Oakland snuffed out a Dodger rally in the fifth and final game. Oakland thus became the first team in 21 years to win three consecutive World Series.

Sports and Athletics. Among the notable sporting events during the last quarter of 1974 were the following:

Automobile Racing

Emerson Fittipaldi of Brazil won the 1974 Grand Prix Formula I championship by finishing fourth in the U.S. Grand Prix, held October 6 in Watkins Glen, New York, to edge Clay Regazzoni of Switzerland. The race was won by Carlos Reutemann of Argentina.

David Pearson won the American 500 stock-car race in October at Rockingham, North Carolina. But Richard Petty clinched an unprecedented fifth Grand National driving title for his performances during the year.

Baseball

The Oakland Athletics became the first team in 21 years to win three consecutive World Series by defeating the Los Angeles Dodgers, four games to one, in the first all-California series. Oakland relief pitcher Rollie Fingers was selected the most valuable player in the series by *Sport* magazine.

Fingers won the first game, which was decided by a 3-2 score—as were all but one of the games. Reggie Jackson of the A's and Jim Wynn of LA hit homers.

The Dodgers won the second game, 3-2, behind Don Sutton's pitching. Bob Ferguson hit a home run for the Dodgers; Steve Garvey scored ahead of him and later batted in another run. Mike Marshall, in ninth-inning relief for LA, gave up a two-run single to Joe Rudi but picked pinch-runner Herb Washington off first base to end the game.

Oakland won the third game, 3-2, behind Jim Hunter. The A's also won the fourth game, 5-2. A's pitcher Ken Holtzman hit a home run to start the scoring; Bill Russell tripled in two runs for the Dodgers, but Oakland exploded for four runs.

The final game, played in Oakland on October 17, was won by the A's, 3-2. Rudi homered off Marshall in the seventh inning for the deciding run.

En route to the series, Oakland defeated the Baltimore Orioles, three games to one, to win the American League pennant. Los Angeles won the National League pennant by beating the Pittsburgh Pirates, three games to one.

Steve Garvey of the Dodgers and Jeff Burroughs of the Texas Rangers were named most valuable players in their respective leagues. The Dodgers' Mike Marshall and the A's Catfish Hunter won Cy Young Awards as the top pitchers in their respective leagues. Outfielders Bake McBride of the St. Louis Cardinals and Mike Hargrove of Texas were voted rookies of the year in the NL and AL, respectively.

Boxing

Heavyweight. Muhammad Ali became only the second heavyweight champion to regain his title, knocking out defending champ George Foreman in the eighth round of their bout in Kinshasa, Zaïre, on October 30. The fight, Africa's first heavyweight title bout, began at 4 A.M. in predawn humid heat so that Americans could see it during the evening in theaters via closed-circuit television. Ali, the 3-to-1 underdog, abandoned his usual dancing movements and hung on or near the ropes, daring Foreman to connect. The defending champion punched himself weary, and in the eighth round Ali suddenly put him on the canvas for the count with right-left combinations.

Each fighter earned $5 million. The government of Zaïre reportedly lost $4 million because closed-circuit television in the United States and Canada fell far below the $30 million estimated by the promoters. The contest, scheduled for September, had been postponed when Foreman was cut over one eye during a sparring session.

Light Heavyweight. John Conteh of Great Britain won a 15-round decision from Jorge Ahumada of Argentina October 1 in Wembley, England, to win the World Boxing Council title vacated by Bob Foster's retirement.

Victor Galindez of Argentina won the World Boxing Association title from Lee Hutchins of Detroit on December 8 in Buenos Aires, Argentina, when Hutchins failed to answer the bell for the 13th round.

Middleweight. Carlos Monzon of Argentina retained the World Boxing Association championship October 5 by knocking out Tony Mundine of Australia in the seventh round of their fight, which was

Muhammad Ali recaptured boxing's heavyweight title, knocking out George Foreman in the eighth round of their championship bout in Zaïre. Ali, the 3-to-1 underdog, let Foreman punch himself weary, then suddenly put the defending champion on the canvas for the count.

Pittsburgh Steelers, sparked by outstanding defense and the running of Franco Harris and Rocky Bleier (20), upset the Oakland Raiders, 24-13, to win the American Football Conference championship. Minnesota won the National Football Conference title.

held in Buenos Aires, Argentina.

Rodrigo Valdes of Colombia retained the WBC version of the title in Paris in November by knocking out Gratien Tonna of France in the 11th round of their bout.

Welterweight. José Napoles of Mexico retained his title in December with a third-round knockout of Argentina's Horacio Saldano in Mexico City.

Lightweight. Gattu Ishimatsu of Japan kept his WBC crown by knocking out Rodolfo Gonzalez of Mexico in the 12th round of their bout, held in Osaka, Japan, in November.

Roberto Duran of Panama successfully defended his WBA title December 21 by knocking out Masataka Takayama in the first round of their fight in San José, Costa Rica.

Featherweight. Alexis Arguello of Nicaragua won the WBA title in November from Ruben Olivares of Mexico, KO'ing Olivares in the 13th round of their fight in Los Angeles.

Flyweight. Shoji Oguma of Japan won the WBC flyweight title from Betulio Gon-

zalez of Venezuela in a split decision. The fight was held in Tokyo on October 1.

Football

Miami, Oakland, Pittsburgh, Buffalo, Minnesota, St. Louis, Los Angeles, and Washington qualified for the National Football League playoffs. Otis Armstrong of the Denver Broncos led the league in yards gained rushing. Five-foot-five Mack Herron of the New England Patriots set a new record with 2,444 yards gained during the season rushing, catching passes, and running back kickoffs and punts.

In the playoff finals December 29, the Minnesota Vikings defeated the Los Angeles Rams, 14-10, to win the National Football Conference championship, while the Pittsburgh Steelers defeated the Oakland Raiders, 24-13, to win the American Football Conference title.

The first World Football League World Bowl was won December 5 by the Birmingham Americans, 22-21, over the Florida Blazers in Birmingham, Alabama. Neither team had been paid for three months, and as the Americans were celebrating, sheriff's deputies were seizing the uniforms for nonpayment of debts to the supplier. Birmingham quarterback George Mira said the league had no problems "on the field."

Oklahoma, which was barred from post-season play by the NCAA for recruiting violations, and Alabama were the only major college teams to go through the season undefeated. Running back Archie Griffin of Ohio State was awarded the Heisman Trophy as the outstanding college player of 1974.

Golf

South Africa, represented by Bobby Cole and Dale Haynes, won the World Cup in Caracas, Venezuela, with a 144-hole total of 554. Cole won the individual title with a score of 271.

Gymnastics

Ludmilla Turischeva of the Soviet Union won the women's all-round competition in October as the Russians retained their world team title in Varna, Bulgaria. Japan won the men's competition.

Hockey

The Soviet national team defeated Team Canada, which was composed of World Hockey Association players, four games to one with three ties, in October.

Horse Racing

Allez France, a filly, won the $500,000 Prix de l'Arc de Triomphe in Paris in October.

Admetus, a 31-to-1 French longshot, won the Washington, D.C., International in Laurel, Maryland, November 9, defeating heavily favored Dahlia, who finished third.

Waymaker won the Kentucky Futurity, the last leg of trotting's triple crown, on October 4 in Lexington, Kentucky. In the first four-heat Futurity in 17 years, Waymaker defeated Dancing Party and Nevele Diamond.

Delmonica Hanover was named harness horse of the year in a poll. Forego was chosen thoroughbred horse of the year.

Chris McCarron, a rookie jockey, set a record by bringing home 547 winners during 1974.

Tennis

South Africa won the Davis Cup by default October 4 when India refused to play in the finals because of South Africa's policy of apartheid.

Britain won the Wightman Cup from the United States, 6-1. The annual contest between women was held in October at Deeside, Wales.

Guillermo Vilas of Argentina, who began the year as an obscure tennis pro, finished first in Grand Prix standings for 1974, winning seven tournaments. He topped off the year in Melbourne, Australia, December 15 by winning the Grand Prix Masters, defeating defending champion Ilie Nastase of Rumania, 7-6, 6-2, 3-6, 3-6, 6-4.

United Nations. With the United Nations entering into its 30th year in 1975, crucial decisions as to its role in world politics had come to the fore. Consequently, there was less talk of anniversaries and more thoughts about the special conference to be held in the summer of 1975 to discuss proposals to revise the United Nations Charter, which was signed in San Francisco on June 26, 1945.

The questions facing this session would center on the role of the third world, or the developing countries, in the world body. The United States—as well as France, Britain, and West Germany—charged that the militancy of developing countries and their tendency to pass unenforceable General Assembly resolutions, was robbing the body of its power and transforming it into a lobby for resentful developing nations. The third-world countries replied that no such complaints were heard from the West when in earlier years the General Assembly was dominated by the United States.

The debate found its symbol in Yasir Arafat's November 13 speech to 1974's annual autumn session of the General Assembly. The head of the Palestinian guerrilla movement, a gun holster under his windbreaker, was offered the chair normally reserved for visiting heads of state. It was the symbolism of this act, as well as the Assembly's attitude towards Israel and its expulsion of South Africa's delegation (see MIDDLE EAST and SOUTH AFRICA in this section), that precipitated what might become the UN's most critical debate, one that could well define its future.

"Tyranny of the Majority"

On December 6, John A. Scali, chief of the United States delegation, told the General Assembly that support for the UN in Congress and among the American people was eroding because of the dominance in the Assembly of a broad coalition of developing countries, including many very small ones, which were backed by the Communist powers. Scali explained that this manipulation was disruptive in that "the minority which is so often offended may in fact be a practical majority, in terms of its capacity to support this organization and implement its decisions."

Reminding the Assembly that it is not a legislature and that its resolutions are only advisory, Scali warned that when majority rule becomes "the tyranny of the majority, the minority will cease to respect or obey it."

But the third-world nations were quick to point out that the United States had held the same dominance over the General Assembly. During the UN's early years following World War II, the Assembly consisted of only 51 members, and Washington could count on a majority from its allies. In 1974, however, membership stood at 138, including more than 50 African countries.

Further, the developing countries claim that their "new majority" is the best method by which they can organize the political leverage which oil and other natural-resource holdings have given them. Their actions, they say, are designed to stress the need for global interdependence, a theme which President Ford struck during his first UN speech, when he linked the world food and energy crises. The third-world bloc also claims that the United States is exaggerating the threat of its united front, pointing to two votes in particular: a vote saving the Assembly seat of the American-backed Cambodian government, and the rejection of a proposal asking that all foreign troops—in effect American troops—be removed from South Korea.

U.S. Reaction

Nevertheless, the United States and the western European countries have found themselves at odds with the new majority, particularly in the area of the Middle East. In his speech, Scali cited a ruling during the November debate on the Palestinian question that curbed the Israeli delegation's right to speak. Scali also said that many Americans were alarmed by a recent decision of the United Nations Educational, Scientific and Cultural Organi-

John Scali, chief of the U.S. delegation to the United Nations, told the General Assembly that support for the UN in Congress and among the American people was eroding.

zation (UNESCO) which denied Israel cultural aid and also excluded Israel from the agency's regional groupings. In reaction to this move, the Senate passed riders to the foreign-aid bill that would curtail American funds for UNESCO and other United Nations bodies. (The United States provides 25 per cent of the UN budget.)

The United States also announced that it would boycott a special fund being set up to give emergency relief and development aid to economically hard-hit countries. The decision marked the first time the United States had declined to participate in a major new UN undertaking. Washington expressed the belief that the fund, which was to be financed by voluntary contributions, would not attract enough support to help countries hurt by quadrupled oil prices and similar rises in other commodity prices.

While the decision was seen by some as a reflection of dissatisfaction with the "tyranny of the majority," some observers also saw it as part of a plan to bypass the United Nations aid programs for needy nations and instead funnel aid through the World Bank and the International Monetary Fund, which have headquarters in Washington. In these organizations, power is concentrated among Western members, owing to weighed voting rights. By contrast, the new special UN fund would be controlled by a committee made up of both donor and recipient countries.

Even as the United States expressed disenchantment with the workings of the UN, it was still felt in Washington that the organization is important in implementing and administering compromises between the superpowers in such trouble spots as the Middle East and Cyprus. Thus, observers saw the United States coping as best it could with the voting blocs in the General Assembly while scaling down its monetary support of the UN bureaucracy. Diplomatically, the United States would continue to concentrate its efforts in the Security Council, the 15-nation core of the UN where the five major powers—the United States, Soviet Union, China, Britain, and France—have veto powers.

United States of AMERICA. Foreign affairs was the principal focus of President Ford's activities during the last quarter of 1974. The new president topped off a Far Eastern tour with an arms agreement in the Soviet Union and held talks with a number of other foreign leaders.

Vladivostok Agreement. Ford and Soviet Communist party leader Leonid Brezhnev conferred in a suburb of Vladivostok on November 23 and 24 and reached a tentative agreement to limit the numbers of all strategic offensive nuclear weapons and delivery systems through 1985. U.S. Secretary of State Henry Kissinger, who accompanied Ford and had conducted talks in Moscow with Brezhnev in October, described the agreement as a "breakthrough" which would "mean that a cap has been put on the arms race for a period of 10 years." He said that there was a strong possibility that a final pact could be reached for signing in the summer of 1975, when Brezhnev was scheduled to visit the United States.

Details of the agreement were disclosed by Ford on December 2. Each side, he said, agreed to put a ceiling of 2,400 on the total number of its land-based intercontinental ballistic missiles (ICBM's), submarine-launched ballistic missiles, and strategic bombers. By contrast, the 1972 interim agreement had left the Soviets with a lead in the number of missiles, but had not covered strategic bombers bearing nuclear weapons.

The new agreement limited the number of missiles that could be armed with MIRV's—multiple independently targeted reentry vehicles, carried on a single missile—to 1,320 of the 2,400. The United States has 750 MIRV missiles already deployed; the Soviet Union has none but reportedly has developed the capacity to MIRV its missiles.

The agreement established the principle of equivalency in strategic forces; because of their larger missile force, the Soviets have roughly 2,600 nuclear-weapon delivery vehicles compared to 2,200 for the United States. Kissinger noted that the Soviet Union had made a basic concession in ceasing to insist that U.S. forward-based fighter-bombers deployed in Europe be in-

Ford Abroad. The president conferred with French President Valéry Giscard d'Estaing on the Caribbean island of Martinique, *left*. In Japan, he tried eating with chopsticks. *Bottom*, Ford and Soviet Communist party leader Leonid Brezhnev, meeting in the Siberian city of Vladivostok, signed a tentative agreement to limit strategic offensive nuclear weapons and delivery systems.

cluded in the total of U.S. strategic delivery vehicles.

However, critics of the agreement felt that the ceiling on delivery vehicles and MIRV's was too high. They also pointed out that the number of warheads mounted on a MIRV missile was not restricted and that the agreement left the Soviet Union with a substantial advantage in throw weight, and the total amount of explosive material that all warheads can deliver.

Brezhnev took Ford on a tour of Vladivostok on November 24. No U.S. visitors reportedly had seen the port city since 1922, and the city has been closed to Soviet tourists as well for almost three decades because it is the chief Soviet naval base in the Far East.

Japan and Korea. Ford arrived in Tokyo November 18 on the first leg of his Far Eastern tour, becoming the first U.S. president to visit Japan. He was formally welcomed the following day by Emperor Hirohito and Premier Kakuei Tanaka.

An 11-point joint communiqué was signed November 20 by Ford and Tanaka, who resigned his office shortly after. (See JAPAN in this issue.) It outlined their positions on bilateral and international problems without mentioning any specific agreements.

After leaving Japan, Ford stopped in Seoul, South Korea, for a 24-hour stay. A communiqué issued after talks with South Korean President Chung Hee Park stated that the United States has "no intention" of withdrawing its forces from South Korea and supported Seoul's moves to conduct negotiations with North Korea aimed at unifying the peninsula. Anti-government demonstrations staged in Seoul before Ford's arrival protested his visit and emphasized opposition to Park's repressive government. (See KOREA in the third section.)

France. Ford and French President Valéry Giscard d'Estaing conferred on the French Caribbean island of Martinique December 15 and 16 and reached compromise agreements on energy, gold, and other issues. In the joint communiqué issued December 16, the United States agreed to participate in a French-proposed conference of oil-producing and -exporting nations "at the earliest possible date," while France agreed to "intensive consultations among consumer countries" prior to such a conference. (See also ENERGY in this section.)

The presidents also agreed it would be "appropriate" for any government which wished to do so to adopt "current market prices as the basis of valuation for its gold holdings." Such a change in valuation could quadruple the value of government gold holdings, since the official price of gold for dealings between governments is $42.22 an ounce, whereas the free-market price was about $180 an ounce in December.

Resolving a long dispute between the two nations, France agreed to pay the United States $100 million to compensate for financial losses incurred in 1966, when France expelled U.S. forces and bases from its territory.

Economic Affairs. President Ford presented an anti-inflation program to the nation October 8 before a joint session of

(W)hip (I)nflation (N)ow. Wearing a WIN button, President Ford called on all Americans to enlist in the fight against inflation. His message emphasized voluntary action rather than mandatory features.

Congress. A call for a "temporary surcharge" of 5 per cent on the incomes of corporations and many families and individuals was later dropped because of growing recession in the United States. (See BUSINESS AND FINANCE in this section.)

Ford's economic package emphasized voluntary action rather than mandatory features. He urged Americans to grow

Nelson Rockefeller met with Ford in the White House Oval Office after being sworn in as vice president. Rockefeller was appointed vice chairman of the Domestic Council and vice chairman of the National Security Council.

more food and waste less, and to save fuel by driving less and heating their homes less. He said that Congress would be asked to remove all remaining acreage limits on rice, peanuts, and cotton, and promised to see to it that farmers received all necessary fuel and fertilizer supplies.

Ford also proposed to Congress a number of other measures designed to increase energy supplies, contain inflation by combating restrictive business practices, avoid a "credit crunch," aid the jobless and thrift institutions, stimulate housing, and reduce federal spending. Tax benefits proposed for business included a generous revision of the investment tax credit that would have provided a saving more than offsetting the surcharge. Ford also proposed that dividends on preferred stock be fully deductible by the issuing company, as a means of attracting new capital.

In the midst of the worsening recession, Ford sent Congress a message November 26 setting a new federal-spending goal of $302.2 billion for fiscal 1975. Earlier, he had sought to hold spending to $300 billion.

Appointments and Resignations. Attorney General William Saxbe resigned December 13, the first cabinet member to do so during the Ford Administration. Saxbe was nominated ambassador to India, replacing Daniel Patrick Moynihan, who had resigned.

Claude Brinegar resigned December 18 as secretary of transportation, effective February 1, 1975.

Kenneth R. Cole, Jr. resigned December 13 as executive director of the Domestic Council but was expected to remain until March, 1975, to help draft legislative proposals.

The resignation of a number of Nixon White House staffers was announced during the fall. Those leaving the Administration included counselors Anne L. Armstrong and Dean Burch; public-relations adviser Patrick Buchanan; and legal counsel Fred Buzhardt. Others leaving the federal government included Assistant Attorney General Henry Petersen and Clay Whitehead, director of the White House Office of Telecommunications Policy.

Congress

Rockefeller Confirmed. Nelson Rockefeller was sworn in as the 41st vice president of the United States on December 20. It was the first time in U.S. history that both a president and vice president had not been elected to their offices.

The House of Representatives voted to confirm Rockefeller's nomination by 287 to 128. Earlier, the Senate had approved the nomination by 90 to 7. Much of the opposition was in reaction to Rockefeller's wealth and his use of his wealth for political purposes. (See UNITED STATES in the third section.) White House Press Secretary Ron Nessen said Rockefeller would serve as vice chairman of the Domestic Council, vice chairman of the National Security Council, and as a member of a special commission overseeing foreign policy.

Among the legislation passed in the last quarter of 1974 was the following:

Campaign Reform. Congress cleared on October 10, and President Ford signed, a major reform of federal election-campaign funding. The bill provided for public financing of presidential primaries and elections and set ceilings on contributions and spending in House, Senate, and presidential campaigns. It was designed to eliminate undue influence of large contributors and special-interest groups.

Key provisions included the following:

• A presidential nominee of a major party would receive a maximum of $20 million from a $1 income-tax check-off fund established in 1971. If the fund were short of the full amount, the nominee could raise the difference from private sources, but $20 million would be the total spending ceiling.

• Major parties would receive $2 million each from the check-off for their national conventions.

• Minor parties would receive public funding in proportion to the votes they polled in previous elections, if at least 5 per cent of the total.

• Public funding for a presidential primary would be available on a matching basis to candidates who raised at least $100,000 from private sources in a way that indicated broad national support. The federal government would also match subsequent private contributions up to a $5-million total. Spending ceilings were established for presidential candidates in any one primary.

• Spending ceilings were established for House and Senate candidates, but there was no provision for public financing.

• Ceilings were established on contributions by individuals and organizations to political candidates. Cash contributions of more than $100, and foreign contributions, were prohibited.

• An independent six-member commission would be established with authority to oversee enforcement of the law. Regular reports by political candidates on contributions and exepnditures would be required.

Rail Pensions. Congress enacted into law October 16 a bill revising the railroad retirement system and refinancing it with an annual infusion of $285 million through the year 2000. The bill became law when a veto by President Ford was overridden. The railroad retirement system was in arrears by $4.5 billion. Ford, in vetoing the bill, said he preferred reduction of benefits or the railway industry financing the deficit.

"No-Knock" Laws Repealed. Ford signed into law a bill cleared by Congress October 16 repealing 1970 laws permitting federal and District of Columbia agents to make "no-knock" drug searches of private dwellings—searches in which the agents did not knock and identify themselves before entry. The bill also made it a federal crime to kill an agent of the Drug Enforcement Administration.

Commodity Trading. A bill to strengthen federal regulation of commodity-futures trading was passed by Congress October 10 and signed into law October 23. An independent commission was to be established to regulate the exchanges in order to halt abuses and to intervene directly in markets to curb threatened or actual manipulation.

Veterans' Benefits. Congress on October 10 approved legislation increasing educational benefits for post-Korean War and Vietnam-era veterans. Monthly educational benefits were increased 22.7 per cent

Mass-Transit Aid. Ford chatted with Senator Harrison Williams of New Jersey, *center*, and Secretary of Transportation Claude Brinegar after signing a bill establishing a six-year, $11.8-billion mass-transit federal-aid program.

and monthly allowances for veterans receiving on-the-job training or vocational rehabilitation for the disabled were increased 18.2 per cent. Ford vetoed the bill, calling it inflationary, but the veto was easily overridden by both houses of Congress on December 3.

Access to Information. On October 7, Congress passed a bill providing freer public access to government data. It gave courts authority to declassify documents, with the burden of proof on the government to justify a secrecy classification. It also provided that federal-agency investigatory files, including those of the Federal Bureau of Investigation, become public on request unless the agency could prove that disclosure would be harmful to the national interest. Ford vetoed the bill October 17, charging that it was unconstitutional and a threat to U.S. "military or intelligence secrets and diplomatic relations." But Congress overrode the veto, making it law on November 21.

Mass-Transit Aid. Congress passed on November 21, and President Ford signed, a six-year, $11.8-billion mass-transit program. About two-thirds of the funds were allotted to capital improvements, such as purchase of new buses and subway cars, with the remainder to be distributed according to local choice, either for additional capital improvements or for operating expenses.

Drinking Water. A $156-million, three-year program to safeguard drinking water was cleared by Congress December 3. National standards for safe drinking water were to be set at the federal level by the Environmental Protection Agency, which could seek compliance by court action if the primary enforcement, assigned to the states, were neglected.

Nixon Tapes. A bill assigning permanent custody of former president Nixon's White House tapes and papers to the federal government was passed by Congress December 9. (See WATERGATE SCANDAL in this section.)

Strip-Mining. A bill to regulate strip-mining of coal on federal lands was cleared by Congress on December 16 but was pocket-vetoed by Ford after Congress had adjourned. Some 260,000 acres of federal lands estimated to contain about 6 million tons of coal are under lease to coal companies, which also were seeking to obtain consent from surface owners for the future leasing of underlying coal by the Interior Department. The bill required the coal companies to obtain the consent of farmers and ranchers with surface rights prior

Trade Bill. Ford signed a comprehensive foreign-trade bill that gave him authority to reduce or eliminate tariffs. But Moscow rejected as unacceptable a provision that would grant trade concessions to the Soviet Union only if Soviet emigration curbs were eased.

to any mining. The bill also required strip miners to prevent environmental damage and restore mine land to its "approximate original contour" and applied a fee on all coal mined in the United States, the revenue to be used to reclaim already strip-mined land, to reimburse local communities for adverse mining impact, and to build miners' facilities. In declining to sign the bill, Ford said December 31 that the measure would have hurt coal production at a time "when the nation can ill-afford significant losses from this critical energy source."

Germ Warfare. The Senate unanimously ratified December 16 the 1925 Geneva protocol banning chemical and biological warfare. The Ford Administration had pledged to "renounce as a matter of national policy" the use of tear gas and herbicides except in certain limited circumstances. The vote also applied to a 1972 convention that prohibited development, production, and stockpiling of bacteriological and toxic weapons.

Foreign Trade. Congress passed on December 20, and President Ford signed, a comprehensive foreign-trade bill that gave the president the authority to eliminate tariffs of 5 per cent or lower and to reduce by three-fifths tariffs above 5 per cent.

The president could also negotiate elimination of tariffs on an industry-by-industry basis, subject to congressional approval.

Tariffs could be eliminated on goods from developing nations, with exceptions for Communist countries (excluding Rumania and Yugoslavia), any country restricting supplies to the United States in a cartel-like operation, and countries discriminating against the United States on trade or refusing compensation for expropriation of property. Exceptions also were provided for certain goods, such as shoes, electronics, and watches. The bill called for relief to industries hurt by imports unless the president found it not in the national interest.

A major provision of the bill would grant trade concessions to the Soviet Union if Soviet emigration curbs were eased. Senator Henry Jackson of Washington told the Senate December 13 that he and Secretary of State Henry Kissinger had agreed that the standard would be an increase in the level of Soviet emigration from about 35,000 a year to 60,000.

However, the Soviet Union December 18 asserted that it would "flatly reject as unacceptable" any attempts to attach conditions to the extension of trade benefits or otherwise "interfere in the internal affairs" of the Soviet Union. Moscow was also reportedly disappointed in a companion bill cleared December 19 that extended the lending authority of the Export-Import Bank for four years at a $25-billion level but set a $300-million ceiling on credit to the Soviet Union (though the president was authorized to raise the ceiling if he found it in the national interest, subject to congressional approval). The bill also barred any Export-Import Bank credit for production, transport, or distribution of energy from the Soviet Union and set a $40-million ceiling on loans or guarantees for exploration of energy sources in the Soviet Union.

The most-favored-nation tariff treatment granted to the Soviet Union and other Communist countries assures a country that tariffs on its goods will be no higher than those levied on goods of the country receiving the best such terms. State Department officials said, however, that Soviet Ambassador Anatoly Dobrynin had told Kissinger that Moscow regarded the trade-bill restrictions as a failure of the United States to live up to its side of détente.

Jobs and Unemployment. On December 18, Congress cleared a bill, later signed by Ford, authorizing $2.5 billion in fiscal 1975 for state and local governments to hire jobless workers for community-service work in education, health, sanitation, day care, recreation, and similar programs. The bill also extended unemployment compensation to about 12 million workers not heretofore covered. Companion legislation, cleared December 19, provided an additional 13 weeks of emergency unemployment compensation benefits—to a total of 52 weeks—for unemployed workers who had exhausted their regular benefits. A bill to appropriate $4 billion in fiscal 1975 to fund the emergency programs was passed December 19.

Foreign Aid. Congress completed work December 18 on a foreign-aid authorization bill of $2.69 billion for fiscal 1975. It contained a provision to suspend military aid to Turkey immediately unless there was substantial progress toward a Cyprus settlement, but the president was

permitted to delay the cutoff until February 5 if he determined it would aid negotiations. Special restrictions were put on aid to Cambodia, Chile, South Korea, South Vietnam, and India.

Oil Shipments. President Ford pocket-vetoed, by refusing to sign, a bill passed just before congressional adjournment that would have required that 20 per cent of the oil imported into the United States be carried on U.S. tankers. Ford said December 31 that the bill, which was promoted by the maritime industry and maritime unions, would have created serious inflationary pressures by increasing the price of oil and would have hurt foreign relations by encouraging other countries to increase protection of their industries.

Supreme Court

Wiretapping. The Supreme Court declined October 15 to hear a challenge to the president's right to authorize warrantless wiretaps to gather foreign intelligence. The court's refusal to hear a case that involved the 1964 espionage conviction of a Soviet national had the effect of permitting federal agents to continue the practice if the surveillance were found to be reasonably related to the exercise of presidential powers in the area of foreign affairs.

Commuting Aliens. By a 5 to 4 margin, the high court on November 25 upheld U.S. Immigration and Naturalization Service rules permitting thousands of Canadians and Mexicans to commute freely into the United States, where they hold daily or seasonal jobs. The INS treats commuting aliens as U.S. residents returning from a visit abroad. At least 42,500 Mexican and 10,000 Canadians commute daily to jobs in the United States.

Rail Reorganization. By a vote of 7 to 2, the Supreme Court December 16 upheld the constitutionality of a 1973 act that reorganized the Penn Central Railroad and several other bankrupt Northeast railways into a single, self-sustaining system. In a ruling that reversed a decision by a special federal district-court panel, the high court rejected arguments by creditors of the Penn Central that the act failed to provide them with sufficient compensation. The majority opinion held that creditors had available to them under another act adequate means for recovering losses not specifically covered by the reorganization act.

Busing in Boston

Resistance to busing during the 1974-75 school year centered in Boston, where protests, sometimes violent, held down public-school attendance. Tension was highest in the Roxbury-South Boston school district, with attendance in mid-October averaging only 28 per cent of a projected enrollment of 3,361. In all, more than 100 persons were injured and more than 120 arrested.

Under a court order, about 45,000 of the Boston public-school system's 94,000 pupils were assigned to schools that they would not otherwise have attended, in order to improve the racial balance of 80 schools (out of Boston's 200) with enrollment more than 50-per-cent black. The plan called for busing 18,000 pupils—about half of them black, the other half white—out of their neighborhoods. The predominantly white South Boston school district and the predominantly black Roxbury district were merged.

Trouble centered around the South Boston area; at South Boston High School a boycott by white parents and fear of violence kept attendance generally below 400 out of 1,500 pupils who were expected to be enrolled. Buses carrying black students were stoned the first two days of school, although Mayor Kevin White ordered police escorts. In all, about 8,500 Boston pupils remained out; city officials launched a drive in November to crack down on truants.

On October 9, Massachusetts Governor Francis Sargent made available 300 state police, 100 Metropolitan District Commission police, and their supervisory personnel to the city police, following a request by White. On the same day, Ford deplored the violence in Boston but stated his opposition to forced busing to achieve racial

Police Escorts were needed to preserve the peace as thousands of Boston public-school pupils were bused out of their neighborhoods under a court-ordered plan. Hundreds were arrested or injured during racial violence.

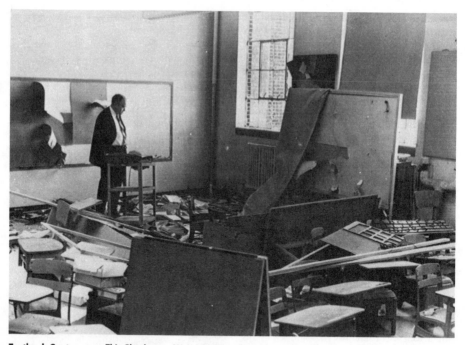

Textbook Controversy. This Charleston, West Virginia, elementary-school classroom was dynamited during a protest campaign by parents and ministers against reading materials that the dissidents characterized as profane, seditious, anti-Christian, and immoral.

balance. White said the next day that Ford had fanned "the flames of resistance" to school integration.

On October 15, Sargent called 450 National Guardsmen (later reduced to 150) to stand-by duty in Boston and called on Ford to send federal troops. He acted after a melee between black and white students at South Boston's Hyde Park High School resulted in the stabbing of a white student. But the call-up was criticized by White, who said the guard comprised "an inept, incompetent, ill-equipped, undisciplined, or undertrained militia." And Ford declined to send troops, saying they should be used only as a "last resort."

South Boston and Roxbury high schools were closed for the remainder of the year December 11 when a crowd of whites, angry over the stabbing of a white student by a black, trapped 135 black students in South Boston High School for four hours. During the following days, supporters and opponents of integration held large rallies.

West Virginia Textbook Controversy

Parents, backed by ministers, protested the introduction of school books in the 121-school system of Kanawha County, West Virginia (including the city of Charleston), that discussed sex, drugs, civil rights, religion, and patriotism in ways that the protestors found offensive. Several elementary schools were dynamited or firebombed in October, and 11 persons were sentenced to 30 days in jail for disruptive activities.

The protest was aimed at removing 325 supplementary reading anthologies, for use mainly in junior and senior high schools, that were alleged to be obscene, blasphemous, and anti-American. The books had been approved in June by the county school board, by a vote of 3 to 2, upon recommendation of a teachers' committee. (A 1970 state law requires all textbooks to reflect religious, racial, and cultural pluralism.)

The protestors objected to selections

from works by, among others, Sigmund Freud, black activists Dick Gregory and Eldridge Cleaver, and poets Allen Ginsberg, E. E. Cummings, and Gwendolyn Brooks. Also attacked was a collection of myths that appeared to challenge the literal interpretation of the Bible. Mrs. Alice Moore, the board member who led the fight, said almost all the new books contained selections that she found "vulgar, profane, violent, critical of parents, depressing, seditious, revolutionary, anti-Christian, and immoral."

The protests, led by fundamentalist ministers, began with the opening of school September 3 and continued despite an antipicketing injunction. A compromise agreement during the second week of demonstrations removed 90 per cent of the disputed texts, subject to review by an 18-member citizens' panel. Nevertheless, members of the United Mine Workers staged occasional wildcat strikes to protest the new textbooks until October 9, when UMW President Arnold Miller ordered them to stop, and federal marshals were called in after not only schools, but also several businesses and coal mines, were closed by disruptive tactics.

On November 8, the school board decided to reinstate all but seven of the books. At the same time it passed resolutions excusing students from using books they or their parents found objectionable for moral or religious reasons, and forbidding teachers to "indoctrinate" students in objectionable moral or religious values. This compromise was unacceptable to the protestors. On November 12, picketers closed down one elementary school and prevented some 30 school buses from leaving their storage yard; three other buses were fired on by snipers.

On November 21, the school board voted to establish four screening committees of teachers and parents in April, 1975. The committees were to remove books that offended or ridiculed the values of various ethnic, religious, or racial groups, contained offensive language, encouraged sedition or revolution against the United States or students to criticize their parents, or, if used to study the English language, did not teach traditional rules of gram-

mar. Nevertheless, the protests continued through December. Many teachers and students threatened counter-demonstrations on behalf of academic freedom, and the Authors League of America urged that action be taken by federal authorities to prevent the forcible censorship of books.

Kent State Trial

U.S. District Court Judge Frank J. Battisti acquitted eight former Ohio National Guardsmen November 8 in Cleveland of charges stemming from the shooting deaths of four students at Kent State University in 1970. Battisti ruled that the prosecution had failed to prove charges that the guardsmen had willfully intended to deprive the slain students and nine other wounded students of their civil rights. The judge cautioned, however, "It is vital that state and National Guard officials not regard this decision as authorizing or approving the use of force against demonstrators."

During the trial, which began October 21, federal prosecutors presented 33 witnesses and 130 exhibits—mostly photographs of the confrontation between the guardsmen and the students. The jury also visited the Kent State campus, where it heard simulated gunshots.

Calley Freed

Former army lieutenant William L. Calley, Jr., the only person convicted in connection with the 1968 massacre at Mylai, South Vietnam, was granted parole effective November 19 by Howard Callaway, secretary of the army. Callaway, who announced his action November 8, described the terms of the parole as routine; Calley had completed serving one-third of his 10-year prison term. On the same day as Callaway's announcement, a U.S. appeals court released Calley on bail from the army disciplinary barracks at Fort Leavenworth, Kansas, while it reviewed a lower-court decision reversing his conviction because of prejudicial pretrial publicity.

See also CUBA; DISASTERS; ELECTIONS; HOUSE PLANTS; LITERATURE; MEDICINE; NEW PRODUCTS; NEWSMAKERS; NOBEL PRIZES; OBITUARIES; PHYSICS; POPULATION; SPORTS AND ATHLETICS; and UNITED NATIONS, in this section.

Watergate Scandal. Congress passed and sent to the White House December 9 a bill nullifying the tapes agreement between President Ford and former president Nixon (see WATERGATE SCANDAL in the third section.) and assigning Nixon's White House tapes and papers to the federal government. Ford later signed the bill.

The bill did not designate ownership of the material, which was to be put in the permanent custody of the General Services Administration. Nixon would have access to the material, which also was to be made available in judicial proceedings. But the measure flatly prohibited the destruction of any Watergate-related tapes without the consent of Congress; the agreement between Ford and Nixon would have permitted Nixon to destroy any of the tapes after five years and specified that all the recordings would be destroyed on September 1, 1984, or on Nixon's death, whichever came earlier.

On November 11, the White House had agreed to modify the tapes agreement with Nixon by letting special prosecutor Henry Ruth have access to all of Nixon's records relating to cases under investigation. It provided that Nixon could not take any of his recordings from the White House without Ruth's approval.

Ford Discusses Pardon

President Ford defended his September 8 pardon of Nixon in an appearance before a House subcommittee on October 17. Ford was not put under oath for his testimony, in which he reiterated he had made "no deal, period" with Nixon on the pardon.

Ford said no conditions were placed on the pardon and no confession sought, although acceptance of the pardon in his mind implied admission of guilt. He said the accompanying tapes agreement was "not a basis" for the decision to grant the pardon.

Historians could cite only one previous instance in U.S. history of a presidential appearance before a congressional committee—Abraham Lincoln's visit to the House Judiciary Committee in 1862 to explain how a newspaper was able to publish his State of the Union message before the speech was delivered. President Wash-

"No Deal, Period." President Ford, in an appearance before a House subcommittee, denied setting any conditions for his pardon of former president Nixon or for the accompanying tapes agreement.

Henry Ruth was named Watergate special prosecutor, succeeding Leon Jaworski, who resigned and recommended Ruth for the job.

ington testified before the Senate in 1789 on Indian treaties.

New Watergate Prosecutor

Henry S. Ruth, Jr. was named Watergate special prosecutor on October 23, succeeding Leon Jaworski, who had resigned. The appointment was made by Attorney General William Saxbe, who said it had been cleared with Ford and congressional leaders.

Ruth, 43, had been deputy special prosecutor for 18 months, and had been recommended by Jaworski for the job. Saxbe said Ruth would "have the same independence as his predecessor in carrying out his duties."

In an interim report to Saxbe accompanying his resignation letter October 12, Jaworski said "the bulk of the work" entrusted to him had been discharged. As remaining tasks, he cited the need for a final report by the special prosecutor's office and access to Nixon's presidential materials for the remaining investigations. A large part of the report was devoted to defending Ford's legal right to grant his pardon to Nixon.

Prize Catch

Catfish Hunter became a New York Yankee December 31, with a five-year contract package estimated to give him $3.75 million, counting deferred payments. Thus, while most experts agree that he is the best pitcher in baseball, everybody agrees that he's the best paid. Nevertheless, he maintains that when his baseball career is over, "I just want to come back to Hertford (North Carolina, population: 2,023) to hunt, fish, farm, and just be a country boy."

Jim "Catfish" Hunter became a free agent when Oakland A's owner Charles Finley reneged on a tax-shelter payment which was part of the pitcher's salary. Though Finley took the matter to court, as soon as Catfish was known to be a free agent 23 out of the 24 major-league teams began bidding for the pitcher, who won 88 games in the last four seasons while helping pitch the A's to three consecutive world championships. Hunter, with a record of 25 wins and 12 losses in 1974, won the Cy Young Award as the best pitcher in the American League.

Oldest Human Fossils

Anthropologists working in Ethiopia have discovered fossilized human remains 3 to 4 million years old, with preliminary dating showing the remains to be as much as 1.5-million years older than those discovered in 1971 by Richard Leakey in Kenya. The new discovery, in the form of a complete upper jaw and half of an upper and lower jaw, all with teeth, was made during an expedition headed by Karl Johanson, an anthropologist from Case Western Reserve University, and Dr. Maurice Taieb of the French Scientific Reserve Center.

The importance of the discovery was capsulized in the expedition's official statement: "These specimens clearly exhibit traits which must be considered as indicative of the genus *Homo*. Taken together they represent the most complete remains of this genus from anywhere in the world at a very ancient time. All previous theories of the origin of the lineage which lead to modern man must now be totally revised. We must throw out many existing theories and consider the possibility that man's origins go back well over 4 million years."

Whether the new fossils are accepted as extending man's antiquity will depend on agreement by other specialists that the jawbones and teeth are sufficiently like modern man's, and on more precise determination of their age. Johanson believes that the small size of the teeth in the jawbones may well mean that *Homo* was "walking, eating meat and probably using tools, perhaps bones, to kill animals" as long ago as 4 million years.

The expedition statement also challenged the widely accepted belief that Africa was the cradle of humankind. The region where the finds were made is little more than 100 miles from the Red Sea and a near-land bridge to the Middle East.

Italy's Revolving Door

Aldo Moro, premier of Italy three times in the past, formed a new government on November 23—the 37th since the fall of Fascism. Formation of the 25-member minority cabinet, composed of Christian Democrats and Republicans, ended a seven-week political crisis. The preceding premier, Mariano Rumor, took over Moro's post as foreign minister.

The Socialists and Social Democrats, both partners in the previous cabinet, promised to support the new government in the Chamber of Deputies, giving it a working majority. Various combinations of the Christian Democratic, Socialist, Social Democratic, and Republican parties have governed Italy in center-left coalitions since 1963, except for a period during 1972 and 1973.

The latest crisis began when the Social Democrats attacked the economic policies of the Socialists and charged they were too accommodating to the Communist party. Besides severe economic difficulties, Italy has been plagued by a wave of political terrorism and persistent rumors of right-wing plots against the state.

Star-Spangled Menace

The United States is intent on looting Canada's natural resources and ultimately plans to invade its northern neighbor, according to two of a half-dozen recent Canadian novels that warn against impending American menace. *Ultimatum* and *Exxoneration*, by Richard Rohmer, have become best-sellers in Canada despite generally poor reviews.

In *Ultimatum*, the president of the United States in 1980 demands that Canada immediately yield to energy-starved Americans the country's huge reserves of natural gas. In *Exxoneration*, the United States launches an invasion after Canada rejects the ultimatum delivered by a tough-talking Texas president patterned on former secretary of the treasury John Connally.

Rohmer, who has written nonfiction books about the development of Canada's vast Arctic North and its mineral wealth, says that his novels are intended to educate as well as entertain. He urges "vigilance and concern" in the face of American "demands for our natural resources [which] are increasing dramatically."

Heading for the Hills

In a surprising switch, the massive exodus from the Appalachian mountain region to the Northern cities has ended, and now more people are moving back to the mountains than are leaving. According to the Appalachian Regional Commission, projected population growth during the 1970's should reach 10 per cent, a dramatic change from the net emigration of 33 per cent in the 1950's and 18 per cent in the 1960's.

Analysts cite several probable reasons for the reversal, the most important being the increase in employment opportunities created by Appalachian development programs and the increases in recreation and retirement homes in the region. The recent coal boom is also fueling the population increase, though analysts are quick to point out that it wasn't the impetus, since the trend dates back to 1970. Other factors include reduced employment and housing opportunities in Northern cities, an increase in Social Security benefits, "black lung" payments for disabled coal miners, and the influx of returning military veterans.

Unbearable!

Smokey the Bear, responding well to recent treatment for his arthritis, is expected to continue stomping around his home in the National Zoo in Washington for another five years, but his many foster parents are anxious about the fate of the bear when he meets his maker. Smokey, who as a small black orphan cub was rescued from a raging fire and nursed back to health, has long been a spokesman warning against man's carelessness in forest areas. Congress recently adopted a resolution declaring that upon the demise of the 25-year-old bear, he should be returned to the Capitan Mountains of New Mexico, where he was found, for "proper disposition."

That last phrase is what worries his ranger friends, since "proper disposition" is not defined. One reporter even asked whether consideration had been made to skin Smokey and stuff the hide so that he could be put on display. A forest ranger who helped rescue Smokey from the burning mountain was shocked at the suggestion. "No," he said, "it don't seem dignified enough."

"Talking" Chimpanzee

Lana, a chimpanzee who has already learned enough of a modified English to converse with people through a computerized keyboard, continues to please her teachers at the Yerkes Regional Primate Research Center in Atlanta. Not only has Lana grasped the concept of referring to animate objects by their names, which were taught to her, but she now asks for the abstractions—that is, she asks for the names of objects whose names she doesn't know. (Each key she presses represents a word.) Thus, Lana has progressed from being a passive learner to a curious student.

Lana's breakthrough marks a major step in the studies under way in several laboratories to determine whether apes have the mental ability to understand a human-like language. Even though apes lack the necessary anatomy for speech, these findings further confirm the results of earlier studies which suggested that man could no longer assume that he was the only animal capable of language.

Dr. Duane M. Rumbaugh, who directs the research on Lana, acknowledges that some scientists doubt whether Lana's skills can be accurately defined as language ability but nevertheless believes that "Lana's skills are clearly related to human skills. They're obviously not equivalent to human skills but it seems to me that we have to admit this is a language ability somewhere on the continuum."

All-Volunteer Army

October 23, 1974, was the first day since before Pearl Harbor that the United States Army was a completely volunteer unit. The plan was put into motion the day the Paris peace agreement was signed, January 28, 1973, when it was announced that there would be no more draft calls. The concept of a volunteer force based on the incentives of higher pay and additional bonuses for enlistees had a hard time in its early stages, but an intense advertising campaign as well as the attractive proposition of guaranteed work during a period of rising unemployment, has apparently made the volunteer concept viable. Between January, 1973, and September, 1974, 350,000 men volunteered for the army, and officers expect the faltering economy to fuel this rate over the next few years.

Stricken by Breast Cancer

By a tragic coincidence, both Betty Ford and Happy Rockefeller underwent surgery for breast cancer in late 1974. Mrs. Ford had a radical mastectomy on September 28 after a cancerous lump had been detected in her right breast. The doctors said they were "optimistic for a prolonged survival."

Mrs. Rockefeller underwent surgery October 17 for the removal of her left breast, 32 adjacent lymph nodes, and part of the underlying chest-wall muscle; on November 25, she underwent a second mastectomy. The prospect for recovery was considered excellent.

The operations resulted in widespread public discussion of breast cancer, which afflicted 90,000 U.S. women in 1973 and resulted in the deaths of 30,000. In announcing the surgery on his wife, Nelson Rockefeller said that she had been prompted to examine herself for possible malignant lumps because of the heightened consciousness that followed Mrs. Ford's operation.

Christmas Presence

The saying goes that lightning doesn't strike the same place twice, but White House security men must be wondering. First there was the February, 1974, incident in which an army private buzzed the executive mansion in a stolen helicopter and finally landed amid a hail of gunfire. Then, on Christmas Day, Marshall H. Fields, 25, smashed his car through the closed White House gate and positioned himself, cloaked in Arab garb and seemingly wired with explosives, just 10 feet from the West Wing.

And that's where he stayed for the next four hours, demanding that he see the Pakistani ambassador, who later reported that he did not know Fields and had no intention of meeting him. Finally, Fields surrendered.

The Secret Service later reported that it had a file on Fields but did not consider him a direct threat to the president. Further, it said it did not have the manpower to keep an eye on every potential threat. A more embarrasing revelation however, was the fact that the White House gate was not completely locked. Nevertheless, Secret Service agents asserted that, had Ford family members been in the White House (they were skiing in Colorado), the man would have been shot during his attempt to get near the mansion.

Southern Exposure

On October 18, the largest telescope ever trained on the southern heavens produced its first photograph at the Cerro Tololo Inter-American Observatory in Chile's Andes Mountains. The 158-inch reflecting telescope, which is said to have the light-gathering power of more than 1 million eyes, is financed by the Ford Foundation and the National Science Foundation and is operated by an association of several universities. Viewing conditions are ideal, since the observatory is located above a virtually cloudless desert.

Almost all the world's large telescopes have been built in the Northern Hemisphere, although many of the most significant astronomical objects can only be observed from the Southern Hemisphere—for example, the Magellanic Clouds, the nearest galaxies to our own. In October, Prince Charles dedicated the 150-inch reflecting Anglo-Australian Telescope near Siding Spring, Australia.

One Way to Win

In November, Little League Baseball, Inc. settled on a way to bring the championship back to the United States—it restricted the annual world-series competition to teams from the continental United States. Teams from Taiwan and Japan had won the annual competition, which is held in Williamsport, Pennsylvania, in August, for seven of the last eight years.

Little League baseball, for youngsters 8 to 12, is the leading spectator sport on Taiwan. The island's semitropical climate allows boys to play the year round, and they drill hard under strict coaching.

In 1974, a Taiwanese team won the Little League championship for the fourth consecutive year. So completely did the team dominate the series that it surrendered only one run in 46 innings, defeating Red Bluff, California, 12-1, in the final game.

Don't Drink the Water

On November 7, the Environmental Defense Fund reported the results of its studies, which showed a possible link between certain cancers and the consumption of Mississippi River water in Louisiana. There were two immediate results: consumption of bottled water in Louisiana increased by twenty-fold and the Safe Drinking Water Act, already approved by the Senate, flew through the House of Representatives by a 296 to 85 vote.

On November 8, the Environmental Protection Agency entered the picture by announcing that, using new sophisticated measuring equipment, its researchers had discovered 68 organic chemicals in New Orleans water, 38 of which are known to be toxic. Further, among the 38 are chemicals which are known to have caused cancer in animals. Some of the organic chemicals are known to occur naturally while others are the results of pollution. Still others, ironically, are the result of the chlorination process used by the city to purify its water.

Russell Train, administrator of the EPA, has ordered a nationwide survey of water supplies in representative cities. With these results in hand, the EPA plans to locate the specific cause of the given contamination and then evaluate the methods for either eliminating the source of the pollutant or determining the most effective means of purifying the water.

An American Saint

Mother Elizabeth Ann Bayley Seton became the United States' first native-born saint on December 9, when Pope Paul VI approved a decree of canonization. (Mother Frances Xavier Cabrini, a naturalized U.S. citizen born in Italy, was canonized in 1946.)

Born in New York City in 1774, Mother Seton organized the Sisters of Charity of St. Joseph, the first U.S. religious order for women. She also started the first U.S. Catholic free school and established a number of other charitable institutions, including orphanages, hospitals, and institutions for lepers. She took a special interest in teaching and was known for her wide intellectual interests. She was beatified in 1963 by Pope John XXIII.

Scotch and Shoulder

Next time you wander into a tavern in Racine, Wisconsin, don't expect a heady conversation over beers on new behaviorist approaches to psychology, but also don't be surprised if you find just that. The fact is that many tavern-keepers in Racine have participated in a new mental-health program which seeks to acquaint bartenders, taxi drivers, barbers, and others whose occupations make them social listening posts, with the psychological needs of their patrons as well as the available help the troubled can obtain. North Dakota already requires a certificate from such a course before granting state certification as a cosmetician.

Since alcohol was recently named in a federal report as the worst U.S. drug problem, the neighborhood tavern is logically a hotbed for such a program. The Racine course involves 16 hours of discussions and lectures which emphasize three rules which the bartender must follow. First, he must never moralize to the patron, he must wait for the customer to express interest in help, and finally, he must not make contact with the professional counsellors to whom he referred the patron. In order to spot those who may need help, the course teaches the bartender to be on the lookout for unusual behavior—a usually quiet person who suddenly becomes aggressive, a noticeable change in someone's drinking habits, or a talkative person who suddenly become quiet and withdrawn.

Enter the Beefalo

The beefalo, a cross between buffalo (actually American bison) and cattle, was introduced in November to curious New Yorkers outside Mama Leone's restaurant in midtown Manhattan by J. D. Basolo, who developed the animal after 17 years of trial-and-error breeding. Since beefalo reach maturity faster than cattle and, unlike cattle, reach desired weight on grass alone, consumers may find the breed a solution to the ever-increasing food budget.

Basolo, who lives in Tracy, California, said it took more than 1,000 different matches to perfect the hybrid. (The buffalo itself is too cantankerous for large-scale raising.) The biggest problem was overcoming the sterility of the offspring, which often occurs when two different species mate. Regular breeding cows are now being inseminated artificially with beefalo semen. There are about 10,000 beefalo in the country—not enough to sell yet for food—but about 500,000 should be bred in 1975, according to Basolo.

Reaction to the taste of beefalo meat sold in a delicatessen was generally favorable. Store tests indicated that the meat has as much protein content as beef and far less fat.

Two-Way Streetwalking

Oregon, a state which has gained a national reputation for its pioneering environmental laws and liberal treatment of victimless crimes, has moved into controlling the world's oldest profession—prostitution. True to its spirit of equal treatment under the law, Oregon has begun prosecuting the male customer as well as the prostitute. Under the new law, a man can be jailed up to a year or fined up to $1,000 if he commits the misdemeanor of paying, or offering to pay, a fee to engage in sexual conduct.

Though other states have enacted similar laws, most policeman look the other way when it comes to enforcement. Even when the law is enforced, though, there is a serious question of equity; during a nine-month period, police in Portland arrested 245 prostitutes compared to only 45 customers. There is also the matter of entrapment. The American Civil Liberties Union, which opposes the prosecution of prostitutes, claiming the right of sexual privacy, believes the use of undercover agents is a violation of civil liberties.

New Mormon Temple

A $15-million temple for the Church of Jesus Christ of Latter-day Saints was completed in September in Kensington, Maryland, to serve as a center for some 300,000 Mormons who live on the east coast of the United States and Canada. It was dedicated in November, after which it was closed to nonmembers.

The temple, the first to be opened east of the Rocky Mountains, symbolizes the rapidly expanding influence of the Mormon church, which has doubled its membership since 1960 to about 3.3 million. Visiting rights are restricted to tithing members, who must dress entirely in white clothing. It is in the temples —there are 16 around the world—that Mormons perform baptisms for dead ancestors, engage in marriages that they believe will endure for eternity, and go through secret rituals known as "endowment ceremonies."

DIAL for Help

More than 60,000 callers are expected to phone the University of Wisconsin's Digital Information Access Line (DIAL) during the 1974-75 academic year. The round-the-clock messages, classified by number, embrace 220 different topics, including how to write a resume, registering with the Selective Service System, and improving one's memory. But the most popular ones pertain to "delicate" subjects such as birth control, rape, venereal disease, drug abuse, and coping with depression.

DIAL was devised because the office hours of the Campus Assistance Center—DIAL's parent institution—were too limited to serve such a large university community. Cooperating college departments and service centers research, write, and update the 2½-minute to 4½-minute tape scripts. Messages are recorded by assistance-center personnel onto tape casettes, which are stored at the University's telecommunications center. Assistant dean of students Stephen Saffian says, "Students aren't offended at hearing a tape so long as they know beforehand that that's what they are calling. What they resent is calling a person and getting a tape."

Top Secret

A third of a century after the fact, the most important intelligence coup of World War II is coming to light, thanks to *The Ultra Secret* by Fred W. Winterbotham, which tells the story of how Britain broke the Third Reich's secret code (actually a cipher). For 5½ years, Ultra, as the operation was called, provided British and United States leaders with the contents of messages sent to top-level German command. The secrecy with which the program was developed and maintained would make James Bond jealous.

The British first learned of the cipher when a Polish mechanic who had been working in a factory manufacturing the cipher machine before being deported when the Gestapo discovered his nationality, contacted British intelligence, which had him attempt to reconstruct the decoder. It was found that the machine was a sophisticated mechanical cipher which the Germans called Enigma. The Enigma was a system of electrically connected revolving drums which created so many possible permutations of the letters of the alphabet, that it was estimated that it would take a month for mathematicians to find the right answer for a single cipher setting. Not long after, the British succeeded in duplicating Enigma and thus possessed what Winston Churchill termed Ultra, "my most secret source."

The actual cracking of the cipher was only half the job though, for now that Britain could obtain top-level information, it had to devise ways to use it without letting the Germans discover that their cipher had been cracked. Secrecy was maintained, and throughout the war, Western leaders were able to learn of the composition, strength, and location of enemy forces as well as what their plans were. For example, Ultra enabled the Allies to destroy a large part of the German forces in Normandy after D-Day. Ultra also paid large dividends in North Africa, Sicily and Italy, and the Pacific theater.

Such knowledge did not avert tragedy, however. The most painful instance occurred as the Germans were bombing British cities in 1940. Normally, the Germans used code names in identifying British cities, but on November 15, someone in Berlin slipped and let the name Coventry come through Ultra. This gave Churchill four hours to decide whether to evacuate the city before the Germans struck. If he did, of course, the Germans would realize their communications system was worthless and the Allies' preemptory advantage would disappear. Taking the tough choice, Churchill alerted the air force, the fire and ambulance services, and the police, but did not evacuate the city, which was devastated.

"This is the sort of terrible decision that sometimes has to be made on the highest levels in war," writes Winterbotham. "It was unquestionably the right one, but I am glad it was not I who had to make it."

"Burn, Baby, Burn"

The image of the lone forest ranger in his lookout tower, ready at a moment's notice to summon firefighters to the source of a blaze, is about to undergo significant revision. The National Park Service has concluded that natural—as opposed to man-made—fires are good for forests and has decided to let them burn. The policy was first tested in California in 1968 and is now in effect in many of the heavily forested U.S. national parks.

Natural fires, usually set off by lightning, clear patches of land for new generations of trees and make way for a prodigious growth of succulent sprouts for animals to feed on. Moreover, they eliminate accumulated deadwood and underbrush—fuel for more dangerous fires. Forest rangers are actually starting fires in places where old trees have been attacked by diseases and pests.

Fighting natural fires can be ultimately destructive. In California's Sequoia National Park, for example, natural fires would have burned young firs, but since the fires were rigorously controlled, the firs have grown so tall that a fire now would probably also ignite the redwoods—the very trees that the park was designed to protect.

The Park Service faces difficulty, however, in explaining the new policy. In the summer of 1974, a forest fire in Wyoming's Grand Teton National Park was allowed to burn thousands of acres. A tourist complained, "I thought I'd see beautiful mountains up there and all I saw was a bunch of smoke." And nearby residents complained of massive air pollution from the blaze.

CUMULATIVE INDEX